TUTTLE
LEARNING
JAPANESE
KANJI

The innovative method for learning the 520 most essential Japanese kanji characters

Glen Nolan Grant

Illustrations by Ya-Wei Lin

TUTTLE Publishing

Tokyo | Rutland, Vermont | Singapore

The Tuttle Story: "Books to Span the East and West"

Many people are surprised to learn that the world's largest publisher of books on Asia had its humble beginnings in the tiny American state of Vermont. The company's founder, Charles E. Tuttle, belonged to a New England family steeped in publishing.

Immediately after WW II, Tuttle served in Tokyo under General Douglas MacArthur and was tasked with reviving the Japanese publishing industry. He later founded the Charles E. Tuttle Publishing Company, which thrives today as one of the world's leading independent publishers.

Though a westerner, Tuttle was hugely instrumental in bringing a knowledge of Japan and Asia to a world hungry for information about the East. By the time of his death in 1993, Tuttle had published over 6,000 books on Asian culture, history and art—a legacy honored by the Japanese emperor with the "Order of the Sacred Treasure," the highest tribute Japan can bestow upon a non-Japanese.

With a backlist of 1,500 titles, Tuttle Publishing is more active today than at any time in its past—inspired by Charles Tuttle's core mission to publish fine books to span the East and West and provide a greater understanding of each.

Published by Tuttle Publishing, an imprint of Periplus Editions (HK) Ltd.

www.tuttlepublishing.com

Library of Congress Cataloging-in-Publication Data

Grant, Glen Nolan.
Tuttle Learning Japanese Kanji : the innovative method to learn the 520 most essential Japanese kanji characters / by Glen Nolan Grant ; illustrations by Ya-Wei Lin.
    p. cm.
ISBN 978-4-8053-1168-4 (pbk.)
1. Japanese language--Writing. 2. Chinese characters--Japan. 3. Japanese language--Textbooks for foreign speakers--English. I. Lin, Ya-Wei. II. Title.
PL528.G723 2012
495.6'82421--dc23

                                        2012018073

ISBN: 978-4-8053-1168-4

Distributed by

North America, Latin America & Europe
Tuttle Publishing
364 Innovation Drive
North Clarendon, VT 05759-9436 U.S.A.
Tel: 1 (802) 773-8930; Fax: 1 (802) 773-6993
info@tuttlepublishing.com; www.tuttlepublishing.com

Japan
Tuttle Publishing
Yaekari Building, 3rd Floor
5-4-12 Osaki
Shinagawa-ku
Tokyo 141 0032
Tel: (81) 3 5437-0171 Fax: (81) 3 5437-0755
sales@tuttle.co.jp; www.tuttle.co.jp

Asia Pacific
Berkeley Books Pte. Ltd.
61 Tai Seng Avenue #02-12
Singapore 534167
Tel: (65) 6280-1330; Fax: (65) 6280-6290
inquiries@periplus.com.sg; www.periplus.com

First edition
17 16 15 14   5 4 3 2   1408RP
Printed in China

TUTTLE PUBLISHING® is a registered trademark of Tuttle Publishing, a division of Periplus Editions (HK) Ltd.

ACKNOWLEDGMENTS

This book is the result of a collaborative effort. Sincere thanks to Eric Oey of Periplus Editions for steering everything in the right direction, as well as to Bob Graham, Calvert Barksdale, Sandra Korinchak, William Notte, Nancy Goh, Angie Ang and the entire editorial and design departments of Tuttle Publishing for their stellar work with the manuscript. Watai Yuko, Niimi Emiko, Nakano Mariko, Watai Fumiko, Murray Grant, Cathy Grant, Damon Vignale, as well as Numamura Shimpei, Rick Havlak and Shaun Culham all offered welcome assistance. Special thanks are also owed to Junko Lucas and Fujitake Rika, for lending their voices to the sound recordings, Matt Pinneo, for his excellent job designing the accompanying 💿, and to the very talented Ya-Wei Lin, whose wonderful illustrations helped bring each of the stories to life.

This book is dedicated to Mr. H.B. (Henry Barrie) and Mrs. Wilma Grant, for their incredible support and encouragement.

Contents

Chapter 4

Chapter 5

Chapter 6

Chapter 7

Chapter 14

Chapter 15

Chapter 16

Chapter 17

Chapter 18

Chapter 19

Chapter 20

Chapter 21

Chapter 22

Appendices

 The **software** offers you animated stroke-order information and pronunciations for all 520 kanji.

 Visit the Learning Japanese Kanji page at **www.tuttlepublishing.com** to download Index 4 and other updates and bonus items.

INTRODUCTION

This book can help you greatly reduce the time and effort involved in learning to read Japanese. It does so by introducing a method that is both effective and easy to use in memorizing the meanings and pronunciations of *kanji*, the array of characters that are used in the language to symbolize everything from abstract ideas to concrete nouns.

Learning any of the kanji, you will find, is a two-step process, requiring that you remember both the *visual* aspect of a character (so you can recognize it when you see it) and the *aural* aspect (so you will know how to say and, thus, read it). The method presented here will show you how to tackle both of these aspects from the outset, and by so doing enable you to immediately get down to the practical (and fun!) business of recognizing and reading kanji on everything from street signs to newspapers. By the time you finish this book, in fact, you will be able to boast of a Japanese vocabulary numbering in the thousands of words.

Kanji and the Japanese Writing System

Kanji (literally, "Chinese characters") arrived in Japan along with Buddhism and other aspects of Chinese culture approximately 1,500 years ago. As with many concepts introduced into the country from abroad, this writing system was gradually shaped and modified over the centuries to better suit the Japanese themselves. Kanji today comprise one part of written Japanese, being used alongside a pair of much simpler phonetic syllabaries, *katakana* and *hiragana*. Katakana are generally employed to denote foreign words, as well as various technical and scientific terms. Hiragana, on the other hand, have a largely grammatical function, and are used for everything from verb endings to particles. As you can see from the examples below, katakana and hiragana are visually similar; they never contain more than four strokes. Kanji, however, are more varied; they can have anywhere from one to more than 20 strokes.

Hiragana:	か	き	く	け	こ
Katakana:	カ	キ	ク	ケ	コ
Kanji:	東	曜	秋	語	意

Written Japanese is thus a mixture of three elements, and a single sentence can have all three present, as in the following example.

アフリカで水牛とキリンを見ました。

I saw a water buffalo and a giraffe in Africa.

Number and Frequency of Kanji

As katakana and hiragana can be learned quickly (there are only around fifty of each), this book will focus exclusively on learning kanji. It's worth keeping in mind that the Japanese Ministry of Education has stipulated that high school students in Japan are expected to learn 2,136 characters (the so-called "general-use" kanji) by the time they graduate. Magazines and newspapers can employ upwards of 3,000 kanji, although these "extra" characters are often accompanied by hiragana showing how they are to be pronounced; without this, most Japanese would often be unsure of both the meaning of the character in question and its pronunciation.

Despite there being so many kanji, it is important to understand that some are used far more frequently than others. The 500 most common, for example, make up approximately 80% of the kanji you will see. The 1,000 most common bring this figure to over 90%. Learning the 520 kanji presented in this volume, therefore, will offer great immediate benefit.

The Composition of Kanji

In general, kanji dictionaries divide characters into groups that share a common part (called a "radical"). As you can see below, the kanji in the first row all share the same left-hand radical 亻. The kanji in the second row share the same top 宀, while the radical in the third row (攵) appears in various positions.

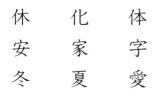

At times this book will break kanji apart into fragments smaller than radicals. To keep things simple, all radicals and parts that make up a kanji – *but are not themselves kanji* – are called components, and will always be presented in a separate text box immediately before the first character in which they appear.

Stroke Order

Stroke order refers to the sequence of lines that are used to correctly write out a kanji. Knowing this order is important for several reasons. First, it will help train you to quickly count the number of strokes in a character, and thus make it easier to locate unfamiliar kanji (or those for which pronunciations may have been forgotten) in a kanji dictionary. It will also aid you in breaking down characters visually, making it easier to see the components that will help you recall a kanji's meaning. Stroke order diagrams accompany each entry in this book. The accompanying 🐾, in addition, provides an animated graphic showing each character being written in its proper order.

An Overview of *On-yomi* and *Kun-yomi*

On-yomi and kun-yomi are the two main branches of pronunciation (or "readings", as they are called) that are present in modern day Japanese. On-yomi are sometimes called the "Chinese readings" of the kanji, as these were the initial pronunciations attached to the characters when they first arrived from China. The kun-yomi, on the other hand, developed from within Japan, and are thus referred to as "Japanese readings". This, along with the fact that different on-yomi for the same character sometimes arrived from China centuries later, helps explain how a single kanji in Japanese can sometimes have more than one of each type of reading.

Clearly, memorizing these various pronunciations and knowing when to use them are two of the most difficult tasks in learning Japanese.

There are, however, reasons to be optimistic. Over 60% of the kanji have only a single **on-yomi**, or one **on-yomi** and one **kun-yomi**. In addition, when multiple **on-** or **kun-yomi** are present, there is usually only one dominant reading for each. This book will help you determine the most important pronunciations to be learned by classifying every reading as either "common" or "less common". Those that are less common do not merit being learned at this stage of your language study; they are presented only for future reference.

An interesting aspect of Japanese (and an unlucky one for us in this volume!) is that the most complex kanji in terms of pronunciation are often amongst the most simple to write. Do not get discouraged, therefore, when thorny characters such as "person" (Entry 2), "one" (Entry 3), "sun" (Entry 6), and "large" (Entry 17) all show up in the first chapter, as these can be classified with the most difficult in the language. Be patient with such characters, and take comfort in knowing that by the time you finish this book you will have dealt with the trickiest entries in the entire range of the general-use kanji.

Rules for Using *On-yomi* and *Kun-yomi*

There are some useful ground rules that you should keep in mind when learning to read single kanji and compounds (words formed from several kanji put together):

1. Kanji in most compounds are usually read with their **on-yomi**. Note, that when the pronunciations for **on-yomi** are given, these are conventionally written in katakana, and indicated by uppercase letters in English.

KANJI	PRONUNCIATION	MEANING
火山	**KA·ZAN** カ・ザン	*volcano*
家具	**KA·GU** カ・グ	*furniture*
弓道	**KYŪ·DŌ** キュ・ウ・ドウ	*(Japanese) archery*
同時	**DŌ·JI** ドウ・ジ	*simultaneous*

2. Compounds only rarely mix **on-yomi** and **kun-yomi**. Note here that **kun-yomi** are conventionally written in hiragana, and indicated by lowercase letters in English.

KANJI	PRONUNCIATION	MEANING
中古車	**CHŪ·KO·SHA** チュウ·コ·シャ	*used car*
十二月	**JŪ·NI·GATSU** ジュウ·ニ·ガツ	*December*
小春	**ko·haru** こ·はる	*Indian summer*
花見	**hana·mi** はな·み	*cherry blossom viewing*

3. Kanji in compounds that are accompanied by hiragana are almost always read with their **kun-yomi**.

KANJI (+ HIRAGANA)	PRONUNCIA-TION	MEANING
切り下げる	**ki·ri sa·geru** き·り さ·げる	*to devalue*
売り家	**u·ri ie** う·り いえ	*"House for sale"*
名高い	**na daka·i** な だか·い	*renowned*
立ち止まる	**ta·chi do·maru** た·ち ど·まる	*to stand still*

4. Kanji that appear alone (that is, they are not part of a compound in a sentence) are usually read with their **kun-yomi**.

KANJI (+ HIRAGANA)	PRONUNCIATION	MEANING
小さい	**chii·sai** ちい·さい	*small*
犬	**inu** いぬ	*dog*
東	**higashi** ひがし	*east*
来る	**ku·ru** く·る	*to come*

You may have noticed words such "usually" and "almost always" in the abo rules. One thing you will soon learn about ka is that they seem to take delight in turning exceptions to every rule. The best thing to is make use of these exceptions as a means memorize the words in which they appear. P another way, you will be much further ahead you learn to love headstrong words that live their own rules!

Voiced and Unvoiced Sounds

An important consideration in learning read Japanese is understanding the diffe ence between voiced and unvoiced consona sounds. Think of this difference by sayi aloud the English words "brink" and "bring the "k" of "brink" is unvoiced, while the " of "bring" is voiced (you need to vibrate yo vocal cords to say it). This is the same distin tion, for example, between the Japanese soun "**ka**" and "**ga**" (か and が). What you need know is that certain kanji can turn from bein unvoiced to voiced, depending on where the appear in a compound. The first entry of th previous section above provides an exampl the unvoiced **on-yomi SAN** (サン) chang to the voiced **ZAN** (ザン) in the first samp word shown. Although there are an assortme of rules that explain when such changes tak place, it is best to develop a "feel" for whe these phonetic transformations might occu Once this happens, your ear will develop to th point where certain compounds begin soundi more natural with one of their kanji voiced.

Irregular Readings

It sometimes occurs in Japanese that a kan compound has an irregular reading. Known *jukujikun*, such readings have no relation the normal **on-** or **kun-yomi** of their comp nent kanji. Rather, these irregular readings a assigned to entire compounds rather than their component kanji.

You will encounter the first of these in Entry In all three such irregular readings shown ther the reading of the kanji "人" is complete different from what we would expect it to normally. In a sense, this is much like the prol lem foreigners face when learning English; the pronunciation of the word "cough", for example, has little connection with the normal sound of the letters from which it is made. Fortunately there are not many irregular readings to be learned (less than fifty appear in this book), but as they are all in common use it is best to come to grips with them the moment they are encountered, by memorizing them as individual words. All irregular readings in this book will be presented separately from the "Common words and compounds" section, to make it clear that these are some truly oddball pronunciations.

A Method for Memorizing the Visual and Aural Aspects of Kanji

As we have seen, kanji are typically more visually complex than hiragana and katakana. Because of this, a good way to simplify the task of committing kanji to memory is to look at their constituent parts. We will do just that, breaking the characters down piece-by-piece and assigning meanings to these components based exclusively on *how they look*. When these various components then join together to build kanji, we will make use of short stories featuring the pieces as "actors", accompanied by drawings to help solidify the appearance of the characters in a unique way. This part of our memorization approach, therefore, will focus exclusively on the visual aspect of each kanji.

For the aural side of the equation, we need to take one other difference between the **on-** and **kun-yomi** into account when devising our memorization strategy: there are far fewer **on-yomi** to learn than **kun-yomi**. This is because **on-yomi** are not often complete words on their own – it helps to think of them as short "blocks" of sound that in most cases form words only when they are strung together. (It is worth keeping in mind, though, that the kanji for numbers are a notable exception to this.) Given that roughly 300 **on-yomi** suffice to cover the entire range of Japan's 2,136 general-use characters, a single reading can be attached to many different kanji. **SHŌ** (ショウ), for example, is an **on-yomi** for more than 60 characters. We will be taking advantage of this aspect of Japanese to cut down on the work involved in memorizing

these readings.

Our basic plan for committing both the **on-yomi** and **kun-yomi** to memory will be to come up with English keywords that approximate their sounds as closely as possible, and to use these in sentences that also contain a word encompassing the general meaning of the character. As an example, the kanji for "two" has an **on-yomi** of **NI** (二), and a **kun-yomi** of **futa** (ふた). If we choose the word "knee" to suggest **NI**, and the phrase "**who tans**" for **futa**, a possible sentence might be the following: "**TWO knees? Who ta**ns only those?". This second side to our approach, therefore, will focus exclusively on the aural aspect of a kanji.

A useful shortcut will involve using the same **on-yomi** keyword every time a kanji having that reading appears (recall that many kanji can share the same **on-yomi**). In the preceding example, therefore, the word "knee" will be used each time a kanji with the **on-yomi** "NI" crops up, and will simply be combined with the different **kun-yomi** and meaning of the new kanji. A major advantage of this approach is that it will make easily confused **on-yomi** such as **HŌ** (ホウ) and **HO** (ホ) absolutely distinctive in your mind, as you will have assigned different keywords to each of these. Given their importance (they will need to be used over and over again with different kanji), the creation of **on-yomi** keywords will be left up to you once a few examples have been provided at the beginning of Chapter 1 – your sentences will be more memorable if these words have a distinct personal meaning for you. The **On-Yomi Keyword Table** at the end of the book will help you manage your list of these keywords as it grows, and is designed to be filled in as you encounter each **on-yomi** in the pages ahead. By keeping all these readings in one place, you can refer to them quickly when needed.

The **kun-yomi**, on the other hand, are far greater in number, and therefore best learned individually. Fortunately, they tend to be more distinctive than the **on-yomi**, and are, as a result, often easier to remember once a unique keyword phrase has been created. In order to help with the workload in this respect, suggestions for

kun-yomi keywords are provided through the first ten chapters of this book, but you should not hesitate to use an idea of your own should one spring immediately to mind.

Presentation of the Entries in This Book

Each entry will offer one kanji along with a word embracing its broadest possible meaning, followed by a grid showing its stroke order. Next, you'll see a list of the components making up the character, together with reference numbers indicating the points at which these have been introduced earlier in the book. After a short background section describes the various shades of meaning the character conveys, a story (when required) and illustration are presented to help you memorize the kanji visually. A pronunciation section then lists the most common **on-** and **kun-yomi** for the character followed by readings that you will encounter less frequently. Entries conclude with a section showing the character's use in a number of common Japanese words, and a sample sentence in which the kanji is featured.

There is an important point to keep in mind with respect to the "Common words and compounds" table in each entry: any word or compound consisting of kanji you have already learned will be shown in **bold face**. This will allow you to focus on reviewing those words you have previously encountered. One useful way to review would involve covering up the right-hand columns in the table with your hand or a piece of paper, then drawing it back to reveal the individual kanji meanings, pronunciation, and the overall meaning of the word in question.

In order to make your task a bit more manageable – you'll be mastering 520 of the most important kanji in Japanese, after all! – the book is divided into chapters of 20 to 30 entries

each. This will allow you to periodically review a reasonable number of characters before proceeding onward. Short review sections at the end of each chapter will help you check your learning, along with cumulative exercises following Chapters 5, 10, 16 and 22. Use these reviews to see exactly how far you've come in your mastery of the kanji, and to find out which entries to return to for more practice, if you need it. You'll find answer keys, along with indices listing kanji by stroke count, English meaning and pronunciation at the end of the book. Remember that all of the **on-yomi** are presented in katakana and employ upper-case Roman letters for romaji. The **kun-yomi** are written with hiragana, and have lower-case Roman letters for romaji.

To add an audio aspect to your kanji learning, the accompanying 🎧 contains pronunciations for all the **on-** and **kun-yomi** found in this book, as well as for the sample sentences and common words in each entry; it will be particularly useful in helping you to select your **on-yomi** keywords. An animated graphic is also provided to show you how each kanji is written using the proper stroke order.

Learning to read kanji is fascinating; the characters, so different from those used in our own writing system, have a mysterious quality that attracts everyone who studies Japanese. As you progress through this book and see how kanji are easily able to present even the most complex ideas, it is worth keeping in mind that you are not only setting out to learn a new means of written communication, but another way of conceptualizing the world around you. It's an exciting task and by using the present book as your guide you will find this process to be not only interesting but fun. So let's jump right in – and start learning Japanese kanji!

Kanji #1—20

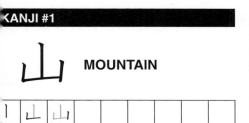 **MOUNTAIN**

Meaning

Mountain. Our first kanji is one of those wonderful characters whose meaning is obvious at a glance. As kanji such as these are best learned from a simple picture, there is no need for an accompanying story. A number of characters in the book will fall into this category.

Common Pronunciations

Common **ON** reading: **SAN** (サン)
Common **kun** reading: **yama** (やま)

This kanji has only one **on-yomi** and one **kun-yomi** (the pronunciation of which – together with all others in this book – can be heard on the accompanying ). To suggest these sounds, let's use the word "**SANDWICH**" for **SAN**, and "**yam appetizer**" for **yama**. As "sandwich" will now be a permanent keyword for all kanji sharing the read-

ing **SAN**, turn to the **on-yomi** table in the back of the book and write "Sandwich" in the space next to **SAN**. Remember that only **on-yomi** (not **kun-yomi**) should be entered in the table.

We now need to link the *meaning* of the kanji to its *sounds* by using the words "mountain", "sandwich", and "yam appetizer" in a sentence. Let's try this: I had a **yam a**ppetizer and a **SAN**DWICH on the Mountain. For future review, write this sentence in the box below.

Now for some common words that make use of this kanji. There's no need to worry for the moment about being unable to recognize the other characters, as they will all be learned over the course of the book; at this stage, try to see how the meanings of individual kanji combine to form more complex words (look especially at the fourth example below). This is a useful skill, as it will help foster an intuitive feel for the meanings of unfamiliar compounds that you encounter in the future. It is also one of the most rewarding aspects of learning to read the language. Understanding the logic that went into the formation of a compound not only makes it easier to remember, but offers fascinating insight into the minds of the people who devised it hundreds – if not thousands – of years earlier.

Remember that the uppercase letters and *katakana* here indicate **on-yomi**, with lowercase letters and *hiragana* indicating **kun-yomi**. Recall as well from the introduction that this is our first instance of a character whose unvoiced reading can sometimes become voiced (in examples 3 - 4, where the **on-yomi** changes from **SAN** to **ZAN**). Note how the first kanji of the entry below is presented in bold face – indicating that this is a word you now know.

Common Words and Compounds		
山	*mountain*	**yama** や ま
一山	one + mountain = *a pile of something*	hito·**yama** ひ と・や ま
高山	tall + mountain = *alpine*	**KŌ·ZAN** コ ウ・ザ ン
火山	fire + mountain = *volcano*	**KA·ZAN** カ・ザ ン
山村	mountain + village = *mountain village*	**SAN·SON** サ ン・ソ ン

Each entry concludes with a sample senten featuring the character under discussion; a unfamiliar kanji in these sentences are introduc later in the book.

SAMPLE SENTENCE:

山　に　木　が　あ り ま せ ん。

yama　ni　ki　ga　　arimasen.

mountain　tree　　are not

= *There are no trees on the mountain.*

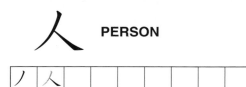

KANJI #2

人 **PERSON**

ノ	人						

Meaning

Person/Human being. Another visually simple kanji for which no story is required. When appearing at the end of country names, this kanji denotes an individual's nationality.

Common Pronunciations

Common **ON** reading: **JIN** (ジ ン); **NIN** (ニ ン)
Common **kun** reading: **hito** (ひ と)

As mentioned in the introduction, 人 is a character that challenges every student of Japanese. As

there are few patterns to its distribution of rea ings, words containing it often need to be mem rized individually. **JIN**, however, tends to signi that a person belongs to a certain subgroup humanity, while **NIN** indicates a person engag in an activity specified by the kanji preceding Look for **JIN** in the first position and at the end words signifying countries, and be aware that t **kun-yomi** is always voiced (changes from **hito bito**) when it appears outside of the first positic as it does in the sixth compound below.

We now need our keywords and sentence the three readings. For **JIN** and **NIN** let's choo "JEANS" and "NINCOMPOOP". As you did the previous entry for 山, turn to the **on-yomi** tat at the end of the book, but this time write "Jean in the space next to **JIN** and "Nincompoop" the space next to **NIN**. For the **kun-yomi** "hit we'll use **heat open**. We can now throw ever thing together into the sentence "That Pers is a **NIN**compoop because they **heat** open the **JEANS**". For future review, write this senten in the box below.

Here are our initial encounters with irregular readings. Note that the irregular reading in the first two examples belongs to 人; as you will learn in the next two entries, "一" and "二" are read with their normal **kun-yomi**. In the final compound, both readings are irregular. All three of these words are best thought of as special cases, and memorized individually.

IRREGULAR READINGS		
一人	one + person = *one person*	**hito·ri** ひと・り
二人	two + person = *two people*	**futa·ri** ふた・り
大人	large + person = *adult*	**otona** おとな

COMMON WORDS AND COMPOUNDS		
人	*person*	**hito** ひと
白人	white + person = *caucasian*	**HAKU·JIN** ハク・ジン
人口	person + mouth = *population*	**JIN·KŌ** ジン・コウ
三人	three + person = *three people*	**SAN·NIN** サン・ニン
四人	four + person = *four people*	**yo·NIN** よ・ニン
村人	village + person = *villager*	**mura·bito** むら・びと
外国人	outside + country + person = *foreigner*	**GAI·KOKU·JIN** ガイ・コク・ジン

SAMPLE SENTENCE:

あ の 人 の 手 は 小さい です。
ano hito no te wa chii·sai desu.
that person hand small
= *That person's hands are small.*

一 — **ONE**

一								

Meaning
One. It's hard to find an easier kanji to remember than this!

Remembering this kanji
Despite its simplicity, we need to complicate things a little in order to make use of this character in other kanji. As a result, this character will mean the "top of a hamburger bun" when appearing over all other parts of another character, and the "bottom of a hamburger bun" when it shows up beneath them. But what of a horizontal line found in the middle of a character? Well, that would be the patty (which vegetarians may wish to picture being made of tofu).

shows up beneath them. But what of a horizontal line found in the middle of a character? Well, that would be the patty (which vegetarians may wish to picture being made of tofu).
"*In the beginning, there was* ONE *shapeless… bun.*"

Common Pronunciations
Common **ON** readings: ICHI (イ チ); ITSU (イ ツ)
Common **kun** reading: hito (ひ と)

Though this is the simplest kanji in a visual sense, knowing when to use which of its readings can be tricky. Now that we have some understanding of the difference between voiced and unvoiced consonant sounds, however, it's much easier for us to make sense of it all. Basically, whenever this kanji appears as the first character in a compound it is almost always read with its **on-yomi**, and its pronunciation of **ICHI** or **ITSU** will depend on whether the initial sound of the following kanji is voiced or voiceless (look closely at the sixth compound of the common words section below to see how the sound of **ITSU** "doubles up" with the sound of the next kanji in this situation). Don't worry if this sounds complicated for now; rest assured it will soon become intuitive as compounds begin sounding more natural with one reading or the other.

We now need a sentence with all three common readings together with the word "one". To suggest the sounds **ICHI** and **ITSU**, let's use "**EACH EEL**" and "**EAT SOUP**". Write these in their respective places in the **on-yomi** table at the back of the book. For the **kun-yomi "hito"**, we'll use "**he to**ld". Let's choose the following sentence: "**One**," **he to**ld us, "**EACH EEL** must **EAT SOUP**." As before, write this sentence in the box below for future reference.

Less Common Pronunciations
Less common **ON** reading: none
Less common **kun** reading: none

Here is another irregular reading; the word "day" appears in brackets to make the logic behind the compound clearer by indicating a secondary meaning of 日 (Entry 6).

IRREGULAR READING		
一日	one + sun (day) = *first day of the month*	**tsuitachi** ついたち

Note that the same compound is shown below with a different pronunciation and meaning. Context will determine which is the appropriate

reading to apply; when 一日 is seen at the top of a newspaper page, for example, it clearly refers to the first day of the month and would thus be read "**tsuitachi**" (ついたち).

COMMON WORDS AND COMPOUNDS		
一	*one*	**ICHI** イチ
一つ	*one (general counter)*	**hito·tsu** ひと・つ
一日	one + sun (day) = *one day*	**ICHI·NICHI** イチ・ニチ
一月	one + moon (month) = *January*	**ICHI·GATSU** イチ・ガツ
同一	same + one = *identical*	**DŌ·ITSU** ドウ・イツ
一回	one + rotate = *once*	**IK·KAI** イッ・カイ
一時	one + time = *one o'clock*	**ICHI·JI** イチ・ジ

SAMPLE SENTENCE:

一時　　に　会いましょう。
ICHI·JI　　**ni**　　**a·imashō.**
One o'clock　　　　let's meet
= *Let's meet at one o'clock.*

KANJI #4

一二　**TWO**

一	二							

BUILDING THIS KANJI
one 一 (3) + one 一 (3) = 二

Meaning
All things to do with two, including the ideas of "double" and "**bi-**", etc. Note that the top line is drawn slightly shorter.

Remembering this kanji
On day TWO, things began to emerge in the form of a hamburger-like object.

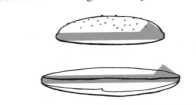

Common Pronunciations
Common **ON** reading: **NI** (二)
Common **kun** reading: **futa** (ふた)

After that bruising encounter with the pronunciation of 一, things become much simpler with 二, although as you can see below there are also three irregular readings that need to be learned with this character. To suggest our **on-yomi**, let's use "**KNEE**", and for our **kun-yomi**, "**who tans**"

After entering KNEE in your **on-yomi** table, write the following sentence in the box below: "Two **KNEES**? **Who ta**ns only those?"

Less Common Pronunciations
Less common **ON** reading: none
Less common **kun** reading: none

Here are three irregular readings that will be frequently encountered.

IRREGULAR READINGS		
二日	two + sun (day) = *second day of the month*	**futsuka** ふつか
二十日	two + ten + sun (day) = *twentieth day of the month*	**hatsuka** はつか
二十歳	two + ten + annual = *twenty years old*	**hatachi** はたち

COMMON WORDS AND COMPOUNDS		
二	*two*	**NI** ニ
二つ	*two (general counter)*	**futa**·tsu ふた·つ
二月	two + moon (month) = *February*	**NI·GATSU** ニ·ガツ
二十	two + ten = *twenty*	**NI·JŪ** ニ·ジュウ
二百	two + hundred = *two hundred*	**NI·HYAKU** ニ·ヒャク
二時	two + time = *two o'clock*	**NI·JI** ニ·ジ
二週間	two + week + interval = *two weeks*	**NI·SHŪ·KAN** ニ·シュウ·カン

SAMPLE SENTENCE:

二月　　　の　オーストラリア　は
NI·GATSU **no** **ōsutoraria** **wa**
February　　　　Australia
美しい。
utsuku·shii.
beautiful
= *Australia is beautiful in February.*

 **THREE**

一	二	三					

BUILDING THIS KANJI
one 一(3) + one 一(3) + one 一(3) = 三

Meaning
Three/Triple/Tri-, etc.

Remembering this kanji
On day THREE, the full hamburger - in all its glory - came into being.

Common Pronunciations
Common **ON** reading: **SAN** (サン)
Common **kun** reading: none

It's now time to begin making use of our key short-cut for learning the **on-yomi**. As we have already created a keyword for **SAN** (recall the **on-yomi** for "山" in Entry 1), we will now use that same word here. Let's keep things simple and have "Three **SANDWICHES**" as our phrase. As always, write this in the box below.

Less Common Pronunciations
Less common **ON** reading: none
Less common **kun** readings: **mi-** (みつ); **mi** (み)

Here we have our first examples of some less common readings, in this case the two **kun-yomi** "mi-" and "mi". Keep in mind that "less common" does not equate with "unimportant," as to read Japanese fluently these pronunciations will all have to be learned in time. At this stage, however, it is far more useful to solidify the common readings in your memory and take up the others when they are encountered in the future. When you reach that stage, the appropriate phrase for the respective kanji (e.g. "Three SANDWICHES") can simply be extended to accommodate additional mnemonic words.

In the present example, the first **kun-yomi** appears in only two words, and always "doubles up" in the same way "**ITSU**" (the **on-yomi** for "一") does when preceding voiceless consonant sounds (this is indicated by the short dash after mi). In a sense, this reading is unusual enough to merit the words being learned as if they were irregular readings: 三日 [**mik·ka** (みっ·か)] "the third day of the month", and 三つ [**mit·tsu** (みっ·つ)] the general counter for "three". The second less common reading is more typical of the pronunciations you will find in this section. The words in which it occurs are

obscure; it is enough to be aware that such less common readings exist for some of the kanji in this book, but that you don't need to worry about them for now.

COMMON WORDS AND COMPOUNDS		
三	*three*	**SAN** サン
三人	three + person = *three people*	**SAN·NIN** サン・ニン
三月	three + moon (month) = *March*	**SAN·GATSU** サン・ガツ
三時	three + time = *three o'clock*	**SAN·JI** サン・ジ
三十	three + ten = *thirty*	**SAN·JŪ** サン・ジュウ
三千	three + thousand = *three thousand*	**SAN·ZEN** サン・ゼン

SAMPLE SENTENCE:

三人　　が　早く　来ました。
SAN·NIN　　ga　haya·ku　ki·mashita.
Three people　　early　　came.
= *Three people came early.*

KANJI #6

日 SUN

丨	冂	日	日					

Meaning

This is a kanji with two primary meanings that are clearly related: "sun" and "day". The character will become most familiar to you through its use in the days of the week, and as the initial kanji in the compound for Japan.

This is another character, incidentally, for which we do not need to make use of a story.

Common Pronunciations
Common **ON** reading: **NICHI** (ニチ); **JITSU** (ジツ)
Common **kun** reading: **hi** (ひ)

日 is another example of a simple-looking kanji that can cause a bit of trouble when it comes to pronunciation. As all three of these readings occur frequently, the best approach is to look for patterns: **NICHI** will be encountered overwhelmingly in the first position (**hi** makes only a few appearances), **JITSU** in the second, and **hi** in the third – where it becomes voiced and pronounced **bi** (び). A perfect example of this odd behavior can be seen in the word Sunday, the final example below. Note also that **NICHI** acts like **ITSU** (from 一) by doubling up any unvoiced consonant sounds that follow it, as can be seen in the more formal rendering of the pronunciation for "Japan", **NIP·PON** (ニッ・ポン), from which the more common **NI·HON** (ニ・ホン) has been derived.

At this point we will now start building our own sentences to memorize pronunciations. First, think of a word to approximate the **on-yomi NICHI** (a

German philosoper, perhaps?) and the **on-yomi** JUTSU (a martial art, maybe?). Whichever words you decide to use, don't forget to write them in the **on-yomi** table at the back of the book. When it comes to the **kun-yomi**, suggestions will be provided for each one ahead (they can be tough to dream up at times). Don't hesitate, however, to use your own ideas if another word springs immediately to mind. For the present character, try "**helium**"; use this together with "sun" and your **on-yomi** keywords to create the sentence you will write in the box below.

COMMON WORDS AND COMPOUNDS		
日	*sun; day*	**hi** ひ
一日	one + day = *one day*	**ICHI·NICHI** イチ・ニチ
日本	sun + main = *Japan*	**NI·HON** ニ・ホン **NIP·PON** ニッ・ポン
休日	rest + day = *holiday*	**KYŪ·JITSU** キュウ・ジツ
毎日	every + day = *daily*	**MAI·NICHI** マイ・ニチ
朝日	morning + sun = *morning sun*	asa·**hi** あさ・ひ
日曜日	sun + day of the week + day = *Sunday*	**NICHI·YŌ·bi** ニチ・ヨウ・び

Less Common Pronunciations

Less common **ON** reading: none
Less common **kun** reading: **ka** (か)

ka is used only to identify the days of the month from 2-10, 14, 17, 20, 24 and 27.

Here are four irregular readings (the most that will appear for any character in this book). You've already seen the first.

IRREGULAR READINGS		
一日	one + day = *first day of the month*	**tsuitachi** ついたち
昨日	past + day = *yesterday*	**kinō** きのう
今日	now + day = *today*	**kyō** きょう
明日	bright + day = *tomorrow*	**asu** あす **ashita** あした

SAMPLE SENTENCE:

　　毎日　　　日本語　の　本　を
MAI·NICHI   NI·HON·GO   no   HON   o
　daily　　　　Japanese　　　book

読みます。
yo·mimasu.
　read

= *(I) read Japanese books every day.*

COMPONENT #7

JELLY BEAN

Here we have our initial "component". These will always be introduced directly before the first character in which they appear, and will be set apart in a separate text box to indicate that they are **not** themselves kanji on their own.

This little guy, incidentally, can appear at various places and on various angles in a kanji. It can also show up with not only one friend, as in Entry 60, but with two, as in Entry 25.

KANJI #7

白 **WHITE**

BUILDING THIS KANJI
Jelly Bean ヽ + Sun 日 (6) = 白

Meaning
White. To the Japanese, this color symbolizes cleanliness and purity (which helps explain the presence of so many white cars in the country!). As a result, the kanji can appear in words with this shade of meaning. The fourth compound is an example.

Remembering this kanji
As this kanji is composed of a separate character and a component, our first story will help you to memorize it:

I think it's safe to say that any **jelly bean**, no matter what color it is, will turn WHITE if thrown into the **sun**.

Common Pronunciations
Common **ON** reading: **HAKU** (ハク)
Common **kun** reading: **shiro** (しろ)

kun-yomi suggestion: "**she wro**te"

Create your **on-yomi** keyword and enter it in the table at the back of the book. After that, write your sentence to remember the **on-yomi** and **kun-yomi** readings in the box below.

Less Common Pronunciations
Less common **ON** reading: **BYAKU** (ビャク)
Less common **kun** readings: **shira** (しら)

COMMON WORDS AND COMPOUNDS		
白	*white (noun)*	**shiro** しろ
白い	*white (adjective)*	**shiro·i** しろ・い
白人	white + person = *caucasian*	**HAKU·JIN** ハク・ジン
明白	bright + white = *obvious*	**MEI·HAKU** メイ・ハク
白鳥	white + bird = *swan*	**HAKU·CHŌ** ハク・チョウ
白米	white + rice = *polished rice*	**HAKU·MAI** ハク・マイ

SAMPLE SENTENCE:

この 白い 馬 の 名前 は "雪"
kono shiro·i uma no na·mae wa "yuki"
this white horse name "snow"
です。
desu.
= *This white horse's name is "Snow".*

KANJI #8

口   **MOUTH**

丨	冂	口					

Meaning
Along with the literal meaning of "mouth" and things oral, the kanji also relates to openings in general, from caves and harbors to taps and bottles, for instance.

Remembering this kanji
Has there ever been a more famous MOUTH than that of Dracula? We will use this image of a vampire to suggest the word "mouth" in our stories from now on; a few other simple characters will be treated like this as well.

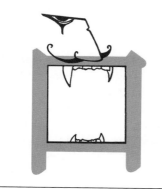

Common Pronunciations
Common **ON** reading: **KŌ** (コウ)
Common **kun** reading: **kuchi** (くち)

Note how the **kun-yomi** for this kanji can become voiced when it appears in the second position, as it does in the fifth example below.

kun-yomi suggestion: "**coochie** coochie coo"

Create your **on-yomi** keyword and enter it in the table at the back of the book. After that, write your sentence to remember the **on-yomi** and **kun-yomi** readings in the box below.

Less Common Pronunciations
Less common **ON** reading: **KU** (ク)
Less common **kun** readings: none

COMMON WORDS AND COMPOUNDS		
口	*mouth*	**kuchi** くち
人口	person + mouth = *population*	**JIN·KŌ** ジン・コウ
早口	early (fast) + mouth = *rapid speaking*	haya·**kuchi** はや・くち
口語	mouth + words = *colloquial language*	**KŌ**·GO コウ・ゴ
出口	exit + mouth = *exit*	de·**guchi** で・ぐち
口先	mouth + precede = *lip service*	**kuchi**·saki くち・さき

SAMPLE SENTENCE:

この 国 の 人口 は 少ない。
kono kuni no JIN·KŌ wa suku·nai.
this country   population   few
= *This country has a small population.*

COMPONENT #9

PRISON

Though it looks similar to the kanji for "mouth", this component is larger and always completely surrounds whatever happens to be inside it (like a prison should!); this difference can be seen clearly in Entry 9.

KANJI #9

ROTATE

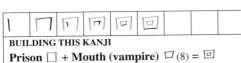

BUILDING THIS KANJI
Prison □ + Mouth (vampire) 口 (8) = 回

Meaning
Here we see the difference between the "prison" component and the kanji for "mouth". Note that the interior part of this kanji is written following the first two strokes of the prison walls, and becomes enclosed by the final stroke at the bottom. All characters of this type have the same pattern.

The general sense of this kanji relates to the ideas of rotation and going around in both space and time. It can also refer to the vicinity of things (neighborhoods and surroundings, etc), and is well-known to Japanese baseball fans as the character used to denote innings.

Remembering this kanji
It was a great relief for everyone when the **vampire** was finally put in **prison**. It soon became obvious, though, that he could not be kept with the rest of the cons; his offer to "ROTATE the blood" of everyone made them suspicious. The end result, as might be expected, was solitary confinement, a bad enough development for the **vampire** that became even worse when he turned into a bat; flying in endless ROTATIONS apparently brought on some nasty dizzy spells.

Common Pronunciations
Common **ON** reading: **KAI** (カイ)
Common **kun** reading: **mawa** (まわ)

kun-yomi suggestion: "llama wagon"

Create your **on-yomi** keyword and enter it in the table at the back of the book. After that, write your sentence to remember the **on-yomi** and **kun-yomi** readings in the box below.

Less Common Pronunciations
Less common **ON** reading: none
Less common **kun** reading: none

This is a good place to highlight another important aspect of Japanese: the difference between intransitive (intr) and transitive (tr) verbs. Basically, an intransitive verb does not require an object, whereas a transitive verb does. This can be more easily understood by comparing the first two examples given below; a person or thing "goes around" on their own (intransitive), but must have an object to "send around" (transitive). As many Japanese verbs come in such intransitive/transitive pairs (the same kanji accompanied by different *hiragana* attached to the end), it is worth noticing how certain endings often indicate the type of verb; for "-ru/-su" pairs such as in the example here, the -su verb will always be the transitive.

COMMON WORDS AND COMPOUNDS		
回る (intr)	*to go around*	**mawa·ru** まわ·る
回す (tr)	*to send around*	**mawa·su** まわ·す
一回	one + rotate = *one time*	**IK·KAI** イッ·カイ
二回	two + rotate = *twice*	**NI·KAI** ニ·カイ
引き 回す	pull + rotate = *to pull around*	hi·ki **mawa·su** ひ·き まわ·す
言い 回し	say + rotate = *(turn of) expression*	i·i **mawa·shi** い·い まわ·し

SAMPLE SENTENCE:

私	は	二回	カナダ	へ
watashi	wa	NI·KAI	Canada	e
I		twice	Canada	

行きました。
i·kimashita.
went.
= *I went to Canada twice.*

COMPONENT #10

BALLET

We'll be using this component to mean anything to do with the world of ballet.

KANJI #10

四 **FOUR**

冂	冂	冊	四			

BUILDING THIS KANJI
Prison □ + Ballet 儿 = 四

Meaning

Four/Quad-, etc. Recall what was noted in Entry 9 regarding the proper stroke order for such characters: the inner part is written after the first two strokes of the prison walls, and enclosed by the final line at the bottom.

Remembering this kanji

Look, I'm not able to say for certain why they threw the **ballet** dancer into **prison**, but I do know one thing: they didn't break him. How could I tell? Well, every afternoon during our exercise period, while the rest of us inmates were either pumping iron or sharpening our shivs, there he'd be, dancing to the FOUR corners of the **prison** walls. We all respected him for it, I suppose; not a single con in those FOUR corners ever laughed at his tights.

Common Pronunciations
Common **ON** reading: **SHI** (シ)
Common **kun** reading: yon (よん); yo (よ)

Do not choose the word "SHE" for your **on-yomi**, as we will be needing it far more for **kun-yomi**, and a word less abstract (try to think of things, places or people) will always be more memorable and make your sentences easier to create. As you can see from the examples below, this character has a tendency to appear in compounds having a mix of **kun-yomi** and **on-yomi**; this makes it a little trickier than the other kanji for numbers.

kun-yomi suggestions: "try only"; "yodel"

Create your **on-yomi** keyword and enter it in the table at the back of the book. After that, write your sentence to remember the **on-yomi** and **kun-yumi** readings in the box below.

Less Common Pronunciations
Less common **ON** reading: none
Less common **kun** reading: yo- (よっ)

This reading is like the less common **kun-yomi** for "three" in that it appears in only two words: 四日 [**yok·ka** (よっ·か)] "the fourth day of the month", and 四つ [**yot·tsu** (よっ·つ)] the general counter for "four". These words are best memorized as is.

COMMON WORDS AND COMPOUNDS		
四	*four*	**SHI** シ
四人	four + person = *four people*	**yo·NIN** よ・ニン
四月	four + moon (month) = *April*	**SHI·GATSU** シ・ガツ
四時	four + time = *four o'clock*	**yo·JI** よ・ジ
四十	four + ten = *forty*	**yon·JŪ** よん・ジュウ
四百	four + hundred = *four hundred*	**yon·HYAKU** よん・ヒャク

SAMPLE SENTENCE:

四月　　に　は　雨　が　多い。

SHI·GATSU ni wa ame ga ō·i.
  April   rain   many.

= *There's a lot of rain in April.*

KANJI #11

 MOON

Meaning
As with the kanji for "sun", this character carries two meanings that are clearly related, in this case "moon" and "month." You will become very familiar with this kanji through its use in the names of the months. This is another visually simple character for which no story is required.

Common Pronunciations
Common **ON** reading: **GETSU** (ゲツ); **GATSU** (ガツ)
Common **kun** reading: **tsuki** (つき)

Like **ITSU** (with the kanji "一") and other readings ending in "-TSU", the two **on-yomi** double up any unvoiced consonant sounds that follow. You will encounter **GATSU** primarily in the names of the months.

kun-yomi suggestion: "bought **Sioux kee**psake

Create your **on-yomi** keyword and enter it in t table at the back of the book. After that, write yo sentence to remember the **on-yomi** and **kun-yo** readings in the box below.

Less Common Pronunciations
Less common **ON** reading: none
Less common **kun** readings: none

COMMON WORDS AND COMPOUNDS		
月	*moon; month*	**tsuki** つき
一月	one + month = *January*	ICHI·**GATSU** イチ・ガツ
二月	two + month = *February*	NI·**GATSU** ニ・ガツ
三月	three + month = *March*	SAN·**GATSU** サン・ガツ
四月	four + month = *April*	SHI·**GATSU** シ・ガツ
先月	precede + month = *last month*	SEN·**GETSU** セン・ゲツ
月見	moon + see = *moon viewing*	**tsuki**·mi つき・み

SAMPLE SENTENCE:

九月　　に　　月見　　に行きました

KU·GATSU ni tsuki·mi ni i·kimashita.
September   moon viewing   went

= *I went moon viewing in September.*

KANJI #12

明   **BRIGHT**

冂	刖	日	日)	朋	明	明

BUILDING THIS KANJI

Sun 日 (6) + Moon 月 (11) = 明

Meaning

Bright/Clear/Light.

Remembering this kanji

"I'm far more BRIGHT than you are," said the moon.

"Really?" answered the sun, smiling. "I find that hard to believe. I'm so BRIGHT people have to wear shades; how many people do you notice wearing moonglasses."

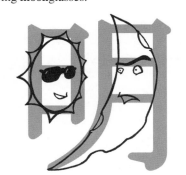

Common Pronunciations

Common **ON** reading: **MEI** (メイ)

Common **kun** reading: **a** (あ); **aka** (あ か)

kun-yomi suggestions: "apt"; "stack a…".

Create your **on-yomi** keyword and enter it in the table at the back of the book. After that, write your sentence to remember the **on-yomi** and **kun-yomi** readings in the box below.

Less Common Pronunciations

Less common **ON** reading: **MYŌ** (ミョウ); **MIN** (ミン)

Less common **kun** reading: **aki** (あ き)

COMMON WORDS AND COMPOUNDS		
明るい	*bright*	**aka**·rui あ か・る い
明かり	*clearness*	**a**·kari あ・か り
明白	bright + white = *obvious*	**MEI**·HAKU メイ・ハク
不明	not + bright = *unclear*	**FU**·**MEI** フ・メイ

SAMPLE SENTENCE:

月　は　明るい　です。

tsuki　wa　aka·rui　desu.
moon　　　bright

= *The moon is bright.*

KANJI #13

木   **TREE**

一	十	才	木		

Meaning

Tree/Wood. No story required.

Common Pronunciations

Common **ON** reading: **MOKU** (モク); **BOKU** (ボク)

Common **kun** reading: **ki** (き)

This is another kanji that will require patience to learn. Look for **MOKU** to show up in the first position, however, and **BOKU** in the second. **ki** occurs less often, but appears with equal frequency in the first or second position.

kun-yomi suggestion: "**keel**" (do not use "key", as this will have far more value as an **on-yomi** keyword).

Create your **on-yomi** keywords and enter them in the table at the back of the book. After that, write your sentence to remember the **on-yomi** and **kun-yomi** readings in the box below.

Less Common Pronunciations
Less common **ON** reading: none
Less common **kun** readings: **ko** (こ)

Here is a common irregular reading you will often see on clothing tags, etc. The second kanji, incidentally, is not covered in this book.

Such characters will be included only when they form common words in which the pronun-

ciation of the character we are considering has irregular reading. Irregular readings contain these kanji will be identified with an asterisk (

IRREGULAR READINGS		
木綿 *	tree + cotton = *cotton (cloth)*	mo·MEN も・メン

COMMON WORDS AND COMPOUNDS		
木	*tree*	ki き
木曜日	tree + day of the week + sun (day) = *Thursday*	MOKU·YŌ·bi モク・ヨウ・て
木星	tree + star = *Jupiter (planet)*	MOKU·SEI モク・セイ
大木	large + tree = *large tree*	TAI·BOKU タイ・ボク
土木	earth + tree = *civil engineering*	DO·BOKU ド・ボク

SAMPLE SENTENCE:

ano   taka·i   ki   no   na·mae   ga   wa·karimas
that   tall   tree   name   understand
か。
ka.
= *Do you know the name of that tall tree?*

KANJI #14

   FIVE

一	丁	五	五				

Meaning
Five.

Remembering this kanji
This is how most people feel when their wor day ends at FIVE o'clock.

Common Pronunciations
Common **ON** reading: **GO** (ゴ)
Common **kun** reading: none

Create your **on-yomi** keyword and enter it in the table at the back of the book. After that, write your sentence to remember the **on-yomi** reading in the box below.

COMMON WORDS AND COMPOUNDS		
五	*five*	**GO** ゴ
五人	five + person = *five people*	**GO·NIN** ゴ・ニン
五月	five + moon (month) = *May*	**GO·GATSU** ゴ・ガツ
五十	five + ten = *fifty*	**GO·JŪ** ゴ・ジュウ
五時	five + time = *five o'clock*	**GO·JI** ゴ・ジ

Less Common Pronunciations
Less common **ON** reading: none
Less common **kun** reading: **itsu** (いつ)

As you might expect, this reading is of most use because of its appearance in two words: 五日 [**itsu·ka** (いつ・か)] "the fifth day of the month," and 五つ [**itsu·tsu** (いつ・つ)] the general counter for "five."

SAMPLE SENTENCE:

五十人 で 山 へ 行きました。
GO·JŪ·NIN de yama e i·kimashita.
fifty people   mountain   went

= *Fifty (of us) went to the mountain.*

KANJI #15

目 **EYE**

〡 冂 冃 冃 目

Meaning
The general meaning is eye. An important secondary usage of the character, however, can be seen when it comes at the end of a number compound such as in the third example below. In these instances it is read with its **kun-yomi** and indicates the "-th" suffix in words such as "fourth" and "seventh" (it also expresses the related endings of "first", "second" and "third" in such compounds).

Remembering this kanji
In the interests of full disclosure, it should be said that the Cyclops lobbied long and hard to be this book's representative for "EYE". Well, it looks like his efforts—which included a few thoughtfully chosen gifts—have paid off. Cyclops, you have been placed on an equal footing with Dracula!

Common Pronunciations
Common **ON** reading: **MOKU** (モク)
Common **kun** reading: **me** (め)

me is the more common of the two readings. Remember to use the keyword for **MOKU** that you entered into the **on-yomi** table earlier (from the kanji "木", Entry 13).

kun-yomi suggestion: "**metric**"

Write your sentence to remember the **on-yomi** and **kun-yomi** readings in the box below.

COMMON WORDS AND COMPOUNDS

目	*eye*	**me** め
目玉	eye + jewel = *eyeball*	**me**·dama め·だ ま
八回目	eight + rotate + eye = *the eighth time*	HACHI·KAI·**me** ハ チ·カ イ·め
目立つ	eye + stand = *to stand out*	**me** da·tsu め だ·つ
注目	pour + eye = *notice*	CHŪ·**MOKU** チュウ·モク

Less Common Pronunciations
Less common **ON** reading: **BOKU** (ボ ク)
Less common **kun** reading: **ma** (ま)

SAMPLE SENTENCE:

王子　の　目　は　青い　です。
Ō·JI　no　me　wa　ao·i　desu.
prince　　　eye　　blue
= *The prince's eyes are blue.*

KANJI #16

女　**WOMAN**

Meaning
Woman/Female. No story required.

Common Pronunciations
Common **ON** reading: **JO** (ジ ョ)
Common **kun** reading: **onna** (お ん な)

kun-yomi suggestion: "**own NASA**"

Create your **on-yomi** keyword and enter it in the table at the back of the book. After that, write your

sentence to remember the **on-yomi** and **kun-yom[i]** readings in the box below.

Less Common Pronunciations
Less common **ON** reading: **NYO** (ニ ョ);
NYŌ (ニ ョ ウ)
Less common **kun** reading: **me** (め)

COMMON WORDS AND COMPOUNDS

女	woman	**onna** お ん な
女王	woman + king = *queen*	**JO·Ō** ジ ョ·オ ウ
少女	few + woman = *girl*	**SHŌ·JO** ショ ウ·ジ ョ
女心	woman + heart = *a woman's heart*	**onna**·gokoro お ん な·ご こ ろ
雪女	snow + woman = *snow fairy*	yuki·**onna** ゆ き·お ん な
男女	man + woman = *men and women*	**DAN·JO** ダ ン·ジ ョ

女	の	人	は	木	の	下	で
onna	no	hito	wa	ki	no	shita	de
woman		person		tree		under	

止まりました。
to·marimashita.
　　stopped
= *The woman stopped under a tree.*

KANJI #17

LARGE

一 ナ 大

Meaning
Large/Big. The meanings of "important" and "great (not always in a positive sense)" can also be implied in words containing this kanji.

Remembering this kanji
Not many things are LARGER than a sumo wrestler, so we'll use this image as our connection to the character from now on.

Common Pronunciations
Common **ON** reading: **DAI** (ダイ); **TAI** (タイ)
Common **kun** reading: **ō** (おお)

As **DAI** and **TAI** occur with equal frequency (ō much less often) when this kanji appears in the first position, this character presents a special challenge for students of Japanese. When it occupies other positions in a compound, however, **DAI** is far and away the more common reading.

kun-yomi suggestion: "oboe"

Create your **on-yomi** keywords and enter them in the table at the back of the book. After that, write your sentence to remember the **on-yomi** and **kun-yomi** readings in the box below.

Less Common Pronunciations
Less common **ON** reading: none
Less common **kun** reading: none

Here is the irregular reading we met earlier in Entry 2.

IRREGULAR READINGS		
大人	large + person = *adult*	**otona** おとな

COMMON WORDS AND COMPOUNDS		
大きい	*large*	**ō·kii** おお・きい
大木	large + tree = *large tree*	**TAI·BOKU** タイ・ボク
大好き	large + like = *to really like*	**DAI** su·ki ダイ す・き
大体	large + body = *in general*	**DAI·TAI** ダイ・タイ
大雨	large + rain = *heavy rain*	**ō·ame** おお・あめ
大切	large + cut = *important*	**TAI·SETSU** タイ・セツ
大学	large + study = *university*	**DAI·GAKU** ダイ・ガク

SAMPLE SENTENCE:

あの	森	に	は	大木	が	多い。
ano	**mori**	**ni**	**wa**	**TAI·BOKU**	**ga**	**ō·i.**
that	forest			large trees		many

= *There are many large trees in that forest.*

COMPONENT #18

POLE | 

KANJI #18

中 MIDDLE

丶	冂	口	中					

BUILDING THIS KANJI
Mouth (vampire) 口 (8) + **Pole** | = 中

Meaning
A versatile character that expresses the ideas of "middle", "medium", and "average", etc. This kanji can also serve as an abbreviation for China; " 日 " is used as the equivalent with respect to Japan.

Remembering this kanji
I approached the sleeping **vampire** with the **pole** shaking in my hands: it was now or never. Raising the weapon over his feet I prepared to bring it down, but at the last moment the master's words came back: "How many times must we go over this? Drive it through the MIDDLE of the **vampire**! The MIDDLE!" Yes, I thought, placing the **pole** over the **vampire's** stomach, it would all go perfectly now.

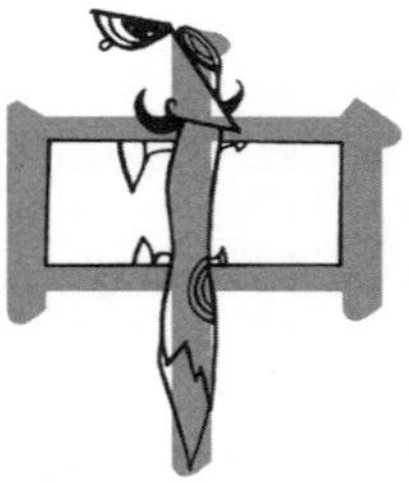

Common Pronunciations
Common **ON** reading: **CHŪ** (チュウ)
Common **kun** reading: **naka** (なか)

kun-yomi suggestion: **"knack 'a"**

Create your **on-yomi** keyword and enter it in t table at the back of the book. After that, write yo sentence to remember the **on-yomi** and **kun-yo** readings in the box below.

Less Common Pronunciations
Less common **ON** reading: **JŪ** (ジュウ)
Less common **kun** reading: none

COMMON WORDS AND COMPOUNDS		
中	*middle*	**naka** なか
中心	middle + heart = *center*	**CHŪ·SHIN** チュウ·シ
中米	middle + rice (America) = *Central America*	**CHŪ·BEI** チュウ·ベ
中国	middle + country = *China*	**CHŪ·GOKU** チュウ·ゴ
中立	middle + stand = *neutrality*	**CHŪ·RITSU** チュウ·リ
中古	middle + old = *secondhand*	**CHŪ·KO** チュウ·コ
水中	water + middle = *underwater/in the water*	**SUI·CHŪ** スイ·チュ

SAMPLE SENTENCE:
車 の 中 に なにが ありますか
kuruma no naka ni nani ga arimasu k
car middle what is
= *What is in your car?*

EIGHT

ノ	八						

Meaning
Eight.

Remembering this kanji
This is another kanji in the manner of "one" and "mouth" for which it is useful to assign an external meaning, in this case, a volcano: *"I can't be sure, but I think the Krakatoa volcano (which erupted in the 1880's) was one of the* EIGHT *wonders of the ancient world."*

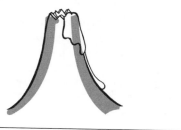

Common Pronunciations
Common **ON** reading: **HACHI** (ハチ)
Common **kun** reading: none

Create your **on-yomi** keyword and enter it in the table at the back of the book. After that, write your sentence to remember the **on-yomi** reading in the box below.

Less Common Pronunciations
Less common **ON** reading: none
Less common **kun** reading: **yō** (よう); **ya-** (や つ); **ya** (や)

Interestingly, the first two **kun-yomi** readings are like the less common **kun-yomi** for "three" and "four" (Entries 5 and 10, respectively), and are found in only one word each: 八日 [**yō·ka** (よう·か)] "the eighth day of the month," and 八つ [**yat·tsu** (やっ·つ)] the general counter for "eight."

COMMON WORDS AND COMPOUNDS		
八	*eight*	**HACHI** ハチ
八月	eight + moon (month) = *August*	**HACHI·GATSU** ハチ·ガツ
八人	eight + person = *eight people*	**HACHI·NIN** ハチ·ニン
八円	eight + circle (yen) = *eight yen*	**HACHI·EN** ハチ·エン
八時	eight + time = *eight o'clock*	**HACHI·JI** ハチ·ジ

SAMPLE SENTENCE:

八月　　に　秋田　へ　行きましょう。
HACHI·GATSU ni Aki·ta e　　i·kimashō.
　August　　　Akita　　　let's go
= *Let's go to Akita in August.*

COMPONENT #20

HARPOON 亅 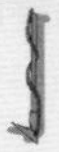

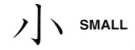

Note how the barbed hook on the bottom of this component distinguishes it from the pole (Component 18).

KANJI #20

小 SMALL

亅	𠃌	小						

BUILDING THIS KANJI
Harpoon 亅 + **Eight (volcano)** 八(19) = 小

Meaning
Small/Little.

Remembering this kanji
The dwarf spoke, his words SMALL comfort: "If you be going after the miniature lava whale," he said, "you'd best toss your **harpoon** in that **volcano** over yonder. Your chances of landing him are SMALL, though, given that he's so… SMALL."

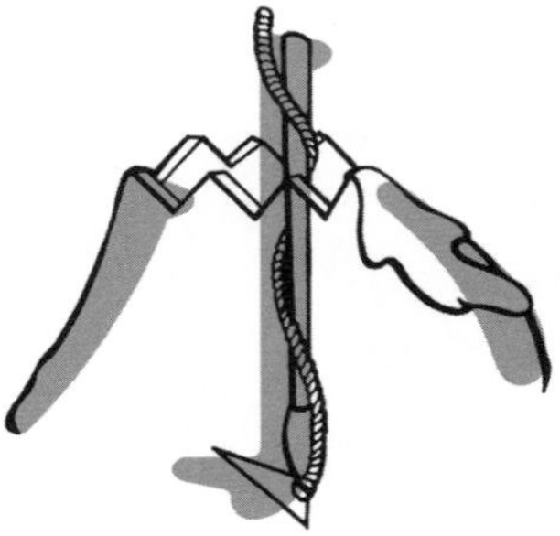

Common Pronunciations
Common **ON** reading: **SHŌ** (ショウ)
Common **kun** reading: **chii** (ちい); **ko** (こ)

SHŌ and **ko** are the readings most often foun in compounds, **chii** only being used in the firs example below.

kun-yomi suggestions: "**chee**eese!"; "**co**at"

Create your **on-yomi** keyword and enter it in th table at the back of the book. After that, write you sentence to remember the **on-yomi** and **kun-yom** readings in the box below.

Less Common Pronunciations
Less common **ON** reading: none
Less common **kun** reading: **o** (お)

COMMON WORDS AND COMPOUNDS		
小さい	*small*	**chii**·sai ちい·さい
小春	small + spring = *Indian summer*	**ko**·haru こ·はる
小国	small + country = *small country*	**SHŌ**·**KOKU** ショウ·コク
小高い	small + tall = *slightly elevated*	**ko** daka·i こ だか·い
最小	most + small = *smallest*	**SAI**·**SHŌ** サイ·ショウ

SAMPLE SENTENCE:
あの 車 はとても小さい です ね。
ano kuruma wa totemo chii·sai desu ne.
that car really small isn't it
= *That car is really small, isn't it?*

CHAPTER 1 REVIEW EXERCISES

A. Please match the following kanji to their meanings.

1. 人
2. 女
3. 月
4. 木
5. 大
6. 二
7. 回
8. 小
9. 三
10. 口

a. Rotate
b. Large
c. Woman
d. Mouth
e. Person
f. Two
g. Moon
h. Three
i. Tree
j. Small

B. Please match the following meanings to their kanji, and these to their **on** or **kun-yomi**.

1. Bright
2. Five
3. White
4. Four
5. Eye
6. Middle
7. Mountain
8. One
9. Eight
10. Sun

a. 白
b. 目
c. 山
d. 八
e. 日
f. 一
g. 明
h. 中
i. 四
j. 五

1. **yama** (やま)
2. **ICHI** (イチ)
3. **me** (め)
4. **hi** (ひ)
5. **GO** (ゴ)
6. **HACHI** (ハチ)
7. **SHI** (シ)
8. **aka** (あか)
9. **naka** (なか)
10. **HAKU** (ハク)

C. Please choose the best answer(s) to the following questions.

1. Which of the following readings apply to the kanji 人?
   a. **Ō** (オウ)
   b. **hito** (ひと)
   c. **NIN** (ニン)
   d. **JIN** (ジン)
   e. **hi** (ひ)

2. Where is the most appropriate place to go in a spaceship?
   a. 人
   b. 目
   c. 月
   d. 口
   e. 木

3. Which of the following readings apply to the kanji 女?
   a. **ZEN** (ゼン)
   b. **SHUN** (シュン)
   c. **uchi** (うち)
   d. **JO** (ジョ)
   e. **onna** (おんな)

4. Which of the following readings apply to the kanji 口?
   a. **KŌ** (コウ)
   b. **haru** (はる)
   c. **SHI** (シ)
   d. **kuchi** (くち)
   e. **Ō** (オウ)

5. Which of the following readings apply to the kanji 日?
   a. **hi** (ひ)
   b. **to** (と)
   c. **KOKU** (コク)
   d. **JITSU** (ジツ)
   e. **NICHI** (ニチ)

D. Please answer the following questions.

1. Which is the correct reading of 回る?
   a. **mi·ru** (み・る)
   b. **sube·ru** (すべ・る)
   c. **haka·ru** (はか・る)
   d. **mawa·ru** (まわ・る)

2. What is the reading for 一日 when it indicates the first day of a month?
   a. **tama** (たま)
   b. **kuni** (くに)
   c. **uchi** (うち)
   d. **kuchi** (くち)
   e. **tsuitachi** (ついたち)

3. Given that **hitori** (ひとり) is the reading for 一人, what is the reading for 二人?
   a. **hatsuka** (はつか)
   b. **futari** (ふたり)
   c. **hatachi** (はたち)
   d. **futsuka** (ふつか)

4. Which of the following does not belong with the others?
   a. 一
   b. 八
   c. 四
   d. 小
   e. 三

5. Which is the correct reading of 白い?
   a. **furu·i** (ふ る·い)
   b. **shiro·i** (し ろ·い)
   c. **maru·i** (ま る·い)
   d. **hiro·i** (ひ ろ·い)

E. Please match the following compound and words to their meanings and pronunciations.

1. 三月	a. Twice	1. **hito·tsu** (ひ と·つ)	
2. 白人	b. Obvious	2. **JIN·KŌ** (ジン·コウ	
3. 二回	c. White	3. **shiro·i** (し ろ·い)	
4. 小さい	d. Five people	4. **SAN·GATSU** (サ ン·ガ ツ	
5. 明白	e. Small	5. **chii·sai** (ち い·さ い	
6. 人口	f. March	6. **NI·KAI** (ニ·カ イ)	
7. 一つ	g. Large tree	7. **GO·NIN** (ゴ·ニ ン)	
8. 五人	h. One	8. **TAI·BOKU** (タ イ·ボ ク	
9. 白い	i. Population	9. **HAKU·JIN** (ハ ク·ジ ン	
10. 大木	j. Caucasian	10. **MEI·HAKU** (メ イ·ハ ク	

Kanji #21—40

KANJI #21

貝 **SHELLFISH**

| 丨 | 冂 | 冂 | 目 | 目 | 貝 | 貝 | |

BUILDING THIS KANJI
Eye (Cyclops) 目 (15) + Eight (volcano) 八 (19) = 貝

Meaning

Shellfish/Seashell. As the lack of common words and compounds in the table indicates, this is not the most useful character to learn for its own sake. It often appears as a component in other kanji, however, and for this reason needs to be learned here.

Remembering this kanji

Celebrating his inclusion in this book, the **Cyclops** decided to throw an enormous SHELL-FISH barbecue for all his friends. Minotaurs, griffins, nymphs and satyrs…even the sirens showed up (after agreeing to refrain from singing, of course). It was quite a crowd, but the grill the **Cyclops** stretched over a nearby **volcano** was more than enough to accommodate the food. And what a variety of SHELLFISH there was! Oysters, mussels, abalone, scallops…everyone agreed it was the best spread since Zeus' clambake on Mt. Etna.

Common Pronunciations

Common **ON** reading: none
Common **kun** reading: **kai** (かい)

This character is always unvoiced (**kai**) in the first position, and becomes voiced (**gai**) elsewhere.
    kun-yomi suggestion: "**Kai**ser roll". If you are choosing your own keywords for the **kun-yomi**, do not use the same word you selected for **KAI** (カイ), the **on-yomi** for "回" in Entry 9; it is best to keep the two types of readings separate. Create your sentence to remember the **kun-yomi** reading in the box below.

| |
| |

Less Common Pronunciations

Less common **ON** reading: **BAI** (バイ)
Less common **kun** reading: none

COMMON WORDS AND COMPOUNDS		
貝	*shellfish*	**kai** かい
生貝	life + shellfish = *raw shellfish*	nama·**gai** なま・がい
赤貝	red + shellfish = *ark shell*	aka·**gai** あか・がい

SAMPLE SENTENCE:

この レストラン の 赤貝 は 有名
kono resutoran no aka·gai wa YŪ·MEI
this restaurant   ark shell   famous
です。
desu.
is
= *The ark shell in this restaurant is famous.*

COMPONENT #22

POLICE

Our hat will symbolize the police, or any other authority from sheriffs to park rangers.

KANJI #22

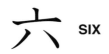 **SIX**

BUILDING THIS KANJI
Police 亠 + Eight (volcano) 八 (19) = 六

Meaning
Six.

Remembering this kanji
Something tells me that if you throw a police hat into a volcano, it will burn. Don't ask me how I know this; it's my SIXTH sense.

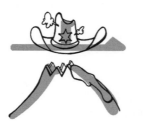

Common Pronunciations
Common **ON** reading: **ROKU** (ロ ク)
Common **kun** reading: none

Create your **on-yomi** keyword and enter it in the table at the back of the book. After that, write your sentence to remember the **on-yomi** reading in the box below.

Less Common Pronunciations
Less common **ON** reading: **RIKU** (リ ク)
Less common **kun** reading: **mui** (む い); **mu-**
(む っ); **mu** (む)

You may have guessed that these first two **kun-yomi** are found in only one word each: 六日 [**mui·ka** (む い・か)] "the sixth day of the month," and 六つ [**mut·tsu** (む っ・つ)] the general counter for "six."

COMMON WORDS AND COMPOUNDS		
六	*six*	**ROKU** ロ ク
六人	six + person = *six people*	**ROKU·NIN** ロ ク・ニ ン
六月	six + moon (month) = *June*	**ROKU·GATSU** ロ ク・ガ ツ
六円	six + circle (yen) = *six yen*	**ROKU·EN** ロ ク・エ ン
六時	six + time = *six o'clock*	**ROKU·JI** ロ ク・ジ

SAMPLE SENTENCE:

六人　 は 　日本　 へ 行きました。
ROKU·NIN wa NI·HON e   i·kimashita.
  six people   Japan   went
= *The six people went to Japan.*

KANJI #23

王　KING

Meaning
Crowns, scepters, long purple robes…think of kings and royalty when you see this kanji. No story required.

Common Pronunciations
Common **ON** reading: Ō（オウ）
Common **kun** reading: none

Only one reading to deal with here — wouldn't it be nice if all the kanji were this well-behaved? Create your **on-yomi** keyword and enter it in the table at the back of the book. After that, write your sentence to remember the **on-yomi** reading in the box below.

Less Common Pronunciations
Less common **ON** reading: none
Less common **kun** reading: none

COMMON WORDS AND COMPOUNDS		
女王	woman + king = *queen*	JO·Ō ジョ・オウ
王国	king + country = *kingdom*	Ō·KOKU オウ・コク
王朝	king + morning = *dynasty*	Ō·CHŌ オウ・チョウ
王子	king + child = *prince*	Ō·JI オウ・ジ
海王星	sea + king + star = *Neptune (planet)*	KAI·Ō·SEI カイ・オウ・セイ

SAMPLE SENTENCE:

女王 が 日本 へ 行きました。
JO·Ō ga NIHON e i·kimashita.
Queen　　Japan　　　　went.
= *The queen went to Japan.*

KANJI #24

玉　JEWEL

BUILDING THIS KANJI
King 王(23) + Jelly Bean ヽ = 玉

Meaning
This character appears in the names of a variety of precious stones, including the compounds for rubies, sapphires, and emeralds. It also incorporates the sense of a "ball-like" object, a meaning evident in the final examples below.

Take note of the correct stroke order for this kanji ("King" + "Jelly bean"); the three horizontal lines are **not** written first.

Remembering this kanji
"I wish to reward you for your faithful service," the **king** said to his minister. "There is a **jelly bean** for you at my feet; you may take it if you wish." The man was a little confused by this, of course, until he bent down and saw a JEWEL shaped like a **jelly bean** next to the **king's** shoes. "You might not want to eat that," smiled the **king**. "After all, JEWELS aren't particularly tasty."

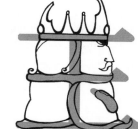

Common Pronunciations

Common **ON** reading: none
Common **kun** reading: **tama** (た ま)

Note how often this character changes from the voiceless "**tama**" (た ま) to its corresponding voiced form "**dama**" (だ ま) when in the second position.

kun-yomi suggestion: "hot **tama**le"

Create your sentence to remember the **kun-yomi** reading in the box below.

COMMON WORDS AND COMPOUNDS		
玉	*jewel*	**tama** た ま
玉ねぎ	*onion*	**tama·negi** た ま·ね ぎ
目玉	eye + jewel = *eyeball*	me·**dama** め·だ ま
水玉	water + jewel = *drop of water*	mizu·**tama** み ず·た ま
火玉	fire + jewel = *fireball*	hi·**dama** ひ·だ ま
雪玉	snow + jewel = *snowball*	yuki·**dama** ゆ き·だ ま

SAMPLE SENTENCE:
玉ねぎ を 切って 下さい。
tama·negi o   ki·tte   kuda·sai.
onion(s)   cut   please
= *Please cut the onions.*

Less Common Pronunciations

Less common **ON** reading: **GYOKU** (ギ ョ ク)
Less common **kun** reading: none

HOOK

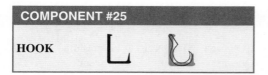 **HEART**

BUILDING THIS KANJI
Jelly Bean ＼ + Hook ∟ + Jelly Bean ＼ +
Jelly Bean ＼ = 心

Meaning

This unique-looking character conveys the idea of heart in all its shades of meaning, be it the actual physical organ, the sense of "feelings," or the concept of something's "core."

Remembering this kanji

There are a couple of ways to capture a HEART. The first is by using kindness; giving gifts such as a trio of **jelly beans** is an example of this method. The second is to simply use a **hook**.

Common Pronunciations

Common **ON** reading: **SHIN** (シ ン)
Common **kun** reading: **kokoro** (こ こ ろ)

The **kun-yomi** for this kanji always becomes voiced (**gokoro**) when not in the first position (as in the second and fourth examples).

kun-yomi suggestion: "**cocoa ro**ast"

Create your **on-yomi** keyword and enter it in the table at the back of the book. After that, write your sentence to remember the **on-yomi** and **kun-yomi** readings in the box below.

Less Common Pronunciations
Less common **ON** reading: none
Less common **kun** reading: none

Here is a common irregular reading containing this character, composed of both **kun** and **on-yomi**.

IRREGULAR READINGS		
心地	heart + ground = *feeling*	**koko·CHI** ここ・チ

COMMON WORDS AND COMPOUNDS		
心	*heart*	**kokoro** こころ
女心	woman + heart = *a woman's heart*	**onna·gokoro** おんな・ごころ
中心	middle + heart = *center*	**CHŪ·SHIN** チュウ・シン
下心	lower + heart = *ulterior motive*	**shita·gokoro** した・ごころ
安心	ease + heart = *peace of mind*	**AN·SHIN** アン・シン
愛国心	love + country + heart = *patriotism*	**AI·KOKU·SHIN** アイ・コク・シン

SAMPLE SENTENCE:

女王　　　　によると　　　愛国心　　　　は
JO·Ō　　**ni yoru to**　**AI·KOKU·SHIN**　**wa**
queen　　　according to　　patriotism
大切　　　だ　そう　です。
TAI·SETSU da　sō　desu.
important
= *According to the queen, patriotism is important.*

KANJI #26

国 **COUNTRY**

BUILDING THIS KANJI
Prison □ + Jewel 玉(24) = 国

Meaning
Think of "country" here in the sense of a nation state.

Remembering this kanji
Most folks will state that their COUNTRY is like a **jewel**, one that must be protected from external dangers. And so they build walls. But is there a difference between being protected and being in **prison**? It's a thorny question, but perhaps the philosopher Epicurus answered it best: "There may be a **jewel** of a COUNTRY within **prison** walls somewhere, but I'd be willing to bet they'd have lousy food."

Common Pronunciations
Common **ON** reading: **KOKU** (コク)
Common **kun** reading: **kuni** (くに)

kun-yomi suggestion: "ty**coon** **e**ra"

Create your **on-yomi** keyword and enter it in the table at the back of the book. After that, write your sentence to remember the **on-yomi** and **kun-yomi** readings in the box below.

COMMON WORDS AND COMPOUNDS		
国	*country*	**kuni** くに
王国	king + country = *kingdom*	**Ō·KOKU** オウ·コク
全国	complete + country = *the whole country/ nationwide*	**ZEN·KOKU** ゼン·コク
入国	enter + country = *to enter a country*	**NYŪ·KOKU** ニュウ·コク
国内	country + inside = *domestic*	**KOKU·NAI** コク·ナイ
外国人	outside + country + person = *foreigner*	**GAI·KOKU·JIN** ガイ·コク·ジン
愛国心	love + country + heart = *patriotism*	**AI·KOKU· SHIN** アイ·コク·シン

Less Common Pronunciations
Less common **ON** reading: none
Less common **kun** reading: none

SAMPLE SENTENCE:

あの 国 には 外国人 が 多い。
ano kuni ni wa GAI·KOKU·JIN ga ō·i.
that country foreigners many
= *There are many foreigners in that country.*

COMPONENT #27

UMBRELLA

KANJI #27

全 **COMPLETE**

ノ	人	𠆢	仐	仐	全		

BUILDING THIS KANJI
Umbrella 𠆢 + King 王(23) = 全

Meaning
This kanji expresses the idea of wholeness and completion. Note in the sample compounds how both the first and third entries can have different connotations. Although the context will usually make the meaning clear, such ambiguity is a common feature of Japanese.

Remembering this kanji
"You might imagine that the **king's umbrella** bearer has a job that even a COMPLETE idiot could do. Well, you're wrong, because you'd better not let the **king** get wet. Sadly, I learned this the hard way, for one afternoon the **umbrella** I chose had a hole, and a drop of moisture sprinkled the **king's** robe. That was enough to leave me dangling in the dungeon for a week. A tyrant **king**, you say? Perhaps, but the lesson I learned that day has remained with me forever: the **umbrella** must COMPLETELY cover the **king**."

Common Pronunciations
Common **ON** reading: **ZEN** (ゼン)
Common **kun** reading: none

iven that "Zen" (as in Buddhism) is one of the ew Japanese words to have entered the English nguage, feel free to take advantage of this y using it to remember this reading. For the entence, then, you might employ some Zen-like implicity: "Complete ZEN".

Create your **on-yomi** keyword and enter it in ie table at the back of the book. After that, write our sentence to remember the **on-yomi** reading a the box below.

COMMON WORDS AND COMPOUNDS		
全国	complete + country = *the whole country/ nationwide*	**ZEN·KOKU** ゼン・コク
安全	ease + complete = *safety*	**AN·ZEN** アン・ゼン
全校	complete + school = *the whole school/ all schools*	**ZEN·KŌ** ゼン・コウ
全力	complete + strength = *all one's power*	**ZEN·RYOKU** ゼン・リョク
全体	complete + body = *the whole*	**ZEN·TAI** ゼン・タイ
全部	complete + part = *all*	**ZEN·BU** ゼン・ブ

SAMPLE SENTENCE:

田中さん は　　全国　　を　回る。
Ta·naka-san wa　ZEN·KOKU　o　mawa·ru.
Tanaka-san　　　whole country　　go around
= *Tanaka-san is going around the whole country.*

ess Common Pronunciations
ess common **ON** reading: none
ess common **kun** reading: **matta** (まった); natto (まっと)

KANJI #28

十

TEN

一	十								

Meaning
Ten. The first two examples of Entry 176 show another use for this character, an interesting application based entirely on its shape.

Remembering this kanji
This is another simple character for which we will assign an external meaning: scarecrow. In case you're wondering why this particular scarecrow was chosen, the answer is simple: he was rated a perfect TEN in terms of style and poise.

Common Pronunciations
Common **ON** reading: **JŪ** (ジュウ)
Common **kun** reading: none

Say hello to the first character for which you should know all the compounds in the main table below. You've already come a long way!

Create your **on-yomi** keyword and enter it in the table at the back of the book. After that, write your sentence to remember the **on-yomi** reading in the box below.

Less Common Pronunciations
Less common **ON** reading: **JITSU** (ジツ)
Less common **kun** reading: **tō** (とお); **to** (と)

tō appears with only one word, 十日 [**tō·ka** (とお·か)] "the tenth day of the month".

Two common irregular readings, found earlier with the kanji 二.

IRREGULAR READINGS		
二十日	two + ten + sun (day) = *twentieth day of the month*	**hatsuka** はつか
二十歳	two + ten + annual = *twenty years old*	**hatachi** はたち

COMMON WORDS AND COMPOUNDS		
十	*ten*	**JŪ** ジュウ
十月	ten + moon (month) = *October*	**JŪ·GATSU** ジュウ·ガツ
十一月	ten + one + moon (month) = *November*	**JŪ·ICHI·GATSU** ジュウ·イチ·ガツ
十二月	ten + two + moon (month) = *December*	**JŪ·NI·GATSU** ジュウ·ニ·ガツ
十六	ten + six = *sixteen*	**JŪ·ROKU** ジュウ·ロク
十八	ten + eight = *eighteen*	**JŪ·HACHI** ジュウ·ハチ

SAMPLE SENTENCE:

十月　に は あ の 木 は 　美しく
JŪ·GATSU ni wa ano ki wa utsuku·shik
October　　　　　　that tree　　　beautiful
なります。
narimasu.
becomes
= *That tree becomes beautiful in October.*

KANJI #29

早 **EARLY**

BUILDING THIS KANJI
Sun 日 (6) + Ten (scarecrow) 十 (28) = 早

Meaning
Early/Fast. It is important to remember that this kanji expresses both of these ideas.

Remembering this kanji
There isn't much a **scarecrow** can do for exercise, but ours is determined to stay in shape. How so? Well, EARLY each day, once the **sun** is up, he'll launch into a vigorous routine of finger stretches, toe curls, and head rolls. As it's too hot to do this later on, it's fortunate he's an EARLY riser.

Common Pronunciations
Common **ON** reading: **SŌ** (ソウ)
Common **kun** reading: **haya** (はや)

Note the intransitive/transitive verb pair in th table.

kun-yomi suggestion: "hi ya!"

Create your **on-yomi** keyword and enter it in th table at the back of the book. After that, write you sentence to remember the **on-yomi** and **kun-yom** readings in the box below.

Less Common Pronunciations
Less common **ON** reading: **SATSU** (サツ)
Less common **kun** reading: none

COMMON WORDS AND COMPOUNDS

早い	early; fast	**haya**·i は や·い
早まる (intr)	to be in a hurry	**haya**·maru は や·ま る
早める (tr)	to hurry (something)	**haya**·meru は や·め る
早口	early (fast) + mouth = *rapid speaking*	**haya**·kuchi は や·く ち
早春	early + spring = *early spring*	**SŌ**·SHUN ソ ウ·シ ュ ン
早朝	early + morning = *early morning*	**SŌ**·CHŌ ソ ウ·チ ョ ウ

SAMPLE SENTENCE:

どうして そんな に　早く　来た の
dōshite　sonna　ni　haya·ku　ki·ta　no
why　　　so　　　　　early　come
です か。
desu　ka.
= *Why did you come so early?*

GOOD FIGURE SKATER

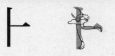

A good figure skater always keeps her leg straight in this position.

KANJI #30

上　　**UPPER**

丨	上	上						

BUILDING THIS KANJI
Good Figure Skater ├ + One (bottom of a bun)
一 (3) = 上

Meaning
This simple-looking character expresses a broad range of ideas relating to the words "upper", "on", and "over", among others; it can refer to anything from goods of high quality to superiors at work. It's a fascinating kanji that is widely used, and one that rewards patient study.

Remembering this kanji
Look at the beautiful posture, with the outstretched leg held perfectly straight; this is a **good figure skater** with complete confidence in her abilities, skating as if the ice were the **bottom of a bun** that would not hurt her if she fell. This is clearly an UPPER-class athlete.

Common Pronunciations
Common **ON** reading: **JŌ** (ジ ョ ウ)
Common **kun** reading: **kami** (か み); **ue** (う え); **nobo** (の ぼ); **a** (あ); **uwa** (う わ)

Take a deep breath, as this kanji contains the second largest number of common readings for any character you will encounter in Japanese (you won't have long to wait for the one with the most!). The **on-yomi JŌ**, however, is by far the most frequently used, and the **kun-yomi** readings will often appear with **hiragana** accompaniment (which will offer a clue as to which pronunciation should be used for the kanji).

The verb **a·geru** (あ·げ る) in example 5 below, incidentally, is almost always used in a transitive sense (that is, it "lifts" some object in either a physical or symbolic way), and is best thought of as being paired with the intransitive **a·garu** (あ·がる).

Before proceeding with your sentence, it is useful now to consider one of the most important benefits of the **on-yomi** table: because you will have chosen different keywords for each of the readings, there will be no danger of confusing pronunciations differing only in their use of a "long" versus "short" vowel sound. We encounter the first example of this here, with **JŌ** sounding much like **JO** (the **on-yomi** for "女" in Entry 16), but needing to be memorized as a separate reading.

kun-yomi suggestions: "make a meal;" "true age;" "no bones;" "anaconda;" "new wok"

Create your **on-yomi** keyword and enter it in the table at the back of the book. After that, write your sentence to remember the **on-yomi** and **kun-yomi** readings in the box below.

Less Common Pronunciations
Less common **ON** reading: **SHŌ** (ショウ)
Less common **kun** reading: none

COMMON WORDS AND COMPOUNDS		
上	*upper*	**kami** かみ
上	*over; on*	**ue** うえ
上る (intr)	*to climb*	**nobo·ru** のぼ·る
上がる (intr)	*to rise*	**a·garu** あ·がる
上げる (tr/intr)	*to lift*	**a·geru** あ·げる
上手	*upper + hand = skillful*	**JŌ·ZU** ジョウ·ズ

SAMPLE SENTENCE:

肉 は テーブル の 上 に あります。
NIKU wa TĒBURU no ue ni   arimasu.
meat   table   on   is
= *The meat is on the table.*

POOR FIGURE SKATER   ト

A poor figure skater lets her leg droop in this position.

下   **LOWER**

一	丁	下					

BUILDING THIS KANJI
One (top of a bun) 一(3) + **Poor Figure Skater** ト
= 下

Meaning
This obvious partner to the preceding kanji expresses a similarly wide range of ideas, with words in this case relating to the notions of "lower", "under", and "below".

Remembering this kanji
No doubt about it: figure skating crowds are tough, and will not tolerate LOWER-class skaters. In one competition, all it took was a **poor figure skater**'s drooping leg to make the audience hurl the **tops of their buns** at her in disgust.

Common Pronunciations

Common **ON** reading: **KA** (カ); **GE** (ゲ)
Common **kun** reading: **shita** (した); **shimo** (しも); **o** (お); **sa** (さ); **kuda** (くだ)

Here it is: the kanji with the most common readings of all. Although it can be a bit of work trying to come to grips with this character's many angles, keep in mind that the final three **kun-yomi** above are all verb stems, and will thus be accompanied by **hiragana** hinting at the correct pronunciation. When it comes to the readings used for compounds, **KA** or **GE** will be encountered far more than the others, although there are no easily discernible patterns as to when each of these is used.

This kanji illustrates well the difference between intransitive/transitive verb pairs. Refer back to "早" and "上" (Entries 29 and 30). Notice similarity between the verbs presented there and examples four and five shown here.

Suggestions for **kun-yomi**: "**she** tackled"; "**she** loped"; "**o**rangutan"; "**sa**t"; "barra**cuda**"

Create your **on-yomi** keywords and enter them in the table at the back of the book. After that, write your sentence to remember the **on-yomi** and **kun-yomi** readings in the box below.

Less Common Pronunciations

Less common **ON** reading: none
Less common **kun** reading: **moto** (もと)

IRREGULAR READINGS		
下手	lower + hand = to be poor at (something)	**he·ta** へ・た

COMMON WORDS AND COMPOUNDS		
下	low; below; under	**shita** した
下りる (intr)	to come down	**o·riru** お・りる
下ろす (tr)	to take down	**o·rosu** お・ろす
下がる (intr)	to hang down (on one's own)	**sa·garu** さ・がる
下げる (tr)	to lower (something)	**sa·geru** さ・げる
下さる	to oblige	**kuda·saru** くだ・さる
上下	upper + lower = high and low	**JŌ·GE** ジョウ・ゲ
天下	heaven + lower = the whole land	**TEN·KA** テン・カ

SAMPLE SENTENCE:

木 から 下りて 下さい。
ki   kara   o·rite   kuda·sai.
tree from come down please
= *Please come down from the tree.*

COMPONENT #32

RABBIT

KANJI #32

 RICE

`		`´	一	半	半	米		

BUILDING THIS KANJI
Rabbit `´ + Tree 木(13) = 米

Meaning

(Uncooked) rice. As can be seen in the last five compounds below, this character is used, curiously, to symbolize the Americas (recall how 中 is used in a similar way for China, and 日 for Japan). Note how the fourth example combines two such characters; this occurs frequently in written Japanese.

Remembering this kanji

Interesting fact: Japan has the equivalent of an Easter Bunny! The difference is that this **rabbit** will sneak around behind **trees** until he can dart out and hide RICE for children to find. Unfortunately, as the grains are really small and a lot less interesting than colored eggs, many kids have grown bored with the custom. As a result of this, the tradition of the Japanese RICE **rabbit** is not well-known today.

Common Pronunciations

Common **ON** reading: **MAI** (マ イ); **BEI** (ベ イ)
Common **kun** reading: **kome** (こ め)

BEI is used as the reading in compounds when this kanji relates to the Americas, with **MAI** the primary choice when it refers to rice.

kun-yomi suggestion: "**comb** acres"

Create your **on-yomi** keywords and enter them i the table at the back of the book. After that, writ your sentence to remember the **on-yomi** and **kun yomi** readings in the box below.

Less Common Pronunciations

Less common **ON** reading: none
Less common **kun** reading: none

COMMON WORDS AND COMPOUNDS		
米	*rice (uncooked)*	**kome** こ め
白米	white + rice = *polished rice*	HAKU·**MAI** ハク·マイ
米国	rice (America) + country = *the United States*	**BEI**·KOKU ベイ·コク
日米	sun + rice (America) = *Japan – U.S.*	NICHI·**BEI** ニチ·ベイ
中米	middle + rice (America) = *Central America*	CHŪ·**BEI** チュウ·ベイ
北米	north + rice (America) = *North America*	HOKU·**BEI** ホク·ベイ
南米	south + rice (America) = *South America*	NAN·**BEI** ナン·ベイ

SAMPLE SENTENCE:

米国　　の　　牛肉　　は　　高い。
BEI·KOKU no GYŪ·NIKU wa   taka·i.
United States   beef   expensive
= *U.S. beef is expensive.*

KANJI #33

自   SELF

´	亻	冂	卢	自	自		

BUILDING THIS KANJI
Jelly Bean ⟍ + Eye (Cyclops) 目 (15) = 自

Meaning
This character conveys the important idea of self. Its function becomes clearer if you think of such English words as "self-confidence" and "self-government". When these and other words beginning with "self-" are translated into Japanese, the resulting compound will usually begin with this kanji.

Remembering this kanji
Everyone is aware of a **Cyclops'** weakness for **jelly beans**. It was this, in fact, that saved Hercules; dangling a **jelly bean** over the **Cyclops'** head was enough to make the monster drop his club and lose all sense of SELF. "It was sad, actually," Hercules said at a later press conference. "No SELF-respecting **Cyclops** should act that way. He needs more SELF-control."

Common Pronunciations
Common **ON** reading: **JI** (ジ)
Common **kun** reading: none

Create your **on-yomi** keyword and enter it in the table at the back of the book. After that, write your sentence to remember the **on-yomi** reading in the box below.

Less Common Pronunciations
Less common **ON** reading: **SHI** (シ)
Less common **kun** reading: **mizuka** (みずか)

SHI appears only in the compound 自然 (Self/Nature), the Japanese word for "nature": **SHI·ZEN** (シ・ゼン).

COMMON WORDS AND COMPOUNDS		
自国	self + country = *one's homeland*	**JI·KOKU** ジ・コク
自立	self + stand = *independence*	**JI·RITSU** ジ・リツ
自分	self + part = *oneself*	**JI·BUN** ジ・ブン
自体	self + body = *in itself*	**JI·TAI** ジ・タイ

SAMPLE SENTENCE:
自分 の 車 が 買いたい。
JI·BUN no kuruma ga   ka·itai.
oneself   car   want to buy
= *I want to buy my own car.*

COMPONENT #34

GORILLA

KANJI #34

内 **INSIDE**

丨	冂	内	内				

BUILDING THIS KANJI

Gorilla 冂 + Person 人(2) = 内

Meaning
Inside/Interior/Within. This character can also convey the idea of "home."

Remembering this kanji
"You can know nothing of the **gorilla's** ways unless you are INSIDE its world. To truly understand, each **person** must get INSIDE an Acme™ **gorilla** suit—available for a limited time at this low introductory price—and head immediately into the jungle. It is then a simple matter of being accepted by a **gorilla** pod; once this has been done, a **person** can delve easily INSIDE the consciousness of our greatest primate."

Common Pronunciations
Common **ON** reading: **NAI** (ナイ)
Common **kun** reading: **uchi** (うち)

kun-yomi suggestion: "**ooh, chee**tahs"

Create your **on-yomi** keyword and enter it in the table at the back of the book. After that, write your sentence to remember the **on-yomi** and **kun-yomi** readings in the box below.

Less Common Pronunciations
Less common **ON** reading: **DAI** (ダイ)
Less common **kun** reading: none

COMMON WORDS AND COMPOUNDS		
内	*inside*	uchi うち
国内	country + inside = *domestic*	KOKU·NAI コク·ナイ
市内	city + inside = *within the city*	SHI·NAI シ·ナイ
内海	inside + sea = *inland sea*	NAI·KAI ナイ·カイ
車内	car + inside = *inside the car*	SHA·NAI シャ·ナイ
町内	town + inside = *in the town*	CHŌ·NAI チョウ·ナイ

SAMPLE SENTENCE:

その 人 は 国内 で 有名です
sono hito wa KOKU·NAI de YŪ·MEI desu
that person　　　domestic　　famous
= *That person is famous domestically.*

COMPONENT #35

SUPERHERO

KANJI #35

右 **RIGHT**

ノ ナ 大 右 右

BUILDING THIS KANJI
Superhero ナ + Mouth (vampire) 口 (8) = 右

Meaning
Right/right-hand side.

Remembering this kanji
Vampires are extremely RIGHT wing, demanding unconditional obedience to their authority and strict adherence to traditional ways. Even **superheroes** can turn to the RIGHT under their hypnotic influence; they invariably develop a tougher stance on crime and become less likely to wear skin-tight costumes.

Common Pronunciations
Common **ON** reading: none
Common **kun** reading: **migi** (み ぎ)

kun-yomi suggestion: "fo**amy gee**se"

Create your sentence to remember the **kun-yomi** reading in the box below.

Less Common Pronunciations
Less common **ON** reading: **YŪ** (ユ ウ); **U** (ウ)
Less common **kun** reading: none

COMMON WORDS AND COMPOUNDS		
右	*right*	**migi** み ぎ
右回り	right + rotate = *clockwise*	**migi** mawa·ri み ぎ まわ·り
右上	right + upper = *upper right*	**migi**·ue み ぎ·う え
右下	right + lower = *lower right*	**migi**·shita み ぎ·し た
右手	right + hand = *right hand*	**migi**·te み ぎ·て
右足	right + leg = *right leg*	**migi**·ashi み ぎ·あ し

SAMPLE SENTENCE:

山口さん は 右 の 目 がかゆい。

Yama·guchi-san wa migi no me ga kayui.
Yamaguchi-san　　right　eye　itchy
= *Yamaguchi-san's right eye is itchy.*

KANJI #36

有 **HAVE**

ノ	ナ	十	冇	有	有			

BUILDING THIS KANJI
Superhero ナ + Moon 月 (11) = 有

Meaning
Have/Possess.

Remembering this kanji
"Help me!" yelled the **moon**. "I'm going down!"
And indeed he was. But just then a **superhero**
arrived on the scene.
"I HAVE you, **moon**," he said, flying him higher
into the sky before returning to Earth with a
smile. "Citizens," he declared before us, "you
HAVE your **moon** back."
"Geez," I heard someone whisper, "how many
times should we tell this guy that the **moon's**
supposed to go down?"

Common Pronunciations
Common **ON** reading: **YŪ** (ユウ)
Common **kun** reading: **a** (あ)

kun-yomi suggestion: "Atilla"

Create your **on-yomi** keyword and enter it in the
table at the back of the book. After that, write your
sentence to remember the **on-yomi** and **kun-yomi**
readings in the box below.

Less Common Pronunciations
Less common **ON** reading: **U** (ウ)
Less common **kun** reading: none

COMMON WORDS AND COMPOUNDS		
有る	*to have*	a·ru あ・る
有力	have + strength = *powerful*	YŪ·RYOKU ユウ・リョク
有名	have + name = *famous*	YŪ·MEI ユウ・メイ
私有	private + have = *privately owned*	SHI·YŪ シ・ユウ
公有	public + have = *publicly owned*	KŌ·YŪ コウ・ユウ
国有化	country + have + change = *nationalization*	KOKU·YŪ·KA コク・ユウ・カ

SAMPLE SENTENCE:

エジプト の ピラミッド は 有名
Ejiputo **no** **piramiddo** **wa** **YŪ·MEI**
Egypt pyramids famous
です。
desu.
= *The Egyptian pyramids are famous.*

KANJI #37

肉 **MEAT**

	冂	内	内	内	肉		

BUILDING THIS KANJI
Inside 内 (34) + Person 人 (2) = 肉

Meaning
Meat/Flesh. In addition to its literal meaning, this kanji also has a sexual connotation through its appearance in words such as "lust" and "sensuality."

Remembering this kanji
"What is really **inside** a **person**?" Troubled by this question, I embarked on an extended spiritual quest that eventually led me to a remote Himalayan summit. There I fasted, growing weak and delirious until a talking leopard appeared one day and laid a paw on my shoulder. "What are you, nuts?" it said. "Take it from me: there's nothing but MEAT in there."

Common Pronunciations
Common **ON** reading: **NIKU** (ニク)
Common **kun** reading: none

Create your **on-yomi** keyword and enter it in the table at the back of the book. After that, write your sentence to remember the **on-yomi** reading in the box below.

Less Common Pronunciations
Less common **ON** reading: none
Less common **kun** reading: none

COMMON WORDS AND COMPOUNDS		
肉	*meat*	**NIKU** ニク
人肉	person + meat = *human flesh*	**JIN·NIKU** ジン・ニク
牛肉	cow + meat = *beef*	**GYŪ·NIKU** ギュウ・ニク
肉親	meat + parent = *blood relative*	**NIKU·SHIN** ニク・シン
肉体	meat + body = *the body*	**NIKU·TAI** ニク・タイ

SAMPLE SENTENCE:

あの　四人　は　牛肉　が
ano　yo·NIN　wa　GYŪ·NIKU　ga
those four people　　　beef
大好き　です。
DAI su·ki　desu.
really like.
= *Those four people really like beef.*

KANJI #38

半 **HALF**

丶	丶丿	丷	丷	半			

BUILDING THIS KANJI

Rabbit 丶丿 + Two 二(4) + Pole 丨 = 半

Meaning

Half. This character also incorporates a sense of "partial," forming many words that English conveys with the prefix "semi-."

Remembering this kanji

I remember a chef answering a question I once posed. "Yes," she said, "a **pole** *could* split a **rabbit** into **two** HALF sections." I also recall her noting that there would only be HALF the **rabbit** left if it were prepared in such a ridiculous way.

Common Pronunciations

Common **ON** reading: **HAN** (ハン)
Common **kun** reading: none

Create your **on-yomi** keyword and enter it in the table at the back of the book. After that, write your sentence to remember the **on-yomi** reading in the box below.

Less Common Pronunciations

Less common **ON** reading: none
Less common **kun** reading: **naka** (なか)

COMMON WORDS AND COMPOUNDS		
上半	upper + half = *upper half*	JŌ·HAN ジョウ・ハン
下半	lower + half = *lower half*	KA·HAN カ・ハン
半日	half + sun (day) = *half a day*	HAN·NICHI ハン・ニチ
半分	half + part = *half*	HAN·BUN ハン・ブン
九時半	nine + time + half = *nine-thirty*	KU·JI·HAN ク・ジ・ハン
半円	half + circle = *semicircle*	HAN·EN ハン・エン

SAMPLE SENTENCE:

木口さん は 半日 ぐらい
Ki·guchi-san wa HAN·NICHI gurai
Kiguchi-san   half a day   about
新聞 を 読みました。
SHIN·BUN o yo·mimashita.
newspaper   read
= *Kiguchi-san read the newspaper for about half a day.*

九 NINE

ノ	九						

Meaning
Nine.

Remembering this kanji
This is clearly someone dressed to the NINES.

Common Pronunciations
Common **ON** reading: **KYŪ** (キュウ); **KU** (ク)
Common **kun** reading: none

KYŪ is the general reading for this kanji. You
are only likely to encounter **KU** in the third and
fourth examples below.

Create your **on-yomi** keywords and enter them in
the table at the back of the book. After that, write
your sentence to remember the **on-yomi** readings
in the box below.

Less Common Pronunciations
Less common **ON** reading: none
Less common **kun** reading: **kokono** (ここの)

This is another reading of most use because of
its appearance in two words: 九日 [**kokono·ka**
(ここの・か)] "the ninth day of the month," and
九つ [**kokono·tsu** (ここの・つ)] the general
counter for "nine."

COMMON WORDS AND COMPOUNDS		
九	*nine*	**KYŪ** キュウ
九十	nine + ten = *ninety*	**KYŪ·JŪ** キュウ・ジュウ
九月	nine + moon (month) = *September*	**KU·GATSU** ク・ガツ
九時	nine + time = *nine o'clock*	**KU·JI** ク・ジ

SAMPLE SENTENCE:

中山さん　は　　九月　　に　　日本
Naka·yama-san wa KU·GATSU ni NI·HON
Nakayama-san　　　　September　　　Japan
へ　行きました
e　i·kimashita.
　　went
= *Nakayama-san went to Japan in September.*

KANJI #40

春 **SPRING**

一	二	三	声	夫	表	春	春	春

BUILDING THIS KANJI

Three (full hamburger) 三 (5) + Person 人 (2) + Sun 日 (6) = 春

Meaning

This elegant-looking character refers to the season of spring. Interestingly, it also carries a hint of sexuality and amorousness, a meaning apparent by its presence in the Japanese word for "puberty," as well as in one of the compounds below. Make sure in writing this kanji to follow the order of the components as they are listed above (three + person + sun).

Remembering this kanji

It's doubtful any **person** looks forward to SPRING more than I do. As a matter of fact, on the first day of the season you'll surely see me in the backyard before dawn, firing up my barbecue to make the most enormous **full hamburger** possible. And why do I do that? Well, it's simple: I'm a **person** who wants to welcome the SPRING **sun** properly when it rises!

Common Pronunciations

Common **ON** reading: **SHUN** (シュン)
Common **kun** reading: **haru** (はる)

kun-yomi suggestion: "**haru**mph"

Create your **on-yomi** keyword and enter it in th[e] table at the back of the book. After that, write you[r] sentence to remember the **on-yomi** and **kun-yom**[i] readings in the box below.

Less Common Pronunciations

Less common **ON** reading: none
Less common **kun** reading: none

COMMON WORDS AND COMPOUNDS		
春	spring	**haru** はる
小春	small + spring = *Indian summer*	ko·**haru** こ·はる
青春	blue + spring = *youth*	**SEI·SHUN** セイ·シュン
売春	sell + spring = *prostitution*	**BAI·SHUN** バイ·シュン
春分	spring + part = *vernal equinox*	**SHUN·BUN** シュン·ブン
来春	come + spring = *next spring*	**RAI·SHUN** ライ·シュン

SAMPLE SENTENCE:

日本 の 春 は 美しい。
NI·HON no haru wa utsuku·shii.
　Japan　　　spring　　　beautiful.
= *Japan's spring is beautiful.*

CHAPTER 2 REVIEW EXERCISES

A. Please match the following kanji to their meanings.

1.	玉	a.	Ten
2.	全	b.	Country
3.	米	c.	Jewel
4.	貝	d.	Right
5.	肉	e.	Meat
6.	十	f.	Rice
7.	心	g.	Upper
8.	上	h.	Shellfish
9.	右	i.	Heart
10.	国	j.	Complete

B. Please match the following meanings to their kanji, and these to their **on** or **kun-yomi**.

1.	Nine	a.	内	1.	**HAN** (ハン)
2.	Have	b.	春	2.	**uchi** (うち)
3.	Inside	c.	早	3.	**haru** (はる)
4.	King	d.	九	4.	**YŪ** (ユウ)
5.	Half	e.	下	5.	**ROKU** (ロク)
6.	Spring	f.	有	6.	**haya** (はや)
7.	Self	g.	自	7.	**shita** (した)
8.	Lower	h.	半	8.	**JI** (ジ)
9.	Early	i.	六	9.	**Ō** (オウ)
10.	Six	j.	王	10.	**KYŪ** (キュウ)

C. Please choose the best answer(s) to the following questions.

1. Which of the following readings apply to the kanji 米?
   a. **MAI** (マイ)
   b. **kome** (こめ)
   c. **SHŪ** (シュウ)
   d. **BEI** (ベイ)
   e. **to** (と)

2. Which of the following readings apply to the kanji 上?
   a. **nobo** (のぼ)
   b. **ue** (うえ)
   c. **naka** (なか)
   d. **JŌ** (ジョウ)
   e. **kami** (かみ)

3. Which of the following readings apply to the kanji 心?
   a. **migi** (みぎ)
   b. **SHIN** (シン)
   c. **tsuki** (つき)
   d. **kokoro** (こころ)
   e. **HAN** (ハン)

4. Which of the following is a sushi chef most likely to put on rice?
   a. 王
   b. 自
   c. 早
   d. 貝
   e. 国

5. Which of the following readings apply to the kanji 下?
   a. **kuda** (くだ)
   b. **KA** (カ)
   c. **shita** (した)
   d. **o** (お)
   e. **GE** (ゲ)

D. Please choose the best answer to the following questions.

1. Which is the correct reading of 上がる?
   a. **to·garu** (と・がる)
   b. **a·garu** (あ・がる)
   c. **ma·garu** (ま・がる)
   d. **sa·garu** (さ・がる)

2. Which answer best captures the meaning of the compound 米国?
   a. Wednesday　　　　d. Oatmeal
   b. Vampire　　　　　e. Heart failure
   c. The United States

3. Which is the correct reading for 九月?
   a. **KU·GATSU** (ク·ガツ)
   b. **kokono·GATSU** (ここの·ガツ)
   c. **KYŪ·GATSU** (キュウ·ガツ)
   d. **kokono·tsuki** (ここの·つき)

4. Which of the following does not belong with the others?
   a. 十
   b. 九
   c. 六
   d. 右

5. Which is the correct reading of 早い?
   a. **aru·i** (ある·い)
   b. **maru·i** (まる·い)
   c. **haya·i** (はや·い)
   d. **ara·i** (あら·い)

E. Please match the following compounds and words to their meanings and pronunciations.

1.	六月	a. Rapid speaking	1.	**ROKU·GATSU** (ロク·ガツ)
2.	中国	b. Ulterior motive	2.	**JO·Ō** (ジョ·オウ)
3.	早口	c. Queen	3.	**GO·JŪ** (ゴ·ジュウ)
4.	五十	d. Early spring	4.	**migi·ue** (みぎ·うえ)
5.	中米	e. Upper right	5.	**SŌ·SHUN** (ソウ·シュン)
6.	女王	f. Fifty	6.	**CHŪ·GOKU** (チュウ·ゴク)
7.	上下	g. June	7.	**CHŪ·BEI** (チュウ·ベイ)
8.	早春	h. High and low	8.	**shita·gokoro** (した·ごころ)
9.	下心	i. Central America	9.	**JŌ·GE** (ジョウ·ゲ)
10.	右上	j. China	10.	**haya·kuchi** (はや·くち)

Kanji #41—60

KANJI #41

CAPITAL

| ' | 一 | 亠 | 亡 | 古 | 宁 | 亨 | 京 | |

BUILDING THIS KANJI

Police 亠 + Mouth (vampire) 口 (8) + Small 小 (20) = 京

Meaning

Think of "capital" in the sense of a large metropolis. Though it's not the most common of characters, it is useful to learn this kanji because of its appearance in the compound for Tokyo and other cities.

Remembering this kanji

The CAPITAL can be a pretty intimidating place if you don't know it, and as a **police** officer here I'm always having to help folks with directions. Even **vampires**, who normally wouldn't go near anyone in a **police** uniform, come up to me now and then. It's not surprising, I suppose, that they're overwhelmed by all the buildings and traffic after having come from such **small** Transylvanian villages. But then, it's only natural that everyone – **vampires** included – feels a bit **small** in the CAPITAL.

Common Pronunciations

Common **ON** reading: **KYŌ** (キョウ)
Common **kun** reading: none

Create your **on-yomi** keyword and enter it in the table at the back of the book. After that, write your sentence to remember the **on-yomi** reading in the box below.

Less Common Pronunciations

Less common **ON** reading: **KEI** (ケイ)
Less common **kun** reading: none

COMMON WORDS AND COMPOUNDS		
上京	upper + capital = *come/go to Tokyo*	**JŌ·KYŌ** ジョウ·キョウ
東京	east + capital = *Tokyo*	**TŌ·KYŌ** トウ·キョウ

SAMPLE SENTENCE:

中山さん は 上京 しました。
Naka·yama-san wa　JŌ·KYŌ　shimashita.
　Nakayama-san　　went to Tokyo
　= *Nakayama-san went to Tokyo.*

KANJI #42

見 **SEE**

| 丨 | 冂 | 冂 | 月 | 目 | 尸 | 見 | | |

BUILDING THIS KANJI
Eye (Cyclops) 目 (15) + Ballet ル = 見

Meaning

See/Watch. The idea of "show" can also be expressed. Make sure you notice the difference between this kanji and "貝" (Entry 21).

Remembering this kanji

"I'm tired of living a lie," said the **Cyclops**, throwing down his club before emerging in a tutu. "People need to SEE me for who I really am. They need to SEE I'm not some slob who lounges around belching in a cave littered with sailor bones. They need to SEE the truth: that I…am a **ballerina**!"

Common Pronunciations

Common **ON** reading: **KEN** (ケン)
Common **kun** reading: **mi** (み)

Expect to use the **kun-yomi** when this kanji appears in the first position. The **on-yomi** occurs more often in the second.

kun-yomi suggestion: "**mean**"

Write your sentence to remember the reading below.

Less Common Pronunciations

Less common **ON** reading: none
Less common **kun** reading: none

COMMON WORDS AND COMPOUNDS		
見える (intr)	*to be visible*	mi·eru み・える
見る (tr)	*to see; to watch*	mi·ru み・る
見せる (tr)	*to show (something)*	mi·seru み・せる
見上げる	see + upper = *to look up (to/at)*	mi a·geru み あ・げる
月見	moon + see = *moon viewing*	tsuki·mi つき・み
見失う	see + lose = *to lose sight of*	mi ushina·u み・うしな・う
外見	outside + see = *external appearance*	GAI·KEN ガイ・ケン

SAMPLE SENTENCE:

山　　の　上　に　小さい　木　が
yama　no　ue　ni　chii·sai　ki　ga
mountain　　upper　　small　tree
見えます。
mi·emasu.
is visible
= *A small tree is visible on top of the mountain*

KANJI #43

止 **STOP**

| 丨 | ⊢ | ⼘ | 止 | | | | |

BUILDING THIS KANJI

Good Figure Skater ⼘ + Pole 丨 + One (bottom of a bun) 一 (3) = 止

Meaning

All senses of the meaning "stop". Take care with the stroke sequence of this kanji; the components should be written in the order shown above.

Remembering this kanji

"STOP! STOP!" the audience screamed. It was horrible. The **good figure skater's** posture was perfect, she was skating as if on the **bottom of a bun**, yet was oblivious to the **pole** sticking out of the ice in front of her. To be sure, no one could figure out what a **pole** was doing there in the first place, but no matter; the story must STOP here, as what happened next is too painful to relate.

Common Pronunciations

Common **ON** reading: **SHI** (シ)
Common **kun** reading: **to** (と)

Remember to use the **on-yomi** keyword for **SHI** that you applied to the kanji "四" (Entry 10). Note also how the **kun-yomi** can become voiced when it is used (as in the fourth and fifth examples) in second position, something that occurs frequently with this kanji.

kun-yomi suggestion: "total"

Write your sentence to remember the **on-yomi** and **kun-yomi** readings in the box below.

Less Common Pronunciations

Less common **ON** reading: none
Less common **kun** reading: none

COMMON WORDS AND COMPOUNDS		
止まる (intr)	*to stop*	**to**·maru と・まる
止める (tr)	*to stop (an object)*	**to**·meru と・める
中止	middle + stop = *discontinue*	CHŪ·**SHI** チュウ・シ
立ち止 まる	stand + stop = *to stand still*	ta·chi **do**·maru た・ち ど・まる
車止め	car + stop = *closed to vehicles*	kuruma **do**·me くるま ど・め

SAMPLE SENTENCE:

こちら に 止まって 下さい。

kochira ni to·matte   kuda·sai.
 here   stop   please
= *Please stop here.*

COMPONENT #44

COMET

Much like a wandering comet, our friend can appear in a variety of locations: as a slanted or curved line (as opposed to the horizontal "one") on top of a character, at the bottom, or right through the middle. One thing worth keeping in mind is that you should always draw this component from its head to its tail (i.e., in this case, from left to right).

KANJI #44

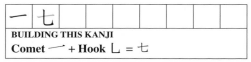 Seven

一	七								

BUILDING THIS KANJI
Comet ⼁ + Hook ∟ = 七

Meaning
Seven. Only two strokes here, but they should be written as the components are listed.

Remembering this kanji
Using a **comet** as his guide, Captain **Hook** sailed the SEVEN seas.

Common Pronunciations
Common **ON** reading: **SHICHI** (シ チ)
Common **kun** reading: **nana** (な な)

Note the mix of **on** and **kun** readings in the fourth and fifth examples.

kun-yomi suggestion: "**Nana**"

Create your **on-yomi** keyword and enter it in th table at the back of the book. After that, write you sentence to remember the **on-yomi** and **kun-yon** readings in the box below.

Less Common Pronunciations
Less common **ON** reading: none
Less common **kun** reading: **nano** (な の)

This reading appears with only one word (an guesses?): 七日 [**nano·ka** (な の·か)] "th seventh day of the month".

COMMON WORDS AND COMPOUNDS		
七	*seven*	**SHICHI** シチ
七つ	*seven (general counter)*	**nana·tsu** なな·つ
七月	seven + moon (month) = *July*	**SHICHI· GATSU** シチ·ガツ
十七	ten + seven = *seventeen*	**JŪ·nana** ジュウ·なな
七十	seven + ten = *seventy*	**nana·JŪ** なな·ジュウ
七時	seven + time = *seven o'clock*	**SHICHI·JI** シチ·ジ

SAMPLE SENTENCE:
高木さん　が　　七月　　に
Taka·gi-san　ga　SHICHI·GATSU　ni
Takagi-san　　　　July
中米　　　から　　来ます。
CHŪ·BEI　　kara　　ki·masu.
Central America　　will come
= *Takagi-san will come from Central Americ in July.*

KANJI #45

少 **FEW**

⺌	⺌	小	少				

BUILDING THIS KANJI
Small 小 (20) + Comet 一 = 少

Meaning
Few/Little (in terms of quantity).

Remembering this kanji
"That's not true," said the **comet**. "I mean, let's face it: I'm **small**, and have only a FEW opportunities to meet others. Everyone knows a planet because of its size and where it lives, but I move all over the place; that's why I have so FEW friends. It's got nothing to do with my tail leaving a mess on people's carpets."

Common Pronunciations
Common **ON** reading: **SHŌ** (ショウ)
Common **kun** reading: **suku** (すく); **suko** (すこ)

HŌ will appear in compounds. **Suku** and **suko** are only found in the first and second exam-

ples below. Note the special symbol in example three; Japanese uses this to indicate that a kanji is repeated.

kun-yomi suggestion: "**scoo**ter"; "**sco**ld"

Using your **on-yomi** keyword for 小 (Kanji 20), write your sentence to remember the **on-yomi** and **kun-yomi** readings in the box below.

Less Common Pronunciations
Less common **ON** reading: none
Less common **kun** reading: none

COMMON WORDS AND COMPOUNDS		
少ない	*few*	**suku·**nai すく・ない
少し	*a little; a few*	**suko·**shi すこ・し
少々	few + few = *a little*	**SHŌ·SHŌ** ショウ・ショウ
少女	few + woman = *girl*	**SHŌ·JO** ショウ・ジョ
少年	few + year = *boy*	**SHŌ·NEN** ショウ・ネン
最少	most + few = *fewest*	**SAI·SHŌ** サイ・ショウ

SAMPLE SENTENCE:

この 家 に は 物 が 少ない。
kono ie ni wa mono ga suku·nai.
this house   thing   few
= *There are few things in this house.*

COMPONENT #46

SNOWBOARD

KANJI 46

南 **SOUTH**

BUILDING THIS KANJI
Ten (scarecrow) 十(28) + Gorilla 冂 +
Snowboard 丷 + Ten (scarecrow) 十(28) = 南

Meaning
South.

Remembering this kanji
Stepchildren can often be a problem. The **gorilla** knew this, of course, when she married the **scarecrow**, for all the **scarecrow's** son wanted to do was **snowboard**. Because of this, there was a predictable response when the **gorilla** suggested they travel SOUTH for their vacation.
  "I don't want to go SOUTH," said Junior, pouting. "How can I **snowboard** there?"
"Now don't be like that, son," said his father. "You know **gorillas** like warm weather. We're going SOUTH, and that's all there is to it."
  Junior said nothing to this, but the **gorilla** knew very well what he was thinking: "I wish Dad had married the polar bear."

Common Pronunciations
Common **ON** reading: **NAN** (ナン)
Common **kun** reading: **minami** (みなみ)

kun-yomi suggestion: "**mean a me**al"

Create your **on-yomi** keyword and enter it in the table at the back of the book. After that, write your sentence to remember the **on-yomi** and **kun-yomi** readings in the box below.

Less Common Pronunciations
Less common **ON** reading: none
Less common **kun** reading: none

COMMON WORDS AND COMPOUNDS		
南	*south*	**minami** みなみ
南口	south + mouth = *south exit/entrance*	**minami**·guchi みなみ・ぐち
南米	south + rice (America) = *South America*	**NAN**·BEI ナン・ベイ
最南	most + south = *southernmost*	**SAI**·NAN サイ・ナン
南西	south + west = *southwest*	**NAN**·SEI ナン・セイ
南東	south + east = *southeast*	**NAN**·TŌ ナン・トウ

SAMPLE SENTENCE

バスターミナル　の　　南口　　て
basutāminaru　**no**　**minami·guchi**　**d**
bus terminal　　south entrance
会いましょう。
a·imashō.
let's meet
= *Let's meet at the south entrance of the bu*
terminal.

KANJI 47

工 **CRAFT**

| 一 | 丁 | 工 | | | | | | |

A final reminder about our major timesaving shortcut: your keyword for **KŌ** in this sentence will be the one you have entered in the **on-yomi** table, and that you have already applied to the kanji "ロ" (Entry 8). Write your sentence to remember the **on-yomi** reading in the box below.

Meaning
Have in mind the ideas of construction and manufacturing when you see this kanji; it's a versatile character that encompasses everything from handicrafts to industrial products. When found at the end of a compound (as in the final example below), this kanji can take on the meaning of "worker", and usually implies a person engaged in some type of manual labor.

Remembering this kanji
There's no better symbol for CRAFT than an anvil.

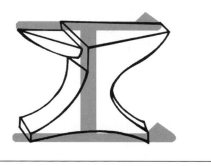

Common Pronunciations
Common ON reading: **KŌ** (コ ウ)
Common kun reading: none

Less Common Pronunciations
Less common ON reading: **KU** (ク)
Less common kun reading: none

COMMON WORDS AND COMPOUNDS		
人工	person + craft = *artificial*	JIN·KŌ ジン・コウ
人工林	person + craft + grove = *planted forest*	JIN·KŌ·RIN ジン・コウ・リン
工学	craft + study = *engineering*	KŌ·GAKU コウ・ガク
工学士	craft + study + gentleman = *Bachelor of Engineering*	KŌ·GAKU·SHI コウ・ガク・シ
刀工	sword + craft = *swordmaker*	TŌ·KŌ トウ・コウ

SAMPLE SENTENCE

これ は 人工 の 島 です ね。
kore wa JIN·KŌ no shima desu ne.
this　　artificial　　island　isn't it
= *This is an artificial island, isn't it?*

左 LEFT

| 一 | ナ | た | た | 左 | | | | |

BUILDING THIS KANJI
Superhero ナ + Craft 工(47) = 左

Common Pronunciations
Common **ON** reading: none
Common **kun** reading: **hidari** (ひだり)
kun-yomi suggestion: "**heed a reef**"

Create a sentence to remember the **kun-yomi** reading below.

Meaning
Left/Left-hand side. Take note: the writing order of the first two lines differs from that of Entries 35 and 36 ("右" and "有"). It may help to note that in all three cases, the direction of the first stroke matches that of the third.

Less Common Pronunciations
Less common **ON** reading: **SA** (サ)
Less common **kun** reading: none

Remembering this kanji
Craft workers are traditionally LEFT wing, and when united can neutralize even a **superhero**, as the illustration makes clear.

COMMON WORDS AND COMPOUNDS		
左	*left*	**hidari** ひだり
左回り	left + rotate = *counter-clockwise*	**hidari** mawa·ri ひだり まわ·り
左上	left + upper = *upper left*	**hidari**·ue ひだり·うえ
左下	left + lower = *lower left*	**hidari**·shita ひだり·した
左手	left + hand = *left hand*	**hidari**·te ひだり·て
左足	left + leg = *left leg*	**hidari**·ashi ひだり·あし

SAMPLE SENTENCE

あ の 人 の 左手 を 見 て 下さい。
ano hito no hidari·te o mi·te kuda·sai.
that person   left hand   see   please
= *Please watch that person's left hand.*

KANJI 49

高

TALL

亠	宀	宁	宁	宁	高	高	高

| 高 | | | | | | | |

BUILDING THIS KANJI

Police 亠 + Mouth (vampire) 口 (8) + Gorilla 冂 + Mouth (vampire) 口 (8) = 高

Meaning

Tall/High/Best. This kanji is also used to express the idea of "expensive."

Remembering this kanji

The story of King Kong the **gorilla** is well known. What most people don't realize, however, is that is based on an obscure Transylvanian legend. In it, the angry **gorilla** kidnaps a baby **vampire** and climbs the TALLEST hut in the land. Unfortunately for him, the baby's father is none other than Dracula; the famous **vampire** dons his **police** hat (he is, for reasons yet to be understood, a part-time deputy in this legend) and flies to the rescue. Even today there are inhabitants in the region who hold this story to be true, although most people, to be sure, consider it a TALL tale.

Common Pronunciations

Common **ON** reading: **KŌ** (コウ)
Common **kun** reading: **taka** (たか)

Note the intransitive/transitive verb pair below, and how the **kun-yomi** becomes voiced in the sixth example. This often occurs with 高 when it appears in the second or third position.

kun-yomi suggestion: "**tack a**pples"

Write your sentence to remember the **on-yomi** and **kun-yomi** readings in the box below.

Less Common Pronunciations

Less common **ON** reading: none
Less common **kun** reading: none

COMMON WORDS AND COMPOUNDS		
高い	*tall*; *expensive*	**taka·i** たか・い
高まる (intr)	*to rise*	**taka·maru** たか・まる
高める (tr)	*to raise*	**taka·meru** たか・める
高山	tall + mountain = *alpine*	**KŌ·ZAN** コウ・ザン
高校	tall + school = *high school*	**KŌ·KŌ** コウ・コウ
円高	circle (yen) + tall = *strong yen*	**EN·daka** エン・だか
最高	most + tall = *highest*; *the best*	**SAI·KŌ** サイ・コウ

SAMPLE SENTENCE

あの 高い 山 は 美しい です ね。

ano taka·i yama wa utsuku·shii desu ne.
that tall mountain beautiful isn't it
= *That tall mountain is beautiful, isn't it?*

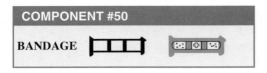

COMPONENT #50

BANDAGE

KANJI 50

買 **BUY**

| ノ | 冖 | 冖 | 罒 | 罒 | 罒 | 罒 | 胃 | 胃 |
| 胃 | 買 | 買 | | | | | | |

BUILDING THIS KANJI

Bandage 罒 + Shellfish 貝 (21) = 買

Meaning

Buy.

Remembering this kanji

As an animal rights activist, I regularly BUY **shellfish** in order to set them free. It's heartbreaking for me to go into a store and find them suffering in the tanks, their shells chipped and scarred. I BUY as many as possible, naturally, and do my best to help heal them by placing **bandages** on their wounds. But there are so many needing rescue… My only wish is for others to join the cause; after all, I can't BUY all the **shellfish** in the world.

Common Pronunciations

Common **ON** reading: none
Common **kun** reading: **ka** (か)

As nice as it is to have only one main reading to remember for this kanji, mention must be made of a particular quirk in written Japanese that occurs when certain verb stems are used to form nouns. The easiest way to understand this is by comparing the second and third examples below. As you can see, the noun in example 3 has "lost" the **i** (い) that would be present if the kanji were in its **-masu** verb form, **kaimasu**. (買います). It is,

in a sense, implied, based on the **hiragana** endin[g] after 上. Unfortunately, there are no hard and fa[st] rules for this aspect of the language, and it c[an] be frustrating when such words are encountere[d.] Our example, for instance, can be seen variou[sly] as "買い上げ," "買上げ," or even "買上" [in] different dictionaries!

It is worth keeping in mind, however, that n[ot] many kanji present such difficulties, and that on[ce] a "primary" word (usually the **-masu** form o[f a] verb) has been learned, its related nouns will [be] easily recognized. Another consolation shou[ld] be the following: by having reached the sta[ge] where you are dealing with such intricacies of t[he] language, you are navigating among the deep[er] levels of written Japanese.

kun-yomi suggestion: "**cap**"

Create your sentence to remember the **kun-yo[mi]** reading in the box below.

Less Common Pronunciations

Less common **ON** reading: **BAI** (バイ)
Less common **kun** reading: none

COMMON WORDS AND COMPOUNDS		
買う	to buy	**ka·u** か・う
買い上げる	buy + upper = *to buy (up/out)*	**ka·i a·geru** か・い あ・げる
買上げ	buy + upper = *a purchase*	**kai a·ge** かい あ・げ
買い物	buy + thing = *shopping*	**ka·i mono** か・い もの
買い入れる	buy + enter = *to stock up on*	**ka·i i·reru** か・い い・れる
買い手	buy + hand = *buyer*	**ka·i te** か・い て

SAMPLE SENTENCE

山中さん	は	高い	物	を	買う
Yama·naka-san	**wa**	**taka·i**	**mono**	**o**	**ka·u**
Yamanaka-san		expensive	thing		buy

つもり　です。
tsumori desu.
 plans

= *Yamanaka-san plans to buy something expensiv[e.]*

KANJI 51

百 **HUNDRED**

一	丆	丆	丆	百	百			

BUILDING THIS KANJI
One (top of a bun) 一 (3) + White 白 (7) = 百

Meaning
Hundred. In a few instances, the idea of "many" is conveyed.

Remembering this kanji
A recent survey found that ONE HUNDRED percent of **white bun tops** are **white**. ONE HUNDRED percent! Rarely is scientific research so conclusive.

Common Pronunciations
Common **ON** reading: **HYAKU** (ヒャク)
Common **kun** reading: none

The thing to watch for here is how **HYAKU** changes phonetically with different numbers.

Note also the **kun-yomi** in examples four and seven. Create your **on-yomi** keyword and enter it in the table at the back of the book. After that, write your sentence to remember the **on-yomi** reading in the box below.

Less Common Pronunciations
Less common **ON** reading: none
Less common **kun** reading: none

COMMON WORDS AND COMPOUNDS		
百	*one hundred*	**HYAKU** ヒャク
二百	two + hundred = *two hundred*	NI·**HYAKU** ニ・ヒャク
三百	three + hundred = *three hundred*	SAN·**BYAKU** サン・ビャク
四百	four + hundred = *four hundred*	yon·**HYAKU** よん・ヒャク
五百	five + hundred = *five hundred*	GO·**HYAKU** ゴ・ヒャク
六百	six + hundred = *six hundred*	ROP·**PYAKU** ロッ・ピャク
七百	seven + hundred = *seven hundred*	nana·**HYAKU** なな・ヒャク
八百	eight + hundred = *eight hundred*	HAP·**PYAKU** ハッ・ピャク
九百	nine + hundred = *nine hundred*	KYŪ·**HYAKU** キュウ・ヒャク

SAMPLE SENTENCE
肉 を 五百 グラム買いました。
NIKU o GO·HYAKU guramu ka·imashita.
meat   five hundred grams   bought
= *(I) bought five hundred grams of meat.*

CIRCLE

丨	冂	冃	円			

BUILDING THIS KANJI
Gorilla 冂 + Police ⺍ = 円

Meaning
Circle/Round. This kanji is also used to denote the yen, Japan's currency. The connection originated from round one-yen coins.

Remembering this kanji
Every **gorilla** in the park hated the **ranger**, for his snide comments about their grooming habits were known to animals far and wide. It was not surprising, therefore, to hear that he had found himself surrounded by a CIRCLE of angry silverbacks on emerging from his tent one day. No one will know for certain what actually happened to the **ranger**, of course, because the **gorillas** CIRCLED their wagons and refused to cooperate with any investigation.

Common Pronunciations
Common **ON** reading: **EN** (エ ン)
Common **kun** reading: **maru** (ま る)

kun-yomi suggestion: "llama ruins"

Create your **on-yomi** keyword and enter it in the table at the back of the book. After that, write your sentence to remember the **on-yomi** and **kun-yomi** readings in the box below.

Less Common Pronunciations
Less common **ON** reading: none
Less common **kun** reading: none

COMMON WORDS AND COMPOUNDS		
円い	*circular*	**maru·i** まる·い
円高	yen + tall = *strong yen*	**EN·daka** エン·だか
二円	two + yen = *two yen*	**NI·EN** ニ·エン
半円	half + circle = *semicircle*	**HAN·EN** ハン·エン
円安	yen + ease = *weak yen*	**EN·yasu** エン·やす
円周	circle + around = *circumference*	**EN·SHŪ** エン·シュウ

SAMPLE SENTENCE
あ の 子 は　　百 円　 を　な く し た 。
ano ko wa HYAKU·EN o　nakushita.
that child　　one hundred yen　　　lost
= *That child lost a hundred yen.*

元 BASIS

一	二	テ	元				

BUILDING THIS KANJI
Two 二(4) + Ballet 儿 = 元

Meaning
This character expresses the idea of a basis or original state of something. When used with its **kun-yomi** before words such as "president," it can be translated as "ex-," or "former."

Remembering this kanji
Two ballet legs are the BASIS of any good performance of Swan Lake. I mean, no one likes to be rude, but every time I watch a one-legged swan take on the role of Princess Odette…well, the very BASIS of the play is called into question for me.

Common Pronunciations
Common **ON** readings: **GEN** (ゲン); **GAN** (ガン)
Common **kun** reading: **moto** (もと)

GAN occurs only in the first position with a few common words.

kun-yomi suggestion: "**moto**cross"

Create your **on-yomi** keywords and enter them in the table at the back of the book. After that, write your sentence to remember the **on-yomi** and **kun-yomi** readings in the box below.

Less Common Pronunciations
Less common **ON** reading: none
Less common **kun** reading: none

COMMON WORDS AND COMPOUNDS		
元々	basis + basis = *from the first*	**moto·moto** もと・もと
元日	basis + sun (day) = *New Year's Day*	**GAN·JITSU** ガン・ジツ
手元	hand + basis = *at hand*	**te·moto** て・もと
元気	basis + spirit = *high spirits*	**GEN·KI** ゲン・キ
火元	fire + basis = *origin of a fire*	**hi·moto** ひ・もと
元来	basis + come = *by nature*	**GAN·RAI** ガン・ライ

SAMPLE SENTENCE

元日　　な　の　で　人　が　少ない。
GAN·JITSU na   no   de hito ga suku·nai.
New Year's Day because   person   few
= *It's New Year's Day, so there aren't many people.*

首   NECK

`	`	一	一	广	广	首	首	首	首

BUILDING THIS KANJI
Snowboard ⼍ + Self 自 (33) = 首

Meaning
Neck in its physical sense, as well as the ideas of leader or chief.

Remembering this kanji
His sense of **self** became so wrapped up in his **snowboard** that things started getting weird. After all, carrying a **snowboard** on your NECK at the ski slope is one thing, but wearing it around your NECK at work is another. When this started happening, even his colleagues in the office were concerned enough to seek advice.

"It all has to do with his sense of **self**-worth," said the company psychologist. "What with the recent demotion, his **self** confidence is shaken. He'll get over it eventually."

Common Pronunciations
Common **ON** reading: **SHU** (シュ)
Common **kun** reading: **kubi** (くび)

kun-yomi suggestion: "Scooby doo"

Create your **on-yomi** keyword and enter it in t table at the back of the book. After that, write yo sentence to remember the **on-yomi** and **kun-yom** readings in the box below.

Less Common Pronunciations
Less common **ON** reading: none
Less common **kun** reading: none

COMMON WORDS AND COMPOUNDS		
首	*neck*	**kubi** くび
自首	self + neck = *surrender*	**JI·SHU** ジ・シュ
手首	hand + neck = *wrist*	te·**kubi** て・くび
足首	leg + neck = *ankle*	ashi·**kubi** あし・くび

SAMPLE SENTENCE

高木さん	は	首	に	水
Takagi-san	**wa**	**kubi**	**ni**	**miz**
Takagi-san		neck		wat

を　かけました。
o   **kakemashita.**
       put
= *Takagi-san put some water on his neck.*

歩 WALK

| 1 | ⊢ | ⺊ | 止 | 牛 | 步 | 步 | 歩 | |

BUILDING THIS KANJI
Stop 止 (43) + Few 少 (45) = 歩

Meaning
Walking/Step/Pace. A secondary meaning of "rate" (as used in a financial sense) is found only with **BU** (ブ), a less-common **on-yomi**.

Remembering this kanji
My WALKING style is a little unorthodox in that I'll **stop**, take a **few** steps, then **stop** once more. It can be frustrating for those WALK-ING with me, I suppose, for what with **stopping** every **few** steps, I rarely make it far beyond my front door.

Common Pronunciations
Common **ON** reading: **HO** (ホ)
Common **kun** reading: **aru** (ある)

kun-yomi suggestion: "a rou**te**"

Create your **on-yomi** keyword and enter it in the table at the back of the book. After that, write your sentence to remember the **on-yomi** and **kun-yomi** readings in the box below.

Less Common Pronunciations
Less common **ON** readings: **BU** (ブ); **FU** (フ)
Less common **kun** reading: **ayu** (あゆ)

COMMON WORDS AND COMPOUNDS		
歩く	to walk	aru·ku ある·く
一歩	one + walk = one step	IP·PO イッ·ポ
歩き回る	walk + rotate = to ramble about	aru·ki mawa·ru ある·き ま わ·る
歩道	walk + road = sidewalk	HO·DŌ ホ·ドウ
歩行	walk + go = walking	HO·KŌ ホ·コウ
歩行者	walk + go + individual = pedestrian	HO·KŌ·SHA ホ·コウ·シャ

SAMPLE SENTENCE
家　から　山　まで　歩きました。
ie　kara　yama　made　aru·kimashita.
house　from　mountain　until　　　walked
= *(We) walked from the house to the mountain.*

KANJI 56

子 **CHILD**

⁊	了	子					

Meaning
Child. As seen in the final compound below, this character can also be used to suggest something small. No story required.

Common Pronunciations
Common ON reading: **SHI** (シ)
Common kun reading: **ko** (こ)

Interestingly, both of these readings can at times become voiced (pronounced **JI** and **go**) in the second position, as seen in the third examples of this entry and that of Entry 167. Japanese parents often choose this kanji for a suffix when naming their children (eg. **Aki·ko**); it is read "**SHI**" in the case of males, and "**ko**" when applied to females.

kun-yomi suggestion: "coat"

Write your sentence to remember the **on-yomi** and **kun-yomi** readings in the box below.

Less Common Pronunciations
Less common ON reading: **SU** (ス)
Less common kun reading: none

COMMON WORDS AND COMPOUNDS		
子	*child*	**ko** こ
女子	woman + child = *women's*	**JO·SHI** ジョ・シ
王子	king + child = *prince*	**Ō·JI** オウ・ジ
男子	man + child = *men's*	**DAN·SHI** ダン・シ
子牛	child + cow = *calf*	**ko·ushi** こ・うし
電子	electric + child = *electron*	**DEN·SHI** デン・シ

SAMPLE SENTENCE

五月　に女王と王子が　　米国
GO·GATSU ni JO·Ō to Ō·JI ga BEI·KOKU
　May　　　queen　prince　　America
へ　　行きました。
e　　　i·kimashita.
　　　　　went
= *In May, the queen and prince went to America.*

好 LIKE

| く | ク | 女 | 女 | 好 | 好 | | | |

BUILDING THIS KANJI
Woman 女(16) + Child 子(56) = 好

Meaning
To like/Good/Favorable…nothing but positive feelings are associated with this gentle character!

Remembering this kanji
This is one of those kanji that is so logically constructed as to need no story at all.

Common Pronunciations
Common **ON** reading: **KŌ** (コ ウ)
Common **kun** reading: **su** (す)

The **kun-yomi** is often voiced when in the second position (becoming "**zu**"), as below in examples three and four.

kun-yomi suggestion: "**soon**"

Write your sentence to remember the **on-yomi** and **kun-yomi** readings in the box below.

Less Common Pronunciations
Less common **ON** reading: none
Less common **kun** reading: **kono** (こ の)

COMMON WORDS AND COMPOUNDS		
好き	like	su·ki す.き
大好き	large + like = to really like	DAI su·ki ダイ す.き
人好き	person + like = amiability	hito zu·ki ひと ず.き
話し好き	speak + like = talkative	hana·shi zu·ki はな.し ず.き
友好	friend + like = friendship	YŪ·KŌ ユウ.コウ
同好	same + like = same tastes	DŌ·KŌ ド ウ.コウ

SAMPLE SENTENCE

山口さん はあそこ の 女 の 人
Yama·guchi-san wa asoko no onna no hito
 Yamaguchi-san   over there   woman   person
が 大好き です。
ga DAI su·ki desu.
   really likes
= *Yamaguchi-san really likes that woman over there.*

KANJI 58

古 **OLD**

| 一 | 十 | 古 | 古 | 古 | | | |

BUILDING THIS KANJI

Ten (scarecrow) 十 (28) + Mouth (vampire)
口 (8) = 古

Meaning
Old/Ancient/Antique.

Remembering this kanji
Even though **vampires** never die, they do grow
OLD and suffer the same deterioration of mental
faculties as the rest of us. The **scarecrow** can
attest to this; as he lives in a field next to an
OLD folks home, he'll often look down to find
an elderly **vampire** bravely fastening its gums
onto his ankle. It's more of a nuisance for him
than anything, of course, but he's always nice
enough to show respect for those OLDER by
acting scared.

Common Pronunciations
Common ON reading: KO (コ)
Common kun reading: furu (ふる)

Remember that your **on-yomi** keyword here will
be different from that used in the preceding entry
(for 好).

kun-yomi suggestion: "**who ru**es…"

Create your **on-yomi** keyword and enter it in the
table at the back of the book. After that, write your
sentence to remember the **on-yomi** and **kun-yomi**
readings in the box below.

Less Common Pronunciations
Less common ON reading: none
Less common kun reading: none

COMMON WORDS AND COMPOUNDS		
古い	old	**furu·i** ふる·い
中古	middle + old = *secondhand*	**CHŪ·KO** チュウ·コ
最古	most + old = *oldest*	**SAI·KO** サイ·コ
古語	old + words = *archaic word*	**KO·GO** コ·ゴ
古来	old + come = *time honored*	**KO·RAI** コ·ライ
古里	old + hamlet = *the old hometown*	**furu·sato** ふる·さと

SAMPLE SENTENCE

山下さん は 中古 の 品 をよく
Yama·shita-san wa CHŪ·KO no shina o yoku
Yamashita-san　　secondhand　goods　often
買います。
ka·imasu.
　buys
= *Yamashita-san often buys secondhand goods.*

火 FIRE

Meaning

This beautifully simple character encompasses all things to do with fire. No story required, although you can imagine the illustration as a **FIRE person** with a couple of flaming **jelly beans**.

Common Pronunciations

Common **ON** reading: **KA** (カ)
Common **kun** reading: **hi** (ひ)

The kun-yomi is always voiced (becomes **bi**) when in the second position, as seen here in example five.

kun-yomi suggestion: "**heat**"

Write your sentence to remember the **on-yomi** and **kun-yomi** readings in the box below.

Less Common Pronunciations

Less common **ON** reading: none
Less common **kun** reading: **ho** (ほ)

COMMON WORDS AND COMPOUNDS		
火	*fire*	**hi** ひ
火元	fire + basis = *origin of a fire*	**hi·moto** ひ・もと
大火	large + fire = *conflagration*	TAI·**KA** タイ・カ
火山	fire + mountain = *volcano*	**KA**·ZAN カ・ザン
花火	flower + fire = *fireworks*	hana·**bi** はな・び
火曜日	fire + day of the week + sun (day) = *Tuesday*	**KA**·YŌ·bi カ・ヨウ・び
火星	fire + star = *Mars (planet)*	**KA**·SEI カ・セイ

SAMPLE SENTENCE

日本 に は 火山 が あります。
NI·HON ni wa KA·ZAN ga arimasu.
Japan   volcano   are
= *There are volcanoes in Japan.*

COMPONENT #60

RUNNING CHICKEN

Common Pronunciations
Common **ON** reading: **TŌ** (ト ウ)
Common **kun** reading: **fuyu** (ふ ゆ)

kun-yomi suggestion: "**who u**ses…"

Create your **on-yomi** keyword and enter it in the table at the back of the book. After that, write your sentence to remember the **on-yomi** and **kun-yomi** readings in the box below.

KANJI 60

冬 **WINTER**

ノ	ク	夂	冬	冬				

BUILDING THIS KANJI
Running Chicken 夂 + Jelly Bean 丶 + Jelly Bean 丶 = 冬

Less Common Pronunciations
Less common **ON** reading: none
Less common **kun** reading: none

Meaning
Winter.

COMMON WORDS AND COMPOUNDS		
冬	*winter*	**fuyu** ふゆ
冬休み	winter + rest = *winter vacation*	**fuyu** yasu·mi ふゆ やす·み
立冬	stand + winter = *first day of winter*	RIT·**TŌ** リッ·トウ
冬物	winter + thing = *winter clothing*	**fuyu**·mono ふゆ·もの
冬空	winter + empty (sky) = *winter sky*	**fuyu**·zora ふゆ·ぞら

Remembering this kanji
WINTER is such a drab time of year. To add a bit of color to the season, therefore, I enjoy strapping bags of **jelly beans** to **chickens running** in the yard, as the **beans** spill out and make everything more cheerful. It's a mystery to me why more people don't do this; even the grayest WINTER would be tolerable if everyone followed my lead.

SAMPLE SENTENCE

冬　に　なる　と　スイス　の　　山　に
fuyu　ni　naru　to　suisu　no　yama w
winter　becomes　Switzerland　mountain
美しい。
utsuku·shii.
　beautiful
= *The mountains of Switzerland are beautiful in winter.*

CHAPTER 3 REVIEW EXERCISES

A. Please match the following kanji to their meanings.

1.	高	a.	Few
2.	止	b.	Hundred
3.	古	c.	Basis
4.	百	d.	Tall
5.	南	e.	Winter
6.	京	f.	Left
7.	元	g.	Capital
8.	左	h.	Stop
9.	少	i.	South
10.	冬	j.	Old

B. Please match the following meanings to their kanji, and these to their on- or kun-yomi.

1.	Like (kun-yomi)	a. 步	1.	HO (ホ)	
2.	Child	b. 火	2.	ko (こ)	
3.	Neck	c. 工	3.	kubi (くび)	
4.	Craft	d. 首	4.	ka (か)	
5.	Walk	e. 七	5.	EN (エン)	
6.	See	f. 子	6.	SHICHI(シチ)	
7.	Fire (kun-yomi)	g. 見	7.	KŌ (コウ)	
8.	Buy	h. 円	8.	mi (み)	
9.	Circle	i. 好	9.	hi (ひ)	
10.	Seven	j. 買	10.	su (す)	

C. Please choose the best answer(s) to the following questions.

1. Which of the following readings apply to the kanji 南?
   a. NAN (ナン)
   b. fuyu (ふゆ)
   c. HYAKU (ヒャク)
   d. minami (みなみ)
   e. hidari (ひだり)

2. What is the worst thing you can hear someone say from behind while you're standing on a plank of a ship?
   a. 子
   b. 七
   c. 好
   d. 元
   e. 步

3. Which of the following readings apply to the kanji 高?
   a. hi (ひ)
   b. GETSU (ゲツ)
   c. KŌ (コウ)
   d. taka (たか)
   e. TAI (タイ)

4. Which of the following readings apply to the kanji 元?
   a. GEN (ゲン)
   b. moto (もと)
   c. furu (ふる)
   d. GAN (ガン)
   e. HAN (ハン)

5. Which of the following readings apply to the kanji 少?
   a. KŌ (コウ)
   b. SHŌ (ショウ)
   c. suko (すこ)
   d. suku (すく)
   e. to (と)

D. Please choose the best answer to the following questions.

1. Which is the correct reading of 少し?
   a. **mawa·shi** (ま わ・し)
   b. **suko·shi** (す こ・し)
   c. **de·shi** (で・し)
   d. **suku·shi** (す く・し)

2. Which kanji would precede 口 to form the compound for "volcanic crater"?
   a. 冬
   b. 火
   c. 左
   d. 首
   e. 止

3. Which is the correct reading of 古い?
   a. **furu·i** (ふ る・い)
   b. **ka·i** (か・い)
   c. **yuru·i** (ゆ る・い)
   d. **futo·i** (ふ と・い)

4. Which of the following kanji has the most number of strokes?
   a. 見
   b. 好
   c. 南
   d. 歩
   e. 京

5. Which is the correct reading of 少ない?
   a. **aka·nai** (あ か・な い)
   b. **to·nai** (と・な い)
   c. **aga·nai** (あ が・な い)
   d. **suku·nai** (す く・な い)

E. Please match the following compounds and words to their meanings and pronunciations

1. 南米	a. To really like	1. **CHŪ·SHI** (チュウ·シ
2. 中古	b. Secondhand	2. **JŌ·KYŌ** (ジョウ· キョウ)
3. 上京	c. Semicircle	3. **JIN·KŌ** (ジン·コウ
4. 大火	d. South America	4. **CHŪ·KO** (チュウ·コ
5. 半円	e. Artificial	5. **IP·PO** (イッ·ポ)
6. 中止	f. Discontinue	6. **NAN·BEI** (ナン·ベイ
7. 一歩	g. Seven hundred	7. **TAI·KA** (タイ·カ)
8. 七百	h. Come/ Go to Tokyo	8. **DAI su·ki** (ダイ す·き
9. 人工	i. One step	9. **HAN·EN** (ハン·エン
10. 大好き	j. Conflagration	10. **nana· HYAKU** (なな· ヒャク)

Kanji #61—80

KANJI 61

水 **WATER**

| 亅 | 기 | 가 | 水 | | | | | 亅 |

Meaning
Another gracefully balanced character, this one suggesting water. The "wavy" effect in the illustration will be easier to remember if you imagine the harpoon being pulled upward. No story required.

Common Pronunciations
Common **ON** reading: **SUI** (スイ)
Common **kun** reading: **mizu** (みず)

un-yomi suggestion: "make **me zoo**m"

reate your **on-yomi** keyword and enter it in the ble at the back of the book. After that, write your

sentence to remember the **on-yomi** and **kun-yomi** readings in the box below.

Less Common Pronunciations
Less common **ON** reading: none
Less common **kun** reading: none

COMMON WORDS AND COMPOUNDS		
水	*water*	**mizu** みず
水中	water + middle = *underwater;* *in the water*	**SUI·CHŪ** スイ・チュウ
下水	lower + water = *sewage*	**GE·SUI** ゲ・スイ
水玉	water + jewel = *drop of water*	**mizu·tama** みず・たま
水星	water + star = *Mercury (planet)*	**SUI·SEI** スイ・セイ
水曜日	water + day of the week + sun (day) = *Wednesday*	**SUI·YŌ·bi** スイ・ヨウ・び
水死	water + death = *drowning*	**SUI·SHI** スイ・シ

SAMPLE SENTENCE:

あの ダム には 水 が ありません。
ano damu ni wa mizu ga arimasen.
that dam water isn't
= *There is no water at that dam.*

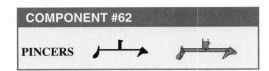

COMPONENT #62

PINCERS

KANJI 62

安 **EASE**

' ` 宀 灾 安 安

BUILDING THIS KANJI
Pincers 宀 + Woman 女 (16) = 安

Meaning
The general sense is of "ease", "peacefulness," and "stability." An important secondary meaning is "inexpensive." In this regard, the kanji's opposite is "高" (Entry 49).

Remembering this kanji
Pincers have always allowed the legendary **women** of history to lead lives of EASE. Nefertiti and Cleopatra had **pincers** deposit them into cushiony boats on the Nile; Catherine the Great had **pincers** EASE her onto a bed strewn with sable… Even Joan of Arc, after a tiring day on the battlefield, would always have **pincers** set her gently into a bubble bath.

Common Pronunciations
Common **ON** reading: **AN** (アン)
Common **kun** reading: yasu (やす)

kun-yomi suggestion: "try a suit"

Create your **on-yomi** keyword and enter it in the table at the back of the book. After that, write your sentence to remember the **on-yomi** and **kun-yomi** readings in the box below.

Less Common Pronunciations
Less common **ON** reading: none
Less common **kun** reading: none

COMMON WORDS AND COMPOUNDS		
安い	easy; cheap	yasu·i やす・い
円安	circle (yen) + ease = weak yen	EN·yasu エン・やす
安心	ease + heart = peace of mind	AN·SHIN アン・シン
安全	ease + complete = safety	AN·ZEN アン・ゼン
不安	not + ease = uneasiness	FU·AN フ・アン
公安	public + ease = public peace	KŌ·AN コウ・アン

SAMPLE SENTENCE:

安心　　　して　下さい。
AN·SHIN   shite   kuda·sai.
peace of mind   do   please
= *Please don't worry.*

KANJI 63

力 **STRENGTH**

フ	カ						

Meaning
Strength/Power/Force. No story required.

Common Pronunciations
Common **ON** readings: **RYOKU** (リョク);
RIKI (リキ)
Common **kun** reading: **chikara** (ちから)

RYOKU will be encountered far more often than
RIKI; the kun-yomi is a common word on its own.

kun-yomi suggestion: "in my **cheek a rat**..."

Create your **on-yomi** keywords and enter them in
the table at the back of the book. After that, write
your sentence to remember the **on-yomi** and **kun-
yomi** readings in the box below.

Less Common Pronunciations
Less common **ON** reading: none
Less common **kun** reading: none

COMMON WORDS AND COMPOUNDS		
力	*strength*	**chikara** ちから
全力	complete + strength = *all one's power*	**ZEN·RYOKU** ゼン・リョク
有力	have + strength = *powerful*	**YŪ·RYOKU** ユウ・リョク
水力	water + strength = *hydro power*	**SUI·RYOKU** スイ・リョク
火力	fire + strength = *thermal power*	**KA·RYOKU** カ・リョク
電力	electric + strength = *electric power*	**DEN·RYOKU** デン・リョク
力士	strength + gentleman = *sumo wrestler*	**RIKI·SHI** リキ・シ

SAMPLE SENTENCE:

中山さん は 車 のビジネスで
Naka·yama-san wa kuruma no bijinesu de
Nakayama-san　　　car　　　business
とても 有力 な 人 です。
totemo YŪ·RYOKU na hito desu.
very　　　powerful　　　person　　　is
= *In the automotive business, Nakayama-san is
a very powerful person.*

KANJI 64

夏 **SUMMER**

一	一	厂	丆	百	百	百	頁	夏
夏								

BUILDING THIS KANJI
One (top of a bun) 一 (3) + Self 自 (33) +
Running Chicken 夂 = 夏

Meaning
Summer.

Remembering this kanji

When SUMMER rolls around I enjoy throwing parties, but like most farming folk, I don't stand on ceremony. After all, what with it being so darn hot in the SUMMER, the last thing I want to do is cook! So you'd better be prepared if you drop by. I'll give you the **top of a bun**, of course, but you'll be heading straight to the coop after that. "Go catch yourself a **running chicken**," I'll say. "This here's a **self**-serve party."

Common Pronunciations
Common **ON** reading: **KA** (カ)
Common **kun** reading: **natsu** (なつ)

kun-yomi suggestion: "**gnat soup**"

Write your sentence to remember the **on-yomi** and **kun-yomi** readings in the box below.

Less Common Pronunciations
Less common **ON** reading: **GE** (ゲ)
Less common **kun** reading: none

COMMON WORDS AND COMPOUNDS		
夏	*summer*	**natsu** なつ
夏休み	summer + rest = *summer vacation*	**natsu** yasu·**mi** なつ やす·み
夏物	summer + thing = *summer clothing*	**natsu**·mono なつ·もの
立夏	stand + summer = *first day of summer*	RIK·KA リッ·カ

SAMPLE SENTENCE:
この 夏 には 東京 へ 行きます。
kono natsu ni wa TŌ·KYŌ e i·kimasu.
this summer   Tokyo   go
= *(We'll) be going to Tokyo this summer.*

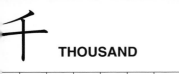

千

THOUSAND

BUILDING THIS KANJI

Comet 一 + Ten (scarecrow) 十(28) = 千

Meaning

Thousand. Like the character for "hundred" (Entry 51), this kanji sometimes conveys a general idea of "many".

Remembering this kanji

My favorite story in the "THOUSAND and One Nights" is the tale in which a comet on a THOUSAND-year journey has a chat with a scarecrow.

"What's up?" he asks.

"Nothing much besides my getting sick of this view," answers the scarecrow. "I must say, I'd sure love to take a trip like yours."

"Well, why don't you go, then?" says the comet, smiling. "Remember: a journey of a THOUSAND miles starts with a single step."

"Gee, thanks for that pearl of wisdom," says the scarecrow sarcastically. "In case you haven't noticed, I'm tied to a couple of boards here."

Common Pronunciations

Common **ON** reading: SEN (セン)

Common **kun** reading: none

As seen with the kanji "百," note how SEN changes phonetically with different numbers, and how **kun-yomi** are used in examples four and seven.

Create your **on-yomi** keyword and enter it in the table at the back of the book. After that, write your sentence to remember the **on-yomi** reading in the box below.

Less Common Pronunciations

Less common **ON** reading: none

Less common **kun** reading: **chi** (ち)

COMMON WORDS AND COMPOUNDS		
千	*one thousand*	**SEN** セン
二千	two + thousand = *two thousand*	**NI·SEN** ニ·セン
三千	three + thousand = *three thousand*	**SAN·ZEN** サン·ゼン
四千	four + thousand = *four thousand*	yon·**SEN** よん·セン
五千	five + thousand = *five thousand*	**GO·SEN** ゴ·セン
六千	six + thousand = *six thousand*	**ROKU·SEN** ロク·セン
七千	seven + thousand = *seven thousand*	nana·**SEN** なな·セン
八千	eight + thousand = *eight thousand*	**HAS·SEN** ハッ·セン
九千	nine + thousand = *nine thousand*	**KYŪ·SEN** キュウ·セン

SAMPLE SENTENCE:

米	は	七千円	なので
kome	**wa**	**nana·SEN·EN**	**na no de**
rice	wa	seven thousand yen	because

安くない。

yasu·kunai.

not cheap

= *At seven thousand yen, rice isn't cheap.*

COMPONENT #66

GIRAFFE

You will notice this component used extensively in written Japanese, as it appears in almost one hundred kanji.

KANJI 66

休 **REST**

BUILDING THIS KANJI
Giraffe 亻 + Tree 木(13) = 休

Meaning
Rest.

Remembering this kanji
One of the surprises of my trip to Africa was learning that **giraffes** RESTED in trees. The safari leader mentioned that this was natural behavior. "They prefer baobabs," he said. "The branches are lower, so when the **giraffes** make a running leap at them they can jump higher into the **tree**. But this is not done simply for REST," he then added. "It also serves as an effective way for any **giraffe** to avoid its natural creditors."

Common Pronunciations
Common **ON** reading: **KYŪ** (キュウ)
Common **kun** reading: **yasu** (やす)

kun-yomi suggestion: "try a souffle"

Create your **on-yomi** keyword and enter it in th table at the back of the book. After that, write yo sentence to remember the **on-yomi** and **kun-yo** readings in the box below.

Less Common Pronunciations
Less common **ON** reading: none
Less common **kun** reading: none

COMMON WORDS AND COMPOUNDS		
休む	*to rest*	**yasu**·mu やす·む
お休み	"Good night!"	o·**yasu**·mi お·やす·み
休日	rest + sun (day) = *holiday*	**KYŪ**·JITSU キュウ·ジツ
夏休み	summer + rest = *summer vacation*	natsu **yasu**·mi なつ やす·み
冬休み	winter + rest = *winter vacation*	fuyu **yasu**·mi ふゆ やす·み
休火山	rest + fire + mountain = *dormant volcano*	**KYŪ**·KA·ZAN キュウ·カ·ザン

SAMPLE SENTENCE:

山口さん　　　は　　　半日
Yama·guchi-san　**wa**　　**HAN·NICHI**
Yamaguchi-san　　　　　　　half a day
休みました。
yasu·mimashita.
　　rested
= *Yamaguchi-san rested for half a day.*

HAND

`	⼆	三	手				

Meaning
Hand. No story required.

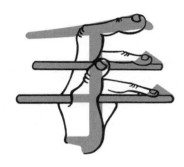

Common Pronunciations
Common **ON** reading: **SHU** (シュ)
Common **kun** reading: **te** (て)

The **kun-yomi** is by far the most common reading.

kun-yomi suggestion: "tent"

Write your sentence to remember the **on-yomi** and **kun-yomi** readings in the box below.

Less Common Pronunciations
Less common **ON** reading: none
Less common **kun** reading: **ta** (た)

ta (た) is an extremely rare reading, although it does show up in 下手, a common irregular reading we learned back in Chapter 2. It is presented again below following its companion; the two words are best learned as a pair.

IRREGULAR READINGS		
上手	upper + hand = to be good at (something)	JŌ·zu ジョウ・ず
下手	lower + hand = to be poor at (something)	he·ta へ・た

COMMON WORDS AND COMPOUNDS		
手	hand	te て
右手	right + hand = right hand	migi·te みぎ・て
左手	left + hand = left hand	hidari·te ひだり・て
手元	hand + basis = at hand	te·moto て・もと
手首	hand + neck = wrist	te·kubi て・くび
手話	hand + speak = sign language	SHU·WA シュ・ワ
空手	empty + hand = karate	kara·te から・て

SAMPLE SENTENCE:

あの ピアニスト の 手 は 美しい
ano   pianisuto   no   te   wa   utsuku·shii
that   pianist   hands   beautiful
です ね。
desu   ne.
aren't they
= *That pianist's hands are beautiful, aren't they?*

KANJI 68

本 **MAIN**

一	十	才	木	本			

BUILDING THIS KANJI
Tree 木(13) + One (hamburger patty) 一(3) = 本

Meaning

This intriguing character encompasses a range of meanings from "main" to "origin," and is also used to emphasize the idea of "this". When encountered alone, however, it often indicates a book. It is also one of the more common of an infamous group of kanji that Japanese uses for counting, being employed for long, cylindrical objects such as pencils and bottles. The sense of "origin," incidentally, is evident in the compound for Japan itself, the "Land of the Rising Sun."

Remembering this kanji

Despite cultural differences, there is a surprising amount of commonality in the world's MAIN myths. The people of Ur, for example, clearly tell Enkidu in the "Epic of Gilgamesh" that the MAIN race of people was conceived from a "union between **hamburger patty** and **tree**." Beowulf, too, quotes Norse mythology to explain the MAIN purpose of mankind: "Go forth, so that from **patties** will sprout mighty **trees**…" Coincidence? In the MAIN, it's unlikely.

Common Pronunciations

Common **ON** reading: **HON** (ホン)
Common **kun** reading: **moto** (もと)

The **kun-yomi** is common in Japanese family and place names; the fifth compound below provides an example. Create your **on-yomi** keyword and enter it in the table at the back of the book. After that, write your sentence to remember the **on-yomi** and **kun-yomi** readings in the box below.

Less Common Pronunciations

Less common **ON** reading: none
Less common **kun** reading: none

COMMON WORDS AND COMPOUNDS		
本	*book*	**HON** ホン
日本	sun + main = *Japan*	**NI·HON** ニ・ホン **NIP·PON** ニッ・ポン
全日本	complete + sun + main = *all Japan*	**ZEN·NI·HON** ゼン・ニ・ホン
日本人	sun + main + person = *a Japanese* *(person)*	**NI·HON·JIN** ニ・ホン・ジン
山本 さん	mountain + main = *Yamamoto-san*	yama·**moto**·san やま・もと・さん
日本語	sun + main + words = *Japanese* *(language)*	**NI·HON·GO** ニ・ホン・ゴ
本土	main + earth = *mainland*	**HON·DO** ホン・ド

SAMPLE SENTENCE:

山下さん　は　　高い　　本　を
Yama·shita-san　wa　　taka·i　　HON　o
Yamashita-san　　　　expensive　book
買いました。
ka·imashita.
　bought
= *Yamashita-san bought an expensive book.*

COMPONENT #69

BEGGAR   ヒ

KANJI 69

化 **CHANGE**

イ	イ	化				

BUILDING THIS KANJI
Giraffe イ + Beggar ヒ = 化

Meaning
Change/Transform. When used as a suffix (as in several of the compounds below), this character expresses a variety of English words ending in "-ification" or "-ization."

Remembering this kanji
Grandpa liked nothing more than to help those down on their luck. But he never gave money. I learned this when I saw him carrying a stuffed **giraffe** down to skid row one day.

"This is for you," he said to a **beggar**, passing him the toy. "A companion to share your woe."

The **beggar** nodded, and after taking his gift started immediately across the street.

"Where are you going?" Grandpa asked.

"This **giraffe** is so wonderful," said the **beggar**, "that I want to show it to all my friends in the pawn shop."

Grandpa smiled. "Now do you understand?" he said to me. "Giving money CHANGES nothing. It is only through stuffed **giraffes** that a **beggar's** life can truly be CHANGED."

Common Pronunciations

Common **ON** reading: **KA** (カ)

Common **kun** reading: none

Write your sentence to remember the **on-yomi** reading in the box below.

Less Common Pronunciations

Less common **ON** reading: **KE** (ケ)

Less common **kun** reading: **ba** (ば)

COMMON WORDS AND COMPOUNDS		
国有化	country + have + change = *nationalization*	KOKU·YŪ·KA コク・ユウ・カ
美化	beautiful + change = *beautification*	BI·KA ビ・カ
化学	change + study = *chemistry*	**KA·GAKU** カ・ガク
気化	spirit + change = *vaporize*	KI·KA キ・カ
電化	electric + change = *electrification*	DEN·KA デン・カ
同化	same + change = *assimilation*	DŌ·KA ドウ・カ

SAMPLE SENTENCE:

山本さん　　は　　化学　　が
Yama·moto-san   wa   KA·GAKU   ga
Yamamoto-san   chemistry
大好き　です。
DAI su·ki   desu.
really likes
= *Yamamoto-san really likes chemistry.*

KANJI 70

川 **RIVER**

ノ	ﾉﾄ	川						

Meaning
River. No story required.

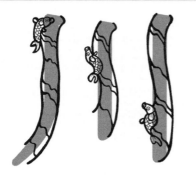

Common Pronunciations
Common **ON** reading: none
Common **kun** reading: **kawa** (かわ)

When appearing as the final character in the names of rivers, this kanji is invariably voiced (becomes "**gawa**").

kun-yomi suggestion: "lack **a wa**x"

Create your sentence to remember the **kun-yo**
reading in the box below.

Less Common Pronunciations
Less common **ON** reading: **SEN**
Less common **kun** reading: none

COMMON WORDS AND COMPOUNDS		
川	*river*	**kawa** かわ
川上	river + upper = *upstream*	**kawa**·kami かわ·かみ
川下	river + lower = *downstream*	**kawa**·shimo かわ·しも
川口	river + mouth = *river mouth*	**kawa**·guchi かわ·ぐち
川本さん	river + main = *Kawamoto-san*	**kawa**·moto·san かわ·もと· さん

SAMPLE SENTENCE:

山　の　上　に　行く　と　川　ガ
yama　no　ue　ni　i·ku　to　kawa　g
mountain　upper　　　go　　river
見えます　か。
mi·emasu　ka.
can see
= *Can you see the river if you go to the top of t.
mountain?*

KANJI 71

体 **BODY**

| 亻 | 仁 | 什 | 伓 | 休 | 体 | | |

BUILDING THIS KANJI

Giraffe 亻 + Main 本(68) = 体

Meaning

The physical body (of a person or object), as well as secondary ideas of "substance" and "style." Make sure to keep this character distinct in your mind from "休" (Entry 66).

Remembering this kanji

As the **main** part of a **giraffe's** identity is tied to its statuesque BODY, all **giraffes** have a tendency to be vain. This naturally breeds conflict on the savanna. It is a rare wildebeest, for example, who hasn't been left with crippling BODY issues after watching a **giraffe** stride nobly along in the distance. As cats, however, it is the lions who are especially BODY conscious and apt to take a slight personally. Though the **main** part of their diet lies elsewhere, they will attack any **giraffe** who looks down on them.

Common Pronunciations

Common **ON** reading: **TAI** (タイ)
Common **kun** reading: **karada** (からだ)

kun-yomi suggestion: "ma**ke a rad a**mbulance"

Write your sentence to remember the **on-yomi** and **kun-yomi** readings in the box below.

Less Common Pronunciations

Less common **ON** reading: **TEI** (テイ)
Less common **kun** reading: none

COMMON WORDS AND COMPOUNDS		
体	*body*	karada からだ
大体	large + body = *in general*	DAI·TAI ダイ・タイ
全体	complete + body = *the whole*	ZEN·TAI ゼン・タイ
肉体	meat + body = *the body*	NIKU·TAI ニク・タイ
体力	body + strength = *physical strength*	TAI·RYOKU タイ・リョク
自体	self + body = *in itself*	JI·TAI ジ・タイ
団体	group + body = *organization*	DAN·TAI ダン・タイ

SAMPLE SENTENCE:

あの　人　は　すごく　　体力
ano　hito　wa　sugoku　TAI·RYOKU
that person　　incredible　physical strength
が　有ります。
ga　a·rimasu.
　　　has
= *That person has incredible physical strength.*

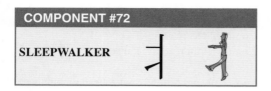

COMPONENT #72

SLEEPWALKER

KANJI 72

北 **NORTH**

BUILDING THIS KANJI
Sleepwalker ㇰ + Beggar ヒ = 北

Meaning
North. Note that in the more calligraphic font used above, the second stroke is slightly shortened at the bottom.

Remembering this kanji
Once upon a time, a **sleepwalker** heading NORTH passed a **beggar**. "I'd better follow," thought the **beggar**. "This **sleepwalker** might be on her way to Santa's workshop, and I hear that guy gives away lots of free stuff."

Common Pronunciations
Common **ON** reading: **HOKU** (ホ ク)
Common **kun** reading: **kita** (き た)

As the final example shows, **HOKU** can doub up with unvoiced consonant sounds.

kun-yomi suggestion: "**ski tax**"

Create your **on-yomi** keyword and enter it in t table at the back of the book. After that, write yo sentence to remember the **on-yomi** and **kun-yo** readings in the box below.

Less Common Pronunciations
Less common **ON** reading: none
Less common **kun** reading: none

COMMON WORDS AND COMPOUNDS		
北	*north*	**kita** き た
北米	north + rice (America) = *North America*	**HOKU·BEI** ホ ク ・ ベ イ
北口	north + mouth = *north exit/entrance*	**kita·guchi** き た ・ ぐ ち
北東	north + east = *northeast*	**HOKU·TŌ** ホ ク ・ ト ウ
北西	north + west = *northwest*	**HOKU·SEI** ホ ク ・ セ イ
北海道	north + sea + road = *Hokkaido*	**HOK·KAI·DŌ** ホ ッ ・ カ イ ・ ド ウ

SAMPLE SENTENCE:

北日本　の　冬　はとても美しい。

kita·NI·HON no fuyu wa totemo utsuku·shi
northern Japan   winter   very   beautiful
= *Northern Japan's winter is very beautiful.*

KANJI 73

RICE FIELD

| 冂 | 𠘨 | 甲 | 田 | | | |

Meaning

Rice field," or a "field" in general. No story required.

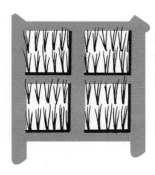

Common Pronunciations

Common **ON** reading: **DEN** (デン)
Common **kun** reading: **ta** (た)

This kanji is commonly used in Japanese family names; it is often voiced, as in the fourth and fifth examples below, the latter of which has a mix of on and **kun-yomi**.

kun-yomi suggestion: "**tack**"

Create your **on-yomi** keyword and enter it in the table at the back of the book. After that, write your sentence to remember the **on-yomi** and **kun-yomi** readings in the box below.

Less Common Pronunciations

Less common **ON** reading: none
Less common **kun** reading: none

Here is a common irregular reading:

IRREGULAR READING		
田舎*	rice field + building = *the countryside*	**inaka** いなか

COMMON WORDS AND COMPOUNDS		
田	*rice field*	**ta** た
水田	water + rice field = *rice paddy*	**SUI·DEN** スイ·デン
田中さん	rice field + middle = *Tanaka-san*	**ta**·naka·san た·なか·さん
山田さん	mountain + rice field = *Yamada-san*	yama·**da**·san やま·だ·さん
本田さん	main + rice field = *Honda-san*	HON·**da**·san ホン·だ·さん

SAMPLE SENTENCE:

水田 を 見 に 行きました。
SUI·DEN o mi ni i·kimashita.
rice paddy   see   went
= *(She) went to see the rice paddies.*

KANJI 74

男 **MAN**

| ㇒ | 冂 | 冊 | 田 | 田 | 罗 | 男 | | |

BUILDING THIS KANJI
Rice field 田 (73) + Strength 力 (63) = 男

Meaning
Man/Male.

Remembering this kanji
There is a story from feudal Japan in which a
lord asks a group of MEN to demonstrate their
strength. The task he sets them is simple: to
lift up as much of a **rice field** as possible. Each
MAN in the competition does his best, of course,
but none save the last can pull up more than
an armful of muck. What is this final MAN'S
secret, you ask? It should be obvious: he was the
only one with enough sense to use a bulldozer.

Common Pronunciations
Common **ON** reading: **DAN** (ダン)
Common **kun** reading: otoko (おとこ)

kun-yomi suggestion: "**O! Toe cold**"

Create your **on-yomi** keyword and enter it in the
table at the back of the book. After that, write your
sentence to remember the **on-yomi** and **kun-yomi**
readings in the box below.

Less Common Pronunciations
Less common **ON** reading: **NAN** (ナン)
Less common **kun** reading: none

COMMON WORDS AND COMPOUNDS		
男	*man*	**otoko** おとこ
男女	man + woman = *men and women*	**DAN·JO** ダン・ジョ
男子	man + child = *men's*	**DAN·SHI** ダン・シ
大男	large + man = *large man*	**ō·otoko** おお・おとこ
雪男	snow + man = *the abominable snowman*	yuki·**otoko** ゆき・おとこ

SAMPLE SENTENCE:

あの　男　の　人　は　　五千円
ano　otoko　no　hito　　wa　　GO·SEN·EN
that　man　　　person　　　five thousand yen
を　なくした。
o　nakushita.
　　　lost
= *That man lost five thousand yen.*

COMPONENT #75

PIG

KANJI 75

家 **HOUSE**

'	ハ	宀	宀	宇	宇	宇	宇	家
家								

BUILDING THIS KANJI

Pincers 宀 + Pig 豕 = 家

Meaning

This character generally imparts some sense of relation to a house or family. When used as a suffix, however, it denotes a person having some degree of skill or interest with respect to the kanji preceding it. The final compound below illustrates this aspect of its meaning.

Remembering this kanji

People told me I was crazy when they learned I was moving from my farm to the metropolis. 'The people are cold there, and you won't make any friends', they all said. Well, I went anyway, and to prove them wrong I got out my **pincers** and hung an enormous **pig** outside my HOUSE in order to welcome people as they walked by. And yet this is the strange thing: despite all the squealing for days on end, nobody visited, and when I told people my HOUSE was the one with the **pincers** and **pig**, they quit talking to me altogether! I guess everyone was right to say folks wouldn't be very friendly, 'cause they sure weren't when it came to my HOUSE.

Common Pronunciations

Common **ON** reading: **KA** (カ)
Common **kun** reading: **ie** (いえ)

kun-yomi suggestion: "Canadian"

Write your sentence to remember the **on-yomi** and **kun-yomi** readings in the box below.

Less Common Pronunciations

Less common **ON** reading: **KE** (ケ)
Less common **kun** reading: **ya** (や)

COMMON WORDS AND COMPOUNDS		
家	house	ie いえ
人家	person + house = *dwelling*	JIN·KA ジン・カ
売り家	sell + house = *"house for sale"*	u·ri ie う・り いえ
家具	house + tool = *furniture*	KA·GU カ・グ
愛鳥家	love + bird + house = *bird lover*	AI·CHŌ·KA アイ・チョウ・カ

SAMPLE SENTENCE:

本田さん の 家 を 見ました か。

HON·da-san no ie o mi·mashita ka.

Honda-san house see

= *Did you see Honda-san's house?*

KANJI 76

東 **EAST**

| 一 | 一 | 冂 | 戸 | 戸 | 車 | 東 | 東 |

BUILDING THIS KANJI
Tree 木(13) + Sun 日(6) = 東

Meaning
East.

Remembering this kanji
Note that the writing order for this kanji does not follow that of the components as listed. This will happen only rarely; the image of a **sun** rising behind a **tree** in the EAST, however, is clearly the logical way to remember this character.

Common Pronunciations
Common **ON** reading: **TŌ** (トウ)
Common **kun** reading: **higashi** (ひがし)

kun-yomi suggestion: "**he gash ea**sy…"

Write your sentence to remember the **on-yomi** and **kun-yomi** readings in the box below.

Less Common Pronunciations
Less common **ON** reading: none
Less common **kun** reading: none

COMMON WORDS AND COMPOUNDS		
東	east	**higashi** ひがし
東口	east + mouth = *east exit/entrance*	**higashi**·guchi ひがし・ぐち
中東	middle + east = *the Middle East*	**CHŪ·TŌ** チュウ・トウ
東京	east + capital = *Tokyo*	**TŌ·KYŌ** トウ・キョウ
南東	south + east = *southeast*	**NAN·TŌ** ナン・トウ
北北東	north + north + east = *north-northeast*	**HOKU·HOKU·TŌ** ホク・ホク・トウ

SAMPLE SENTENCE:

東口　　　の　　キオスク　で　　　本
higashi·guchi　no　kiosuku　de　　HON
　east exit　　　　　kiosk　　　　　book
を　買いました。
o　　ka·imashita.
　　　bought
= *(I) bought a book at the east exit kiosk.*

思 THINK

| 丶 | 冂 | 冖 | 用 | 田 | 田 | 甲 | 思 | 思 | 思 |

BUILDING THIS KANJI
Rice field 田 (73) + Heart 心 (25) = 思

Meaning
Think.

Remembering this kanji
And so I took the **heart** and buried it in a **rice field**. But soon I began to THINK: What if it rises to the surface? What if a thrifty animal digs it up for food? Horrors! All I could do was THINK...THINK of what I had done, until there was nothing in my head but the beating of that hideous **heart** in the **rice field**. But I know what you THINK: you either THINK I'm mad, or that this story sounds awfully familiar.

Common Pronunciations
Common **ON** reading: **SHI** (シ)
Common **kun** reading: **omo** (おも)

kun-yomi suggestion: "**o, mow**..."

Write your sentence to remember the **on-yomi** and **kun-yomi** readings in the box below.

Less Common Pronunciations
Less common **ON** reading: none
Less common **kun** reading: none

COMMON WORDS AND COMPOUNDS		
思う	*to think*	**omo·u** おも·う
思い出す	think + exit = *to remember*	**omo·i** da·su おも·い だ·す
物思い	thing + think = *pensiveness*	mono **omo·i** もの おも·い
思い切る	think + cut = *to make up one's mind*	**omo·i** ki·ru おも·い き·る
意思	mind + think = *(one's) intent*	**I·SHI** イ·シ

SAMPLE SENTENCE:

テーブル の 上 に 四百円
tēburu   no   ue   ni   yon·HYAKU·EN
table   above   four hundred yen
ある と 思います。
aru   to   omo·imasu.
 is   think
= *(I) think there's four hundred yen on the table.*

KANJI 78

耳
EAR

Meaning
Ear. No story required.

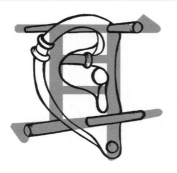

Common Pronunciations
Common **ON** reading: none
Common **kun** reading: **mimi** (みみ)

kun-yomi suggestion: "Me! Me!"

Create your sentence to remember the **kun-yo**▸
reading in the box below.

Less Common Pronunciations
Less common **ON** reading: **JI** (ジ)
Less common **kun** reading: none

COMMON WORDS AND COMPOUNDS		
耳	*ear*	**mimi** みみ
耳元	ear + basis = *close to one's ear*	**mimi**·moto みみ·もと
空耳	empty + ear = *mishearing; feigned deafness*	sora·**mimi** そら·みみ

SAMPLE SENTENCE:

田中さん　の　　耳　が　赤い。
Ta·naka-san　no　mimi　ga　aka·i.
Tanaka-san　　　　ears　　　red
= *Tanaka-san's ears are red.*

COMPONENT #79

WISHBONES

KANJI 79

父 **FATHER**

ノ	ハ	グ	父				

BUILDING THIS KANJI
Eight (volcano) ハ(19) + Wishbones メ = 父

Meaning
Father.

Remembering this kanji
Jupiter, as FATHER of the gods, can do whatever he wants. Unfortunately, he's not as environmentally conscious as he should be, and often uses the nearest **volcano** to dump **wishbones** and other scraps from his plate. Jupiter's son Vulcan, the god of **volcanoes**, naturally takes exception to this behavior. "So help me, FATHER," he says, "if I wake up with any more **wishbones** on my rug, I might just erupt."

Common Pronunciations
Common **ON** reading: FU (フ)
Common **kun** reading: chichi (ち ち)

The various words for father shown below reflect differing levels of familiarity and politeness; most terms used for addressing people in Japan have multiple forms such as these.

kun-yomi suggestion: "**Chichi** Rodriguez"

Create your **on-yomi** keyword and enter it in the table at the back of the book. After that, write your sentence to remember the **on-yomi** and **kun-yomi** readings in the box below.

Less Common Pronunciations
Less common **ON** reading: none
Less common **kun** reading: none

These two irregular readings are extremely common.

IRREGULAR READINGS		
お父さん	father = *father*	otōsan おとうさん
伯父さん*	related + father = *uncle*	ojisan おじさん

COMMON WORDS AND COMPOUNDS		
父	father	**chichi** ち ち
父の日	father + sun (day) = *Father's Day*	**chichi**·no·hi ち ち·の·ひ
父母	father + mother = *father and mother*	**FU·BO** フ·ボ
父親	father + parent = *father*	**chichi**·oya ち ち·おや

SAMPLE SENTENCE:

父 は ビジネス で 東京
chichi wa bijinesu de TŌ·KYŌ
Father business Tokyo
へ 行きました。
e i·kimashita.
went
= *Father went to Tokyo on business.*

KANJI 80

言 **SAY**

Meaning

"Saying," and things of a verbal nature. This character, incidentally, will become very familiar; it appears in more than sixty other kanji.

Remembering this kanji

"I vant...to drink...yours...blood." Isn't this what a **vampire** like Dracula always SAYS? Sure, you SAY, but what's with the bad grammar? Well, give Dracula a break; he's from Transylvania, and English isn't his first language. Notice, by the way, that the second stroke from the top is longer than those above or below it. Also note that in some more calligraphic fonts (such as that used above), the first stroke transforms into our "jelly bean" component.

Common Pronunciations

Common **ON** reading: **GEN** (ゲン)
Common **kun** reading: **i** (い)

kun-yomi suggestion: **"eager"**

Write your sentence to remember the **on-yomi** and **kun-yomi** readings in the box below.

Less Common Pronunciations

Less common **ON** reading: **GON** (ゴン)
Less common **kun** reading: **koto** (こと)

The reading **koto** will be encountered primarily in the Japanese term for "word": **koto·ba** (こと ば), composed of the kanji 言葉 (Say/Leaf *).

COMMON WORDS AND COMPOUNDS		
言う	*to say*	i·u い・う
言い回し	say + rotate = *(turn of)* *expression*	i·i mawa·shi い・い まわ・し
明言	bright + say = *declaration*	**MEI·GEN** メイ・ゲン
言語	say + words = *language*	**GEN·GO** ゲン・ゴ
言い出す	say + exit = *to begin to say*	i·i da·su い・い だ・す
言い切る	say + cut = *to say* *definitively*	i·i ki·ru い・い き・る

SAMPLE SENTENCE:

川本さん	も	"はい"	と
Kawa·moto-san	**mo**	**"hai"**	**to**
Kawamoto-san	also	"yes"	

言いました。
i·imashita.
said
= *Kawamoto-san also said "yes."*

CHAPTER 4 REVIEW EXERCISES

A. Please match the following kanji to their meanings.

1.	父	a.	Body
2.	川	b.	Hand
3.	安	c.	Father
4.	東	d.	Thousand
5.	手	e.	Main
6.	男	f.	Ease
7.	千	g.	Man
8.	力	h.	East
9.	体	i.	Strength
10.	本	j.	River

B. Please match the following meanings to their kanji, and these to their **on** or **kun-yomi**.

1.	Rest	a. 田	1.	**GEN** (ゲン)	
2.	Change	b. 耳	2.	**HOKU** (ホク)	
3.	North	c. 化	3.	**SHI** (シ)	
4.	House **(kun-yomi)**	d. 言	4.	**yasu** (やす)	
5.	Rice field	e. 夏	5.	**SUI** (スイ)	
6.	Think	f. 休	6.	**ta** (た)	
7.	Summer **(kun-yomi)**	g. 家	7.	**natsu** (なつ)	
8.	Say	h. 水	8.	**ie** (いえ)	

9.	Water	i. 北	9. **KA** (カ)
10.	Ear	j. 思	10. **mimi** (みみ)

C. Please choose the best answer(s) to the following questions.

1. Which of the following readings apply to the kanji 東?
   a. **TŌ** (トウ)
   b. **higashi** (ひがし)
   c. **KA** (カ)
   d. **kita** (きた)
   e. **minami** (みなみ)

2. Which of the following readings apply to the kanji 男?
   a. **onna** (おんな)
   b. **DAN** (ダン)
   c. **otoko** (おとこ)
   d. **KYŪ** (キュウ)
   e. **SUI** (スイ)

3. Which of the following kanji have an **on-yomi** of **KA** (カ)?
   a. 夏
   b. 北
   c. 思
   d. 家
   e. 化

4. What would make a nice gift for a pair of newlyweds?
   a. 手
   b. 体
   c. 耳
   d. 家
   e. 北

5. Which of the following readings apply to the kanji 体?
   a. **SHŌ** (ショウ)
   b. **TAI** (タイ)
   c. **omo** (おも)
   d. **DAI** (ダイ)
   e. **karada** (からだ)

D. Please choose the best answer to the following questions.

1. Which of the following kanji has the most number of strokes?
   a. 東
   b. 男
   c. 言
   d. 思
   e. 体

2. Which is the correct reading of 安い?
   a. **omo·i** (おも・い)
   b. **yasu·i** (やす・い)
   c. **taka·i** (たか・い)
   d. **ō·i** (おお・い)

3. Which is the correct reading of 思う?
   a. **ka·u** (か・う)
   b. **ko·u** (こ・う)
   c. **omo·u** (おも・う)
   d. **o·u** (お・う)

4. Which kanji would precede 力 to form the compound for "physical strength"?
   a. 休
   b. 本
   c. 東
   d. 体
   e. 耳

5. Which is the correct reading of 言う?
   a. **i·u** (い・う)
   b. **o·u** (お・う)
   c. **a·u** (あ・う)
   d. **omo·u** (おも・う)

E. Please match the following compounds and words to their meanings and pronunciations.

1.	大体	a. Close to one's ear	1.	**SUI·CHŪ** (スイ・チュウ)
2.	全日本	b. Peace of mind	2.	**te·kubi** (て・くび)
3.	北米	c. In general	3.	**mimi·moto** (みみ・もと)
4.	耳元	d. Summer vacation	4.	**i·i mawa·shi** (い・い まわ・し)
5.	水中	e. Powerful	5.	**AN·SHIN** (アン・シン)
6.	有力	f. North America	6.	**ZEN·NI·HON** (ゼン・ニ・ホン)
7.	言い回し	g. Wrist	7.	**natsu yasu·mi** (なつ やす・み)
8.	夏休み	h. All Japan	8.	**HOKU·BEI** (ホク・ベイ)
9.	手首	i. (Turn of) expression	9.	**DAI·TAI** (ダイ・タイ)
10.	安心	j. Underwater/ In the water	10.	**YŪ·RYOKU** (ユウ・リョク)

CHAPTER FIVE

Kanji #81 — 100

KANJI 81

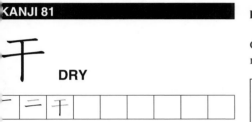

DRY

一	二	千						

Meaning
Dry/Ebb. This character will not be encountered frequently. It does figure as a component in other more common kanji, however, and because of this is presented here. Take a moment to note the difference between this character and 千 (Entry 65). No story required.

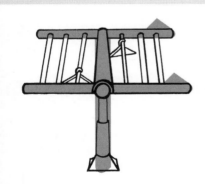

Common Pronunciations
Common **ON** reading: none
Common **kun** readings: **hi** (ひ); **ho** (ほ)

As seen in the third example below, the **kun-yomi** "**ho**" can become voiced in the second position.

kun-yomi suggestions: "**heat**"; "**hose**"

Create your sentence to remember the **kun-yomi** readings in the box below.

Less Common Pronunciations
Less common **ON** reading: **KAN** (カン)
Less common **kun** reading: none

COMMON WORDS AND COMPOUNDS		
干る (intr)	to dry *(on its own)*	**hi**·ru ひ・る
干す (tr)	to dry *(something)*	**ho**·su ほ・す
日干し	sun + dry = *sun-dried*	hi **bo**·shi ひ ぼ・し
干上がる	dry + upper = *to dry up*	**hi** a·garu ひ あ・がる
干物	dry + thing = *dried fish*	**hi**·mono ひ・もの

SAMPLE SENTENCE:
干物　を　買って　下さい。
hi·mono　o　kat·te　kuda·sai.
dried fish　　　buy　　　please
= *Please buy dried fish.*

KANJI 82

金 **GOLD**

ノ	𠆢	厶	今	全	全	金	金

BUILDING THIS KANJI
Umbrella 𠆢 + Dry 千 (81) + Snowboard ⼆ = 金

Meaning
Depending on the context in which it appears, this common character signifies either "gold," "metal," or "money." It clearly means "gold", for instance, when referring to the status of an Olympic champion. When functioning as a component, however, it hints that the kanji involved has some connection to metal in general

Remembering this kanji
Following a quick break with his buddies, the **snowboarder** had another vision. This time, however, the genie was very specific: "Dude, unless this GOLDEN snowboard is kept **dry** at all times, it will immediately turn back into fiberglass. You must, therefore, always use an **umbrella**, even on the gnarliest runs. Should you not keep it **dry**…well, it would still be a decent enough board, it just wouldn't be GOLD anymore. And GOLD is like, really valuable."

Common Pronunciations
Common **ON** reading: **KIN** (キ ン)
Common **kun** reading: **kane** (か ね)

kun-yomi suggestion: "**Khan** ate"

Create your **on-yomi** keyword and enter it in th
table at the back of the book. After that, write yo
sentence to remember the **on-yomi** and **kun-yor**
readings in the box below.

Less Common Pronunciations
Less common **ON** reading: **KON** (コ ン)
Less common **kun** reading: **kana** (か な)

COMMON WORDS AND COMPOUNDS		
金	gold; metal; money	**KIN** キン
金	metal; money	**kane** かね
金山	gold + mountain = *gold mine*	**KIN·ZAN** キン・ザン
年金	year + gold (money) = *annuity/pension*	**NEN·KIN** ネン・キン
金曜日	gold + day of the week + sun (day) = *Friday*	**KIN·YŌ·bi** キン・ヨウ・び
金星	gold + star = *Venus (planet)*	**KIN·SEI** キン・セイ

SAMPLE SENTENCE:

内田さん は あまり お金 が ない。
Uchi·da-san wa amari o·kane ga nai.
Uchida-san   not much money   not
= *Uchida-san doesn't have much money.*

KANJI 83

語 **WORDS**

`	゛	⸍	≡	≡	言	言	言	訂
訢	語	語	語	語				

BUILDING THIS KANJI
Say 言 (80) + Five 五 (14) + Mouth (vampire) 口 (8) = 語

Meaning
Words. This kanji will become familiar as the character used to indicate languages; a pair of examples can be seen in the compounds below.

Remembering this kanji
Mark my WORDS: despite what **vampires** everywhere will **say**, you do not want to go to a pentagon party with **five** of them. Their reassuring WORDS of such events being "normal Transylvanian hospitality" are far from the truth.

I VANT
TO DRINK
YOURS
BLOOD

Common Pronunciations
Common **ON** reading: **GO** (ゴ)
Common **kun** reading: **kata** (か た)

Note the importance of long and short vowel sounds in Japanese by looking closely at the second and third examples below. Also note the presence of an irregular reading (上手) in the sample sentence.

kun-yomi suggestion: "**cat a**cne"

Write your sentence to remember the **on-yomi** and **kun-yomi** readings in the box below.

Less Common Pronunciations
Less common **ON** reading: none
Less common **kun** reading: **katari** (か た り)

COMMON WORDS AND COMPOUNDS		
語る	to talk	**kata·ru** か た・る
口語	mouth + words = *colloquial language*	**KŌ·GO** コ ウ・ゴ
古語	old + words = *archaic word*	**KO·GO** コ・ゴ
日本語	sun + main + words = *Japanese (language)*	**NI·HON·GO** ニ・ホ ン・ゴ
言語	say + words = *language*	**GEN·GO** ゲ ン・ゴ
英語	English + words = *English (language)*	**EI·GO** エ イ・ゴ
語学	words + study = *linguistics*	**GO·GAKU** ゴ・ガ ク

SAMPLE SENTENCE:
あ な た の　 日 本 語　 は 上 手 で す よ 。
anata   no NI·HON·GO wa JŌ·zu desu   yo.
you   Japanese   good at
= *Your Japanese is good!*

KANJI 84

士 **GENTLEMAN**

Meaning
The sense is of a gentleman, or of a man who has attained status in a military or academic field. No story required.

Common Pronunciations
Common **ON** reading: **SHI** (シ)
Common **kun** reading: none

Write your sentence to remember the **on-yon** reading in the box below.

Less Common Pronunciations
Less common **ON** reading: none
Less common **kun** reading: none

COMMON WORDS AND COMPOUNDS		
力士	strength + gentleman = *sumo wrestler*	RIKI·**SHI** リ キ·シ
士気	gentleman + spirit = *morale*	**SHI**·KI シ·キ
工学士	craft + study + gentleman = *Bachelor of Engineering*	KŌ·GAKU·**SHI** コ ウ·ガ ク·シ

SAMPLE SENTENCE:

あの 力士 はとても大きいですよ。

 ano RIKI·SHI wa totemo ō·kii desu yo
that sumo wrestler very large is
= *That sumo wrestler is really large!*

KANJI 85

朝 **MORNING**

一	十	亠	古	吉	甴	直	卓	龺
朝	朝	朝						

BUILDING THIS KANJI
Ten (scarecrow) 十 (28) + Early 早 (29) +
Moon 月 (11) = 朝

Meaning
Morning. A secondary meaning relates to royal dynasties.

Remembering this kanji
As always, each MORNING the **moon** gave a wink to the **scarecrow**. "You're up **early**," he said.

  "For godsakes," said the **scarecrow**. "When are you going to get tired of that joke?"

Common Pronunciations

Common **ON** reading: **CHŌ** (チョウ)
Common **kun** reading: **asa** (あさ)

Note the mix of **on** and **kun-yomi** in the final example below.

kun-yomi suggestion: "**Casa**nova"

Create your **on-yomi** keyword and enter it in the table at the back of the book. After that, write your sentence to remember the **on-yomi** and **kun-yomi** readings in the box below.

Less Common Pronunciations

Less common **ON** reading: none
Less common **kun** reading: none

IRREGULAR READING		
今朝	now + morning = *this morning*	**kesa** けさ

COMMON WORDS AND COMPOUNDS		
朝	*morning*	**asa** あさ
朝日	morning + sun = *morning sun*	**asa·hi** あさ・ひ
王朝	king + morning = *dynasty*	**Ō·CHŌ** オウ・チョウ
早朝	early + morning = *early morning*	**SŌ·CHŌ** ソウ・チョウ
毎朝	every + morning = *every morning*	**MAI·asa** マイ・あさ

SAMPLE SENTENCE:

上田さんは　朝　が　大好き　です。
Ue·da-san wa　asa　ga　DAI su·ki　desu.
Ueda-san　　　morning　　really likes
= *Ueda-san really likes mornings.*

CANDLESTICK HOLDER

青 **BLUE**

BUILDING THIS KANJI
Candlestick Holder 圭 + Moon 月 (11) = 青

Meaning

Blue. Interestingly, this character is also applied to a few objects that Westerners invariably consider green, so prepare yourself to be confronted with blue traffic lights and blue vegetables, amongst other things. As in English, the sense of youth and immaturity is tied up with this idea of "green"; the third compound below provides an example.

Remembering this kanji

Even the **moon** can get depressed, and on those occasions when he's feeling BLUE he doesn't give off his normal amount of light. To cover up for this he'll take out a **candlestick holder**, but as there's nothing in it, his ploy doesn't fool anyone. Luckily for us, he only feels this way once in a BLUE **moon**.

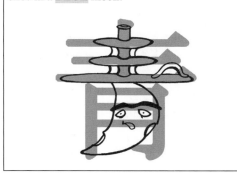

Common Pronunciations

Common **ON** reading: **SEI** (セイ)
Common **kun** reading: **ao** (あお)

kun-yomi suggestion: "**Lao**s"

Create your **on-yomi** keyword and enter it in the table at the back of the book. After that, write your sentence to remember the **on-yomi** and **kun-yomi** readings in the box below.

COMMON WORDS AND COMPOUNDS		
青	*blue; green (noun)*	**ao** あお
青い	*blue; green (adjective)*	**ao·i** あお・い
青春	blue + spring = *youth*	**SEI·SHUN** セイ・シュン
青物	blue + thing = *green vegetables*	**ao·mono** あお・もの
青空	blue + empty (sky) = *blue sky*	**ao·zora** あお・ぞら

Less Common Pronunciations
Less common **ON** reading: **SHŌ** (ショウ)
Less common **kun** reading: none

SAMPLE SENTENCE:

山田さん　の　家　は　青い　です。
Yama·da-san　no　ie　wa　ao·i　desu.
Yamada-san　　　　house　　blue
= *Yamada-san's house is blue.*

KANJI 87

土 **EARTH**

一	十	土					

Meaning
Think of earth here as in "dirt," not the planet on which we live. Take a moment to note the subtle difference between this kanji and "士" (Entry 84); you've developed a practiced eye if you're now able to take such variations into account! No story required.

Common Pronunciations
Common **ON** reading: **DO** (ド)
Common **kun** reading: **tsuchi** (つち)

Note the mixture of **on-** and **kun-yomi** in the second example (and in the last, as expected).

kun-yomi suggestion: "got **Sioux chee**tahs"

Create your **on-yomi** keyword and enter it in the table at the back of the book. After that, write your sentence to remember the **on-yomi** and **kun-yomi** readings in the box below.

Less Common Pronunciations
Less common **ON** reading: **TO** (ト)
Less common **kun** reading: none

IRREGULAR READING		
土産	earth + produce = *souvenir*	**miyage** みやげ

COMMON WORDS AND COMPOUNDS

土	earth	tsuchi つち
土手	earth + hand = embankment	DO·te ド·て
本土	main + earth = mainland	HON·DO ホン·ド
土木	earth + tree = civil engineering	DO·BOKU ド·ボク
土星	earth + star = Saturn (planet)	DO·SEI ド·セイ
土曜日	earth + day of the week + sun (day) = Saturday	DO·YŌ·bi ド·ヨウ·び

SAMPLE SENTENCE:

川　の　　土手　　を　上がる　と
kawa　no　　DO·te　　o　　a·garu　to
river　　embankment　　　go up
　水田　　　が　　見えます。
SUI·DEN　　ga　　mi·emasu.
rice paddies　　　　　can see
= *If you go up the river embankment, you can
　see rice paddies.*

INGER

ring and a string for a finger. There will be
ttle chance of forgetting this component,
cidentally, as it is present in nearly a hundred
anji—most relating in some way to hands and
rms.

KANJI 88

掛　**HANG**

扌	扌	扌	扩	扩	拃	拌	挂
卦	掛						

UILDING THIS KANJI
inger 扌 + **Earth** 土(87) + **Earth** 土(87) +
oor Figure Skater ト = 掛

Meaning
ang. Note how the last stroke of the bottom
earth" component leads into the next line by
eing drawn on an upward angle.

Remembering this kanji
Fingers can indicate harsh criticism, especially
when it comes to bad figure skating. "HANG up
your skates!" people will scream while pointing, making the **bad figure skater** want to hide
behind a **couple piles of earth**. Some skaters,
apparently, can do nothing but HANG their
heads in shame.

Common Pronunciations
Common **ON** reading: none
Common **kun** reading: **ka** (か)

As the final example below shows, this kanji can
act similarly to 買う (Entry 50).

kun-yomi suggestion: "cat"

There is no **on-yomi** reading for this character. Create your sentence to remember the **kun-yomi** reading in the box below.

COMMON WORDS AND COMPOUNDS		
掛かる (intr)	to hang (by oneself)	**ka**·karu か・かる
掛ける (tr)	to hang (something)	**ka**·keru か・ける
掛金	hang + gold (money) = *installment*	kake·KIN かけ・キン

Less Common Pronunciations
Less common **ON** reading: none
Less common **kun** reading: none

SAMPLE SENTENCE:

シャツ を あそこ に 掛けて 下さい。

shatsu o asoko ni ka·kete kuda·sai.
shirts   over there   hang   please
= *Please hang the shirts over there.*

COMPONENT #89

CHAIR

KANJI 89

万 **TEN THOUSAND**

一	丁	万				

BUILDING THIS KANJI
One (top of a bun) 一 (3) + Chair 刀 = 万

Meaning
Ten thousand. More so than "百" and "千" (Entries 51 and 65), this character can express the general idea of a "countless amount" of something.

Remembering this kanji
The ancient writer Xenophon tells the story of TEN THOUSAND Greek mercenaries marching against Persia in 401 B.C. What is interesting is that each of the TEN THOUSAND carries a lawn **chair**, together with a shield shaped like the **top of a bun**.

Common Pronunciations
Common **ON** reading: **MAN** (マン)
Common **kun** reading: none

As we saw for the kanji "百" and "千," note how the numbers four and seven appear with their **kun-yomi**.

Create your **on-yomi** keyword and enter it in the table at the back of the book. After that, write your sentence to remember the **on-yomi** reading in the box below.

Less Common Pronunciations
Less common **ON** reading: **BAN** (バン)
Less common **kun** reading: none

BAN shows up in Japan's famous word for "hurrah!", 万歳 (Ten thousand/Annual) **BAN·ZAI** (バン・ザイ)

COMMON WORDS AND COMPOUNDS		
一万	one + ten thousand = *ten thousand*	ICHI·MAN イチ・マン
二万	two + ten thousand = *twenty thousand*	NI·MAN ニ・マン
三万	three + ten thousand = *thirty thousand*	SAN·MAN サン・マン
四万	four + ten thousand = *forty thousand*	yon·MAN よん・マン
五万	five + ten thousand = *fifty thousand*	GO·MAN ゴ・マン
六万	six + ten thousand = *sixty thousand*	ROKU·MAN ロク・マン
七万	seven + ten thousand = *seventy thousand*	nana·MAN なな・マン
八万	eight + ten thousand = *eighty thousand*	HACHI·MAN ハチ・マン
九万	nine + ten thousand = *ninety thousand*	KYŪ·MAN キュウ・マン

SAMPLE SENTENCE:

あの　　　国　　　の　　　人口　　　は
ano　　kuni　　no　　JIN·KŌ　　wa
that　　country　　　　population
八万人　　　　です。
HACHI·MAN·NIN　　desu.
eighty thousand people　　　　is
= *That country's population is eighty thousand.*

KANJI 90

RAIN

Meaning

Rain. This wonderfully distinctive character is more easily learned without being broken into components. Because of this, no story is required.

Common Pronunciations
Common ON reading: none
Common kun readings: ame (あめ); ama (あま)

The **kun-yomi** "ama" only appears in the first position.

kun-yomi suggestions: "scam age"; "amaretto"

Create your sentence to remember the **kun-yomi** readings in the box below.

Less Common Pronunciations
Less common ON reading: U (ウ)
Less common kun reading: none

The following word can be read with its normal **on-yomi**, but is often heard with the irregular reading pronunciation below.

IRREGULAR READING		
梅雨*	plum tree + rain = *the rainy season*	tsuyu つゆ

COMMON WORDS AND COMPOUNDS		
雨	rain	**ame** あめ
雨上がり	rain + upper = *after the rain*	**ame** a·gari あめ あ·がり
大雨	large + rain = *heavy rain*	**ō·ame** おお·あめ
雨空	rain + empty (sky) = *a rainy sky*	**ama**·zora あま·ぞら

SAMPLE SENTENCE:

九月　に　は　日本　で　大雨の
KU·GATSU ni wa NI·HON de ō·ame n
September　　　　　Japan　　heavy rain
日　が　多い　です。
hi　ga　ō·i　desu.
day　　many
=*In September, Japan has many days with hea*
rain.

 ELECTRIC

一	一	戸	币	币	雨	雨	雨	雨
雨	雷	雷	電					

BUILDING THIS KANJI
Rain 雨 (90) + Sun 日 (6) + Hook ∟ = 電

Meaning
Electric/Electricity.

Remembering this kanji
The atmosphere was ELECTRIC: **rain** and **sun**
were on a collision course! At the last moment,
however, a **hook** was used to hold the **sun** back,
saving either it from being extinguished or the
rain from being evaporated. As the kanji shows,
the elements remain in this state even now, so
close than an ELECTRIC current would have
difficulty passing between them.

Common Pronunciations
Common **ON** reading: **DEN** (デン)
Common **kun** reading: none

Write your sentence to remember the **on-yo**
reading in the box below.

Less Common Pronunciations
Less common **ON** reading: none
Less common **kun** reading: none

COMMON WORDS AND COMPOUNDS		
電化	electric + change = *electrification*	**DEN·KA** デン·カ
電力	electric + strength = *electric power*	**DEN·RYOKU** デン·リョク
電子	electric + child = *electron*	**DEN·SHI** デン·シ
電気	electric + spirit = *electricity*	**DEN·KI** デン·キ
電話	electric + speak = *telephone*	**DEN·WA** デン·ワ
電車	electric + car = *(electric) train*	**DEN·SHA** デン·シャ

SAMPLE SENTENCE:

田中さん　は　電車　を　下りました
Ta·naka-san wa DEN·SHA o　o·rimashita.
Tanaka-san　　　　train　　descended
= *Tanaka-san got off the train.*

Component 92

UFO

Make sure you clearly see the difference between this component and the "pincers" 宀.

KANJI 92

売 **SELL**

| 一 | 十 | 士 | 声 | 声 | 売 | 売 | | |

BUILDING THIS KANJI
Gentleman 士(84) + UFO 宀 + Ballet ル = 売

Meaning
Sell.

Remembering this kanji
It is common knowledge that the statues of Easter Island relate to the visit of a UFO. What is less well known is that the **gentleman** piloting this UFO chose to SELL **ballet** gear to the locals. What was the purpose of this? Were the natives to put tutus on the monoliths? Wear the slippers themselves? Given the lack of **ballet** dancers or practice facilities on Easter Island at the time, anthropologists wonder why this **gentleman** didn't SELL the locals something more useful.

Common Pronunciations
Common **ON** reading: **BAI** (バイ)
Common **kun** reading: **u** (う)

As the final example below shows, this is another kanji that can function similarly to "買" (Entry 50).

kun-yomi suggestion: "**oo**dles"

Create your **on-yomi** keyword and enter it in the table at the back of the book. After that, write your sentence to remember the **on-yomi** and **kun-yomi** readings in the box below.

Less Common Pronunciations
Less common **ON** reading: none
Less common **kun** reading: none

COMMON WORDS AND COMPOUNDS		
売る	*to sell*	**u·ru** う・る
売り歩く	sell + walk = *to peddle*	**u·ri aru·ku** う・り ある・く
売春	sell + spring = *prostitution*	**BAI·SHUN** バイ・シュン
売り家	sell + house = *"house for sale"*	**u·ri ie** う・り いえ
売り切れる	sell + cut = *to be sold out*	**u·ri ki·reru** う・り き・れる
売切れ	sell + cut = *"sold out"*	**uri ki·re** うり き・れ

SAMPLE SENTENCE:

田口さん は 日本語 の 本 を
Ta·guchi-san wa NI·HON·GO no HON o
Taguchi-san   Japanese   books
売って います。
u·tte   imasu.
sells

= *Taguchi-san sells Japanese books.*

KANJI 93

者 **INDIVIDUAL**

一 十 土 耂 耂 者 者 者

BUILDING THIS KANJI
Earth 土(87) + Comet 一 + Sun 日(6) = 者

Meaning
Think of individual in the sense of a human being. The characters in a compound that precede this kanji (it never comes first) define the person.

Remembering this kanji
It's never a good idea to generalize, but let's face it: you can tell a lot about an INDIVIDUAL by the way they look. A heap of **earth**, for example, tends to be dirty; it clearly doesn't care about appearances and is thus down to **earth**. **Suns**, on the other hand, are obviously outgoing INDIVIDUALS with blazing style. **Comets**, however, have personalities that lie between these extremes (as the kanji shows); with qualities of **earth** and **sun**, each must be considered a separate INDIVIDUAL.

Common Pronunciations
Common **ON** reading: **SHA** (シャ)
Common **kun** reading: none

Create your **on-yomi** keyword and enter it in the table at the back of the book. After that, write your sentence to remember the **on-yomi** reading in the box below.

Less Common Pronunciations
Less common **ON** reading: none
Less common **kun** reading: **mono** (もの)

COMMON WORDS AND COMPOUNDS		
有力者	have + strength + individual = *powerful person*	YŪ·RYOKU·SHA ユウ·リョク· シャ
前者	before + individual = *the former*	ZEN·SHA ゼン·シャ
後者	after + individual = *the latter*	KŌ·SHA コウ·シャ
学者	study + individual = *scholar*	GAKU·SHA ガク·シャ

SAMPLE SENTENCE:

あの 国 で 王子 は 有力者
ano kuni de Ō·JI wa YŪ·RYOKU·SHA
that country prince powerful person
です。
desu.
= *The prince is a powerful person in that country*

KANJI 94

入 **ENTER**

| ノ | 入 | | | | | |

Meaning
Entering/Putting in. Make sure that you clearly see the difference between this kanji and those for "人" (Entry 2), and "八" (Entry 19). No story required.

Common Pronunciations
Common **ON** reading: **NYŪ** (ニュウ)
Common **kun** readings: **hai** (はい); **i** (い)

It is worth looking carefully at the first three entries below. The word "**hai·ru**" expresses the **intransitive** meaning of the verb "enter" (that is, to enter some type of place); it is rarely used in compounds. "**i·ru**", on the other hand, is most commonly found in compounds, primarily when the other kanji is read with **kun-yomi** (**NYŪ** performs this function when the other kanji is read with **on-yomi**). The word **i·reru** is simply the transitive companion of **hai·ru**.

One last twist is that the kanji can behave on rare occasions like 買; this can be seen in the fourth example.

kun-yomi suggestions: "**high**way"; "**ether**"

Create your **on-yomi** keyword and enter it in the table at the back of the book. After that, write your sentence to remember the **on-yomi** and **kun-yomi** readings in the box below.

Less Common Pronunciations
Less common **ON** reading: none
Less common **kun** reading: none

COMMON WORDS AND COMPOUNDS		
入る (intr)	to enter	**hai**·ru はい・る
入る (intr)	to enter	**i**·ru い・る
入れる (tr)	to put (something) into	**i**·reru い・れる
入口	enter + mouth = entrance	**iri**·guchi いり・ぐち
入国	enter + country = to enter a country	**NYŪ**·KOKU ニュウ・ コク
入金	enter + gold (money) = payment	**NYŪ**·KIN ニュウ・ キン
買い入 れる	buy + enter = to stock up on	ka·i **i**·reru か・い い・ れる

SAMPLE SENTENCE:

お金　を　入れて　下さい。
o·kane　**o**　**i·rete**　**kuda·sai.**
money　　　put in　　please
= *Please insert the money.*

Component 95

COMB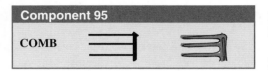

KANJI 95

雪 **SNOW**

一　厂　冖　示　示　雪　雪　雪　雪

雪　雪

BUILDING THIS KANJI
Rain 雨(90) + Comb ヨ = 雪

Meaning
Snow.

Remembering this kanji
I've come in from the **rain** and need to straighten my hair for a date. I do this, of course, but looking down moments later I tremble like a kitten: my **comb** is now covered with dandruff! I start to panic…until realizing that the **rain** had at some point become SNOW.

Common Pronunciations
Common **ON** reading: none
Common **kun** reading: **yuki** (ゆき)

Note that the sample sentence contains an irregular reading (明日).

kun-yomi suggestion: "**you kee**p"

Create your sentence to remember the **kun-yom** reading in the box below.

Less Common Pronunciations
Less common **ON** reading: **SETSU** (セツ)
Less common **kun** reading: none

Here are two irregular readings that make use of this character.

IRREGULAR READINGS		
吹雪*	blow + snow = *blizzard*	**fubuki** ふぶき
雪崩*	snow + crumble = *avalanche*	**nadare** なだれ

COMMON WORDS AND COMPOUNDS		
雪	*snow*	**yuki** ゆき
雪玉	snow + jewel = *snowball*	**yuki**·dama ゆき・だま
雪女	snow + woman = *snow fairy*	**yuki**·onna ゆき・おんな
雪男	snow + man = *the Abominable Snowman*	**yuki**·otoko ゆき・おとこ
大雪	large + snow = *heavy snow*	ō·**yuki** おお・ゆき
小雪	small + snow = *light snow*	ko·**yuki** こ・ゆき

SAMPLE SENTENCE:

テレビ　の　ニュース　に　よる　と
terebi　no　nyūsu　ni　yoru　to
television　　　news　　　according to
明日　　から　　大雪　　です。
ashita　kara　ōyuki　desu.
tomorrow　from　heavy snow
= *According to the TV news, heavy snow will b*
starting tomorrow.

KANJI 96

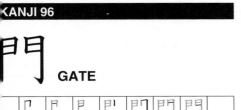

門
GATE

| 冖 | 冂 | 冋 | 冋ˈ | 冋コ | 門 | 門 | |

Meaning

Gate. No story required.

Common Pronunciations

Common **ON** reading: **MON** (モン)
Common **kun** reading: **kado** (か ど)

Note that this kanji is usually read with its **on-yomi** when appearing alone.

kun-yomi suggestion: "**cod o**ver"

Create your **on-yomi** keyword and enter it in the table at the back of the book. After that, write your sentence to remember the **on-yomi** and **kun-yomi** readings in the box below.

Less Common Pronunciations

Less common **ON** reading: none
Less common **kun** reading: none

COMMON WORDS AND COMPOUNDS		
門	gate	**MON** モ ン
門口	gate + mouth = *front door*	**kado·**guchi か ど・ぐ ち
水門	water + gate = *sluice gate*	**SUI·MON** ス イ・モ ン
校門	school + gate = *school gate*	**KŌ·MON** コ ウ・モ ン

SAMPLE SENTENCE:

あそこ　の　高い　門　は　とても
asoko　no　taka·i　MON　wa　totemo
over there　　tall　gate　　very

古い　です　ね。
furu·i　desu　ne.
old

= *That tall gate over there is very old, isn't it?*

KANJI 97

間
INTERVAL

| 冖 | 冂 | 冋 | 冋ˈ | 門 | 門 | 門 | 門 |
| 門 | 間 | 間 | | | | | |

BUILDING THIS KANJI
Gate 門(96) + Sun 日 (6) = 間

Meaning
This character indicates an interval in time or space, and thus incorporates the ideas of "during", "between" and "among". When used with the **kun-yomi** "ma", it can also mean a room.

Remembering this kanji

If the **sun** in this kanji is rising (as every fiber in my being leads me to believe), it will pass, after a short INTERVAL, through that INTERVAL between the **gates**.

Common Pronunciations

Common **ON** reading: **KAN** (カ ン)
Common **kun** readings: **aida** (あ い だ); **ma** (ま)

kun-yomi suggestions: "**Ida**ho;" "**ma**p"

Create your **on-yomi** keyword and enter it in the table at the back of the book. After that, write your sentence to remember the **on-yomi** and **kun-yomi** readings in the box below.

Less Common Pronunciations

Less common **ON** reading: **KEN** (ケ ン)
Less common **kun** reading: none

COMMON WORDS AND COMPOUNDS		
間	*interval*	**aida** あ い だ
手間	hand + interval = *labor; trouble*	te·**ma** て · ま
中間	middle + interval = *midway*	CHŪ·**KAN** チ ュ ウ · カ ン
時間	time + interval = *time*	JI·**KAN** ジ · カ ン
空間	empty + interval = *space*	KŪ·**KAN** ク ウ · カ ン

SAMPLE SENTENCE:

ア メ リ カ に い る 間 英 語

Amerika   ni   iru   aida   EI·GO
America   be   interval English

話 し ま す 。
hana·shimasu.
speak
= *I'll speak English while I'm in America.*

COMPONENT #98

GARBAGE CAN

KANJI 98

出 **EXIT**

BUILDING THIS KANJI
Pole | + **Garbage Can** └┘ + **Garbage Can** └┘
= 出

Meaning

Leave/Let out. Take care with the stroke order of this character.

Remembering this kanji

All right, so maybe I misunderstood my boss; putting a couple of **garbage cans** on a **pole** an standing at the EXIT of the voting station wasn the right thing to do. But asking people to pu "yes" votes in one **can** and "no" votes in th other…wouldn't anyone have thought that' what she meant by an EXIT poll?

Common Pronunciations

Common **ON** reading: **SHUTSU** (シュツ)
Common **kun** readings: **de** (で); **da** (だ)

Note how the on-yomi "doubles up" with an unvoiced consonant sound in the last example below.

kun-yomi suggestions: "**date**"; "**dash**"

Create your **on-yomi** keyword and enter it in the table at the back of the book. After that, write your sentence to remember the **on-yomi** and **kun-yomi** readings in the box below.

Less Common Pronunciations

Less common **ON** reading: **SUI** (スイ)
Less common **kun** reading: none

COMMON WORDS AND COMPOUNDS		
出る (intr)	to leave	**de**·ru で・る
出す (tr)	to let out	**da**·su だ・す
出かける	to leave (for somewhere)	**de**·kakeru で・かける
思い出す	think + exit = to remember	omo·i **da**·su おも・い だ・す
出口	exit + mouth = exit	**de**·guchi で・ぐち
出国	exit + country = to leave a country	**SHUK**·KOKU シュッ・コク

SAMPLE SENTENCE:

すみません、　　出口　　は　　どこ
sumimasen　　　**de·guchi**　　**wa**　　**doko**
　excuse me　　　　exit　　　　　　where
です　か。
desu　**ka.**
= *Excuse me, where's the exit?*

LIFE

BUILDING THIS KANJI
Jelly Bean ヽ + Candlestick Holder ≖ = 生

Meaning

One of the most fascinating characters in the language, this kanji deals with life in all its guises. Along with the ideas of "birth", "production", and "growing", it also incorporates the notions of "pure", "raw", and "fresh", in everything from beer to silk. When used as a suffix, it will often indicate "student".

Remembering this kanji

"Is there a better symbol of LIFE," asked Sartre, "than a **jelly bean** stuck to the side of a **candlestick holder**, one that sits there alone and grows brittle with each passing year?"

It's an interesting question. From what I've heard, though, **jelly beans** hold their flavor quite well, even when stuck to **candlestick holders**. So who knows, maybe LIFE isn't so bad after all.

Common Pronunciations

Common **ON** reading: **SEI** (セイ)
Common **kun** readings: **i** (い); **u** (う); **nama** (なま)

In terms of its variety of pronunciations, kanji do not come any more complicated than this. Perhaps it's appropriate, though: life itself can be complicated, so shouldn't the character representing it be as well? Fortunately, the two initial **kun-yomi** are verb stems (as are "**o**" and "**ha**" of the less common **kun-yomi** below), and **nama** appears only in the first position. This will always belong to the ranks of the toughest kanji, however, so allow yourself time to learn it, while not forgetting to enjoy a few of the fifth example below along the way.

kun-yomi suggestions: "**eag**le;" "**oo**dles;" "Viet**nam a**pple"

Write your sentence to remember the **on-yomi** and **kun-yomi** readings in the box below.

Less Common Pronunciations

Less common **ON** reading: **SHŌ** (ショウ)
Less common **kun** readings: **o** (お); **ha** (は); **ki** (き

IRREGULAR READING		
芝生*	lawn + life = *lawn*	**shiba·fu** しば・ふ

COMMON WORDS AND COMPOUNDS		
生きる (intr)	to live	**i·kiru** い・きる
生かす (tr)	to give life to	**i·kasu** い・かす
生まれる (intr)	to be born	**u·mareru** う・まれる
生む (tr)	to give birth to	**u·mu** う・む
生ビール	life + beer = *draft beer*	**nama·bīru** なま・ビール
人生	person + life = *(human) life*	**JIN·SEI** ジン・セイ
学生	study + life = *student*	**GAKU·SEI** ガク・セイ
先生	precede + life = *teacher*	**SEN·SEI** セン・セイ

SAMPLE SENTENCE:

生ビール は 好き です か。
nama bīru wa su·ki desu ka.
draft beer like
= *Do you like draft beer?*

KANJI 100

 COW

Meaning
Cow/Ox/Bull. Note the difference in stroke order between this character and that of "生" (Entry 99). No story required.

Common Pronunciations
Common **ON** reading: **GYŪ** (ギュウ)
Common **kun** reading: **ushi** (うし)

kun-yomi suggestion: "**true sheen**"

reate your **on-yomi** keyword and enter it in the
ble at the back of the book. After that, write your
ntence to remember the **on-yomi** and **kun-yomi**
adings in the box below.

COMMON WORDS AND COMPOUNDS		
牛	*cow*	**ushi** うし
子牛	child + cow = *calf*	ko·**ushi** こ·うし
水牛	water + cow = *water buffalo*	**SUI·GYŪ** スイ·ギュウ
牛肉	cow + meat = *beef*	**GYŪ·NIKU** ギュウ·ニク
牛馬	cow + horse = *cattle and horses*	**GYŪ·BA** ギュウ·バ

SAMPLE SENTENCE:

アフリカ　で　　　　水牛　　　と　キリン
Afurika　de　SUI·GYŪ　to　kirin
Africa　　　　　water buffalo　　giraffe
を　見ました。
o　mi·mashita.
　　saw
= *(I) saw a water buffalo and a giraffe in Africa.*

ess **Common Pronunciations**

ess common **ON** reading: none

ess common **kun** reading: none

HAPTER 5 REVIEW EXERCISES

. Please match the following kanji to their meanings.

1. 土 　　　　　a. Words

2. 士 　　　　　b. Gentleman

3. 雨 　　　　　c. Sell

4. 間 　　　　　d. Exit

5. 売 　　　　　e. Rain

6. 干 　　　　　f. Life

7. 生 　　　　　g. Interval

8. 電 　　　　　h. Earth

9. 出 　　　　　i. Electric

10. 語 　　　　　j. Dry

. Please match the following meanings to their
kanji, and these to their **on** or **kun-yomi**.

1. Hang 　　a. 者 　　1. **SHA** (シャ)

2. Snow 　　b. 牛 　　2. **MAN** (マン)

3. Individual 　c. 青 　　3. **asa** (あさ)

4. Morning 　d. 掛 　　4. **GYŪ** (ギュウ)

5. Gold 　　e. 雪 　　5. **yuki** (ゆき)

6. Gate 　　f. 入 　　6. **MON** (モン)

7. Cow 　　g. 金 　　7. **ao** (あお)

8. Enter 　　h. 万 　　8. **KIN** (キン)

9. Ten thousand 　i. 門 　　9. **NYŪ** (ニュウ)

10. Blue 　　j. 朝 　　10. **ka** (か)

C. Please choose the best answer(s) to the following questions.

1. Which of the following kanji have an
on-yomi of **SEI** (セイ)?

a. 士

b. 者

c. 生

d. 朝

e. 青

2. Which of the following readings apply to the kanji 出?
   a. **da** (だ)
   b. **SHUTSU** (シュツ)
   c. **MON** (モン)
   d. **de** (で)
   e. **u** (う)

3. I went to the Himalayas and saw the Abominable ___ Man.
   a. 牛
   b. 雨
   c. 青
   d. 土
   e. 雪

4. Which of the following kanji have an **on-yomi** of **KAN** (カン)?
   a. 士
   b. 金
   c. 語
   d. 間
   e. 電

5. Which of the following readings apply to the kanji 生?
   a. **de** (で)
   b. **i** (い)
   c. **kado** (かど)
   d. **nama** (なま)
   e. **u** (う)

D. Please choose the best answer to the following questions.

   1. Which of the following kanji has the most number of strokes?
      a. 間
      b. 語
      c. 掛
      d. 朝
      e. 電

   2. Which is the correct reading of 売る?
      a. **de·ru** (で・る)
      b. **i·ru** (い・る)
      c. **u·ru** (う・る)
      d. **kata·ru** (かた・る)

   3. Which is the correct reading of 入れる?
      a. **ka·reru** (か・れる)
      b. **omo·reru** (おも・れる)
      c. **kama·reru** (かま・れる)
      d. **i·reru** (い・れる)

4. Which answer best captures the meaning of the compound 電化?
   a. Toast
   b. Electrification
   c. Cactus
   d. Lawnmower
   e. Yogurt

5. Which is the most common reading of る when it appears alone (is not part of a compound)?
   a. **i·ru** (い・る)
   b. **kata·ru** (かた・る)
   c. **u·ru** (う・る)
   d. **hai·ru** (はい・る)
   e. **hi·ru** (ひ・る)

E. Please match the following compounds and words to their meanings and pronunciations.

1. 朝日	a. Entrance	1. **DEN·RYOKU** (デン・リョク)
2. 掛金	b. Snow fairy	2. **DO·te** (ド・て)
3. 口語	c. Midway	3. **KŌ·GO** (コウ・ゴ)
4. 入口	d. Installment	4. **asa·hi** (あさ・ひ)
5. 中間	e. Youth	5. **yuki·onna** (ゆき・おんな)
6. 大雨	f. Morning sun	6. **CHŪ·KAN** (チュウ・カン)
7. 青春	g. Electric power	7. **kake·KIN** (かけ・キン)
8. 電力	h. Colloquial language	8. **ō·ame** (おお・あめ)
9. 雪女	i. Embankment	9. **iri·guchi** (いり・ぐち)
10. 土手	j. Heavy rain	10. **SEI·SHUN** (セイ・シュン)

UMULATIVE REVIEW EXERCISES FOR

HAPTER 1 - 5

Please match the following kanji to their meanings.

1.	京	a.	Self
2.	北	b.	Summer
3.	玉	c.	Half
4.	自	d.	North
5.	化	e.	Spring
6.	半	f.	Capital
7.	朝	g.	Like
8.	春	h.	Change
9.	好	i.	Jewel
10.	夏	j.	Morning

Which kanji does not belong in the group?

1. a. 耳   b. 目   c. 北   d. 手   e. 首

2. a. 土   b. 女   c. 王   d. 男   e. 子

3. a. 川   b. 回   c. 山   d. 木   e. 田

4. a. 木   b. 牛   c. 米   d. 貝   e. 玉

5. a. 子   b. 上   c. 左   d. 右   e. 下

6. a. 二   b. 九   c. 七   d. 工   e. 三

7. a. 万   b. 干   c. 十   d. 千   e. 百

8. a. 川   b. 雪   c. 全   d. 水   e. 雨

9. a. 肉   b. 出   c. 歩   d. 回   e. 入

10. a. 日   b. 月   c. 火   d. 水   e. 木
    f. 金   g. 土   h. 夏

C. Identify the kanji having the most number of strokes.

1. a. 山   b. 日   c. 工   d. 万   e. 女

2. a. 男   b. 貝   c. 回   d. 金   e. 体

3. a. 冬   b. 木   c. 子   d. 五   e. 元

4. a. 言   b. 者   c. 東   d. 南   e. 売

5. a. 早   b. 出   c. 耳   d. 全   e. 見

6. a. 家   b. 雪   c. 買   d. 掛   e. 高

7. a. 夏   b. 歩   c. 首   d. 雨   e. 思

8. a. 家   b. 掛   c. 明   d. 国   e. 青

9. a. 生   b. 本   c. 白   d. 古   e. 肉

10. a. 電   b. 朝   c. 語   d. 間   e. 雪

D. Please list the following kanji in the order indicated (alphabetical).

1. Body / Main / Rest / Rice / Tree
   a. 休   b. 木   c. 本   d. 体   e. 米

2. Dry / Earth / Gentleman / Ten thousand / Thousand
   a. 士   b. 干   c. 千   d. 土   e. 万

3. Cow / Half / Jewel / King / Life
   a. 王   b. 生   c. 牛   d. 玉   e. 半

4. Buy / Eye / See / Self / Shellfish
   a. 自   b. 目   c. 買   d. 貝   e. 見

5. Early / Hundred / Individual / Sun / White
   a. 早   b. 白   c. 日   d. 者   e. 百

6. Capital / Early / Morning / Old / Tall
    a. 高 b. 京 c. 早 d. 朝 e. 古

7. Eight / Enter / Gentleman / Large /
    Person
    a. 士 b. 人 c. 入 d. 大 e. 八

8. Basis / Hand / Ten thousand / Thousand /
    Three
    a. 元 b. 万 c. 三 d. 手 e. 千

9. Circle / Ear / Inside / Meat / Moon
    a. 肉 b. 耳 c. 円 d. 内 e. 月

10. Change / Lower / North / Stop / Upper
    a. 下 b. 化 c. 上 d. 北 e. 止

E. Please choose the best answer to the following
    questions.

1. I went on a nice vacation to the _____.
    a. 日 b. 火 c. 耳 d. 牛 e. 南

2. What is the best thing to take on a desert
    crossing?
    a. 木 b. 水 c. 火 d. 門 e. 掛

3. I bought some boots and took up _____
    climbing.
    a. 米 b. 肉 c. 雨 d. 山 e. 口

4. A country would be run most poorly by a

    _____.
    a. 王 b. 男 c. 女 d. 牛
    e. All of the preceding

5. The vampire bat flew in and went
    straight for my ___.
    a. 目 b. 貝 c. 首 d. 手 e. Wallet

F. Please choose the best answer(s) to the follow
    ing questions.

1. Which of the following are readings for
    the kanji 木?
    a. **BOKU** (ボク)
    b. **ki** (き)
    c. **SETSU** (セツ)
    d. **haru** (はる)
    e. **MOKU** (モク)

2. Which of the following are readings for
    the kanji 下?
    a. **shita** (した)
    b. **o** (お)
    c. **kado** (かど)
    d. **kuda** (くだ)
    e. **KA** (カ)
    f. **sa** (さ)
    g. **GE** (ゲ)

3. Which of the following are readings for
    the kanji 米?
    a. **MAI** (マイ)
    b. **kome** (こめ)
    c. **BEI** (ベイ)
    d. **HOKU** (ホク)
    e. **yuki** (ゆき)

4. Which of the following are readings for
    the kanji 上?
    a. **kami** (かみ)
    b. **ue** (うえ)
    c. **JŌ** (ジョウ)
    d. **nobo** (のぼ)
    e. **a** (あ)
    f. **ie** (いえ)
    g. **uwa** (うわ)

5. Which of the following are readings for
    the kanji 生?
    a. **i** (い)
    b. **nama** (なま)
    c. **SEI** (セイ)
    d. **haru** (はる)
    e. **u** (う)

G. Please choose the best answer to the following questions.

1. Which is the correct reading of 歩く?
   a. **haba·ku** (は ば・く)
   b. **aru·ku** (あ る・く)
   c. **fu·ku** (ふ・く)
   d. **kata·ku** (か た・く)

2. Which is the correct reading of 高い?
   a. **taka·i** (た か・い)
   b. **kata·i** (か た・い)
   c. **ara·i** (あ ら・い)
   d. **usu·i** (う す・い)

3. Which is the correct reading of 休む?
   a. **kara·mu** (か ら・む)
   b. **i·mu** (い・む)
   c. **u·mu** (う・む)
   d. **yasu·mu** (や す・む)

4. Which is the correct reading of 入れる?
   a. **de·reru** (で・れ る)
   b. **u·reru** (う・れ る)
   c. **kata·reru** (か た・れ る)
   d. **i·reru** (い・れ る)

5. Which is the correct reading of 二つ?
   a. **mi·tsu** (み・つ)
   b. **futa·tsu** (ふ た・つ)
   c. **hito·tsu** (ひ と・つ)
   d. **u·tsu** (う・つ)

6. Which is the correct reading of 古い?
   a. **taka·i** (た か・い)
   b. **omo·i** (お も・い)
   c. **furu·i** (ふ る・い)
   d. **haya·i** (は や・い)

7. Which is the correct reading of 早い?
   a. **haya·i** (は や・い)
   b. **yasu·i** (や す・い)
   c. **ao·i** (あ お・い)
   d. **furu·i** (ふ る・い)

8. Which is the correct reading of 小さい?
   a. **ka·sai** (か・さ い)
   b. **ko·sai** (こ・さ い)
   c. **chii·sai** (ち い・さ い)
   d. **uru·sai** (う る・さ い)

9. Which is the correct reading of 少ない?
   a. **de·nai** (で・な い)
   b. **suku·nai** (す く・な い)
   c. **taka·nai** (た か・な い)
   d. **kata·nai** (か た・な い)

10. Which is the correct reading of 少し?
    a. **ma·shi** (ま・し)
    b. **saga·shi** (さ が・し)
    c. **u·shi** (う・し)
    d. **suko·shi** (す こ・し)

H. Please match the following compounds and words to their meanings and pronunciations.

1. 東京	a. To stock up on	1.	**HON·DO** (ホン·ド)
2. 見上げる	b. To remember	2.	**AN·ZEN** (アン· ゼン)
3. 休日	c. Five hundred	3.	**TŌ·KYŌ** (トウ· キョウ)
4. 人生	d. Mainland	4.	**JŪ·ICHI· GATSU** (ジュウ· イチ·ガツ)
5. 思い出す	e. To look up (to/at)	5.	**ka·i i·reru** (か·い い·れ る)
6. 十一月	f. November	6.	**JIN·SEI** (ジン· セイ)

7. 五百	g. To enter a country	7. **ko·haru** (こ·はる)	
8. 下水	h. Holiday	8. **GYŪ· NIKU** (ギュウ· ニク)	
9. 小春	i. Safety	9. **GO· HYAKU** (ゴ·ヒ ャク)	
10. 入国	j. One time	10. **mi a·geru** (み あ· げる)	
11. 安全	k. Tokyo	11. **IK·KAI** (イッ· カイ)	

12. 牛肉	l. Indian summer	12. **omo·i da·su** (おも· い だ· す)	
13. 買い入 れる	m. (Human) Life	13. **NYŪ· KOKU** (ニュウ· コク)	
14. 一回	n. Sewage	14. **KYŪ· JITSU** (キュウ· ジツ)	
15. 本土	o. Beef	15. **GE·SUI** (ゲ·スイ)	

Kanji #101—120

BEAUTIFUL

`	`	`	`	`	`	`	`
丶	一	丷	半	羊	羊	羊	美

BUILDING THIS KANJI

Rabbit ` ´ + King 王(23) + Large (sumo wrestler) 大(17) = 美

Meaning

Used for all things beautiful, this character lives up to its name in a visual sense as well. Take care with the stroke order by writing the components as listed.

Remembering this kanji

The Zulu, along with several other tribes in southern Africa, equate **large** size with being BEAUTIFUL. A **king**, therefore, will make good use of the region's **rabbit** population to grow as **large** as possible, through eating incredible amounts of a filling **rabbit** stew. In being read from the top down, the kanji shows this process clearly: **rabbit** goes into **king**... king becomes as **large** as a sumo wrestler... large is BEAUTIFUL.

Common Pronunciations

Common **ON** reading: **BI** (ビ)
Common **kun** reading: **utsuku** (うつく)

kun-yomi suggestion: "fr**uits cool**ing"

Create your **on-yomi** keyword and enter it in the table at the back of the book. After that, write your sentence to remember the **on-yomi** and **kun-yomi** readings in the box below.

Less Common Pronunciations

Less common **ON** reading: none
Less common **kun** reading: none

The following is a very common irregular reading.

IRREGULAR READING		
美味しい	beautiful + taste = *delicious*	**oi·shii** おい・しい

COMMON WORDS AND COMPOUNDS		
美しい	*beautiful*	**utsuku·**shii うつく・しい
美人	beautiful + person = *beautiful woman*	**BI·JIN** ビ・ジン
美化	beautiful + change = *beautification*	**BI·KA** ビ・カ
美学	beautiful + study = *aesthetics*	**BI·GAKU** ビ・ガク

SAMPLE SENTENCE:

山	の	木	が	美しい	です。
yama	**no**	**ki**	**ga**	**utsuku·shii**	**desu.**
mountain		trees		beautiful	

= *The trees on the mountain are beautiful.*

COMPONENT #102	
DINOSAUR 鳥	

KANJI 102

島 ISLAND

′	⺁	⼢	⼾	白	白	鳥	鳥	島
島								

BUILDING THIS KANJI
Dinosaur 鳥 + Mountain 山(1) = 島

Meaning
Island.

Remembering this kanji
OK, so I have this great idea for a movie. It's set on an ISLAND, but what makes this ISLAND interesting is that some **dinosaurs** are still living on one of its **mountains**! It's a blockbuster concept, and though I'm still working out the details, I've already decided on a title: "Jurassic ISLAND".

Common Pronunciations
Common **ON** reading: **TŌ** (トウ)
Common **kun** reading: **shima** (しま)
The **kun-yomi** for this kanji is often voiced wh in the final position, as in the second compoun below. Note also the voiced reading for 国 in t third example.

kun-yomi suggestion: "**she ma**ps"

Write your sentence to remember the **on-yomi a kun-yomi** readings in the box below.

Less Common Pronunciations
Less common **ON** reading: none
Less common **kun** reading: none

COMMON WORDS AND COMPOUNDS		
島	*island*	**shima** しま
小島	small + island = *small island*	**ko·jima** こ·じま
島国	island + country = *island nation*	**shima·guni** しま·ぐに
半島	half + island = *peninsula*	**HAN·TŌ** ハン·トウ
本島	main + island = *main island*	**HON·TŌ** ホン·トウ

SAMPLE SENTENCE:

オーストラリア	と	日本	は
Ōsutoraria	**to**	**NI·HON**	**wa**
Australia		Japan	

島国	です。
shima·guni	**desu.**
island nation	

= *Australia and Japan are island nations.*

KANJI 103

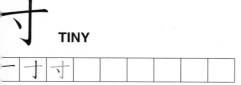

寸

TINY

| 一 | 寸 | 寸 | | | | | |

Meaning

Tiny.

Remembering this kanji

How TINY, you ask? Well, given that the soccer player in this illustration is life-size... pretty TINY. This kanji, as the lack of compounds below makes clear, will be much more important for us as a component than a character on its own; the tiny soccer player will be used to suggest it in all future stories.

Common Pronunciations

Common **ON** reading: **SUN** (スン)
Common **kun** reading: none

Create your **on-yomi** keyword and enter it in the table at the back of the book. After that, write your sentence to remember the **on-yomi** reading in the box below.

Less Common Pronunciations

Less common **ON** reading: none
Less common **kun** reading: none

COMMON WORDS AND COMPOUNDS		
一寸	one + tiny = *a tiny bit*	**IS·SUN** イッ・スン
寸前	tiny + before = *immediately before*	**SUN·ZEN** スン・ゼン

SAMPLE SENTENCE:

出かける　　　寸前　　に 高木さん
de·kakeru　　**SUN·ZEN**　　**ni Taka·gi-san**
　leave　　immediately before　　Takagi-san
を　　見ました。
o　　**mi·mashita.**
　　　　　saw
= *I saw Takagi-san just before I left.*

KANJI 104

寺

TEMPLE

| 一 | 十 | 土 | 士 | 寺 | 寺 | | |

BUILDING THIS KANJI

Earth 土(87) + Tiny (soccer player) 寸(103)
= 寺

Meaning

(Buddhist) temple.

Remembering this kanji

Tiny soccer players are always in danger of being pushed around by their opponents. As a result of this, they usually become known as fearless defenders who protect their positions at all costs — treating even the **tiniest** piece of **earth** they occupy like a TEMPLE that must not be defiled. A TEMPLE in which it is permitted to wear cleats, of course.

Common Pronunciations

Common **ON** reading: **JI** (ジ)
Common **kun** reading: **tera** (て ら)

The **kun-yomi** becomes voiced when not in the first position, as it does below in the third example. The final compound can also be read by the respective **kun-yomi**: **furu·dera** (ふ る · で ら).

kun-yomi suggestion: "**tear a**pples"

Write your sentence to remember the **on-yomi** and **kun-yomi** readings in the box below.

COMMON WORDS AND COMPOUNDS		
寺	*temple*	**tera** て ら
寺田 さん	temple + rice field = *Terada-san*	**tera·da·san** て ら · だ · さ ん
山寺	mountain + temple = *mountain temple*	**yama·dera** や ま · で ら
古寺	old + temple = *old temple*	**KO·JI** コ · ジ

SAMPLE SENTENCE:

山寺		の	古い	門	の
yama·dera		**no**	**furu·i**	**MON**	**no**
mountain temple			old	gate	

下 で 休みました。
shita de yasu·mimashita.
under   rested

= *(We) rested under the old gate of the mountai
temple.*

Less Common Pronunciations

Less common **ON** reading: none
Less common **kun** reading: none

KANJI 105

PRECEDE

ノ	⺊	屮	生	牛	先		

BUILDING THIS KANJI
Jelly Bean ヽ + Earth 土(87) + Ballet 儿 = 先

Meaning

This character has a multitude of meanings, all of them derived from the general sense of "preceding", or the idea of an object "ahead" in a literal or figurative way. Depending on the context in which it appears, this kanji can signify the "tip" or "point" of something, the general future (or the specific past, when used as in the third compound), or a destination. It can also refer to people in the sense of "the other party".

Remembering this kanji

Most people are unaware that Tchaikovsky deleted a **jelly bean** character from his **ballet** "The Nutcracker". This **jelly bean** was to always PRECEDE the Sugar Plum Fairy onstage, then be pinned to the **earth** and devoured by her at the end of the work (she by this time having been driven wild with sugar cravings). It was an edgy scene, but fortunately for **ballet** lovers everywhere, Tchaikovsky concluded it was incompatible with what PRECEDED, and decided to remove the **jelly bean** character altogether.

Common Pronunciations

Common **ON** reading: **SEN** (セン)
Common **kun** reading: **saki** (さき)

kun-yomi suggestion: "**sack ee**ls". If using your own idea for this **kun-yomi**, keep in mind that Japan's famous rice wine is pronounced **saké** (さけ), and should not be confused with the reading of this character.

Write your sentence to remember the **on-yomi** and **kun-yomi** readings in the box below.

COMMON WORDS AND COMPOUNDS		
先	*precede; point; tip*	saki さき
先生	precede + life = *teacher*	**SEN·SEI** セン・セイ
先月	precede + moon (month) = *last month*	**SEN·GETSU** セン・ゲツ
口先	mouth + precede = *lip service*	kuchi·**saki** くち・さき

SAMPLE SENTENCE:

先生　　は　　冬休み　　に
SEN·SEI　wa　fuyu yasu·mi　ni
teacher　　　　　winter vacation
日本アルプス　　へ　　行きました。
NI·HON arupusu　e　i·kimashita.
　Japanese Alps　　　　　went
=*(Our) teacher went to the Japanese Alps for winter vacation.*

Less Common Pronunciations

Less common **ON** reading: none
Less common **kun** reading: none

PICNIC TABLE

Admittedly, this is not the most comfortable-looking picnic table.

KANJI 106

OPEN

「	ア	ア	ア	門	門	門	門
閂	閈	開					

BUILDING THIS KANJI
Gate 門 (96) + Picnic Table 开 = 開

Meaning

Open. Secondary meanings include "starting", and the idea of "developing" things (in the sense of opening or reclaiming land, for example).

Remembering this kanji

Their picnic thrown into chaos by the sight of Visigoths on the horizon, the partiers ran desperately back to the castle. "OPEN the **gates**!", "OPEN the **gates**!" they yelled to no avail, for nobody on the other side could hear them. It was only when the **picnic table** was used as a battering ram (thus breaking it) that the **gates** finally flew OPEN to let them in.

Common Pronunciations

Common **ON** reading: **KAI** (カイ)
Common **kun** readings: **a** (あ); **hira** (ひら)

As a glance at the first three examples below suggests, this character can be a little tricky. In the general physical sense of "to open", however, **a·ku** (あ・く) and **a·keru** (あ・ける) function as a normal intransitive/transitive verb pair. The word **hira·ku**, on the other hand, is more concerned with a metaphorical or non-physical sense of "opening", and appears primarily in certain expressions (in the "opening", for example, of a conference, of new lands, or of cherry blossoms). Expressing the sense of a shop's front door being open would thus call for the verb **a·ku**, while conveying the idea of opening a business would require **hira·ku**.

In the first position, this kanji invariably takes the **on-yomi**.

kun-yomi suggestions: "**appetite**"; "**he ra**pidly"

Write your sentence to remember the **on-yomi** and **kun-yomi** readings in the box below.

Less Common Pronunciations
Less common **ON** reading: none
Less common **kun** reading: none

COMMON WORDS AND COMPOUNDS		
開く (intr)	*to be open*	**a·ku** あ・く
開ける (tr)	*to open (something)*	**a·keru** あ・ける
開く (intr/tr)	*to open; to develop*	**hira·ku** ひら・く
開化	open + change = *becoming civilized*	**KAI·KA** カイ・カ
開国	open + country = *to open up a country*	**KAI·KOKU** カイ・コク
開会	open + meet = *to open a meeting*	**KAI·KAI** カイ・カイ
公開	public + open = *open to the public*	**KŌ·KAI** コウ・カイ

SAMPLE SENTENCE:

水門　を　開けて　下さい。

SUI·MON   o   a·kete   kuda·sai.
sluice gate   open   please
= *Please open the sluice gate.*

COMPONENT #107

GAS STOVE

KANJI 107

鳥 BIRD

´	亠	冖	冖	冎	自	鸟	鳥	鳥
鳥	鳥							

BUILDING THIS KANJI
Dinosaur 鳥 + Gas Stove 灬 = 鳥

Meaning
Bird.

Remembering this kanji
As recent archaeological evidence has shown, BIRDS were an important part of a **dinosaur's** diet. Numerous cave drawings, in fact, show **dinosaurs** cooking BIRDS over **gas stoves**. This is interesting, for it has led some scholars to theorize that it was the **dinosaurs'** clumsy use of **gas stoves** that led to their extinction. If this is true, it explains nicely how BIRDS have managed to survive to the present day.

Common Pronunciations

Common **ON** reading: **CHŌ** (チョウ)
Common **kun** reading: **tori** (とり)

kun-yomi suggestion: "lava**tory**"

Write your sentence to remember the **on-yomi** and **kun-yomi** readings in the box below.

COMMON WORDS AND COMPOUNDS		
鳥	*bird*	**tori** とり
白鳥	white + bird = *swan*	**HAKU·CHŌ** ハク・チョウ
小鳥	small + bird = *small bird*	**ko·tori** こ・とり
夜鳥	night + bird = *nocturnal bird*	**YA·CHŌ** ヤ・チョウ
愛鳥家	love + bird + house = *bird lover*	**AI·CHŌ·KA** アイ・チョウ・カ

Less Common Pronunciations

Less common **ON** reading: none
Less common **kun** reading: none

SAMPLE SENTENCE:

あの　青い　　小鳥　　の　　名前　　が
ano   ao·i   ko·tori   no   na·mae   ga
that   blue   little bird   no   name
分かります　　か。
wa·karimasu   ka.
understand
= *Do you know the name of that little blue bird?*

KANJI 108

EVENING

ノ	ク	夕					

Meaning

Evening. At this time of day, our friend the moon is not yet entirely visible through the evening mist. No story required.

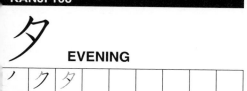

Common Pronunciations

Common **ON** reading: none
Common **kun** reading: **yū** (ゆう)

kun-yomi suggestion: "ukulele"

Create your sentence to remember the **kun-yomi** reading in the box below.

Less Common Pronunciations

Less common **ON** reading: **SEKI** (セキ)
Less common **kun** reading: none

COMMON WORDS AND COMPOUNDS		
夕べ	*evening*	**yū·be** ゆう・べ
夕日	evening + sun = *setting sun*	**yū·hi** ゆう・ひ
夕立	evening + stand = *late afternoon (rain) shower*	**yū·dachi** ゆう・だち

SAMPLE SENTENCE:

山　　から見る　夕日　が　美しい。
yama   kara mi·ru   yū·hi   ga utsuku·shii.
mountain from see setting sun   beautiful
= *The setting sun is beautiful when seen from the mountain.*

KANJI 109

外 **OUTSIDE**

ノ	ク	タ	夘	外			

BUILDING THIS KANJI
Evening 夕 (108) + **Poor Figure Skater** ト = 外

Meaning
Outside. The idea of "foreign" or "other" is also present, as the third example below makes clear. The less common readings convey some secondary meanings of removal and disconnection.

Remembering this kanji
There is a very rigid hierarchy in the world of figure skating. When **evening** arrives, for instance, the arenas are often so full that the **poor figure skaters** are forced OUTSIDE. Unfortunately, the frozen puddles on the OUTSIDE parking lot do not provide nearly enough room for jumps.

Common Pronunciations
Common **ON** reading: **GAI** (ガイ)
Common **kun** reading: **soto** (そと)

kun-yomi suggestion: "**so to**asty"

Create your **on-yomi** keyword and enter it in the table at the back of the book. After that, write your sentence to remember the **on-yomi** and **kun-yomi** readings in the box below.

Less Common Pronunciations
Less common **ON** reading: **GE** (ゲ)
Less common **kun** readings: **hoka** (ほか); **hazu** (はず)

COMMON WORDS AND COMPOUNDS		
外	*outside*	**soto** そと
外見	outside + see = *external appearance*	**GAI·KEN** ガイ・ケン
外国人	outside + country + person = *foreigner*	**GAI·KOKU·JIN** ガイ・コク・ジン
外出	outside + exit = *going out*	**GAI·SHUTSU** ガイ・シュツ
海外	sea + outside = *overseas*	**KAI·GAI** カイ・ガイ

SAMPLE SENTENCE:

日本   には   外国人   が 多い。
NI·HON ni wa **GAI·KOKU·JIN** ga ō·i.
 Japan   foreigners   many
= *There are many foreigners in Japan.*

KANJI 110

TONGUE

BUILDING THIS KANJI
Thousand 千 (65) + Mouth (vampire) 口 (8) = 舌

Meaning
Tongue.

Remembering this kanji
Interesting fact: a survey showed that **Thousand** Island dressing was a favorite amongst **vampires**. "It's very pleasing to the TONGUE," said one, "and it doesn't have any…unfortunate ingredients." Manufacturers of garlic-based dressings, it seems, need to take the TONGUES of **vampires** more into account if they want access to this market segment.

Common Pronunciations
Common **ON** reading: none
Common **kun** reading: **shita** (した)

kun-yomi suggestion: "**she taps**"

Create your sentence to remember the **kun-yomi** reading in the box below.

Less Common Pronunciations
Less common **ON** reading: ZETSU (ゼ ツ)
Less common **kun** reading: none

COMMON WORDS AND COMPOUND		
舌	*tongue*	**shita** した

SAMPLE SENTENCE:

内田さん は 舌 に ピアス を
Uchi·da-san wa shita ni piasu o
Uchida-san   tongue   piercing
しました。
shimashita.
did
= *Uchida-san got her tongue pierced.*

COMPONENT #111

BANANA PEELS

Note to subtle different between this component and the "Wishbones" of Component 79.

KANJI 111

BUILDING THIS KANJI
Prison 囗 + Jelly Bean ヽ + Jelly Bean ヽ +
Banana Peels メ = 図

Meaning
Diagram/Drawing. By extension comes the idea of "planning".

DIAGRAM

Remembering this kanji

"You have to be sly if you're going to break out of this **prison**," my cellmate told me as I settled in. "The guards won't allow us any pens so there's no way to draw up an escape DIAGRAM. That's why I have these." He placed a couple of moldy **jelly beans** and some rotting **banana peels** on my bunk. "These **jelly beans** will be us," he whispered, "and the **banana peels** will represent the guards. It's not much, but we can plan our break using these as a DIAGRAM."

I nodded. My time in **prison**, it seemed, was not only going to be long, but more boring than I could have possibly imagined.

Common Pronunciations

Common **ON** readings: **ZU** (ズ); **TO** (ト)
Common **kun** reading: none

ZU is the more common reading. Note in the second example below how effectively Japanese can express complex English words.

Create your **on-yomi** keywords and enter them the table at the back of the book. After that, wri your sentence to remember the **on-yomi** readin, in the box below.

Less Common Pronunciations

Less common **ON** reading: none
Less common **kun** reading: **haka** (は か)

	COMMON WORDS AND COMPOUNDS	
図工	diagram + craft = *drawing and manual arts*	ZU·KŌ ズ・コウ
心電図	heart + electric + diagram = *electrocardiogram*	SHIN·DEN·ZU シン・デン・ズ
海図	sea + diagram = *nautical chart*	KAI·ZU カイ・ズ
意図	mind + diagram = *(one's) aim*	I·TO イ・ト

SAMPLE SENTENCE:

心電図　　モニター　を
SHIN·DEN·ZU　　monitā　　o
electrocardiogram　monitor
見せて　下さい。
mi·sete　　kuda·sai.
show　　　please
= *Please show me the electrocardiogram monitc*

KANJI 112

 **STAND**

| ' | 一 | 亠 | 立 | 立 | | | |

Meaning
Stand/Rise. No story required.

...mmon Pronunciations

...mmon **ON** reading: **RITSU** (リ ツ)
...mmon **kun** reading: **ta** (た)

...nsistent with other **on-yomi** ending in **TSU**
(ﾂ), **RITSU** "doubles up" with unvoiced conso-
...nt sounds that follow it, as the fifth example
...low demonstrates. It can also act like 買 (Entry
...) and absorb its accompanying hiragana, as the
...al example shows.

...n-yomi** suggestion: "**tax**"

...eate your **on-yomi** keyword and enter it in the
...ble at the back of the book. After that, write your
...ntence to remember the **on-yomi** and **kun-yomi**
...adings in the box below.

COMMON WORDS AND COMPOUNDS		
立つ (intr)	*to stand*	**ta**·tsu た·つ
立てる (tr)	*to set up*	**ta**·teru た·てる
自立	self + stand = *independence*	**JI·RITSU** ジ·リツ
中立	middle + stand = *neutrality*	**CHŪ·RITSU** チュウ·リツ
立春	stand + spring = *first day of spring*	**RIS·SHUN** リッ·シュン
立ち入る	stand + enter = *to go into*	**ta**·chi i·ru た·ち い·る
夕立	evening + stand = *late afternoon (rain) shower*	**yū·dachi** ゆう·だち

SAMPLE SENTENCE:

女　の　人　が　美しい　月
onna　no　hito　ga　utsuku·shii　tsuki
woman　　person　　　　beautiful　moon
の　下　に　立っています。
no　shita　ni　tat·te imasu.
　under　　　　is standing
=*The woman is standing under a beautiful moon.*

...ess Common Pronunciations

...ess common **ON** reading: **RYŪ** (リ ュ ウ)
...ess common **kun** reading: none

KANJI 113

親 PARENT

亠	竒	产	立	立	辛	亲	亲
新	新	新	親	親	親		

BUILDING THIS KANJI

Stand 立(112) + **Tree** 木(13) + **See** 見(42) = 親

Meaning

"Parent", together with the senses of intimacy
...nd closeness.

Remembering this kanji

When she was young, her PARENTS would
often sing the following ditty:

> "**Stand** on a **tree**,
> And what do you **see**?
> Your PARENTS! Your PARENTS!"

It was cute, of course, but they really should
have stopped at some point. After all, it wasn't
easy for her as a university student having to
answer the question "What's up with your
PARENTS and that dumb song?"

Common Pronunciations
Common **ON** reading: **SHIN** (シ ン)
Common **kun** reading: **oya** (おや)

kun-yomi suggestion: "**coy a**bout"

Write your sentence to remember the **on-yomi** and **kun-yomi** readings in the box below.

Less Common Pronunciations
Less common **ON** reading: none
Less common **kun** reading: **shita** (し た)

COMMON WORDS AND COMPOUNDS		
親	*parent*	**oya** おや
父親	father + parent = *father*	chichi·**oya** ち ち · おや
親子	parent + child = *parent and child*	**oya**·ko おや · こ
肉親	meat + parent = *blood relative*	NIKU·**SHI**」 ニ ク · シ ン
母親	mother + parent = *mother*	haha·**oya** は は · おや
親切	parent + cut = *kindhearted*	**SHIN**·SET! シ ン · セ ツ

SAMPLE SENTENCE:

中川さん の 父親 は 山
Naka·gawa-san no chichi·oya wa yama
Nakagawa-san　　　　father　mountai
大好き です。
DAI su·ki　desu.
really likes
=*Nakagawa-san's father really likes the m*
tains.

KANJI 114

星 **STAR**

丶	冂	冂	日	尸	尸	早	早	星

BUILDING THIS KANJI
Sun 日 (6) + **Life** 生 (99) = 星

Meaning
Star.

Remembering this kanji
When the **sun** is shining over your **life**, impossible not to feel like a STAR. A fam STAR like Sirius, mind you, not one of th dim ones nobody cares about.

Common Pronunciations

Common **ON** reading: **SEI** (セイ)

Common **kun** reading: **hoshi** (ほし)

on-yomi suggestion: "tally **ho, Sheeb**a!"

Write your sentence to remember the **on-yomi** and **kun-yomi** readings in the box below.

COMMON WORDS AND COMPOUNDS		
星	*star*	**hoshi** ほし
水星	water + star = *Mercury (planet)*	**SUI·SEI** スイ・セイ
金星	gold + star = *Venus (planet)*	**KIN·SEI** キン・セイ
火星	fire + star = *Mars (planet)*	**KA·SEI** カ・セイ
木星	tree + star = *Jupiter (planet)*	**MOKU·SEI** モク・セイ
土星	earth + star = *Saturn (planet)*	**DO·SEI** ド・セイ

SAMPLE SENTENCE:

あの　明るい　星　は　金星　だ
ano　aka·rui　hoshi　wa　KIN·SEI　da
that　bright　star　　　Venus
と　思います　か。
to　omo·imasu　ka.
　　think
= *Do you think that bright star is Venus?*

Less Common Pronunciations

Less common **ON** reading: **SHŌ** (ショウ)

Less common **kun** reading: none

COMPONENT #115

CROPS

When this component appears it usually indicates a kanji with some connection to crops and harvesting.

KANJI 115

秋 **AUTUMN**

二 千 禾 禾 禾 禾 秒 秋

BUILDING THIS KANJI

Crops 禾 + Fire 火(59) = 秋

Meaning

Autumn.

Remembering this kanji

No need for a long story here, given that the origin of this graceful character is clearly apparent, AUTUMN being the time when the stubble of **crops** was set on **fire** after harvesting.

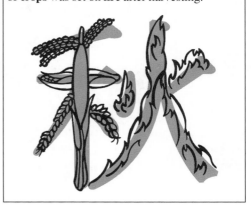

Common Pronunciations

Common **ON** reading: **SHŪ** (シュウ)

Common **kun** reading: **aki** (あき)

Note the great four-kanji compound in the third example below.

kun-yomi suggestion: "st**ack ea**sily"

Create your **on-yomi** keyword and enter it in the table at the back of the book. After that, write your sentence to remember the **on-yomi** and **kun-yomi** readings in the box below.

COMMON WORDS AND COMPOUNDS		
秋	*autumn*	**aki** あ き
立秋	stand + autumn = *first day of* *autumn*	RIS·**SHŪ** リッ・シュウ
春夏 秋冬	spring + summer + autumn + winter = *the four seasons;* *year round*	SHUN·KA·**SHŪ**·T シュン・カ・ シュウ・トウ
秋空	autumn + empty (sky) = *autumn sky*	**aki**·zora あ き・ぞ ら
秋分	autumn + part = *autumnal* *equinox*	**SHŪ**·BUN シュウ・ブン

Less Common Pronunciations
Less common **ON** reading: none
Less common **kun** reading: none

SAMPLE SENTENCE:

秋 に は　日 本　の　山　が　美 し

aki ni wa　NI·HON　no　yama　ga　utsuku·
autumn　Japan　　mountain　beauti

=*Japan's mountains are beautiful in autumn*

WHISKEY JUG

It's hard to imagine many whiskey drinkers being happy about the stopper for this jug taking up so much room!

KANJI 116

西   **WEST**

| 一 | 丆 | 厂 | 丙 | 西 | 西 | | |

Meaning
West.

Remembering this kanji
Everyone knows there were a lot of alco problems in the wild WEST. Fittingly, a drai **whiskey jug** is used to show this.

Common Pronunciations
Common **ON** reading: **SEI** (セイ)
Common **kun** reading: **nishi** (にし)

kun-yomi suggestion: "honey shield"

rite your sentence to remember the **on-yomi** and
n-yomi readings in the box below.

COMMON WORDS AND COMPOUNDS		
西	*west*	**nishi** にし
西口	west + mouth = *west exit/entrance*	**nishi**·guchi にし・ぐち
北西	north + west = *northwest*	HOKU·**SEI** ホク・セイ
北北西	north + north + west = *north-northwest*	HOKU·HOKU·**SEI** ホク・ホク・セイ
南西	south + west = *southwest*	NAN·**SEI** ナン・セイ
南南西	south + south + west = *south-southwest*	NAN·NAN·**SEI** ナン・ナン・セイ

ss Common Pronunciations
ss common **ON** reading: **SAI** (サイ)
ss common **kun** reading: none

SAMPLE SENTENCE:

西口	から	出て	父	に
nishi·guchi	**kara**	**de·te**	**chichi**	**ni**
west exit		exit	father	

会いました。
   a·imashita.
        met
=*(She) left by the west exit and met her father.*

刀

SWORD

フ	刀							

Meaning
word. No story required.

Common Pronunciations
Common **ON** reading: **TŌ** (トウ)
Common **kun** reading: **katana** (かたな)

kun-yomi suggestion: "ma**k**e **a** **t**a**n** **a**pple"

Write your sentence to remember the **on-yomi** and
kun-yomi readings in the box below.

Less Common Pronunciations
Less common **ON** reading: none
Less common **kun** reading: none

COMMON WORDS AND COMPOUNDS		
刀	sword	**katana** か た な
刀工	sword + craft = *sword maker*	**TŌ·KŌ** ト ウ·コ ウ
日本刀	sun + main + sword = *Japanese sword*	NI·HON·**TŌ** ニ·ホ ン·ト ウ

SAMPLE SENTENCE:

先月　　　東京　で　　日本刀
SEN·GETSU　TŌ·KYŌ　de　NI·HON·TŌ
last month　　Tokyo　　　Japanese sword
買いました。
ka·imashita.
　　bought
=*Last month I bought a Japanese sword in To*

KANJI 118

　CUT

一	七	切	切				

BUILDING THIS KANJI
Seven 七 (44) + Sword 刀 (117) = 切

Meaning
Cut. When the **kun-yomi** is used as a suffix it can impart a sense of completely finishing something, or acting in a decisive manner. The final compound provides an example.

Remembering this kanji
Seven samurai means **seven swords**, and **seven swords** can mean trouble on the set:
　"For the last time," said the director, exasperated, "when I yell 'CUT', it does *not* mean to CUT each other."

Common Pronunciations
Common **ON** reading: **SETSU** (セ ツ)
Common **kun** reading: **ki** (き)

As can be seen in the fourth example, thi another kanji that behaves like 買.

kun-yomi suggestion: "**qui**che"

Create your **on-yomi** keyword and enter it in table at the back of the book. After that, write y sentence to remember the **on-yomi** and **kun-y** readings in the box below.

Less Common Pronunciations
Less common **ON** reading: **SAI** (サ イ)
Less common **kun** reading: none

As the **kun-yomi** of 切 "doubles up" with kanji following it in this next pair of words, th compounds are best learned as irregular readi

IRREGULAR READINGS		
切手	cut + hand = *postage stamp*	**kit·te** きっ·て
切符*	cut + symbol = *ticket*	**kip·pu** きっ·プ

COMMON WORDS AND COMPOUNDS

切れる (intr)	to break (by itself)	**ki**·reru き・れる
切る (tr)	to cut (something)	**ki**·ru き・る
切り下げる	cut + lower = to devalue	**ki**·ri sa·geru き・り さ・げる
切下げ	cut + lower = devaluation	**kiri** sa·ge き り さ・げ
親切	parent + cut = kindhearted	**SHIN·SETSU** シン・セツ
大切	large + cut = important	**TAI·SETSU** タイ・セツ
思い切る	think + cut = to make up one's mind	omo·i **ki**·ru おも・い き・る

SAMPLE SENTENCE:

水力　と　火力　は　大切
SUI·RYOKU to KA·RYOKU wa TAI·SETSU
hydro power　　thermal power　　important
です ね。
desu ne.
= *Hydro and thermal power are important, aren't they?*

COMPONENT #119

**SQUIRRELS
(ON A BRICK WALL)**

隹 蓶

Why are they hanging out on a brick wall?
'Cause they're tough, that's why.

KANJI 119

DAY OF THE WEEK

| 冂 | 日 | 日 | 日⌐ | 日⌐ | 日⌐ | 日⌐⌐ | 日⌐⌐ |
| 日⌐ | 日⌐⌐ | 日⌐⌐ | 日⌐⌐ | 日⌐⌐ | 日⌐⌐ | 曜 | 曜 |

BUILDING THIS KANJI

Sun 日 (6) + Comb ≡ + Comb ≡ + Squirrels
隹 = 曜

Meaning

Day of the week.

Remembering this kanji

Every DAY OF THE WEEK the squirrels sit on
their brick wall and wait for the **sun** to come up.
Once it does, it becomes light enough for each
to grab a **comb** and start slicking back his fur in
order to look tough. This is always necessary.
After all, every DAY OF THE WEEK is a struggle if you're a **squirrel**.

Common Pronunciations
Common **ON** reading: **YŌ** (ヨ ウ)
Common **kun** reading: none

Remember that the final kanji in each compound below is read with its **kun-yomi** (in voiced form). Create your **on-yomi** keyword and enter it in the table at the back of the book. After that, write your sentence to remember the **on-yomi** reading in the box below.

Less Common Pronunciations
Less common **ON** reading: none
Less common **kun** reading: none

COMMON WORDS AND COMPOUNDS		
日曜日	sun + day of the week + sun (day) = *Sunday*	NICHI·**YŌ**·b ニチ・ヨウ・
月曜日	moon + day of the week + sun (day) = *Monday*	GETSU·**YŌ**· ゲツ・ヨウ・
火曜日	fire + day of the week + sun (day) = *Tuesday*	KA·**YŌ**·bi カ・ヨウ・ひ
水曜日	water + day of the week + sun (day) = *Wednesday*	SUI·**YŌ**·bi スイ・ヨウ・
木曜日	tree + day of the week + sun (day) = *Thursday*	MOKU·**YŌ**· モク・ヨウ・
金曜日	gold + day of the week + sun (day) = *Friday*	KIN·**YŌ**·b キン・ヨウ・
土曜日	earth + day of the week + sun (day) = *Saturday*	DO·**YŌ**·bi ド・ヨウ・ひ

SAMPLE SENTENCE:

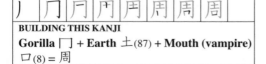

土曜日　に　パーティー　が　あります
DO·YŌ·bi ni   pātī   ga   arimas
Saturday   party   is
=*There's a party on Saturday.*

KANJI 120

周 **AROUND**

丿 冂 冂 冂 用 用 周 周

BUILDING THIS KANJI
Gorilla 冂 + **Earth** 土 (87) + **Mouth (vampire)**
口 (8) = 周

Meaning
"Around", as in the sense of a lap or circuit.

Remembering this kanji
If a **gorilla** and **vampire** show up at your lo square dance, you'd best be gettin' outta th way. Reason being that they'll spin AROU and AROUND, tramplin' the **earth** and anyth else that gets between 'em. Yup, there's gettin' AROUND it: they ain't exactly grace

ommon Pronunciations

ommon **ON** reading: **SHŪ** (シュウ)

ommon **kun** reading: none

rite your sentence to remember the **on-yomi**
ading in the box below.

COMMON WORDS AND COMPOUNDS		
円周	circle + around = *circumference*	EN·**SHŪ** エン・シュウ
周回	around + rotate = *going around*	**SHŪ**·KAI シュウ・カイ
一周	one + around = *once around*	IS·**SHŪ** イッ・シュウ

SAMPLE SENTENCE:

寺田さん　　は　　ニュージーランド

Tera·da-san　　**wa**　　　　**Nyūjīrando**

Terada-san　　　　　　　　New Zealand

を　　　一周　　　しました。

o　　**IS·SHŪ**　　**shimashita.**

　　　once around　　　did

=*Terada-san did a circuit of New Zealand.*

ess Common Pronunciations

ess common **ON** reading: none

ess common **kun** reading: none

CHAPTER 6 REVIEW EXERCISES

A. Please match the following kanji to their meanings.

1. 立   a. Bird

2. 星   b. Autumn

3. 切   c. Star

4. 鳥   d. Temple

5. 秋   e. Outside

6. 外   f. Stand

7. 美   g. Cut

8. 先   h. West

9. 寺   i. Beautiful

10. 西   j. Precede

B. Please match the following meanings to their kanji, and these to their **on** or **kun-yomi**.

1. Island   a. 刀   1. **ZU** (ズ)

2. Parent   b. 図   2. **oya** (おや)

3. Day of the week   c. 寸   3. **SHŪ** (シュウ)

4. Tiny   d. 夕   4. **shita** (した)

5. Sword   e. 開   5. **katana** (かたな)

6. Around   f. 親   6. **YŌ** (ヨウ)

7. Evening   g. 舌   7. **shima** (しま)

8. Open   h. 曜   8. **yū** (ゆう)

9. Tongue   i. 島   9. **a** (あ)

10. Diagram   j. 周   10. **SUN** (ス

C. Please choose the best answer(s) to the following questions.

1. Which of the following readings appl
the kanji 鳥?
a. **AI** (アイ)
b. **tori** (とり)
c. **hoshi** (ほし)
d. **SHŪ** (シュウ)
e. **CHŌ** (チョウ)

2. Which of the following readings appl
the kanji 星?
a. **SEI** (セイ)
b. **soto** (そと)
c. **BUN** (ブン)
d. **hoshi** (ほし)
e. **ZU** (ズ)

3. Which of the following presents the grea
danger to a newly-washed car?
a. 夕
b. 星
c. 鳥
d. 外
e. 舌

4. Which of the following readings appl
the kanji 秋?
a. **BI** (ビ)
b. **a** (あ)
c. **tera** (てら)
d. **SHŪ** (シュウ)
e. **aki** (あき)

5. Which of the following readings appl
the kanji 先?
a. **saki** (さき)
b. **YŌ** (ヨウ)
c. **SEN** (セン)
d. **yū** (ゆう)
e. **JI** (ジ)

D. Please choose the best answer(s) to the following questions.

   1. Which is the correct reading of 美しい?
     a. **ara·shii** (あら・しい)
     b. **tama·shii** (たま・しい)
     c. **mawa·shii** (まわ・しい)
     d. **utsuku·shii** (うつく・しい)

   2. Which answer best captures the meaning of the compound 月曜日?
     a. Sunday
     b. Thursday
     c. Monday
     d. Saturday
     e. All of the preceding

   3. Which of the following kanji has the most number of strokes?
     a. 開
     b. 鳥
     c. 美
     d. 秋
     e. 星

   4. Which is the correct reading of 立つ?
     a. **ta·tsu** (た・つ)
     b. **u·tsu** (う・つ)
     c. **ma·tsu** (ま・つ)
     d. **ka·tsu** (か・つ)

   5. Which are the correct readings of 開く? (There are two possible answers.)
     a. **o·ku** (お・く)
     b. **a·ku** (あ・く)
     c. **ama·ku** (あま・く)
     d. **hira·ku** (ひら・く)

E. Please match the following compounds and words to their meanings and pronunciations.

1. 木曜日	a. Setting sun	1.	**SHIN·SETSU** (シン・セツ)
2. 自立	b. Mars (planet)	2.	**HAN·TŌ** (ハン・トウ)
3. 親切	c. Beautiful woman	3.	**MOKU·YŌ·bi** (モク・ヨウ・び)
4. 先生	d. Independence	4.	**yū·hi** (ゆう・ひ)
5. 西口	e. Foreigner	5.	**nishi·guchi** (にし・ぐち)
6. 火星	f. Peninsula	6.	**KA·SEI** (カ・セイ)
7. 夕日	g. Thursday	7.	**SEN·SEI** (セン・セイ)
8. 外国人	h. Kindhearted	8.	**GAI·KOKU·JIN** (ガイ・コク・ジン)
9. 半島	i. West exit/entrance	9.	**BI·JIN** (ビ・ジン)
10. 美人	j. Teacher	10.	**JI·RITSU** (ジ・リツ)

CHAPTER SEVEN

Kanji #121—140

KANJI 121

読 **READ**

丶	亠	亖	言	言	言	言	言	言
訃	訐	誄	誎	読				

BUILDING THIS KANJI
Say 言 (80) + Sell 売 (92) = 読

Meaning
Read.

Remembering this kanji
The sales manager rose to address her staff. It was time for the READING.

"And lo, I **say** unto you who **sell**," she intoned. "READ carefully the customer's face. READ their gestures and clothes. But READ not, I **say**, our price protection guarantee; this let them READ for themselves."

Common Pronunciations
Common **ON** reading: **DOKU** (ドク)
Common **kun** reading: **yo** (よ)

kun-yomi suggestion: "yoga"

Create your **on-yomi** keyword and enter it in t[...] table at the back of the book. After that, write yo[...] sentence to remember the **on-yomi** and **kun-yo**[...] readings in the box below.

Less Common Pronunciations
Less common **ON** readings: **TOKU** (トク); T[...] (トウ)
Less common **kun** reading: none

COMMON WORDS AND COMPOUNDS		
読む	*to read*	yo·mu よ・む
読み切る	read + cut = *to finish reading*	yo·mi ki·ru よ・み き・る
読者	read + individual = *reader*	**DOKU·SHA** ド ク・シャ
読み物	read + thing = *reading matter*	yo·mi mono よ・み もの
多読家	many + read + house = *well-read person*	TA·**DOKU·K**[...] タ・ド ク・カ[...]

SAMPLE SENTENCE:

この 古い 本 を 読んでいますか

kono furu·i HON o　　yo·nde imasu[...]
this　old　book　　　are reading
= *Are you reading this old book?*

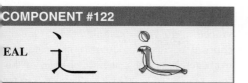

COMPONENT #122

EAL

KANJI 122

道 **ROAD**

`	ソ	ヽ	丷	广	产	芦	首	首

首	渞	道					

BUILDING THIS KANJI

Neck 首 (54) + Seal 辶 = 道

Meaning

Road/Way. This interesting kanji can signify both a physical road and a spiritual "path". In this latter sense it is often translated as "the Way".

Remembering this kanji

Being so poor growing up, we had to use our imaginations when it came time for fun. That's why it was so lucky for us when the **seal** washed up on the beach that day; once some yellow lines were painted down the back of its **neck**, we had ourselves a nice ROAD on which to race our toys. And did we ever get good mileage out of that ROAD! We played on it for ages, and only quit using it when our wheels started getting stuck.

Common Pronunciations

Common **ON** reading: **DŌ** (ドウ)
Common **kun** reading: **michi** (みち)
kun-yomi suggestion: "give **me chee**se"

Create your **on-yomi** keyword and enter it in the table at the back of the book. After that, write your sentence to remember the **on-yomi** and **kun-yomi** readings in the box below.

Less Common Pronunciations

Less common **ON** reading: **TŌ** (トウ)
Less common **kun** reading: none

TŌ is extremely rare, although it is found in a common word formed by the characters "God" and "Road" to indicate the Japanese religion Shinto (神道): **SHIN·TŌ** (シン·トウ).

COMMON WORDS AND COMPOUNDS		
道	road; way	**michi** みち
小道	small + road = path	ko·**michi** こ·みち
水道	water + road = water supply system	**SUI·DŌ** スイ·ドウ
下水道	lower + water + road = sewer system	**GE·SUI·DŌ** ゲ·スイ·ドウ
歩道	walk + road = sidewalk	**HO·DŌ** ホ·ドウ
国道	country + road = national highway	**KOKU·DŌ** コク·ドウ

SAMPLE SENTENCE:

あの　国　に　は　安全　な
ano　kuni　ni　wa　AN·ZEN　na
that　country　　　　safe
水道水　　が　ありません。
SUI·DŌ·SUI　ga　　arimasen.
tap water　　　　　isn't
=*There is no safe tap water in that country.*

天 HEAVEN

BUILDING THIS KANJI
One (top of a bun) 一 (3) + **Large (sumo wrestler)** 大 (17) = 天

Meaning
Heaven/The heavens. This character can indicate both the spiritual sense of heaven as well as the more down to earth notions of sky and air.

Remembering this kanji
The Japanese believe that **sumo wrestlers** in HEAVEN live in mansions built of food. The ceilings of these are made from the **tops of buns** that exude various types of mustards and sauces when they leak. Such living conditions must truly be HEAVEN for a **sumo wrestler**.

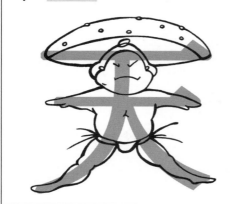

Common Pronunciations
Common **ON** reading: **TEN** (テン)
Common **kun** reading: none

Note how the **on-yomi** for "country" (国 voiced in the first example below. One m curiosity occurs in the fourth compound; in word, note how 天 changes the **on-yomi** of "k from **Ō** (オ ウ) to **NŌ** (ノ ウ) in order to n the pronunciation smoother. This type of pho change is extremely rare. Note that the sar sentence contains an irregular reading (明 E

Create your **on-yomi** keyword and enter it in table at the back of the book. After that, v your sentence to remember the **on-yomi** rea in the box below.

Less Common Pronunciations
Less common **ON** reading: none
Less common **kun** readings: **ame** (あ め);
(あ ま)

COMMON WORDS AND COMPOUNDS		
天国	heaven + country = *heaven*	**TEN·GOKU** テン・ゴ ク
天下	heaven + lower = *the whole land*	**TEN·KA** テン・カ
天体	heaven + body = *heavenly body*	**TEN·TAI** テン・タ イ
天王星	heaven + king + star = *Uranus (planet)*	**TEN·NŌ·SI** テン・ノ ウ セ イ
天気	heaven + spirit = *the weather*	**TEN·KI** テン・キ

SAMPLE SENTENCE:
明日 の 天気 は 雨 だそうで
ashita no TEN·KI wa ame da sō de
tomorrow weather rain seems
=*It seems the weather will be rainy tomorro*

KANJI 124

分 **PART**

| ノ | 八 | 分 | 分 | | | | |

BUILDING THIS KANJI
Eight (volcano) 八 (19) + Sword 刀 (117) = 分

Meaning
This important character suggests the ideas of "dividing" and "portion". It appears in a wide range of words, but the sense of division is always present in some way; the first example below, for instance, can be thought of as "parting" the unknown to arrive at understanding

Remembering this kanji
Modern scientists may scoff at the notion, but a lot of people still believe that **volcanoes** show how the underground dwellers made their way to the surface. By PARTING the rock and magma with **swords** on the way up, it is thought, they created the **volcanoes** we have today. Though the kanji clearly shows a **sword** beneath the missing PART of a **volcano**, it is impossible to verify this theory until the underground dwellers themselves shed more light on their past.

Common Pronunciations
Common **ON** reading: **BUN** (ブン)
Common **kun** reading: **wa** (わ)

kun-yomi suggestion: "**watch**"

Create your **on-yomi** keyword and enter it in the table at the back of the book. After that, write your sentence to remember the **on-yomi** and **kun-yomi** readings in the box below.

Less Common Pronunciations
Less common **ON** readings: **FUN** (フン);
BU (ブ)
Less common **kun** reading: none

As these readings are both used following numbers, it is important to know the context in which each is employed. **FUN** relates to minutes (of time or arc), as in the example 五分 **GO·FUN** (ゴ・フン): five minutes. **BU** deals with percentages and rates; 五分 in this sense would be pronounced **GO·BU** (ゴ・ブ), and mean either five (or fifty) percent. It merits learning the words for minutes as irregular readings, as they will be needed for telling time.

Note also that 大分 **DAI·BUN** (ダイ・ブン), one of many Japanese words expressing the idea of "much" or "very", is often pronounced **DAI·BU** (ダイ・ブ).

COMMON WORDS AND COMPOUNDS		
分かる (intr)	*to understand*	**wa·**karu わ・かる
分ける (tr)	*to part; to divide*	**wa·**keru わ・ける
自分	self + part = *oneself*	**JI·BUN** ジ・ブン
半分	half + part = *half*	**HAN·BUN** ハン・ブン
春分	spring + part = *vernal equinox*	**SHUN·BUN** シュン・ブン
秋分	autumn + part = *autumnal equinox*	**SHŪ·BUN** シュウ・ブン

SAMPLE SENTENCE:
日本語　が　分かります　か。
NI·HON·GO　ga　wa·karimasu　ka.
Japanese　　　　understand
= *Do you understand Japanese?*

COMPONENT #125

STOOPING

Labor Code regulations require the following disclaimer be inserted: "This is not an appropriate method of lifting heavy objects."

KANJI 125

物 **THING**

BUILDING THIS KANJI
Cow 牛(100) + **Stooping** 勹 = 物

Meaning
Thing/Object. Note that the writing order for "cow" differs when it is used as a component; slanting the final stroke upward makes for a smoother transition to the next part of the character.

Remembering this kanji
"What's that THING?" asked a guy **stooping** next to a **cow**.
  "That's my tail," said the **cow**, irritated.
  "And what's that THING?"
  "It's a hoof, OK? Everyone knows it's a hoof."
  "And what about those THINGS?"
  "What?! How dare you **stoop** so low as to question me about my udder!"

  Though THINGS had started out well, relations between **cows** and tourists had slowly become strained.

Common Pronunciations
Common **ON** reading: BUTSU (ブツ)
Common **kun** reading: mono (もの)

Pronunciation-wise, this is a tough kanji to down; both readings are found extensively, there are no easy rules to fall back on as to w each is used in compounds. This is a character has to be taken on a word-for-word basis.

kun-yomi suggestion: "**moan o**ver"

Create your **on-yomi** keyword and enter it in table at the back of the book. After that, write y sentence to remember the **on-yomi** and **kun-y** readings in the box below.

Less Common Pronunciations
Less common **ON** reading: MOTSU (モツ)
Less common **kun** reading: none

COMMON WORDS AND COMPOUNDS		
物	*thing*	**mono** もの
買い物	buy + thing = *shopping*	ka·i **mono** か·い もの
読み物	read + thing = *reading matter*	yo·mi **mono** よ·み もの
人物	person + thing = *one's character*	**JIN·BUTSU** ジン·ブツ
見物	see + thing = *sightseeing*	**KEN·BUTSU** ケン·ブツ
物体	thing + body = *an object*	**BUT·TAI** ブッ·タイ

SAMPLE SENTENCE:

本田さん　は　どんな　　人物
Hon·da-san　**wa**　**donna**　**JIN·BUTS**
Honda-san　　　what kind of　　charactei
です　か。
desu　**ka.**
= *What kind of person is Honda-san?*

KANJI 126

AXE

一	厂	斤	斤					

Meaning

Axe. Though rarely encountered on its own, this character serves as a component in several important kanji (an example being Entry 127). No story required.

Common Pronunciations

Common **ON** reading: **KIN** (キン)
Common **kun** reading: none

Write your sentence to remember the **on-yomi** reading in the box below.

Less Common Pronunciations

Less common **ON** reading: none
Less common **kun** reading: none

COMMON WORDS AND COMPOUND		
斤	*axe*	**KIN** キン

SAMPLE SENTENCE:

"斤" が 読めます か。
"KIN" **ga** **yo·memasu** **ka.**
KIN   can read
= *Can you read "斤"?*

KANJI 127

新

NEW

一	一	一	立	立	辛	辛	亲
辛	新	新	新				

BUILDING THIS KANJI

Stand 立(112) + **Tree** 木(13) + **Axe** 斤(126)
= 新

Meaning

New.

Remembering this kanji

Standing in the **tree**, I felt safe from the **axe**-wielding maniac.

"Come on down," he said. "I'll give you my **axe**."

I thought about this for a moment and realized I needed to split some wood behind the barn. "Is it NEW?" I asked warily.

"Brand NEW," he said. "I just got it."

"What's that stuff on the blade, then?"

"Oh, that? That's from the wrapper. Trust me, it's totally NEW."

"Well, OK then," I said, climbing down from the **tree**. "I suppose you can't hurt me if you don't have your **axe**."

Common Pronunciations

Common **ON** reading: **SHIN** (シ ン)
Common **kun** reading: **atara** (あ た ら)

kun-yomi suggestion: "**at a raffle**"

Write your sentence to remember the **on-yomi** and **kun-yomi** readings in the box below.

Less Common Pronunciations

Less common **ON** reading: none
Less common **kun** readings: **ara** (あ ら);
nii (に い)

COMMON WORDS AND COMPOUNDS		
新しい	*new*	**atara**·shii あ た ら · し
一新	one + new = *complete renewal*	**IS**·**SHIN** イ ッ · シ ン
新月	new + moon = *new moon*	**SHIN**·GETS シ ン · ゲ ツ
新星	new + star = *nova*	**SHIN**·SEI シ ン · セ イ
最新	most + new = *newest*	SAI·**SHIN** サ イ · シ ン

SAMPLE SENTENCE:

新しい　　日本刀　　を　買いまし
atara·shii　NI·HON·TŌ　o　ka·imashi
　new　　Japanese sword　　　bought
= *(I) bought a new Japanese sword.*

COMPONENT #128

WREATH

This component figures prominently in characters related to grasses and plants.

KANJI 128

花 **FLOWER**

BUILDING THIS KANJI
Wreath 艹 + **Change** 化(69) = 花

Meaning
Flower.

Remembering this kanji

Crowned with a **wreath**, Caesar strode i
Rome.
　"Everything has **changed**," whispered a se
tor. "Look how the masses throw **FLOWE**
It bodes ill."
　"Perhaps," said another, slowly, "but
FLOWERS in that **wreath** – be they sweet sm
ing roses – will also **change**, and become as th
that are now trampled underfoot."

Common Pronunciations

Common **ON** reading: **KA** (カ)
Common **kun** reading: **hana** (は な)

s the second example below shows, **hana** can
come voiced when not in the first position. Also
te the interesting juxtaposition of characters in
e fourth and fifth examples as well as the irregu-
r reading (上手) used in the sample sentence.

n-yomi suggestion: "**Han a**mulet"

rite your sentence to remember the **on-yomi** and
n-yomi readings in the box below.

COMMON WORDS AND COMPOUNDS		
花	*flower*	**hana** は な
生け花	life + flower = *flower arrangement*	i·ke **bana** い·け ばな
花見	flower + see = *cherry blossom viewing*	**hana**·mi はな·み
花火	flower + fire = *fireworks*	**hana**·bi はな·び
火花	fire + flower = *sparks*	hi·**bana** ひ·ばな
開花	open + flower = *bloom*	KAI·**KA** カイ·カ

ess Common Pronunciations
ess common **ON** reading: none
ess common **kun** reading: none

SAMPLE SENTENCE:

西田さん は 生け花 が 上手ですね。
Nishi·da san wa i·ke bana ga JŌ·zu desu ne.
Nishida-san   ikebana   good at
= *Nishida-san is good at ikebana isn't (she)?*

KANJI 129

NAME

ノ	ク	タ	タ	名	名		

BUILDING THIS KANJI
Evening 夕 (108) + Mouth (vampire) 口 (8)
= 名

Meaning
Name. By extension, this kanji also includes
he ideas of "reputation" and "fame".

Remembering this kanji
Dracula, of course, is a **vampire** whose NAME
is synonymous with **evening**. This is the real
reason he comes out only then; his NAME and
reputation would suffer, after all, if someone
were to spot him at a coffee shop in broad
daylight.

Common Pronunciations
Common **ON** reading: **MEI** (メイ)
Common **kun** reading: **na** (な)

kun-yomi suggestion: "**na**pkin"

Write your sentence to remember the **on-yomi** and **kun-yomi** readings in the box below.

Less Common Pronunciations
Less common **ON** reading: **MYŌ** (ミョウ)
Less common **kun** reading: none

COMMON WORDS AND COMPOUNDS		
名高い	name + tall = *renowned*	**na** daka·i な だ か·い
有名	have + name = *famous*	**YŪ·MEI** ユウ·メイ
名山	name + mountain = *famous mountain*	**MEI·ZAN** メイ·ザン
名物	name + thing = *famous regional product*	**MEI·BUTSU** メイ·ブツ
名前	name + before = *name*	**na**·mae な·まえ

SAMPLE SENTENCE:

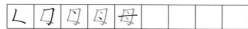

日本　の　　　　名山　　　の 一つ
NI·HON no　　MEI·ZAN　　no hito·tsu
　Japan　　famous mountains　　　one
見ました　か。
mi·mashita　ka.
　seen
= *Have you seen one of Japan's famous mountains?*

KANJI 130

MOTHER

㇄	刁	刄	彑	母			

Meaning
Mother. No story required.

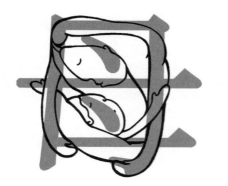

Common Pronunciations
Common **ON** reading: **BO** (ボ)
Common **kun** reading: **haha** (はは)

As with the kanji for father (Entry 79), the var of words for mother shown below reflect diffe levels of familiarity and politeness.

kun-yomi suggestion: "**Ha! Ha!**"

Create your **on-yomi** keyword and enter it in table at the back of the book. After that, write y sentence to remember the **on-yomi** and **kun-y** readings in the box below.

Less Common Pronunciations
Less common **ON** reading: none
Less common **kun** reading: none

These two irregular readings correspond to th we learned earlier for "father".

IRREGULAR READINGS

お母さん	mother	**okāsan** おかあさん
伯母 さん*	related + mother = *aunt*	**obasan** おばさん

COMMON WORDS AND COMPOUNDS

母	mother	**haha** はは
母親	mother + parent = *mother*	**haha·oya** はは・おや
母国語	mother + country + words = *mother tongue*	**BO·KOKU·GO** ボ・コク・ゴ
母の日	mother + sun (day) = *Mother's Day*	**haha·no·hi** はは・の・ひ
父母	father + mother = *father and mother*	**FU·BO** フ・ボ

SAMPLE SENTENCE:

新しい　　先生　　の　　母国語　　は
atara·shii   SEN·SEI   no   BO·KOKU·GO   wa
new   teacher   mother tongue
英語　です。
EI·GO   desu.
English
= *The new teacher's mother tongue is English.*

COMPONENT #131

BROKEN CRUTCH

Although this component appears to have three strokes, it is actually written with two; this is shown in the following kanji.

KANJI 131

 PRIVATE

BUILDING THIS KANJI
Crops 禾 + Broken Crutch 厶 = 私

Meaning
Private. This character is also used for the first person singular, "I".

Remembering this kanji
Nobody could figure out what was going on with the **crops**. The oats were acting wilder than ever, and rumor had it that gangs of wheat were causing trouble amongst the barley. PRIVATELY we began to worry about the harvest, especially when stalks of rye began showing up with bruises and **broken crutches**. Several of us tried to ask the **crops** what was going on, but nobody got very far. "What happens between us **crops** is none of your business," they always replied. "It's PRIVATE, you got that? PRIVATE!"

Common Pronunciations
Common **ON** reading: **SHI** (シ)
Common **kun** reading: **watashi** (わたし)

kun-yomi suggestion: "**what a shee**r"

Write your sentence to remember the **on-yomi** and **kun-yomi** readings in the box below.

Less Common Pronunciations
Less common **ON** reading: none
Less common **kun** reading: **watakushi** (わた
くし)

COMMON WORDS AND COMPOUNDS		
私	*I*	**watashi** わたし
私有	private + have = *privately owned*	**SHI·YŪ** シ・ユウ
私道	private + road = *private road*	**SHI·DŌ** シ・ドウ
私物	private + thing = *private property*	**SHI·BUTS** シ・ブツ
私学	private + study = *private school*	**SHI·GAKU** シ・ガク

SAMPLE SENTENCE:

私 は 本 を 読んでいます。
watashi wa HON o yo·nde imasu.
I book reading
= *I'm reading a book.*

KANJI 132

夜 **NIGHT**

BUILDING THIS KANJI
Police 亠 + Giraffe 亻 + Evening 夕 (108) +
Comet 一 = 夜

Meaning
Night. Make sure to write this character in the order given.

Remembering this kanji
After a long day policing the savanna,
ranger went to her local watering hole fo
drink. Surprisingly, the **giraffes** were alrea
there, and seemed well on the way to mak
a NIGHT of it.

"It's safe to come here the moment a **come**
visible in the **evening**," said one, slurring o
a gin and tonic. "That means it's NIGHT, a
dark enough so that nothing can hunt."

"I wouldn't be so sure about that," said
ranger. "The leopards I just passed on the w
over didn't look like they were coming here
a NIGHTCAP."

Common Pronunciations
Common **ON** reading: **YA** (ヤ)
Common **kun** reading: **yoru** (よる); **yo** (よ

oru is only used when this kanji appears lone; **yo** and **YA** are distributed evenly through ompounds.

un-yomi suggestions: "**you're oo**zing"; "**yo**gurt"

reate your **on-yomi** keyword and enter it in the ble at the back of the book. After that, write your ntence to remember the **on-yomi** and **kun-yomi** adings in the box below.

COMMON WORDS AND COMPOUNDS		
夜	*night*	**yoru** よる
夜中	night + middle = *middle of the night*	**yo·naka** よ・なか
夜明け	night + bright = *dawn*	**yo a·ke** よ あ・け
月夜	moon + night = *moonlit night*	**tsuki·yo** つき・よ
夜間	night + interval = *night time*	**YA·KAN** ヤ・カン

SAMPLE SENTENCE:

夜明け に 家 を 出ました。

yo a·ke ni ie o de·mashita.
  dawn   house   exit

= *I left the house at dawn.*

ess Common Pronunciations

ess common **ON** reading: none
ess common **kun** reading: none

HISEL   リ   

前 **BEFORE**

丶 丷 亠 亠 肯 肯 肯 前 前 前

BUILDING THIS KANJI

Snowboard 亠 + Moon 月 (11) + Chisel リ
= 前

Meaning

3efore/Front. It is worth comparing the ompounds below to those for "先" (Entry 105) o get a sense of the subtle differences between hese two characters.

Remembering this kanji

We all know that a waxing **moon** comes BEFORE a full **moon**, but how many know where the expression "waxing **moon**" originated? It's an interesting story, in that the **moon** used to work at a **snowboard** shop long BEFORE he took his place in the sky. Using a **chisel**, he would wax the **snowboards** as carefully as possible, trying not to let the **chisel** slip and add yet another crater to his face. He was, by all accounts, a conscientious worker, one who always reminded customers to prep their boards BEFORE they hit the slopes.

Common Pronunciations
Common **ON** reading: **ZEN** (ゼン)
Common **kun** reading: **mae** (まえ)

kun-yomi suggestion: "llama ate"

Write your sentence to remember the **on-yomi** and **kun-yomi** readings in the box below.

Less Common Pronunciations
Less common **ON** reading: none
Less common **kun** reading: none

COMMON WORDS AND COMPOUNDS		
前	*before*	**mae** まえ
名前	name + before = *name*	na·**mae** な・まえ
手前	hand + before = *this side of*	te·**mae** て・まえ
前半	before + half = *first half*	**ZEN·HAN** ゼン・ハン
前者	before + individual = *the former*	**ZEN·SHA** ゼン・シャ
午前	noon + before = *A.M.; morning*	**GO·ZEN** ゴ・ゼン

SAMPLE SENTENCE:

門 の 前 に 美しい 花
MON no mae ni utsuku·shii hana
gate before beautiful flower
が あります。
ga arimasu.
are
= *There are beautiful flowers in front of the gate*

KANJI 134

MANY

ノ	ク	夕	夕	多	多			

BUILDING THIS KANJI
Evening 夕 (108) + Evening 夕 (108) = 多

Meaning
Many/Much.

Remembering this kanji
Evening after **evening**, MANY **evenings** ago, something happened…to MANY.

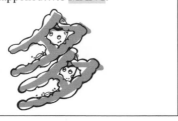

Common Pronunciations
Common **ON** reading: **TA** (タ)
Common **kun** reading: **ō** (おお)

kun-yomi suggestion: "oboe"

Create your **on-yomi** keyword and enter it in table at the back of the book. After that, write y sentence to remember the **on-yomi** and **kun-y** readings in the box below.

Less Common Pronunciations
Less common **ON** reading: none
Less common **kun** reading: none

COMMON WORDS AND COMPOUNDS		
多い	*many*	**ō·**i おお・い
多少	many + few = *more or less*	**TA·**SHŌ タ・ショウ
多分	many + part = *perhaps*	**TA·**BUN タ・ブン
多大	many + large = *great quantity*	**TA·**DAI タ・ダイ
多読家	many + read + house = *well-read person*	**TA·**DOKU·KA タ・ドク・カ

SAMPLE SENTENCE:

この　国　には　お金　が　大好き　な
kono　kuni　ni wa　o kane　ga　DAI su·ki　na
this　country　　　money　　　really like
人　が　多い。
hito　ga　ō·i.
person　　many
= *In this country, there are a lot of people who really like money.*

KANJI 135

HOLD

	十	扌	扩	扌	扫	拌	持	持

BUILDING THIS KANJI
Finger 扌 + Temple 寺(104) = 持

Meaning
Hold/Possess.

Remembering this kanji
I saw a **finger** emerge from a **temple** I was passing one day. "HOLD me," came a shaky voice from behind a curtain.
For some reason, I decided not to.

Common Pronunciations
Common **ON** reading: none
Common **kun** reading: **mo** (も)

As the fourth example below shows, this kanji can act like 買.

kun-yomi suggestion: "**mo**cha"

Create your sentence to remember the **kun-yomi** reading in the box below.

Less Common Pronunciations
Less common **ON** reading: **JI** (ジ)
Less common **kun** reading: none

COMMON WORDS AND COMPOUNDS		
持つ	*to hold*	**mo·tsu** も・つ
金持ち	gold + hold = *rich person*	kane **mo·**chi かね も・ち
持ち上げる	hold + upper = *to lift up*	**mo·**chi a·geru も・ち あ・げる
持物	hold + thing = *one's belongings*	**mochi·**mono もち・もの
気持ち	spirit + hold = *feeling*	KI **mo·**chi キ も・ち

SAMPLE SENTENCE:

雪男　　　　は　　田中さん
yuki·otoko　　wa　　Tanaka-san
The Abominable Snowman　　Tanaka-san
を　持ち上げました。
o　　mo·chi a·gemashita.
　　　　lifted up
= *The Abominable Snowman lifted up Tanaka-san.*

COMPONENT #136

PITCHFORK

Fittingly for a pitchfork, this component will always be stabbing through at least one other line in the kanji. The next entry provides an example.

KANJI 136

書 **WRITE**

ㄱ	乛	彐	彐	彐	聿	書	書	書
書								

BUILDING THIS KANJI
Pitchfork 彐 + Two 二(4) + Pole │ + Sun 日 (6) = 書

Meaning
Write. This character has to do with all matters related to writing, and can suggest such things as books, notes, documents, and calligraphy, amongst others.

Remembering this kanji
Even if you dip them in ink, it is simply not possible to WRITE the Japanese kanji for "**two**" using a **pitchfork** (it makes a triple line) or a **pole** (a single line). Using the **sun** is even worse; it burns the paper and is thus unsuitable for any kind of WRITING.

Common Pronunciations
Common **ON** reading: **SHO** (ショ)
Common **kun** reading: **ka** (か)

The third and fifth examples below show how this kanji can act like 買. Be aware that the **kun-yomi** is always voiced when it appears in the second position, as it is in the final compound.

kun-yomi suggestion: "**ca**lendar"

Create your **on-yomi** keyword and enter it in the table at the back of the book. After that, write your sentence to remember the **on-yomi** and **kun-yomi** readings in the box below.

Less Common Pronunciations
Less common **ON** reading: none
Less common **kun** reading: none

COMMON WORDS AND COMPOUNDS		
書く	to write	**ka·ku** か・く
書き入れる	write + enter = to write in	**ka·ki i·reru** か・き い・れる
書入れ	write + enter = an entry	**kaki i·re** かき い・れ
書道	write + road = calligraphy	**SHO·DŌ** ショ・ドウ
前書	before + write = preface	**mae·gaki** まえ・がき

SAMPLE SENTENCE:

お名前 を こちら へ 書いて 下さい
o na·mae o kochira e ka·ite kuda·sa
name   here   write   please
= *Please write your name here.*

KANJI 137

音 **SOUND**

`	一	一	立	立	产	音	音	音

BUILDING THIS KANJI
Stand 立(112) + Sun 日(6) = 音

Meaning
Sound.

Remembering this kanji
Crackling, sizzling, hissing…it's easy, unfortunately, to imagine the SOUNDS that would be produced if someone were **standing** on the **sun**.

Common Pronunciations
Common **ON** reading: **ON** (オン)
Common **kun** reading: **oto** (おと)

Although it is a mixture of **on-** and **kun-yomi**, the second example below is probably very familiar to you by now. Note also how the meaning

of the same compound changes in the example following this, when both kanji are read with their on-yomi.

kun-yomi suggestion: "guano **to**ast"

Create your **on-yomi** keyword and enter it in the table at the back of the book. After that, write your sentence to remember the **on-yomi** and **kun-yomi** readings in the box below.

Less Common Pronunciations
Less common **ON** reading: **IN** (イン)
Less common **kun** reading: **ne** (ね)

COMMON WORDS AND COMPOUNDS		
音	sound	oto おと
音読み	sound + read = the **on-yomi**	**ON** yo·mi オン よ·み
音読	sound + read = reading aloud	**ON·DOKU** オン·ドク
物音	thing + sound = a noise	mono·oto もの·おと
足音	leg + sound = sound of footsteps	ashi·oto あし·おと

SAMPLE SENTENCE:
あれ は 水 の 音 だ と 思います。
are wa mizu no oto da to omo·imasu.
that   water   sound   think
= (I) think that's the sound of water.

COMPONENT #138

SPY

As with the broken crutch in ム, the bottom of this component is written with two strokes, not three.

KANJI 138

 MEET

BUILDING THIS KANJI
Umbrella 𠆢 + Spy 云 = 会

Meaning

Meet/Meeting. When found at the end of compounds, this kanji often expresses English words such as "society", "association" and "party".

Remembering this kanji

"What's with the **umbrella**?" she asked on MEETING the **spy**, looking around nervously.

"What do you mean?"

"What do I mean!? The weather's perfect, so why in the world are you under an **umbrella**? Everyone's staring at us!"

"That's enough!" interrupted the **spy**. "You obviously don't know the rules; if you MEET a **spy**, you MEET under an **umbrella**. Everyone knows it's more stylish that way."

Common Pronunciations

Common **ON** reading: **KAI** (カイ)
Common **kun** reading: **a** (あ)

kun-yomi suggestion: "ambassador"

Write your sentence to remember the **on-yomi** and **kun-yomi** readings in the box below.

Less Common Pronunciations

Less common **ON** reading: **E** (エ)
Less common **kun** reading: none

COMMON WORDS AND COMPOUNDS		
会う	to meet	a·u あ・う
会見	meet + see = interview	KAI·KEN カイ・ケン
大会	large + meet = convention; tournament	TAI·KAI タイ・カイ
開会	open + meet = to open a meeting	KAI·KAI カイ・カイ
入会金	enter + meet + gold (money) = enrollment fee	NYŪ·KAI·KIN ニュウ・カイ・ キン

SAMPLE SENTENCE:

米国大会　　は　　九月　　に
BEI·KOKU·TAI·KAI　wa　KU·GATSU　ni
　U.S. tournament　　　September

あります　か。
arimasu　ka.
　is

= *Is the U.S. tournament in September?*

HEAR

BUILDING THIS KANJI
Gate 門(96) + Ear 耳(78) = 聞

Meaning

Hear/Ask. Like "早" (Entry 29), this is another kanji with two unrelated and distinct meanings.

Remembering this kanji

I pressed my **ear** against the **gate**.
   "What do you HEAR?" she asked.
   "'HEAR ye', 'HEAR ye'," I answered.
   "How can I?" she said. "You're in my way."
   "No," I said. "I HEAR 'HEAR ye…' oh, forget it."

Common Pronunciations

Common **ON** reading: **BUN** (ブン)
Common **kun** reading: **ki** (き)

Only the **kun-yomi** appears in the first position.

kun-yomi suggestion: "**key**note address"

Write your sentence to remember the **on-yomi** and **kun-yomi** readings in the box below.

Less Common Pronunciations

Less common **ON** reading: **MON** (モン)
Less common **kun** reading: none

COMMON WORDS AND COMPOUNDS		
聞こえる (intr)	*to be heard*	**ki**·koeru き・こえる
聞く (tr)	*to hear; to ask*	**ki**·ku き・く
聞き出す	hear + exit = *to find out about*	**ki**·ki da·su き・き だ・す
聞き入れる	hear + enter = *to comply with*	**ki**·ki i·reru き・き い・れる
新聞	new + hear = *newspaper*	**SHIN·BUN** シン・ブン
見聞	see + hear = *information*	**KEN·BUN** ケン・ブン

SAMPLE SENTENCE:

夜中 に 物音 を
yo·naka   ni mono·oto   o
middle of the night   sound

聞きました。
ki·kimashita.
heard
= *(She) heard a sound in the middle of the night.*

COMPONENT #140

GOAL POSTS

KANJI 140

央 **CENTER**

ノ	冖	冖	央	央			

BUILDING THIS KANJI
Goal Posts 冂 + Large (sumo wrestler)
大(17) = 央

Meaning
Center. Other than the first example (and words derived from it), this kanji is rarely used.

Remembering this kanji
You put a **sumo wrestler** dead CENTER between the **goal posts**, and chances are your team will give up fewer goals. Your opponent, quite simply, will never hit the CENTER of the net.

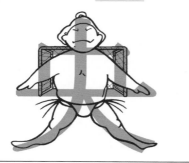

Common Pronunciations
Common **ON** reading: Ō (オウ)
Common **kun** reading: none

Write your sentence to remember the **on-yom** reading in the box below.

Less Common Pronunciations
Less common **ON** reading: none
Less common **kun** reading: none

COMMON WORDS AND COMPOUNDS		
中央	middle + center = *center*	CHŪ·Ō チュウ·オ ウ
中央口	middle + center + mouth = *central exit/entrance*	CHŪ·Ō·guchi チュウ· オウ·ぐ ち

SAMPLE SENTENCE:

中央口　　で　秋山さん　を
CHŪ·Ō·guchi   de   Aki·yama-san   o
central entrance   Akiyama-san
見ました。
mi·mashita.
　　saw
= *(He) saw Akiyama-san at the central entrance*

HAPTER 7 REVIEW EXERCISES

Please match the following kanji to their meanings.

1.	多	a.	Many
2.	物	b.	Mother
3.	音	c.	Heaven
4.	天	d.	Read
5.	花	e.	Write
6.	書	f.	Thing
7.	読	g.	Hear
8.	私	h.	Flower
9.	母	i.	Private
10.	聞	j.	Sound

Please match the following meanings to their kanji, and these to their **on** or **kun-yomi**.

1.	New	a. 会	1.	**Ō** (オウ)
2.	Hold	b. 前	2.	**wa** (わ)
3.	Center	c. 新	3.	**KIN** (キン)
4.	Road	d. 分	4.	**mo** (も)
5.	Meet	e. 夜	5.	**SHIN** (シン)
6.	Axe	f. 央	6.	**yoru** (よる)
7.	Before	g. 名	7.	**a** (あ)
8.	Part	h. 持	8.	**MEI** (メイ)
9.	Name	i. 道	9.	**mae** (まえ)
10.	Night	j. 斤	10.	**DŌ** (ドウ)

C. Please choose the best answer(s) to the following questions.

1. Which of the following kanji have an **on-yomi** of **BUN** (ブ ン)?
   a. 読
   b. 聞
   c. 分
   d. 母
   e. 物

2. Which of the following readings apply to the kanji 多 ?
   a. **TA** (タ)
   b. **hana** (は な)
   c. **DŌ** (ド ウ)
   d. **michi** (み ち)
   e. **ō** (お お)

3. Which of the following readings apply to the kanji 花 ?
   a. **YA** (ヤ)
   b. **na** (な)
   c. **hana** (は な)
   d. **KA** (カ)
   e. **ON** (オ ン)

4. I planted a beautiful ___ in a corner of my garden.
   a. 斤
   b. 母
   c. 道
   d. 花
   e. 音

5. Which of the following readings apply to the kanji 物 ?
   a. **mono** (も の)
   b. **SHŌ** (シ ョ ウ)
   c. **SHITSU** (シ ツ)
   d. **na** (な)
   e. **BUTSU** (ブ ツ)

D. Please choose the best answer(s) to the following questions.

1. Which is the correct reading of 聞く?
   a. **yu·ku** (ゆ·く)
   b. **ki·ku** (き·く)
   c. **a·ku** (あ·く)
   d. **ka·ku** (か·く)

2. Which is the correct reading of 読む?
   a. **o·mu** (お·む)
   b. **ka·mu** (か·む)
   c. **u·mu** (う·む)
   d. **yo·mu** (よ·む)

3. Which of the following kanji has the most number of strokes?
   a. 前
   b. 物
   c. 書
   d. 夜
   e. 持

4. Which is the correct reading of 書く?
   a. **ka·ku** (か·く)
   b. **ama·ku** (あま·く)
   c. **ki·ku** (き·く)
   d. **shi·ku** (し·く)

5. Which is the correct reading of 新しい?
   a. **atara·shii** (あたら·しい)
   b. **mawa·shii** (まわ·しい)
   c. **utsuku·shii** (うつく·しい)
   d. **ara·shii** (あら·しい)

E. Please match the following compounds and words to their meanings and pronunciations.

1. 金持ち   a. National highway   1. **i·ke bana** (い·け ばな)

2. 新聞   b. An entry   2. **ka·i mono** (か·い もの)

3. 生け花   c. Oneself   3. **na·mae** (な·まえ)

4. 国道   d. Center   4. **kane mo·chi** (かね も·ち)

5. 自分   e. Flower arrangement   5. **JI·BUN** (ジ·ブン)

6. 書入れ   f. Name   6. **NYŪ· KAI·KIN** (ニュウ· カイ·キン)

7. 名前   g. Newspaper   7. **KOKU·DŌ** (コク·ドウ)

8. 中央   h. Enrollment fee   8. **kaki i·re** (かき い·れ)

9. 買い物   i. Rich person   9. **SHIN·BUN** (シン·ブン)

10. 入会金   j. Shopping   10. **CHŪ·Ō** (チュウ· オウ)

Kanji #141—160

NEAR

| ʼ | ｢ | ｢ | 斤 | ʼ斤 | 近 | 近 | | |

BUILDING THIS KANJI
Axe 斤 (126) + Seal 辶 = 近

Meaning
Near. The sense of "recent" is also incorporated.

Remembering this kanji
Brandishing an **axe**, the **seal** came NEARER and NEARER the waiter's station.
"Don't come NEAR me!" I screamed.
"You ever gonna slip me farmed salmon again?" he said threateningly.
I shouldn't have tried to be sneaky; any **seal** would have known that farmed salmon didn't taste NEARLY as good as wild.

Common Pronunciations
Common **ON** reading: **KIN** (キン)
Common **kun** reading: **chika** (ちか)

kun-yomi suggestion: "**chica**"

Write your sentence to remember the **on-yomi** and **kun-yomi** readings in the box below.

Less Common Pronunciations
Less common **ON** reading: none
Less common **kun** reading: none

COMMON WORDS AND COMPOUNDS		
近い	*near*	**chika**·i ちか·い
近づく	*to approach*	**chika**·zuku ちか·づく
近道	near + road = *shortcut*	**chika**·michi ちか·みち
近親	near + parent = *close relative*	**KIN**·SHIN キン·シン
最近	most + near = *recently*	SAI·**KIN** サイ·キン

SAMPLE SENTENCE:

新しい 家 は 川 の 近く に
atara·shii ie wa kawa no chika·ku ni
new house river near
あります。
  arimasu.
    is
= *The new house is near a river.*

COMPONENT #142

HAMMER

KANJI 142

失 **LOSE**

| ノ | ⺧ | ⺧ | 牛 | 失 | | | |

BUILDING THIS KANJI
Hammer ⺧ + Large (sumo wrestler) 大(17)
= 失

Meaning
Lose, in the sense of "mislay". This character often conveys a hint of failure and error, so guard against becoming depressed on seeing it.

Remembering this kanji
LOSING one's belt is obviously the worst thing that can happen to a **sumo wrestler**. Should this occur, the **wrestler** is to strike himself repeatedly with a **hammer** to atone for LOSING face.

Common Pronunciations
Common **ON** reading: **SHITSU** (シツ)
Common **kun** reading: **ushina** (うしな)

kun-yomi suggestion: **"ooh, she napped"**

Create your **on-yomi** keyword and enter it in the table at the back of the book. After that, write your sentence to remember the **on-yomi** and **kun-yomi** readings in the box below.

Less Common Pronunciations
Less common **ON** reading: none
Less common **kun** reading: none

COMMON WORDS AND COMPOUNDS		
失う	*to lose*	ushina·u うしな·う
見失う	see + lose = *to lose sight of*	mi ushina·u み うしな·う
失言	lose + say = *slip of the tongue*	SHITSU·GEN シツ·ゲン

SAMPLE SENTENCE:

大会　で　失言　しました。
TAI·KAI de SHITSU·GEN shimashita.
convention　　slip of the tongue　　did
= *(I) made a slip of the tongue at the convention*

KANJI 143
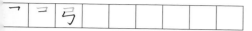

弓 **BOW**

ㄱ	ㄱ	弓					

Meaning
Bow (the partner to an arrow).

Remembering this kanji
It's a shame about this **BOW** having been run over by a tractor.

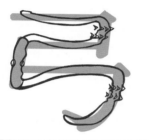

Common Pronunciations
Common **ON** reading: **KYŪ** (キュウ)
Common **kun** reading: **yumi** (ゆみ)

kun-yomi suggestion: "**you, me** and…"

Write your sentence to remember the **on-yomi** and **kun-yomi** readings in the box below.

Less Common Pronunciations
Less common **ON** reading: none
Less common **kun** reading: none

COMMON WORDS AND COMPOUNDS		
弓	*bow*	**yumi** ゆみ
弓道	bow + road = *(Japanese) archery*	**KYŪ·DŌ** キュウ・ドウ

SAMPLE SENTENCE:

前田さん は 古い 弓 と 美しい
Mae·da-san wa furu·i yumi to utsuku·shii
Maeda-san　　　old　bow　　beautiful
日本刀　　を 買いました。
NI·HON·TŌ　o　ka·imashita.
Japanese sword　　　bought
= *Maeda-san bought an old bow and a beautiful Japanese sword.*

COMPONENT #144

SADDLE 馬

丨	厂	厂	下	軍	馬	馬	馬	馬
馬								

BUILDING THIS KANJI
Saddle 馬 + Gas Stove 灬 = 馬

Meaning
Horse.

KANJI 144

馬 **HORSE**

Remembering this kanji

I was devastated when Trigger slipped his **saddle** and bolted off with another HORSE. I waited for him to return, naturally, but it was all in vain: he had left for greener pastures. In the end I hurled his **saddle** onto a **gas stove**; it was hateful to me now, and I didn't want anything to remind me of how fickle a HORSE could be.

Common Pronunciations

Common **ON** reading: **BA** (バ)
Common **kun** reading: **uma** (う ま)

kun-yomi suggestion: "**zoo**m **a**round"

Create your **on-yomi** keyword and enter it in the table at the back of the book. After that, write your sentence to remember the **on-yomi** and **kun-yo**▮ readings in the box below.

Less Common Pronunciations

Less common **ON** reading: none
Less common **kun** reading: **ma** (ま)

COMMON WORDS AND COMPOUNDS		
馬	*horse*	**uma** う ま
子馬	child + horse = *colt; pony*	ko·**uma** こ・う ま
牛馬	cow + horse = *cows and horses*	GYŪ·**BA** ギュ ウ・バ
馬具	horse + tool = *harness*	**BA**·GU バ・グ

SAMPLE SENTENCE:

馬　と　牛　の　どちら　が　好き
uma　to　ushi　no　dochira　ga　su·ki
horse　　cow　　　which　　　like
です　か。
desu　ka.
= *Which do you like, horses or cows?*

KANJI 145

 WEEK

丿	刀	刀	冂	円	用	周	周	`周
週	週							

BUILDING THIS KANJI
Around 周 (120) + Seal 辶 = 週

Meaning
Week.

Remembering this kanji

"It's the same routine every WEEK here at th aquarium," said the **seal**, shrugging. "I swir **around** and **around** 'cause there's nothing els to do."

I nodded. Digging up stories for my magazin "**Seal** WEEKLY", it seemed, was going to b harder than I had thought.

Common Pronunciations

Common **ON** reading: **SHŪ** (シュウ)
Common **kun** reading: none

Write your sentence to remember the **on-yomi**
reading in the box below.

Less Common Pronunciations

Less common **ON** reading: none
Less common **kun** reading: none

COMMON WORDS AND COMPOUNDS		
週間	week + interval = *week*	**SHŪ·KAN** シュウ・カン
一週間	one + week + interval = *one week*	**IS·SHŪ·KAN** イッ・シュウ・カン
二週間	two + week + interval = *two weeks*	**NI·SHŪ·KAN** ニ・シュウ・カン
週日	week + sun (day) = *weekday*	**SHŪ·JITSU** シュウ・ジツ
先週	precede + week = *last week*	**SEN·SHŪ** セン・シュウ
来週	come + week = *next week*	**RAI·SHŪ** ライ・シュウ

SAMPLE SENTENCE:

月曜日　　から　　二週間　　の
GETSU·YŌ·bi   kara   NI·SHŪ·KAN   no
Monday   from   two weeks
夏休み　　　です
natsu yasu·mi   desu.
summer vacation
= *There's a two-week summer vacation from
Monday.*

KANJI 146

弓| **PULL**

フ	コ	弓	引				

BUILDING THIS KANJI
Bow 弓 (143) + Pole | = 引|

Meaning

Pull. This character also conveys the idea of
"attraction" (best seen in the fourth example)
and the senses of receding and withdrawing.
You will notice it frequently on signs; it indicates "pull" on doors, and "discount" when used
with numbers.

Remembering this kanji

A **bow** obviously needs to be PULLED in order
to work effectively as a weapon, and the same
is true for a **pole**. How so? Well, a catapult is
basically a **pole**, and if you think about it, the
sound "PULL" is actually found in "catapult".

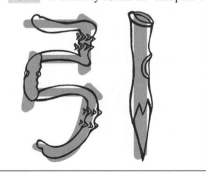

Common Pronunciations

Common **ON** reading: **IN** (イン)
Common **kun** reading: **hi** (ひ)

As seen in the third example, this is another kanji that can act like 買. The **kun-yomi** can also become voiced in the second position, as happens in the fifth compound.

kun-yomi suggestion: "**hea**ve"

Create your **on-yomi** keyword and enter it in the table at the back of the book. After that, write your sentence to remember the **on-yomi** and **kun-yomi** readings in the box below.

	COMMON WORDS AND COMPOUNDS	
引く	*to pull*	**hi·ku** ひ・く
引き 出す	pull + exit = *to withdraw (something)*	**hi·ki** da·su ひ・き だ・す
引出し	pull + exit = *a withdrawal; a drawer*	**hiki** da·shi ひき だ・し
引力	pull + strength = *gravitation*	**IN·RYOKU** イン・リョク
万引き	ten thousand + pull = *shoplifter*	**MAN** bi·ki マン び・き
引き受 ける	pull + receive = *to undertake*	**hi·ki** u·keru ひ・き う・ける
引き 上げる	pull + upper = *to pull up*	**hi·ki** a·geru ひ・き あ・げる

Less Common Pronunciations
Less common **ON** reading: none
Less common **kun** reading: none

SAMPLE SENTENCE:

やっと　牛　を　　川　　から
  yatto ushi o kawa kara
  finally cow   river from
引き上げました。
hi·ki a·gemashita.
  pulled up
= *(We) finally pulled the cow from the river.*

KANJI 147

秒   **SECOND**

´	二	千	禾	禾	利	利	秒	秒

BUILDING THIS KANJI
Crops 禾 + Few 少 (45) = 秒

Meaning
Second (of time or arc).

Remembering this kanji
"When **crops** are **few**," said the aid worker, "SECONDS count. Food needs to be rushed in, as the population will be growing weaker SECOND by SECOND."

ommon Pronunciations

ommon **ON** reading: **BYŌ** (ビョウ)

ommon **kun** reading: none

ote that the sample sentence contains one of the
ss common **on-yomi** for "分" (Entry 124) in the
mpound "十五分".

eate your **on-yomi** keyword and enter it in the
ble at the back of the book. After that, write
ur sentence to remember the **on-yomi** reading
the box below.

Less Common Pronunciations

Less common **ON** reading: none

Less common **kun** reading: none

COMMON WORDS AND COMPOUNDS		
一秒	one + second = *one second*	ICHI·BYŌ イチ·ビョウ
五秒	five + second = *five seconds*	GO·BYŌ ゴ·ビョウ
秒読み	second + read = *countdown*	BYŌ yo·mi ビョウ よ·み

SAMPLE SENTENCE:

十五分　　二十秒 かかりました。

JŪ·GO·FUN　　NI·JŪ·BYŌ　kakarimashita.

fifteen minutes twenty seconds　　took

= *It took fifteen minutes and twenty seconds.*

KANJI 148

SHELL

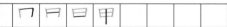

Meaning

hell. This is another character that rarely
ppears on its own. Like similar kanji we have
ncountered, however, it proves valuable as a
omponent.

Remembering this kanji

his is another kanji to which we will give an
xternal meaning – in this case, a fly swatter.
Vhy a fly swatter? Well, you'll need one if you
ver go down to the seashore to get SHELLS;
ies are all over them at low tide.

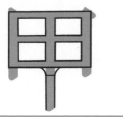

Common Pronunciations

Common **ON** reading: **KŌ** (コウ)

Common **kun** reading: none

Write your sentence to remember the **on-yomi**
reading in the box below.

Less Common Pronunciations

Less common **ON** reading: **KAN** (カン)

Less common **kun** reading: none

COMMON WORDS AND COMPOUND		
手の甲	hand + shell = *back of the hand*	te·no·KŌ て·の·コウ

SAMPLE SENTENCE:

上田さん は　　手の甲　　が かゆい。

Ue·da-san　wa　te·no·KŌ　ga　kayui.

Ueda-san　　back of the hand　　itchy

= *The back of Ueda-san's hand is itchy.*

COMPONENT #149

SKI JUMP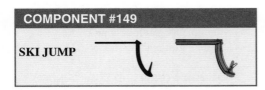

KANJI 149

気 **SPIRIT**

| ′ | ⌐ | ⌐ | 气 | 気 | 気 | | | |

BUILDING THIS KANJI
Hammer ⌐ + One (hamburger patty) 一(3) +
Ski Jump ⌐ + Banana Peels ㄨ = 気

Meaning
This fascinating character encompasses a range
of meanings, including the ideas of "spirit",
"air", "feeling", and "mood". It is worth spending some time getting to know this kanji; it is
found in many common words and expressions.

Remembering this kanji
I wanted to be a **ski-jumper**, but the national
team crushed my SPIRIT when they left me off
the squad. Oddly, it wasn't long after this that I
grew to dislike everything about the sport, and
began sabotaging all the facilities I could find.
My method was simple: use a **hammer** to drive
hamburger patties into the **ski jump** so that the
athletes would be thrown off course, and leave
banana peels on the side so that the spectators
would slip. Isn't it strange what happens when
the SPIRIT moves you?

Common Pronunciations
Common **ON** reading: **KI** (キ)
Common **kun** reading: none

The sample sentence is an extremely commo
greeting/question in Japanese. Create yo
on-yomi keyword and enter it in the table at t
back of the book. After that, write your sentence
remember the **on-yomi** reading in the box belo

Less Common Pronunciations
Less common **ON** reading: **KE** (ケ)
Less common **kun** reading: none

COMMON WORDS AND COMPOUNDS		
気	*spirit*	**KI** キ
元気	basis + spirit = *high spirits*	**GEN·KI** ゲン・キ
人気	person + spirit = *popularity*	**NIN·KI** ニン・キ
電気	electric + spirit = *electricity*	**DEN·KI** デン・キ
天気	heaven + spirit = *the weather*	**TEN·KI** テン・キ
気持ち	spirit + hold = *feeling*	**KI** mo·chi キ も・ち

SAMPLE SENTENCE:

元気 です か。
GEN·KI desu ka.
high spirits
= *How are you?*

KANJI 150

時

TIME

冂	冃	日	日⁻	日⁺	旹	旹	時	
寺								

BUILDING THIS KANJI
un 日 (6) + **Temple** 寺 (104) = 時

Meaning

Time. This character will become familiar to you through its use in the hours of the day (the third and fourth compounds below are examples).

Remembering this kanji

The Incas developed a remarkable system of measuring TIME. The **sun temple** at Machu Picchu was of great importance in this respect, for it marked the exact TIME of the solstices.

Common Pronunciations

Common **ON** reading: **JI** (ジ)
Common **kun** reading: **toki** (と き)

Note how the final half of the second compound becomes voiced; this is an occasional feature of repeated compounds.

kun-yomi suggestion: "**stoke ee**ls"

Write your sentence to remember the **on-yomi** and **kun-yomi** readings in the box below.

Less Common Pronunciations

Less common **ON** reading: none
Less common **kun** reading: none

This irregular reading is very common.

IRREGULAR READING		
時計	time + measure = *watch; clock*	**to·KEI** と・ケイ

COMMON WORDS AND COMPOUNDS		
時	*time*	**toki** と き
時々	time + time = *sometimes*	**toki·doki** と き・ど き
四時	four + time = *four o'clock*	**yo·JI** よ・ジ
九時半	nine + time + half = *nine-thirty*	**KU·JI·HAN** ク・ジ・ハン
同時	same + time = *simultaneous*	**DŌ·JI** ド ウ・ジ

SAMPLE SENTENCE:

八時半　に　東口　の
HACHI·JI·HAN　ni　higashi·guchi　no
eight-thirty　　　east entrance
近く　で　会いましょう。
chika·ku　de　a·imashō.
near　　　let's meet
= *Let's meet near the east entrance at eight-thirty.*

KANJI 151

話 SPEAK

` ｀ 亠 三 言 言 言 言 言
訐 訐 話 話

BUILDING THIS KANJI
Say 言 (80) + Tongue 舌 (110) = 話

Meaning
Speak, along with the ideas of conversations and stories.

Remembering this kanji
"SPEAK freely."
  "Though it is on the tip of my **tongue**, pharaoh, I dare not **say** it."
  "Then I order you: SPEAK!"
  I shriveled inwardly, knowing I would have to **say** it to avoid a **tongue**-lashing, or worse. "All right," I answered, shaking, "if you must know then, yes, it's true: those pants *do* tend to make you look big in the hips."
  Pharaoh approached me with his headgear swaying menacingly. "I **say** to you this," he warned. "You will lose that **tongue** should you SPEAK of this further."

I VANT
TO DRINK
YOURS
BLOOD

Common Pronunciations
Common **ON** reading: **WA** (ワ)
Common **kun** readings: **hanashi** (はなし); **hana** (はな)

As in the final example below, the **kun-yomi** for this kanji is always voiced in the second position.

kun-yomi suggestions: "**Hannah shielded**"
                          "**Han a**mbassador"

Create your **on-yomi** keyword and enter it in the table at the back of the book. After that, write your sentence to remember the **on-yomi** and **kun-yomi** readings in the box below.

Less Common Pronunciations
Less common **ON** reading: none
Less common **kun** reading: none

COMMON WORDS AND COMPOUNDS		
話	*story*	**hanashi** はなし
話す	*to speak*	**hana·su** はな・す
話し好き	speak + like = *talkative*	**hana·shi zu·ki** はな・し ず・き
電話	electric + speak = *telephone*	**DEN·WA** デン・ワ
会話	meet + speak = *conversation*	**KAI·WA** カイ・ワ
立ち話	stand + speak = *chatting while standing*	**ta·chi banashi** た・ち ばなし

SAMPLE SENTENCE:
田中さん は フランス語 を 上手 に
Tana·ka-san wa Furansu·GO o JO·zu ni
Tanaka-san   French   well
話せます。
hana·semasu.
  can speak
= *Tanaka-san can speak French well.*

KANJI 152

英 **ENGLISH**

一	十	艹	艹	苆	苩	苪	英

BUILDING THIS KANJI
Wreath 艹 + **Center** 央(140) = 英

Meaning
Although a secondary meaning relates to "briliance", this character will be far more familiar to you through its connection with all things English.

Remembering this kanji
To the ENGLISH, there can be only one object at the center of a wreath: the ENGLISH rose.

Common Pronunciations
Common **ON** reading: **EI** (エイ)
Common **kun** reading: none

Create your **on-yomi** keyword and enter it in the table at the back of the book. After that, write your sentence to remember the **on-yomi** reading in the box below.

Less Common Pronunciations
Less common **ON** reading: none
Less common **kun** reading: none

COMMON WORDS AND COMPOUNDS		
英語	English + words = *English (language)*	**EI·GO** エイ·ゴ
英国	English + country = *England*	**EI·KOKU** エイ·コク
英会話	English + meet + speak = *English conversation*	**EI·KAI·WA** エイ·カイ·ワ
日英	sun + English = *Japan and England*	**NICHI·EI** ニチ·エイ

SAMPLE SENTENCE:

英会話　　は　日本　で
EI·KAI·WA　　wa　NI·HON　de
English conversation　　Japan
人気　が　あります。
NIN·KI　ga　arimasu.
popular　　is
= *English conversation is popular in Japan.*

KANJI 153

訓 **INSTRUCTION**

、	二	二	主	言	言	言	訓	訓
訓								

BUILDING THIS KANJI
Say 言(80) + **River** 川(70) = 訓

Meaning
Instruction. This kanji tends to give a more serious or spiritual sense of teaching to the compounds in which it appears.

Remembering this kanji

INSTRUCTION for **rivers**: "All right everyone, listen carefully to what I **say**. What you want to do is head for the ocean; that means going downhill. Also, keep up a good pace or you'll either turn into a swamp or one of those **rivers** without a current that everyone laughs at. Oh, and don't be afraid to overflow your banks now and then; if anyone asks what's going on, just **say** "that's what **rivers** are supposed to do". Follow these INSTRUCTIONS and you'll be fine."

The first compound below presents another reading with which you may have become famili... Now create your **on-yomi** keyword and enter it ... the table at the back of the book. After that, wr... your sentence to remember the **on-yomi** readi... in the box below.

Less Common Pronunciations

Less common **ON** reading: none
Less common **kun** reading: none

COMMON WORDS AND COMPOUNDS		
訓読み	instruction + read = *the kun-yomi*	**KUN** yo·mi クン よ・み
訓話	instruction + speak = *moral discourse*	**KUN·WA** クン・ワ

SAMPLE SENTENCE:

これ を 訓読み で 読んで 下さい。
kore o KUN yo·mi de yo·nde kuda·sa
this kun-yomi read please
= *Please read this with kun-yomi.*

Common Pronunciations

Common **ON** reading: **KUN** (クン)
Common **kun** reading: none

KANJI 154

押 **PUSH**

BUILDING THIS KANJI
Finger 扌 + Shell (Fly swatter) 甲 (148) = 押

Meaning

"Push", together with the ideas of "suppression" and "restraint". This kanji also serves as the partner to "引" (Entry 146) on door signs.

Remembering this kanji

OK, then, your **fingers** are now gripping the f... swatter. Excellent. The next step is simple: i... order to kill the fly, PUSH the **fly swatter** awa... from you with a PUSHING motion.

Common Pronunciations

Common **ON** reading: none
Common **kun** reading: **o** (お)

s indicated by the last two examples below, this
another kanji that often shows up in the manner
買.

un-yomi suggestion: "orangutan"

reate your sentence to remember the **kun-yomi**
ading in the box below.

ess Common Pronunciations
ess common **ON** reading: **Ō** (オ ウ)
ess common **kun** reading: none

COMMON WORDS AND COMPOUNDS		
押す	*to push*	o·su お・す
押し出す	push + exit = *to push out*	o·shi da·su お・し だ・す
押し上 げる	push + upper = *to push up*	o·shi a·geru お・し あ・げる
押し開 ける	push + open = *to push open*	o·shi a·keru お・し あ・ける
押入れ	push + enter = *closet*	oshi i·re おし い・れ
押売	push + sell = *high-pressure sales*	oshi·uri おし・うり

SAMPLE SENTENCE:

押入れ の 中 に 物 が 少ない。
oshi i·re no naka ni mono ga suku·nai.
closet   middle   things   few
= *There aren't many things in the closet.*

COMPONENT #155

WHIRLING
DERVISH

Remembering this kanji
One of the events at the track and field champi-
onships is starting to become controversial: the
hammer toss. Why? Simply because a **whirling
dervish** wins it every YEAR. Athletes unable
to whirl as quickly have complained that the
dervishes have an unfair advantage. YEAR after
YEAR of winning, it seems, can bring YEAR
after YEAR of envy.

KANJI 155

年 **YEAR**

丿 ト ヒ 午 牛 年

BUILDING THIS KANJI
Hammer 丿 + Whirling Dervish 牛 = 年

Meaning
Year.

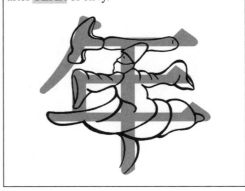

Common Pronunciations
Common **ON** reading: **NEN** (ネ ン)
Common **kun** reading: **toshi** (と し)

kun-yomi suggestion: "lot**to sheet**"

Create your **on-yomi** keyword and enter it in the table at the back of the book. After that, write your sentence to remember the **on-yomi** and **kun-yomi** readings in the box below.

Less Common Pronunciations
Less common **ON** reading: none
Less common **kun** reading: none

COMMON WORDS AND COMPOUNDS		
年	*year*	**toshi** と し
年上	year + upper = *older*	**toshi**·ue と し・う え
年下	year + lower = *younger*	**toshi**·shita と し・し た
新年	new + year = *the New Year*	**SHIN·NEN** シ ン・ネ ン
中年	middle + year = *middle age*	**CHŪ·NEN** チ ュ ウ・ネ ン
一年生	one + year + life = *first-year student*	**ICHI·NEN·SEI** イ チ・ネ ン・セ

SAMPLE SENTENCE:

青木さん は 三年生 です。
Ao·ki-san wa SAN·NEN·SEI desu.
Aoki-san third-year student
= *Aoki-san is a third-year student.*

KANJI 156

来 **COME**

| 一 | 一 | 冖 | 立 | 平 | 来 | 来 | | |

BUILDING THIS KANJI
One (hamburger patty) 一(3) + Rice 米(32)
= 来

Meaning
Come. As the final four compounds below make clear, the related meaning of "next" is also included.

Remembering this kanji
"COME on, everyone, dig in!"
  I didn't want to be rude, but a **hamburger patt** on a pile of uncooked **rice**? COME on! Not t mention the noise we all made as we crunche our way through the grains… Really, it wa enough to make me wish I hadn't COME to th **patty** and **rice** festival at all.

Common Pronunciations
Common **ON** reading: **RAI** (ラ イ)
Common **kun** reading: **ku** (く)

his character is infamous for being one of only
vo irregular verbs in Japanese, but whereas "to
ɔ" (為る) is rarely presented with its kanji (it is
ɔw universally written in **hiragana**), "to come"
ill is. What this means for us is that the char-
cter can be read variously as "**ku**" (く), "**ki**"
き) or "**ko**" (こ), depending on which tense
f the verb is being used. The sample sentence
fers an example of the polite past tense. Note,
ɔwever, an important exception in the second
ɔmpound below (an extremely common word);
hen following the kanji " 出 ", 来 is always read
ɪi". Lucky for us there are only two odd verbs
ı Japanese!

un-yomi suggestion: "**cool**"

reate your **on-yomi** keyword and enter it in the
ble at the back of the book. After that, write your
ɪntence to remember the **on-yomi** and **kun-yomi**
ɪadings in the box below.

This reading applies to only a pair of words:
ki·tasu (来たす) "to be forthcoming", and
ki·taru (来たる) "coming". This latter word is
used as an adjective.

COMMON WORDS AND COMPOUNDS		
来る	*to come*	ku·ru く・る
出来る	exit + come = *to be able to*	de ki·ru で き・る
来週	come + week = *next week*	**RAI**·SHŪ ライ・シュウ
来月	come + moon = *next month*	**RAI**·GETSU ライ・ゲツ
来年	come + year = *next year*	**RAI**·NEN ライ・ネン
来春	come + spring = *next spring*	**RAI**·SHUN ライ・シュン

SAMPLE SENTENCE:

先生　　は　　　一週間　　　前　　　に
SEN·SEI　wa　　IS·SHŪ·KAN　　mae　　ni
teacher　　　　　one week　　　before
来ました。
ki·mashita.
　came
= *The teacher came a week ago.*

ess Common Pronunciations
ιess common **ON** reading: none
ιess common **kun** reading: **ki** (き)

COMPONENT #157

CLAW

KANJI 157

学 **STUDY**

丶	丷	丷	⺍	兴	学	学	学

BUILDING THIS KANJI
Claw 丷 + UFO 冖 + Child 子 (56) = 学

Meaning
This character appears in words related to study and learning. When used as a suffix, it is often equivalent to the English "-ology". The final compound offers such an example.

Remembering this kanji
"I don't want to STUDY," the **child** said. "You can't make me."

"Oh, really?" the teacher replied. "Don't you know what happens to a **child** who doesn't STUDY? A **UFO** flies down to get them."

"Is that so?" said the **child**, now sauntering to the blackboard. "And when the **UFO** arrives, will my screams be like this? Like **claws** scraping down a blackboard?"

"No! Don't do that!"

"Then what happens if I refuse to STUDY?"

"Nothing! You become very successful!"

So it was true, then, thought the other students: there really was no need to STUDY.

Common Pronunciations
Common **ON** reading: **GAKU** (ガク)
Common **kun** reading: **mana** (まな)

kun-yomi suggestion: "**man a**nswer"

Create your **on-yomi** keyword and enter it in th table at the back of the book. After that, write you sentence to remember the **on-yomi** and **kun-yor** readings in the box below.

Less Common Pronunciations
Less common **ON** reading: none
Less common **kun** reading: none

COMMON WORDS AND COMPOUNDS		
学ぶ	to study	**mana**·bu まな·ぶ
大学	large + study = university	DAI·**GAKU** ダイ·ガク
学生	study + life = student	**GAKU**·SEI ガク·セイ
休学	rest + study = absence from school	KYŪ·**GAKU** キュウ·ガク
語学	words + study = linguistics	GO·**GAKU** ゴ·ガク
生物学	life + thing + study = biology	SEI·BUTSU·**GAKU** セイ·ブツ·ガク

SAMPLE SENTENCE:

この 家 には 大学生 が 多い。
kono ie ni wa DAI·GAKU·SEI ga ō·i.
this house   university students   man〉
= *There are many university students in th house.*

KANJI 158

意 **MIND**

`	一	亠	立	立	产	咅	音	音
音	意	意	意					

BUILDING THIS KANJI
Sound 音(137) + **Heart** 心(25) = 意

Meaning
Mind/Thought. This abstract character appears in many compounds conveying the ideas of "will", "intention" and "opinion", etc.

Remembering this kanji
Juliet :   Take me in your arms, Romeo.
Romeo: My darling.
Juliet :   The **sound** of your **heart**…it fills my MIND.
Romeo: Sorry, what's that?
Juliet :   My MIND, it's filled with the **sound** of your **heart**.
Romeo: Oh…um…that's great.
Juliet :   What do you mean "that's great"?
(stepping   Is that the best you can do? Doesn't
back)   this moment inspire anything more eloquent than that?
Romeo: Hey look, I've got a lot on my MIND, OK? Finals are coming up, I've got an important stag hunt this weekend, my cousin's wedding is just around the corner…oh, never MIND.

Common Pronunciations
Common **ON** reading: **I** (イ)
Common **kun** reading: none

Create your **on-yomi** keyword and enter it in the table at the back of the book. After that, write your sentence to remember the **on-yomi** reading in the box below.

Less Common Pronunciations
Less common **ON** reading: none
Less common **kun** reading: none

COMMON WORDS AND COMPOUNDS		
意思	mind + think = *(one's) intent*	I·SHI イ・シ
意図	mind + diagram = *(one's) aim*	I·TO イ・ト
意外	mind + outside = *unforeseen*	I·GAI イ・ガイ
意見	mind + see = *opinion*	I·KEN イ・ケン
意気	mind + spirit = *morale*	I·KI イ・キ
注意	pour + mind = *attention*	CHŪ·I チュウ・イ

SAMPLE SENTENCE:
あなた の 意見 が 分かりません。
anata no I·KEN ga wa·karimasen.
you   opinion   don't understand
= *I don't understand your opinion.*

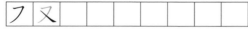

又 AGAIN

フ	又						

Meaning
Again/Also. Though this character will rarely be encountered on its own (indeed, it is often written in **hiragana**), it does serve as a component in several important kanji. Like other characters we have encountered of this type, we will assign a meaning with a more immediate visual connection: an ironing board.

Remembering this kanji
"Do it AGAIN," ordered the headmistress.
  AGAIN and AGAIN I brought out the **ironing board**; AGAIN and AGAIN I failed to get rid of the wrinkles.

Common Pronunciations
Common **ON** reading: none
Common **kun** reading: **mata** (ま た)

kun-yomi suggestion: "**mat a**ctivity"

Note how the second kanji in the final examp[le]
below is voiced. The pronunciation of "来 な か
っ た" in the sample sentence, incidentally, [is]
the informal past tense reading of "来". The[re]
is no **on-yomi** reading for this character. Crea[te]
your sentence to remember the **kun-yomi** readi[ng]
in the box below.

Less Common Pronunciations
Less common **ON** reading: none
Less common **kun** reading: none

COMMON WORDS AND COMPOUNDS		
又	*again*	**mata** ま た
又々	again + again = *once again*	**mata·mata** ま た・ま た
又聞き	again + hear = *hearsay*	**mata·giki** ま た・ぎ き

SAMPLE SENTENCE:

北川さん　は　又　来なかったよ。

Kita·gawa-san wa mata   ko·nakatta yo.

Kitagawa-san   again   didn't come

= *Kitagawa-san didn't come again!*

COMPONENT #160

ANTEATER 小

KANJI 160

赤 **RED**

| 一 | 十 | 土 | 亍 | 赤 | 赤 | 赤 | | |

BUILDING THIS KANJI
Earth 土(87) + Anteater 小 = 赤

Meaning
Red.

Remembering this kanji
It's pretty obvious what this **anteater** is doing:
looking for RED ants in the RED, RED **earth**.

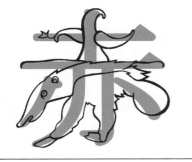

Common Pronunciations
Common **ON** reading: **SEKI** (セキ)
Common **kun** reading: **aka** (あか)

kun-yomi suggestion: "**st**ack **a**pples"

Create your **on-yomi** keyword and enter it in the
table at the back of the book. After that, write your
sentence to remember the **on-yomi** and **kun-yomi**
readings in the box below.

Less Common Pronunciations
Less common **ON** reading: **SHAKU** (シャク)
Less common **kun** reading: none

COMMON WORDS AND COMPOUNDS		
赤	red (noun)	**aka** あか
赤い	red (adjective)	**aka·i** あか・い
赤ちゃん	baby	**aka·chan** あか・ちゃん
赤道	red + road = equator	**SEKI·DŌ** セキ・ドウ

SAMPLE SENTENCE:
あの 赤い 花 は 美しい です ね。
ano aka·i hana wa utsuku·shii desu ne.
that red flower beautiful isn't it
= *That red flower is beautiful, isn't it?*

CHAPTER 8 REVIEW EXERCISES

A. Please match the following kanji to their meanings.

1.	又	a.	Horse
2.	話	b.	Again
3.	馬	c.	Shell
4.	赤	d.	Speak
5.	近	e.	Push
6.	訓	f.	Pull
7.	引	g.	Near
8.	甲	h.	Study
9.	押	i.	Red
10.	学	j.	Instruction

B. Please match the following meanings to their kanji, and these to their **on** or **kun-yomi**.

1.	Time	a. 失	1.	**toshi** (と し)
2.	Year	b. 年	2.	**EI** (エ イ)
3.	Bow	c. 気	3.	**SHŪ** (シ ュ ウ)
4.	Mind	d. 秒	4.	**I** (イ)
5.	Spirit	e. 来	5.	**ushina** (う し な)
6.	Come	f. 弓	6.	**BYŌ** (ビ ョ ウ)
7.	Lose	g. 英	7.	**RAI** (ラ イ)
8.	Week	h. 意	8.	**KI** (キ)
9.	Second	i. 週	9.	**yumi** (ゆ み)
10.	English	j. 時	10.	**toki** (と き)

C. Please choose the best answer(s) to the following questions.

1. Which of the following readings apply the kanji 赤?
   a. **KAN** (カ ン)
   b. **aka** (あ か)
   c. **ON** (オ ン)
   d. **o** (お)
   e. **SEKI** (セ キ)

2. I wasn't popular on my tug-of-war team because I always liked to ___.
   a. 秒
   b. 赤
   c. 近
   d. 押
   e. 年

3. Which of the following readings apply the kanji 馬?
   a. **BA** (バ)
   b. **NEN** (ネ ン)
   c. **uma** (う ま)
   d. **KI** (キ)
   e. **hana** (は な)

4. Which of the following readings apply the kanji 近?
   a. **TA** (タ)
   b. **toki** (と き)
   c. **hi** (ひ)
   d. **chika** (ち か)
   e. **KIN** (キ ン)

5. Which of the following readings apply the kanji 話?
   a. **hana** (は な)
   b. **YŪ** (ユ ウ)
   c. **hanashi** (は な し)
   d. **WA** (ワ)
   e. **mi** (み)

D. Please choose the best answer(s) to the following questions.

1. Which is the correct reading of 引く?
   a. **o·ku** (お・く)
   b. **ki·ku** (き・く)
   c. **yu·ku** (ゆ・く)
   d. **hi·ku** (ひ・く)

2. Which is the correct reading of 学ぶ?
   a. **a·bu** (あ・ぶ)
   b. **mana·bu** (まな・ぶ)
   c. **kara·bu** (から・ぶ)
   d. **yo·bu** (よ・ぶ)

3. Which of the following kanji has the most number of strokes?
   a. 週
   b. 馬
   c. 訓
   d. 時
   e. 秒

4. Which is the correct reading of 押す?
   a. **o·su** (お・す)
   b. **ama·su** (あま・す)
   c. **ko·su** (こ・す)
   d. **hi·su** (ひ・す)

5. Which kanji would come next in the following series: 日....週....月....?
   a. 秒
   b. 来
   c. 年
   d. 弓
   e. 引

E. Please match the following compounds and words to their meanings and pronunciations.

1. 週間　　a. English (language)　　1. **o·shi da·su** (お・し だ・す)

2. 生物学　　b. Week　　2. **MAN bi·ki** (マン び・き)

3. 英語　　c. Conversation　　3. **SEI·BUTSU·GAKU** (セイ・ブツ・ガク)

4. 押し出す　d. Four o'clock　　4. **KAI·WA** (カイ・ワ)

5. 来年　　e. Feeling　　5. **SHŪ·KAN** (シュウ・カン)

6. 四時　　f. To push out　　6. **RAI·NEN** (ライ・ネン)

7. 赤道　　g. Equator　　7. **KI mo·chi** (キ も・ち)

8. 万引き　　h. Biology　　8. **SEKI·DŌ** (セキ・ドウ)

9. 会話　　i. Shoplifter　　9. **EI·GO** (エイ・ゴ)

10. 気持ち　j. Next year　　10. **yo·JI** (よ・ジ)

Kanji #161—180

KANJI 161

 PUBLIC

ノ	八	公	公				

BUILDING THIS KANJI
Eight (volcano) 八(19) + Broken Crutch ム
= 公

Meaning
Public. In many instances, this character serves
as the opposite to "私" (Entry 131).

Remembering this kanji
The eruption of a **volcano** is a very PUBLIC
event, but nobody suffers more than those on
crutches who are blown off their feet. After all,
if you're hobbling along with **broken crutches**
as a result of this, you might as well carry a
sign that announces "Stay Away: I'm Really
Unlucky". It's a very PUBLIC humiliation.

Common Pronunciations
Common ON reading: **KŌ** (コ ウ)
Common kun reading: none

Write your sentence to remember the **on-yo**
reading in the box below.

Less Common Pronunciations
Less common ON reading: **KU** (ク)
Less common kun reading: **ōyake** (お お や け

COMMON WORDS AND COMPOUNDS		
公有	public + have = *publicly owned*	**KŌ·YŪ** コウ・ユウ
公安	public + ease = *public peace*	**KŌ·AN** コウ・アン
公開	public + open = *open to the public*	**KŌ·KAI** コウ・カイ
公金	public + gold (money) = *public funds*	**KŌ·KIN** コウ・キン
公道	public + road = *public road*	**KŌ·DŌ** コウ・ドウ
公会	public + meet = *public meeting*	**KŌ·KAI** コウ・カイ

SAMPLE SENTENCE:
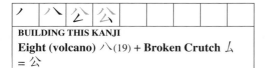
ここ は 公道 です。
koko wa KŌ·DŌ desu.
 this public road
= *This is a public road.*

ANJI 162

巾 **CLOTH**

冂	巾					

UILDING THIS KANJI
orilla 冂 + Pole ｜ = 巾

eaning
loth, rag. As the lack of compounds below
dicates, this character will prove to be of more
e to us as a component in other kanji.

emembering this kanji
nd so the **gorilla** won the **pole**-vaulting
mpetition and was given a CLOTH as a prize.
hy a CLOTH? Well, a medal or trophy was
dged to be of no use at all to a **gorilla**, whereas
CLOTH, at the very least, could be used to
ipe the **pole**.

Common Pronunciations
Common **ON** reading: **KIN** (キン)
Common **kun** reading: none

Write your sentence to remember the **on-yomi**
reading in the box below.

Less Common Pronunciations
Less common **ON** reading: none
Less common **kun** reading: **haba** (はば)

COMMON WORDS AND COMPOUNDS		
巾	*cloth, rag*	**KIN** キン
巾着	cloth + wear = *pouch (for coins, etc.)*	**KIN·CHAKU** キン・チャク

SAMPLE SENTENCE:

あそこ	に	巾着	を	掛けて
asoko	**ni**	**KIN·CHAKU**	**o**	**ka·kete**
over there		pouch		hang

下さい。
kuda·sai
　please
= *Please hang the pouch over there.*

ANJI 163

市 **CITY**

一	亠	市	市			

UILDING THIS KANJI
olice 亠 + Cloth 巾 (162) = 市

Meaning
City. A secondary meaning relates to "market";
in this sense the character can refer to anything
from a simple fair to the idea of a general "business" market. This will be the first of four kanji
in Chapter 9 connected with groups of people
living in a defined area; moving from larger to
smaller units will provide a sense of their rela-
tive sizes.

Remembering this kanji

One of the **policeman** grabbed a **cloth**. "All right, guys," he said, "you all heard what the captain said: let's get out there and clean up this CITY!" Numamura could only sigh as he watched his officers hurriedly picking up **cloths**. The CITY crime sweep, it seemed, was already off to a rocky start.

Common Pronunciations

Common **ON** reading: **SHI** (シ)
Common **kun** reading: none

Write your sentence to remember the **on-yomi** reading in the box below.

Less Common Pronunciations

Less common **ON** reading: none
Less common **kun** reading: **ichi** (い ち)

This **kun-yomi** occurs in compounds when kanji carries its secondary meaning of "mark or "fair".

COMMON WORDS AND COMPOUNDS		
市	*city*	**SHI** シ
市内	city + inside = *within the city*	**SHI·NAI** シ・ナ イ
市外	city + outside = *outside the city*	**SHI·GAI** シ・ガ イ
市立	city + stand = *municipal*	**SHI·RITSU** シ・リ ツ
市有	city + have = *city-owned*	**SHI·YŪ** シ・ユ ウ

SAMPLE SENTENCE:

夜　は　一人　で　市内
yoru　wa　hito·ri　de　SHI·NAI
night　　one person　　within the city
歩かないで　下さい。
aru·kanaide　kuda·sai.
don't walk　　please
= *Please don't walk alone at night in the city.*

KANJI 164

主　PRIMARY

ﾉ	宀	丁	干	主				

BUILDING THIS KANJI
Jelly Bean ﾉ + King 王(23) = 主

Meaning

This character conveys a sense of importance and authority; it is used in this vein with both concrete objects and abstract ideas. Note the difference between this kanji and that for "Jewel" in Entry 24 (玉).

Remembering this kanji

The PRIMARY reason a **king** puts a **jelly be** on his head is to learn from the reaction generates amongst his subjects. If no one dar tell him it's there, the **king** knows he is rulir PRIMARILY by fear. If it is pointed out to hi with a smile, however, he knows he is viewe PRIMARILY with kindness.

ommon Pronunciations
ommon **ON** reading: **SHU** (シ ュ)
ommon **kun** reading: **nushi** (ぬ し)

n-yomi suggestion: "**new shears**"

rite your sentence to remember the **on-yomi** and
n-yomi readings in the box below.

COMMON WORDS AND COMPOUNDS		
主力	primary + strength = *main force*	SHU·RYOKU シュ・リョク
主人公	primary + person + public = *main character*	SHU·JIN·KŌ シュ・ジン・コウ
売主	sell + primary = *seller*	uri·**nushi** うり・ぬし
持主	hold + primary = *owner*	mochi·**nushi** もち・ぬし

SAMPLE SENTENCE:

主人公　　は　有名　な
SHU·JIN·KŌ wa YŪ·MEI na
main character　　famous
　　美人　　　　です。
　　BI·JIN　　　**desu.**
beautiful woman
= *The main character is a famously beautiful woman.*

ss Common Pronunciations
ss common **ON** reading: **SU** (ス)
ss common **kun** reading: **omo** (お も)

丁

BLOCK

ー	丁							

Meaning

he main sense is of a city "block", although
ore obscure meanings can range from "pages"
 "polite". This is a quirky character that shows
p often as a component in other kanji.

Remembering this kanji
Let's face it: this looks like a capital "T", so best
think of it as an overhead view of a "T" junction
marking the intersection of BLOCKS.

Common Pronunciations
Common **ON** reading: **CHŌ** (チ ョ ウ)
Common **kun** reading: none

Write your sentence to remember the **on-yomi**
reading in the box below.

Less Common Pronunciations
Less common **ON** reading: **TEI** (テイ)
Less common **kun** reading: none

COMMON WORDS AND COMPOUNDS		
丁目	block + eye = *city block area*	**CHŌ**·me チョウ·め
二丁目	two + block + eye = *City Block 2*	NI·**CHŌ**·me ニ·チョウ·め
四丁目	four + block + eye = *City Block 4*	yon·**CHŌ**·me よん·チョウ·め

SAMPLE SENTENCE:

私　の　新しい　家　は
watashi　no　atara·shii　ie　wa
my　　　　new　　house
五丁目　に　あります。
GO·CHŌ·me　ni　arimasu.
City Block 5　　　　　is
= *My new house is in City Block 5.*

 FRIEND

一 ナ 方 友

BUILDING THIS KANJI
Superhero ナ + **Again (ironing board)** 又
(159) = 友

Meaning
Friend. The first two strokes are written in the same order as Entry 48 ("左").

Remembering this kanji
"I just think you're taking me for granted as a FRIEND," said the **superhero**.
  "What do you mean? All I asked you to do was pick up an **ironing board** for me. That's something any FRIEND would do."
  "Yeah, but I mean…it's embarrassing to fly with an **ironing board**. I look ridiculous."
  "You need to quit worrying about the opinions of others. And don't make that face; I'm telling you this as a FRIEND."

Common Pronunciations
Common **ON** reading: **YŪ** (ユウ)
Common **kun** reading: **tomo** (とも)

kun-yomi suggestion: "lot**to mo**ment"

Write your sentence to remember the **on-yomi a**
kun-yomi readings in the box below.

Less Common Pronunciations
Less common **ON** reading: none
Less common **kun** reading: none

COMMON WORDS AND COMPOUNDS		
友	*friend*	**tomo** とも
友人	friend + person = *friend*	**YŪ·JIN** ユウ·ジン
友好	friend + like = *friendship*	**YŪ·KŌ** ユウ·コウ

SAMPLE SENTENCE:

西山さん　の　友人　は　南米
Nishi·yama-san　no　YŪ·JIN　wa　NAN·BEI
Nishiyama-san　　　friend　　South Americ
から　来ました。
kara　ki·mashita.
from　　came
= *Nishiyama-san's friend came from South Am*
rica

KANJI 167

団

GROUP

| 冂 | 冂 | 冂 | 団 | 団 | | | |

BUILDING THIS KANJI

Prison 囗 + Tiny (soccer player) 寸 (103) = 団

Meaning

Group. Good luck making sense of the third example below!

Remembering this kanji

When they first arrive in **prison**, **tiny** soccer players will always huddle together in a GROUP. This behavior draws the attention of the regular cons, and a GROUP of them will soon approach the newcomers with welcoming smiles.

Common Pronunciations

Common **ON** reading: **DAN** (ダン)
Common **kun** reading: none

Write your sentence to remember the **on-yomi** reading in the box below.

Less Common Pronunciations

Less common **ON** reading: **TON** (トン)
Less common **kun** reading: none

TON is found only in the well-known Japanese word for bedding: **FU·TON** (フ・トン), composed of the kanji 布団 (Spread* + Group).

COMMON WORDS AND COMPOUNDS		
一団	one + group = *a group*	**ICHI·DAN** イチ・ダン
団体	group + body = *organization*	**DAN·TAI** ダン・タイ
団子	group + child = *dumpling*	**DAN·**go ダン・ご
入団	enter + group = *joining (a group)*	**NYŪ·DAN** ニュウ・ダン

SAMPLE SENTENCE:

内田さん は 団子 が 好き です。
Uchi·da-san wa DAN·go ga su·ki desu.
Uchida-san   dumplings   likes
= *Uchida-san likes dumplings.*

COMPONENT #168

ROWER

KANJI 168

毎

EVERY

| ノ | ⺊ | ⺈ | 勹 | 毎 | 毎 | | | |

BUILDING THIS KANJI
Hammer ⺊ + Rower 毋 = 毎

Meaning
Every.

Remembering this kanji

"How long you been a **rower**?"

"A while. I was on the crew that took Caesar to North Africa. You?"

"Just started."

"Well, all you have to remember is this: when the **hammer** comes down, you row. EVERY minute of EVERY hour of EVERY boring day. Not that I'm bitter, though. Like EVERY other guy here, all I want is a little variety in the beat."

Common Pronunciations

Common **ON** reading: **MAI** (マイ)
Common **kun** reading: none

Note the mix of readings in the last three exam‑ ples. Write your sentence to remember th **on-yomi** reading in the box below.

Less Common Pronunciations

Less common **ON** reading: none
Less common **kun** reading: **goto** (ごと)

COMMON WORDS AND COMPOUNDS		
毎日	every + sun (day) = *daily*	**MAI**·NICHI マイ・ニチ
毎週	every + week = *weekly*	**MAI**·SHŪ マイ・シュウ
毎月	every + moon (month) = *monthly*	**MAI**·tsuki マイ・つき
毎年	every + year = *yearly*	**MAI**·toshi マイ・とし
毎朝	every + morning = *every morning*	**MAI**·asa マイ・あさ

SAMPLE SENTENCE:

私	は	毎朝	父	と
watashi	**wa**	**MAI·asa**	**chichi**	**to**
I		every morning	my father	
話	を	します。		
hanashi	**o**	**shimasu.**		
speak				

= *I speak with my father every morning.*

WEIGHTLIFTER

KANJI 169

空 EMPTY

'	ハ	⼧	⼧	灾	空	空	空

BUILDING THIS KANJI
Weightlifter 灾 + **Craft** 工(47) = 空

Meaning

Empty/Sky. As in English, "empty" can incor porate suggestions of uselessness and futility.

Remembering this kanji

Like a lot of students, I became a **weightlifter** at college and practiced my **craft** well. First up were EMPTY cans – I could curl a lot of those. Next came EMPTY bottles, followed by EMPTY kegs. It was only later that I realized how EMPTY the **craft** of **weightlifting** beer really was.

Common Pronunciations

Common **ON** reading: **KŪ** (ク ウ)
Common **kun** readings: **sora** (そ ら); **kara** (か ら)

This kanji takes a bit of work, although **KŪ** is by far the most common reading in compounds. **sora**, as shown in the first example, means "sky"; it becomes voiced in the second position (as in the compound following). **kara** occasionally appears in first position with a meaning of "empty", and is a reading you will no doubt be familiar with from the third example.

kun-yomi suggestions: "**soar a**lbatross"; "**kara**mba"

Create your **on-yomi** keyword and enter it in the table at the back of the book. After that, write your sentence to remember the **on-yomi** and **kun-yomi** readings in the box below.

Less Common Pronunciations

Less common **ON** reading: none
Less common **kun** reading: **a** (あ)

This reading is used to make the verbs 空く and 空ける (**a·ku and a·keru**). Meaning "to open", these can be thought of as interchangeable with the more common 開く and 開ける (also **a·ku and a·keru**) from Entry 106. A few nouns, however, make use of this kanji exclusively: 空き缶* (**a·ki KAN**) "an empty can", and 空き瓶* (**a·ki BIN**) "an empty bottle", are two examples.

COMMON WORDS AND COMPOUNDS		
空	*sky*	**sora** そら
青空	blue + empty (sky) = *blue sky*	ao·**zora** あお·ぞら
空手	empty + hand = *karate*	**kara**·te から·て
空間	empty + interval = *space*	**KŪ·KAN** クウ·カン
空気	empty + spirit = *air*	**KŪ·KI** クウ·キ

SAMPLE SENTENCE:

朝 の 空 は きれい です よ。
asa no sora wa kirei desu yo.
morning sky   lovely
= *The morning sky is lovely!*

KANJI 170

町 **TOWN**

| 一 | 冂 | 冂 | 用 | 田 | 田 | 町 | | |

BUILDING THIS KANJI
Rice Field 田 (73) + Block 丁 (165) = 町

Meaning
Town. One size smaller than a city is the town, making this the second of our four kanji related to people living in defined locations. This character can also refer on occasion to a "street" or an "alley".

Remembering this kanji
"TOWN! TOWN!"
   Strong and clear it resounded over the **rice fields**. From **block** to **block** it was heard in the neighborhoods.
   "TOWN! TOWN!"
   In all honesty, though, nobody could really see the point of the TOWN crier.

Common Pronunciations
Common **ON** reading: **CHŌ** (チョウ)
Common **kun** reading: **machi** (まち)

Write your sentence to remember the **on-yomi** a
kun-yomi readings in the box below.

Less Common Pronunciations
Less common **ON** reading: none
Less common **kun** reading: none

COMMON WORDS AND COMPOUNDS		
町	town	**machi** まち
町内	town + inside = *in the town*	**CHŌ·NAI** チョウ·ナ
町立	town + stand = *established by the town*	**CHŌ·RITSU** チョウ·リ
町会	town + meet = *town assembly*	**CHŌ·KAI** チョウ·カ

SAMPLE SENTENCE:

この　町　の　ラーメン　は　有名
kono　machi　no　rāmen　wa　YŪ·MI
this　town　　　ramen　　　famou
です。
desu.
= *This town's ramen is famous.*

KANJI 171

犬 **DOG**

| 一 | ナ | 大 | 犬 | | | | |

BUILDING THIS KANJI
Large (sumo wrestler) 大 (17) + Jelly Bean ヽ
= 犬

Meaning
Dog.

Remembering this kanji

Only a **jelly bean** dangled next to his head could make a **sumo wrestler** jump up like a DOG.

Common Pronunciations

Common **ON** reading: **KEN** (ケン)
Common **kun** reading: **inu** (いぬ)

kun-yomi suggestion: "**enu**merate"

Write your sentence to remember the **on-yomi** and **kun-yomi** readings in the box below.

Less Common Pronunciations

Less common **ON** reading: none
Less common **kun** reading: none

COMMON WORDS AND COMPOUNDS		
犬	dog	**inu** いぬ
子犬	child + dog = *puppy*	ko·**inu** こ・いぬ
秋田犬	autumn + rice field + dog = *an Akita dog*	aki·ta·**KEN** あき・た・ケン
愛犬	love + dog = *pet dog*	AI·**KEN** アイ・ケン
愛犬家	love + dog + house = *dog lover*	AI·**KEN**·KA アイ・ケン・カ

SAMPLE SENTENCE:

古川さん　が　子犬　を　買いました
Furu·kawa-san ga ko·inu o   ka·imashita.
Furukawa-san   puppy   bought
= *Furukawa-san bought a puppy.*

死 DEATH

一	厂	歹	歹	歹ヽ	死		

BUILDING THIS KANJI
One (top of a bun) 一 (3) + Evening 夕 (108) + Beggar ヒ = 死

Meaning
Death.

Remembering this kanji

"So how did DEATH arrive for you?" she asked the **beggar**.

"It was weird," he said. "I was begging on my usual corner when I noticed it starting to get dark. "Is it **evening** already?" I wondered. I looked up to check, but realized I was mistaken, that what I had thought was **evening** was actually the **top of a bun** settling over me. Now, you would have thought I'd be scared by this, but I wasn't; the bun was really warm and smelled great, and for the first time in ages I didn't feel hungry. I wasn't afraid of DEATH at all."

Common Pronunciations
Common **ON** reading: **SHI** (シ)
Common **kun** reading: **shi** (し)

It is a welcome event when both types of reading for a kanji are identical like this; truly, death can sometimes be kind!

kun-yomi suggestion: "**sheet**"

Write your sentence to remember the **on-yomi** and **kun-yomi** readings in the box below.

Less Common Pronunciations
Less common **ON** reading: none
Less common **kun** reading: none

COMMON WORDS AND COMPOUNDS		
死ぬ	*to die*	**shi**·nu し·ぬ
水死	water + death = *drowning*	**SUI**·**SHI** スイ·シ
死体	death + body = *dead body*	**SHI**·TAI シ·タイ
死火山	death + fire + mountain = *extinct volcano*	**SHI**·KA·ZAN シ·カ·ザン

SAMPLE SENTENCE:

私　　の　　好き　な　　馬　　は
watashi　no　　su·ki　na　　uma　wa
　my　　　　　like　　　　horse
五年前　　　に　　死にました。
GO·NEN·mae　　ni　　shi·nimashita.
five years ago　　　　　　died
= *My horse that I liked died five years ago.*

KANJI 173

 GO

BUILDING THIS KANJI
Razor 彳 + One (hamburger patty) 一 (3) +
Block 丁 (165) = 行

Meaning
"Go" is the primary meaning of this character, along with related ideas of "carrying out" or "doing". Far less common is the secondary sense of a "stroke" or "line" of text.

Remembering this kanji
When the **razor** moved into our neighborhood, no one in the **block** knew quite what to do. "How can it fit in with us?" I asked my wife. "**GO** and invite it to our **block** party," she said. I didn't want to do this, of course, but this turned out to be a great idea, for the **razor** was a big hit when it came time to prepare the **hamburger patties** that day. Shaving each one perfectly, it soon had everyone cheering "**GO! GO! GO!**" as it worked faster and faster. "You know something, honey?" I said to my wife. "Looks like the **razor's** going to fit in well with our **block** after all. You were right telling me to **GO** and invite it here."

Common Pronunciations
Common **ON** reading: **KŌ** (コウ)
Common **kun** readings: **i** (い); **yu** (ゆ)

This is another character for our rogues' gallery of troublesome kanji, and one that merits added attention from the outset. For the general sense of the verb "to go", **i·ku** (い・く) is the choice; **yu·ku** (ゆ・く) is employed far less often and is of most use in a few specific compounds (such as in the second example), or as a suffix meaning "bound for" (as in the third). It can also act like 買, albeit strangely in that on rare occasions it will incorporate **yuku** as opposed to **yuki**. This is seen in the well-known compound **yuku·e·FU·MEI** (ゆく・え・フ・メイ) 行方不明: "Missing", built from the two words "whereabouts" (Go/Direction) and "unclear" (Not/Bright).

kun-yomi suggestions: "Egypt"; "Unicorn"

Write your sentence to remember the **on-yomi** and **kun-yomi** readings in the box below.

Less Common Pronunciations

Less common **ON** readings: **GYŌ** (ギョウ); **AN** (アン)

Less common **kun** reading: **okona** (おこな)

GYŌ is found primarily in compounds relating to this kanji's secondary meaning of "line" or "stroke". Note the irregular compound used at the beginning of the sample sentence (今日); we encountered this word back in Entry 6 (日).

COMMON WORDS AND COMPOUNDS		
行く	*to go*	i·ku い・く
行き先	go + precede = *destination*	**yu·ki** saki ゆ・き さき
東京行き	east + capital + go = *bound for Tokyo*	TŌ·KYŌ **yu·ki** トウ・キョウ ゆ・き
夜行	night + go = *night travel*	YA·KŌ ヤ・コウ
歩行	walk + go = *walking*	HO·KŌ ホ・コウ
歩行者	walk + go + individual = *pedestrian*	HO·KŌ·SHA ホ・コウ・シャ

SAMPLE SENTENCE:

今日　は　　歩行者　　が　多い。
kyō　**wa**　**HO·KŌ·SHA**　**ga**　**ō·i.**
today　　　　pedestrians　　　many
= *There are many pedestrians today.*

KANJI 174

取 **TAKE**

BUILDING THIS KANJI
Ear 耳 (78) + Again (ironing board) 又 (159)
= 取

Meaning
Take.

Remembering this kanji
The **ear** was nervous.
　"Um…I was wondering…" he said to the **ironing board**, "if, uh…"
　"Yes?"
　"If I could, uh…you know, TAKE you…"
　"TAKE me where?"
　"TAKE you on a…stroll or something."
　The **ironing board** smiled, and for the first time noticed the **ear's** wrinkles; she understood now that he needed her.
　"That would be nice," she said. "I'd love for you to TAKE me out."

Common Pronunciations

Common **ON** reading: none
Common **kun** reading: **to** (と)

As the second example below shows, this kanji acts like 買. It can also become voiced in the second position, as shown here in the final compound.

kun-yomi suggestion: "**to**ll"

Create your sentence to remember the **kun-yomi** reading in the box below.

COMMON WORDS AND COMPOUNDS		
取る	*to take*	**to·ru** と・る
取引	take + pull = *transactions*	**tori·hiki** とり・ひき
取り上 げる	take + upper = *to pick up*	**to·ri a·geru** と・り あ・げる
取り入 れる	take + enter = *to take in*	**to·ri i·reru** と・り い・れる
取り出 す	take + exit = *to take out*	**to·ri da·su** と・り だ・す
気取る	spirit + take = *to put on airs*	KI **do·ru** キ ど・る

SAMPLE SENTENCE:

赤とうがらし を 取り出して 下さい。
aka·tōgarashi o to·ri da·shite kuda·sa
red peppers   take out   please
= *Please take out the red peppers.*

Less Common Pronunciations

Less common **ON** reading: **SHU** (シュ)
Less common **kun** reading: none

KANJI 175

村 **VILLAGE**

| 一 | 十 | 才 | 木 | 朩 | 村 | 村 | | |

BUILDING THIS KANJI
Tree 木(13) + **Tiny (soccer player)** 寸(103)
= 村

Meaning

Village. Here we have the third of our four "community" kanji. Keep in mind that this character implies something smaller than a city or town.

Remembering this kanji

As the population of our VILLAGE is **tiny**, the **tiny** soccer players have no one to play with. A suggestion that they use **trees** for opponents, however, was dismissed by everyone. This was hardly surprising given that it was proposed by the VILLAGE idiot.

Common Pronunciations

Common **ON** reading: **SON** (ソン)
Common **kun** reading: **mura** (むら)

Note that the reading for " 人 " in the second example is voiced.

kun-yomi suggestion: "**moor** alongside"

Create your **on-yomi** keyword and enter it in the table at the back of the book. After that, write your sentence to remember the **on-yomi** and **kun-yomi** readings in the box below.

COMMON WORDS AND COMPOUNDS

村	*village*	**mura** むら
村人	village + person = *villager*	**mura·bito** むら・びと
山村	mountain + village = *mountain village*	SAN·SON サン・ソン

SAMPLE SENTENCE:

村人　は　小道　に立っています。
mura·bito wa ko·michi ni　　ta·tte imasu.
villager　　　path　　　　is standing
= *A villager is standing in the path.*

Less Common Pronunciations
Less common **ON** reading: none
Less common **kun** reading: none

KANJI 176

CHARACTER

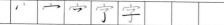

BUILDING THIS KANJI
Pincers 宀 + Child 子 (56) = 字

Meaning
"Character", in the sense of a Chinese character or letter of an alphabet.

Remembering this kanji
There are various ways of teaching Japanese CHARACTERS to a **child**, but a controversial method in days gone by involved the use of **pincers**. In it, a set of pincers would be suspended menacingly over a **child** practicing kanji. Should a mistake be made with any CHARACTER, the **pincers** would...well, best not describe what happened. Learning CHARACTERS today, quite simply, is a lot less stressful.

Common Pronunciations
Common **ON** reading: **JI** (ジ)
Common **kun** reading: none

Note that the reading for "引" is voiced in the final example.

Write your sentence to remember the **on-yomi** reading in the box below.

Less Common Pronunciations
Less common **ON** reading: none
Less common **kun** reading: **aza** (あ ざ)

COMMON WORDS AND COMPOUNDS

十字	ten + character = *a cross*	JŪ·JI ジュウ・ジ
赤十字	red + ten + character = *the Red Cross*	SEKI·JŪ·JI セキ・ジュウ・ジ
字引	character + pull = *dictionary*	JI·biki ジ・びき

SAMPLE SENTENCE:

多く　の　国　で　は　赤十字　は
ō·ku no　kuni　de　wa　SEKI·JŪ·JI wa
many　country　　　　Red Cross
大切　です。
TAI·SETSU　desu.
important
= *The Red Cross is important in many countries.*

COMPONENT #177

SEESAW

KANJI 177

具 **TOOL**

一	冂	冃	冃	目	目	具	具

BUILDING THIS KANJI
Eye (Cyclops) 目 (15) + Seesaw 六 = 具

Meaning
Tool/Equipment.

Remembering this kanji
I once got on a **seesaw** with a **Cyclops** and soon found myself stuck in the air. As he was in no hurry to let me down I had to endure watching him eat his lunch as I sat there dangling, which was unpleasant given his manners. Instead of cutlery, he used the only TOOL he had – his club – to do everything from spread butter to roll up pasta. That being said, though, it did work well as a cheese grater, so I suppose he had a point in describing it as a multi-purpose TOOL.

Common Pronunciations
Common **ON** reading: **GU** (グ)
Common **kun** reading: none

Create your **on-yomi** keyword and enter it in the table at the back of the book. After that, write your sentence to remember the **on-yomi** reading in the box below.

Less Common Pronunciations
Less common **ON** reading: none
Less common **kun** reading: none

COMMON WORDS AND COMPOUNDS		
道具	road + tool = *tool*	DŌ·GU ド ウ・グ
家具	house + tool = *furniture*	KA·GU カ・グ
具体	tool + body = *definite; concrete*	GU·TAI グ・タイ
馬具	horse + tool = *harness*	BA·GU バ・グ

SAMPLE SENTENCE:

山下先生　　は　新しい　　家具　を
Yama·shita-sensei　wa　atara·shii　KA·GU　o
(teacher) Yamashita　　new　　furniture
買いました。
　　ka·imashita.
　　　bought
= *Yamashita-sensei bought new furniture.*

COMPONENT #178

PLASH

This important component usually indicates a character having some connection to water. It will be encountered frequently, being present in more than one hundred of the general-use kanji.

KANJI 178

注 **POUR**

BUILDING THIS KANJI
Splash 氵 + Primary 主(164) = 注

Meaning
Pour. In addition to the literal meaning, there is often an implied sense of "directing" something (a gaze or one's attention, for instance) toward an object.

Remembering this kanji
This is how I was taught to POUR:

"When you POUR, your **primary** objective is not to let anything **splash** out. POUR carefully, but POUR confidently. **Splashes** are the **primary** indication that someone does not know how to POUR properly."

Common Pronunciations
Common **ON** reading: **CHŪ** (チュウ)
Common **kun** reading: **soso** (そそ)

kun-yomi suggestion: "**so-so**"

Write your sentence to remember the **on-yomi** and **kun-yomi** readings in the box below.

Less Common Pronunciations
Less common **ON** reading: none
Less common **kun** reading: none

COMMON WORDS AND COMPOUNDS		
注ぐ	*to pour*	soso·gu そそ・ぐ
注意	pour + mind = *attention*	CHŪ·I チュウ・イ
注水	pour + water = *watering*	CHŪ·SUI チュウ・スイ
注入	pour + enter = *infusion*	CHŪ·NYŪ チュウ・ニュウ
注目	pour + eye = *notice*	CHŪ·MOKU チュウ・モク

SAMPLE SENTENCE:
犬 に 注意 して 下さい。
inu ni CHŪ·I shite kuda·sai.
dog   attention   do   please
= *Watch out for the dog.*

KANJI 179

品 **GOODS**

＼	⼝	口	口	口口	口口	口口	口口	品

BUILDING THIS KANJI
Mouth (vampire) 口 (8) + Mouth (vampire) 口 (8) + Mouth (vampire) 口 (8) = 品

Meaning
This character expresses the idea of "goods" or "articles" in the majority of compounds in which it appears. It can occasionally have the more abstract notion of "refinement"; the fourth and fifth examples below illustrate this aspect of its meaning.

Remembering this kanji
You can imagine the GOODS a trio of **vampires** might have: capes, coffins, hair gel, teeth whiteners, blood pudding...all manner of GOODS, really.

Common Pronunciations
Common **ON** reading: **HIN** (ヒ ン)
Common **kun** reading: **shina** (し な)

Note how the second character in example three below has become voiced.

kun-yomi suggestion: "**she na**bbed"

Create your **on-yomi** keyword and enter it in the table at the back of the book. After that, write your sentence to remember the **on-yomi** and **kun-yomi** readings in the box below.

Less Common Pronunciations
Less common **ON** reading: none
Less common **kun** reading: none

COMMON WORDS AND COMPOUNDS		
品	*goods*	**shina** し な
品物	goods + thing = *merchandise*	**shina·mono** し な・も の
品切れ	goods + cut = *"out of stock"*	**shina** gi·re し な ぎ・れ
上品	upper + goods = *elegant*	**JŌ·HIN** ジ ョ ウ・ヒ ン
下品	lower + goods = *vulgar*	**GE·HIN** ゲ・ヒ ン
中古品	middle + old + goods = *secondhand goods*	CHŪ·KO·HIN チ ュ ウ・コ・ヒ ン

SAMPLE SENTENCE:

下 品 な 人 で す ね。
GE·HIN   na   hito   desu   ne.
 vulgar   person   is
= *(He's) a vulgar person, isn't he?*

ANJI 180

里

HAMLET

| 冂 | 冂 | 日 | 甲 | 甲 | 里 | | |

UILDING THIS KANJI
hell (Fly swatter) 甲 (148) + **Two** 二 (4) = 里

eaning
amlet. Here we have the fourth and smallest
our populated units. This character can also
gnify the countryside in general; not surpris-
gly, given how small a settlement this kanji
plies.

emembering this kanji
Vhen Hamlet came to our HAMLET, me 'n the
her resident were pretty darn excited; the guy
as the prince of Denmark, after all. Unfortu-
ately, with only **two** of us in the HAMLET we
ly had **two fly swatters**, and what with all the
es buzzin' everywhere, I wasn't in any mood
lend him mine. Anyway, rumor has it he told
lks back in Elsinore that he didn't much care
r our HAMLET. Which strikes me as kind
f ironic.

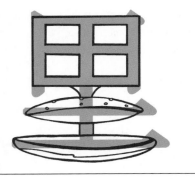

Common Pronunciations
Common **ON** reading: none
Common **kun** reading: **sato** (さ と)
The final compound below reminds us once again
that this reading of " 人 " is always voiced when it
appears in the second position

kun-yomi suggestion: "**sat o**penly"

Create your sentence to remember the **kun-yomi**
reading in the box below.

Less Common Pronunciations
Less common **ON** reading: **RI** (リ)
Less common **kun** readings: none

COMMON WORDS AND COMPOUNDS		
里	*hamlet*	**sato** さ と
古里	old + hamlet = *the old hometown*	furu·**sato** ふ る・さ と
里人	hamlet + person = *country folk*	**sato**·bito さ と・び と

SAMPLE SENTENCE:
先週　は　古里　へ　行きました。
SEN·SHŪ wa　furu·sato　e　i·kimashita.
last week　　old hometown　　　went
= *Last week I went to my old hometown.*

CHAPTER 9 REVIEW EXERCISES

A. Please match the following kanji to their meanings.

1. 丁   a. Hamlet

2. 死   b. Death

3. 村   c. Take

4. 行   d. Pour

5. 主   e. Goods

6. 取   f. Village

7. 友   g. Block

8. 注   h. Primary

9. 品   i. Friend

10. 里   j. Go

B. Please match the following meanings to their kanji, and these to their **on** or **kun-yomi**.

1. Dog   a. 犬   1. **KŌ** (コウ)

2. Cloth   b. 巾   2. **KIN** (キン)

3. Group   c. 公   3. **kara** (から)

4. Every   d. 町   4. **MAI** (マイ)

5. Public   e. 具   5. **GU** (グ)

6. Character   f. 市   6. **SHI** (シ)

7. City   g. 毎   7. **machi** (まち)

8. Tool   h. 字   8. **inu** (いぬ)

9. Empty   i. 団   9. **DAN** (ダン)

10. Town   j. 空   10. **JI** (ジ)

C. Please choose the best answer(s) to the following questions.

1. Which of the following readings apply the kanji 村?
   a. **mura** (むら)
   b. **CHŌ** (チョウ)
   c. **SON** (ソン)
   d. **machi** (まち)
   e. **SHI** (シ)

2. Which of the following readings apply the kanji 友?
   a. **sato** (さと)
   b. **YŪ** (ユウ)
   c. **YŌ** (ヨウ)
   d. **minato** (みなと)
   e. **tomo** (とも)

3. Which of the following readings apply the kanji 品?
   a. **SHŪ** (シュウ)
   b. **shina** (しな)
   c. **hana** (はな)
   d. **HIN** (ヒン)
   e. **IN** (イン)

4. It became really hot that day, and I needed to wipe my face with a ___.
   a. 犬
   b. 友
   c. 巾
   d. 具
   e. 注

5. Which of the following readings apply the kanji 行?
   a. **i** (い)
   b. **KŌ** (コウ)
   c. **yu** (ゆ)
   d. **to** (と)
   e. **KA** (カ)

D. Please choose the best answer(s) to the following questions.

  1. Which kanji would come next in the following series: 市....町....村....?
    a. 行
    b. 丁
    c. 空
    d. 里
    e. 具

  2. Which is the correct reading of 死ぬ?
    a. **shi·nu** (し・ぬ)
    b. **a·nu** (あ・ぬ)
    c. **chi·nu** (ち・ぬ)
    d. **u·nu** (う・ぬ)

  3. Which of the following kanji has the most number of strokes?
    a. 具
    b. 品
    c. 取
    d. 里
    e. 注

  4. Which is the correct reading of 注ぐ?
    a. **ama·gu** (あ ま・ぐ)
    b. **shi·gu** (し・ぐ)
    c. **soso·gu** (そ そ・ぐ)
    d. **o·gu** (お・ぐ)

  5. Which is the correct reading of 取る?
    a. **mawa·ru** (ま わ・る)
    b. **shi·ru** (し・る)
    c. **hi·ru** (ひ・る)
    d. **to·ru** (と・る)

E. Please match the following compounds and words to their meanings and pronunciations.

1.	取り上げる	a. Daily	1.	**CHŌ·KAI** (チ ョ ウ・カ イ)
2.	注意	b. Drowning	2.	**KA·GU** (カ・グ)
3.	家具	c. Blue sky	3.	**CHŪ·I** (チ ュ ウ・イ)
4.	青空	d. Attention	4.	**shina·mono** (し な・も の)
5.	毎日	e. Organization	5.	**MAI·NICHI** (マ イ・ニ チ)
6.	主人公	f. Town assembly	6.	**DAN·TAI** (ダ ン・タ イ)
7.	品物	g. Furniture	7.	**SUI·SHI** (ス イ・シ)
8.	団体	h. Merchandise	8.	**to·ri a·geru** (と・り あ・げ る)
9.	町会	i. Main character	9.	**SHU·JIN·KŌ** (シ ュ・ジ ン・コ ウ)
10.	水死	j. To pick up	10.	**ao·zora** (あ お・ぞ ら)

Kanji #181—200

KANJI 181

 **GROVE**

| 一 | 十 | 才 | 木 | 村 | 村 | 材 | 林 | |

BUILDING THIS KANJI
Tree 木(13) + Tree 木(13) = 林

Meaning
Grove.

Remembering this kanji
No story needed, as it's easy to see how this character could stand for a small group of trees!

Common Pronunciations
Common **ON** reading: **RIN** (リン)
Common **kun** reading: **hayashi** (はやし)

As the common Japanese family name in the second example below shows, this reading becomes voiced when not in the first position.

kun-yomi suggestion: "**high ash e**vent"

Create your **on-yomi** keyword and enter it in the table at the back of the book. After that, write your sentence to remember the **on-yomi** and **kun-yomi** readings in the box below.

Less Common Pronunciations
Less common **ON** reading: none
Less common **kun** reading: none

COMMON WORDS AND COMPOUNDS		
林	*grove*	**hayashi** はやし
小林 さん	small + grove = *Kobayashi-san*	ko·**bayashi**·san こ・ばやし・さん
林道	grove + road = *woodland trail;* *road*	**RIN**·DŌ リン・ドウ
人工林	person + craft + grove = *planted forest*	JIN·KŌ·**RIN** ジン・コウ・リン
公有林	public + have + grove = *public woodland*	KŌ·YŪ·**RIN** コウ・ユウ・リン

SAMPLE SENTENCE:

あの	国	に	は	公有林	が
ano	**kuni**	**ni**	**wa**	**KŌ·YŪ·RIN**	**ga**
that	country			public woodland	

少ない。
suku·nai.
　few
= *That country has little public woodland.*

KANJI 182

森 **FOREST**

| 一 | 十 | 才 | 木 | 杢 | 杢 | 森 | 森 | 森 |
| 森 | 森 | 森 | | | | | | |

BUILDING THIS KANJI
Tree 木(13) + Grove 林(181) = 森

Meaning
Forest.

Remembering this kanji
Another wonderfully simple character! You've probably guessed that this kanji implies a larger area of trees than that of the preceding entry.

Common Pronunciations
Common **ON** reading: **SHIN** (シン)
Common **kun** reading: **mori** (もり)

kun-yomi suggestion: "Ne**mo** **re**alized"

Write your sentence to remember the **on-yomi** and **kun-yomi** readings in the box below.

Less Common Pronunciations
Less common **ON** reading: none
Less common **kun** reading: none

COMMON WORDS AND COMPOUNDS		
森	*forest*	**mori** もり
森林	forest + grove = *forests*	**SHIN·RIN** シン・リン
森林学	forest + grove + study = *forestry*	**SHIN·RIN·GAKU** シン・リン・ガク

SAMPLE SENTENCE:

森	に	入る	時	は	注意	して
mori	**ni**	**hai·ru**	**toki**	**wa**	**CHŪ·I**	**shite**
forest	enter	time		attention	do	

下さい。
kuda·sai.
　please
= *Please be careful when going into the forest.*

KANJI 183

旦 **DAWN**

| 丨 | 冂 | 冂 | 日 | 旦 | | | | |

BUILDING THIS KANJI
Sun 日(6) + One (bottom of a bun) 一(3) = 旦

Meaning
Dawn. You will see this character figure more prominently as a component in other kanji than on its own.

Remembering this kanji

When the rays of the **sun** hit the **bottom of a bun**, it's DAWN.

Common Pronunciations

Common **ON** reading: **TAN** (タン)
Common **kun** reading: none

Create your **on-yomi** keyword and enter it in the table at the back of the book. After that, write your

sentence to remember the **on-yomi** reading in the box below.

Less Common Pronunciations

Less common **ON** reading: **DAN** (ダン)
Less common **kun** reading: none

COMMON WORDS AND COMPOUNDS		
一旦	one + dawn = *once*	IT·TAN イッ·タン
元旦	basis + dawn = *New Year's Day*	GAN·TAN ガン·タン

SAMPLE SENTENCE:

元旦　　に　お寺　へ　行きました。
GAN·TAN   ni o·tera e   i·kimashita
New Year's Day   temple   went
= *(I) went to a temple on New Year's Day.*

KANJI 184

黒　**BLACK**

⼁	⼞	⺜	⽇	甲	甲	里	里	黒
黒	黒							

BUILDING THIS KANJI
Hamlet 里 (180) + Gas Stove ⺗ = 黒

Meaning

Black.

Remembering this kanji

The introduction of **gas stoves** was problematic for our **hamlet**; nobody was sure how to cook with them, and a lot of food was burnt beyond recognition. The inevitable result was that BLACK smoke drifted everywhere, covering the landscape and **hamlet** with soot. Residents began to grumble. "We should go back to the old ways," some said, "because these **gas stoves** are nothing but trouble. It was a BLACK day when they arrived here".

Common Pronunciations

Common **ON** reading: **KOKU** (コク)
Common **kun** reading: **kuro** (くろ)

With the exception of the third example, the **kun-yomi** is always voiced in the second position (as it appears in the fourth compound).

kun-yomi suggestion: "**coo ro**sily"

Write your sentence to remember the **on-yomi** and **kun-yomi** readings in the box below.

COMMON WORDS AND COMPOUNDS		
黒	black (noun)	**kuro** くろ
黒い	black (adjective)	**kuro·**i くろ·い
白黒	white + black = black-and-white	shiro·**kuro** しろ·くろ
赤黒い	red + black = dark red	aka **guro·**i あか ぐろ·い
黒人	black + person = a black person	**KOKU·JIN** コク·ジン

SAMPLE SENTENCE:

この 黒い 馬 は 美しい です ね。
kono kuro·i uma wa utsuku·shii desu ne.
this   black horse   beautiful isn't it
= *This black horse is beautiful, isn't it?*

KANJI 185

交 **MIX**

'	一	亠	六	亣	交			

BUILDING THIS KANJI
Police 亠 + Father 父(79) = 交

Meaning
This character conveys a general sense of things mixing in both physical and figurative ways ("associating" with people or "exchanging" words are examples of the latter).

Remembering this kanji
My **father** was a **police** officer who enjoyed throwing MIXERS. Such occasions would always draw an interesting MIX of ranks: corporals, constables, inspectors…they all attended. My **father**, however, would not let anyone else MIX the drinks. "The last thing you want," he said to me, "is a MIX-up with all these guns around."

Common Pronunciations
Common **ON** reading: **KŌ** (コ ウ)
Common **kun** reading: **ma** (ま)

kun-yomi suggestion: "**match**"

Write your sentence to remember the **on-yomi** and **kun-yomi** readings in the box below.

Less Common Pronunciations
Less common **ON** reading: none
Less common **kun** readings: **maji** (ま じ) ; **ka** (か)

COMMON WORDS AND COMPOUNDS		
交ざる (intr)	to mingle	**ma·**zaru ま·ざる
交ぜる (tr)	to mix (something)	**ma·**zeru ま·ぜる
外交	outside + mix = foreign policy	**GAI·KŌ** ガイ·コウ

Less Common Pronunciations
Less common **ON** reading: none
Less common **kun** reading: none

SAMPLE SENTENCE:

あの　　国　　の　　　外交　　　が

ano　　kuni　　no　　GAI·KŌ　　ga

that　　country　　　foreign policy

分かりません。

wa·karimasen.

don't understand

= *(I) don't understand that country's forei[g]*
policy.

KANJI 186

NOT

| 一 | フ | 不 | 不 | | | | |

Meaning

Expressing the idea of "not" or "un-", this is an important negating prefix in Japanese.

Remembering this kanji

What is this, you ask? Well, it's NOT a super-hero, it's NOT a giraffe, and it's NOT a figure skater. It's just…NOT like anything, really.

Common Pronunciations

Common **ON** reading: **FU** (フ)

Common **kun** reading: none

Note how this kanji can function as a prefix with complete words, as it does below in the final

example [the base compound for this word (親
切) was presented in Entry 118].

Write your sentence to remember the **on-yo[n]** reading in the box below.

Less Common Pronunciations

Less common **ON** reading: **BU** (ブ)

Less common **kun** readings: none

COMMON WORDS AND COMPOUNDS		
不意	not + mind = *unexpectedly*	**FU·I** フ・イ
不安	not + ease = *uneasy*	**FU·AN** フ・アン
不明	not + bright = *unclear*	**FU·MEI** フ・メイ
不死	not + death = *immortal*	**FU·SHI** フ・シ
不親切	not + parent + cut = *unkind*	**FU·SHIN·SETSU** フ・シン・セツ

SAMPLE SENTENCE:

小林さん　　の　意図　は　　不明 です。

Ko·bayashi·san　no　I·TO　wa　FU·MEI desu

Kobayashi-san　　　aim　　　unclear

= *Kobayashi-san's aim is unclear.*

COMPONENT #187

FRUSTRATION

As will be seen in the following entry, this component is written with three strokes.

KANJI 187

後 **AFTER**

| ー | イ | 彳 | 彳 | 彳 | 移 | 移 | 後 |

BUILDING THIS KANJI

Razor 彳 + Frustration 厶 + Running Chicken 夂 = 後

Meaning

After/Later/Behind. These meanings apply to the ideas of both physical location and time.

Remembering this kanji

A butcher's lament:

"Am I **frustrated**? Yeah, I'm **frustrated**. I just spent an hour chasing AFTER a **running chicken** with a **razor**. Why? 'Cause a customer wanted shaved chicken, that's why! And then AFTER I got it for them, they complained about the taste of the AFTER shave!"

Common Pronunciations

Common **ON** readings: **KŌ** (コウ); **GO** (ゴ)
Common **kun** readings: **ato** (あと); **ushi** (うし)

This can be a tough character to master, but is not as fearsome as might be expected given its many readings. Look for **KŌ** in the first position; **ato** and **ushi·ro** (this reading is always accompanied by **ro**) appear far less frequently here, and **GO** pops up in only a few words. In second position, moreover, the reading will invariably be **GO**.

It is worth having another look at the compounds for "前" in Chapter 7 (Entry 133), to see how the fourth, fifth and sixth examples given there "pair up" with the three below.

kun-yomi suggestions: "**at O**klahoma"; "**Ooh, she**…"

Write your sentence to remember the **on-yomi** and **kun-yomi** readings in the box below.

Less Common Pronunciations

Less common **ON** reading: none
Less common **kun** readings: **nochi** (のち); **oku** (おく)

COMMON WORDS AND COMPOUNDS		
後	*after*	**ato** あと
後ろ	*behind*	**ushi·**ro うし・ろ
後年	after + year = *in later years*	**KŌ**·NEN コウ・ネン
後半	after + half = *second half*	**KŌ**·HAN コウ・ハン
後者	after + individual = *the latter*	**KŌ**·SHA コウ・シャ
午後	noon + after = *P.M.; afternoon*	**GO·GO** ゴ・ゴ

SAMPLE SENTENCE:

後 で 友人 と 東京 へ 行きます。
ato de YŪ·JIN to TŌ·KYŌ e   i·kimasu.
after   friend with Tokyo   go
= *Afterward, I'll go to Tokyo with a friend.*

KANJI 188

最 **MOST**

一	冂	曱	冃	甼	且	畠	畠	畠	畠
畠	最	最							

BUILDING THIS KANJI
Sun 日 (6) + Take 取 (174) = 最

Meaning
Most. Note how the first stroke of "ear" has been lengthened.

Remembering this kanji
So the ear was finally able to **take** the ironing board on a date, and luckily for him it turned out to be the MOST wonderful, MOST picturesque day. Not to mention the MOST romantic, too, for when the **sun** grew overly hot, the ear stretched himself out so that the ironing board would be shaded. He really was a MOST chivalrous ear when it came to **taking** care of a date.

Common Pronunciations
Common **ON** reading: **SAI** (サイ)
Common **kun** reading: none

Create your **on-yomi** keyword and enter it in the table at the back of the book. After that, write your sentence to remember the **on-yomi**.

Less Common Pronunciations
Less common **ON** reading: none
Less common **kun** readings: **motto** (もっと)
mo (も)

COMMON WORDS AND COMPOUNDS		
最小	most + small = *smallest*	**SAI·SHŌ** サイ・ショウ
最少	most + few = *fewest*	**SAI·SHŌ** サイ・ショウ
最高	most + tall = *highest; the best*	**SAI·KŌ** サイ・コウ
最古	most + old = *oldest*	**SAI·KO** サイ・コ
最新	most + new = *newest*	**SAI·SHIN** サイ・シン
最後	most + after = *the last*	**SAI·GO** サイ・ゴ

SAMPLE SENTENCE:
この 天気 は 最高 です よ。
kono TEN·KI wa SAI·KŌ desu yo.
this weather the best is
= *This weather is fantastic!*

KANJI 189

太 **FAT**

一	ナ	大	太				

BUILDING THIS KANJI
Large (sumo wrestler) 大 (17) + **Jelly Bean** 丶
= 太

Meaning
Fat/Thick. Note the difference between this character and "犬" (Entry 171).

Remembering this kanji

This is what happens when a **sumo wrestler** gets too FAT: try as he might, he can't even bend down to pick up a **jelly bean** lying between his feet.

Common Pronunciations

Common **ON** reading: **TAI** (タ イ)
Common **kun** reading: **futo** (ふ と)

un-yomi suggestion: "**who to**ld"

Write your sentence to remember the **on-yomi** and **kun-yomi** readings in the box below.

Less Common Pronunciations

Less common **ON** reading: **TA** (タ)
Less common **kun** reading: none

COMMON WORDS AND COMPOUNDS		
太い	fat; thick	**futo·i** ふ と・い
太る	to grow fat	**futo·ru** ふ と・る
太子	fat + child = crown prince	**TAI·SHI** タ イ・シ

SAMPLE SENTENCE:

私	は	冬休み	に	とても
watashi	**wa**	**fuyu yasu·mi**	**ni**	**totemo**
I		winter vacation		really

太った。
futo·tta.
grew fat
= *I really put on weight during winter vacation.*

KANJI 190

車

CAR

一 厂 厂 厄 百 亘 車

Meaning

Car. As the compounds below indicate, this character can also refer to a wide range of other vehicles. No story required.

Common Pronunciations

Common **ON** reading: **SHA** (シ ャ)
Common **kun** reading: **kuruma** (く る ま)

kun-yomi suggestion: "**coo rheuma**tism"

Write your sentence to remember the **on-yomi** and **kun-yomi** readings in the box below.

Less Common Pronunciations

Less common **ON** reading: none
Less common **kun** reading: none

COMMON WORDS AND COMPOUNDS		
車	car; vehicle	**kuruma** くるま
電車	electric + car = (electric) train	**DEN·SHA** デン·シャ
空車	empty + car = (taxi) "for hire"	**KŪ·SHA** クウ·シャ
車内	car + inside = inside the car	**SHA·NAI** シャ·ナイ
中古車	middle + old + car = used car	CHŪ·KO·SHA チュウ·コ·シャ

SAMPLE SENTENCE:

中村さん　　は　　　中古車　　を
Naka·mura-san   wa   CHŪ·KO·SHA   o
Nakamura-san   used car
買いました。
ka·imashita.
   bought
= *Nakamura-san bought a used car.*

STROLLER

KANJI 191

受 **RECEIVE**

一	一	ア	爫	爫	严	受	受

BUILDING THIS KANJI
Stroller 爫 + UFO 冖 + Again (ironing
board) 又 (159) = 受

Meaning

Receive/Accept. This interesting character
encompasses a wide range of meanings having
to do with the idea of reception; "taking" an
exam, "undergoing" an operation, or "suffering"
injuries are several examples.

Remembering this kanji

The **ironing board** longed to have a miniatur
ironing board in the worst way, but still hadn
RECEIVED the adoption papers. As the wa
dragged on, she began to have visions of a UFO
descending with a **stroller** on top of it: "We hav
your **ironing board**," a voice would announce
"will you RECEIVE it?". "I will RECEIVE i
yes" she always answered, "I will".

Common Pronunciations

Common **ON** reading: **JU** (ジュ)
Common **kun** reading: **u** (う)

the third and fourth examples below show this to
another kanji sharing the pronunciation char-
teristics of 買.

n-yomi suggestion: "**oo**long tea"

eate your **on-yomi** keyword and enter it in the
ble at the back of the book. After that, write your
ntence to remember the **on-yomi** and **kun-yomi**
adings in the box below.

COMMON WORDS AND COMPOUNDS		
受ける	*to receive; to accept*	**u·**keru う・ける
受け 取る	receive + take = *to receive*	**u·**ke to·ru う・け と・る
受取	receive + take = *receipt*	**uke·**tori うけ・とり
受取人	receive + take + person = *recipient*	**uke·**tori·NIN うけ・とり・ ニン
引き受 ける	pull + receive = *to undertake*	hi·ki **u·**keru ひ・き う・ける
受注	receive + pour = *receipt of an order*	**JU·**CHŪ ジュ・チュウ

SAMPLE SENTENCE:

田中さん は 新しい 本 を
Ta·naka-san wa atara·shii HON o
Tanaka-san   new   book
受け取りました。
  u·ke to·rimashita.
      received
= *Tanaka-san received a new book.*

ss **Common Pronunciations**
ss common **ON** reading: none
ss common **kun** reading: none

KANJI 192

EVIL

ノ ㄨ 凶 凶

BUILDING THIS KANJI
Banana Peels ㄨ + **Garbage Can** └┘ = 凶

Meaning
Take care: this unpleasant character relates
exclusively to evil and misfortune.

Remembering this kanji
EVIL comes in all forms. Environmentalists,
for example, regard **banana peels** in a **garbage
can** as EVIL, as this is a telltale sign of someone
being uninterested in composting.

Common Pronunciations
Common **ON** reading: **KYŌ** (キョウ)
Common **kun** reading: none

Write your sentence to remember the **on-yomi** reading in the box below.

COMMON WORDS AND COMPOUNDS

凶年	evil + year = *a bad year*	**KYŌ**·NEN キョウ・ネン
凶行	evil + go = *violence*	**KYŌ**·**KŌ** キョウ・コウ

SAMPLE SENTENCE:

凶年　　だ　そう　です。
KYŌ·NEN da 　sō　 **desu.**
 bad year 　　　　seems
= *Apparently it's a bad year.*

Less Common Pronunciations
Less common **ON** reading: none
Less common **kun** reading: none

KANJI 193

 **SEA**

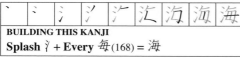

BUILDING THIS KANJI
Splash 氵 + **Every** 毎 (168) = 海

Meaning
Sea.

Remembering this kanji
Q. Which SEA **splashes every** shoreline in the Caribbean?
A. a) The SEA of Confusion?
　 b) The SEA of Tranquility?
　 c) The Caribbean SEA?

Common Pronunciations
Common **ON** reading: **KAI** (カイ)
Common **kun** reading: **umi** (うみ)

Recall that the fourth example below was presented early in Chapter 2; we've come a long way since then!

kun-yomi suggestion: **"ooh, me!"**

Write your sentence to remember the **on-yomi** and **kun-yomi** readings in the box below.

Less Common Pronunciations
Less common **ON** reading: none
Less common **kun** reading: none

COMMON WORDS AND COMPOUNDS

海	*sea*	**umi** うみ
海水	sea + water = *sea water*	**KAI**·SUI カイ・スイ
海図	sea + diagram = *nautical chart*	**KAI**·ZU カイ・ズ
海王星	sea + king + star = *Neptune (planet)*	**KAI**·Ō·SEI カイ・オウ・セ
北海道	north + sea + road = *Hokkaido*	HOK·**KAI**·DŌ ホッ・カイ・ド

SAMPLE SENTENCE:

夏休み　　に　　北海道　　へ
natsu yasu·mi　 ni　 HOK·KAI·DŌ　 e
summer vacation 　　　　Hokkaido
行きました。
　i·kimashita.
　　went
= *(We) went to Hokkaido for summer vacation*

校 **SCHOOL**

†	才	木	木'	朴	栌	栌	校
交							

BUILDING THIS KANJI

Tree 木(13) + **Mix** 交(185) = 校

Meaning

School. A secondary meaning related to "proof-reading" shows up in only a few compounds.

Remembering this kanji

When **trees** attend SCHOOL, they are often required to **mix** with other species. This can be problematic; maple **trees** refuse to take exams with evergreens, for example, and thus drag down test scores for the SCHOOL as a whole. This, as we know, is a traditional source of tension; when it comes to SCHOOL, some argue, coniferous and deciduous **trees** simply cannot **mix**.

Common Pronunciations

Common **ON** reading: **KŌ** (コ ウ)
Common **kun** reading: none

Note how "学" in the second example "doubles up" with 校, and how this remains constant in the other compounds in which this word occurs.

Write your sentence to remember the **on-yomi** reading in the box below.

Less Common Pronunciations

Less common **ON** reading: none
Less common **kun** reading: none

COMMON WORDS AND COMPOUNDS		
校外	school + outside = *off-campus*	**KŌ**·GAI コウ·ガイ
学校	study + school = *school*	GAK·**KŌ** ガッ·コウ
小学校	small + study + school = *elementary school*	SHŌ·GAK·**KŌ** ショウ·ガッ· コウ
中学校	middle + study + school = *junior high school*	CHŪ·GAK·**KŌ** チュウ·ガッ· コウ
高校	tall + school = *high school*	**KŌ**·**KŌ** コウ·コウ
女学校	woman + study + school = *girls' school*	JO·GAK·**KŌ** ジョ·ガッ· コウ

SAMPLE SENTENCE:

あの	女	の	子	は	高校
ano	**onna**	**no**	**ko**	**wa**	**KŌ·KŌ**
that	woman		child		high school

二年生   です。
NI·NEN·SEI   **desu.**
second year student

= *That girl is a second-year high school student.*

足 LEG

ヽ	丶	口	口	甲	足	足	足		

BUILDING THIS KANJI
Mouth (vampire) 口 (8) + Good Figure Skater
卜 + Person 人 (2) = 足

Meaning
Confusingly for English speakers, this character can signify both "leg" and "foot". A secondary meaning relates to the sense of "suffice".

Remembering this kanji
Even a **good figure skater** can mess up on occasion, and the kanji here provides an example of this happening. The steps are easy to follow: 1. **Vampire** flies onto **good figure skater**; 2. Figure skater is distracted, lands awkwardly on the **person** skating with her (this takes place during a pairs competition); 3. Said **person** breaks LEG.

Common Pronunciations
Common **ON** reading: SOKU (ソク)
Common **kun** reading: ashi (あし)

Note that "取" is voiced in the fouth example.
kun-yomi suggestion: "**ash ea**ting"

Create your **on-yomi** keyword and enter it in the table at the back of the book. After that, write your sentence to remember the **on-yomi** and **kun-yomi** readings in the box below.

Less Common Pronunciations
Less common **ON** reading: none
Less common **kun** reading: ta (た)

IRREGULAR READING		
裸足 *	naked + leg = *barefoot*	**hadashi** は だ し

COMMON WORDS AND COMPOUNDS		
足	*leg; foot*	**ashi** あ し
足首	leg + neck = *ankle*	**ashi·kubi** あ し・く び
足音	leg + sound = *sound of footsteps*	**ashi·oto** あ し・お と
足取り	leg + take = *one's gait*	**ashi do·ri** あ し ど・り
土足	earth + leg = *with shoes on*	**DO·SOKU** ド・ソ ク
足元 注意	leg + basis + pour + mind = *"watch your step"*	**ashi·moto·CHŪ·I** あ し・も と・チ ュ ウ・イ

SAMPLE SENTENCE:

足音　　を　聞きました　か。
ashi·oto　o　**ki·kimashita**　**ka.**
sound of footsteps　　heard
= *Did you hear footsteps?*

COMPONENT #196

TRIPOD

KANJI 196

  THREAD

| 丶 | 乡 | 幺 | 糸 | 糸 | 糸 | | |

BUILDING THIS KANJI
Frustration 幺 + Tripod 八 = 糸

Meaning
Thread. You will become very familiar with this character over time; it appears as a component in more than sixty other kanji.

Remembering this kanji
If you want to get a sense of **frustration**, try doing anything with a **tripod** made out of THREAD. The moment you use it with a camera, the THREAD collapses and ruins your shot. As a support for painting, though, it's even worse: the **tripod** falls over and leaves a bunch of THREAD stuck in your masterpiece.

Common Pronunciations
Common **ON** reading: none
Common **kun** reading: ito (いと)

Note that "口" is voiced in the second example.

kun-yomi suggestion: "**eat o**nly"

From this point on, the "create your own" reminders will only be presented for those kanji that feature new **on-yomi**. The absence of this reminder and blank box will indicate that you have already created an **on-yomi** keyword for that reading. In such instances, try to recall your keyword without having to look it up in the table at the back of the book.

Less Common Pronunciations
Less common **ON** reading: **SHI** (シ)
Less common **kun** reading: none

COMMON WORDS AND COMPOUNDS		
糸	*thread*	**ito** いと
糸口	thread + mouth = *beginning; clue*	**ito**·guchi いと・ぐち

SAMPLE SENTENCE:

青い　　糸　　が　あります　か。
ao·i　　ito　　ga　arimasu　　ka.
blue　　thread　　　　is
= *Is there any blue thread?*

KANJI 197

  SAME

| 丨 | 冂 | 冂 | 冂 | 同 | 同 | | |

BUILDING THIS KANJI
Gorilla 冂 + One (hamburger patty) 一 (3) +
Mouth (vampire) 口 (8) = 同

Meaning
Same.

Remembering this kanji

As a vegetarian, a **gorilla's** diet is always the SAME: fruits, nuts and berries. A **vampire**, too, is only interested in having the SAME meal over and over: the blood of living creatures. It should come as no surprise, therefore, that a **gorilla** and **vampire** will react the SAME way if a **hamburger patty** is placed between them – neither will want it.

Common Pronunciations

Common **ON** reading: **DŌ** (ド ウ)
Common **kun** reading: ona (おな)

Remember that **ona** (おな) differs from **onna** (お ん な), a reading for "女" in Entry 16.

kun-yomi suggestion: "**o, na**sty!"

Less Common Pronunciations

Less common **ON** reading: none
Less common **kun** reading: none

COMMON WORDS AND COMPOUNDS		
同じ	*same*	**ona**·ji おな·じ
同意	same + mind = *agreement*	**DŌ**·I ド ウ·イ
同一	same + one = *identical*	**DŌ**·ITSU ド ウ·イ ツ
同時	same + time = *simultaneous*	**DŌ**·JI ド ウ·ジ
同化	same + change = *assimilation*	**DŌ**·KA ド ウ·カ
同行者	same + go + individual = *traveling companion*	**DŌ**·KŌ·SHA ド ウ·コ ウ·シ ャ

SAMPLE SENTENCE:

私　　と　　中村さん　　は　　　同時
watashi   to   Naka·mura-san   wa   DŌ·JI
　I　　　　　　Nakamura-san　　　　simultaneo
に　　来ました。
ni　　ki·mashita.
　　　　came
= *Nakamura-san and I arrived at the same tim*

KANJI 198

午

NOON

ノ	仁	仁	午				

BUILDING THIS KANJI
Hammer 仁 + **Ten (scarecrow)** 十(28) = 午

Meaning
Noon.

Remembering this kanji

Everyone feels sorry for a **scarecrow** at NOO[N] as NOON is when the heat starts to pound (him like a **hammer**.

Common Pronunciations
Common **ON** reading: **GO** (ゴ)
Common **kun** reading: none

Less Common Pronunciations
Less common **ON** reading: none
Less common **kun** reading: none

COMMON WORDS AND COMPOUNDS		
午前	noon + before = A.M.; morning	**GO**·ZEN ゴ・ゼン
午後	noon + after = P.M.; afternoon	**GO**·GO ゴ・ゴ
午前中	noon + before + middle = all morning	**GO**·ZEN·CHŪ ゴ・ゼン・チュウ

SAMPLE SENTENCE:

午前　　　八時　　に　　高校　　へ
GO·ZEN　HACHI·JI　ni　KŌ·KŌ　e
A.M.　　eight o'clock　　high school
行きます。
i·kimasu.
　　go
= I go to high school at 8 A.M.

KANJI 199

愛 LOVE

丶	´	⺌	⺌	⺍	⺍	⺌	杰	愛
愛	愛	愛	愛					

BUILDING THIS KANJI

Stroller ⼍ + UFO ⼍ + Heart 心(25) + Running Chicken 夂 = 愛

Meaning

Love. After an entry for "evil", space had to be made for this character!

Remembering this kanji

LOVE, as we know, is profound, and the components in this kanji all have a connection to its secrets. A **stroller** can be filled through LOVE, a **UFO** is as mysterious as LOVE, a **heart** is the symbol of LOVE, and a **running chicken**...well, a **running chicken** has clearly been set free by someone who LOVES chickens.

Common Pronunciations

Common ON reading: **AI** (アイ)
Common kun reading: none

Create your **on-yomi** keyword and enter it in the table at the back of the book. After that, write your sentence to remember the **on-yomi** reading in the box below.

[blank box]

Less Common Pronunciations

Less common ON reading: none
Less common kun reading: none

The following is a very common irregular reading.

IRREGULAR READING		
可愛い	possible + love = cute	KA·**WAI**·i カ・ワイ・い

COMMON WORDS AND COMPOUNDS		
愛好	love + like = love; like	**AI**·KŌ アイ・コウ
愛犬	love + dog = pet dog	**AI**·KEN アイ・ケン
愛犬家	love + dog + house = dog lover	**AI**·KEN·KA アイ・ケン・カ
愛鳥家	love + bird + house = bird lover	**AI**·CHŌ·KA アイ・チョウ・カ
愛国心	love + country + heart = patriotism	**AI**·KOKU·SHIN アイ・コク・シン

SAMPLE SENTENCE:

本田さん　は　愛鳥家　として　有名
Hon·da-san　wa　AI·CHŌ·KA　toshite　YŪ·MEI
Honda-san　　bird lover　　as　　famous
です。
desu.
= Honda-san is famous as a bird lover.

KANJI 200

離 **SEPARATE**

丶	亠	六	文	产	卤	卤	离	离
离	斎	离	斎'	離	離	離	離	離

BUILDING THIS KANJI

Police 亠 + Evil 凵 (192) + Gorilla 冂 + Broken Crutch 厶 + Squirrels 隹 = 離

Meaning

Separate/Leave. This is one the most compli-cated-looking of all the kanji, but as you are now familiar with each its components, even a ferocious character like this can be tackled with confidence.

Remembering this kanji

A warning: *never* try to SEPARATE the **squirrels**, as they will offer violent resist-ance should you try. The **police** once made an effort, of course, but the **squirrels** SEPARATED them from their weapons and committed an act of such unspeakable **evil** that it cannot be related here. The **police** then sent in a **gorilla** to do their dirty work, but as the **broken crutch** indicates, this maneuver failed miser-ably as well. In the end, everyone was forced to agree that it was best not to SEPARATE the **squirrels** at all.

Common Pronunciations

Common **ON** reading: **RI** (リ)
Common **kun** reading: **hana** (はな)
Note how the reading of this character has becom▮ voiced in the third compound.

kun-yomi suggestions: "**Han a**mulet"

Create your **on-yomi** keyword and enter it in t▮ table at the back of the book. After that, write yo▮ sentence to remember the **on-yomi** and **kun-yo▮** readings in the box below.

Less Common Pronunciations

Less common **ON** reading: none
Less common **kun** reading: none

COMMON WORDS AND COMPOUNDS		
離れる (intr)	to separate; to leave	**hana**·reru はな·れる
離す (tr)	to separate (something)	**hana**·su はな·す
離れ 離れ	separate + separate = *scattered; separated*	**hana**·re **bana**·re はな·れ ばな·▮
切り 離す	cut + separate = *to cut off*	ki·ri **hana**·su き·り はな·す
分離	part + separate = *separation*	**BUN·RI** ブン·リ
離村	separate + village = *rural exodus*	**RI·SON** リ·ソン

SAMPLE SENTENCE:

山	で	その	親子	は
yama	**de**	**sono**	**oya·ko**	**wa**
mountain		that	parent and child	

離れ離れ　　に なってしまいました
hana·re bana·re ni natte shimaimashita.
separated ended up
= *That parent and child ended up getting sep▮ rated on the mountain.*

CHAPTER 10 REVIEW EXERCISES

. Please match the following kanji to their meanings.

1.	旦	a.	Separate
2.	午	b.	After
3.	交	c.	Sea
4.	後	d.	Same
5.	海	e.	Mix
6.	太	f.	Black
7.	離	g.	Receive
8.	受	h.	Dawn
9.	黒	i.	Noon
10.	同	j.	Fat

. Please match the following meanings to their
kanji, and these to their **on** or **kun-yomi**.

1.	Not	a. 林	1.	**SAI** (サイ)
2.	School	b. 最	2.	**ashi** (あし)
3.	Grove	c. 足	3.	**KŌ** (コウ)
4.	Car	d. 不	4.	**mori** (もり)
5.	Love	e. 凶	5.	**AI** (アイ)
6.	Leg	f. 糸	6.	**hayashi** (はやし)
7.	Forest	g. 車	7.	**KYŌ** (キョウ)
8.	Evil	h. 愛	8.	**ito** (いと)
9.	Most	i. 森	9.	**FU** (フ)
10.	Thread	j. 校	10.	**kuruma** (くるま)

C. Please choose the best answer(s) to the following questions.

1. Which of the following readings apply to
the kanji 離?
a. **YŪ** (ユウ)
b. **mori** (もり)
c. **RYŌ** (リョウ)
d. **hana** (はな)
e. **RI** (リ)

2. Which of the following readings apply to
the kanji 太?
a. **futo** (ふと)
b. **DAI** (ダイ)
c. **inu** (いぬ)
d. **TAI** (タイ)
e. **ō** (おお)

3. I was going to win the marathon, but got a
massive cramp in my ____.
a. 旦
b. 車
c. 森
d. 愛
e. 足

4. Which of the following readings apply to
the kanji 海?
a. **mizu** (みず)
b. **umi** (うみ)
c. **KAI** (カイ)
d. **kawa** (かわ)
e. **KŌ** (コウ)

5. Which of the following readings apply to
the kanji 後?
a. **ushi** (うし)
b. **KŌ** (コウ)
c. **SHŌ** (ショウ)
d. **ato** (あと)
e. **GO** (ゴ)

D. Please choose the best answer(s) to the following questions.

1. . Which is the correct reading of 交ぜる?
   a. **ora·zeru** (おら·ぜる)
   b. **ko·zeru** (こ·ぜる)
   c. **ma·zeru** (ま·ぜる)
   d. **a·zeru** (あ·ぜる)

2. Which is the correct reading of 同じ?
   a. **ona·ji** (おな·じ)
   b. **ara·ji** (あら·じ)
   c. **aka·ji** (あか·じ)
   d. **u·ji** (う·じ)

3. Which of the following kanji has the most number of strokes?
   a. 後
   b. 森
   c. 最
   d. 愛
   e. 黒

4. Which is the correct reading of 受ける?
   a. **a·keru** (あ·ける)
   b. **u·keru** (う·ける)
   c. **tata·keru** (たた·ける)
   d. **oda·keru** (おだ·ける)

5. Which is the correct reading of 黒い?
   a. **shiro·i** (し ろ·い)
   b. **ao·i** (あお·い)
   c. **aka·i** (あか·い)
   d. **kuro·i** (く ろ·い)

E. Please match the following compounds and words to their meanings and pronunciations

1. 分離   a. Smallest   1. **DŌ·I**
                                       (ドウ·イ)

2. 赤黒い   b. To undertake   2. **ashi·kubi**
                                       (あし·くび)

3. 同意   c. Afternoon   3. **KAI·Ō·SEI**
                                       (カイ·オウ
                                       セイ)

4. 海王星   d. Unclear   4. **GO·GO**
                                       (ゴ·ゴ)

5. 引き受   e. Agreement   5. **KŌ·KŌ**
   ける   (コウ·コウ

6. 最小   f. High school   6. **SAI·SHŌ**
                                       (サイ·
                                       ショウ)

7. 足首   g. Neptune   7. **BUN·RI**
               (planet)   (ブン·リ)

8. 不明   h. Dark red   8. **hi·ki u·keru**
                                       (ひ·き う·
                                       ける)

9. 午後   i. Separation   9. **FU·MEI**
                                       (フ·メイ)

10. 高校   j. Ankle   10.**aka guro·i**
                                       (あか ぐろ·
                                       い)

CUMULATIVE REVIEW EXERCISES FOR
CHAPTERS 1 - 10

A. Please match the following kanji to their meanings.

1. 家		a. Electric
2. 干		b. Country
3. 先		c. Mother
4. 母		d. Spirit
5. 空		e. Dry
6. 国		f. House
7. 太		g. Precede
8. 有		h. Fat
9. 電		i. Empty
10. 気		j. Have

B. Which kanji does not belong in the group?

1. a. 日   b. 週   c. 年   d. 首   e. 秒
2. a. 赤   b. 外   c. 青   d. 白   e. 黒
3. a. 春   b. 秋   c. 注   d. 冬   e. 夏
4. a. 市   b. 里   c. 高   d. 町   e. 村
5. a. 金   b. 馬   c. 牛   d. 鳥   e. 犬
6. a. 東   b. 南   c. 西   d. 北   e. 干
7. a. 舌   b. 売   c. 目   d. 足   e. 耳
8. a. 鳥   b. 午   c. 夕   d. 朝   e. 夜
9. a. 車   b. 寺   c. 門   d. 花   e. 道
10. a. 美   b. 好   c. 愛   d. 天   e. 凶

C. Identify the kanji having the most number of strokes.

1. a. 出   b. 主   c. 右   d. 央   e. 百
2. a. 車   b. 学   c. 持   d. 押   e. 周
3. a. 道   b. 週   c. 島   d. 黒   e. 校
4. a. 字   b. 図   c. 来   d. 英   e. 糸
5. a. 秋   b. 思   c. 書   d. 品   e. 前
6. a. 森   b. 鳥   c. 開   d. 新   e. 朝
7. a. 年   b. 私   c. 気   d. 甲   e. 母
8. a. 注   b. 夜   c. 音   d. 訓   e. 具
9. a. 掛   b. 時   c. 雪   d. 海   e. 最
10. a. 親 b. 離   c. 読   d. 語   e. 一

D. Please list the following kanji in the order indicated (alphabetical).

1. Dog / Fat / Heaven / Large / Lose
   a. 大   b. 犬   c. 太   d. 天   e. 失

2. Come / Half / Mix / Rice / Tree
   a. 来   b. 米   c. 木   d. 半   e. 交

3. Block / Dry / Noon / Not / Thousand
   a. 午   b. 干   c. 丁   d. 不   e. 千

4. Father / Heaven / Mix / School / Stand
   a. 天   b. 交   c. 父   d. 校   e. 立

5. Complete / Jewel / King / Pour / Primary
   a. 主   b. 注   c. 玉   d. 王   e. 全

6. Basis / Meet / Part / Public / Same
   a. 同   b. 公   c. 分   d. 会   e. 元

7. Precede / Read / Receive / Red / Sell
    a. 受   b. 売   c. 先   d. 読   e. 赤

8. Mind / New / Parent / Sound / Stand
    a. 親   b. 新   c. 音   d. 意   e. 立

9. Character / City / Ease / House / Study
    a. 学   b. 字   c. 安   d. 家   e. 市

10. Buy / Neck / Road / Shellfish / Tool
    a. 具   b. 道   c. 首   d. 買   e. 貝

E. Please choose the best answer to the following
    questions.

1. I often see monks when I walk past that
    ____.
    a. 星   b. 馬   c. 足   d. 電   e. 寺

2. The samurai made a menacing gesture
    with his ___.
    a. 花   b. 車   c. 刀   d. 川   e. 牛

3. What is the worst thing to find waiting
    for you on your doorstep?
    a. 金   b. 品   c. 親   d. 鳥   e. 死

4. Romeo was troubled. How could he
    demonstrate his ___ for Juliet?
    a. 凶   b. 太   c. 具   d. 愛   e. 田

5. It's so quiet and peaceful in the middle of
    this ___!
    a. 森   b. 犬   c. 月   d. 肉   e. 火

F. Please choose the best answer(s) to the follow-
    ing questions.

1. As 小 is to 大, 少 is to ___.
    a. 多   b. 人   c. 名   d. 外   e. 主

2. As 読 is to 書, 押 is to ___.
    a. 有   b. 交   c. 買   d. 引   e. 休

3. As 内 is to 外, 私 is to ___.
    a. 毎   b. 公   c. 不   d. 元   e. 取

4. As 上 is to 下, 前 is to ___.
    a. 本   b. 生   c. 最   d. 山   e. 後

5. As 林 is to 森, 好 is to ___.
    a. 赤   b. 愛   c. 心   d. 先   e. 図

G. Please choose the best answer to the following
    questions.

1. Which is the correct reading of 行く?
    a. a·ku (あ・く)
    b. i·ku (い・く)
    c. fu·ku (ふ・く)
    d. ta·ku (た・く)

2. Which is the correct reading of 切る?
    a. tabe·ru (たべ・る)
    b. ino·ru (いの・る)
    c. a·ru (あ・る)
    d. ki·ru (き・る)

3. Which is the correct reading of 会う?
    a. a·u (あ・う)
    b. o·u (お・う)
    c. muka·u (むか・う)
    d. i·u (い・う)

4. Which is the correct reading of 近い?
    a. chika·i (ちか・い)
    b. ao·i (あお・い)
    c. kata·i (かた・い)
    d. aka·i (あか・い)

5. Which is the correct reading of 話す?
    a. wata·su (わた・す)
    b. furu·su (ふる・す)
    c. hana·su (はな・す)
    d. ta·su (た・す)

6. Which is the correct reading of 赤い?
    a. furu·i (ふる・い)
    b. taka·i (たか・い)
    c. ō·i (おお・い)
    d. aka·i (あか・い)

7. Which is the correct reading of 少し?
   a. **suko·shi** (すこ・し)
   b. **haya·shi** (はや・し)
   c. **ara·shi** (あら・し)
   d. **hana·shi** (はな・し)

8. Which is the correct reading of 古い?
   a. **kuro·i** (くろ・い)
   b. **shiro·i** (しろ・い)
   c. **furu·i** (ふる・い)
   d. **usu·i** (うす・い)

9. Which is the correct reading of 聞く?
   a. **hi·ku** (ひ・く)
   b. **ki·ku** (き・く)
   c. **a·ku** (あ・く)
   d. **ara·ku** (あら・く)

10. Which is the correct reading of 押す?
    a. **hana·su** (はな・す)
    b. **u·su** (う・す)
    c. **ama·su** (あま・す)
    d. **o·su** (お・す)

Please match the following compounds and words to their meanings and pronunciations.

1. 有名　　a. Exit　　1. **TA·DOKU·KA** (タ・ドク・カ)

2. 多読家　b. Talkative　2. **NYŪ·KAI·KIN** (ニュウ・カイ・キン)

3. 出口　　c. Famous　　3. **BI·KA** (ビ・カ)

4. 同行者　d. The four seasons　4. **ta·chi i·ru** (た・ち い・る)

5. 書き入れる　e. "Watch Your Step"　5. **ka·ki i·reru** (か・き い・れる)

6. 午前　　f. Traveling companion　6. **GAI·KŌ** (ガイ・コウ)

7. 立ち入る　g. Patriotism　7. **GO·ZEN** (ゴ・ゼン)

8. 春夏秋冬　h. Well-read person　8. **YŪ·MEI** (ユウ・メイ)

9. 美化　　i. Beautification　9. **hana·shi zu·ki** (はな・しず・き)

10. 足元注意　j. Fireworks　10. **hana·bi** (はな・び)

11. 外交　　k. Morning (a.m.)　11. **de·guchi** (で・ぐち)

12. 愛国心　l. Enrollment fee　12. **SHUN·KA·SHŪ·TO** (シュン・カ・シュウ・トウ)

13. 話し好き　m. To go into　13. **AI·KOKU·SHIN** (アイ・コク・シン)

14. 入会金　n. Foreign policy　14. **DŌ·KŌ·SHA** (ドウ・コウ・シャ)

15. 花火　　o. To write in　15. **ashi·moto·CHŪ·I** (あし・もと・チュウ・イ)

Kanji #201—225

KANJI 201

信 **TRUST**

BUILDING THIS KANJI
Giraffe イ + Say 言 (80) + = 信

Meaning

Trust. As can be seen in the final entry of the "Common Words and Compounds" section below, a secondary meaning relates to the ideas of messages and correspondence. This will be the first entry, incidentally, for which there is no sample sentence. In its place, a short passage of written Japanese in the chapter review section will enable you to better test your comprehension skills.

Remembering this kanji

Can you TRUST what a **giraffe says**? Well, m̶ neighbor's a **giraffe**, and here's what he sa̶ yesterday: "TRUST me, I won't chew on yo̶ new shrubs", "TRUST me, I'll have your law̶ mower back next week", "TRUST me, I'll giv̶ you that money soon."

I sure as heck hope you can TRUST what̶ **giraffe says**.

Common Pronunciations

Common **ON** reading: **SHIN** (シン)
Common **kun** reading: none

Less Common Pronunciations

Less common **ON** reading: none
Less common **kun** reading: none

COMMON WORDS AND COMPOUNDS		
信じる	believe	**SHIN**·jiru シン·じる
自信	self + trust = *self confidence*	**JI·SHIN** ジ·シン
信号	trust + title = *signal*	**SHIN**·GŌ シン·ゴウ
通信	passage + trust = *correspondence*	TSŪ·**SHIN** ツウ·シン

KANJI 202

文 **LITERATURE**

`	一	ナ	文				

BUILDING THIS KANJI
Police ⼇ + Wishbones 乂 = 文

Meaning
This character relates to writing and composition, from grand literary works to sentences and individual letters.

Remembering this kanji
Crime (as symbolized by the **police** hat) and cooking (as symbolized by the **wishbones**) have always been popular topics in LITERATURE. So why, then, is my novel about a **policeman's** desperate search for a missing **wishbone** not considered high LITERATURE?

Common Pronunciations
Common **ON** reading: **BUN** (ブ ン); **MON** (モ ン)
Common **kun** reading: none
BUN is the far more common reading.

Less Common Pronunciations
Less common **ON** reading: none
Less common **kun** reading: **fumi** (ふ み)

IRREGULAR READING		
文字	literature + character = *character/letter (of an alphabet)*	**MO·JI** モ・ジ

COMMON WORDS AND COMPOUNDS		
文化	literature + change = *culture*	**BUN·KA** ブ ン・カ
文明	literature + bright = *civilization*	**BUN·MEI** ブ ン・メ イ
注文	pour + literature = *order; request*	**CHŪ·MON** チ ュ ウ・モ ン
天文学	heaven + literature + study = *astronomy*	**TEN·MON·GAKU** テ ン・モ ン・ガ ク

KANJI 203

進 **ADVANCE**

ノ	イ	イ′	亻	什	件	隹	隹	ˋ隹
隹	進							

BUILDING THIS KANJI
Squirrels 隹 + Seal 辶 = 進

Meaning
Advance, along with the idea of progressing in figurative sense.

Remembering this kanji
Criticize if you want, but my opinion is this: **squirrels** and **seals** have yet to ADVANCE. They have not invented the wheel, are unable to use cutlery, and their communication skills remain minimal. And don't tell me that **squirrels** ADVANCE with whiskers twitching and **seals** ADVANCE by bellying over beaches; such statements in no way ADVANCE this discussion.

Common Pronunciations
Common **ON** reading: **SHIN** (シン)
Common **kun** reading: **susu** (すす)

kun-yomi suggestion: "Sue! Sue!"

This is the last time a suggestion will be given for a **kun-yomi**. Using your **on-yomi** keyword and the **kun-yomi** suggestion above, write your sentence to remember these readings in the box below.

Less Common Pronunciations
Less common **ON** reading: **JIN** (ジン)
Less common **kun** reading: none

COMMON WORDS AND COMPOUNDS		
進む (intr)	*advance; progress*	**susu·**mu すす・む
進める (tr)	*lead; promote (something)*	**susu·**meru すす・める
進行	advance + go = *advance; proceed*	**SHIN·KŌ** シン・コウ
先進国	precede + advance + country = *developed nation*	SEN·**SHIN·**KOKﾞ セン・シン・コ ﾗ

KANJI 204

 SAKÉ

`	`	ﾝ	ﾝ	沂	沂	沔	沔	酒
酒								

BUILDING THIS KANJI
Splash ⺡ + Whiskey Jug 西 = 酒

Meaning
This kanji can refer to Japan's famous rice wine specifically, as well as to alcoholic drinks in general.

Remembering this kanji
"Hey you, gimme a **splash** out of that there **whiskey jug**," the grizzled prospector said with a scowl. Fearing trouble, the bartender quickly set out a shot glass, but had it slapped away the moment it was filled.

"What in tarnation!" the oldtimer yelled. "This is SAKÉ! If I'm havin' SAKÉ, I want it in a dainty cup on a lacquered tray!"

Common Pronunciations
Common **ON** reading: **SHU** (シュ)
Common **kun** reading: **saké** (さけ); **saka** (さか

Saké and saka are always voiced (becoming za and zaké) when they appear outside of first position. Using your **on-yomi** keyword for シュ a your ideas for words or sounds that approxima the two **kun-yomi**, write your sentence to remember the **on-yomi** and **kun-yomi** readings in th box below.

Less Common Pronunciations
Less common **ON** reading: none
Less common **kun** reading: none

COMMON WORDS AND COMPOUNDS		
酒	*saké; liquor*	**saké** さけ
日本酒	Japan + saké = *(Japanese) saké*	NI·HON·**SHU** ニ・ホン・シュ
酒屋	saké + roof = *liquor store*	**saka·**ya さか・や
飲酒	drink + saké = *to drink alcohol*	IN·**SHU** イン・シュ

COMPONENT #205

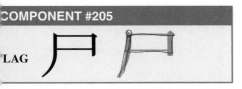

FLAG

KANJI 205

DOOR

一	⼁	⼎	尸				

BUILDING THIS KANJI

One (top of a bun) 一 (3) + Flag 尸 = 尸

Meaning

Door. This kanji is also used as a counter for buildings and houses.

Remembering this kanji

Let's assume you've moved into an apartment that has no DOOR. What would be better in its place, the **top of a bun**, or a **flag**? I can't help feeling that the **top of a bun** wouldn't do a very good job, as it would tear easily off the hinges and leave sesame seeds on the carpet whenever you moved it. A **flag** would be better, offering more privacy and having the added advantage of being shaped like a DOOR.

Common Pronunciations

Common **ON** reading: KO (コ)
Common **kun** reading: **to** (と)

The **kun-yomi** is almost always voiced when not in first position; the third compound below offers an example. The only instance where the **on-yomi** becomes voiced is shown in the final compound.

After creating a keyword to remember the **kun-yomi**, write your sentence to remember the **on-yomi** and **kun-yomi** readings in the box below.

Less Common Pronunciations

Less common **ON** reading: none
Less common **kun** reading: none

COMMON WORDS AND COMPOUNDS		
戸	door	**to** と
戸外	door + outside = *outdoors; open air*	**KO·GAI** コ·ガイ
雨戸	rain + door = *sliding door; shutter*	ama·**do** あま·ど
泣き 上戸	cry + upper + door = *a weepy drunk*	na·ki JŌ·**GO** な·き ジョウ·ゴ

KANJI 206

MATTER

一	⼀	⼀	⼀	彐	亭	事	事	事

BUILDING THIS KANJI

One (hamburger patty) 一 (3) + Mouth (vampire) 口 (8) + Pitchfork ⼀ + Harpoon ⼁ = 事

Meaning

A matter. This is an important kanji that appears in a number of common words.

Remembering this kanji

"What's the MATTER honey?" she asked, concerned. "You haven't even touched your **hamburger patty**."

"Nothing's the MATTER dear," said the **vampire**.

"I don't believe you. Something's definitely the MATTER."

"OK, maybe there is. I'm just starting to suspect that you don't understand me very well. I mean, really, a **hamburger patty**? I can't have that in my diet. And the **pitchfork** you gave me yesterday? As much as I'd like to help out around the farm, I can't be out there pitching hay in broad daylight. And do I even have to go into the **harpoon** you gave me for my birthday? I wouldn't go after my victims with that as a MATTER of principle."

Common Pronunciations

Common **ON** reading: **JI** (ジ)
Common **kun** readings: **koto** (こ と)

The **kun-yomi** is always voiced when not in fir position, as shown in the final compound belo (an extremely common word composed of a m of on and **kun-yomi**).

After creating a kun-yomi keyword, write yo sentence to remember the **on-yomi** and **kun-yo** readings in the box below.

Less Common Pronunciations

Less common **ON** reading: **ZU** (ズ)
Less common **kun** reading: none

COMMON WORDS AND COMPOUNDS		
事	*matter*	koto こ と
工事	craft + matter = *construction work*	KŌ·JI コ ウ · ジ
大事	large + matter = *serious/important matter*	DAI·JI ダ イ · ジ
仕事	serve + matter = *job; work*	SHI·goto シ · ご と

KANJI 207

待 **WAIT**

BUILDING THIS KANJI
Razor 彳 + **Temple** 寺 (104) = 待

Meaning

Wait. A secondary meaning relates to the sense o how someone or something is treated or handled

Remembering this kanji

"WAIT! WAIT!"

Once more the **razor** was drawn away from the girl's head. "Look," the **temple** priestess laughed, "if you wish to be one of us your hair must be shaved off."

She nodded and tried to steel herself, but as soon as the **razor** approached her scalp, she broke down as before: "WAIT! WAIT!"

"I may be wrong," one of the other initiates whispered, "but something tells me this might not be the right career choice for Rapunzel."

Common Pronunciations

Common **ON** reading: **TAI** (タ イ)
Common **kun** reading: **ma** (ま)

As the final compound shows, this is another common verb that can "absorb" its hiragana accompaniment in the manner of 買.

After creating a **kun-yomi** keyword, write your sentence to remember the **on-yomi** and **kun-yomi** readings in the box below.

Less Common Pronunciations

Less common **ON** reading: none
Less common **kun** reading: none

COMMON WORDS AND COMPOUNDS		
待つ	*wait*	**ma**·tsu ま·つ
ちょっと待って	*Just a moment!*	chotto **ma**·tte ちょっと ま·って
期待	period + wait = *expectation*	**KI·TAI** キ·タイ
待合室	wait + match + room = *waiting room*	**machi**·ai·SHITSU まち·あい·シツ

兄 ELDER BROTHER

BUILDING THIS KANJI
Mouth (vampire) 口 (8) + Ballet 儿 = 兄

Meaning
Elder brother.

Remembering this kanji

Q. Why is an ELDER BROTHER more likely to attend a **vampire ballet**?

A. A **vampire ballet** has to take place long after nightfall, which is past the bedtimes of an ELDER BROTHER'S siblings.

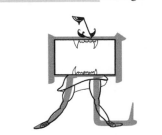

Common Pronunciations
Common **ON** reading: **KEI** (ケ イ)
Common **kun** reading: **ani** (あ に)

Create your **on-yomi** keyword and enter it in the table at the back of the book. Then, after creating your **kun-yomi** keyword, write your sentence to remember the **on-yomi** and **kun-yomi** readings in the box below.

IRREGULAR READING		
お兄さん	*elder brother*	o·nii·san お・にい・さん

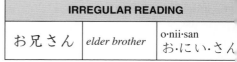

This is a more polite form of address.

COMMON WORDS AND COMPOUNDS		
兄	*elder brother*	**ani** あに
父兄会	father + elder brother + meet = *parents' association*	FU·KEI·KAI フ・ケイ・カ

Less Common Pronunciations
Less common ON reading: **KYŌ** (キョウ)
Less common **kun** reading: none

COMPONENT #209

FORKLIFT

KANJI 209

県 **PREFECTURE**

| 丨 | 冂 | 冃 | 目 | 目 | 但 | 県 | 県 | 県 |

BUILDING THIS KANJI
Eye (Cyclops) 目 (15) + Forklift ∟ + Tripod ハ = 県

Meaning
Prefecture.

Remembering this kanji
The **Cyclops** paused a moment. "I'm attemptin to uncover the essence of the Japanese **forklift** he said finally, folding up his **tripod**. This that PREFECTURE has its own variation; for**l** lifts in Aomori PREFECTURE, for exampl are slightly smaller due to the frigid climat while those in Okinawa PREFECTURE tend have a tanned complexion. I'm wandering fro PREFECTURE to PREFECTURE with m trusty **tripod** so that I can capture these subtl ties. You obviously need a good eye to do this

Common Pronunciations
Common ON reading: **KEN** (ケン)
Common kun reading: none

Less Common Pronunciations
Less common ON reading: none
Less common kun readings: none

COMMON WORDS AND COMPOUNDS		
県	*prefecture*	**KEN** ケン
県立	prefecture + stand = *prefectural*	**KEN**·RITSU ケン・リツ
山口県	mountain + mouth + prefecture = *Yama-guchi prefecture*	yama·guchi·**KEN** やま・ぐち・ケ
愛知県	love + know + prefecture = *Aichi prefecture*	AI·CHI·**KEN** アイ・チ・ケン

KANJI 210

BACK

㇀	㇉	㇉⸍	北⸍	北	背	背	背

BUILDING THIS KANJI

North 北(72) + **Moon** 月(11) = 背

Meaning

The 'back' of someone or something. This character is commonly used to refer to a person's height, but also has a secondary meaning related to disobedience or betrayal (think of "turning one's back" on someone).

Remembering this kanji

With his BACK against the wall of our igloo, the ancient one would tell tales of the **north**, of an age when the **moon** trod over the tundra. "We often hunted, the **moon** and I," he said, "sitting BACK to BACK so that crafty musk-ox could not surprise us. But the **moon** eventually left, turning his BACK on the ways of the **north** so that he could take his place in the sky."

Common Pronunciations

Common **ON** reading: **HAI** (ハイ)
Common **kun** reading: **se** (せ); **sei** (せい)

This kanji takes a bit of work to pin down. **sei** refers only to one's height, and appears in very few words. **se** and **HAI** are more common, but whereas **se** refers primarily to the 'back' of someone or something, **HAI** not only incorporates this meaning, but also the sense of betrayal mentioned above. Both **kun-yomi** can become voiced when not in first position.

Create your **on-yomi** keyword and enter it in the table at the back of the book. After that, create your **kun-yomi** keywords and write your sentence to remember the **on-yomi** and **kun-yomi** readings in the box below.

Less Common Pronunciations

Less common **ON** reading: none
Less common **kun** reading: **somu** (そむ)

COMMON WORDS AND COMPOUND		
背	*back*	**se** せ
背	*one's height*	**sei** せい
背中	back + middle = *one's back*	**se**·naka せ·なか
背後	back + after = *back; rear*	**HAI**·GO ハイ·ゴ

KANJI 211

CLEAR

ㄇ	日	日	日㇀	日㇇	晴	晴	晴

| 晴 | 晴 | 晴 | | | | | |

BUILDING THIS KANJI

Sun 日(6) + **Blue** 青(86) = 晴

Meaning

Clear, as in weather.

Remembering this kanji

"Hmm...**sun** and **blue** sky. Unless I miss my guess, we got us some CLEAR weather here.

Common Pronunciations
Common **ON** readings: **SEI** (セイ)
Common **kun** reading: **ha** (は)

The **kun-yomi** becomes voiced when not in first position, as it does in the second example below.

Less Common Pronunciations
Less common **ON** reading: none
Less common **kun** reading: none

COMMON WORDS AND COMPOUNDS		
晴れ	*clear skies*	**ha**·re は·れ
秋晴れ	autumn + clear = *fine autumn weather*	aki **ba**·re あき ば·
晴天	clear + heaven = *fine weather*	**SEI**·TEN セイ·テン

COMPONENT #212

SURFER 疋

KANJI 212

走 **RUN**

一	十	土	キ	キ	走	走	

BUILDING THIS KANJI
Ten (scarecrow) 十(28) + Surfer 疋 = 走

Meaning
Run.

Remembering this kanji
I was really upset when those cool **surfer** dudes showed up at my local beach. "RUN along, **scarecrow**," they said, "us **surfers** are taking over here. You don't belong around our rippling abs and easygoing ways."

Well, I thought, I may have a saggy physique and be a bit uptight, but I'm not going to RUN anywhere. Which isn't surprising, I suppose, given that I really am a **scarecrow**.

Common Pronunciations
Common **ON** reading: **SŌ** (ソウ)
Common **kun** reading: **hashi** (はし)

The **kun-yomi** becomes voiced when not in first position, as it is in the third example below.

Less Common Pronunciations
Less common **ON** reading: none
Less common **kun** reading: none

COMMON WORDS AND COMPOUNDS		
走る	*run*	**hashi**·ru はし·る
走り 回る	run + rotate = *run around*	**hashi**·ri mawa·ru はし·り まわ·る
口走る	mouth + run = *blurt out*	kuchi **bashi**·ru くち ばし·る
走行 時間	run + go + time + interval = *travel time*	**SŌ**·KŌ·JI·KAN ソウ·コウ·ジ·カ

KANJI 213

 **WASH**

⟍	⟍	⟍	⟍	⟍	⟍	⟍	⟍

BUILDING THIS KANJI

Splash 氵 + Precede 先(105) = 洗

Meaning

Wash.

Remembering this kanji

OK, so you've showered and thus had a WASH. Well done. But what exactly does it mean to WASH? According to physicists, when the process is slowed down sufficiently, a WASH is nothing more than a set of **splashes** – one **splash precedes** another **splash**, which **precedes** another **splash**, and so on. When linked, these isolated **splashes** form what is known as a WASH.

Common Pronunciations

Common **ON** reading: **SEN** (セン)
Common **kun** reading: **ara** (あら)

Less Common Pronunciations

Less common **ON** reading: none
Less common **kun** reading: none

COMMON WORDS AND COMPOUNDS		
洗う	wash	**ara·u** あら·う
お手洗い	hand + wash = *washroom; lavatory*	o·te **ara·i** お·て あら·い
洗車	wash + car = *car wash*	**SEN·SHA** セン·シャ
皿洗い	dish + wash = *dishwashing*	sara **ara·i** さら あら·い

KANJI 214

 **ONESELF**

⟋	⟂	己					

Meaning

Oneself. Though close in meaning to "自" ("self", from Entry 33), this character is much less common—you are only likely to encounter it in the two compounds shown below. It does, however, show up frequently as a component in other kanji, so as we have done with other such characters ("寸", "又", etc.) we will assign it an external meaning having a more immediate visual connection: "whip".

Remembering this kanji

A **whip** is an excellent symbol for ONESELF, as it can be used to **whip** ONESELF into a frenzy or **whip** ONESELF into shape. And, as any hardcore medieval sinner will tell you, nothing beats a **whip** when it comes time to literally **whip** ONESELF.

Common Pronunciations

Common **ON** reading: **KO** (コ)
Common **kun** reading: none

Less Common Pronunciations

Less common **ON** reading: **KI** (キ)
Less common **kun** reading: **onore** (おのれ)

COMMON WORDS AND COMPOUNDS		
自己	self + oneself = *oneself*	JI·KO ジ·コ
利己的	profit + oneself + target = *selfish; egoistic*	RI·KO·TEK リ·コ·テキ

KANJI 215

転 **ROLL**

一	厂	冂	戸	自	亘	車	車'	車二
転	転							

BUILDING THIS KANJI
Car 車 (190) + Spy 云 = 転

Meaning

Roll, tumble. This character can also imply a sense of change or transition when it appears in certain compounds.

Remembering this kanji

I grew nervous as I watched the **car** ROLL up. "Get in," said the **spy**. I did as told, and asked him to let me ROLL a cigarette. He looked at me warily. "All right," he said at last, "but ROLL down the window. I don't want you smelling up my **car**."

Common Pronunciations

Common **ON** reading: **TEN** (テン)
Common **kun** reading: **koro** (ころ)

Note the interesting difference between the tw intransitive verbs below.

Less Common Pronunciations

Less common **ON** reading: none
Less common **kun** reading: none

COMMON WORDS AND COMPOUNDS		
転ぶ (intr)	*roll; tumble (by accident)*	**koro**·bu ころ·ぶ
転がる (intr)	*roll; tumble (on purpose)*	**koro**·garu ころ·がる
転がす (tr)	*to roll (something)*	**koro**·gasu ころ·がす
自転車	self + roll + car = *bicycle*	JI·TEN·SHA ジ·テン·シャ

COMPONENT #216

IRECRACKER

Common Pronunciations

Common **ON** readings: **GAKU** (ガク);
RAKU (ラク)
Common **kun** reading: **tano** (たの)

GAKU is used when the compound relates to
music, **RAKU** when referring to pleasure and
comfort.

After entering your **on-yomi** keyword for ラク
in the table at the back of the book and creating a **kun-yomi** keyword, write your sentence to
remember the **on-yomi** and **kun-yomi** readings in
the box below.

KANJI 216

 **MUSIC**

ʼ	⸍	冂	白	白	⸌白	泊	泊ʼ	泊⸌
毕	楽	楽	楽					

BUILDING THIS KANJI
White 白 (7) + Firecracker ﱞ + 木 (13) = 楽

Meaning
This beautiful character can mean two things:
music, or a sense of comfort and pleasure.

Remembering this kanji
The **white** bark of the birch **tree** had great signifi-
cance for the elders, as the **firecracker** noises it
made when burning were believed to be MUSIC
sent from the beyond. Indeed, the distinctive
patterns on the trunk of this **white tree** are still
thought to represent the notations of this other-
worldly MUSIC.

Less Common Pronunciations
Less common **ON** reading: none
Less common **kun** reading: none

COMMON WORDS AND COMPOUNDS		
楽しい	*fun*	**tano**·shii たの·しい
音楽	sound + music = *music*	**ON·GAKU** オン·ガク
楽団	music + group = *band; orchestra*	**GAKU·DAN** ガク·ダン
楽園	music (pleasure) + garden = *paradise*	**RAKU·EN** ラク·エン

KANJI 217

 **REASON**

一	丁	干	王	刲	玏	玾	珇	理
理	理							

BUILDING THIS KANJI
King 王 (23) + Hamlet 里 (180) = 理

Meaning
The idea of 'reason'. This is an important character that appears in many common words.

Remembering this kanji

"What REASON did the **king** have for visiting such a humble **hamlet**?" she asked me.

"A very important REASON," I answered, playing it cool.

"Well, what was it? No one can come up with any REASON why he went there."

I smiled knowingly, paused for effect, then told her in a hushed tone.

"That's a really dumb REASON," she said.

Common Pronunciations

Common **ON** reading: **RI** (リ)
Common **kun** reading: none

Less Common Pronunciations

Less common **ON** reading: none
Less common **kun** reading: none

COMMON WORDS AND COMPOUNDS		
心理学	heart + reason + study = *psychology*	SHIN·**RI**·GAKU シン·リ·ガ ク
理由	reason + cause = *reason; cause*	**RI**·YŪ リ·ユウ
無理	without + reason = *unreasonable; impossible*	MU·**RI** ム·リ
代理	substitute + reason = *representation; proxy*	DAI·**RI** ダイ·リ

KANJI 218

番

ORDER

一	㇒	㇆	立	平	乑	釆	釆	番
釆	番	番						

BUILDING THIS KANJI

Comet 一 + **Rice** 米 (32) + **Rice field** 田 (73) = 番

Meaning

This kanji can appear in a variety of seemingly unrelated compounds, but there will usually be some sense of 'order' present, from the order of a person's turn in line, to the order of numbers, to the keeping of order by overseeing something.

Remembering this kanji

There is an ORDER to everything, as the ORDER of building this kanji demonstrates: a **comet** passes above **rice**, which can only grow out of a **rice field**.

Common Pronunciations

Common **ON** reading: **BAN** (バン)
Common **kun** reading: none

Create your **on-yomi** keyword and enter it in the table at the back of the book. After that, write your sentence to remember the **on-yomi** reading in the box below.

Less Common Pronunciations

Less common **ON** reading: none
Less common **kun** reading: none

COMMON WORDS AND COMPOUNDS		
一番	one + order = *number one; the best*	ICHI·**BAN** イチ·バン
交番	mix + order = *police box/stand*	KŌ·**BAN** コウ·バン
番号	order + title = *number*	**BAN**·GŌ バン·ゴウ
番組	order + association = *(television, etc.) program*	**BAN**·gumi バン·ぐみ

KANJI 219

両 **BOTH**

一 厂 冂 币 両 両

BUILDING THIS KANJI
One (top of a bun) 一(3) + Gorilla 冂 +
Mountain 山(1) = 両

Meaning
Both. This kanji is also used as a counter for such
vehicles as railway cars and carriages.

Remembering this kanji
That's enough! BOTH of you!" said the **gorilla**,
placing herself between the **top of the bun** and
the **mountain**. "Can't you understand that I'm
fond of you BOTH? That BOTH of you are
important to me?" Sighing, she turned at last to
the **top of the bun**. "I'm sorry," she said. "You're
delicious, but you have to realize that I'll always
be a **mountain gorilla**."

Common Pronunciations
Common **ON** reading: **RYŌ** (リ ョ ウ)
Common **kun** reading: none

Create your **on-yomi** keyword and enter it in the
table at the back of the book. After that, write
your sentence to remember the **on-yomi** reading
in the box below.

Less Common Pronunciations
Less common **ON** reading: none
Less common **kun** reading: none

COMMON WORDS AND COMPOUNDS		
両親	both + parent = *parents*	**RYŌ**·SHIN リ ョ ウ・シ ン
両者	both + individual = *both people*	**RYŌ**·SHA リ ョ ウ・シ ャ
両面	both + mask = *both sides*	**RYŌ**·MEN リ ョ ウ・メ ン

COMPONENT #220

GHOST

This is the first in a 'family' of five components
that you will meet in this book. Each one that
follows will be built on the one preceding it
through the addition of an extra stroke.

KANJI 220

民 **PEOPLE**

フ ⁊ 尸 尸 民

BUILDING THIS KANJI
Flag 尸 + Ghost 七 = 民

Meaning
People. This is the only character in the 2,136
general-use kanji in which the flag component
is bent.

Remembering this kanji

"PEOPLE, PEOPLE, listen!" yelled the **ghost**. "I'm claiming this land for... Oh, come on, PEOPLE!"

"Give it up," said another **ghost**. "PEOPLE can't tell we're here. And anyway, that **ghost flag** is so flimsy the staff's already bent."

Common Pronunciations

Common **ON** reading: **MIN** (ミ ン)
Common **kun** reading: none

Create your **on-yomi** keyword and enter it in t table at the back of the book. After that, wr your sentence to remember the **on-yomi** readi in the box below.

Less Common Pronunciations

Less common **ON** reading: none
Less common **kun** reading: **tami** (た み)

COMMON WORDS AND COMPOUNDS		
市民	city + people = *citizen*	SHI·**MIN** シ・ミ ン
国民	country + people = *the people (of a nation)*	KOKU·**MIN** コ ク・ミ ン
民主	people + primary = *democratic*	**MIN**·SHU ミ ン・シ ュ
住民	reside + people = *residents; inhabitants*	JŪ·**MIN** ジ ュ ウ・ミ ン

KANJI 221

質 **QUALITY**

´	ﾉ	ｾ	斤	斤´	斤ﾉ	斤斤	斤斤	斤斤 丨
斤斤	所	質	質	質	質			

BUILDING THIS KANJI

Axe 斤 (126) + Axe 斤 (126) + Shellfish 貝 (21) = 質

Meaning

The quality or intrinsic nature of something. A secondary meaning, curiously, relates to pawning and pawnshops.

Remembering this kanji

"How's the QUALITY of these **shellfish**?" sh asked the merchant.

"Fantastic! You couldn't break 'em apart wit a **couple of axes**."

"Uh...that's not what I meant."

"Oh. Well then, what kind of weird QUALITY are you looking for?"

Common Pronunciations

Common **ON** reading: **SHITSU** (シ ツ), **SHICHI** (シ チ)
Common **kun** reading: none

SHITSU is the most common reading, and i used when this kanji relates to the idea of qua ity. **SHICHI** is used with respect to pawnshops and pawned objects; the third compound below (note the mixture of on and **kun-yomi**) provides an example and is the only time this reading becomes voiced.

Less Common Pronunciations
Less common **ON** readings: **CHI** (チ)
Less common **kun** reading: none

COMMON WORDS AND COMPOUNDS		
本質	main + quality = *essence*	HON·**SHITSU** ホン・シツ
体質	body + quality = *(physical) constitution*	TAI·**SHITSU** タイ・シツ
人質	person + quality (pawn) = *hostage*	hito·**JICHI** ひと・ジチ
質問	quality + question = *question*	**SHITSU**·MON シツ・モン

KANJI 222

正 **PROPER**

一	丁	F	止	正			

BUILDING THIS KANJI
One (top of a bun) 一 (3) + Stop 止 (43) = 正

Meaning
Proper. This versatile kanji can convey a sense of 'formality', as well as the ideas of what is correct or just, etc.

Remembering this kanji
Using the **top of a bun** will not help you **stop** in a PROPER way, as it will quickly crumble under stress. No, it's far more PROPER to have PROPER brakes.

Common Pronunciations
Common **ON** reading: **SEI** (セイ);
SHŌ (ショウ)
Common **kun** reading: **tada** (ただ)

SEI is the more common of the **on-yomi**. **tada** appears in only the first example below.

Less Common Pronunciations
Less common **ON** reading: none
Less common **kun** reading: **masa** (まさ)

COMMON WORDS AND COMPOUNDS		
正しい	*proper; correct*	**tada**·shii た だ・し い
正午	proper + noon = *noon*	**SHŌ**·GO ショウ・ゴ
正式	proper + type = *formal; official*	**SEI**·SHIKI セイ・シキ

DIRECTION

'	一	丁	方				

BUILDING THIS KANJI

Police 宀 + Chair 刀 = 方

Meaning

This commonly-used kanji has to do with direction. It can refer to both physical directions as well as to the idea of directions as a method for doing something. In this latter sense it attaches to verb stems and can be translated as "how to …"; the final compound below provides an example. Ensure that you can clearly see the difference between this kanji and that for "ten thousand" (万), from Entry 89.

Remembering this kanji

"What with all the budget cutbacks," said the **police** chief, "we've needed to do things a little differently around here. Instead of inter-rogations, for example, we just spin this swivel **chair** in front of a bunch of suspects; whichever DIRECTION it points in tells us who the criminal is. We believe we're taking **police** work in an innovative DIRECTION."

Common Pronunciations

Common ON reading: HŌ (ホウ)
Common kun reading: kata (かた)

Note that **kata** can become voiced when not in first position. When the kanji is attached to verb stems in the sense of "how to…", though (as in the final example), it is always read **kata**.

Create your **on-yomi** keyword and enter it in the table at the back of the book. Then, after creating your **kun-yomi** keyword, write your sentence to remember the **on-yomi** and **kun-yomi** readings in the box below.

Less Common Pronunciations

Less common ON reading: none
Less common kun reading: none

IRREGULAR READING
Recall the following irregular reading from Entry 173, constructed from the words "whereabouts" and "unclear". Remember also that the first kanji has an unusual reading as well (**yuku** as opposed to **yuki**):

行方不明	go + direction + not + bright = *"Missing"*	yuku·e·FU·MEI ゆく・え・フ・メイ

COMMON WORDS AND COMPOUNDS		
一方	one + direction *one side; on the other hand*	IP·PŌ イッ・ポウ
地方	ground + direction = *district; region*	CHI·HŌ チ・ホウ
方法	direction + law = *method; way*	HŌ·HŌ ホウ・ホウ
作り方	make + direction = *how to make (something)*	tsuku·ri·kata つく・り かた

COMPONENT #224

HEATER GLASSES 尸

KANJI 224

声 VOICE

| 一 | 十 | 士 | 吉 | 吉 | 吉 | 声 | | |

BUILDING THIS KANJI

Gentleman 士(84) + Theater Glasses 尸 = 声

Meaning

Voice.

Remembering this kanji

"Sssh! Keep your VOICE down!"

The **gentleman** with the **theater glasses** was growing irritable. "Please, miss," the **gentleman** said once more, "your VOICE. I can't concentrate on the performance."

"Look," she said. "In case you haven't noticed, I'm a beer vendor at a baseball game. I *have* to raise my VOICE."

Common Pronunciations

Common **ON** reading: **SEI** (セイ)
Common **kun** reading: **koe** (こえ)

With the exception of the second compound below, the **kun-yomi** is always voiced when not in first position (as in the third compound). It is worth noting that when 一 is read with its **kun-yomi** of ひと, no kanji following it ever becomes voiced.

Less Common Pronunciations

Less common **ON** reading: **SHŌ** (ショウ)
Less common **kun** reading: **kowa** (こわ)

COMMON WORDS AND COMPOUNDS		
声	voice	koe こえ
一声	one + voice = *a voice; a cry*	hito·koe ひと・こえ
大声	large + voice = *a loud voice*	ō·goe おお・ごえ
声明	voice + bright = *declaration; proclamation*	SEI·MEI セイ・メイ

KANJI 225

住 RESIDE

| イ | イ | 仁 | 仁 | 住 | 住 | | |

BUILDING THIS KANJI

Giraffe イ + Primary 主(164) = 住

Meaning

Reside.

Remembering this kanji

"As real estate marketers, we need to understand the **giraffe**, in particular his **primary** motive in choosing where to RESIDE. I believe they need to:

a) RESIDE in wide open spaces,
b) RESIDE where there's fine grazing, and
c) RESIDE where it's safe.

For their **primary** residence, therefore, I suggest we tell our **giraffe** clients to RESIDE in that subdivision on the savanna."

Common Pronunciations

Common **ON** reading: **JŪ** (ジュウ)
Common **kun** reading: **su** (す)

The **kun-yomi** is voiced when not in first positi

Less Common Pronunciations

Less common **ON** reading: none
Less common **kun** reading: none

COMMON WORDS AND COMPOUNDS		
住む	*reside; live*	**su·mu** す·む
住民	reside + people = *residents*	**JŪ·MIN** ジュウ·ミン
住所	reside + location = *address*	**JŪ·SHO** ジュウ·ショ

CHAPTER 11 REVIEW EXERCISES

A. Please match the following kanji to their meanings.

1.	声	a.	Wait
2.	待	b.	Proper
3.	民	c.	Run
4.	酒	d.	Literature
5.	正	e.	Voice
6.	文	f.	Elder brother
7.	清	g.	Music
8.	走	h.	Clear
9.	楽	i.	Saké
10.	兄	j.	People

B. Please match the following meanings to their kanji, and these to their **on** or **kun-yomi**.

1.	Advance (**kun-yomi**)	a. 理	1.	**su** (す)	
2.	Trust	b. 県	2.	**susu** (すす)	
3.	Reside	c. 進	3.	**koto** (こと)	
4.	Wash	d. 両	4.	**SEN** (セン)	
5.	Direction	e. 事	5.	**koro** (ころ)	
6.	Reason	f. 信	6.	**HŌ** (ホウ)	
7.	Matter	g. 洗	7.	**RYŌ** (リョウ)	
8.	Prefecture	h. 住	8.	**KEN** (ケン)	

9. Both   i. 転   9. **SHIN** (シン)
10. Roll   j. 方   10. **RI** (リ)

C. Please choose the best answer(s) to the follow ing questions.

1. Which is the correct reading of 走る ?
   a. **ha·ru** (は·る)
   b. **hashi·ru** (はし·る)
   c. **u·ru** (う·る)
   d. **shi·ru** (し·る)

2. Which of the following readings apply the kanji 正 ?
   a. **a** (あ)
   b. **SEI** (セイ)
   c. **SHŌ** (ショウ)
   d. **tada** (ただ)
   e. **HŌ** (ホウ)

3. Which of the following kanji has the mo number of strokes?
   a. 背
   b. 番
   c. 進
   d. 質
   e. 転

4. I was trapped in a burning house, but managed to open a(n) ___ and get out.
   a. 兄
   b. 背
   c. 戸
   d. 酒
   e. 声

5. Which is the correct reading of 洗う?
   a. **ara·u** (あら·う)
   b. **ka·u** (か·う)
   c. **uba·u** (うば·う)
   d. **chiga·u** (ちが·う)

D. Please match the following compounds to their meanings and pronunciations.

1. 雨戸   a. Sliding door/   1. **ICHI·BAN** (イチ· バン)
      Shutter

2. 県立   b. Oneself   2. **ō·goe** (おお· ごえ)

3. 人質   c. Noon   3. **SHŌ·GO** (ショウ·ゴ)

4. 大声   d. One's back   4. **se·naka** (せ· なか)

5. 正午   e. Prefectural   5. **KEN·RITSU** (ケン·リツ)

6. 一番   f. The best   6. **JI·KO** (ジ·コ)

7. 自己   g. Hostage   7. **BUN·MEI** (ブン·メイ)

8. 音楽   h. Music   8. **ama·do** (あま·ど)

9. 背中   i. Civilization   9. **ON·GAKU** (オン·ガク)

10. 文明   j. Loud voice   10. **hito·JICHI** (ひと·ジチ)

E. Please read the passage below and answer the questions that follow.

私は午前九時に兄を見た。。。

"お兄さん、ちょっと待って、"
と声をかけた。"どこへ行くのですか"と聞きました。
"大学です。両親と大学の門の前で会います。"
"車で行くのですか。"
"いいえ。自転車で。"

1. At what time did I see my older brother?
2. Where is he going?
3. Who is he going to meet?
4. Where will he meet them?
5. How will he get there?

Kanji #226—250

KANJI 226

付 ATTACH

ノ	イ	仁	付	付				

BUILDING THIS KANJI

Giraffe 亻 + **Tiny (soccer player)** 寸(103) = 付

Meaning

Attach, in both physical and figurative senses. It's worth learning this kanji well, as it conveys the meanings of many English words — from 'setting' something on fire to 'turning on' a light or an electrical device.

Remembering this kanji

Let's be honest: a **giraffe** doesn't have arms, so it could never ATTACH anything to a **tiny soccer player**. To be fair, though, a **tiny soccer player** couldn't ATTACH much to a **giraffe** either; the moment he tried to ATTACH a leash or a poster, for example, the **giraffe** would simply bolt off.

Common Pronunciations

Common **ON** reading: **FU** (フ)
Common **kun** reading: **tsu** (つ)

Knowing when the **kun-yomi** becomes voic[ed] in second position is a bit tricky, but as this ka[nji] appears in many common words, it pays to spe[nd] some extra time with it. In general the reading [in] second position will be **tsu**, and it always is wh[en] this kanji is preceded by another kanji that is re[ad] with its verb stem: 見付ける (mi **tsu**·keru / [み]つ·ける: 'to find') is one example, as 'mi' [is] the stem of the verb 見る. It is only when t[he] preceding reading does *not* form a verb with [the] kanji that 付 will sometimes become voiced [as] **zu**: 気付く (KI **zu**·ku / キ づ·く: 'to notice'[)] and 名付ける (na **zu**·keru / な づ·ける: '[to] name') are examples of this, as 気 and 名 do n[ot] form standalone verbs with **KI** and **na** in the w[ay] 見 does with **mi**. This character can also act li[ke] 買 in absorbing its hiragana ending when form[-] ing nouns (as shown in the final example belo[w].

Less Common Pronunciations

Less common **ON** reading: none
Less common **kun** reading: none

COMMON WORDS AND COMPOUND[S]		
付く (intr)	*be attached; stick to*	**tsu**·ku つ·く
付ける (tr)	*attach; put on*	**tsu**·keru つ·ける
付近	attach + near = *neighborhood; nearby*	**FU·KIN** フ·キン
受付	receive + attach = *receipt; reception desk*	uke·**tsuke** うけ·つ[け]

KANJI 227

 LIGHT

一	厂	亓	亓	百	亘	車	軒	軒
軽	軽	軽						

BUILDING THIS KANJI
Car 車(190) + Again(ironing board) 又(159) +
Earth 土(87) = 軽

Meaning
Light, in terms of weight or feeling.

Remembering this kanji
She was all about being LIGHT. Her **car**? A
LIGHT-duty pickup. Her **ironing board**? Used
with a LIGHT touch from the iron. Her way of
patting down **earth**? You've probably guessed:
LIGHTLY.

Common Pronunciations
Common **ON** reading: **KEI** (ケイ)
Common **kun** reading: **karu** (かる)

The **kun-yomi** is voiced when not in first position,
as seen in the second and third compounds (the
latter a mix of on and **kun-yomi**).

Less Common Pronunciations
Less common **ON** reading: none
Less common **kun** readings: **karo** (かろ)

COMMON WORDS AND COMPOUNDS		
軽い	*light*	**karu·i** かる・い
手軽	hand + light = *simple; easy*	te·**garu** て・がる
気軽	spirit + light = *lighthearted*	**KI**·garu キ・がる
軽食	light + eat = *light meal; snack*	**KEI**·SHOKU ケイ・ショク

KANJI 228

 MOURN

ㄱ	ㄱ	弓	弔					

BUILDING THIS KANJI
Bow 弓(143) + Pole 丨 = 弔

Meaning
Mourn.

Remembering this kanji
If you want to write the character for 'pull'
(引), don't scrunch it up and write 弔. It'll mean
you've made a mistake, and that will make you
MOURN.

Common Pronunciations

Common **ON** reading: **CHO** (チョウ)
Common **kun** reading: none

Less Common Pronunciations

Less common **ON** reading: none
Less common **kun** readings: **tomura** (とむら)

COMMON WORDS AND COMPOUNDS		
弔意	mourn + mind = *condolence*	**CHŌ·I** チョウ・イ
弔文	mourn + literature = *funeral address*	**CHŌ·BUN** チョウ・ブン
弔問	mourn + question = *sympathy call*	**CHŌ·MON** チョウ・モン

KANJI 229

 CRY

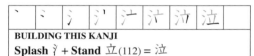

BUILDING THIS KANJI
Splash 氵 + **Stand** 立 (112) = 泣

Meaning
Cry.

Remembering this kanji
"For CRYING out loud, don't CRY like that! I told you you'd get a **splash** if you continued to **stand** next to that puddle."

Common Pronunciations

Common **ON** reading: none
Common **kun** reading: **na** (な)

Less Common Pronunciations

Less common **ON** reading: **KYŪ** (キュウ)
Less common **kun** readings: none

COMMON WORDS AND COMPOUNDS		
泣く	*cry*	**na·ku** な・く
泣き出す	cry + exit = *burst out crying*	**na·ki da·su** な・き だ・す
泣き声	cry + voice = *tearful voice*	**na·ki goe** な・き ご・え
泣き虫	cry + insect = *crybaby*	**na·ki mushī** な・き むし

COMPONENT #230

FROG

Note that the long vertical line and bottom left-most line are written as one stroke.

KANJI 230

 **SILVER**

ノ	ハ	ム	台	牟	牟	金	金	金ㄱ
金ㄱ	金ㄱ	銀	銀	銀				

BUILDING THIS KANJI
Metal 金 (82) + **Frog** 艮 = 銀

Meaning
Silver. Recall from Entry 82 that when the character for gold functions as a component in other kanji, it means 'metal' in general.

Remembering this kanji

"Congratulations! You won the SILVER!"
"Oh, big deal. It's just a hunk of **metal** to me.
Nobody cares who gets the SILVER."
"What are you talking about? This '**metal**'
means you're the runner-up. SILVER's great!"
"Maybe for you. But I'm a **frog**, and you can't
imagine what it's like for a **frog** to be beaten
by a toad."

Common Pronunciations

Common **ON** reading: **GIN** (ギ ン)
Common **kun** reading: none

Create your **on-yomi** keyword and enter it in the
table at the back of the book. After that, write
your sentence to remember the **on-yomi** reading
in the box below.

Less Common Pronunciations

Less common **ON** reading: none
Less common **kun** readings: none

COMMON WORDS AND COMPOUNDS		
銀	*silver*	**GIN** ギ ン
銀行	silver + go = *bank*	**GIN·KŌ** ギ ン · コ ウ
銀世界	silver + society + world = *snow-covered scene*	**GIN·SE·KAI** ギ ン · セ · カ イ

KANJI 231

QUESTION

冂	冂	冂	冂'	冂	冂	冂	冂
冐	問						

BUILDING THIS KANJI

Gate 門 (96) + Mouth (vampire) 口 (8) = 問

Meaning

Question, inquiry. In some words (the second
compound below is an example), this kanji can
convey the sense of 'problem'.

Remembering this kanji

As both of the components making up this
character have now been encountered numerous times, this will be our first kanji presented
without an illustration. The absence of a drawing
will aid you in progressing to the next stage of
kanji recognition—identifying a character on
its own.

"I have a QUESTION, ma'am."
"What is it, Jeeves?"
"There's someone at the **gate**. A **vampire**, I
believe, who wishes to ask you a QUESTION.
What should I do?"
"Well, let him in."
"Are you sure that's wise?"
"How dare you QUESTION me!"

Common Pronunciations

Common **ON** reading: **MON** (モ ン)
Common **kun** reading: **to** (と)

Less Common Pronunciations

Less common **ON** reading: none
Less common **kun** readings: none

IRREGULAR READING		
問屋	question + roof = *wholesale dealer*	**ton**·ya とん·や

COMMON WORDS AND COMPOUNDS		
質問	quality + question = *question*	SHITSU·MON シツ·モン
問題	question + topic = *problem; issue*	**MON**·DAI モン·ダイ
問い合わせる	question + match = *inquire; apply to*	**to**·i a·waseru と·い あ·わ せる

KANJI 232

暗 **DARK**

丨	冂	日	日	日'	日亠	日亠	日立	日立
暗	暗	暗	暗					

BUILDING THIS KANJI
Sun 日 (6) + Sound 音 (137) = 暗

Meaning
Dark, with its various implications.

Remembering this kanji
A DARK thought: If we ever heard the **sun** make a **sound**, it would probably be the **sound** of the **sun** exploding. Boy, would it ever be DARK after that happened.

Common Pronunciations
Common **ON** reading: **AN** (アン)
Common **kun** reading: **kura** (くら)

Less Common Pronunciations
Less common **ON** reading: none
Less common **kun** readings: none

COMMON WORDS AND COMPOUNDS		
暗い	*dark*	**kura**·i くら·い
暗黒	dark + black = *darkness; blackness*	**AN**·KOKU アン·コク
暗記	dark + note = *memorization*	**AN**·KI アン·キ

KANJI 233

絵 **PICTURE**

㇀	幺	幺	糸	糸	糸	紹	紷	絵
絵	絵	絵						

BUILDING THIS KANJI
Thread 糸 (196) + Meet 会 (138) = 絵

Meaning
Picture.

Remembering this kanji
"OK, this **thread** is to **meet** this **thread**, and tha **thread** is to **meet** that **thread**. Do you notice th PICTURE emerging? Still no? Well, what kin of quilters are you? You're just going to have t PICTURE it, then."

Common Pronunciations
Common **ON** reading: **E** (エ)
Common **kun** reading: none

Create your **on-yomi** keyword and enter it in the table at the back of the book. After that, write your sentence to remember the **on-yomi** reading in the box below.

This reading appears in only one compound. The word, however, is commonly used: 絵画 (**KAI**·GA / カイ・ガ) "pictures and paintings", composed of, naturally enough, the kanji for "picture" and "painting" (Entry 251).

Less Common Pronunciations
Less common **ON** reading: **KAI** (カイ)
Less common **kun** readings: none

COMMON WORDS AND COMPOUNDS		
絵	*picture*	E エ
絵本	picture + main (book) = *picture book*	E·HON エ・ホン

COMPONENT #234

COAT RACK

KANJI 234

氏 **SURNAME**

BUILDING THIS KANJI
Coat Rack 厂 + Ghost 弋 = 氏

Meaning
Surname. This kanji can also mean 'clan' in some instances, as well as convey a more official-sounding form of "Mr." when it is attached to a family name (as in the final compound below).

Remembering this kanji
"Allow me to put that on the **coat rack**, sir."
"Thank you."
"I'll also need to sign you in. Your SURNAME?"
"Host."
"Ah, I recognize that SURNAME. Mr. **G. Host**, I presume?"

Common Pronunciations
Common **ON** reading: **SHI** (シ)
Common **kun** reading: none

Less Common Pronunciations
Less common **ON** reading: none
Less common **kun** readings: **uji** (うじ)

COMMON WORDS AND COMPOUNDS		
氏名	surname + name = *one's full name*	SHI·MEI シ・メイ
中村氏	middle + village + surname = *Mr. Nakamura*	naka·mura·SHI なか・むら・シ

KANJI 235

若 **YOUNG**

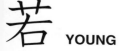

BUILDING THIS KANJI
Wreath 艹 + Right 右 (35) = 若

Meaning
Young.

Remembering this kanji
The ancient Olympics celebrated the accomplishments of those who were YOUNG. A **wreath** was presented to a YOUNG champion, with the runner-up (who was also YOUNG) given the position of honor to his **right**.

Common Pronunciations
Common **ON** reading: none
Common **kun** reading: **waka** (わか)

Note that the second compound uses the less common pronunciation of 者.

Less Common Pronunciations
Less common **ON** reading: **JAKU** (ジャク
NYAKU (ニャク)
Less common **kun** readings: none

IRREGULAR READING		
若人	young + person = *young person*	**wakō**·do わこう・ど

COMMON WORDS AND COMPOUNDS		
若い	*young*	**waka**·i わか・い
若者	young + individual = *young person*	**waka**·mono わか・もの
若々 しい	young + young = *youthful*	**waka·waka**·shii わか・わか・しい

KANJI 236

 **CAUSE**

This is written in the same order as the kanji for "rice field" (Entry 73), but with the third stroke lengthened.

Meaning
Cause, reason.

Remembering this kanji
"Oh-oh, he's let his **rice field** grow over its border. What would CAUSE him to be so negligent?"

"Who can tell with that guy? This is going to CAUSE trouble, though."

Common Pronunciations
Common **ON** reading: **YU** (ユ); **YŪ** (ユウ)
Common **kun** reading: none

This character only appears in roughly ten Japanese compounds, which makes the large number of readings for it seem extreme. The examples below, however, are all very common.

Create your **on-yomi** keyword for ユ and enter it in the table at the back of the book. After that, write your sentence to remember the **on-yomi** readings in the box below.

Less Common Pronunciations
Less common **ON** reading: **YUI** (ユイ)
Less common **kun** readings: **yoshi** (よし)

COMMON WORDS AND COMPOUNDS		
由来	cause + come = *origin*	**YU·RAI** ユ・ライ
自由	self + cause = *freedom*	**JI·YŪ** ジ・ユウ
理由	reason + cause = *reason*	**RI·YŪ** リ・ユウ

KANJI 237

申 **DECLARE**

| | 口 | 日 | 日 | 申 | | | |

BUILDING THIS KANJI

Sun 日 (6) + Pole | = 申

Ensure that you are able to see the difference between this kanji and the preceding entry for 日, as well as between these two and the character for "shell" (甲), our "fly swatter" from Entry 148.

Meaning

Declare, in the sense of a more humble way to say the verb "say".

Common Pronunciations

Common **ON** reading: **SHIN** (シン)
Common **kun** reading: **mō** (もう)

Less Common Pronunciations

Less common **ON** reading: none
Less common **kun** readings: none

COMMON WORDS AND COMPOUNDS		
申す	*say (humble form)*	**mō**·su もう・す
申し 上げる	declare + upper = *inform; tell* *(humble form)*	**mō**·shi a·geru もう・し あ・げる
内申	inside + declare = *confidential report*	**NAI·SHIN** ナイ・シン

Remembering this kanji

"Anything to DECLARE?"

"Yes. I have a sun on a **pole**."

"Well, I DECLARE! I'm afraid I'll have to confiscate that, sir; we can't have an extra **sun** in this solar system."

COMPONENT #238

SUITCASE   西

KANJI 238

要 **ESSENTIAL**

| 一 | 厂 | 厅 | 襾 | 襾 | 西 | 覀 | 要 | 要 |

BUILDING THIS KANJI

Suitcase 西 + Woman 女 (16) = 要

Meaning

Essential, necessary.

Remembering this kanji

The **suitcase** of any **woman** taking a trip will be packed with what is ESSENTIAL: important documents, business suits (if needed), guide books and maps, for instance. That's a lot of stuff, making a sturdy **suitcase** pretty much ESSENTIAL.

Common Pronunciations

Common ON reading: **YŌ** (ヨ ウ)
Common kun reading: **i** (い)

Less Common Pronunciations

Less common ON reading: none
Less common kun readings: none

COMMON WORDS AND COMPOUNDS		
要る	*need; be needed*	i·ru い・る
要する	*require; need*	YŌ·suru ヨ ウ・す る
必要	certain + essential = *essential; necessary*	HITSU·YŌ ヒ ツ・ヨ ウ
重要	heavy + essential = *importance*	JU·YŌ ジ ュ ウ・ヨ ウ

KANJI 239

REACH

一	乙	云	云	至	至		

BUILDING THIS KANJI
One (top of a bun) 一 (3) + **Broken crutch** ム + **Earth** 土 (87) = 至

Meaning
Reach, in the sense of 'arrive at' or 'extend to'.

Remembering this kanji

"Must...REACH...the condiments," she gasped.

You wonder why she's let the situation REACH this stage. The **top of the bun** is where she's left it, of course, but with her **broken crutch** littering the **earth** it might as well be miles away. And yet somehow she much REACH that spot...

Common Pronunciations

Common ON reading: **SHI** (シ)
Common kun reading: **ita** (い た)

The second compound below is the only word in which the **on-yomi** becomes voiced.

Less Common Pronunciations

Less common ON reading: none
Less common kun readings: none

COMMON WORDS AND COMPOUNDS		
至る	*reach; extend*	ita·ru い た・る
冬至	winter + reach = *winter solstice*	TŌ·JI ト ウ・ジ
至る所	reach + location = *everywhere*	ita·ru tokoro い た・る と こ ろ
至急	reach + hasten = *urgent*	SHI·KYŪ シ・キ ュ ウ

KANJI 240

比 **COMPARE**

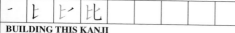

-	ヒ	ヒ′	比				

BUILDING THIS KANJI
Beggar ヒ + Beggar ヒ = 比

Meaning
Compare. The sense of 'ratio' is also present in a few compounds.

Remembering this kanji
Let's COMPARE these beggars. COMPARE the arms: the ones of the first are held level (and written left to right)! COMPARE the postures: one sits on his calves! Isn't it exciting to COMPARE them?

Common Pronunciations
Common ON reading: **HI** (ヒ)
Common kun reading: **kura** (く ら)

Create your **on-yomi** keyword and enter it in the table at the back of the book. After that, write your sentence to remember the **on-yomi** and **kun-yomi** readings in the box below.

Less Common Pronunciations
Less common ON reading: none
Less common kun readings: none

COMMON WORDS AND COMPOUNDS		
比べる	*compare*	kura·beru く ら·べ る
背比べ	back + compare = *compare heights*	sei kura·be せ い く ら·べ
見比べる	see + compare = *comparison*	mi kura·beru み く ら·べ る
対比	versus + compare = *contrast; compare*	TAI·HI タ イ·ヒ

KANJI 241

計 **MEASURE**

`	⺦	⺀	亖	言	言	言	言一	計

BUILDING THIS KANJI
Say 言 (80) + Ten (scarecrow) 十 (28) = 計

Meaning
To measure, estimate.

Remembering this kanji
What can you **say** to a **scarecrow** to get the MEASURE of him as a comedian? I'd suggest "What are you doing?", for when I said that to a **scarecrow** once he answered me with "Oh, I'm just posing like this because my tailor's about to MEASURE me for a jacket."

Common Pronunciations
Common ON reading: **KEI** (ケ イ)
Common kun reading: **haka** (は か)

Don't forget that the reading of 時 in the third compound is irregular.

Less Common Pronunciations
Less common **ON** reading: none
Less common **kun** readings: none

COMMON WORDS AND COMPOUNDS		
計る	*measure; estimate*	**haka·ru** は か・る
会計	meet + measure = *accounts;* *accounting*	KAI·**KEI** カイ・ケイ
時計	time + measure = *watch; clock*	to·**KEI** と・ケイ
温度計	warm + degree + measure = *thermometer*	ON·DO·**KEI** オン・ド・ケイ

KANJI 242

所 **LOCATION**

一	�	ｚ	尸	戸	所	所	所

BUILDING THIS KANJI
Door 戸 (205) + **Axe** 斤 (126) = 所

Meaning
Location.

Remembering this kanji
Panicking, she crouches behind the bathroom
door with a baseball bat. Is it a safe LOCA-
TION? Unfortunately no, for all too soon he
is there, and the **axe** chops through the door…
Don't worry though, this is just a scene from a
B-movie filmed on LOCATION.

Common Pronunciations
Common **ON** reading: **SHO** (ショ)
Common **kun** reading: **tokoro** (と こ ろ)

We'll need to bring out our work gloves for this
one. In first position, **SHO** is by far the more
common reading; it's after this, however, that

things can get confusing. In second position, th
kun-yomi is always voiced, with the exception o
only a few words in which this kanji is precede
by a verb in its "ru" form (such as 至る所, th
third example in Entry 239). The **on-yomi**, b
contrast is almost never voiced in second positior
the only time you are likely to encounter it voice
here is in the second example below. In the thir
position and beyond, however, there is no way t
predict on first encountering a compound whethe
or not the **on-yomi** is voiced (the **kun-yomi** neve
appears after second position). Since **SHO** an
JO occur equally here, you may wish to asso
ciate your **on-yomi** keyword with each of thes
compounds as you learn them. In other words, i
you can link your keyword for **SHO** to "powe
station" (発電所: HATSU·DEN·**SHO** / ハツ・テ
ン・ショ) from the kanji for "discharge", "elec
tric" and "location", it will help you to remembe
that 所 is unvoiced here.

Less Common Pronunciations
Less common **ON** reading: none
Less common **kun** readings: none

COMMON WORDS AND COMPOUNDS		
所	*location; place*	**tokoro** と こ ろ
近所	near + location = *neighborhood; vicinity*	KIN·**JO** キン・ジョ
台所	platform + location = *kitchen*	DAI·**dokoro** ダイ・どころ
場所	place + location = *place*	ba·**SHO** ば・ショ

COMPONENT #243

MACHINE GUNS

KANJI 243

第

NO. (NUMBER)

ノ	仁	仁'	ケー	ケケ	竹	竺	笁
第	第						

BUILDING THIS KANJI
Machine Guns ⺮ + Mourn 弔 (228) + Comet
一 = 第

Meaning
This kanji is usually used as a prefix for numbers, such as English uses 'No.' or '#'. In a few compounds it can also mean 'exam'.

Remembering this kanji
Due to the classified nature of this document, all NO.'s have been removed.

Case NO. xxxx:

Machine guns (serial NO.'s xxxx and xxxx) were employed to shoot down the **comet**. Those firing said **machine guns** (personnel NO.'s xxxx and xxxx) did not survive the **comet**'s impact. We **mourn** their passing.

Agent NO. xxxx

Common Pronunciations
Common **ON** reading: **DAI** (ダイ)
Common **kun** reading: none
Recall that 'ease' plus 'complete' in the second compound below gives us 'safety'.

Less Common Pronunciations
Less common **ON** reading: none
Less common **kun** readings: none

COMMON WORDS AND COMPOUNDS		
第一	*No. 1*	**DAI**·ICHI ダイ・イチ
安全 第一	safety + No. + one = *"safety first"*	AN·ZEN·**DAI**·ICHI アン・ゼン・ダイ・ イチ
次第	next + No. = *order; circumstances*	SHI·**DAI** シ・ダイ

KANJI 244

旨

GIST

一	ヒ	ヒ	匕	旨	旨		

BUILDING THIS KANJI
Beggar 匕 + Sun 日 (6) = 旨

Meaning
Gist. Though rarely encountered on its own, this kanji figures in other more common characters.

Remembering this kanji

"Look, I'm in a big hurry. Just give me the GIST of it."

"The GIST? Well…a **beggar** sat on the **sun**, I guess."

"Really? Hmm… It would seem, then, that the GIST isn't enough to explain this."

Common Pronunciations

Common **ON** reading: none
Common **kun** reading: **mune** (むね)

Less Common Pronunciations

Less common **ON** reading: **SHI** (シ)
Less common **kun** readings: none

COMMON WORDS AND COMPOUNDS		
旨	*gist; meaning*	**mune** むね

KANJI 245

着   **WEAR**

ヽ	ヽ	ソ	ソ	平	羊	羊	羊	着
着	着	着						

BUILDING THIS KANJI
Rabbit ヽ′ + King 王(23) + Comet ⌐ + Eye (Cyclops) 目(15) = 着

Meaning

This important kanji has two main meanings: to wear, and to arrive. It may help to think that, in a sense, a person "wears" their surroundings when they arrive at a place. This kanji, in fact, consistently has this idea of things coming together in certain ways.

Remembering this kanji

A rabbit on a **king**? Well sure, if he wants to WEAR a **rabbit** fur collar. A **comet** on a **Cyclops**? Not unless he's found some pajamas with **comets** on them. Because let's not kid ourselves: **kings** WEAR sable robes, and a **Cyclops** always seems to WEAR that smelly toga-like outfit.

Common Pronunciations

Common **ON** reading: **CHAKU** (チャク)
Common **kun** reading: **ki** (き); **tsu** (つ)

As the famous word in the third example make[s] clear, **ki** is used when this kanji refers to wearing clothes; it is always voiced in second and third position. **tsu** is used in the sense of "arrive", and is never voiced in second position. **CHAKU** i[s] the most common of these readings and has the overarching meaning of things coming together.

Create your **on-yomi** keyword and enter it in the table at the back of the book. Then, after creating your **kun-yomi** keywords, write your sentence t[o] remember the **on-yomi** and **kun-yomi** readings i[n] the box below.

Less Common Pronunciations

Less common **ON** reading: **JAKU** (ジャク)
Less common **kun** readings: none

COMMON WORDS AND COMPOUNDS		
着る	*wear*	**ki·ru** き・る
着く	*arrive*	**tsu·ku** つ・く
着物	*wear + thing = kimono*	**ki·mono** き・もの
接着	*join + thing = adhesion*	**SET·CHAKU** セッ・チャク

COMPONENT #246

LITTLE RED RIDING HOOD

Hey, your arms would be a bit long too if you were carrying a basket like this all day.

KANJI 246

 **LACK**

ノ	┝	ケ	欠				

BUILDING THIS KANJI
Little Red Riding Hood ┝ + Person 人(2) = 欠

Meaning
Lack.

Remembering this kanji
"Hey, there goes **Little Red Riding Hood**."
"She's a strange **person**, isn't she?"
"How so?"
"She seems to LACK common sense. Look at how she traipses around everywhere with that basket."
"Well if she LACKS anything, it's good judgment. That hairy guy she's chatting with over here looks an awful lot like a wolf."

Common Pronunciations
Common **ON** reading: **KETSU** (ケ ツ)
Common **kun** reading: **ka** (か)

Create your **on-yomi** keyword and enter it in the table at the back of the book. Then, after creating your **kun-yomi** keyword, write your sentence to remember the **on-yomi** and **kun-yomi** readings in the box below.

Less Common Pronunciations
Less common **ON** reading: none
Less common **kun** readings: none

COMMON WORDS AND COMPOUNDS		
欠く	*lack*	**ka·ku** か・く
欠点	lack + point = *defect; shortcoming*	**KET·TEN** ケッ・テン
欠員	lack + member = *vacancy; post*	**KETSU·IN** ケツ・イン

KANJI 247

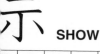 **SHOW**

ー	二	丁	亓	示			

BUILDING THIS KANJI
Two 二(4) + Small 小(20) = 示

Meaning
To show.

Remembering this kanji

"Psst! Hey you **two**, I wanna SHOW you something."

"What is it?"

"These. Look how **small** they are. And I've only got **two**."

"Are you crazy? You can't SHOW stuff like that!"

Common Pronunciations

Common **ON** reading: **JI** (ジ)

Common **kun** reading: **shime** (しめ)

Less Common Pronunciations

Less common **ON** reading: **SHI** (シ)

Less common **kun** readings: none

COMMON WORDS AND COMPOUNDS		
示す	show	shime·su しめ・す
暗示	dark + show = *hint*	AN·JI アン・ジ
指示	finger + show = *indication; direction*	SHI·JI シ・ジ
展示	display + show = *display; exhibition*	TEN·JI テン・ジ

KANJI 248

 **SERVE**

ノ	亻	仁	什	仕			

BUILDING THIS KANJI

Giraffe 亻 + Gentleman 士(84) = 仕

Meaning

Serve, work.

Remembering this kanji

It would not SERVE to have a **giraffe** SERVE a **gentleman**; its hoofs would clatter noisily over the floor of the **gentleman's** club and make any **gentleman** look up in annoyance. No, it simply would not SERVE.

Common Pronunciations

Common **ON** reading: **SHI** (シ)

Common **kun** reading: none

This kanji is unusual in that its **on-yomi** almost always forms compounds with the **kun-yomi** of other characters, as in the examples below.

Less Common Pronunciations

Less common **ON** reading: **JI** (ジ)

Less common **kun** readings: **tsuka** (つか)

COMMON WORDS AND COMPOUNDS		
仕方	serve + direction = *way; method*	SHI·kata シ・かた
仕事	serve + matter = *job; work*	SHI·goto シ・ごと
仕切り	serve + cut = *partition; dividing line*	SHI·ki·ri シ・き・り
仕上げる	serve + upper = *finish; complete*	SHI a·geru シ あ・げ

COMPONENT #249

POGO STICK

一	一	一	一	一	一	一	一	一

BUILDING THIS KANJI

Pogo Stick 甫 + Two 二(4) = 重

Meaning

Heavy, in both the literal and the figurative sense.

KANJI 249

 **HEAVY**

emembering this kanji

A single **pogo stic**k wasn't enough. We had to
et her **two**."

Why?"

Well, she's a bit…HEAVY."

ommon Pronunciations

ommon **ON** reading: **JŪ** (ジュウ)

ommon **kun** reading: **omo** (おも)

JŪ is by far the more common reading.

Less Common Pronunciations

Less common **ON** reading: **CHŌ** (チョウ)

Less common **kun** readings: **kasa** (かさ); **e** (え)

COMMON WORDS AND COMPOUNDS		
重い	*heavy*	omo·i おも・い
重大	heavy + large = *important; grave*	JŪ·DAI ジュウ・ダイ
重要	heavy + essential = *important; essential*	JŪ·YŌ ジュウ・ヨウ

KANJI 250

MATCH

ノ 人 △ 合 合 合

BUILDING THIS KANJI

Umbrella 𠆢 + One (hamburger patty) 一 (3)
+ Mouth (vampire) 口 (8) = 合

Meaning

Match, combine. This is a kanji you will encounter frequently, as it forms many compound verbs
(such as in the third example) that suggest
some kind of reciprocal action between people
or things. These words are often translated
into English with the phrase "each other": 押
し合う (o·shi **a**·u / お・し あ・う) "to push
each other", is one example. As they can be
confused, make sure you clearly see the difference between this kanji and that of 'same' (同),
from Entry 197.

Remembering this kanji

The centuries-old fingerprints on the **umbrella**?
A MATCH!

The fang marks on the **hamburger patty**?
Another MATCH!

Yup, it looked like we'd be able to MATCH the
vampire to the crime scenes of the **umbrella**
vendor *and* the butcher.

Common Pronunciations

Common **ON** reading: **GŌ** (ゴウ)

Common **kun** reading: **a** (あ)

This is another tough kanji when it comes to knowing which reading should be used in compounds.
GŌ is the most common choice in first position,
but both it and **a** occur frequently in second. This
kanji can also act like 買 in absorbing its hiragana
accompaniment in certain compounds.

Create your **on-yomi** keyword and enter it in the
table at the back of the book. Then, after creating
your **kun-yomi** keyword, write your sentence to
remember the **on-yomi** and **kun-yomi** readings in
the box below.

Less Common Pronunciations

Less common **ON** reading: **GA-** (ガ ッ);
KA- (カ ッ)

Less common **kun** readings: none

These two readings only occur in a few words, and always "double up" with the **on-yomi** of the kanji that follows them (as the small katakana " ッ " indicates). The compound 合宿 (**GAS·SHUKU** / ガッ・シュク) "to lodge together", from the kanji "match" and "lodging" is an example. When the time comes to memorize these **on-yomi** you can do one of two things: come up with new keywords for each (incorporating some way to account for their pronunciation being "clipped"),

or simply use your existing keywords for **GAT!** and **KATSU** (you will create one for this late **on-yomi** in Entry 300) while remembering th they always change phonetically like this.

COMMON WORDS AND COMPOUNDS		
合う (intr)	*match; fit*	**a·u** あ・う
合わせる (tr)	*put together;* *combine*	**a·waseru** あ・わせる
話し合う	speak + match = *discuss; talk*	hana·shi **a·u** はな・し あ・
合意	match + mind = *mutual agreement*	**GŌ·I** ゴウ・イ

CHAPTER 12 REVIEW EXERCISES

A. Please match the following kanji to their meanings.

1. 第
2. 旨
3. 由
4. 軽
5. 銀
6. 合
7. 欠
8. 至
9. 若
10. 計

  a. Young
  b. Match
  c. Silver
  d. Reach
  e. Light
  f. No.
  g. Cause
  h. Measure
  i. Lack
  j. Gist

B. Please match the following meanings to their kanji, and these to their **on** or **kun-yomi**.

1. Attach a. 所
2. Surname b. 氏
3. Location c. 申
4. Heavy d. 比
   (kun-yomi)
5. Picture e. 絵
6. Mourn f. 付
7. Cry g. 泣
8. Declare h. 重
9. Show i. 弔
   (kun-yomi)
10. Compare j. 示

1. **omo** (おも)
2. **CHŌ** (チョウ)
3. **tokoro** (ところ)
4. **na** (な)
5. **kura** (くら)
6. **SHIN** (シン)
7. **tsu** (つ)
8. **E** (エ)
9. **SHI** (シ)
10. **shime** (しめ)

C. Please choose the best answer(s) to the follow ing questions.

1. Which of the following readings apply the kanji 着?
  a. **tsu** (つ)
  b. **CHAKU** (チャク)
  c. **SHŌ** (ショウ)
  d. **ko** (こ)
  e. **ki** (き)

2. He hit his thumb with a hammer, but acte tough and didn't ____ .
  a. 至 b. 欠 c. 付 d. 泣 e. 計

3. Which is the correct reading of 思い付く
  a. **omo·i zu·ku** (おも・い づ・く)
  b. **omo·i tsu·ku** (おも・い つ・く)

4. Which of the following kanji has the mo number of strokes?
  a. 絵 b. 計 c. 要 d. 第 e. 問

5. Which is the correct reading of 軽い?
  a. **karu·i** (かる・い)
  b. **maru·i** (まる・い)
  c. **shiro·i** (しろ・い)
  d. **kura·i** (くら・い)

D. Please match the following compounds to their meanings and pronunciations.

1. 銀行	a. Job / Work	1. **ki·mono** (き·もの)	
2. 質問	b. Winter solstice	2. **JI·YŪ** (ジ·ユウ)	
3. 時計	c. Important	3. **TŌ·JI** (トウ·ジ)	
4. 重要	d. Hint	4. **AN·JI** (アン·ジ)	
5. 着物	e. Bank	5. **JŪ·YŌ** (ジュウ·ヨウ)	
6. 冬至	f. Question	6. **to·KEI** (と·ケイ)	
7. 自由	g. Freedom	7. **GIN·KŌ** (ギン·コウ)	
8. 仕事	h. Kimono	8. **SHI·goto** (シ·ごと)	
9. 合意	i. Mutual agreement	9. **SHITSU·MON** (シツ·モン)	
10. 暗示	j. Watch/ Clock	10. **GŌ·I** (ゴウ·イ)	

E. Please read the passage below and answer the questions that follow.

金本さんは銀行で受付の仕事をしています。銀行付近に住んでいて、毎朝歩いて十分で着きます。本日正午に重要な会見があります。

1. Where does Kanemoto-san work?
2. What job does she do?
3. How long does it take her to walk to work?
4. What is happening at work today?
5. What time will it happen?

Kanji #251—280

KANJI 251

PAINTING

BUILDING THIS KANJI
One (top of a bun) 一 (3) + **Cause** 由 (236) +
Garbage Can ⊔ = 画

Meaning
This character relates primarily to painting. A
secondary meaning has to do with kanji strokes
(think of how they are "painted" in calligraphy)
and things being drawn up, from dividing lines
to plans.

Remembering this kanji
Did you realize that the **top of a bun** was the
underlying **cause** of DaVinci's Mona Lisa being
created? A recently discovered interview unrav-
els the mystery.

  "I was broke back then," DaVinci said, "as
nobody wanted my PAINTINGS. But one day I
was digging through a **garbage can** for food, and
saw the **top of a bun**. It was magnificent, and I
thought that if I could reproduce the curve of that
bun top in a smile...well, I'd have a PAINTING
I could really be proud of."

Common Pronunciations
Common **ON** reading: **GA** (ガ); **KAKU** (カ ゛
Common **kun** reading: none

GA is the reading used when this kanji refers
painting, **KAKU** when it refers to such things
kanji strokes and plans. Recall from Entry
how 家 can refer to a skilled person when us
as a suffix (as it is in the first compound below

Create your **on-yomi** keywords and enter them
the table at the back of the book. After that, wr
your sentence to remember the **on-yomi** readin
in the box below.

Less Common Pronunciations
Less common **ON** reading: none
Less common **kun** readings: none

COMMON WORDS AND COMPOUNDS		
画家	painting + house = *painter; artist*	**GA·KA** ガ・カ
計画	measure + painting = *plan; scheme*	**KEI·KAKU** ケイ・カク
映画	reflect + painting = *movie*	**EI·GA** エイ・ガ

POSSIBLE

一	丁	可	可				

UILDING THIS KANJI
ne (top of a bun) 一 (3) + **Mouth (vampire)**
口 (8) + **Harpoon** 亅 = 可

eaning
ssible. It's important to learn the proper stroke
der of this kanji so as not to confuse it with
milar-looking characters we will meet in the
ture.

emembering this kanji
listen guys, you're not locked into doing these
bs. Anything is POSSIBLE."
eah, right. I'm the **top of a bun**. What else
uld I do?"
Why not let yourself go stale and become a
isbee? That's POSSIBLE. And you, **vampire**:
s POSSIBLE for you to be a night watchman.
nd don't tell me, **harpoon**, that you couldn't
d something as a javelin; you know darn well
at's POSSIBLE.

Common Pronunciations
Common **ON** reading: **KA** (カ)
Common **kun** reading: none

Recall from Entry 199 that the reading for 愛 is
irregular in the first compound below.

Less Common Pronunciations
Less common **ON** reading: none
Less common **kun** readings: none

COMMON WORDS AND COMPOUNDS		
可愛い	possible + love = *cute*	**KA**·WAI·i カ・ワイ・い
不可欠	not + possible + lack = *indispensable*	FU·**KA**·KETSU フ・カ・ケ・ツ
可動	possible + move = *movable; mobile*	**KA**·DŌ カ・ド・ウ

HITTLING 示 示

 GOD

`	フ	示	礻	礻	初	袘	袙	神

BUILDING THIS KANJI
Whittling 礻 + **Declare** 申 (237) = 神

Meaning
God.

Remembering this kanji

"The **whittling** is done: I **declare** the birth of the universe."

So spoke GOD.

SHIN is by far the most common of these re[a]ings, although the others do show up in so[m]e important words. Recall that this kanji popp[ed] up in the "Less Common Pronunciations" secti[on] of 道 (Entry 122).

Less Common Pronunciations

Less common **ON** reading: none
Less common **kun** readings: **kan** (か ん);
kō (こ う)

Common Pronunciations

Common **ON** reading: **SHIN** (シ ン); **JIN** (ジ ン)
Common **kun** reading: **kami** (か み)

COMMON WORDS AND COMPOUNDS		
神	God	**kami** か み
神話	God + speak = *myth; mythology*	**SHIN·WA** シ ン · ワ
神社	God + company = *Shinto shrine*	**JIN·JA** ジ ン · ジ ャ

KANJI 254

亡 **PERISH**

¹	一	亡					

BUILDING THIS KANJI
Police ⼇ + Forklift ∟ = 亡

Meaning
Perish, die.

Remembering this kanji

"The load must have been too great," said the **policewoman**, laying her hat over the **forklift**. "It's always tragic when a **forklift** PERISHES," said her partner. "Especially when it has to PERISH on duty."

Common Pronunciations

Common **ON** reading: **BŌ** (ボ ウ)
Common **kun** reading: **na** (な)

Create your **on-yomi** keyword and enter it in [the] table at the back of the book. Then, after creati[ng] your **kun-yomi** keyword, write your sentence [to] remember the **on-yomi** and **kun-yomi** readings [in] the box below.

Less Common Pronunciations
Less common **ON** reading: none **MŌ** (モ ウ)
Less common **kun** readings: **horo** (ほ ろ)

COMMON WORDS AND COMPOUNDS		
亡くなる	*die; pass away*	**na·kunaru** な · く な [る]
死亡	death + perish = *death*	**SHI·BŌ** シ · ボ ウ

KANJI 255

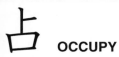

占   OCCUPY

| 丨 | 卜 | 丄 | 占 | 占 | | | |

BUILDING THIS KANJI
Good Figure Skater 卜 + Mouth (vampire)
ロ (8) = 占

Meaning
This character appears in only a few words (although it figures prominently in the makeup of several more common kanji), but has two meanings that are oddly unrelated: "occupy" and "fortune telling".

Remembering this kanji
A **good figure skater** always wants to OCCUPY the top of the podium. In a sense, this is like a **vampire** striving to OCCUPY the best coffin.

Common Pronunciations
Common **ON** reading: **SEN** (セン)
Common **kun** reading: **urana** (うらな)

Less Common Pronunciations
Less common **ON** reading: none
Less common **kun** readings: **shi** (し)

COMMON WORDS AND COMPOUNDS		
占う	*tell fortunes*	**urana·u** うらな・う
占有	occupy + have = *occupy*	**SEN·YŪ** セン・ユウ

COMPONENT #256

STRAW

KANJI 256

世   SOCIETY

| 一 | 十 | 卅 | 卋 | 世 | | | |

BUILDING THIS KANJI
Straw 廿 + Forklift └ = 世

Meaning
This interesting kanji encompasses the idea of society. It finds expression in such terms as 'the age', 'the times' and 'the era'.

Remembering this kanji

Marx, on SOCIETY:

SOCIETY is conflict. Some elements are content to siphon from SOCIETY what they will (the so-called "**straws**"), while others strive to raise it to a higher plane (those whom I have termed "**forklifts**").

Common Pronunciations
Common **ON** reading: **SE** (セ); **SEI** (セイ)
Common **kun** reading: none

SE is the overwhelming choice in first position, **SEI** in second. Note the second compound below: this is one of only two words in which 間 carries its less common **on-yomi** of **KEN** (ケン). The other compound, incidentally, means 'humanity', and sees the reading voiced: 人間 NIN·GEN (ニ ン・ゲン), from the kanji 'person' and 'interval'.

Create your **on-yomi** keyword for SE (セ) and enter it in the table at the back of the book. Then, write your sentence to remember the **on-yomi** readings in the box below.

COMMON WORDS AND COMPOUNDS		
世話	society + speak = *help; service*	**SE·WA** セ・ワ
世間	society + interval = *society; life*	**SE·KEN** セ・ケン
中世	middle + society = *the Middle Ages*	CHŪ·**SEI** チュウ・セイ

Less Common Pronunciations
Less common **ON** reading: none
Less common **kun** readings: **yo** (よ)

KANJI 257

FIXED

'	' '	'	'	'	'	'	'

BUILDING THIS KANJI
Pincers 宀 + **Surfer** 疋 = 定

Meaning
Fixed in time or place. Regular, definite.

Remembering this kanji
The **pincers** were carefully lowered, and another novice **surfer** was FIXED onto his board. "Yeah, it's risky," said one of the laid-off surfing instructors, "but the management of that surf school is really FIXED on reducing expenses."

Common Pronunciations
Common **ON** reading: **TEI** (テイ)
Common **kun** reading: **sada** (さだ)

Create your **on-yomi** keyword and enter it in the table at the back of the book. Then write your sentence to remember the **on-yomi** and **kun-yomi** readings in the box below.

Less Common Pronunciations
Less common **ON** reading: **JŌ** (ジョウ)
Less common **kun** readings: none

COMMON WORDS AND COMPOUNDS		
定まる (intr)	*to be fixed / determined*	**sada**·maru さだ・まる
定める (tr)	*to decide; determine*	**sada**·meru さだ・める
安定	ease + fixed = *stability*	AN·**TEI** アン・テイ
定食	fixed + eat = *set meal*	**TEI**·SHOKU テイ・ショ〈

KANJI 258

PAPER

￲	￳	￴	￵	￶	￷	￸	￹	紅
紙								

BUILDING THIS KANJI
Thread 糸 (196) + **Surname** 氏 (234) = 紙

Meaning
paper.

Common Pronunciations
Common **ON** reading: **SHI** (シ)
Common **kun** reading: **kami** (か み)

Remembering this kanji
PAPER runs like a **thread** through your family,"
e said, bringing out a dusty roll of PAPER.
Just look at this **surname**: that was your great
ncle, a PAPER manufacturer. And follow the
thread to this **surname** here: your grandfather,
PAPER miller. So do you understand? Your
PAPER obsession is nothing to worry about."

The **kun-yomi** is almost always voiced when
not in first position (as it appears in the second
compound below).

Less Common Pronunciations
Less common **ON** reading: none
Less common **kun** readings: none

COMMON WORDS AND COMPOUNDS		
紙	*paper*	kami か み
手紙	hand + paper = *letter*	te·**gami** て·が み
和紙	harmony (Japan) + paper = *Japanese paper*	WA·**SHI** ワ·シ

  APPEARANCE

一	丷	爫	爫	平	平	采	采	

BUILDING THIS KANJI
Stroller 爫 + Tree 木(13) = 采

Meaning
Appearance, the look of something.

Remembering this kanji
'I can't believe it, the **stroller** landed on top of
a **tree**!"
'Yes, he really is the best at **stroller** toss. His
gaze, his bearing - everything in his APPEAR-
ANCE suggests it."

Common Pronunciations
Common **ON** reading: **SAI** (サ イ)
Common **kun** reading: none

Less Common Pronunciations
Less common **ON** reading: none
Less common **kun** readings: none

COMMON WORDS AND COMPOUNDS		
采	*Appearance*	SAI サ イ
風采	wind + appearance = *appearance; bearing*	FŪ·**SAI** フ ウ·サ イ

KANJI 260

ARMY

BUILDING THIS KANJI
UFO ⌐ + **Car** 車 (190) = 軍

Meaning
Army, military.

Remembering this kanji
"Look at their ARMY," sneered one of the aliens in the **UFO**. They still have **cars**!"
"Don't underestimate their ARMY because of that," said another. "I tried to drive a **car** once, and never could figure out how to use the clutch."

Common Pronunciations
Common **ON** reading: **GUN** (グン)
Common **kun** reading: none

Create your **on-yomi** keyword and enter it in th table at the back of the book. After that, writ your sentence to remember the **on-yomi** readin in the box below.

Less Common Pronunciations
Less common **ON** reading: none
Less common **kun** readings: none

COMMON WORDS AND COMPOUNDS		
軍人	army + person = *military person; soldier*	**GUN**·JIN グン・ジン
海軍	sea + army = *navy*	**KAI·GUN** カイ・グン
空軍	empty (sky) + army = *air force*	**KŪ·GUN** クウ・グン

KANJI 261

 ELDER SISTER

〈	丿	女	女'	女⁻	女⁻	女市	姉

BUILDING THIS KANJI
Woman 女 (16) + **City** 市 (163) = 姉

Meaning
Elder sister.

Remembering this kanji
"Why does Charlotte always get to visit the **city**?" they asked, pouting.
"Because she's your ELDER SISTER, that's why."
"That's right," said Charlotte. "I'm your ELDER SISTER, which means that I'm a **woman**, and you're still babies."
Even if she was their ELDER SISTER, there was no need for Charlotte to be so mean to the other Brontë girls.

Common Pronunciations
Common **ON** reading: **SHI** (シ)
Common **kun** reading: **ane** (あね)

Less Common Pronunciations
Less common **ON** reading: none
Less common **kun** readings: none

IRREGULAR READING		
お姉さん	*elder sister*	**o·nē**·san お・ねえ・さん

As we saw with a similar word for 兄, this is a more polite form of address.

COMMON WORDS AND COMPOUNDS		
姉	*elder sister*	**ane** あね
姉妹	elder sister + younger sister = *sister (city/company, etc.)*	**SHI·MAI** シ・マイ
姉妹 都市	sister + metropolis + city = *sister city*	**SHI·MAI·TO·SHI** シ・マイ・ト・シ

KANJI 262

SHEEP

Meaning
Sheep. No story required.

Common Pronunciations
Common **ON** reading: none
Common **kun** reading: **hitsuji** (ひつぎ)

Less Common Pronunciations
Less common **ON** reading: **YŌ** (ヨウ)
Less common **kun** readings: none

COMMON WORDS AND COMPOUNDS		
羊	*sheep*	**hitsuji** ひつじ
子羊	child + sheep = *lamb*	**ko·hitsuji** こ・ひつじ

COMPONENT #263

MERGING

KANJI 263

介 **INTERVENE**

BUILDING THIS KANJI
Umbrella へ + Merging 八 = 介

Meaning
Intervene, mediate.

Remembering this kanji
So you've noticed that your teenaged daughter is sharing an **umbrella** with her boyfriend, and that they've started **merging**. There's no need to INTERVENE; they're just sheltering from the weather.

Common Pronunciations

Common **ON** reading: **KAI** (カ イ)
Common **kun** reading: none

Less Common Pronunciations

Less common **ON** reading: none
Less common **kun** readings: none

COMMON WORDS AND COMPOUNDS		
介入	intervene + enter = *intervention*	**KAI**·NYŪ カイ·ニュウ
不介入	not + intervene + enter = *nonintervention*	FU·**KAI**·NYŪ フ·カイ·ニュ

KANJI 264

PLATFORM

㇄	㇇	台	台	台			

BUILDING THIS KANJI
Broken Crutch ㇄ + Mouth (vampire) 口 (8)
= 台

Meaning
This kanji relates to objects that tend to be flat and elevated (think of such things as tables, stands, flatlands and stages, etc.) It's also used as a counter for machinery and vehicles.

Remembering this kanji
It had always been a struggle for the **vampire** to blend in at his local disco. So then given he was on **crutches**, why had he taken his moves onto the raised PLATFORM? It was hardly a surprise that he would have an accident and end up with a **broken crutch**, what with his already shaky footing and the ridiculous PLATFORM shoes he'd put on.

Common Pronunciations

Common **ON** reading: **DAI** (ダ イ); **TAI** (タ
Common **kun** reading: none

DAI is the far more common reading. Note t
mix of on and **kun-yomi** in the first compou
below.

Less Common Pronunciations

Less common **ON** reading: none
Less common **kun** readings: none

COMMON WORDS AND COMPOUNDS		
台所	platform + location = *kitchen*	**DAI**·dokoro ダイ·どころ
天文台	heaven + literature + platform = *astronomical observatory*	TEN·MON·D テン·モン·ダイ
台風	platform + wind = *typhoon*	**TAI**·FŪ タイ·フウ

KANJI 265

HASTEN

ノ	㇇	刍	刍	刍	刍	急	急	急

BUILDING THIS KANJI
Little Red Riding Hood ㇇ + Comb ヨ +
Heart 心 (25) = 急

Meaning
Hasten, and the sense of things being urger
or sudden.

Remembering this kanji

"I must HASTEN home," said **Little Red Riding Hood**, HASTENING to run a **comb** through her curly locks.

"Yes, by all means HASTEN," said the surgeon, "but please remember your **heart** condition."

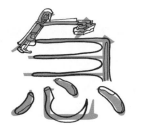

Common Pronunciations

Common **ON** reading: **KYŪ** (キュウ)
Common **kun** reading: **iso** (いそ)

Less Common Pronunciations

Less common **ON** reading: none
Less common **kun** readings: none

COMMON WORDS AND COMPOUNDS		
急ぐ	*hasten; go quickly*	**iso**·gu いそ·ぐ
急変	hasten + alter = *sudden change*	**KYŪ·HEN** キュウ·ヘン
急降下	hasten + descend + lower = *nose dive*	**KYŪ·KŌ·KA** キュウ·コウ·カ

KANJI 266

州   **STATE**

ノ	リ	州	州	州			

BUILDING THIS KANJI

Jelly Beans (3 of them) ヽ + **River** 川(70) = 州

Meaning

The political subdivision of a 'state' or 'province'.

Remembering this kanji

This is another of those rare characters we will learn (recall the kanji for "east" (東) from Entry 76) whose stroke order does not follow that of the components as listed above.

"Which STATE are we in?" asked the tourist, squinting at his map.

"A STATE is an arbitrary political subdivision," answered the philosopher. "They drift away, having as much permanence as a trio of **jelly beans** cast into a **river**."

Common Pronunciations

Common **ON** reading: **SHŪ** (シュウ)
Common **kun** reading: none

With the two compounds below you are now able to read the names of Japan's four main islands – the other two being Hokkaido and Shikoku: 北海道 (HOK·KAI·DŌ·/ホッ·カイ·ドウ), 四国 (SHI·KOKU/シ·コク).

Less Common Pronunciations

Less common **ON** reading: none
Less common **kun** readings: **su** (す)

COMMON WORDS AND COMPOUNDS		
本州	main + state = *Honshu*	**HON·SHŪ** ホン·シュウ
九州	nine + state = *Kyushu*	**KYŪ·SHŪ** キュウ·シュウ

KANJI 267

辛　**SPICY**

'	亠	゙	立	立	辛		

BUILDING THIS KANJI
Stand 立 (112) + Ten (scarecrow) 十 (28) = 辛

Common Pronunciations
Common **ON** reading: none
Common **kun** reading: **kara** (か ら)

Less Common Pronunciations
Less common **ON** reading: **SHIN** (シ ン)
Less common **kun** readings: none

COMMON WORDS AND COMPOUNDS		
辛い	*spicy; hot*	**kara·i** か ら·い
辛口	spicy + mouth = *dry* *(saké / wine)*	**kara·kuchi** か ら·く ち

Meaning
Spicy, pungent. By extension, this kanji is also used in some compounds to express the ideas of hardship and trials.

Remembering this kanji
She could do nothing but **stand** over the **scarecrow** in disbelief, the curry dinner she had made still in her oven mitts. "But…your dating profile said you were fond of SPICY food," she stammered.

"I'm sorry, but you must have confused me with someone else. I'm a **scarecrow**; I'm not into anything, SPICY or otherwise."

COMPONENT #268

FERN　厂

KANJI 268

服　**CLOTHES**

）	刀	月	月	肜	肝	服	服	

BUILDING THIS KANJI
Moon 月 (11) + Fern 厂 + Again (ironing board) 又 (159) = 服

Meaning
Clothes. One secondary meaning relates to the ideas of 'obey' and 'submission', while another, curiously, has to do with a 'dose' of something (the second compound offers an example).

emembering this kanji

s interesting how CLOTHES are important to me and not to others. The **moon**, for instance, s trouble finding his size, so doesn't care much out CLOTHES. **Ferns**, though, grow in damp imates, and because of this insist on having LOTHES that are waterproof and breathable. nd an **ironing board**? Well, an **ironing board** obsessed with CLOTHES, isn't it?

ommon Pronunciations

•mmon **ON** reading: **FUKU** (フク)
mmon **kun** reading: none

call from Entry 157 that the first two kanji in final compound mean 'student' when taken ;ether.

Create your **on-yomi** keyword and enter it in the table at the back of the book. After that, write your sentence to remember the **on-yomi** reading in the box below.

Less Common Pronunciations

Less common **ON** reading: none
Less common **kun** readings: none

COMMON WORDS AND COMPOUNDS		
服	*clothes*	**FUKU** フク
一服	one + clothes (dose) = *a dose; a smoke; a rest*	**IP·PUKU** イッ・プク
学生服	student + clothes = *school uniform*	**GAKU·SEI·FUKU** ガク・セイ・フク

ANJI 269

LUCKY

一	十	士	士	吉	吉		

UILDING THIS KANJI

;entleman 士 (84) + **Mouth (vampire)** 口 (8)
吉

leaning

ucky, fortunate.

emembering this kanji

t would seem, kind **gentleman**," hissed the ampire as he drew off, "that today is your UCKY day."
LUCKY indeed," said the **gentleman**. "But do low me to apologize for having garlic breath."

ommon Pronunciations

•mmon **ON** reading: **KICHI** (キチ);
ITSU (キツ)
•mmon **kun** reading: none

This is another of those quirky kanji that have multiple common readings and only a few compounds.

Create your **on-yomi** keywords and enter them in the table at the back of the book. After that, write your sentence to remember the **on-yomi** readings in the box below.

Less Common Pronunciations

Less common **ON** reading: none
Less common **kun** readings: none

COMMON WORDS AND COMPOUNDS		
吉日	lucky + sun (day) = *lucky day*	**KICHI·JITSU** キチ・ジツ
不吉	not + lucky = *unlucky*	**FU·KITSU** フ・キツ

KANJI 270

用 UTILIZE

|) | 刀 | 月 | 月 | 用 | | | |

BUILDING THIS KANJI
Moon 月 (11) + Pole | = 用

Meaning
Utilize. This important kanji also has the sense of a person's 'business' or 'errands'. It is often translated as "for" when used as the last character in a compound (illustrated by the final example below).

Remembering this kanji
"I don't understand why the **moon** has a **pole**. What could he UTILIZE it for?"
"He could UTILIZE it for **pole** vaulting, he could UTILIZE it for rafting…he could UTILIZE it for lots of stuff."

Common Pronunciations
Common **ON** reading: **YŌ** (ヨ ウ)
Common **kun** reading: none

Note the unusual reading for 心 in the seco
example; it is extremely rare for this kanji
become voiced like this.

Less Common Pronunciations
Less common **ON** reading: none
Less common **kun** readings: **mochi** (も ち)

COMMON WORDS AND COMPOUNDS		
用事	utilize + matter = *business; things to be done*	**YŌ·JI** ヨ ウ・ジ
用心	utilize + heart = *caution; care*	**YŌ·JIN** ヨ ウ・ジン
男子用	man + child + utilize = *for men; men's*	DAN·SHI·YŌ ダン・シ・ヨ

COMPONENT #271

ICE HOCKEY　

KANJI 271

次 NEXT

| ` | 冫 | 冫 | 汐 | 方 | 次 | | |

BUILDING THIS KANJI
Ice Hockey 冫 + Lack 欠 (246) = 次

Meaning
Next, following.

Remembering this kanji
So you want to have a game of **ice hockey**? Wel
it looks as though you **lack** some items. Fir
get some skates and sticks. NEXT, get a puc
NEXT, helmets. NEXT, an arena, and NEXT
couple of teams.

mmon Pronunciations
mmon **ON** reading: **JI** (ジ)
mmon **kun** reading: **tsu** (つ); **tsugi** (つぎ)

is the most common of these readings. **tsu** is und only as the verb in the second example low.

ss Common Pronunciations
ss common **ON** reading: **SHI** (シ)
ss common **kun** readings: none

This reading is found in only one word, 次第, which we met earlier as the last compound for 第 in Entry 243.

COMMON WORDS AND COMPOUNDS		
次	*next*	**tsugi** 次
次ぐ	*come after; follow*	**tsu**·gu つ·ぐ
目次	eye + next = *table of contents*	MOKU·**JI** モク·ジ

ANJI 272

低 **LOW**

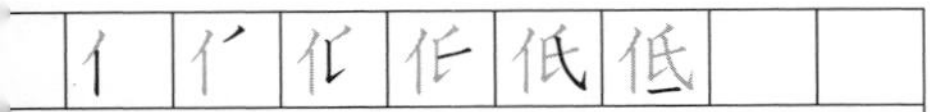

UILDING THIS KANJI
iraffe 亻 + **Surname** 氏(234) + **One hamburger patty)** 一(3) = 低

leaning
ow.

emembering this kanji
LOW! LOW! LOW!" the crowd roared.
Come on, Mrs. Zebra," said the trainer, holding ut a **hamburger patty**.
LOW! LOW! LOW!"
Look at the tasty **hamburger patty**…"
he **giraffe** could take it no longer. "What kind f crazy zoo is this?" she yelled. "My **surname** Giraffe, and **hamburger patties** aren't in my iet. But even if they were, I wouldn't LOWER yself to do a limbo dance to get one."

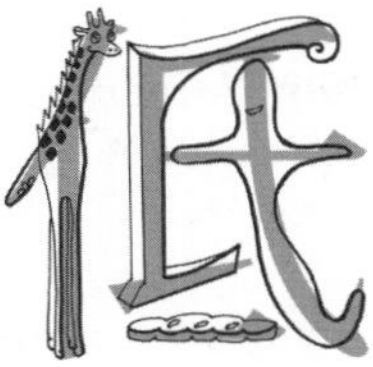

Common Pronunciations
Common **ON** reading: **TEI** (テイ)
Common **kun** reading: **hiku** (ひく)

Less Common Pronunciations
Less common **ON** reading: none
Less common **kun** readings: none

COMMON WORDS AND COMPOUNDS		
低い	*low*	**hiku**·i ひく·い
低下	low + lower = *lowering; decline*	**TEI**·KA テイ·カ
低速	low + fast = *low speed*	**TEI**·SOKU テイ·ソク

KANJI 273

孝 FILIAL PIETY

| 一 | 十 | 土 | 少 | 耂 | 考 | 孝 | | |

BUILDING THIS KANJI
Earth 土(87) + Comet 一 + Child 子(56) = 孝

Meaning
Filial piety, obedience to one's parents.

Remembering this kanji
She was a **child** of the **earth**, and was famed for her FILIAL PIETY. She tended the **earth** carefully, raking it with great affection and sprinkling it gently. It was rumored that a **comet** had once flashed between her and the **earth**, but that even then she had not been distracted. I'm totally serious: the **child** had that much FILIAL PIETY.

Common Pronunciations
Common **ON** reading: **KO** (コウ)
Common **kun** reading: none

Note the mix of **on** and **kun-yomi** in the t
sample compounds.

Less Common Pronunciations
Less common **ON** reading: none
Less common **kun** readings: none

COMMON WORDS AND COMPOUNDS		
親孝行	parent + filial piety + go = *filial piety*	oya·**KŌ**·KŌ おや·コウ·コ
親不孝	parent + not + filial piety = *lack of filial piety*	oya·FU·**KŌ** おや·フ·コウ

COMPONENT #274

ZOMBIE

KANJI 274

茶 TEA

| 一 | 十 | 艹 | 艹 | 芯 | 荟 | 苯 | 茶 | 茶 |

BUILDING THIS KANJI
Wreath 艹 + Umbrella 𠆢 + Zombie 朩 = 茶

Meaning
Tea.

Remembering this kanji
Zombies, I feel, get a bad rap. Why? Wel
with no lust for glory, they shun any **wreat**
given them. And the idea of a **zombie** using a
umbrella? It wouldn't happen in a hurrican
TEA, however, finds favor. As one **zombie** tol
me: "Oh sure, I may rampage as one of th
undead, but that doesn't mean I don't enjoy
spot of TEA in the afternoon".

Common Pronunciations
Common **ON** reading: **CHA** (チャ)
Common **kun** reading: none

Create your **on-yomi** keyword and enter it in th
table at the back of the book. After that, wri

ur sentence to remember the **on-yomi** reading
the box below.

SA·DŌ / サ・ドウ), composed of the kanji 'tea'
and 'road' (in this instance, better translated as
the 'way').

COMMON WORDS AND COMPOUNDS		
茶	*tea*	**CHA** チャ
茶色	tea + color = *brown*	**CHA·iro** チャ・いろ
茶室	tea + room = *tea room*	**CHA·SHITSU** チャ・シツ

ess Common Pronunciations
ess common **ON** reading: **SA** (サ)
ess common **kun** readings: none

hough not common, this reading does show up
the Japanese word for 'tea ceremony' (茶道 :

PROFIT

〟 二 千 禾 禾 利 利

BUILDING THIS KANJI
Crops 禾 + Chisel 刂 = 利

Meaning
Profit, advantage.

Remembering this kanji
"Buck up, farmer," he told himself. "Nobody
said it would be easy making a PROFIT, so grab
hat **chisel** and get every last grain out of those
crops."
    He'd expected it to be tough, but still…how
had he made so much more PROFIT as a sculptor?

Common Pronunciations
Common **ON** reading: **RI** (リ)
Common **kun** reading: **ki** (き)

Less Common Pronunciations
Less common **ON** reading: none
Less common **kun** readings: none

COMMON WORDS AND COMPOUNDS		
利く	*take effect; work*	**ki·ku** き・く
利子	profit + child = *interest (on money)*	**RI·SHI** リ・シ
利口	profit + mouth = *smart; clever*	**RI·KŌ** リ・コウ

NOT YET

一 二 キ 才 未

BUILDING THIS KANJI
One (hamburger patty) 一 (3) + Tree 木 (13)
= 未

Meaning
Not yet. This kanji is invariably used as the first
in a compound to indicate something incomplete
or unfinished.

Remembering this kanji

Because they are so visually similar, we will be learning this character together with that of the next entry in order to focus on how to tell them apart. It would also be wise at this point to review the stroke order of 本 ("Main" from Entry 68), to see clearly how it differs from the present kanji.

"Have you girls seen the **hamburger patty tree**?"
"NOT YET!" they said excitedly.
"Well," he chuckled, "here it is. Look at that cute little **hamburger patty** growing at the top."
"Can we pick it?"
"NOT YET," he cautioned. "It's NOT YET ready."

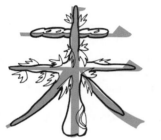

Common Pronunciations

Common **ON** reading: MI (ミ)
Common **kun** reading: none

Create your **on-yomi** keyword and enter it in th table at the back of the book. After that, wri your sentence to remember the **on-yomi** readir in the box below.

Less Common Pronunciations

Less common **ON** reading: none
Less common **kun** readings: none

COMMON WORDS AND COMPOUNDS		
未来	not yet + come = *future; future tense*	**MI·RAI** ミ・ライ
未定	not yet + fixed = *undecided; pending*	**MI·TEI** ミ・テイ
未開発	not yet + open + discharge = *undeveloped*	**MI·KAI·HATSU** ミ・カイ・ハツ

KANJI 277

END

一	二	丰	才	末			

BUILDING THIS KANJI
One (hamburger patty) 一(3) + Tree 木(13) = 末

Meaning
The "end" of things, in space as well as time.

Remembering this kanji

Were you able to quickly spot the difference between this kanji and that of the preceding entry? The story and illustration, hopefully, will help in remembering that the top stroke here is longer than that of 未.

"Here's another **hamburger patty tree**," he said. "Notice how the **hamburger patty** here is fully formed; it's even grown past the END of the **tree** tips."
"Oh, I wish this wasn't the END of the tour," said one of the girls.
"So do I," he murmured, "but we have to realize that to everything there is an END."

Common Pronunciations

Common **ON** reading: **MATSU** (マ ツ)
Common **kun** reading: none

Create your **on-yomi** keyword and enter it in the table at the back of the book. After that, write your sentence to remember the **on-yomi** reading in the box below.

Less Common Pronunciations

Less common **ON** reading: **BATSU** (バ ツ)
Less common **kun** readings: **sue** (す え)

COMMON WORDS AND COMPOUNDS		
週末	week + end = *weekend*	SHŪ·MATSU シュウ·マツ
年末	year + end = *end of the year*	NEN·MATSU ネン·マツ
末期	end + period = *last stage*	MAK·KI マッ·キ

COMPONENT #278

SCISSORS   十   十

KANJI 278

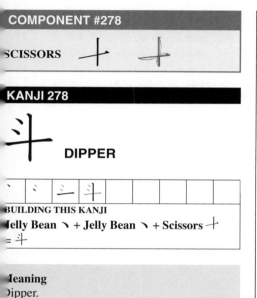

DIPPER

`	`	`	斗				

BUILDING THIS KANJI

Jelly Bean ` + Jelly Bean ` + Scissors 十
= 斗

Meaning

Dipper.

Remembering this kanji

This is another uncommon character that will be encountered far more often as a component in other kanji. It is most easily remembered through the compound below.

This kanji makes it obvious how inadequately **jelly beans** could be gathered with **scissors**. Even a couple of **jelly beans** — like the ones that have slipped through the **scissors** here — could be picked up much more easily with a DIPPER.

Common Pronunciations

Common **ON** reading: **TO** (ト)
Common **kun** reading: none

Less Common Pronunciations

Less common **ON** reading: none
Less common **kun** readings: none

COMMON WORDS AND COMPOUNDS		
北斗 七星	north + dipper + seven + star = *the Big Dipper*	HOKU·TO·SHICHI·SEI ホク·ト·シチ·セイ

KANJI 279

遊 PLAY

BUILDING THIS KANJI
Direction 方 (223) + **Hammer** 𠂉 + **Child** 子 (56) + **Seal** 辶 = 遊

Meaning
Make sure to have fun with this kanji, as it's all about play and amusement. The combination of the 'direction' character and 'hammer' component, incidentally, will show up often in other kanji.

Remembering this kanji
Give the **child** of a **seal** hunter a **hammer** and he'll look in every **direction** for a **seal** to PLAY with. But what about the **seal**? Well, the **seal** will glance in various **directions** too, only a lot more nervously. Because let's be honest, if you're a **seal** and you spot that **child** coming at you with a **hammer**, the last thing you'll want to do is PLAY with him.

Common Pronunciations
Common **ON** reading: **YŪ** (ユウ)
Common **kun** reading: **aso** (あそ)

Less Common Pronunciations
Less common **ON** reading: **YU** (ユ)
Less common **kun** readings: none

COMMON WORDS AND COMPOUNDS		
遊ぶ	*play*	**aso**·bu あそ·ぶ
遊泳	play + swim = *swimming*	**YŪ**·EI ユウ·エイ
遊園地	play + garden + ground = *amusement park; playground*	**YŪ**·EN·CHI ユウ·エン·チ

KANJI 280

豆 BEAN

BUILDING THIS KANJI
One (top of a bun) 一 (3) + **Mouth (vampire)** 口 (8) + **Snowboard** 䒑 = 豆

Meaning
Bean.

Remembering this kanji
If everyone were crazy about BEANS:

a) BEANS, instead of sesame seeds, would b
put on the **top of a bun**.
b) **Vampires** could lure their victims with
promise of BEANS.
c) Those who liked to **snowboard** would rathe
be knee-deep in BEANS than fresh powde

Common Pronunciations
Common **ON** reading: none
Common **kun** reading: **mame** (まめ)

Less Common Pronunciations

Less common **ON** reading: **ZU** (ズ); **TŌ** (ト ウ)
Less common **kun** readings: none

ZU appears only in the word for 'soybean' 大豆 (**DAI·ZU** / ダ イ ・ ズ) made from the kanji for 'large' and 'bean'. **TŌ** is the pronunciation when this kanji shows up in the famous Japanese word 'tofu' 豆腐 * (**TŌ·FU** / ト ウ ・ フ), formed from the kanji 'bean' and 'rot' (the latter character does not appear in this book).

COMMON WORDS AND COMPOUNDS		
豆	*bean*	**mame** まめ

CHAPTER 13 REVIEW EXERCISES

A. Please match the following kanji to their meanings.

1.	神	a.	Bean
2.	利	b.	Next
3.	羊	c.	Sheep
4.	紙	d.	Tea
5.	茶	e.	God
6.	遊	f.	Hasten
7.	急	g.	Paper
8.	世	h.	Play
9.	次	i.	Society
10.	豆	j.	Profit

B. Please match the following meanings to their kanji, and these to their **on** or **kun-yomi**.

1.	Army	a. 画	1.	**FUKU** (フク)
2.	Painting	b. 末	2.	**na** (な)
3.	State	c. 定	3.	**MATSU** (マツ)
4.	Elder sister	d. 軍	4.	**GUN** (グン)
5.	Clothes	e. 姉	5.	**SHŪ** (シュウ)
6.	Fixed	f. 未	6.	**MI** (ミ)
7.	End	g. 服	7.	**ane** (あね)
8.	Perish	h. 辛	8.	**sada** (さだ)
9.	Spicy	i. 州	9.	**GA** (ガ)
10.	Not yet	j. 亡	10.	**kara** (から)

C. Please choose the best answer(s) to the following questions.

1. Which is the correct reading of 低い?
   a. **waka·i** (わか・い)
   b. **hiku·i** (ひく・い)
   c. **ara·i** (あら・い)
   d. **kuro·i** (くろ・い)

2. That falling grand piano just missed you! You're sure ___ .
   a. 辛 b. 台 c. 豆 d. 吉 e. 釆

3. Which of the following readings apply to the kanji 神?
   a. **JIN** (ジン) b. **karu** (かる)
   c. **SHI** (シ) d. **kami** (かみ)
   e. **SHIN** (シン)

4. Which of the following kanji has the m number of strokes?
   a. 画 b. 服 c. 急 d. 定 e. 姉

5. Which of the following readings apply the kanji 世?
   a. **SHŪ** (シュウ) b. **SEI** (セイ)
   c. **SEN** (セン) d. **SE** (セ) e. **SHIN** (シン

D. Please match the following compounds to th meanings and pronunciations.

1.	介入	a. Smart/ Clever	1.	**SHI·BŌ** (シ・ボウ)
2.	用心	b. Kitchen	2.	**HOKU·TO· SHICHI·SEI** (ホク・ト・ シチ・セイ)
3.	利口	c. The Big Dipper	3.	**DAI·dokoro** (ダイ・どこ
4.	台所	d. Myth / Mythology	4.	**SHIN·WA** (シン・ワ)
5.	死亡	e. Occupy	5.	**KAI·NYŪ** (カイ・ニュ
6.	吉日	f. Death	6.	**KICHI·JITSU** (キチ・ジツ
7.	神話	g. Society / Life	7.	**RI·KŌ** (リ・コウ)
8.	占有	h. Intervention	8.	**SE·KEN** (セ・ケン)
9.	世間	i. Lucky day	9.	**YŌ·JIN** (ヨウ・ジン)
10.	北斗 七星	j. Caution / Care	10.	**SEN·YŪ** (セン・ユウ

E. Please read the passage below and answer questions that follow.

姉は茶道が大好きです。週末九 で有名な茶道の大会が有りま だから土曜日に電車で行くつも です。

1. What does this elder sister really like?
2. When is there a famous convention taking place
3. Where will this happen?
4. On which day will she go there?
5. How will she travel?

Kanji #281—305

KANJI 281

ROOF

BUILDING THIS KANJI

Flag 尸 + **Reach** 至 (239) = 屋

Meaning

Roof. When this kanji is the final character in a compound, it will often mean a 'shop' when referring to a building, or a 'dealer' when referring to a person.

Remembering this kanji

If you're able to grab a **flag** by simply making a **reach** for it, there's a decent chance you're on a ROOF.

Common Pronunciations

Common **ON** reading: **OKU** (オク)
Common **kun** reading: **ya** (や)

ya is by far the more common reading, and is invariably used when this kanji appears in the final position of a compound. There is often a mixture of **on** and **kun-yomi** in such words (as in the final two examples below).

Create your **on-yomi** keyword and enter it in the table at the back of the book. Then, after creating your **kun-yomi** keyword, write your sentence to remember the **on-yomi** and **kun-yomi** readings in the box below.

Less Common Pronunciations

Less common **ON** reading: none
Less common **kun** readings: none

COMMON WORDS AND COMPOUNDS		
屋上	roof + upper = *rooftop*	OKU·JŌ オク・ジョウ
本屋	main (book) + roof = *bookstore*	HON·ya ホン・や
料理屋	fee + reason + roof = *restaurant*	RYŌ·RI·ya リョウ・リ・や

KANJI 282

各 **EACH**

ノ	ク	夂	各	各	各		

BUILDING THIS KANJI

Running Chicken 夂 + Mouth (vampire) 口
(8) = 各

Meaning
Each.

Remembering this kanji
EACH **running chicken** behaved differently in the presence of the **vampire**. EACH was running scared, of course, but some zigged while others zagged. Oh well, it was up to EACH to get away, and EACH had their own strategy for doing so.

Common Pronunciations
Common **ON** reading: **KAKU** (カク)
Common **kun** reading: none

Less Common Pronunciations
Less common **ON** reading: none
Less common **kun** readings: **onoono** (おのおの)

COMMON WORDS AND COMPOUNDS		
各人	each + person = *each person*	**KAKU·JIN** カク・ジン
各地	each + ground = *each area*	**KAKU·CH** カク・チ

COMPONENT #283

SCRATCHES 彡

KANJI 283

形 **FORM**

一	二	于	开	开	形	形	

BUILDING THIS KANJI

Picnic Table 开 + Scratches 彡 = 形

Meaning
Form, shape, appearance.

Remembering this kanji
"Hard to tell. It had a weird FORM, though."
"What kind of FORM?"
"A hunched FORM."
She knelt down to examine the broken **picnic table** and noticed a trio of **scratches**. Could i have been done by the picnic-loving three-toed sloth? Perhaps, but a FORM alone wasn't much to go on…

Common Pronunciations
Common **ON** reading: **KEI** (ケイ)
Common **kun** reading: **katachi** (かたち);
kata (かた)

These readings can seem a bit confusing at first, but **katachi** is the choice when this kanji appears on its own; it such a case it means 'form' or 'shape'. In compounds, look for **KEI** in first position (with a notable exception being the second example below), and a split between **KEI** and **kata** after that, keeping in mind that **kata** is almost always voiced in such instances.

Less Common Pronunciations
Less common **ON** reading: **GYŌ** (ギョウ)
Less common **kun** readings: none

This is a very uncommon reading that you are only likely to meet in the word for 'doll', 人形 (NIN·GYŌ / ニン・ギョウ) from the kanji for 'person' and 'form'.

COMMON WORDS AND COMPOUNDS		
形	*form; shape*	**katachi** かたち
形見	form + see = *memento; keepsake*	**kata·mi** かた・み
手形	hand + form = *bill; draft; note*	**te·gata** て・がた
形成	form + become = *formation*	**KEI·SEI** ケイ・セイ

COMPONENT #284

BOWING

KANJI 284

的　**TARGET**

＇｜イ｜ｆ｜白｜白｜白＇｜的｜的

BUILDING THIS KANJI
White 白 (7) + Bowing 勹 + Jelly Bean ◥ =
的

Meaning
Target. This is an important character that is used as a suffix to express such ideas as the English equivalent of '-istic' in words such as 'artistic'. If you spend some time getting to know this kanji, you will quickly notice your vocabulary growing in sophistication.

Remembering this kanji
"What are you watching?" she asked.
He adjusted the binoculars. "I'm not sure. There's a little **white** object, and a guy's **bowing** over it...now he's hit it so high into the sky that it doesn't look any bigger than a **jelly bean**! Oh hang on...it seems he was aiming at a TARGET of some sort."
"Really?" she said. "I wonder what that TARGET could be?"

It would seem, apparently, that not everyone living next to a golf course understands the game.

Common Pronunciations
Common **ON** reading: **TEKI** (テキ)
Common **kun** reading: none

Recall from Entry 202 that 'literature' plus 'change' in the second example below means 'culture', and from Entry 177 that 'tool' plus 'body' in the third example means 'definite; concrete'.

Create your **on-yomi** keyword and enter it in the table at the back of the book. After that, write

your sentence to remember the **on-yomi** reading in the box below.

COMMON WORDS AND COMPOUNDS		
目的	eye + target = *purpose; aim*	MOKU·**TEKI** モク・テキ
文化的	culture + target = *cultural*	BUN·KA·**TEKI** ブン・カ・テキ
具体的	definite + target = *definite; specific; concrete*	GU·TAI·**TEKI** グ・タイ・テキ

Less Common Pronunciations
Less common **ON** reading: none
Less common **kun** readings: **mato** (まと)

KANJI 285

 **ARROW**

ノ	ヒ	ニ	ケ	矢			

BUILDING THIS KANJI
Hammer 宀 + Large (sumo wrestler) 大(17)
= 矢

Meaning
Arrow. As these are the same two components used to make the kanji for "Lose" (Entry 142), ensure that you able to tell them apart (the respective illustrations and stories should help).

Remembering this kanji
I tried to shoot an apple off a **sumo wrestler** wit an ARROW, but it would always be eaten befor the ARROW made it there. A **hammer** on hi head worked better, even if it was hard for hir to balance it and the ARROW never stuck in.

Common Pronunciations
Common **ON** reading: none
Common **kun** reading: **ya** (や)

Less Common Pronunciations
Less common **ON** reading: **SHI** (シ)
Less common **kun** readings: none

COMMON WORDS AND COMPOUNDS		
矢	*arrow*	**ya** や
弓矢	bow + arrow = *bow and arrow*	yumi·**ya** ゆみ・や

KANJI 286

 **WORLD**

丶	冂	冂	用	田	尹	甼	界	界

BUILDING THIS KANJI
Rice Field 田(73) + Intervene 介(263) = 界

Meaning
World, circles (in the sense of 'financial circles' or 'scientific circles', etc).

Remembering this kanji
Who cares if you've got your own **rice field**? There'll always be others wanting to **intervene** in it; that's how it is in this WORLD.

Common Pronunciations
Common **ON** reading: **KAI** (カイ)
Common **kun** reading: none

Less Common Pronunciations
Less common **ON** reading: none
Less common **kun** readings: none

COMMON WORDS AND COMPOUNDS		
世界	society + world = *the world*	**SE·KAI** セ・カイ
業界	business + world = *the business world*	**GYO·KAI** ギョウ・カイ
自然界	self + nature + world = *the world of nature*	**SHI·ZEN·KAI** シ・ゼン・カイ

CLIFF

KANJI 287

反 **AGAINST**

一	厂	厂	反				

BUILDING THIS KANJI
Cliff 厂 + Again (ironing board) 又(159) = 反

Meaning
Against, anti-.

Remembering this kanji
I tumbled down a **cliff** once and hurt myself. Stupid, arrogant **cliff**, soaring over everything else! I'm AGAINST cliffs. Another day I went into my closet and was struck by my **ironing board**. Grrrr. I'm AGAINST **ironing boards** too.

Common Pronunciations
Common **ON** reading: **HAN** (ハン)
Common **kun** reading: none

Less Common Pronunciations
Less common **ON** reading: **TAN** (タン);
HON (ホン)
Less common **kun** readings: **so** (そ)

COMMON WORDS AND COMPOUNDS		
反転	against + roll = *roll over; reverse*	**HAN·TEN** ハン・テン
反動	against + move = *reaction; recoil*	**HAN·DŌ** ハン・ドウ
反対	against + versus = *opposition; resistance*	**HAN·TAI** ハン・タイ

KANJI 288

良 **GOOD**

丶	ㄅ	ㄅ	ㄅ	戶	良	良		

BUILDING THIS KANJI
Jelly Bean 丶 + Frog 艮 = 良

Meaning
Good.

Remembering this kanji
When the 'jelly bean' component looks like
this, we'll think of it as balancing straight up
and down.

"GOOD…GOOD…keep at it…"
It's a GOOD exercise getting a **jelly bean** to
balance straight up and down on a **frog**. GOOD
for developing patience, GOOD for steadying
your movements, and GOOD for honing your
vision. I'm not sure how GOOD it is for the
frog, though.

Common Pronunciations
Common **ON** reading: **RYŌ** (リ ョ ウ)
Common **kun** reading: **yo** (よ)

Less Common Pronunciations
Less common **ON** reading: none
Less common **kun** readings: none

COMMON WORDS AND COMPOUNDS		
良い	good	yo·i よ・い
良心	good + heart = *conscience*	**RYŌ·SHIN** リ ョ ウ・シ)
良好	good + like = *good; satisfactory*	**RYŌ·KO** リ ョ ウ・コ)

KANJI 289

配 **DISTRIBUTE**

一	厂	冂	币	酉	酉	酉	酉⁻	酉⁻
配								

BUILDING THIS KANJI
Whiskey Jug 酉 + Oneself (whip) 己(214) = 配

Meaning
Distribute.

Remembering this kanji

If you've ever seen a **whiskey jug** and taken a **whip** to it, the chances are you're a pretty serious teetotaler. Given that, it wouldn't be smart for you to get a job where you'd have to DISTRIBUTE whiskey jugs. No, you'd likely find it more rewarding to DISTRIBUTE advice to those sorry whiskey drinkers instead.

Common Pronunciations

Common **ON** reading: **HAI** (ハイ)
Common **kun** reading: **kuba** (くば)

Less Common Pronunciations

Less common **ON** reading: none
Less common **kun** readings: none

COMMON WORDS AND COMPOUNDS		
配る	*distribute*	**kuba·ru** くば・る
配水	distribute + water = *water supply*	**HAI·SUI** ハイ・スイ
心配	heart + distribute = *worry; anxiety*	**SHIN·PAI** シン・パイ

SHERPA

KANJI 290

 FAR

一	十	土	士	吉	吉	声	専	寺
袁	袁	遠	遠					

BUILDING THIS KANJI
Earth 土(87) + Sherpa 呆 + Seal 辶 = 遠

Meaning
Far.

Remembering this kanji

"I bring you this **earth** from FAR away," said the **sherpa**, placing his pile next to the **seal**'s flippers.
"How FAR is FAR, **sherpa**?" demanded the **seal**.
"From Nepal."

That *is* FAR, thought the **seal**, grinning. If this keeps up, I'll soon have all the earth I need.

Common Pronunciations

Common **ON** reading: **EN** (エン)
Common **kun** reading: **tō** (とお)

Less Common Pronunciations

Less common **ON** reading: **ON** (オン)
Less common **kun** readings: none

COMMON WORDS AND COMPOUNDS		
遠い	*far; distant*	**tō·i** とお・い
遠足	far + leg = *excursion*	**EN·SOKU** エン・ソク
永遠	eternal + far = *eternity*	**EI·EN** エイ・エン

忘 FORGET

'	一	亡	亡	忘	忘	忘	

BUILDING THIS KANJI
Perish 亡 (254) + Heart 心 (25) = 忘

Meaning
Forget.

Remembering this kanji
"What does it mean to FORGET?" she asked her disciple. "Does everything **perish** in the **heart**?"
"Oh, darn it," he said, "I should be able to get this one. I have a feeling you told me earlier, but I FORGET."

Common Pronunciations
Common **ON** reading: **BŌ** (ボ ウ)
Common **kun** reading: **wasu** (わ す)

Less Common Pronunciations
Less common **ON** reading: none
Less common **kun** readings: none

COMMON WORDS AND COMPOUNDS		
忘れる	*forget*	**wasu**·reru わ す·れ る
忘れ物	forget + thing = *something left behind*	**wasu**·re mono わ す·れ もの
忘年会	forget + year + meet = *year-end party*	**BŌ**·NEN·KAI ボウ·ネン·カ

完 PERFECT

'	'	宀	宁	完	完	完	

BUILDING THIS KANJI
Pincers 宀 + Basis 元 (53) = 完

Meaning
Perfect, complete.

Remembering this kanji
"Hey boss," he asked, "when it comes to **pincers**, what is the **basis** of a PERFECT set?"
The **pincer** maker smiled. "Son, some will tell you the **basis** is PERFECT welding, others that it is PERFECT riveting. But don't be fooled: the **basis** of PERFECT **pincers** has – and always will be – how well they pick stuff up."

Common Pronunciations
Common **ON** reading: **KAN** (カ ン)
Common **kun** reading: none

Less Common Pronunciations
Less common **ON** reading: none
Less common **kun** readings: none

COMMON WORDS AND COMPOUNDS		
完全	perfect + complete = *perfection; completeness*	**KAN**·ZEN カン·ゼン
完成	perfect + become = *completion; accomplishment*	**KAN**·SEI カン·セイ
完結	perfect + bind = *completion; conclusion*	**KAN**·KETSU カン·ケツ

且
BESIDES

丨	冂	丹	且	且			

Meaning
Besides, moreover.

Remembering this kanji
We will assign this character the unrelated meaning of a **filing cabinet**. Why, you ask? Well, like 又 ('Again', which we know from Entry 159 as our 'ironing board'), it's obscure and not very common on its own. BESIDES, it has to be learned given that it pops up as a component in other kanji. BESIDES that, it looks like a **filing cabinet**.

Common Pronunciations
Common **ON** reading: none
Common **kun** reading: **ka** (か)

Less Common Pronunciations
Less common **ON** reading: **SHO** (ショ)
Less common **kun** readings: none

COMMON WORDS AND COMPOUNDS		
且つ	*besides*	**ka**·tsu か・つ

VETERAN YODELER

Just as we met the 'good figure skater' and 'poor figure skater' earlier, we will now meet a pair of yodelers. This present fellow is clearly a veteran yodeler: the raised-leg form and chubby physique are classic, and he projects his voice beautifully into open air. It is this latter fact, actually, that distinguishes the veteran yodeler; he always appears on the right-hand side of a kanji so that nothing interferes with his sound.

都
METROPOLIS

一	十	土	耂	耂	者	者	者	者⁷
者阝	都							

BUILDING THIS KANJI
Individual 者(93) + Veteran Yodeler 阝 = 都

Meaning
Metropolis, large city.

Remembering this kanji
Look, an **individual** can only succeed in getting heard in this METROPOLIS if they're like a **veteran yodeler**. I mean, it's a great big METROPOLIS for goodness sakes, and only a **veteran yodeler** could get noticed in such a noisy environment.

Common Pronunciations
Common **ON** reading: **TO** (ト)
Common **kun** reading: **miyako** (みやこ)

Less Common Pronunciations
Less common **ON** reading: **TSU** (ツ)
Less common **kun** readings: none

You will only meet this **on-yomi** in two compounds, the first being 都合 (**TSU·GŌ** / ツ·ゴウ) 'circumstances, arrangements' composed of the kanji 'metropolis' and 'match', the second 都度 (**TSU·DO** / ツ·ド) 'each time, whenev from the kanji 'metropolis' and 'degree'.

COMMON WORDS AND COMPOUNDS		
都	*metropolis; capital*	**miyako** みやこ
京都	capital + metropolis = *Kyoto*	KYŌ·**TO** キョウ·ト
首都	neck + metropolis = *capital city*	SHU·**TO** シュ·ト

COMPONENT #295

NOVICE YODELER ⻖

What a sorry sight! As we can see by the horrible posture and skinny physique, this is obviously a novice yodeler. And as the next kanji makes clear, he needs to learn not to yodel into other objects; sadly, however, he always does so by only showing up on the left-hand side of any kanji in which he appears.

KANJI 295

降 DESCEND

㇇	阝	阝	阝'	阝ク	阝夂	阝夅	阝夅	阝夅
降								

BUILDING THIS KANJI
Novice Yodeler ⻖ + **Running Chicken** 夂 + **Whirling Dervish** 㐄 = 降

Meaning
Descend, fall, surrender. This is the character used when describing the 'falling' of rain or snow, etc.

Remembering this kanji
You can never tell what will happen whe a plane DESCENDS. On my last flight, fo instance, I was sitting between a terrible **novic yodeler** who started to yodel when a **runnin chicken** flapped by him, and a **whirling dervis** who began to whirl. The whole episode made m a little nervous… I dunno, maybe I'm just on of those guys who doesn't like to DESCEND.

Common Pronunciations
Common **ON** reading: **KŌ** (コウ)
Common **kun** reading: **fu** (ふ)

Less Common Pronunciations
Less common **ON** reading: none
Less common **kun** readings: **o** (お)

This reading forms an intransitive/transitiv verb pair (降りる / 降ろす) that has the sam pronunciation as one we met earlier with th kanji 下 (Entry 31): 下りる / 下ろす. Th characters are sometimes used interchangeabl although you are more likely to see them writte as 下りる and 下ろす.

COMMON WORDS AND COMPOUNDS

降る	fall (rain / snow)	**fu**·ru ふ·る
降下	descend + lower = descent; landing	**KŌ**·KA コウ·カ
降水	descend + water = precipitation	**KŌ**·SUI コウ·スイ

KANJI 296

婚

MARRIAGE

| | 女 | 女 | 女´ | 妒 | 妒 | 姬 | 姬 | 婚 |
| 婚 | 婚 | | | | | | | |

BUILDING THIS KANJI

Woman 女 (16) + Surname 氏 (234) + Sun 日 (6) = 婚

Meaning

Marriage.

Remembering this kanji

MARRIAGE, in a lot of cultures, means that a **woman** essentially tosses her **surname** into the **sun**. She assumes another **surname**, of course, but there is disagreement nowadays as to whether this requirement of MARRIAGE is out-of-date.

Common Pronunciations

Common **ON** reading: **KON** (コ ン)
Common **kun** reading: none

Create your **on-yomi** keyword and enter it in the table at the back of the book. After that, write your sentence to remember the **on-yomi** reading in the box below.

Less Common Pronunciations

Less common **ON** reading: none
Less common **kun** readings: none

COMMON WORDS AND COMPOUNDS

離婚	separate + marriage = divorce	**RI**·**KON** リ·コン
結婚	bind + marriage = marriage	**KEK**·**KON** ケッ·コン
婚期	marriage + period = marriageable age	**KON**·**KI** コン·キ

KANJI 297

FESTIVAL

ノ	ク	タ	タ	タ⁊	癶	祭	祭	祭
祭	祭							

BUILDING THIS KANJI
Moon 月 (11) + **Again (ironing board)** 又 (159)
+ **Show** 示 (247) = 祭

Meaning
Festival. This kanji can also have some religious overtones in the senses of ritual and worship. Note that the first stroke of 'again' is clipped off in some fonts so that it does not pass through the second.

Remembering this kanji
"You here **moon** FESTIVAL? I **show** you. Nic price. No?...What?...**Ironing board** FESTI VAL? There is **ironing board** FESTIVAL No, no, come back! I **show** you **ironing boar** FESTIVAL! Then **moon** FESTIVAL."

Common Pronunciations
Common **ON** reading: **SAI** (サイ)
Common **kun** reading: **matsu** (まつ)

Less Common Pronunciations
Less common **ON** reading: none
Less common **kun** readings: none

COMMON WORDS AND COMPOUNDS		
祭り	*festival*	**matsu·**ri まつ·り
祭日	festival + sun (day) = *festival day*	**SAI·**JITSU サイ·ジツ
百年祭	hundred + year + festival = *centennial*	HYAKU·NEN·SA ヒャク·ネン· サイ

KANJI 298

FINGER

一	十	扌	扩	扗	扗	指	指	指

BUILDING THIS KANJI
Finger 扌 + **Gist** 旨 (244) = 指

Meaning
Finger, along with the senses of indicating and pointing. Note that this kanji never appears as a component in other characters; any reference to "finger" in future stories, therefore, will always be to 扌.

Remembering this kanji
Look, it makes sense for the **finger** component to be in the kanji for FINGER. That's the **gist** of it, anyway.

Common Pronunciations
Common **ON** reading: **SHI** (シ)
Common **kun** reading: **yubi** (ゆび); **sa** (さ)

As the second example shows, **sa** can become voiced outside of the first position.

Less Common Pronunciations
Less common **ON** reading: none
Less common **kun** readings: none

COMMON WORDS AND COMPOUNDS		
指	*finger*	**yubi** ゆび
目指す	eye + finger = *aim at*	me za·**su** め ざ·す
指名	finger + name = *nomination; designation*	**SHI·**MEI シ·メイ

DENTIST LIGHT

Ensure that you note the difference between this component and 厶, the 'broken crutch', introduced prior to Entry 131.

KANJI 299

予

BEFOREHAND

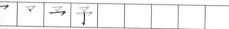

BUILDING THIS KANJI
Dentist Light マ + Harpoon 亅 = 予

Meaning
Beforehand, previously. As you may have guessed, it's unusual for a component to show up in different positions in the same kanji like this.

Remembering this kanji
'd had a sense BEFOREHAND that it wasn't going to be routine, and started to worry the moment my orthodontist turned on the **dentist light**.

"Hmm," she said, holding the **harpoon** first evenly, then straight up and down. My assistant told me BEFOREHAND that you had a whale of a cavity, but I wasn't expecting this. You should have taken care of it BEFOREHAND."

Common Pronunciations
Common **ON** reading: **YO** (ヨ)
Common **kun** reading: none

Create your **on-yomi** keyword and enter it in the table at the back of the book. After that, write your sentence to remember the **on-yomi** reading in the box below.

Less Common Pronunciations
Less common **ON** reading: none
Less common **kun** readings: none

COMMON WORDS AND COMPOUNDS		
予言	beforehand + say = *prediction*	**YO·GEN** ヨ・ゲン
予定	beforehand + fixed = *prearrangement; plan*	**YO·TEI** ヨ・テイ
予期	beforehand + period = *anticipation; expectation*	**YO·KI** ヨ・キ

 **ACTIVE**

`	⸝	⸜	氵	浐	浐	汗	汗	活	活

BUILDING THIS KANJI
Splash 氵 + Tongue 舌 (110) = 活

Meaning
Active, lively.

Remembering this kanji

"Look at that **tongue splash** around in the pool over there."

"Yeah, it does laps to keep ACTIVE."

Common Pronunciations

Common **ON** reading: **KATSU** (カ ツ)

Common **kun** reading: none

Create your **on-yomi** keyword and enter it in the table at the back of the book. After that, write your sentence to remember the **on-yomi** reading in the box below.

Less Common Pronunciations

Less common **ON** reading: none

Less common **kun** readings: none

	COMMON WORDS AND COMPOUNDS	
生活	life + active = *life; livelihood*	SEI·KATSU セイ・カツ
活気	active + spirit = *liveliness; vigor*	KAK·KI カッ・キ
活動	active + move = *activity; action*	KATSU·DŌ カツ・ドウ

KANJI 301

HARMONY

´	二	千	禾	禾	和	和	和

BUILDING THIS KANJI

Crops 禾 + Mouth (vampire) 口 (8) = 和

Meaning

Harmony, peace. This kanji is also used as an abbreviation for Japan in much the same way ' 日 ' is (the final compound offers an example of this usage).

Remembering this kanji

Crops have nothing to fear from **vampires**, since **vampires** have no interest in **crops**. Thus, there is HARMONY between them.

Common Pronunciations

Common **ON** reading: **WA** (ワ)

Common **kun** reading: none

Less Common Pronunciations

Less common **ON** reading: **O** (オ)

Less common **kun** readings: **yawa** (やわ);

nago (な ご)

	IRREGULAR READING	
大和	large + harmony = *ancient Japan*	yamato やまと
日和	sun + harmony = *fine weather*	hi·yori ひ・より

	COMMON WORDS AND COMPOUNDS	
和	*harmony*	WA ワ
平和	flat + harmony = *peace*	HEI·WA ヘイ・ワ
和食	harmony (Japan) + eat = *Japanese food*	WA·SHOKU ワ・ショク

KANJI 302

 経 **VIA**

BUILDING THIS KANJI
Thread 糸 (196) + Again (ironing board) 又 (159) + Earth 土 (87) = 経

Meaning
Via, in the sense of things passing or elapsing. A secondary meaning related to Buddhist sutras makes use of the less common **on-yomi**.

Remembering this kanji
"I will help you find me in the labyrinth," she promised.
"But how?" he asked.
She turned to the **ironing board**. "**VIA** this."
"**VIA** the **ironing board**? I don't get it."
"No. **VIA** this **thread**. I'll let it trail behind me over the **earth** so that you can follow me."
"I'm not sure," he said. "Don't you feel it might be easier to find you **VIA** a trail of **ironing boards** instead?"

Common Pronunciations
Common **ON** reading: **KEI** (ケイ)
Common **kun** reading: **he** (ヘ)

Less Common Pronunciations
Less common **ON** reading: **KYŌ** (キョウ)
Less common **kun** readings: none

COMMON WORDS AND COMPOUNDS		
経る	*elapse; pass through*	**he·ru** ヘ・る
経由	via + cause = *via; by way of*	**KEI·YU** ケイ・ユ
経験	via + test = *experience*	**KEI·KEN** ケイ・ケン

COMPONENT #303

GUY WEARING A BARREL

KANJI 303

頭 **HEAD**

BUILDING THIS KANJI
Bean 豆 (280) + Guy Wearing a Barrel 頁 = 頭

Meaning
Head.

Remembering this kanji
So I gave a **bean** to this **guy wearing** a **barrel**. "What's this for?" he asked. "For your HEAD," I answered. "Why should I put a **bean** on my HEAD?" he said. "Well," I replied, "you have to begin your wardrobe somewhere, don't you? Why not with a beanie for your HEAD?"

Common Pronunciations

Common **ON** reading: **TŌ** (トウ)
Common **kun** reading: **atama** (あたま)

Less Common Pronunciations

Less common **ON** reading: **ZU** (ズ); **TO** (ト)
Less common **kun** readings: **kashira** (かしら)

You are most likely to encounter the first of these **on-yomi** in only a pair of words: 頭上 (**ZU·JŌ** / ズ・ジョウ) "overhead" from the kanji "head" and "upper", and the final sample compound of Entry 461.

COMMON WORDS AND COMPOUNDS		
頭	*head*	**atama** あたま
先頭	precede + head = *at the lead; at the head*	**SEN·TŌ** セン・トウ
店頭	shop + head = *storefront; shopwindow*	**TEN·TŌ** テン・トウ

KANJI 304

魚 **FISH**

BUILDING THIS KANJI
Little Red Riding Hood ﾉｰ + Rice Field 田
(73) + Gas Stove ⺌ = 魚

Meaning
Fish.

Remembering this kanji

"What's **Little Red Riding Hood** doing in that **rice field**?" someone cried. "And there's smoke! Maybe she's the one!"

The mob rushed through the **rice field**, but slowed on catching sight of the **gas stove**. "It's not her, guys," someone said. "She's just grilling a FISH."

Common Pronunciations

Common **ON** reading: **GYO** (ギョ)
Common **kun** reading: **sakana** (さかな)

Create your **on-yomi** keyword and enter it in the table at the back of the book. Then, after creating your **kun-yomi** keyword, write your sentence to remember the **on-yomi** and **kun-yomi** readings in the box below.

Less Common Pronunciations

Less common **ON** reading: none
Less common **kun** readings: **uo** (うお)

COMMON WORDS AND COMPOUNDS		
魚	*fish*	**sakana** さかな
金魚	gold + fish = *goldfish*	**KIN·GYO** キン・ギョ
人魚	person + fish = *mermaid; merman*	**NIN·GYO** ニン・ギョ

KANJI 305

実

ACTUAL

丶 宀 宀 宀 宀 宀 宇 実

BUILDING THIS KANJI

Pincers 宀 + Three (full hamburger) 三(5) +
Person 人(2) = 実

Meaning

This kanji has to do with the actual nature or
reality of things.

Remembering this kanji

So this **person** made an ACTUAL **full hamburger**
that was bigger than he was! Unfortunately, he
had to get lifted up by an ACTUAL set of **pincers**
after he ate it. They had to be ACTUAL **pincers**,
of course, because he was an ACTUAL **person**.

Common Pronunciations
Common **ON** reading: **JITSU** (ジツ)
Common **kun** reading: none

Less Common Pronunciations
Less common **ON** reading: none
Less common **kun** readings: **mi** (み);
mino (み の)

These two readings relate to a secondary meaning of this kanji that has to do with seeds, berries
and nuts, etc.

COMMON WORDS AND COMPOUNDS		
事実	matter + actual = *fact*	**JI·JITSU** ジ·ジツ
実用	actual + utilize = *practical use; utility*	**JITSU·YŌ** ジツ·ヨウ
実行	actual + go = *put into practice; execute*	**JIK·KŌ** ジッ·コウ

CHAPTER 14 REVIEW EXERCISES

A. Please match the following kanji to their meanings.

1.	指	a.	Roof
2.	完	b.	Descend
3.	遠	c.	Perfect
4.	魚	d.	Marriage
5.	婚	e.	Finger
6.	経	f.	Arrow
7.	降	g.	Good
8.	屋	h.	Far
9.	良	i.	Via
10.	矢	j.	Fish

B. Please match the following meanings to their
kanji, and these to their **on** or **kun-yomi**.

1.	Distribute	a.	配	1.	**wasu** (わす)
2.	Metropolis	b.	的	2.	**KATSU** (カツ)
3.	Harmony	c.	実	3.	**atama** (あたま)
4.	Actual	d.	反	4.	**WA** (ワ)
5.	Target	e.	活	5.	**kuba** (くば)
6.	Festival	f.	頭	6.	**JITSU** (ジツ)
7.	Active	g.	和	7.	**TO** (ト)
8.	Forget	h.	祭	8.	**HAN** (ハン)
9.	Against	i.	忘	9.	**TEKI** (テキ)
10.	Head	j.	都	10.	**matsu** (まつ)
	(kun-yomi)				

C. Please choose the best answer(s) to the following questions.

1. Which is the correct reading of 降る?
   a. **ka·ru** (か・る)
   b. **ku·ru** (く・る)
   c. **a·ru** (あ・る)
   d. **fu·ru** (ふ・る)

2. Which of the following readings apply to the kanji 遠?
   a. **kō** (こお)
   b. **KEN** (ケン)
   c. **EN** (エン)
   d. **IN** (イン)
   e. **tō** (とお)

3. Which of the following kanji has the most number of strokes?
   a. 祭 b. 配 c. 屋 d. 降 e. 界

4. I'm afraid of ___ , so please don't make me go to the public aquarium.
   a. 婚 b. 各 c. 界 d. 魚 e. 和

5. Which of the following readings apply to the kanji 形?
   a. **KA**(カ)   b. **KI** (キ)
   c. **KEI** (ケイ)   d. **kata** (かた)
   e. **katachi** (かたち)

D. Please match the following compounds to their meanings and pronunciations.

1. 世界   a. Nomination   1. **KIN·GYO** (キン・ギョ)

2. 予定   b. Kyoto   2. **RYŌ·SHIN** (リョウ・シン)

3. 金魚   c. Conscience   3. **KAK·KI**

4. 目的   d. Prearrangement   4. **KAN·ZE** (カッ·キ)
                                      (カン・ゼン)

5. 指名   e. Liveliness / Vigor   5. **SE·KAI** (セ·カイ)

6. 京都   f. The world   6. **MOKU·TEKI** (モク・テキ)

7. 活気   g. Purpose / Aim   7. **KYŌ·TO** (キョウ・ト)

8. 完全   h. Divorce   8. **SHI·MEI** (シ・メイ)

9. 離婚   i. Perfection   9. **RI·KON** (リ・コン)

10. 良心   j. Goldfish   10. **YO·TEI** (ヨ・テイ)

E. Please read the passage below and answer the questions that follow.

"来月京都のお祭りへ行きま
か。"
"はい。学校の遠足で。あなたも行
きますか。"
"いいえ。ここで大事な用事があり
ます。"

1. What is happening next month?
2. Where is it taking place?
3. Why is one of these people able to go?
4. Will both of these people be going?
5. What does one of these people have to take care of

Kanji #306—330

KANJI 306

ACHIEVE

一	十	土	土	去	去	幸	幸	幸
幸	達	達						

BUILDING THIS KANJI

Earth 土(87) + Sheep 羊(262) + Seal 辶 = 達

Meaning

Achieve, attain. When used as a suffix this kanji also serves to indicate the plural, although the second compound below can refer to only one person as well.

Remembering this kanji

To the extent of what you'd like to ACHIEVE is to put **earth** on a **sheep**? Big deal. Why not do something no one has ever ACHIEVED, and plop that **earth**-covered **sheep** on a **seal**! You do that and you'll have really ACHIEVED something, since you'd not only have to haul the **sheep** over a kelp-covered beach, but chase down the **seal** as well.

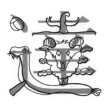

Common Pronunciations

Common **ON** reading: **TATSU** (タ ツ)
Common **kun** reading: **tachi** (た ち)

The second example shows how the **kun-yomi** can become voiced; this reading never appears in first position.

Create your **on-yomi** keyword and enter it in the table at the back of the book. Then, after creating your **kun-yomi** keyword, write your sentence to remember the **on-yomi** and **kun-yomi** readings in the box below.

Less Common Pronunciations

Less common **ON** reading: none
Less common **kun** reading: none

COMMON WORDS AND COMPOUNDS		
上達	upper + achieve = *improvement; progress*	JŌ·TATSU ジョウ·タツ
友達	friend + achieve = *friend(s)*	tomo·**dachi** と も·だ ち
発達	discharge + achieve = *correspondence*	HAT·TATSU ハッ·タツ

KANJI 307

 CONTINUE

⼁	⼄	⼓	⽷	糸	糸	糸⁻	糸⁺	結
結	続	続	続					

BUILDING THIS KANJI
Thread 糸(196) + Sell 売(92) = 続

Meaning
Continue.

Remembering this kanji
If it's **thread** you'd like to **sell**, you must understand this fact: you can only CONTINUE to **sell** it for as long as it CONTINUES to come off the spool.

Common Pronunciations
Common ON reading: ZOKU (ゾク)
Common kun reading: tsuzu (つづ)

Create your **on-yomi** keyword and enter it in the table at the back of the book. Then, after creating your **kun-yomi** keyword, write your sentence to remember the **on-yomi** and **kun-yomi** readings in the box below.

Less Common Pronunciations
Less common ON reading: none
Less common kun reading: none

COMMON WORDS AND COMPOUNDS		
続く (intr)	*continue*	**tsuzu**·ku つづ·く
続ける (tr)	*continue*	**tsuzu**·keru つづ·ける
手続き	hand + continue = *formalities; procedure*	te **tsuzu**·ki て つづ·き
接続	join + continue = *connection; joining*	SETSU·**ZOKU** セツ·ゾク

COMPONENT #308

PINBALL

KANJI 308

弱 WEAK

⼀	⼀	弓	弓	弓	弓ˀ	弓ˀ	弱	弱
弱								

BUILDING THIS KANJI
Bow 弓 (143) + Pinball ⼀ + Bow 弓 (143) +
Pinball ⼀ = 弱

Meaning
Weak.

Remembering this kanji
Note that the story below emphasizes that there are two of each of these components.

Geez, I'm WEAK. I tried to do curls with a couple of **bows** but was too WEAK to lift them. So I went to my **pinball** machine to have some fun, but I couldn't even get the pair of flippers to budge. Yeah, I'm that WEAK.

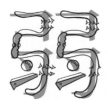

ommon Pronunciations
ommon **ON** reading: **JAKU** (ジャク)
ommon **kun** reading: **yowa** (よわ)

reate your **on-yomi** keyword and enter it in the
ble at the back of the book. Then, after creating
ur **kun-yomi** keyword, write your sentence to
member the **on-yomi** and **kun-yomi** readings in
e box below.

Less Common Pronunciations
Less common **ON** reading: none
Less common **kun** reading: none

COMMON WORDS AND COMPOUNDS		
弱い	*weak*	**yowa·i** よわ·い
弱点	weak + point = *weak point;* *shortcoming*	**JAKU·TEN** ジャク·テン
弱肉強食	weak + meat + strong + eat = *survival* *of the fittest*	**JAKU·NIKU·KYŌ·** **SHOKU** ジャク·ニク· キョウ·ショク

SHORT

㇒	㇑	㇉	矢	矢	矢	矢	短
短	短	短					

BUILDING THIS KANJI
Arrow 矢 (285) + **Bean** 豆 (280) = 短

Meaning
Short.

Remembering this kanji
n SHORT, a SHORT distance makes it easier
o shoot an **arrow** into a **bean**.

Common Pronunciations
Common **ON** reading: **TAN** (タン)
Common **kun** reading: **mijika** (みじか)

Less Common Pronunciations
Less common **ON** reading: none
Less common **kun** reading: none

COMMON WORDS AND COMPOUNDS		
短い	*short*	**mijika·i** みじか·い
最短	most + short = *shortest*	**SAI·TAN** サイ·タン
短期	short + period = *short-term*	**TAN·KI** タン·キ

KANJI 310

 辞 **RESIGN**

| ′ | ニ | 千 | 舌 | 舌 | 舌 | 舌′ | 舌゙ | 舌 |
| 舌゙ | 辞 | 辞 | 辞 | | | | | |

BUILDING THIS KANJI
Tongue 舌 (110) + Spicy 辛 (267) = 辞

Meaning
Resign, quit. A second meaning relates to phrases and words; this sense is reflected in the final two compounds.

Remembering this kanji
"You had to RESIGN?! What happened?"
"It was the curry I had for lunch. It made m
tongue too **spicy** to be a judge in the pie-tastin
competition; I had no choice but to RESIGN.

Common Pronunciations
Common **ON** reading: **JI** (ジ)
Common **kun** reading: **ya** (や)

Less Common Pronunciations
Less common **ON** reading: none
Less common **kun** reading: none

COMMON WORDS AND COMPOUND		
辞める	*resign; quit*	**ya**·meru や・める
辞書	resign (phrase) + write = *dictionary*	**JI**·SHO ジ・ショ
お世辞	society + resign (phrase) = *flattery; compliment*	o SE·**JI** お セ・ジ

COMPONENT #311

BUCKTEETH

KANJI 311

免 **EXEMPTION**

| ′ | ク | ク | ㄅ | 缶 | 色 | 免 | 免 | |

BUILDING THIS KANJI
Little Red Riding Hood 𠂉 + Buckteeth 口 + Ballet 儿 = 免

Meaning
Exemption, permission.

Remembering this kanji
"But **Little Red Riding Hood** doesn't have
buckteeth, so how can she be in our **buckteeth**
ballet?"
"Because I gave her an EXEMPTION, al
right?"
"How come? Without **buckteeth** she can'
even…"
"Don't you realize we're doing "**Little Re**
Riding Hood: The **Ballet**" this season? It make
sense to give her an EXEMPTION!"

Common Pronunciations
Common **ON** reading: **MEN** (メン)
Common **kun** reading: none

Create your **on-yomi** keyword and enter it in th
table at the back of the book. After that, writ

your sentence to remember the **on-yomi** reading in the box below.

Less Common Pronunciations
Less common **ON** reading: none
Less common **kun** reading: **manuka** (ま ぬ か)

COMMON WORDS AND COMPOUNDS		
免じる	*to exempt; dismiss*	**MEN**·jiru メン・じる

KANJI 312

 SONG

一	一	二	三	可	可	可	哥	哥
哥	哥	歌	歌	歌				

BUILDING THIS KANJI
Possible 可 (252) + Possible 可 (252) + Lack 欠 (246) = 歌

Common Pronunciations
Common **ON** reading: **KA** (カ)
Common **kun** reading: **uta** (う た)

The **on-yomi** is the more common reading.

Less Common Pronunciations
Less common **ON** reading: none
Less common **kun** reading: none

Meaning
Song, singing. In a few compounds this character can also mean poetry.

COMMON WORDS AND COMPOUNDS		
歌	*song; poem*	**uta** う た
歌手	song + hand = *singer*	**KA**·SHU カ・シュ
国歌	country + song = *national anthem*	**KOK·KA** コッ・カ

Remembering this kanji
"What's up with that SONG? It seems to **lack** something."
"Is it the **lack** of rhythm?"
"It's **possible**."
"How about the **lack** of melody or nice singing?"
"That's *doubly* **possible**."
"Hmm. Maybe it just **lacks** everything needed to be a decent SONG."

OPERA SINGER

 **SEND**

`	´	亠	亣	关	关	﹆关	送	送

BUILDING THIS KANJI
Opera Singer 关 + Seal 辶 = 送

Meaning
Send.

Remembering this kanji
"SEND it away!" said the **opera singer**. "I've told you countless times: I realize he's a fan, but I don't want that **seal** to SEND me buckets of bait."

Common Pronunciations
Common **ON** reading: **SŌ** (ソウ)
Common **kun** reading: **oku** (おく)

Although there are a few compound verbs (su as the second example below) making use of t **kun-yomi**, the **on-yomi** is the more common rea ing.

Less Common Pronunciations
Less common **ON** reading: none
Less common **kun** reading: none

COMMON WORDS AND COMPOUNDS		
送る	*to send*	**oku**·ru おく・る
見送る	see + send = *see (someone) off*	mi·**oku**·ru み おく・る
送別	send + different = *farewell; send off*	**SŌ**·BETSU ソウ・ベツ

KANJI 314

払 **PAY**

一	十	扌	払	払			

BUILDING THIS KANJI
Finger 扌 + Broken Crutch 厶 = 払

Meaning
Pay. A secondary meaning relates to the idea of 'driving / sweeping away' something.

Remembering this kanji
Recall from Entry 298 that the word 'finger' in this and all future stories indicates the component 扌, not the kanji 指.

"You're gonna PAY for that!" he said, pointing (with his **finger**) at the **broken crutch**.
"I'm not going to PAY for anything," I shot back.
"You asked me to break it!"

Common Pronunciations
Common **ON** reading: none
Common **kun** reading: **hara** (はら)

This **kun-yomi** will often become voiced i second and third position when forming noun as in the final compound. It never becomes voice however, when forming verbs.

Less Common Pronunciations
Less common **ON** reading: **FUTSU** (フツ)
Less common **kun** reading: none

COMMON WORDS AND COMPOUNDS		
払う	*pay; sweep away*	**hara**·u はら・う
先払い	precede + pay = *payment in advance*	saki·**bara**·i さき ばら・い

ʌNJI 315

夫 **HUSBAND**

一	二	夫	夫				

ᴜILDING THIS KANJI

ne (hamburger patty) 一(3) + **Large (sumo restler)** 大(17) = 夫

ᴇaning

usband. This is a good time to ensure that ɒu can clearly distinguish the following five ʌnji based on our sumo wrestler: 大 "large" ɒm Entry 17, 天 "heaven" from Entry 123, ʌ "husband" from here, as well as the two that cluded a hammer component, 失 "lose" from ntry 142, and 矢 "arrow" from Entry 285.

ᴇmembering this kanji

you're looking for a HUSBAND, a quick way ɒ get one is to offer a **hamburger patty** to a **sumo restler**. Do that and you'll have a HUSBAND ght away.

Common Pronunciations

Common **ON** reading: **FU** (フ)
Common **kun** reading: **otto** (おっと)

Less Common Pronunciations

Less common **ON** reading: **FŪ** (フウ)
Less common **kun** reading: none

You are only likely to encounter this reading in the final compound of Entry 504, as well as in the word 工夫 (**KU·FŪ** / ク・フウ) 'device, invention', from the kanji for 'craft' and 'husband' ('工' being read here with its less common **on-yomi**).

COMMON WORDS AND COMPOUNDS		
夫	*husband*	otto おっと
夫人	husband + person = *wife; Mrs.*	**FU·JIN** フ・ジン

COMPONENT #316

ʀISKING

ʌNJI 316

変 **ALTER**

一	一	亠	六	亦	亦	亦	変	変

ʙUILDING THIS KANJI

ʀisking 亦 + **Running Chicken** 夂 = 変

Meaning

Alter, change. In some compounds the idea of an accident or mishap is present.

Remembering this kanji

It's not easy **frisking** a **running chicken**, given how quickly they're able to ALTER their course. And even if you do find contraband on them, you'll need some skill to get a confession; they're famous for being able to ALTER their story on a moment's notice.

Common Pronunciations
Common **ON** reading: **HEN** (ヘ ン)
Common **kun** reading: **ka** (か)

HEN is the overwhelming choice in first position. The **kun-yomi** becomes voiced in second position according to the same rules we learned for 付 back in Entry 226.

Create your **on-yomi** keyword and enter it in the table at the back of the book. Then, after creating your **kun-yomi** keyword, write your sentence to remember the **on-yomi** and **kun-yomi** readings in the box below.

Less Common Pronunciations
Less common **ON** reading: none
Less common **kun** reading: none

COMMON WORDS AND COMPOUNDS		
変わる (intr)	*change; be different*	**ka**·waru か·わる
変える (tr)	*alter; change*	**ka**·eru か·える
変化	alter + change = *change; transformation*	**HEN·KA** ヘン·カ
大変	large + alter = *serious; very*	**TAI·HEN** タイ·ヘン

KANJI 317

食 **EAT**

ノ	𠆢	𠆢	今	今	今	食	食	食

BUILDING THIS KANJI
Umbrella 𠆢 + Good 良(288) = 食

Meaning
Eat.

Remembering this kanji
"**Umbrella good!**"
"Yeah, but don't EAT it."

Common Pronunciations
Common **ON** reading: **SHOKU** (ショク)
Common **kun** reading: **ta** (た)

Create your **on-yomi** keyword and enter it in the table at the back of the book. Then, after creating your **kun-yomi** keyword, write your sentence to remember the **on-yomi** and **kun-yomi** readings in the box below.

Less Common Pronunciations
Less common **ON** reading: **JIKI** (ジキ)
Less common **kun** reading: **ku** (く)

This **kun-yomi** is often found in words conveying a negative aspect of eating.

COMMON WORDS AND COMPOUNDS		
食べる	*eat*	**ta**·beru た·べる
食べ物	eat + thing = *food*	**ta**·be mono た·べ もの
定食	fixed + eat = *set meal*	**TEI·SHOKU** テイ·ショク

KANJI 318

MOVE

一	二	三	三	戸	百	盲	盲	重	重
動	動								

BUILDING THIS KANJI
Heavy 重 (249) + Strength 力 (63) = 動

Meaning
Move.

Remembering this kanji
Advice from a professional mover, on how to MOVE stuff:

"If it's **heavy**, you'll need **strength** to MOVE it."

Common Pronunciations
Common **ON** reading: **DŌ** (ド ウ)
Common **kun** reading: **ugo** (う ご)

Less Common Pronunciations
Less common **ON** reading: none
Less common **kun** reading: none

COMMON WORDS AND COMPOUNDS		
動く (intr)	*move*	**ugo·ku** う ご・く
動かす (tr)	*move*	**ugo·kasu** う ご・か す
動物	move + thing = *animal*	**DŌ·BUTSU** ド ウ・ブ ツ
自動	self + move = *automatic*	**JI·DŌ** ジ・ド ウ

KANJI 319

SPRING(S)

'	'	宀	白	白	白	身	身	泉

BUILDING THIS KANJI
White 白 (7) + Water 水 (61) = 泉

Meaning
Spring(s) (as in a source of water).

Remembering this kanji
"Excuse me, how do I find the SPRINGS?"
"Well, can you spot that **white** froth on the **water** over there? Those are your SPRINGS."

Common Pronunciations
Common **ON** reading: **SEN** (セ ン)
Common **kun** reading: **izumi** (い ず み)

Less Common Pronunciations
Less common **ON** reading: none
Less common **kun** reading: none

COMMON WORDS AND COMPOUNDS		
泉	*spring(s)*	**izumi** い ず み
温泉	warm + springs = *hot spring; spa*	**ON·SEN** オ ン・セ ン

KANJI 320

非 UN-

Meaning

This curious-looking character is another important negating prefix, much like '不' ('Not', from Entry 186). In this and future stories we will assign it the external meaning of "amoebas". Take care with the stroke order—though the first line of the 'merging' component is the initial stroke of this kanji, the second comes after the three amoebas on the left. Also keep in mind that the six amoebas are always written left to right.

Remembering this kanji

What could be more "UN-" than amoebas? They're UNcoordinated, and their blobby physique is UNattractive. They're also UNdisciplined; if told to **merge** in an orderly fashion (as these were), at least one will be UNcooperative and fail to do so. It's obvious from the illustration which one was UNwilling to listen in this case.

Common Pronunciations
Common **ON** reading: **HI** (ヒ)
Common **kun** reading: none

Less Common Pronunciations
Less common **ON** reading: none
Less common **kun** reading: none

COMMON WORDS AND COMPOUNDS		
非売品	un- + sell + goods = *"item not for sale"*	**HI·BAI·HIN** ヒ・バイ・ヒン
是非	approve + un- = *without fail; by any means*	**ZE·HI** ゼ・ヒ
非公式	un- + public + type = *unofficial; informal*	**HI·KŌ·SHIKI** ヒ・コウ・シキ

COMPONENT #321

SPILLING COFFEE

This is the second of our special family of five components (the first being 七). As you can see, it differs from 'ghost' by virtue of an additional stroke at the end. An important thing to keep in mind with this component (and the next two members of the family) is that if anything ever appears underneath the horizontal line (such as 工 in Entry 353), it is always written immediately after it, thus breaking the normal stroke order of the component.

KANJI 321

代 SUBSTITUTE

BUILDING THIS KANJI
Giraffe イ + Spilling Coffee 弋 = 代

Meaning

ubstitute. This interesting kanji also carries ome important secondary meanings—it can ndicate a 'fee' for some type of good or service think of the fee as a 'substitute' for what is eceived), as well as convey the idea of 'genera-ons' in compounds related to eras or reigns (as the third example below).

Remembering this kanji

he **giraffe** slammed down her cup, **spilling** offee on the counter. "You put a SUBSTITUTE this coffee, didn't you?" she said. "I told you ot to do that; you can't imagine what it's like aving a SUBSTITUTE sweetener going down is throat of mine."

Common Pronunciations

Common **ON** reading: **DAI** (ダイ)
Common **kun** reading: **ka** (か)

Though sharing the same pronunciation, note the subtle difference in meaning between the intransitive/transitive verb pair shown here and the pair in Entry 316.

Less Common Pronunciations

Less common **ON** readings: **TAI** (タイ)
Less common **kun** reading: **yo** (よ)

COMMON WORDS AND COMPOUNDS		
代わる (intr)	take the place of	**ka**·waru か・わる
代える (tr)	substitute; exchange	**ka**·eru か・える
時代	time + substitute = *era; age*	**JI·DAI** ジ・ダイ
代表	substitute + express = *representative*	**DAI**·HYŌ ダイ・ヒョウ

KANJI 322

記　**NOTE**

ニ	言	言	言	言	言	記	記
記							

BUILDING THIS KANJI

ay 言 (80) + **Oneself (whip)** 己 (214) = 記

Meaning

ote, write down.

Remembering this kanji

Hey, there's a NOTE on this **whip**."
Really? What's it **say**?"
It **says**: 'This is a **whip**'."
Hmm. That's a very useful NOTE."

Common Pronunciations

Common **ON** reading: **KI** (キ)
Common **kun** reading: none

Less Common Pronunciations

Less common **ON** reading: none
Less common **kun** reading: **shiru** (しる)

COMMON WORDS AND COMPOUNDS		
記者	note + individual = *(newspaper) reporter / writer*	**KI·SHA** キ・シャ
日記	sun (day) + note = *diary; journal*	NIK·**KI** ニッ・キ
暗記	dark + note = *memorization*	AN·**KI** アン・キ

KANJI 323

 **REFLECT**

| 丨 | 冂 | 日 | 日 | 旫 | 旫 | 吅 | 映 | 映 |

BUILDING THIS KANJI
Sun 日 (6) + Center 央 (140) = 映

Meaning
Reflect (an image, etc.), project.

Remembering this kanji
The **sun** is at the **center** of our orbit, so a lot of stuff will REFLECT it.

Common Pronunciations
Common **ON** reading: **EI** (エイ)
Common **kun** reading: **utsu** (うつ)

Less Common Pronunciations
Less common **ON** reading: none
Less common **kun** reading: **ha** (は)

COMMON WORDS AND COMPOUNDS		
映る (intr)	reflect	**utsu·ru** うつ・る
映す (tr)	reflect (something)	**utsu·su** うつ・す
映画	reflect + painting = movie; film	**EI·GA** エイ・ガ

COMPONENT #324

MAGNET

Here we have another component with a 'broken' stroke order similar to that of the 'prison'. In this case, whatever is inside the magnet is always written following the first stroke. It is subsequently enclosed by the final one.

KANJI 324

 DOCTOR

| 一 | 丆 | 亇 | 匸 | 产 | 矢 | 医 | | |

BUILDING THIS KANJI
Magnet 匚 + Arrow 矢 (285) = 医

Meaning
Doctor, healing, cure.

Remembering this kanji
"I should be able to get that **arrow** out with the **magnet**," said the DOCTOR.
"Are you sure that's how it's supposed to be done?" I asked.
"Oh, I didn't realize you were a DOCTOR," he said.
"Sorry, DOCTOR," I replied.

Common Pronunciations
Common **ON** reading: **I** (イ)
Common **kun** reading: none

Less Common Pronunciations
Less common **ON** reading: none
Less common **kun** reading: none

COMMON WORDS AND COMPOUNDS		
医者	doctor + individual = doctor; physician	**I·SHA** イ・シャ
医学	doctor + study = medical science	**I·GAKU** イ・ガク
医院	doctor + institution = doctor's office; clinic	**I·IN** イ・イン

KANJI 325

洋 **OCEAN**

丶 氵 氵 沪 沪 泮 泮 洋

BUILDING THIS KANJI
Splash 氵 + Sheep 羊(262) = 洋

Meaning
Ocean. This kanji is also used to denote things from the 'West' (as opposed to the Orient); the first compound provides an example of this usage.

Remembering this kanji
"Ah, the **splash** of **sheep** in the OCEAN," he sighed.

"Um...those **sheep** look like they're pretty desperate to get back to shore," she said. "Why are you tossing them into the OCEAN anyway?"

Common Pronunciations
Common **ON** reading: **YŌ** (ヨウ)
Common **kun** reading: none

Less Common Pronunciations
Less common **ON** reading: none
Less common **kun** reading: none

COMMON WORDS AND COMPOUNDS		
洋服	ocean (Western) + clothes = *(Western-type) clothes*	**YŌ·FUKU** ヨウ・フク
大西洋	large + west + ocean = *the Atlantic Ocean*	**TAI·SEI·YŌ** タイ・セイ・ヨウ
海洋学	sea + ocean + study = *oceanography*	**KAI·YŌ·GAKU** カイ・ヨウ・ガク

COMPONENT #326

1950'S ROCK STAR 夭

KANJI 326

橋 **BRIDGE**

一 十 十 木 松 杮 扩 桥 桥
桥 梂 桥 桥 橋 橋 橋

BUILDING THIS KANJI
Tree 木(13) + 1950's Rock Star 夭 + Mouth
(vampire) 口(8) + Gorilla 冂 + Mouth
(vampire) 口(8) = 橋

Meaning
Bridge.

Remembering this kanji
Several aspects of BRIDGE are represented in this kanji. Most important is the **tree**, which has long given us wood for BRIDGES. The **1950's rock star** BRIDGES the gap nicely between big band jazz and psychedelic rock, and though we can't fathom what the misunderstanding might be between this **pair of vampires**, the kanji obviously has the **gorilla** acting as a BRIDGE here so that they can BRIDGE their differences.

Common Pronunciations

Common **ON** reading: **KYŌ** (キョウ)
Common **kun** reading: **hashi** (はし)

The **kun-yomi** can become voiced outside of first position (as in the final compound).

Less Common Pronunciations

Less common **ON** reading: none
Less common **kun** reading: none

COMMON WORDS AND COMPOUNDS		
橋	*bridge*	**hashi** はし
歩道橋	walk + road + bridge = *pedestrian bridge*	HO·DŌ·**KYŌ** ホ・ドウ・キョウ
石橋	stone + bridge = *stone bridge*	ishi·**bashi** いし・ばし

KANJI 327

現 **PRESENT**

一	丁	王	王	丑	珂	珇	玥	珇
玥	現							

BUILDING THIS KANJI
King 王 (23) + **See** 見 (42) = 現

Meaning

Present (in terms of time). A related meaning has to do with the ideas of revealing and expressing things. The overall sense is one of things being present or brought into being.

Remembering this kanji

Even the greatest **king** can **see** only what the rest of us **see**: nothing but the PRESENT.

Common Pronunciations

Common **ON** reading: **GEN** (ゲン)
Common **kun** reading: **arawa** (あらわ)

The **kun-yomi** is the usual verb stem for the fir and second examples below. A quirk with th kanji, however, is that you may occasionall see these verbs written as 現われる and 現 わす. Think of these two verbs as things eithe presenting themselves (in the first instance) being presented in some way.

Less Common Pronunciations

Less common **ON** reading: none
Less common **kun** reading: none

COMMON WORDS AND COMPOUNDS		
現れる (intr)	*appear; come out*	**arawa**·reru あらわ・れる
現す (tr)	*reveal*	**arawa**·su あらわ・す
現実	present + actual = *actuality; reality*	**GEN**·JITSU ゲン・ジツ

COMPONENT #328

HUCKLEBERRY FINN 也

KANJI 328

地 GROUND

一	十	土	圹	圸	地

BUILDING THIS KANJI
Earth 土 (87) + **Huckleberry Finn** 也 = 地

Meaning
Ground. Whereas 土 is primarily concerned with the idea of actual earth and soil, this kanji has more to do with the **surface** of things in the sense of 'land', 'district' and 'region', for example. This concept of a 'base' is even extended to include such things as the fabric or texture of objects like cloth, as well as the background of a person's character or voice.

Remembering this kanji
Tom Sawyer: "Golly! Why ya got **earth** on your pants, **Huckleberry Finn**?"

Huckleberry Finn: "Well, look at me in this kanji, Tom: I'm sittin' on the GROUND."

Common Pronunciations
Common **ON** reading: **CHI** (チ); JI (ジ)
Common **kun** reading: none

CHI is by far the more common of these readings, especially in second and third position, where JI appears in only a few compounds primarily related to cloth. In the first position the situation is a bit less precise, although even here **CHI** will be encountered more often. Note that the second compound uses the less common on-yomi of 土 (**TO** / ト); this is the only word in which the kanji has this reading. Recall from Entry 25 that 心 in the first example below has an irregular reading of **koko** / こ こ.

Create your **on-yomi** keyword for "チ" and enter it in the table at the back of the book. After that, write your sentence to remember the **on-yomi** readings in the box below.

Less Common Pronunciations
Less common **ON** reading: none
Less common **kun** reading: none

COMMON WORDS AND COMPOUNDS		
心地	heart + ground = *feeling*	koko·**CHI** こ こ·チ
土地	earth + ground = *land*	**TO·CHI** ト·チ
地所	ground + location = *piece of land*	**JI**·SHO ジ·ショ

KANJI 329

伝 **TRANSMIT**

ｲ	ｲｰ	ｲｰ	伝	伝			

BUILDING THIS KANJI
Giraffe イ + Spy 云 = 伝

Meaning
Transmit, communicate.

Remembering this kanji
"We were shocked," said the **giraffe**." He said he just wanted to graze with us."
"So none of you realized he was a **spy**?"
"Not until we caught him in the act; it seems the lions were having him TRANSMIT our whereabouts."

Common Pronunciations
Common **ON** reading: **DEN** (デ ン)
Common **kun** reading: **tsuta** (つ た)

The kun-yomi can become voiced in second position according to the same rules for 付 (Entry 226).

Less Common Pronunciations
Less common **ON** reading: **TEN** (テン)
Less common **kun** reading: none

COMMON WORDS AND COMPOUNDS		
伝える	*transmit; convey*	**tsuta**·eru つた·える
伝来	transmit + come = *transmission; handing down*	**DEN**·**RAI** デン·ライ
伝記	transmit + note = *biography*	**DEN**·**KI** デン·キ

KANJI 330

結 **BIND**

╰	⼕	⼚	⼤	⼶	糸	糸一	糸十	結
結	結	結						

BUILDING THIS KANJI
Thread 糸 (196) + Lucky 吉 (269) = 結

Meaning
Bind, as well as the senses of 'tying up' such things as a contract or marriage, for example.

Remembering this kanji
"Yeah, I knocked him out with the spool and wa[s] able to BIND him with the **thread**."
"That was sure **lucky**. It sounds like you wer[e] in a real BIND."

Common Pronunciations
Common **ON** reading: **KETSU** (ケツ)
Common **kun** reading: **musu** (むす)

Less Common Pronunciations
Less common **ON** reading: none
Less common **kun** reading: **yu** (ゆ)

COMMON WORDS AND COMPOUNDS		
結ぶ	*bind; connect*	**musu**·bu むす·ぶ
結婚	bind + marriage = *marriage*	**KEK**·**KON** ケッ·コン
結合	bind + match = *union; combination*	**KETSU**·**GŌ** ケツ·ゴウ

CHAPTER 15 REVIEW EXERCISES

A. Please match the following kanji to their meanings.

1.	代	a.	Substitute
2.	変	b.	Ocean
3.	続	c.	Send
4.	映	d.	Reflect
5.	達	e.	Springs
6.	夫	f.	Continue
7.	送	g.	Achieve
8.	洋	h.	Alter
9.	伝	i.	Husband
10.	泉	j.	Transmit

B. Please match the following meanings to the kanji, and these to their **on**- or **kun-yomi**.

1.	Song	a.	非	1.	**I** (イ)
2.	Present	b.	短	2.	**HI** (ヒ)
3.	Weak	c.	医	3.	**ugo** (うご)
4.	Short	d.	歌	4.	**GEN** (ゲン)
5.	Doctor	e.	動	5.	**uta** (うた)

6. Bridge   f. 弱   6. **hashi**（はし）
7. Move   g. 結   7. **mijika**（みじか）
8. Un-   h. 橋   8. **MEN**（メン）
9. Bind   i. 現   9. **musu**（むす）
10. Exemption j. 免   10. **yowa**（よわ）

Please choose the best answer(s) to the following questions.

1. Which of the following readings apply to the kanji 地?
   a. **JI**（ジ）   b. **JO**（ジョ）
   c. **SHI**（シ）   d. **SHO**（ショ）
   e. **CHI**（チ）

2. She needed to relax, so went on a holiday to a hot ___ resort.
   a. 医   b. 夫   c. 泉   d. 記   e. 橋

3. Which is the correct reading of 食べる?
   a. **ka·beru**（か・べる）
   b. **sa·beru**（さ・べる）
   c. **shira·beru**（しら・べる）
   d. **ta·beru**（た・べる）

4. Which of the following kanji has the most number of strokes?
   a. 辞   b. 短   c. 続   d. 歌   e. 達

5. Which is the correct reading of 払う?
   a. **ka·u**（か・う）
   b. **hara·u**（はら・う）
   c. **uba·u**（うば・う）
   d. **kura·u**（くら・う）

. Please match the following compounds to their meanings and pronunciations.

1. 日記   a. Set meal   1. **DŌ·BUTSU**
                        （ドウ・ブツ）

2. 心地   b. Doctor   2. **TEI·SHOKU**
                        （テイ・ショク）
3. 動物   c. Change   3. **I·SHA**
                        （イ・シャ）
4. 時代   d. Diary /   4. **EI·GA**
            Journal   （エイ・ガ）
5. 変化   e. Animal   5. **KEK·KON**
                        （ケッ・コン）
6. 映画   f. Dictionary 6. **JI·DAI**
                        （ジ・ダイ）
7. 辞書   g. Era / Age 7. **HEN·KA**
                        （ヘン・カ）
8. 結婚   h. Feeling   8. **NIK·KI**
                        （ニッ・キ）
9. 定食   i. Movie   9. **JI·SHO**
                        （ジ・ショ）
10. 医者 j. Marriage 10. **koko·CHI**
                        （ここ・チ）

E. Please read the passage below and answer the questions that follow.

先週末、私の小学校からの友達が
結婚しました。"
"だれですか。"
"本田さんです。"
"本田さんは新聞記者ですよね。"
"いいえ。医者です。"

1. What did Honda-san recently do?
2. When did this happen?
3. What is the relationship of the first person to Honda-san?
4. What did the second person believe Honda-san did for a living?
5. What is Honda-san's actual profession?

Kanji #331—360

KANJI 331

味 **TASTE**

㇒	㇄	㇂	㇀	㇁	呋	呋	味

BUILDING THIS KANJI
Mouth (vampire) 口 (8) + **Not yet** 未 (276) = 味

Meaning
Taste, flavor.

Remembering this kanji
"I only want a TASTE," murmured the **vampire**, drawing closer.
"**Not yet**!" she said.
"**Not yet**!?" he cried. "C'mon, there's hardly any cookie dough left!"
"Well, I'm sorry," she said, "but if I give you a TASTE, I'll have to let everyone have a TASTE."

Common Pronunciations
Common **ON** reading: **MI** (ミ)
Common **kun** reading: **aji** (あじ)

Less Common Pronunciations
Less common **ON** reading: none
Less common **kun** reading: none

IRREGULAR READING		
美味しい	beautiful + taste = *delicious*	**oi·**shii おい·しい

COMMON WORDS AND COMPOUNDS		
味	*taste*	**aji** あじ
気味	spirit + taste = *feeling; sensation*	**KI·MI** キ・ミ
意味	mind + taste = *meaning; significance*	**I·MI** イ・ミ

KANJI 332

尺 **MEASUREMENT**

㇕	㇆	尸	尺				

BUILDING THIS KANJI
Flag 尸 + **Comet** 一 = 尺

Meaning

Measurement. This kanji derives from an old Japanese unit of measurement equivalent to about 30.3 cm; it is of most use as a component in other characters.

Remembering this kanji

So you're going to put a **flag** on a **comet**, are you? Well, you better get some MEASUREMENTS. And not just a MEASUREMENT for the **flag**, because that's easy. No, you'll have to get out there and come up with a MEASUREMENT for the **comet**, too.

Common Pronunciations

Common **ON** reading: **SHAKU** (シャク)
Common **kun** reading: none

Create your **on-yomi** keyword and enter it in the table at the back of the book. After that, write your sentence to remember the **on-yomi** reading in the box below.

Less Common Pronunciations

Less common **ON** reading: none
Less common **kun** reading: none

COMMON WORDS AND COMPOUNDS		
尺八	measurement + eight = *shakuhachi flute*	**SHAKU·HACHI** シャク・ハチ
尺度	measurement + degree = *linear measure; scale*	**SHAKU·DO** シャク・ド

KANJI 333

FLAT

BUILDING THIS KANJI

One (top of a bun) 一 (3) + Rabbit `丷` + Ten (scarecrow) 十 (28) = 平

Meaning

Flat, with extended meanings such as ordinary and peaceful.

Remembering this kanji

She laid the blanket out FLAT, and after flattening down the **top of the bun**, bit into her ham and cheese. The noise of crunching lettuce startled a nearby **rabbit**—it held its ears FLAT in surprise. Did she sense this? She looked up, but as always there was only the **scarecrow** watching her, tied FLAT to its boards.

Common Pronunciations

Common **ON** reading: **HEI** (ヘイ)
Common **kun** reading: **hira** (ひら)

HEI is the more common of these readings.

Create your **on-yomi** keyword and enter it in the table at the back of the book. Then, after creating your kun-yomi keyword, write your sentence to remember the **on-yomi** and **kun-yom**i readings in the box below.

COMMON WORDS AND COMPOUNDS		
平たい	*flat; level*	**hira**·tai ひら·たい
平和	flat + harmony = *peace*	**HEI**·WA ヘイ·ワ
太平洋	fat + flat + ocean = *the Pacific Ocean*	TAI·**HEI**·YŌ タイ·ヘイ·ヨウ

Less Common Pronunciations
Less common **ON** reading: **BYŌ** (ビョウ)
Less common **kun** reading: **tai** (たい)

COMPONENT #334

CLIFF DIVER

KANJI 334

度 **DEGREE**

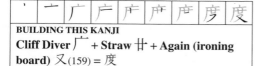

BUILDING THIS KANJI
Cliff Diver 广 + Straw 丗 + Again (ironing board) 又 (159) = 度

Meaning
Degree, extent. As the second compound shows, this kanji can also mean 'times' in the sense of 'how many times'.

Remembering this kanji
"For me it's about the DEGREE of difficulty," said the **cliff diver**.
"For me it's the DEGREE of temperature," said the **ironing board**. "I can't have it too high."
The **straw** had been sitting quietly between them. "I just realized something," he said. "When I get put in a drink I'm always stuck at some angle between 0 and 90 DEGREES. No wonder I'm so bored."

Common Pronunciations
Common **ON** reading: **DO** (ド)
Common **kun** reading: **tabi** (たび)

Less Common Pronunciations
Less common **ON** reading: **TAKU** (タク);
TO (ト)
Less common **kun** reading: none

COMMON WORDS AND COMPOUNDS		
度々	degree + degree = *often; over and over*	**tabi·tabi** たび·たび
一度	one + degree (times) = *once; one time*	**ICHI·DO** イチ·ド
丁度	block + degree = *exactly*	CHŌ·DO チョウ·ド

KANJI 335

祭 **EDGE**

ß	ß	ß'	ß⁷	ßㄅ	ß⁷	ßㄅ	際
又	際	降	際	際			

BUILDING THIS KANJI
Novice Yodeler ß + Festival 祭 (297) = 際

Meaning
Edge, limit. A secondary meaning has to do with an 'occasion'.

Remembering this kanji
"Geez, honey, does it have to be another amateur yodeling **festival**? If I have to listen to any more **novice yodelers** it'll drive me over the EDGE."

Common Pronunciations
Common **ON** reading: **SAI** (サイ)
Common **kun** reading: **kiwa** (きわ)

The **kun-yomi** is always voiced outside of first position with the exception of '一際' (hito·**kiwa** / ひと・きわ), 'remarkably, conspicuously'; recall from Entry 224 that no kanji becomes voiced following 一 when it is read with its **kun-yomi** of **hito** (ひと).

Less Common Pronunciations
Less common **ON** reading: none
Less common **kun** reading: none

COMMON WORDS AND COMPOUNDS		
水際	water + edge = *water's edge; waterside*	mizu·**giwa** みず・ぎわ
国際	country + edge = *international*	KOKU·SAI コク・サイ
実際	actual + edge = *in practice; in actuality*	JIS·SAI ジッ・サイ

KANJI 336

貸 **LEND**

イ	仁	代	代	代	代	貸	貸
貸	貸	貸					

BUILDING THIS KANJI
Substitute 代 (321) + Shellfish 貝 (21) = 貸

Meaning
Lend.

Remembering this kanji
"But there is no **substitute** for **shellfish**. Just LEND me yours."
"All right, then, I'll LEND them to you for tonight. But if you don't have them home at a decent hour I'll never LEND you anything else."

Common Pronunciations
Common **ON** reading: none
Common **kun** reading: **ka** (か)

As the last two examples show, this kanji can absorb its hiragana accompaniment when forming compounds. This reading is also frequently voiced when not in first position.

Less Common Pronunciations
Less common **ON** reading: **TAI** (タイ)
Less common **kun** reading: none

COMMON WORDS AND COMPOUNDS		
貸す	*lend*	**ka·su** か・す
貸切	lend + cut = *reserved; chartered*	**kashi·kiri** かし・き
貸主	lend + primary = *lender; landlord*	**kashi·nush** かし・ぬ

PAINT SPRAYER

This component is unusual in that it is often abbreviated when either handwritten or presented in a more calligraphic font, as in the next entry. In such instances it becomes the "dentist light" component we learned prior to Entry 299. It only appears, incidentally, in the following kanji, although this kanji finds its way into other characters as a component.

KANJI 337

 **COMMAND**

BUILDING THIS KANJI
Umbrella 𠆢 + One (hamburger patty) 一(3)
+ Paint Sprayer ㇇ = 令

Meaning
Command, order. This kanji is also used as an honorific prefix in certain compounds. Note that the kanji appears in the next section (as background for the illustration) in its more formal rendering, and thus contains the hamburger patty and paint sprayer components listed above.

Remembering this kanji
Though his **umbrella** was shielding th **hamburger patty**, he flinched on hearing th COMMAND.

"I COMMAND you to put down you **umbrella** and step away from the **patty**," sai the girl with the **paint sprayer**.

"But it's done nothing wrong!" he cried.

And yet…even he had suspected that thi would happen, and as the **paint sprayer** hisse he knew that somehow, in some way, th COMMAND had needed to be given.

Common Pronunciations
Common **ON** reading: **REI** (レイ)
Common **kun** reading: none

Create your **on-yomi** keyword and enter it in th table at the back of the book. After that, wri your sentence to remember the **on-yomi** readin in the box below.

ss Common Pronunciations
ss common **ON** reading: none
ss common **kun** reading: none

COMMON WORDS AND COMPOUNDS		
指令	finger + command = *order; directive*	SHI·REI シ・レイ
号令	title + command = *command; order*	GŌ·REI ゴウ・レイ

 ANJI 338

野 FIELD

口	日	日	甲	甲	里	野	野	野
予	野							

UILDING THIS KANJI
lamlet 里(180) + **Beforehand** 予(299) = 野

leaning
...eld, the wild. Interestingly, this kanji is used
denote a political party in opposition.

emembering this kanji
...veryone in the **hamlet** came out as I approached.
You'd do well to understand something **before-
and**," said the **hamlet** leader. "We care for our
...IELDS here. We'll tend a FIELD, and if the
...IELD sees fit it'll give us its bounty. So you'd
...etter tell us **beforehand** if you don't get along
...ith FIELDS."

Common Pronunciations
Common **ON** reading: **YA** (ヤ)
Common **kun** reading: **no** (の)

This is a tougher character than might be expected;
both readings will be encountered frequently,
although **YA** appears more often in the second
position.

Less Common Pronunciations
Less common **ON** reading: none
Less common **kun** reading: none

COMMON WORDS AND COMPOUNDS		
野心	field + heart = *ambition*	YA·SHIN ヤ・シン
分野	part + field = *field (of study, etc.)*	BUN·YA ブン・ヤ
野原	field + original = *field(s)*	no·hara の・はら

 KANJI 339

広 WIDE

'	一	广	広	広			

BUILDING THIS KANJI
Cliff Diver 厂 + **Broken Crutch** ム = 広

Meaning
Wide, broad, spacious.

Remembering this kanji

The **cliff diver** peered down and saw a **broken crutch** strewn over a **WIDE** area. "How could anyone have believed they could do this on crutches?" he thought, spreading his arms **WIDE** before diving in a **WIDE** arc.

Common Pronunciations

Common **ON** reading: **KŌ** (コ ウ)
Common **kun** reading: **hiro** (ひ ろ)

Less Common Pronunciations

Less common **ON** reading: none
Less common **kun** reading: none

COMMON WORDS AND COMPOUNDS		
広い	*wide; spacious*	**hiro·i** ひろ・い
広島	wide + island = *Hiroshima*	**hiro·shima** ひろ・し
広大	wide + large = *extensive; immense*	**KŌ·DAI** コウ・ダ

KANJI 340

 STONE

一	厂	石	石	石				

BUILDING THIS KANJI
One (top of a bun) 一 (3) + Comet 一 +
Mouth (vampire) 口 (8) = 石

Meaning
Stone.

Remembering this kanji
If you leave it long enough, the **top of a bun** will eventually turn into a STONE. Like the STONE in a **comet**. Oh, or the STONE that a **vampire** would dislike (since he realizes like everyone else that there are certain things you can't get from a STONE).

Common Pronunciations
Common **ON** reading: **SEKI** (セ キ)
Common **kun** reading: **ishi** (い し)

Both readings are used frequently in compound although **SEKI** is more common outside of fir position.

Less Common Pronunciations
Less common **ON** readings: **SHAKU** (シャク **KOKU** (コ ク)
Less common **kun** reading: none

COMMON WORDS AND COMPOUNDS		
石	*stone*	**ishi** いし
化石	change + stone = *fossil*	**KA·SEKI** カ・セキ
一石二鳥	one + stone + two + bird = *kill two birds with one stone*	**IS·SEKI·NI·CHŌ** イッ・セキ・ニ・チョウ

COMPONENT #341

GIRL WITH A HULA HOOP

KANJI 341

CHINA

⟍	氵	氵	汁	汁	泔	泔	溝

BUILDING THIS KANJI

Splash 氵 + Wreath ⁺⁺ + Girl With A Hula Hoop 罘 = 漢

Meaning

China, the Han dynasty. The first compound below may be familiar to you.

Remembering this kanji

"And this is us **splashing** in the Yangtze…"
"Where's that?"
"It's in CHINA. And here I am laying a **wreath** at a monument to Confucius…"
"Where was he from?"
"From CHINA. And this **girl with a hula hoop**…"
"Where…"
"It was in CHINA, OK! At a circus in CHINA! The slides are all from CHINA!"

Common Pronunciations

Common **ON** reading: KAN (カン)
Common **kun** reading: none

Less Common Pronunciations

Less common **ON** reading: none
Less common **kun** reading: none

COMMON WORDS AND COMPOUNDS		
漢字	China + character = *kanji*	**KAN·JI** カン・ジ
漢方	China + direction = *Chinese medicine*	**KAN·PŌ** カン・ポウ

KANJI 342

別 **DIFFERENT**

⼝	口	弓	号	別	別	

BUILDING THIS KANJI

Mouth (vampire) 口 (8) + Chair 力 + Chisel 刂 = 別

Meaning

Different, as well as the ideas of separation and farewell.

Remembering this kanji

"You're DIFFERENT from my usual customers," she said as the **vampire** took a **chair** in her salon. "I mean, I'm going to need a **chisel** to get through that hair gel!"
"It's Transylvanian," said the **vampire**. "We prefer a DIFFERENT brand there."

Common Pronunciations

Common **ON** reading: BETSU (ベツ)
Common **kun** reading: waka (わか)

Create your **on-yomi** keyword and enter it in the table at the back of the book. Then, after creating your **kun-yomi** keyword, write your sentence to remember the **on-yomi** and **kun-yomi** readings in the box below.

Less Common Pronunciations
Less common **ON** reading: none
Less common **kun** reading: **wa** (わ)

COMMON WORDS AND COMPOUNDS		
別れる	*part company; branch off*	**waka·reru** わか·れる
別々	different + different = *separate; individual*	**BETSU·BETS** ベツ·ベツ
送別	send + different = *farewell; send-off*	**SŌ·BETSU** ソウ·ベツ

KANJI 343

GARDEN

BUILDING THIS KANJI
Prison ☐ + Earth 土(87) + Sherpa 呆 = 園

Meaning
Garden.

Remembering this kanji
"Geez, warden, that **sherpa** hasn't adjusted to our **prison** very well, has he? I mean, what's the deal with him hauling that **earth** everywhere?"
"He said he wants to create a GARDEN so that it'll remind him of the nature in Nepal."
"Isn't that a bit risky? I could be wrong, but something tells me the other cons won't be too thrilled to see their basketball court turned into a GARDEN."

Common Pronunciations
Common **ON** reading: **EN** (エン)
Common **kun** reading: none

Recall from Entry 318 that the first two characte of the final compound mean "animal" when take together.

Less Common Pronunciations
Less common **ON** reading: none
Less common **kun** reading: **sono** (その)

COMMON WORDS AND COMPOUNDS		
公園	public + garden = *park*	**KŌ·EN** コウ·エン
学園	study + garden = *educational institute*	**GAKU·EN** ガク·エン
動物園	animal + garden = *zoo*	**DŌ·BUTSU·E** ドウ·ブツ· エン

KANJI 344

皆 **ALL**

ヒ	ヒ丶	比	比丶	比	皆	皆	皆

BUILDING THIS KANJI
Compare 比(240) + **White** 白(7) = 皆

Meaning
All.

Remembering this kanji
"Listen up, ALL of you," she said. "I want you
ALL to **compare** this **white** stuff."
We stared at her in disbelief.
"That is ALL!" she yelled.

Common Pronunciations
Common **ON** reading: none
Common **kun** reading: **mina** (みな)

In spoken Japanese, this reading is often
pronounced **minna** (みんな) for emphasis.

Less Common Pronunciations
Less common **ON** reading: **KAI** (カイ)
Less common **kun** reading: none

COMMON WORDS AND COMPOUNDS		
皆	*all; everybody*	**mina** みな
皆様	all + manner = *"ladies and gentlemen"*	**mina·sama** みな・さま

BILLIONAIRE 艮

Note the difference between this component
and 艮, our "frog" introduced prior to Entry 230.

Remembering this kanji
If a **billionaire** wants a **fern** it means he needs it
IMMEDIATELY, so take IMMEDIATE action
and get him one. And yes, even if it's for something weird it's still your IMMEDIATE concern.

KANJI 345

即 **IMMEDIATE**

⁊	⁊	⁊	艮	艮	即⁊	即	

BUILDING THIS KANJI
Billionaire 艮 + **Fern** ⌐ = 即

Meaning
Immediate, at once.

Common Pronunciations
Common **ON** reading: **SOKU** (ソク)
Common **kun** reading: none

Less Common Pronunciations
Less common **ON** reading: none
Less common **kun** reading: none

COMMON WORDS AND COMPOUNDS		
即日	immediate + sun (day) = *on the same day*	**SOKU·JITSU** ソク・ジツ
即死	immediate + death = *instant death*	**SOKU·SHI** ソク・シ
即売	immediate + sell = *sale on the spot*	**SOKU·BAI** ソク・バイ

KANJI 346

店 **SHOP**

'	一	广	广	庐	店	店	店

BUILDING THIS KANJI
Cliff Diver 广 + Occupy 占 (255) = 店

Meaning
Shop, store.

Remembering this kanji
"I don't get it. What made the **cliff diver occupy** that SHOP?"

"Hasn't anyone told you? That SHOP makes low-cost artificial **cliff divers**. His livelihood is at stake; he had no choice but to **occupy** it."

Common Pronunciations
Common **ON** reading: **TEN** (テ ン)
Common **kun** reading: **mise** (み せ)

The **on-yomi** is the more common reading.

Less Common Pronunciations
Less common **ON** reading: none
Less common **kun** reading: none

COMMON WORDS AND COMPOUNDS		
店	*shop; store*	**mise** み せ
開店	open + shop = *shop/store opening*	**KAI·TEN** カ イ・テ ン
書店	write + shop = *bookstore*	**SHO·TEN** シ ョ・テ ン

KANJI 347

院 **INSTITUTION**

⁷	了	ß	ß'	ß'	ßⁿ	ßⁿ	ßⁿ	ßⁿ
院								

BUILDING THIS KANJI
Novice Yodeler ß + Perfect 完 (292) = 院

Meaning
Institution, in the sense of public buildings such as a hospitals, or bodies such as legislatures.

Remembering this kanji
For a **novice yodeler** who wants to be **perfec** there is only one INSTITUTION: the INSTITU TION for **Perfect** Yodeling. But what about **novice yodeler** who doesn't want to be **perfect** Well, someone like that belongs in an INST TUTION.

Common Pronunciations

Common **ON** reading: **IN** (イ ン)
Common **kun** reading: none

Less Common Pronunciations

Less common **ON** reading: none
Less common **kun** reading: none

COMMON WORDS AND COMPOUNDS		
入院	enter + institution = *be admitted to hospital*	NYŪ·**IN** ニュウ·イン
学院	study + institution = *academy*	GAKU·**IN** ガク·イン
病院	illness + institution = *hospital*	BYŌ·**IN** ビョウ·イン

COMPONENT #348

SHARK ATTACK

KANJI 348

 **CLIMB**

フ	ヌ	ヌ゛	アト	癶	癶	癶	登	登
登	登	登						

BUILDING THIS KANJI
Shark Attack 癶 + Bean 豆 (280) = 登

Meaning

Climb. An important secondary meaning has to do with attendance (the first compound offers an example).

Remembering this kanji

I kept CLIMBING and CLIMBING, but this was no run-of-the-mill **shark attack**.

"The **beans**, Jack," someone yelled at me from below, "maybe it just wants **beans**!"

It didn't seem likely. I mean, if I was able to CLIMB up a beanstalk, it was only logical that a shark could attack me by CLIMBING one too.

Common Pronunciations

Common **ON** reading: **TŌ** (ト ウ)
Common **kun** reading: none

Less Common Pronunciations

Less common **ON** reading: **TO** (ト)
Less common **kun** reading: **nobo** (のぼ)

You are most likely to encounter the **on-yomi** in one word: 登山 (**TO**·ZAN / ト·ザン) "mountain climbing", with 山 being voiced. The **kun-yomi** for this kanji serves as an alternate form of 上る (**nobo**·ru / のぼ·る), which we met in Entry 30.

COMMON WORDS AND COMPOUNDS		
登校	climb (attend) + school = *attend school*	**TŌ**·KŌ トウ·コウ
登場	climb + place = *make an entrance; show up*	**TŌ**·JŌ トウ·ジョウ

KANJI 349

原 **ORIGINAL**

一	厂	厂	厂	所	盾	盾	原	原
原								

BUILDING THIS KANJI
Cliff 厂 + White 白 (7) + Small 小 (20) = 原

Common Pronunciations
Common **ON** reading: **GEN** (ゲン)
Common **kun** reading: **hara** (は ら)

Less Common Pronunciations
Less common **ON** reading: none
Less common **kun** reading: none

IRREGULAR READING		
川原	river + original = *dry riverbed*	kawa·**ra** か わ·ら

Meaning
Original, in the sense of things in their original or primitive state. Many compounds with this character also convey the idea of a plain or field (the first two examples below, for instance). Think of this in connection to "original" as a place that is unspoiled or wilderness-like.

COMMON WORDS AND COMPOUNDS		
野原	field + original = *field(s)*	no·**hara** の·は ら
高原	tall + original = *plateau; tableland*	**KŌ·GEN** コ ウ·ゲン
原子力	original + child + strength = *atomic energy; nuclear power*	**GEN·SHI·RYOKU** ゲン·シ·リ ョ ク

Remembering this kanji
"It seems that the ORIGINAL inhabitants of this **cliff** not only painted themselves **white**, but were very **small**," said the tour guide. "Can anyone tell me who they were?"
"The **Whites** and the **Smalls**?" someone asked with a smirk.
"Gee, that's ORIGINAL," she said.

KANJI 350

晩 **LATE**

丨	冂	日	日	日′	日⁊	旷	晗	晚
晚	晚	晚						

BUILDING THIS KANJI
Sun 日 (6) + Exemption 免 (311) = 晩

Meaning
Late, evening. This kanji also imparts the idea of late in a number of more poetic words — the first two compounds below offer examples.

Remembering this kanji

The orderly told me it's getting LATE," she said. "I should probably be on my way."

"No, you don't have to," he said. "It won't get LATE until I let it get LATE. If the **sun** doesn't ask me for an **exemption**, it can't set."

So this is it, she thought. This is what the LATE stages will be like.

Common Pronunciations

Common **ON** reading: **BAN** (バン)
Common **kun** reading: none

Less Common Pronunciations

Less common **ON** reading: none
Less common **kun** reading: none

COMMON WORDS AND COMPOUNDS		
晩秋	late + autumn = *late autumn*	**BAN·SHŪ** バン・シュウ
晩年	late + year = *one's later years*	**BAN·NEN** バン・ネン
今晩は	now + late = *"good evening"*	KON·**BAN**·wa コン・バン・は

KANJI 351

ENTWINE

⿱	⿱	⿱	糸	糸	糸	紋	終
終	絡	絡					

BUILDING THIS KANJI

Thread 糸 (196) + **Each** 各 (282) = 絡

Meaning

Entwine, become entangled.

Remembering this kanji

We are as **thread**," he whispered, "in that **each** of our lives will ENTWINE with the other."

Common Pronunciations

Common **ON** reading: **RAKU** (ラク)
Common **kun** reading: **kara** (から)

Less Common Pronunciations

Less common **ON** reading: none
Less common **kun** reading: none

COMMON WORDS AND COMPOUNDS		
絡む	*entwine; become entangled*	**kara·mu** から・む
絡み 付く	entwine + attach = *cling to; coil around*	**kara·mi tsu·ku** から・み つ・く
短絡	short + entwine = *short circuit*	TAN·**RAKU** タン・ラク

COMPONENT #352

SPRINTER

As we will meet a few other components that look similar to this one in the pages ahead, it would be a good idea to spend some time here in order to clearly see how each line contributes to the illustration. You may find it useful to compare this component to the lower half of 呆, the sherpa we learned prior to Entry 290. Keep in mind as well that the sprinter's arms and starting line are written as a single stroke.

KANJI 352

表 **EXPRESS**

BUILDING THIS KANJI
Candlestick Holder 主 + **Sprinter** 衣 = 表

Meaning
To express, often one's feelings and beliefs, etc. This idea of bringing things into the open extends to this kanji's other primary meanings, namely surfaces and charts.

Remembering this kanji
The **candlestick holder** was awarded, and the **sprinter** made an attempt to EXPRESS his feelings. "I'd like to EXPRESS my thanks," he said, but I would rather EXPRESS my gratitude. With this **candlestick holder** I can sprint with candles. It's so…so…I'm sorry, it's more than I can EXPRESS."

Common Pronunciations
Common **ON** reading: **HYŌ** (ヒョウ)
Common **kun** reading: **omote** (おもて);
arawa (あらわ)

HYŌ is the more common of these reading **arawa** forms the two verbs in the second a third examples below; you may recognize the as being pronounced identically to 現れる a 現す from Entry 327. Not surprisingly, the pa here can also be seen written at times as 表 れる and 表わす. Though these characters a similar in some respects, this kanji is used mo for the idea of "expressing" things such as fee ings, thoughts and opinions.

Create your **on-yomi** keyword and enter it in t table at the back of the book. Then, after creatii your **kun-yomi** keywords, write your sentence remember the **on-yomi** and **kun-yomi** readings the box below.

Less Common Pronunciations
Less common **ON** reading: none
Less common **kun** reading: none

COMMON WORDS AND COMPOUNDS		
表	*surface; front*	**omote** おもて
表れる (intr)	*be expressed*	**arawa·reru** あらわ·れる
表す (tr)	*express; reveal*	**arawa·su** あらわ·す
表現	express + present = *expression*	**HYŌ·GEN** ヒョウ·ゲン

KANJI 353

TYPE

| 一 | 二 | 干 | 式 | 式 | 式 | | | |

BUILDING THIS KANJI

Spilling Coffee 弋 + **Craft** 工(47) = 式

Meaning

The primary meaning is that of a type or style of something (as in the second compound). It is also very commonly used, however, in the sense of "ceremony" (as is evident in the final example). Take care with the stroke order of this kanji; recall what was written about the "spilling coffee" component when it was introduced prior to Entry 321.

Remembering this kanji

Hey, watch it! What TYPE of an idiot are you?" The TYPE who **spills coffee** on others. That TYPE."

Oh. Well then, you've really mastered your **craft**. Forgive me for being rude, you're obviously a decent TYPE."

Common Pronunciations

Common **ON** reading: **SHIKI** (シ キ)
Common **kun** reading: none

Create your **on-yomi** keyword and enter it in the table at the back of the book. After that, write your sentence to remember the **on-yomi** reading in the box below.

Less Common Pronunciations

Less common **ON** reading: none
Less common **kun** reading: none

COMMON WORDS AND COMPOUNDS		
形式	form + type = *form; formality*	**KEI·SHIKI** ケイ・シキ
自動式	self + move + type = *automatic*	**JI·DŌ·SHIKI** ジ・ドウ・シキ
成人式	become + person + type = *Coming of Age ceremony*	**SEI·JIN·SHIKI** セイ・ジン・シキ

KANJI 354

PASSAGE

| マ | マ | マ | ㄢ | 予 | 肖 | 甬 | 甬 | 涌 |
| 通 | | | | | | | | |

BUILDING THIS KANJI

Dentist Light マ + **Utilize** 用(270) + **Seal** 辶 = 通

Meaning

The general concept is of passing through and along. This is a very versatile kanji that can mean a variety of things, from "street" (it often appears on road signs), to the ideas of thoroughly getting to know a subject or having things go according to plan.

Remembering this kanji

On hearing that the **dentist light** could finally be **utilized**, she forced her way through the PASSAGE. Moments later she identified the SEAL'S problem: a blocked PASSAGE!

Common Pronunciations

Common **ON** reading: **TSŪ** (ツウ)
Common **kun** reading: **tō** (とお)

In the first position, **TSŪ** is by far the more common reading. Both occur frequently in the second position, and the **kun-yomi** is often voiced (although it never becomes so when forming verbs).

Create your **on-yomi** keyword and enter it in the table at the back of the book. Then, after creating your **kun-yomi** keyword, write your sentence remember the **on-yomi** and **kun-yomi** readings the box below.

Less Common Pronunciations

Less common **ON** reading: **TSU** (ツ)
Less common **kun** reading: **kayo** (かよ)

COMMON WORDS AND COMPOUNDS		
通る (intr)	go along; pass by	**tō·ru** とお・る
通す (tr)	pierce; let through	**tō·su** とお・す
大通り	large + passage = *a main street*	ō **dō·ri** おお どお・り
交通	mix + passage = *traffic; communication*	**KŌ·TSŪ** コウ・ツウ

COMPONENT #355

KOI STREAMERS 乍 乍

KANJI 355

昨 **PAST**

	冂	日	日	日′	日⸍	昨	昨	昨

BUILDING THIS KANJI
Sun 日 (6) + Koi Streamers 乍 = 昨

Meaning

Past.

Remembering this kanji

"The **sun** was dazzling that day…**koi streamers** twirled in the sky…"
"Yes," she said, "but the PAST is the PAST."

Common Pronunciations

Common **ON** reading: **SAKU** (サク)
Common **kun** reading: none

Create your **on-yomi** keyword and enter it in th table at the back of the book. After that, writ your sentence to remember the **on-yomi** readin in the box below.

Less Common Pronunciations

Less common **ON** reading: none
Less common **kun** reading: none

<table>
<thead>
<tr><th colspan="3">IRREGULAR READING</th></tr>
</thead>
<tbody>
<tr><td>昨日</td><td>past + sun (day) = yesterday</td><td>kinō
き の う</td></tr>
</tbody>
</table>

...is compound can also be read using the charters' normal on-yomi (**SAKU**·JITSU / サ ク · ジ ...), giving the word a more formal tone.

COMMON WORDS AND COMPOUNDS		
昨年	past + year = *last year*	**SAKU**·**NEN** サク·ネン
昨夜	past + night = *last night*	**SAKU**·**YA** サク·ヤ
昨今	past + now = *recently;* *nowadays*	**SAK**·**KON** サッ·コン

KANJI 356

BUNDLE

一 厂 冂 曰 申 申 束

BUILDING THIS KANJI
Tree 木(13) + Mouth (vampire) 口(8) = 束

Meaning
...undle, bunch. Note that the writing order of this kanji does not follow the components as listed above, with "mouth" written after the initial horizontal stroke. It is similar in this respect to the character for "east" (東) from Entry 76.

Remembering this kanji
Crouched behind the **tree**, the **vampire** was a BUNDLE of nerves. "They're getting closer," he thought. "I'd better get rid of this BUNDLE."

Common Pronunciations
Common **ON** reading: SOKU (ソ ク)
Common **kun** reading: taba (た ば)

Less Common Pronunciations
Less common **ON** reading: none
Less common **kun** reading: tsuka (つ か)

COMMON WORDS AND COMPOUNDS		
束	*bundle; bunch*	**taba** た ば
花束	flower + bunch = *bouquet*	hana·**taba** は な · た ば
結束	bind + bunch = *union;* *combination*	KES·**SOKU** ケ ッ · ソ ク

KANJI 357

SPECIAL

ヒ 十 牛 牛 牜 牪 牪 特

BUILDING THIS KANJI
Cow 牛(100) + Temple 寺(104) = 特

Meaning
Special.

Remembering this kanji
"There was a **cow** in that **temple** the other day. I didn't realize they were so SPECIAL here." "They are. But speaking of **cows**, the deli downtown has a great SPECIAL on sirloin today."

Common Pronunciations
Common **ON** reading: TOKU (ト ク)
Common **kun** reading: none

Create your **on-yomi** keyword and enter it in the table at the back of the book. After that, write

your sentence to remember the **on-yomi** reading in the box below.

	COMMON WORDS AND COMPOUNDS	
特別	special + different = *special; extraordinary*	**TOKU·BETSU** ト ク・ベ ツ
特売	special + sell = *bargain; special buy*	**TOKU·BAI** ト ク・バ イ
特急	special + hasten = *special express (train)*	**TOKU·KYŪ** トッ・キュウ

Less Common Pronunciations
Less common **ON** reading: none
Less common **kun** reading: none

KANJI 358

真 **TRUE**

一	十	广	市	古	吉	百	直	真
真								

BUILDING THIS KANJI
Ten (scarecrow) 十 (28) + **Tool** 具 (177) = 真

Meaning
True, genuine. This interesting kanji often intensifies the quality of the character that follows it—the irregular readings and first compound below offer examples of this. As this kanji is very similar to some others we will learn, make sure you clearly see that it breaks apart into "ten (scarecrow)" and "tool".

Remembering this kanji
"You are a **scarecrow**?"
"TRUE."
"Then giving you this TOOL would be kind of pointless, wouldn't it?"
"That is also TRUE."

It was looking like he would have to fix the barn on his own; that which he had feared more than anything else was coming TRUE.

Common Pronunciations
Common **ON** reading: **SHIN** (シン)
Common **kun** reading: **ma** (ま)

Less Common Pronunciations
Less common **ON** reading: none
Less common **kun** reading: none

	IRREGULAR READINGS	
真赤	true + red = *deep red*	**mak·ka** まっ・か
真青	true + blue = *deep blue; horribly pale*	**mas·sao** まっ・さお

These are the only two words in which the readings of the kanji that follow 真 change in such radical way. More common examples include 真白 (**mas**·shiro / まっ・しろ) "snow white" and 真暗 (**mak**·kura / まっ・くら) "pitch dark". You may also see these compounds written as 真っ赤, 真っ青, and 真っ白, etc. Keep an eye out as well for a few words such as 真中 (**man**·naka / まん・なか) "right in the middle", which is also sometimes written as 真ん中.

	COMMON WORDS AND COMPOUNDS	
真新しい	true + new = *brand-new*	**ma** atara·shii ま あたら・しい
真実	true + actual = *truth; reality*	**SHIN·JITSU** シン・ジツ

COMPONENT #359

CRANE

KANJI 359

局

OFFICE

フ コ ア 月 月 局 局

BUILDING THIS KANJI

Flag 尸 + Crane コ + Mouth (vampire) 口 (8)
= 局

Meaning

Office, bureau. In a few words this kanji can also mean the "situation", or state of something (the first compound is an example).

Remembering this kanji

"The **flag** is torn," said the foreman. "We gotta replace it."

"Can I get up there with the **crane**, boss?" asked he **vampire**.

"Why do that? Just head through their OFFICE."

The **vampire** took off his hard hat. "Really," he said. "Imagine me strolling by those power suits, cubicles and computers. I'd look ridiculous in an OFFICE."

Common Pronunciations

Common **ON** reading: **KYOKU** (キョク)
Common **kun** reading: none

Recall from Entry 122 that the first two kanji of the second compound mean "water supply system" when taken together

Create your **on-yomi** keyword and enter it in the table at the back of the book. After that, write your sentence to remember the **on-yomi** reading in the box below.

Less Common Pronunciations

Less common **ON** reading: none
Less common **kun** reading: none

COMMON WORDS AND COMPOUNDS		
結局	bind + office (situation) = *after all; in the long run*	KEK·**KYOKU** ケッ·キョク
水道局	water supply system + office = *water bureau*	SUI·DŌ·**KYOKU** スイ·ドウ· キョク
薬局	medicine + office = *pharmacy*	YAK·**KYOKU** ヤッ·キョク

KANJI 360

GATHER

ノ イ イ 广 什 付 住 隹 隹
隼 隼 集

BUILDING THIS KANJI

Squirrels 隹 + Tree 土 (13) = 集

Meaning
Gather, assemble.

Less Common Pronunciations
Less common **ON** reading: none
Less common **kun** reading: **tsudo** (つど)

Remembering this kanji
"**Squirrels** sure like to GATHER in that **tree**, don't they?"
"Yeah, they GATHER nuts and then GATHER afterward to chat about how much they GATHERED."

COMMON WORDS AND COMPOUNDS		
集まる (intr)	*gather; come together*	**atsu**·maru あつ·まる
集める (tr)	*gather; collect*	**atsu**·meru あつ·める
集中	gather + middle = *concentration*	**SHŪ**·CHŪ シュウ·チュ

Common Pronunciations
Common **ON** reading: **SHŪ** (シュウ)
Common **kun** reading: **atsu** (あつ)

CHAPTER 16 REVIEW EXERCISES

A. Please match the following kanji to their meanings.

1.	通	a.	Field
2.	集	b.	Late
3.	晩	c.	Passage
4.	野	d.	True
5.	石	e.	Garden
6.	園	f.	Wide
7.	別	g.	Stone
8.	真	h.	Different
9.	院	i.	Gather
10.	広	j.	Institution

B. Please match the following meanings to their kanji, and these to their on- or kun-yomi.

1.	Special	a. 昨	1.	**GEN** (ゲン)	
2.	Taste	b. 局	2.	**KYOKU** (キョク)	
3.	Flat	c. 特	3.	**mise** (みせ)	
4.	Office	d. 店	4.	**ka** (か)	
5.	Original	e. 味	5.	**TOKU** (トク)	
6.	Shop	f. 貸	6.	**mina** (みな)	
7.	Edge	g. 際	7.	**hira** (ひら)	
8.	All	h. 原	8.	**SAI** (サイ)	
9.	Past	i. 平	9.	**SAKU** (サク)	
10.	Lend	j. 皆	10.	**aji** (あじ)	

C. Please choose the best answer(s) to the follow ing questions.

1. Which of the following kanji has the m number of strokes?
   a. 表   b. 皆   c. 野   d. 通   e. 真

2. Which of the following readings apply the kanji 表?
   a. **arawa** (あらわ)
   b. **kara** (から)
   c. **SHI** (シ)
   d. **JO** (ジョ)
   e. **omote** (おもて)

3. I will not rest until I ___ Mr. Everest!
   a. 味   b. 貸   c. 集   d. 登   e. 絡

4. Which is the correct reading of 通る?
   a. **no·ru** (の·る)
   b. **tō·ru** (とお·る)
   c. **kō·ru** (こお·る)
   d. **so·ru** (そ·る)

5. Which is the correct reading of 広い?
   a. **hira·i** (ひら·い)
   b. **hara·i** (はら·い)
   c. **hiro·i** (ひろ·い)
   d. **kuro·i** (くろ·い)

D. Please match the following compounds to their meanings and pronunciations.

1. 国際   a. Special
2. 動物園   b. Automatic
3. 特別   c. Fossil
4. 丁度   d. Instant death
5. 意味   e. Zoo
6. 漢字   f. Meaning
7. 自動式   g. Exactly
8. 指令   h. Order / Directive
9. 即死   i. Kanji
10. 化石   j. International

1. **KAN·JI** (カン·ジ)
2. **I·MI** (イ·ミ)
3. **SOKU·SHI** (ソク·シ)
4. **DŌ·BUTSU·EN** (ドウ·ブツ·エン)
5. **KOKU·SAI** (コク·サイ)
6. **TOKU·BETSU** (トク·ベツ)
7. **KA·SEKI** (カ·セキ)
8. **SHI·REI** (シ·レイ)
9. **CHŌ·DO** (チョウ·ド)
10. **JI·DŌ·SHIKI** (ジ·ドウ·シキ)

E. Please read the passage below and answer the questions that follow.

先月私は夫と広島へ行きました。県立動物園へ行って付近の山をハイキングしました。とても楽しかったです。来年は北海道へ行く予定です。

1. Where did she go last month?
2. With whom did she go?
3. Where did they visit in the city?
4. What did they do outside the city?
5. Where do they plan to go next year?

CUMULATIVE REVIEW EXERCISES FOR
CHAPTERS 1 - 16

A. Please match the following kanji to their meanings.

1. 若   a. Clothes

2. 界   b. Bundle

3. 可   c. World

4. 服   d. Beforehand

5. 束   e. Filial piety

6. 且   f. Appearance

7. 孝   g. Besides

8. 仕   h. Serve

9. 予   i. Young

10. 采   j. Possible

B. Which kanji does not belong in the group?

1. a.野   b.泉   c.忘   d.石   e.洋

2. a.楽   b.羊   c.牛   d.魚   e.馬

3. a.進   b.動   c.走   d.登   e.県

4. a.姉   b.夫   c.兄   d.医   e.母

5. a.亡   b.死   c.和   d.泣   e.弔

6. a.洋   b.歌   c.海   d.魚   e.泉

7. a.暗   b.低   c.短   d.若   e.番

8. a.弱   b.吉   c.良   d.美   e.完

9. a.指   b.酒   c.足   d.頭   e.耳

10. a.現   b.予   c.昨   d.晩   e.信

C. Identify the kanji n each group having the m...
number of strokes.

1. a.兄   b.反   c.予   d.手   e.

2. a.各   b.州   c.旨   d.令   e.

3. a.県   b.店   c.配   d.即   e.

4. a.姉   b.屋   c.実   d.良   e.

5. a.楽   b.際   c.遠   d.漢   e.

6. a.事   b.形   c.式   d.送   e.

7. a.己   b.亡   c.代   d.文   e.

8. a.理   b.神   c.紙   d.降   e.

9. a.用   b.両   c.払   d.民   e.

10. a.銀   b.遊   c.園   d.質   e.

D. Please list the following kanji in the order in...
cated (alphabetical).

1. Arrow / End / Husband / Not yet / Spicy
   a.辛   b.夫   c.矢   d.未   e.末

2. Against / Door / Measurement / Office /
   Roof
   a.反   b.尺   c.戸   d.局   e.屋

3. Lend / People / Substitute / Surname / Typ...
   a.民   b.式   c.貸   d.氏   e.代

4. Cause / Declare / God / Painting / Utiliz...
   a.神   b.申   c.画   d.用   e.由

5. Bind / Continue / Entwine / Picture / Vi...
   a.続   b.結   c.絵   d.経   e.絡

6. Active / Cry / Ocean / Saké / Wash
   a.洋   b.洗   c.酒   d.活   e.泣

7. Direction / Flat / Literature / Perish / Proper
   a. 方 b. 文 c. 正 d. 平 e. 亡

8. Achieve / Advance / Passage / Play / Send
   a. 進 b. 遊 c. 送 d. 通 e. 達

9. Besides / Prefecture / Quality / True / Wear
   a. 着 b. 且 c. 質 d. 真 e. 県

10. Against / Original / Shop / Stone / Wide
    a. 反 b. 広 c. 店 d. 原 e. 石

Please choose the best answer to the following questions.

1. There's nothing nicer than an afternoon cup of ____.
   a. 洋 b. 魚 c. 茶 d. 民 e. 羊

2. Don't you dare wag your ____ at me!
   a. 神 b. 質 c. 都 d. 野 e. 指

3. Have you ever tasted a more delicious Japanese ____ than this one?
   a. 園 b. 橋 c. 矢 d. 束 e. 酒

4. Congratulations on your recent ____!
   a. 県 b. 婚 c. 軍 d. 味 e. 食

5. My boss wants to speak with me about an important ____.
   a. 洗 b. 非 c. 重 d. 事 e. 至

Please choose the best answer to the following questions.

1. Which is the correct reading of 比べる?
   a. **shira·beru** (しら·べる)
   b. **ara·beru** (あら·べる)
   c. **fu·beru** (ふ·べる)
   d. **kura·beru** (くら·べる)

2. Which is the correct reading of 楽しい?
   a. **tano·shii** (たの·しい)
   b. **taka·shii** (たか·しい)
   c. **tada·shii** (ただ·しい)
   d. **tama·shii** (たま·しい)

3. Which is the correct reading of 付ける?
   a. **a·keru** (あ·ける)
   b. **u·keru** (う·ける)
   c. **tsu·keru** (つ·ける)
   d. **ma·keru** (ま·ける)

4. Which is the correct reading of 辞める?
   a. **de·meru** (で·める)
   b. **shi·meru** (し·める)
   c. **ka·meru** (か·める)
   d. **ya·meru** (や·める)

5. Which is the correct reading of 占う?
   a. **makana·u** (まかな·う)
   b. **urana·u** (うらな·う)
   c. **fuka·u** (ふか·う)
   d. **tama·u** (たま·う)

G. Please choose the best answer to the following questions.

1. Which is the correct reading of 登山?
   a. **KO·ZAN** (コ·ザン)
   b. **O·ZAN** (オ·ザン)
   c. **TO·ZAN** (ト·ザン)
   d. **DO·SAN** (ド·サン)

2. Which is the correct reading of 頭上?
   a. **MU·JŌ** (ム·ジョウ)
   b. **ZU·JŌ** (ズ·ジョウ)
   c. **SU·JŌ** (ス·ジョウ)
   d. **KU·JŌ** (ク·ジョウ)

3. Which is the correct reading of 茶道?
   a. **KA·DŌ** (カ·ドウ)
   b. **TA·DŌ** (タ·ドウ)
   c. **HA·DŌ** (ハ·ドウ)
   d. **SA·DŌ** (サ·ドウ)

4. Which is the correct reading of 大和?
   a. **amato** (あまと)
   b. **sabaku** (さばく)
   c. **yamato** (やまと)
   d. **sabato** (さばと)

5. Which is the correct reading of 文字?
   a. **MO·JI** (モ・ジ)
   b. **FU·JI** (フ・ジ)
   c. **HI·JI** (ヒ・ジ)
   d. **U·JI** (ウ・ジ)

6. Which is the correct reading of 人形?
   a. **hito·GYŌ** (ひと・ギョウ)
   b. **NIN·GYŌ** (ニン・ギョウ)
   c. **NIN·JI** (ニン・ジ)
   d. **NIN·JA** (ニン・ジャ)

7. Which is the correct reading of 気付く?
   a. **KI fu·ku** (キ ふ・く)
   b. **KI zu·ku** (キ づ・く)
   c. **KI chi·ku** (キ ち・く)
   d. **KI ma·ku** (キ ま・く)

8. Which is the correct reading of 美味しい?
   a. **oi·shii** (おい・しい)
   b. **ko·shii** (こ・しい)
   c. **i·shii** (い・しい)
   d. **uru·shii** (うる・しい)

9. Which is the correct reading of 川原?
   a. **kawa·na** (かわ・な)
   b. **kawa·ba** (かわ・ば)
   c. **kawa·sa** (かわ・さ)
   d. **kawa·ra** (かわ・ら)

10. Which is the correct reading of 世間?
    a. **SO·KEN** (ソ・ケン)
    b. **SA·KEN** (サ・ケン)
    c. **SE·KEN** (セ・ケン)
    d. **SE·KAN** (セ・カン)

H. Please match the following compounds to their meanings and pronunciations.

1. 酒屋   a. District / Region   1. **RAKU·EN** (ラク・エン)

2. 活動   b. Definite / Concrete   2. **hana·taba** (はな・たば)

3. 楽園   c. Excursion / Day trip   3. **HO·DŌ·KYŌ** (ホ・ドウ・キョウ)

4. 具体的   d. Form / Formality   4. **KEI·SHIKI** (ケイ・シキ

5. 送別   e. Liquor store   5. **HYAKU·NE SAI** (ヒャク・ネン・サイ

6. 花束   f. Bouquet   6. **saka·ya** (さか・や)

7. 地方   g. Activity   7. **TAI·SEI·YŌ** (タイ・セイ ヨウ)

8. 百年歳   h. Atlantic Ocean   8. **GAKU·IN** (ガク・イン

9. 学院   i. Pacific Ocean   9. **KATSU·DŌ** (カツ・ドウ

10. 大西洋   j. Worry / Anxiety   10. **SHIN·PAI** (シン・パイ

11. 太平洋   k. Farewell / Send-off   11. **EN·SOKU** (エン・ソク

12. 遠足   l. Pedestrian bridge   12. **CHI·HŌ·** (チ・ホウ)

13. 歩道橋   m. Academy   13. **SŌ·BETSU** (ソウ・ベツ

14. 心配   n. Paradise   14. **TAI·HEI·YŌ** (タイ・ヘイ ヨウ)

15. 形式   o. Centennial   15. **GU·TAI· TEKI** (グ・タイ・ テキ)

CHAPTER SEVENTEEN

Kanji #361—385

KANJI 361

HARD

BUILDING THIS KANJI
Prison 囗 + Old 古 (58) = 固

Meaning
Hard, solid.

Remembering this kanji
You don't wanna be in **prison** when you're **old** like me," he said. "The walls are HARD, the cells are HARD, the cots are HARD, even the grub is HARD. I dunno…I'd just like to figure out what it is about being here that makes my attitude so HARD."

Common Pronunciations
Common **ON** reading: **KO** (コ)
Common **kun** reading: **kata** (か た)

Less Common Pronunciations
Less common **ON** reading: none
Less common **kun** reading: none

COMMON WORDS AND COMPOUNDS		
固い	*hard; solid*	**kata·i** か た・い
固体	hard + body = *a solid*	**KO·TAI** コ・タイ
固定	hard + fixed = *fixed; settled*	**KO·TEI** コ・テイ

KANJI 362

COOL

BUILDING THIS KANJI
Ice Hockey 冫 + Command 令 (337) = 冷

Meaning
Cool, cold. The sense here is of objects that are cool or cold to the touch (the idea of cold weather, however, is generally conveyed by the kanji in Entry 446). Remember that the 'paint sprayer' component in the character for command will often change to マ (the 'dentist light') when handwritten or in a more calligraphic-style font.

Remembering this kanji

You're in an **ice hockey** game, and have to take **command**. It's COOL in the arena; you'll need to be even COOLER than that.

Common Pronunciations

Common **ON** reading: **REI** (レイ)
Common **kun** reading: **tsume** (つめ)

Less Common Pronunciations

Less common **ON** reading: none
Less common **kun** reading: **hi** (ひ); **sa** (さ)

COMMON WORDS AND COMPOUNDS		
冷たい	cool	**tsume**·tai つめ·たい
冷気	cool + spirit = chill; cold weather	**REI**·**KI** レイ·キ
寒冷	cold + cool = cold; chilly	**KAN**·**REI** カン·レイ

COMPONENT #363

CHIMNEY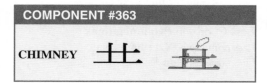

KANJI 363

昔

LONG AGO

一	十	卄	屮	告	昔	昔	昔

BUILDING THIS KANJI
Chimney 屮 + Sun 日 (6) = 昔

Meaning

Long ago, old times.

Remembering this kanji

"LONG AGO," he said, "when Santa used to g[o] down the **chimney** on the **sun**…"
"What are you talking about?" the girl inte[r]rupted. "There could never have been a **chimne[y]** on the **sun**. It's a superheated ball of gas."
"Jeez, I guess you really did give up on fair[y] tales LONG AGO."

Common Pronunciations

Common **ON** reading: none
Common **kun** reading: **mukashi** (むかし)

Less Common Pronunciations

Less common **ON** reading: **SEKI** (セキ); **SHAKU** (シャク)
Less common **kun** reading: none

COMMON WORDS AND COMPOUNDS		
昔	long ago	**mukashi** むかし
昔話	long ago + speak = old story; folklore	**mukashi**·banashi むかし·ばなし

KANJI 364

究 **INQUIRY**

゛	゛	宀	宀	究	究	究		

BUILDING THIS KANJI

Weightlifter 宀 + Nine 九(39) = 究

Meaning

Inquiry, often with the sense of this being done thoroughly or extensively.

Remembering this kanji

Even if a **weightlifter** can raise **99.99%** of the weight given him, he will still have failed in his task. If he wants to succeed, he must make INQUIRY upon INQUIRY into how he can lift up the rest.

Common Pronunciations
Common **ON** reading: **KYŪ** (キュウ)
Common **kun** reading: kiwa (きわ)

Less Common Pronunciations
Less common **ON** reading: none
Less common **kun** reading: none

COMMON WORDS AND COMPOUNDS		
究める	*investigate thoroughly; master*	kiwa·meru きわ·める
研究	polish + inquiry = *research*	KEN·KYŪ ケン·キュウ

KANJI 365

薬 **MEDICINE**

一	十	艹	艹	艹	苩	苩	苩	苩
苩	莁	莁	莁	薬	薬	薬		

BUILDING THIS KANJI

Wreath 艹 + Music 楽(216) = 薬

Meaning

Medicine. In a few compounds this kanji can mean 'chemical'.

Remembering this kanji

If you realize that someone's laying a **wreath** over you, and that the **music** playing is Chopin's funeral march…chances are you didn't get the right MEDICINE.

Common Pronunciations
Common **ON** reading: **YAKU** (ヤク)
Common **kun** reading: kusuri (くすり)

The **kun-yomi** is always voiced outside of first position, as in the second compound below.

Create your **on-yomi** keyword and enter it in the table at the back of the book. After that, write your sentence to remember the **on-yomi** and **kun-yomi** readings in the box below.

Less Common Pronunciations
Less common **ON** reading: none
Less common **kun** reading: none

COMMON WORDS AND COMPOUNDS		
薬	*medicine*	**kusuri** くすり
目薬	eye + medicine = *eye drops*	me·**gusuri** め・ぐすり
薬局	medicine + office = *pharmacy*	**YAK**·KYOKU ヤッ・キョク

 **LINE**

＜	∠	∠	⺰	糸	糸	糹	糹	糹
紛	綿	絹	線	線	線			

BUILDING THIS KANJI
Thread 糸 (196) + **Springs** 泉 (319) = 線

Meaning
Line.

Remembering this kanji
"I really dislike being in LINE to get tickets like this," said the **thread**.
"I don't understand why," said the **springs**. "You *are* a LINE."
"Very funny, but I wouldn't be joking about LINES if I were you; look at the wet LINE you're leaving on the carpet here."

Common Pronunciations
Common **ON** reading: **SEN** (セン)
Common **kun** reading: none

Less Common Pronunciations
Less common **ON** reading: none
Less common **kun** reading: none

COMMON WORDS AND COMPOUNDS		
本線	main + line = *main railway line*	**HON**·SEN ホン・セン
前線	before + line = *front line; (weather) front*	**ZEN**·SEN ゼン・セン
配線	distribute + line = *wiring*	**HAI**·SEN ハイ・セン

VASE

Ensure that you can see how this component differs from 立, the kanji for 'stand' in Entry 112.

 FACE

ヽ	一	ユ	ヴ	立	产	产	彦	彦
彦	彦	產	顏	顏	顏	顏	顏	顏

BUILDING THIS KANJI
Vase ヰ + Cliff 厂 + Scratches 彡 +
Guy Wearing a Barrel 頁 = 顏

Meaning
Face.

Remembering this kanji
So there's this **vase** on the top of a **cliff**, and a
guy wearing a barrel wants to get it. But as he
scratches his way up the FACE of the **cliff** he
gets a lot of **scratches** of his own. Especially
on his FACE. Fortunately for him, the **vase** has
FACE cream in it.

Common Pronunciations
Common **ON** reading: **GAN** (ガン)
Common **kun** reading: **kao** (か お)

The **kun-yomi** is almost always voiced when not
in first position, as in the third compound.

Less Common Pronunciations
Less common **ON** reading: none
Less common **kun** reading: none

COMMON WORDS AND COMPOUNDS		
顏	*face*	**kao** か お
洗顏	wash + face = *washing one's face*	**SEN·GAN** セン・ガン
横顏	sideways + face = *profile*	yoko·**gao** よ こ・が お

KANJI 368

族 **TRIBE**

ヽ	一	方	方	扩	扩	扩	扩	旅
族	族							

BUILDING THIS KANJI
Direction 方 (223) + Hammer 宀 + Arrow 矢
(285) = 族

Meaning
Tribe, family.

Remembering this kanji
In one **direction** was a TRIBE of fierce carpen-
ters, **hammers** at the ready. In another **direction**, a more traditional TRIBE with **arrows**.
Hammers or **arrows**... We weren't afraid
of either, I thought, until I looked back and
wondered where the rest of my TRIBE had gone.

Common Pronunciations
Common **ON** reading: **ZOKU** (ゾク)
Common **kun** reading: none

Less Common Pronunciations
Less common **ON** reading: none
Less common **kun** reading: none

COMMON WORDS AND COMPOUNDS		
家族	house + tribe = *family*	**KA·ZOKU** カ・ゾク
民族	people + tribe = *race; a people*	**MIN·ZOKU** ミン・ゾク
水族館	water + tribe + manor = *(public) aquarium*	**SUI·ZOKU·KAN** スイ・ゾク・カン

COMPONENT #369

CHEERLEADERS

夊

In comparison to our short and squat 'running chicken' component, the 'cheerleaders' presented here are taller and thinner. It's important to remember that this component is written with *four* strokes, not three, and that the feet of the top cheerleader will always poke out a bit on the side.

KANJI 369

 TEACH

一	十	土	耂	耂	孝	孝	孝	孝
教	教							

BUILDING THIS KANJI
Filial piety 孝(273) + Cheerleaders 夊 = 教

Meaning
Teach. A religious element can be present in this kanji, as shown in the second compound below.

Remembering this kanji
Since they're usually so popular and able to ge what they want, **cheerleaders** often have littl **filial piety**…

"We have to TEACH her!"
"Oh, let them TEACH her in the classroom."
"Honey, how could they TEACH anyone no to toss their pom-poms into the gravy on ou dinner table?"

Common Pronunciations
Common **ON** reading: **KYŌ** (キョウ)
Common **kun** reading: **oshi** (おし)

Less Common Pronunciations
Less common **ON** reading: none
Less common **kun** reading: **oso** (おそ)

COMMON WORDS AND COMPOUNDS		
教える	*teach*	**oshi·eru** おし・える
教会	teach + meet = *church*	**KYŌ·KAI** キョウ・カイ
教科書	teach + course + write = *textbook; school book*	**KYŌ·KA·SHO** キョウ・カ・シ

KANJI 370

丙 **THIRD**

一	厂	冂	丙	丙				

BUILDING THIS KANJI
One (top of a bun) 一(3) + Inside 内 (34) = 丙

Meaning
You will rarely meet this kanji on its own; its value for us is as a component in other more common characters. It is, however, found in documents of a more official nature, where it is used to indicate the third item or clause in a list.

Remembering this kanji
Sure, you can look at the **top of a bun** and get sense of its width and height. It is only by being **inside** it, however, that you can appreciate it THIRD dimension.

Common Pronunciations
Common **ON** reading: **HEI** (ヘイ)
Common **kun** reading: none

Less Common Pronunciations
Less common **ON** readings: none
Less common **kun** reading: none

COMMON WORDS AND COMPOUNDS		
丙	*third (in a series)*	**HEI** ヘイ

KANJI 371

宿 **LODGING**

'	ハ	宀	宀	宀	宁	宍	宿	宿
宿	宿							

BUILDING THIS KANJI

Pincers 宀 + Giraffe 亻 + Hundred 百 (51)
= 宿

Meaning

Lodging, from inns to hotels.

Remembering this kanji

Even with **pincers** able to deposit them onto the balconies of their suites, it's still hopeless: **giraffes** are a **hundred** percent likely to be uncomfortable with their LODGING.

Common Pronunciations

Common **ON** reading: **SHUKU** (シュク)
Common **kun** reading: **yado** (やど)

Create your **on-yomi** keyword and enter it in the table at the back of the book. Then, after creating your kun-yomi keyword, write your sentence to remember the **on-yomi** and **kun-yomi** readings in the box below.

Less Common Pronunciations

Less common **ON** reading: none
Less common **kun** reading: none

COMMON WORDS AND COMPOUNDS		
宿	*lodging; inn*	**yado** やど
下宿	lower + lodging = *lodgings; boarding house*	**GE·SHUKU** ゲ・シュク
宿題	lodging + topic = *homework*	**SHUKU·DAI** シュク・ダイ

KANJI 372

試 **TRY**

ゝ	̇	̇	̇	̇	̇	̇	̇	言
訂	訂	試	試					

BUILDING THIS KANJI

Say 言 (80) + Type 式 (353) = 試

Meaning

Try.

Remembering this kanji

"You **say** you're the **type** who will TRY anything. Would you care to TRY this?"
"Uh…I would TRY it, but…"
"But what? If you **say** you're that **type**…"
"OK, OK, I'll TRY it."

Common Pronunciations

Common **ON** reading: **SHI** (シ)
Common **kun** reading: **kokoro** (こころ);
tame (ため)

The two **kun-yomi** are verb stems for the first and second examples below. Though they both mean to 'try', 試す (**tame·su** / ため・す) has the added implication of testing something so as to ascertain its value or validity. Note the mix of **on** and **kun-yomi** in the third compound.

Less Common Pronunciations
Less common **ON** reading: none
Less common **kun** reading: none

KANJI 373

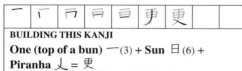

ANEW

一	厂	厅	岂	目	刵	更	

BUILDING THIS KANJI
One (top of a bun) 一 (3) + Sun 日 (6) + Piranha 乂 = 更

Meaning
This kanji conveys a sense of doing things anew, be it through revision, reform or renewal, amongst others. A secondary meaning (expressed with the less common **kun-yomi**) has to do with staying up late or the day growing late.

Remembering this kanji
The **tops of buns** baked ANEW when the su~~n~~ rises, feeding those as hungry as **piranhas**. An~~d~~ so the day begins ANEW…

Common Pronunciations
Common **ON** reading: **KŌ** (コウ)
Common **kun** reading: **sara** (さ ら)

Less Common Pronunciations
Less common **ON** reading: none
Less common **kun** reading: **fu** (ふ)

COMMON WORDS AND COMPOUNDS		
更に	*anew; furthermore*	**sara**-ni さら・に
更生	anew + life = *rebirth; revival*	**KŌ**-SEI コウ・セイ
変更	alter + anew = *alteration; change*	HEN-**KŌ** ヘン・コウ

KANJI 374

SYSTEM

一	乇	玊	幺	糸	糸	糸	

BUILDING THIS KANJI
Comet 一 + Thread 糸 (196) = 系

Meaning
System. As you can see from the final compound below, this kanji also appears in words related t~~o~~ lineage and genealogy.

Remembering this kanji
I asked a **comet** if it was tough to **thread** its way through the space debris of a planetary SYSTEM like ours. "Of course it is," he said, "but what can you do? You can't fight the SYSTEM."

Common Pronunciations

Common **ON** reading: **KEI** (ケイ)
Common **kun** reading: none

Less Common Pronunciations

Less common **ON** reading: none
Less common **kun** reading: none

COMMON WORDS AND COMPOUNDS		
体系	body + system = *system*	**TAI·KEI** タイ・ケイ
系図	system + diagram = *family tree; genealogy*	**KEI·ZU** ケイ・ズ
日系	sun (Japan) + system = *of Japanese descent*	**NIK·KEI** ニッ・ケイ

KANJI 375

去 DEPART

BUILDING THIS KANJI
Earth 土 (87) + **Broken Crutch** ム = 去

Meaning
Depart, leave.

Remembering this kanji

Covered in **earth**, the **broken crutch** looked up.
"You must DEPART from me," it said. "I'm
broken and can no longer do anything for you."
It was a wrenching moment, but she realized the
broken crutch was right. Placing the last of the
earth over it, she turned to DEPART.

Common Pronunciations

Common **ON** reading: **KYO** (キョ)
Common **kun** reading: **sa** (さ)

Create your **on-yomi** keyword and enter it in the
table at the back of the book. Then, after creating
your **kun-yomi** keyword, write your sentence to
remember the **on-yomi** and **kun-yomi** readings in
the box below.

Less Common Pronunciations

Less common **ON** reading: **KO** (コ)
Less common **kun** reading: none

COMMON WORDS AND COMPOUNDS		
去る	*depart; leave*	**sa·ru** さ・る
去年	depart + year = *last year*	**KYO·NEN** キョ・ネン
飛び去る	fly + depart = *fly away*	**to·bi sa·ru** と・び さ・る

COMPONENT #376

BALLROOM DANCERS

Ensure that you can quickly spot the difference
between this component and 开, the "picnic
table" introduced prior to Entry 106.

KANJI 376

NOSE

'	｀	⺧	⺕	白	自	自	畠	鼻
鼻	畠	畠	鼻	鼻				

BUILDING THIS KANJI
Self 自 (33) + **Rice Field** 田 (73) + **Ballroom Dancers** 廾 = 鼻

Meaning
Nose.

Remembering this kanji

"Wow, that guy has a pretty inflated sense of **self**, doesn't he? Look at his NOSE sticking up!"
"No, you're mistaken. He wants to figure out which **rice field** over there got a fresh load of manure; that's why his NOSE is up like that."
"Oh. Well, he still looks like a snooty **ballroom dancer** with his NOSE in the air."

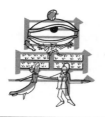

Common Pronunciations
Common **ON** reading: none
Common **kun** reading: **hana** (は な)

Less Common Pronunciations
Less common **ON** reading: **BI** (ビ)
Less common **kun** reading: none

COMMON WORDS AND COMPOUNDS		
鼻	*nose*	**hana** は な
鼻歌	nose + song = *humming*	**hana·uta** は な・う た
鼻水	nose + water = *runny nose*	**hana·mizu** は な・み ず

KANJI 377

ASIA

一 丆 丏 亐 再 冊 亜

Meaning
This kanji can stand for Asia in the same way that 日 does for Japan and 中 does for China. In a few other compounds it can act like the English prefix 'sub-'. It's an uncommon character, however, and will prove more useful as a component.

Remembering this kanji
What does an overhead view of a train track have to do with ASIA? Well, the Trans-Siberian is mostly in ASIA isn't it? And Japan, also in ASIA, is famous for the bullet train.

Common Pronunciations
Common **ON** reading: **A** (ア)
Common **kun** reading: none

After creating your **on-yomi** keyword and entering it in the table at the back of the book, write your sentence to remember the **on-yomi** reading in the box below.

Less Common Pronunciations
Less common **ON** reading: none
Less common **kun** reading: none

COMMON WORDS AND COMPOUNDS		
東亜	east + Asia = *East Asia*	**TŌ·A** ト ウ・ア

KANJI 378

JOIN

一 扌 扌 扩 扩 扩 扩 接
接 接

BUILDING THIS KANJI
Finger 扌 + Stand 立(112) + Woman 女(16)
= 接

eaning

in, contact.

emembering this kanji

.et us JOIN **fingers** and **stand** up for our rights one **woman**!" they cried. "JOIN us! JOIN us!"

ommon Pronunciations

mmon **ON** reading: **SETSU** (セ ツ)
mmon **kun** reading: none

Less Common Pronunciations

Less common **ON** reading: none
Less common **kun** reading: none

COMMON WORDS AND COMPOUNDS		
接続	join + continue = *joining; connection*	**SETSU·ZOKU** セツ·ゾク
接着	join + wear = *adhesion*	**SET·CHAKU** セッ·チャク
面接	mask + join = *interview*	**MEN·SETSU** メン·セツ

OMPONENT #379

ELEVISION 兑

ANJI 379

 **OPINION**

㇒	ニ	三	亖	言	言	言	訁
訁	訃	説	説	説			

UILDING THIS KANJI
ay 言 (80) + **Television** 兑 = 説

eaning

pinion, theory.

Remembering this kanji

They asked me to **say** something on **television**. So I did. Yeah, that's right, I gave them just what they wanted: my OPINION.

Common Pronunciations

Common **ON** reading: **SETSU** (セ ツ)
Common **kun** reading: none

Less Common Pronunciations

Less common **ON** reading: **ZEI** (ゼ イ)
Less common **kun** reading: **to** (と)

COMMON WORDS AND COMPOUNDS		
説明	opinion + bright = *explanation*	**SETSU·MEI** セツ·メイ
伝説	transmit + opinion = *legend*	**DEN·SETSU** デン·セツ
小説	small + opinion = *a novel*	**SHŌ·SETSU** ショウ·セツ

ANJI 380

 **MAKE**

ノ	イ	𠆢	乍	竹	作	作

BUILDING THIS KANJI
Giraffe イ + **Koi Streamers** 乍 = 作

Meaning

Make. A secondary meaning relates to crops and harvesting.

Remembering this kanji

Giraffes are clueless when it comes to **koi streamers**, so don't ask any of them to MAKE one. They can't MAKE the cloth, they can't MAKE the design…they can't even MAKE the wire frame! About the only thing they can MAKE is a giant mess with those clumsy hooves of theirs.

Common Pronunciations

Common **ON** reading: SAKU (サク); SA (サ)
Common **kun** reading: tsuku (つく)

SAKU is by far the more commonly used of these readings. The **kun-yomi** is usually voiced outside of first position.

Create your **on-yomi** keyword for SA (サ) a enter it in the table at the back of the book. The after creating your **kun-yomi** keyword, write yo sentence to remember the **on-yomi** and **kun-yo** readings in the box below.

Less Common Pronunciations

Less common **ON** reading: none
Less common **kun** reading: none

COMMON WORDS AND COMPOUNDS		
作る	*make*	tsuku·ru つく・る
作者	make + individual = *author; writer*	SAKU·SHA サク・シャ
動作	move + make = *action; movement*	DŌ·SA ドウ・サ

節 JOINT

ノ	⸜	⺮	⺊⺮	⺮⺊	⺮⺮	⺮⺊	⺮⺊	⺮⺊
笆	笆	節	節					

BUILDING THIS KANJI
Machine Guns ⺮ + Immediate 即 (345) = 節

Meaning

This interesting character refers to a joint or a section of something. It is used in a variety of words, and can refer to everything from a 'joint' between seasons (the second common word provides an example), a knot in wood, or a melody in music, for instance. It can also convey a sense of moderation or economizing; think of this in terms of a narrowing joint that squeezes off the use of something such as a flow of money.

Remembering this kanji

The **machine guns** went off, and my reactio was **immediate**: they're aiming for my JOIN

Common Pronunciations

Common **ON** reading: SETSU (セツ)
Common **kun** reading: fushi (ふし)

Less Common Pronunciations

Less common **ON** reading: SECHI (セチ)
Less common **kun** reading: none

COMMON WORDS AND COMPOUNDS		
節	*joint; melody; knot*	fushi ふし
節分	joint + part = *last day of winter*	SETSU·BUN セツ・ブン
調節	tone + joint = *adjustment; regulaton*	CHŌ·SETSU チョウ・セツ

KANJI 382

則 **RULE**

丨	冂	月	目	目	貝	貝	則	則

BUILDING THIS KANJI
Shellfish 貝 (21) + Chisel 刂 = 則

Meaning
Rule, in the sense of a law or regulation.

Remembering this kanji
Be careful! There's a very important RULE to remember when prying apart **shellfish** with a **chisel**. Unfortunately, though, I have a RULE not to tell that RULE to anyone.

Common Pronunciations
Common **ON** reading: **SOKU** (ソ ク)
Common **kun** reading: none

Less Common Pronunciations
Less common **ON** reading: none
Less common **kun** reading: none

COMMON WORDS AND COMPOUNDS		
定則	fixed + rule = *established rule*	**TEI·SOKU** テイ・ソク
原則	original + rule = *principle; general rule*	**GEN·SOKU** ゲン・ソク
法則	law + rule = *rule; law*	**HŌ·SOKU** ホウ・ソク

COMPONENT #383

ELBOW コ

KANJI 383

今 **NOW**

ノ	人	今	今					

BUILDING THIS KANJI
Umbrella 𠆢 + One (hamburger patty) 一 (3) + Elbow コ = 今

Meaning
Now.

Remembering this kanji
Even though I was hidden by the **umbrella**, I grew nervous when the **hamburger patty** was placed on my **elbow**. "Get it off me," I was soon pleading, "NOW!" They remained calm, however, and only smiled. "NOW, NOW," one of them said, "don't be like that."

Common Pronunciations
Common **ON** reading: **KON** (コン)
Common **kun** reading: **ima** (いま)

Less Common Pronunciations
Less common **ON** reading: **KIN** (キン)
Less common **kun** reading: none

IRREGULAR READING		
今日	now + sun (day) = *today*	**kyō** きょう
今朝	now + morning = *this morning*	**kesa** けさ
今年	now + year = *this year*	**ko·toshi** こ・とし

We met the first two of these compounds in Entries 6 and 85, as the readings of both kanji were irregular. The third we encounter here, as **toshi** is the normal **kun-yomi** for 年. Also note how the addition of the **hiragana** は in the second example below (which creates the most famous of all Japanese greetings) can change the readings of both kanji from the first example above.

COMMON WORDS AND COMPOUNDS

今	*now*	**ima** いま
今日は	now + sun (day) = *Good morning / afternoon; Hello!*	**KON·NICHI·wa** コン·ニチ·は
今週	now + week = *this week*	**KON·SHŪ** コン·シュウ

KANJI 384

 **ETERNAL**

`	亅	刁	永	永				

BUILDING THIS KANJI
Jelly Bean ﹀ + Water 水(61) = 永

Meaning
Eternal, forever. Much as we did for 未 and 末 (Entries 276 and 277), we will learn this and the next entry as a pair in order to solidify the differences between these easily confused kanji. Refer back to the kanji for "water" (Entry 61) in order to see how the "harpoon" component of that character has become transformed in this one.

Remembering this kanji
How long do you suppose it would take for a **jelly bean** dropping onto the kanji for "**water**" to turn its harpoon into a crane? It's tough to imagine, isn't it? Obviously we're dealing with something ETERNAL here.

Common Pronunciations
Common **ON** reading: **EI** (エイ)
Common **kun** reading: **naga** (なが)

Less Common Pronunciations
Less common **ON** reading: none
Less common **kun** reading: none

COMMON WORDS AND COMPOUNDS

永い	*long (in terms of time)*	**naga·i** なが·い
永遠	eternal + far = *eternity*	**EI·EN** エイ·エン

KANJI 385

 ICE

丿	刁	刁	氺	氷				

BUILDING THIS KANJI
Water 水(61) + Jelly Bean ﹀ = 氷

Meaning
Ice. As you can see, this kanji is very similar visually to 永. The only other thing to keep in mind here is that the stroke order of the 'water' component is broken—the jelly bean is written immediately after the initial harpoon stroke.

remembering this kanji

.stuck on the **water**…hungry…shivering…

'm going to get that **jelly bean** floating over
ere," he told her in a daze.
She barely kept him from jumping out of their
nghy into the frigid **water**. "That's not a **jelly**
ean," she said desperately. "It's not. It's ICE.
othing but ICE."

Common Pronunciations

Common **ON** reading: **HYŌ** (ヒョウ)
Common **kun** reading: **kōri** (こおり)

Less Common Pronunciations

Less common **ON** reading: none
Less common **kun** reading: none

COMMON WORDS AND COMPOUNDS		
氷	ice	**kōri** こおり
氷山	ice + mountain = *iceberg*	**HYŌ·ZAN** ヒョウ·ザン
氷結	ice + bind = *freeze over*	**HYŌ·KETSU** ヒョウ·ケツ

HAPTER 17 REVIEW EXERCISES

Please match the following kanji to their meanings.

1.	薬	a.	Nose
2.	氷	b.	Medicine
3.	永	c.	Long ago
4.	教	d.	Hard
5.	系	e.	Try
6.	昔	f.	Eternal
7.	接	g.	Teach
8.	固	h.	Ice
9.	試	i.	Join
10.	鼻	j.	System

Please match the following meanings to their
kanji, and these to their **on-** or **kun-yomi**.

1.	Face	a. 亜	1.	**REI** (レイ)
2.	Asia	b. 今	2.	**SEN** (セン)
3.	Now	c. 去	3.	**yado** (やど)
4.	Line	d. 顔	4.	**ZOKU** (ゾク)
5.	Cool	e. 線	5.	**sa** (さ)
6.	Opinion	f. 説	6.	**SETSU** (セツ)
7.	Depart	g. 族	7.	**fushi** (ふし)
8.	Lodging	h. 節	8.	**A** (ア)
9.	Joint	i. 宿	9.	**ima** (いま)
	(kun-yomi)			
10.	Tribe	j. 冷	10.	**kao** (かお)

C. Please choose the best answer(s) to the following questions.

1. Which of the following readings apply to
the kanji 作?
a. **tsu** (つ)
b. **SEI** (セイ)
c. **SA** (サ)
d. **tsuku** (つく)
e. **SAKU** (サク)

2. Which is the correct reading of 固い?
a. **ama·i** (あま·い)
b. **kata·i** (かた·い)
c. **kita·i** (きた·い)
d. **kota·i** (こた·い)

3. Which of the following kanji has the most
number of strokes?
a. 接   b. 族   c. 試   d. 宿   e. 教

4. You're darn right it hurt. I got hit smack on
the _____ .
a. 氷   b. 鼻   c. 薬   d. 丙   e. 則

5. Which is the correct reading of 冷たい?
   a. **mika·tai** (み か·た い)
   b. **kami·tai** (か み·た い)
   c. **tsume·tai** (つ め·た い)
   d. **hari·tai** (は り·た い)

D. Please match the following compounds to their meanings and pronunciations.

1.	民族	a. Adhesion	1.	**MIN·ZOKU** (ミ ン·ゾ ク)
2.	今週	b. This week	2.	**TEI·SOKU** (テ イ·ソ ク)
3.	試合	c. Game / Match	3.	**KŌ·SEI** (コ ウ·セ イ)
4.	接着	d. Established rule	4.	**SHI·ai** (シ·あ い)
5.	薬局	e. Humming	5.	**SET·CHAKU** (セ ッ·チ ャ ク)
6.	昔話	f. Old story / Folklore	6.	**hana·uta** (は な·う た)
7.	永遠	g. Race / A people	7.	**EI·EN** (エ イ·エ ン)
8.	鼻歌	h. Rebirth / Revival	8.	**YAK·KYOK** (ヤ ッ·キ ョ ク)
9.	更生	i. Pharmacy	9.	**KON·SHŪ** (コ ン·シ ュ ウ)
10.	定則	j. Eternity	10.	**mukashi·banashi** (む か し·ば な し)

E. Please read the passage below and answer the questions that follow.

今日は冷たい雨が降った。私の小さい家の上に黒い鳥が集まった。晩秋だ。今年も一人です。

1. What happened today?
2. What time of year is it?
3. Do I have a spacious house?
4. What has happened above my house?
5. Am I surrounded by friends this year?

Kanji #386—410

 LAW

| シ | シ | ラ | 汁 | 汁 | 泔 | 法 | 法 |

BUILDING THIS KANJI
Splash 氵 + Depart 去 (375) = 法

Meaning
Law, method. A religious meaning (particularly
Buddhist) is also conveyed in some specialized
compounds that include this kanji.

Remembering this kanji
"I can't believe you'd just **splash** someone like
that and **depart**!" he exclaimed. "Don't you
realize you broke the LAW!?"

Common Pronunciations
Common **ON** reading: **HŌ** (ホウ)
Common **kun** reading: none

Less Common Pronunciations
Less common **ON** reading: **HA-** (ハッ);
HO- (ホッ)
Less common **kun** reading: none

As we saw in the less common **on-yomi** for 合
back in Entry 250 [**GA-** (ガッ) and **KA-** (カッ)],
these two readings always "double up" with the
on-yomi of the kanji that follow. The compounds
in which they appear are obscure.

COMMON WORDS AND COMPOUNDS		
方法	direction + law = *method; way*	HO·HŌ ホウ·ホウ
文法	literature + law = *grammar*	BUN·PŌ ブン·ポウ
立法	stand + law = *legislation; law making*	RIP·PŌ リッ·ポウ

DRAGON

 **PLACE**

| 一 | 十 | 土 | 圵 | 圹 | 圹 | 坦 | 埸 |
| 埸 | 場 | 場 | | | | | |

BUILDING THIS KANJI
Earth 土 (87) + Sun 日 (6) + Dragon 圿 = 場

Meaning
A place.

Remembering this kanji

I grabbed a handful of crumbly **earth** and squinted up at the **sun** as the **dragon** landed nearby. "What is this terrible PLACE?" I asked. "How can you not recognize it?" she said. "It's the PLACE you have always wished to be."

Common Pronunciations

Common **ON** reading: **JŌ** (ジョウ)
Common **kun** reading: **ba** (ば)

As both readings are used extensively, compoun containing this kanji need to be learned on a w by word basis. You may find it useful to emp the same strategy that was suggested for on-yomi of 所 back in Entry 242. Note the m of on- and kun-yomi in the second example belo a very common word.

Less Common Pronunciations

Less common **ON** reading: none
Less common **kun** reading: none

COMMON WORDS AND COMPOUNDS		
工場	craft + place = *factory; plant*	**KŌ·JŌ** コウ・ジョ
場所	place + location = *place; location*	**ba·SHO** ば・ショ
場合	place + match = *circumstances; situation*	**ba·ai** ば・あい

科 **COURSE**

丶	二	千	千	禾	禾	禾	科	科

BUILDING THIS KANJI
Crops 禾 + Dipper 斗 (278) = 科

Meaning

Course (of study), as well as other ideas largely related to scholarly matters. This character is used to denote the departments and faculties of educational institutions, for example.

Remembering this kanji

"You obviously care a lot about **crops**, so take a farming COURSE."
"Yeah, but what about this **dipper** I've got?"
"Well, look at this COURSE: '**Crop** harvesting with a **dipper**'."
"Hey, that does seem like an interesting COURSE!"

Common Pronunciations

Common **ON** reading: **KA** (カ)
Common **kun** reading: none

Less Common Pronunciations

Less common **ON** reading: none
Less common **kun** reading: none

COMMON WORDS AND COMPOUNDS		
科学	course + study = *science*	**KA·GAKU** カ・ガク
科目	course + eye = *academic subject;* *course*	**KA·MOKU** カ・モク
教科書	teach + course + write = *textbook*	**KYŌ·KA·SHO** キョウ・カ・シ

KANJI 389

弟 **YOUNGER BROTHER**

| ` | ` | ⺍ | ⺌ | 弔 | 弟 | 弟 | | |

BUILDING THIS KANJI
Rabbit `´ + Mourn 弔(228) + Comet 一
= 弟

Meaning
Younger brother. This kanji can also refer to the disciples or pupils of an accomplished master. Ensure that you can easily see the difference between this character and 第 ("No.", from Entry 243).

Remembering this kanji
So my YOUNGER BROTHER had this pet **rabbit** that ended up dying on him, and geez did he ever **mourn**. So we got him a **comet** to cheer him up, but he just kept on **mourning** for that silly **rabbit**. I mean, the **comet** took him to other planets and he still wasn't happy! I'm starting to wonder if my YOUNGER BROTHER'S a bit spoiled.

Common Pronunciations
Common **ON** reading: none
Common **kun** reading: **otōto** (お と う と)

Less Common Pronunciations
Less common **ON** reading: **TEI** (テ イ);
DAI (ダ イ); **DE** (デ)
Less common **kun** reading: none

Interestingly, the last two **on-yomi** appear in only one word each, although the words themselves are commonly used. The first is 兄弟 (**KYŌ·DAI** / キョウ・ダイ) 'brothers (as well as sisters)' from the kanji 'elder brother' and 'younger brother'. This is the only compound, incidentally, in which 兄 is read with it's less common **on-yomi** of KYŌ. The only word in which 弟 is read with DE is 弟子 (**DE·SHI** / デ・シ) 'disciple; pupil', from the kanji 'younger brother' and 'child'.

COMMON WORDS AND COMPOUNDS		
弟	= younger brother	otōto おとうと

COMPONENT #390

LONG-TAILED BUTTERFLY

KANJI 390

様 **MANNER**

| ` | 十 | 才 | 木 | 栟 | 栐 | 栐 | 栏 | 栏 |
| 栏 | 栐 | 様 | 様 | 様 | | | | |

BUILDING THIS KANJI
Tree 木(13) + Rabbit `´ + Three (full hamburger) 三(5) + Long-tailed Butterfly 氺
= 様

Meaning
Manner, way. When following a family name, this kanji acts as a very polite form of 'Mr.', 'Mrs.', or 'Miss'.

Remembering this kanji
Beside a **tree**—growing in a gnarled **MANNER**—is a **rabbit** sitting over a **full hamburger**. Yet it is interested only in the lettuce, and chews this in a halting **MANNER**. Until, that is, it is startled by the tail of a **long-tailed butterfly's** fluttery **MANNER**…

Common Pronunciations
Common **ON** reading: **YŌ** (ヨ ウ)
Common **kun** reading: **sama** (さ ま)

The **kun-yomi** is the reading used to convey the polite form of 'Mr.', 'Mrs.' or 'Miss' mentioned above: 山本様 (yama·moto·**sama** / や ま·も と·さ ま), 'Mr. / Mrs. / Miss Yamamoto', for example.

Less Common Pronunciations
Less common **ON** readings: none
Less common **kun** reading: none

	COMMON WORDS AND COMPOUNDS	
皆様	all + manner = *Ladies and Gentlemen!; all (of you)*	mina·**sama** みな·さ ま
神様	God + manner = *God; god*	kami·**sama** か み·さ ま
様式	manner + type = *mode; form*	**YŌ**·SHIKI ヨ ウ·シ キ

虫 **INSECT**

Meaning
Insect. No story required. Take note that the long vertical line is not combined into a single stroke with the horizontal line at the bottom when writing this kanji; there are thus six strokes to the character here, not five.

Common Pronunciations
Common **ON** reading: **CHŪ** (チ ュ ウ)
Common **kun** reading: **mushi** (む し)

The **kun-yomi** is the more common reading.

Less Common Pronunciations
Less common **ON** reading: none
Less common **kun** reading: none

	COMMON WORDS AND COMPOUNDS	
虫	*insect; bug*	mushi む し
泣き虫	cry + insect = *crybaby*	na·ki **mushi** な·き む し
成虫	become + insect = *adult insect*	SEI·**CHŪ** セ イ·チ ュ ウ

駅 **STATION**

BUILDING THIS KANJI
Horse 馬(144) + Measurement 尺(332) = 駅

Meaning
Train station.

Remembering this kanji
"Forelock…mane… Ma'am, will you please keep your **horse** still so that I can take the **measurements**?"

"Look, I don't even understand what the heck you're doing!"

"Hey, you're the one who pulled into a **horse measurement** STATION."

ommon Pronunciations

ommon **ON** reading: **EKI** (エ キ)

ommon **kun** reading: none

ote the mix of **on** and **kun-yom**i in the second
ample.

eate your **on-yomi** keyword and enter it in the
ble at the back of the book. After that, write
ur sentence to remember the **on-yomi** reading
the box below.

Less Common Pronunciations

Less common **ON** reading: none

Less common **kun** reading: none

COMMON WORDS AND COMPOUNDS		
駅	*train station*	**EKI** エ キ
駅前	station + before = *in front of the station*	**EKI**·mae エ キ・まえ
駅伝	station + transmit = *long-distance relay race*	**EKI**·DEN エ キ・デン

OMPONENT #393

IAMOND RING

ANJI 393

商

COMMERCE

`	一	十	ㅗ	产	内	内	冇	商
商	商							

BUILDING THIS KANJI

Diamond Ring 冂 + Ballet 儿 + Mouth
(vampire) 口 (8) = 商

Meaning

Commerce, trade.

Remembering this kanji

Dracula flashed a **diamond ring**, and the **ballet
dancer** came closer. "It goes with your tutu,"
said the **vampire**, "and it's yours for this cheap
introductory price."

"Oh," she replied, "I didn't realize you were so
into COMMERCE."

"You'd be surprised," he said. "What with rent
and the cost of coffins, I'd be crazy not to be
doing at least some COMMERCE."

Common Pronunciations

Common **ON** reading: **SHŌ** (ショウ)

Common **kun** reading: none

Less Common Pronunciations

Less common **ON** reading: none

Less common **kun** reading: **akina** (あ き な)

COMMON WORDS AND COMPOUNDS		
商人	commerce + person = *merchant; dealer*	**SHŌ**·NIN ショウ・ニン
商売	commerce + sell = *commerce; trade*	**SHŌ**·BAI ショウ・バイ
商店	commerce + shop = *shop; store*	**SHŌ**·TEN ショウ・テン

KANJI 394

悪 **BAD**

一	一	一	一	一	一	亜	悪	悪
悪	悪							

BUILDING THIS KANJI
Asia 亜 (377) + **Heart** 心 (25) = 悪

Meaning
Bad, wrong, inferior…this kanji is bad news all around.

Remembering this kanji
Imagine the entire continent of **Asia** weighing down on your **heart**. That would be pretty BAD.

Common Pronunciations
Common **ON** reading: **AKU** (アク)
Common **kun** reading: **waru** (わる)

Create your **on-yomi** keyword and enter it in th table at the back of the book. Then, after creatin your **kun-yomi** keyword, write your sentence t remember the **on-yomi** and **kun-yomi** readings i the box below.

Less Common Pronunciations
Less common **ON** reading: **O** (オ)
Less common **kun** reading: none

COMMON WORDS AND COMPOUNDS		
悪い	*bad*	**waru·i** わる・い
最悪	most + bad = *worst*	**SAI·AKU** サイ・アク
悪意	bad + mind = *evil intention*	**AKU·I** アク・イ

KANJI 395

知 **KNOW**

ノ	一	仁	午	矢	矢	知	知	

BUILDING THIS KANJI
Arrow 矢 (285) + **Mouth (vampire)** 口 (8) = 知

Meaning
Know, information.

Remembering this kanji
Oh yeah? Well, I'll bet you didn't KNOW that an **arrow** is useless on a **vampire**, did you? Oh, you *did* KNOW. Hmm, I wonder why I didn't KNOW that…

Common Pronunciations
Common **ON** reading: **CHI** (チ)
Common **kun** reading: **shi** (し)

Less Common Pronunciations
Less common **ON** reading: none
Less common **kun** reading: none

COMMON WORDS AND COMPOUNDS		
知る	*know*	**shi·ru** し・る
知らせ	*notice; information*	**shi·rase** し・らせ
知人	know + person = *acquaintance*	**CHI·JIN** チ・ジン

ANJI 396

昔

BORROW

亻	仁	仕	什	供	借	借	借
昔							

UILDING THIS KANJI
iraffe 亻 + Long Ago 昔 (363) = 借

eaning
orrow.

emembering this kanji

That **giraffe** really bugs me."

Why's that?"

Oh, it's something that happened **long ago**."

Allow me to guess: you let it BORROW some
f your stuff and you didn't get it back."

Yeah, that's right! Did it BORROW something
om you as well?"

My tennis racket. I learned **long ago** that a
raffe will BORROW anything."

Common Pronunciations
Common **ON** reading: **SHAKU** (シャク)
Common **kun** reading: **ka** (か)

As you can see by the second example, this is
another of those kanji whose verb form can incorporate its **hiragana** ending when forming nouns.

Less Common Pronunciations
Less common **ON** reading: none
Less common **kun** reading: none

COMMON WORDS AND COMPOUNDS		
借りる	*borrow*	**ka·riru** か・りる
借手	borrow + hand = *borrower*	**kari·te** かり・て
借金	borrow + gold (money) = *loan; a debt*	**SHAK·KIN** シャッ・キン

COMPONENT #397

ERISCOPE

KANJI 397

決 **DECIDE**

丶	冫	氵	汀	沪	決	決	

BUILDING THIS KANJI
Splash 氵 + Periscope ユ + Person 人 (2) = 決

Meaning
Decide.

Remembering this kanji

I looked up when hit by the **splash** and found myself right in front of a **periscope**. A **person** appeared moments later. "Are you crazy?!" he yelled. "What the heck made you DECIDE to snorkel through a naval base?"

Common Pronunciations

Common **ON** reading: **KETSU** (ケ ツ)
Common **kun** reading: **ki** (き)

Less Common Pronunciations

Less common **ON** reading: none
Less common **kun** reading: none

COMMON WORDS AND COMPOUNDS		
決まる (intr)	*to be decided / settled*	**ki**·maru き・まる
決める (tr)	*to decide / settle*	**ki**·meru き・める
決心	decide + heart = *determination; resolution*	**KES**·SHIN ケッ・シ ゙

KANJI 398

区 **PARTITION**

一	フ	メ	区			

BUILDING THIS KANJI
Magnet ∟ + Banana Peels メ = 区

Meaning

Partition, division. This character is used to indicate zones or areas. You will often see this kanji in mailing addresses, as it's used to denote a ward or district of a city; the final compound below, a famous area of Tokyo, offers an example.

Remembering this kanji

A **magnet** would only be OK as a PARTITION, as anything not magnetic could get through it. **Banana peels** would do a better job, as they're slippery and would discourage crossings. So why, then, doesn't someone invent a **magnet** made of **banana peels**? I mean, that would obviously be the best PARTITION ever, wouldn't it?

Common Pronunciations

Common **ON** reading: **KU** (ク)
Common **kun** reading: none

Less Common Pronunciations

Less common **ON** reading: none
Less common **kun** reading: none

COMMON WORDS AND COMPOUNDS		
区分	partition + part = *partition; division*	**KU**·BUN ク・ブン
区別	partition + different = *distinction; difference*	**KU**·BETSU ク・ベツ
新宿区	new + lodging + partition = *Shinjuku ward (in Tokyo)*	SHIN·JUKU·KU シン・ジュク・ク

KANJI 399

DISCHARGE

ァ	ヺ	ヺ゙	癶	癶	癶	癶	癶	発

BUILDING THIS KANJI
Shark Attack 癶 + Picnic Table 开 = 発

Meaning
Discharge, break out.

Remembering this kanji
It's necessary here to DISCHARGE an unusual act: this is the only time the '**picnic table**' component will appear with both its legs broken (although this entire character does figure as part of another more complex kanji). That it should look like this is hardly surprising, as there's an enormous DISCHARGE of energy whenever a **shark attack** occurs on a **picnic table**.

Common Pronunciations
Common **ON** reading: **HATSU** (ハツ)
Common **kun** reading: none

Create your **on-yomi** keyword and enter it in the table at the back of the book. After that, write your sentence to remember the **on-yomi** reading in the box below.

Less Common Pronunciations
Less common **ON** reading: **HOTSU** (ホツ)
Less common **kun** reading: none

COMMON WORDS AND COMPOUNDS		
発音	discharge + sound = *pronunciation*	**HATSU·ON** ハツ・オン
出発	exit + discharge = *departure*	**SHUP·PATSU** シュッ・パツ
新発売	new + discharge + sell = "Now on Sale"	**SHIN·HATSU·BAI** シン・ハツ・バイ

COMPONENT #400

KILLER BEE

The addition of another stroke gives us the third member of our special component family, following 七 'ghost', and 弋 'spilling coffee'. Remember that anything appearing underneath the horizontal line (the next entry provides an example), is always written immediately after it, interrupting the stroke order of this component.

KANJI 400

HOW MANY

ˊ	ˊˊ	幺	幺ˊ	幺ˊ	幺幺	絲	絲	絲
幾	幾	幾						

BUILDING THIS KANJI
Frustration 幺 + Frustration 幺 + Killer Bee 戈 + Person 人(2) = 幾

Meaning
How many, how much. Another meaning is conveyed when this character precedes a 'number' kanji (as in the final example); in these cases the character means 'some' or 'several'. Take care with the stroke order of this kanji, remembering that 'person' is written immediately after the horizontal line of the killer bee component. And don't forget that bee!

Remembering this kanji

Oh, **frustration** upon **frustration**. That's right, *double* **frustration**! HOW MANY instances must there be of a **killer bee** scaring a **person**? I ask you: HOW MANY must flee from HOW MANY **killer bees**?

Common Pronunciations

Common **ON** reading: none
Common **kun** reading: **iku** (い く)

Less Common Pronunciations

Less common **ON** reading: **KI** (キ)
Less common **kun** reading: none

You are only likely to meet this reading in on compound: 幾何学 (**KI·KA·GAKU** / キ・カ ガク) 'geometry', from the kanji 'how many' 'what', and 'study' .

COMMON WORDS AND COMPOUNDS		
幾つ	*how many; how much*	**iku**·tsu い く・つ
幾ら	*how much*	**iku**·ra い く・ら
幾百	how many + hundred = *some / several hundreds*	**iku**·HYAKU い く・ヒャ

KANJI 401

 ROOM

'	'	⌐	宀	宀	宏	宝	室	室

BUILDING THIS KANJI
Pincers 宀 + Reach 至 (239) = 室

Meaning

Room, chamber. As they're visually similar, make sure not to confuse this character with 屋, the kanji for 'roof' we learned back in Entry 281.

Remembering this kanji

"What are you doing in this ROOM?"
"Don't you remember? This was the only ROOM the **pincers** couldn't **reach** me."
"Oh, so this is the ROOM!"
"Yes. I'm only alive today because I was able to **reach** this ROOM."

Common Pronunciations

Common **ON** reading: **SHITSU** (シ ツ)
Common **kun** reading: none

Less Common Pronunciations

Less common **ON** reading: none
Less common **kun** reading: **muro** (む ろ)

COMMON WORDS AND COMPOUNDS		
室内	room + inside = *indoor(s)*	**SHITSU·NAI** シ ツ・ナイ
室外	room + outside = *outdoor(s)*	**SHITSU·GAI** シ ツ・ガイ
温室	warm + room = *hothouse; greenhouse*	**ON·SHITSU** オ ン・シ ツ

KANJI 402

FALL

一	十	艹	艹	艹	艿	芐	莎	莈
芐	落	落						

BUILDING THIS KANJI

Wreath 艹 + Splash 氵 + Each 各(282) = 落

Meaning

Fall, fail.

Remembering this kanji

"How could you not have realized that the **wreath** needed care? Did I not tell you to **splash each** day, **each** of you, so that the petals and leaves would not FALL off? But you didn't, and so they did FALL… Oh, the lot of you should FALL to your knees!"

Common Pronunciations

Common **ON** reading: **RAKU** (ラ ク)

Common **kun** reading: **o** (お)

The verbs in the first and second examples below can sometimes absorb their **hiragana** endings when forming words with other kanji.

Less Common Pronunciations

Less common **ON** reading: none

Less common **kun** reading: none

COMMON WORDS AND COMPOUNDS		
落ちる (intr)	to fall	**o**·chiru お·ちる
落とす (tr)	to let fall / drop	**o**·tosu お·とす
急落	hasten + fall = sudden drop/decline	**KYŪ·RAKU** キュウ·ラク

KANJI 403

FAST

一	厂	戸	曰	東	束	束	〵束	涑
速								

BUILDING THIS KANJI

Bundle 束(356) + Seal 辶 = 速

Meaning

Fast, in terms of speed and movement. Recall that 早 ("early", Entry 29) is more concerned with the idea of "fast" in terms of time.

Remembering this kanji

"Look kid, if you're gonna **bundle** up a **seal** at this rodeo, you'd better be FAST. 'Cause believe you me, when they get those flippers flappin', they're FAST."

Common Pronunciations

Common **ON** reading: **SOKU** (ソ ク)

Common **kun** reading: **haya** (は や)

Less Common Pronunciations

Less common **ON** reading: none

Less common **kun** reading: **sumi** (す み)

COMMON WORDS AND COMPOUNDS		
速い	fast	**haya**·i はや·い
高速	tall + fast = high-speed	**KŌ·SOKU** コウ·ソク
速度	fast + degree = speed	**SOKU·DO** ソク·ド

COMPONENT #404

SHOPPING CART 巴

KANJI 404

色 COLOR

BUILDING THIS KANJI
Little Red Riding Hood ⼧ + Shopping Cart
巴 = 色

Meaning
Color. Interestingly, this kanji also conveys a decidedly erotic meaning to many compounds in which it appears (as it does in the second example below).

Remembering this kanji
"Hello, I'm **Little Red Riding Hood**, and I'v got a **shopping cart**! Isn't it a nice COLOR?"
"First of all, miss, **Little Red Riding Hoo**d woul have a basket, not a **shopping cart**. But even she had one it wouldn't be purple; didn't anyon tell you she's only into one COLOR?"

Common Pronunciations
Common **ON** reading: **SHOKU** (ショク)
Common **kun** reading: **iro** (いろ)

Both these readings are used frequently compounds, although **iro** is more common in t first position and **SHOKU** more common in t second and third.

Less Common Pronunciations
Less common **ON** reading: **SHIKI** (シキ)
Less common **kun** reading: none

COMMON WORDS AND COMPOUNDS		
色	*color*	**iro** いろ
色目	color + eye = *amorous glance*	**iro·me** いろ・め
原色	original + color = *primary color*	**GEN·SHOKU** ゲン・ショク

KANJI 405

始 START

BUILDING THIS KANJI
Woman 女 (16) + Platform 台 (264) = 始

Meaning
Start.

Remembering this kanji
"Look, there's a **woman** on the **platform**."
"That means they're ready to START."
"Why's that?"
"Because it's the starter's **platform**. In a momen she'll call out 'START your engines'."

Common Pronunciations
Common **ON** reading: **SHI** (シ)
Common **kun** reading: **haji** (は じ)

Less Common Pronunciations
Less common **ON** reading: none
Less common **kun** reading: none

COMMON WORDS AND COMPOUNDS		
始まる (intr)	to start	**haji**·maru は じ・まる
始める (tr)	to start (something)	**haji**·meru は じ・める
原始	original + start = *primitive*	**GEN·SHI** ゲン・シ

KANJI 406

APPROVE

一	口	日	日	旦	早	导	吊	是

BUILDING THIS KANJI
Sun 日 (6) + Surfer 疋 = 是

Meaning
Approve, to be right.

Remembering this kanji
The **sun** looked down on a **surfer**. "I APPROVE
of how you're surfing," it said.
"Well yeah," said the **surfer**. "I APPROVE of
your approval."

Common Pronunciations
Common **ON** reading: **ZE** (ゼ)
Common **kun** reading: none

Create your **on-yomi** keyword and enter it in the
table at the back of the book. After that, write
your sentence to remember the **on-yomi** reading
in the box below.

Less Common Pronunciations
Less common **ON** reading: none
Less common **kun** reading: none

COMMON WORDS AND COMPOUNDS		
是非	approve + un- = *by any means; without fail*	**ZE·HI** ゼ・ヒ

KANJI 407

直 **STRAIGHT**

一	十	广	市	古	直	直	直

BUILDING THIS KANJI
Ten (scarecrow) 十 (28) + Eye (cyclops) 目 (15)
+ Forklift ∟ = 直

Meaning
Straight, direct, at once. By extension comes the
idea of things being correct or corrected (best
illustrated by the intransitive/transitive verb pair
below). An important aspect of these two verbs
can be seen when they attach to the end of other
kanji as a suffix (as in the third example). In such
cases, this character gives the compound a sense
of 'redoing' whatever the first kanji represents.
Ensure that you can clearly see the difference
between this kanji and 真 ('true', from Entry
358).

Remembering this kanji

If there's a **scarecrow** on top of a **Cyclops**, the only way you can lift them with a **forklift** is if they pose as STRAIGHT as the **forklift**. The **Cyclops** in this illustration is obviously keeping as STRAIGHT as he can, and the **scarecrow** is balancing with his arms out STRAIGHT.

Common Pronunciations

Common **ON** reading: **CHOKU** (チョク)
Common **kun** reading: **nao** (なお)

Create your **on-yomi** keyword and enter it in the table at the back of the book. Then, after creating your **kun-yomi** keyword, write your sentence to remember the **on-yomi** and **kun-yomi** readings in the box below.

Less Common Pronunciations

Less common **ON** reading: **JIKI** (ジキ)
Less common **kun** reading: **tada** (ただ)

You will encounter the **kun-yomi** in only o word: 直ちに (**tada**·chi ni / ただ·ち に 'immediately, at once'.

COMMON WORDS AND COMPOUNDS		
直る (intr)	*to be corrected / repaired*	**nao**·ru なお·る
直す (tr)	*to correct / repair / fix*	**nao**·su なお·す
書き 直す	write + straight = *rewrite; write again*	ka·ki **nao**·su か·き なお·
直線	straight + line = *straight line*	**CHOKU·SEN** チョク·セン

LEMMINGS 疒 疒

Lemmings jumping off a cliff. This component usually appears in characters whose meaning has some connection to illness or disease.

KANJI 408

病 **ILLNESS**

`	一	广	广	疒	疒	疒	病	病
病								

BUILDING THIS KANJI
Lemmings 疒 + Third 丙(370) = 病

Meaning
Illness, disease.

Remembering this kanji

If you couldn't tell from the couple of **lemming** in the illustration who have already gone ove it should be obvious looking at the **third** who about to: these are creatures with an ILLNESS

Common Pronunciations
Common **ON** reading: **BYŌ** (ビョウ)
Common **kun** reading: none

ote that the final compound below uses the less
mmon **on-yomi** for 持.

ess Common Pronunciations
ess common **ON** reading: **HEI** (ヘイ)
ess common **kun** reading: **ya** (や);
amai (やまい)

COMMON WORDS AND COMPOUNDS		
病気	illness + spirit = *illness*	**BYŌ·KI** ビョウ·キ
病院	illness + institution = *hospital*	**BYŌ·IN** ビョウ·イン
持病	hold + illness = *chronic disease*	**JI·BYŌ** ジ·ビョウ

KANJI 409

共 TOGETHER

BUILDING THIS KANJI
Chimney 廾 + **Eight (volcano)** 八(19) = 共

Meaning
Together.

Remembering this kanji
Have you ever noticed that **chimneys** and **volcanoes** are linked TOGETHER? Well they are, because a volcano is simply a **chimney** for a planet. So it's only right that they should be thought of TOGETHER.

Common Pronunciations
Common **ON** reading: **KYŌ** (キョウ)
Common **kun** reading: **tomo** (とも)

Less Common Pronunciations
Less common **ON** reading: none
Less common **kun** reading: none

COMMON WORDS AND COMPOUNDS		
共	*together*	**tomo** とも
共同	together + same = *cooperation; collaboration*	**KYŌ·DŌ** キョウ·ドウ
共和国	together + harmony + country = *republic*	**KYŌ·WA·KOKU** キョウ·ワ·コク

KANJI 410

願 DESIRE

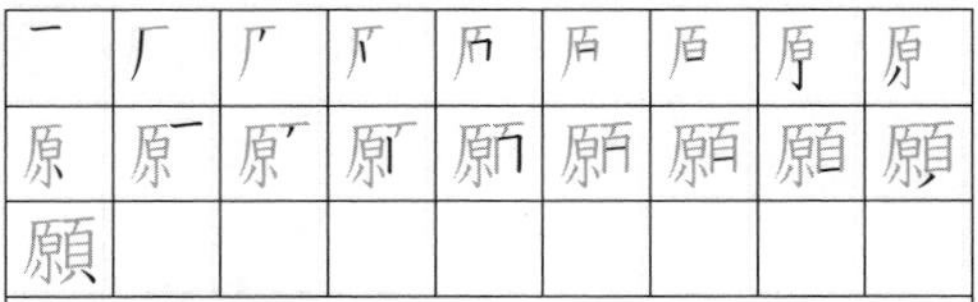

BUILDING THIS KANJI
Original 原(349) + **Guy Wearing a Barrel** 頁 = 願

Meaning

Desire, petition. This character carries a polite tone of entreaty.

Common Pronunciations

Common **ON** reading: **GAN** (ガン)
Common **kun** reading: **nega** (ねが)

Less Common Pronunciations

Less common **ON** reading: none
Less common **kun** reading: none

Remembering this kanji

"We've been told that you're the **original guy wearing a barrel**. We DESIRE to ask you something."

"Oh really? Well, *my* DESIRE is to put on something other than a ridiculous looking barrel; this outfit could only appeal to someone with a DESIRE to get slivers."

COMMON WORDS AND COMPOUNDS		
願う	desire; request politely	**nega·u** ねが・う
お願い します	please	o **nega·i** shimas お ねが・い します
願書	desire + write = written application / request	**GAN·SHO** ガン・ショ

CHAPTER 18 REVIEW EXERCISES

A. Please match the following kanji to their meanings.

1. 落   a. Straight
2. 病   b. Desire
3. 虫   c. Law
4. 科   d. Know
5. 法   e. Fall
6. 知   f. Illness
7. 発   g. Decide
8. 直   h. Course
9. 願   i. Discharge
10. 決   j. Insect

B. Please match the following meanings to their kanji, and these to their **on-** or **kun-yomi**.

1. Place   a. 弟   1. **iku** (いく)
2. Partition   b. 速   2. **haya** (はや)
3. Station   c. 場   3. **SHITSU** (シツ)
4. Younger brother   d. 共   4. **EKI** (エキ)
5. Fast   e. 幾   5. **KU** (ク)

6. How many   f. 様   6. **KYŌ** (キョウ
7. Manner   g. 駅   7. **haji** (はじ)
8. Start   h. 始   8. **YŌ** (ヨウ)
9. Room   i. 室   9. **otōto** (おとうと)
10. Together   j. 区   10. **ba** (ば)

C. Please choose the best answer(s) to the follow ing questions.

1. If you don't hurry up and get to the ____ you'll miss your train.
   a. 虫   b. 願   c. 駅   d. 病   e. 科

2. Which is the correct reading of 落ちる
   a. **a·chiru** (あ・ちる)
   b. **i·chiru** (い・ちる)
   c. **o·chiru** (お・ちる)
   d. **u·chiru** (う・ちる)

3. Which of the following kanji has the mo number of strokes?
   a. 是   b. 病   c. 直   d. 弟   e. 発

4. Which of the following readings apply to the kanji 色?
   a. **iro** (いろ)
   b. **SHŌ** (ショウ)
   c. **kuro** (くろ)
   d. **SHOKU** (ショク)
   e. **SAKU** (サク)

5. Which is the correct reading of 借りる?
   a. **mina·riru** (みな・りる)
   b. **ko·riru** (こ・りる)
   c. **ake·riru** (あけ・りる)
   d. **ka·riru** (か・りる)

D. Please match the following compounds to their meanings and pronunciations.

1. 最悪　a. Speed / Velocity　1. **HATSU·ON** (ハツ・オン)
2. 商店　b. Straight line　2. **BYŌ·KI** (ビョウ・キ)
3. 場所　c. Pronunciation　3. **SHŌ·TEN** (ショウ・テン)
4. 発音　d. Indoor(s)　4. **CHOKU·SEN** (チョク・セン)
5. 是非　e. Shop / Store　5. **SHITSU·NAI** (シツ・ナイ)

6. 直線　f. By any means　6. **KA·GAKU** (カ・ガク)
7. 科学　g. Illness　7. **SOKU·DO** (ソク・ド)
8. 病気　h. Worst　8. **SAI·AKU** (サイ・アク)
9. 速度　i. Place / Location　9. **ZE·HI** (ゼ・ヒ)
10. 室内　j. Science　10. **ba·SHO** (ば・ショ)

E. Please read the passage below and answer the questions that follow.

テレビを買いに新宿駅前の店へ行きました。。。

"すみません、新発売のテレビは幾らですか"
"二十五万円です"

その夜、私は弟に借金をお願いしました。

1. What do I want to buy?
2. Where did I go to find it?
3. About which specific one did I ask?
4. How much was it?
5. What did I do that evening?

Kanji #411—440

KANJI 411

何 **WHAT**

BUILDING THIS KANJI
Giraffe イ + Possible 可 (252) = 何

Meaning

What, although the sense of 'how many' can also be expressed in certain compounds (such as the first example of Entry 488). This is obviously a common word that appears often in the stories of this book. Unless accompanied by a string of exclamation and question marks (as shown below), however, the word "what" in future stories will have no connection to this kanji. There is, incidentally, only one character in the 2,136 general-use list that uses this kanji as a component—you will meet it in Entry 466. Take care with the stroke order of the right-hand side here.

Remembering this kanji

"If you can convince the **giraffe** to do it" he whispered, "it's **possible**."
"WHAT!!!???"

Common Pronunciations

Common **ON** reading: none
Common **kun** reading: **nan** (なん); **nani** (なに

nan is the more common of these readings.

Less Common Pronunciations

Less common **ON** reading: **KA** (カ)
Less common **kun** reading: none

This reading is found in only one compound which we met back in Entry 400: 幾何学 (KI·**KA**·GAKU / キ・カ・ガク) 'geometry', from the kanji 'how many', 'what', and 'study'.

COMMON WORDS AND COMPOUNDS		
何	*what; What!*	**nani** なに
何時	what + time = *What time?*	**nan·JI** なん・ジ

KANJI 412

研 **POLISH**

一	丁	丆	石	石	石	石	矴	研

BUILDING THIS KANJI
Stone 石 (340) + Picnic Table 开 = 研

Meaning
To polish.

Remembering this kanji
"Look what you did to that **picnic table**! Why did you have to POLISH your **stone** on it?"
"Hey, I didn't care about POLISHING the **stone**. I wanted to POLISH the **picnic table**."

Common Pronunciations
Common **ON** reading: **KEN** (ケン)
Common **kun** reading: none

Less Common Pronunciations
Less common **ON** reading: none
Less common **kun** reading: **to** (と)

COMMON WORDS AND COMPOUNDS		
研究	polish + inquiry = *research*	**KEN·KYŪ** ケン・キュウ
研究所	research + location = *laboratory; research institute*	**KEN·KYŪ·JO** ケン・キュウ・ジョ

COMPONENT #413

ACTOR   小

Like any good actor, this component is all about sentiment; it usually shows up in kanji having to do with feelings and emotions.

KANJI 413

忙 **BUSY**

丶	忄	忄	忄	忙	忙			

BUILDING THIS KANJI
Actor 忄 + Perish 亡 (254) = 忙

Meaning
Busy.

Remembering this kanji
"You landed another role? Wow, you sure are BUSY."
"An **actor** must always be BUSY. Those who aren't BUSY, **perish**."

Common Pronunciations
Common **ON** reading: **BŌ** (ボウ)
Common **kun** reading: **isoga** (いそが)

Less Common Pronunciations
Less common **ON** reading: none
Less common **kun** reading: none

COMMON WORDS AND COMPOUNDS		
忙しい	*busy*	**isoga·**shii いそが・しい
多忙	many + busy = *busy; work pressure*	**TA·BŌ** タ・ボウ

KANJI 414

 **SLOW**

⁻	⊐	⼫	⼫	⼫	⼫	⼫	⼫	⼫
犀	遅	遅						

BUILDING THIS KANJI
Flag 尸 + Sheep 羊(262) + Seal 辶 = 遅

Meaning
Slow, and the ideas of being late or delayed.

Remembering this kanji
Ah, it seemed to be SLOW everywhere that day…the **flag** shifted SLOWLY in the air, **sheep** grazed SLOWLY in the pastures, and a **seal** lolled SLOWLY on the tide.

Common Pronunciations
Common **ON** reading: none
Common **kun** reading: **oku** (お く); **oso** (お そ)

Less Common Pronunciations
Less common **ON** reading: **CHI** (チ)
Less common **kun** reading: none

COMMON WORDS AND COMPOUNDS		
遅い	*slow; delayed*	**oso·i** おそ・い
遅れる	*be late / delayed*	**oku·reru** おく・れる

KANJI 415

 FEE

⟍	⟍	⼃	半	半	米	米	米	料
料								

BUILDING THIS KANJI
Rice 米(32) + Dipper 斗(278) = 料

Meaning
Fee, charge. Another meaning relates to 'materials' (the second compound of Entry 440 provides an example). Ensure that you can clearly distinguish this kanji from 科 ('course', Entry 388).

Remembering this kanji
"The **rice** is piled over there with a **dipper** on top. Grab as much as you need."
"Is there a FEE?"
"There's a FEE for the **rice**, but no FEE for getting it with the **dipper**."

Common Pronunciations
Common **ON** reading: **RYŌ** (リョウ)
Common **kun** reading: none

Less Common Pronunciations
Less common **ON** reading: none
Less common **kun** reading: none

COMMON WORDS AND COMPOUNDS		
料金	fee + gold (money) = *fee; charge*	**RYŌ·KIN** リョウ・キン
料理	fee + reason = *cooking; food*	**RYŌ·RI** リョウ・リ
入場料	enter + place + fee = *admission fee*	**NYŪ·JŌ·RYŌ** ニュウ・ジョウ・リョウ

COMPONENT #416

QUICKSAND

KANJI 416

業 **BUSINESS**

ˈ	ˈˈ	ˈˈˈ	ˈˈˈˈ	业	业	业	业	业
业	丵	丵	業					

BUILDING THIS KANJI
Quicksand 业 + Sheep 羊(262) + Umbrella 𠆢 = 業

Meaning
Business, industry.

Remembering this kanji
"Look at that **quicksand**, Rocco. You'd never guess we tossed that **sheep** in there."
"Well, BUSINESS is BUSINESS, ain't it Vinnie?"
"Yeah. He shoulda known better than to butt into our **umbrella** BUSINESS."

Common Pronunciations
Common **ON** reading: **GYŌ** (ギョウ)
Common **kun** reading: none

Create your **on-yomi** keyword and enter it in the table at the back of the book. After that, write your sentence to remember the **on-yomi** reading in the box below.

Less Common Pronunciations
Less common **ON** reading: **GŌ** (ゴウ)
Less common **kun** reading: **waza** (わざ)

COMMON WORDS AND COMPOUNDS		
工業	craft + business = *industry*	**KŌ·GYŌ** コウ・ギョウ
事業	matter + business = *undertakings; tasks*	**JI·GYŌ** ジ・ギョウ
商業	commerce + business = *commerce; business*	**SHŌ·GYŌ** ショウ・ギョウ

KANJI 417

泳 **SWIM**

| ` | ⟍ | ⟍ | ⟍ | ⟍ | ⟍ | ⟍ | 泳 | |

BUILDING THIS KANJI
Splash 氵 + Eternal 永(384) = 泳

Meaning
Swim.

Remembering this kanji
"When you SWIM," she said, "SWIM efficiently by keeping your **splashes** down."
"But what if I'm on an **eternal** SWIM, coach?" someone asked.
"Well, in that case, **splash** away," she answered, "since you'll probably do it out of sheer boredom if you're on an **eternal** SWIM."

Common Pronunciations
Common **ON** reading: **EI** (エイ)
Common **kun** reading: **oyo** (およ)

Less Common Pronunciations
Less common **ON** reading: none
Less common **kun** reading: none

COMMON WORDS AND COMPOUNDS		
泳ぐ	*swim*	oyo·gu およ・ぐ
平泳ぎ	flat + swim = *breaststroke*	hira oyo·gi ひら およ・ぎ
水泳	water + swim = *swimming*	SUI·EI スイ・エイ

KANJI 418

係 **CONNECTION**

| ノ | イ | 亻 | 伫 | 伫 | 伫 | 係 | 係 | 係 |

BUILDING THIS KANJI
Giraffe 亻 + System 系(374) = 係

Meaning
Connection, often with the sense of being concerned with or involved in something. When used on its own or as a suffix, however, this kanji usually indicates a person working at a certain type of job—ticket collectors, tellers, receptionists and sales clerks are a few examples of compounds making use of this character.

Remembering this kanji
"You should ask that **giraffe** over there. He understands the **system** better than I do."
"Really?"
"Yeah. You gotta have CONNECTIONS here. You need a bit of extra food? He has a CONNECTION to the zookeeper. You want your pen hosed down? He has a CONNECTION to the cleaning guy. Believe me, a **giraffe** like you will find this **system** tough without CONNECTIONS."

Common Pronunciations
Common **ON** reading: **KEI** (ケイ)
Common **kun** reading: **kakari** (かかり)

kari is the reading used as a suffix to denote
the types of jobs mentioned above. It is always
voiced when in this final position (as in the second
example below).

Less Common Pronunciations
Less common **ON** reading: none
Less common **kun** reading: none

係	clerk	**kakari** かかり
受付係	receive + attach + connection = *receptionist; information clerk*	uke·tsuke·**gakari** うけ・つけ・がかり
関係	checkpoint + connection = *connection; relationship*	**KAN·KEI** カン・ケイ

COMPONENT #419

GLUTTON

Something tells me that cupcake won't be there
for long. Fittingly, the glutton usually appears
in kanji related to food and drink; he invariably
tries to hide his shameful behavior under an
umbrella, as in the next entry. Make sure to note
the difference between this component and 貝
the 'billionaire' that was introduced prior to
Entry 345.

KANJI 419

 DRINK

	へ	^	今	今	今	飠	飠	飠
飠	飫	飲						

BUILDING THIS KANJI
Umbrella へ + Glutton 良 + Lack 欠 (246) = 飲

Meaning
Drink.

Remembering this kanji
Bring an **umbrella** if you'll be close to a **glutton**
with a DRINK. If you don't, his **lack** of manners
will result in a lot of that DRINK ending up
on you.

Common Pronunciations
Common **ON** reading: **IN** (イン)
Common **kun** reading: **no** (の)

Less Common Pronunciations
Less common **ON** reading: none
Less common **kun** reading: none

飲む	drink	**no**·mu の・む
飲み物	drink + thing = *a drink*	**no**·mi mono の・み もの
飲食	drink + eat = *drinking and eating; food and drink*	**IN·SHOKU** イン・ショク

KANJI 420

黄 YELLOW

一	十	卄	世	芢	芐	苗	苗	苗
黄	黄							

BUILDING THIS KANJI
Chimney 土 + Cause 由 (236) + Eight
(volcano) (19) = 黄

Meaning
Yellow.

Remembering this kanji
"I can't understand why my **chimney's** turning
YELLOW."
"Maybe sulphur's the **cause**."
"How so?"
"Well, it's YELLOW isn't it? Plus, I saw some
on a **volcano** once, and soon after that I came
down with YELLOW fever."

Common Pronunciations
Common **ON** reading: **Ō** (オウ); **KŌ** (コウ)
Common **kun** reading: **ki** (き)

This is an odd character when it comes to pronun‐
ciations, as it has three common readings despite
there being very few compounds containing this
kanji. In addition, several of these compounds
can be read with either of the **on-yomi**; in such
cases, though, one of them will invariably be the
more widely used.

Less Common Pronunciations
Less common **ON** reading: none
Less common **kun** reading: **ko** (こ)

You will only encounter this reading as an alternate
to the second compound below: 黄金 (**ko**·gane
/ こ·がね) 'gold' or 'money'. Nevertheless, it
is far more common for 黄金色 (**ko**·gane-iro
こ·がね·いろ) 'gold color', to be read with the
kun-yomi of these kanji.

COMMON WORDS AND COMPOUNDS		
黄色	*yellow*	**ki**·iro き・いろ
黄金	yellow + gold = *gold; money*	**Ō**·GON オウ・ゴン
黄海	yellow + sea = *the Yellow Sea*	**KŌ**·KAI コウ・カ

KANJI 421

答 ANSWER

ノ	ト	片	竹	竺	笁	笁	笁	笁
答	答	答						

BUILDING THIS KANJI
Machine Guns 竹 + Match 合 (250) = 答

Meaning
Answer.

Remembering this kanji
They fired their **machine guns** and we were
forced to **match** them in ANSWER. "No!" the
peacenik cried, jumping between us. "This is
not the ANSWER!"

Common Pronunciations
Common **ON** reading: **TŌ** (トウ)
Common **kun** reading: **kota** (こた)

…e final compound below is the only instance in …hich the **on-yomi** becomes voiced.

…ess Common Pronunciations
…ss common **ON** reading: none
…ss common **kun** reading: none

	COMMON WORDS AND COMPOUNDS	
答え	*answer; response*	**kota·e** こた・え
答える	*to answer; respond*	**kota·eru** こた・える
問答	question + answer = *questions and answers*	MON·**DŌ** モン・ドウ

COMPONENT #422

CROSSING GATE

…ake some time to review 呆, our 'sherpa' …omponent that preceded Entry 290, and 仪, …he 'sprinter' we met prior to Entry 352 in …rder to solidify the differences between these …hree components.

KANJI 422

旅 **TRAVEL**

一	亠	方	方	方	扩	扩	旅
旅							

BUILDING THIS KANJI
Direction 方 (223) + **Hammer** ー + **Crossing Gate** 仪 = 旅

Meaning
Travel, journey.

Remembering this kanji
So you want to TRAVEL? Great, but you'd better pick a **direction**, because you obviously can't TRAVEL without one. Oh, and you also have to make sure that someone hasn't taken a **hammer** and put up a **crossing gate** somewhere in that **direction**, as that means you probably can't TRAVEL there.

Common Pronunciations
Common **ON** reading: **RYO** (リ ョ)
Common **kun** reading: **tabi** (た び)

Create your **on-yomi** keyword and enter it in the table at the back of the book. Then, after creating your **kun-yomi** keyword, write your sentence to remember the **on-yomi** and **kun-yomi** readings in the box below.

Less Common Pronunciations
Less common **ON** reading: none
Less common **kun** reading: none

	COMMON WORDS AND COMPOUNDS	
旅	*travel; trip*	**tabi** た び
旅人	travel + person = *traveler*	**tabi**·bito た び・び と
旅行	travel + go = *travel; trip*	**RYO**·KŌ リ ョ・コ ウ

KANJI 423

 **DISH**

丨	冂	冊	皿	皿			

Meaning
Dish, plate. No story required.

Common Pronunciations
Common **ON** reading: none
Common **kun** reading: **sara** (さ ら)

Less Common Pronunciations
Less common **ON** reading: none
Less common **kun** reading: none

COMMON WORDS AND COMPOUNDS		
皿	dish	**sara** さ ら
皿洗い	dish + wash = dishwashing	**sara** ara·i さ ら あ ら·い

KANJI 424

治 **GOVERN**

丶	冫	氵	氵	氿	汸	治	治

BUILDING THIS KANJI
Splash 氵 + Platform 台 (264) = 治

Meaning
This interesting kanji conveys a sense of governing or having things under control. It's a meaning that can extend to the idea of managing one's health or having an illness cured. Make sure to clearly distinguish this character from 法 ("law", Entry 386), as the two are visually similar.

Remembering this kanji
The president struggled to GOVERN her emotions. "If you feel you must **splash** me whenever I address you from this **platform**," she said, "how can you expect me to GOVERN?"

Common Pronunciations
Common **ON** reading: CHI (チ); JI (ジ)
Common **kun** reading: osa (お さ); nao (な お)

Though we're dealing with four common readings here, things are much simpler than they appear first glance. The **kun-yomi** are only found in th two intransitive/transitive verb pairs below, and CHI is the more common of the on-yomi.

Less Common Pronunciations
Less common **ON** reading: none
Less common **kun** reading: none

COMMON WORDS AND COMPOUNDS		
治まる (intr)	to be tranquil; calm down	**osa·maru** お さ·ま る
治める (tr)	to govern / administer	**osa·meru** お さ·め る
治る (intr)	to get well / recover	**nao·ru** な お·る
治す (tr)	to heal	**nao·su** な お·す
自治	self + govern = self-government; autonomy	**JI·CHI** ジ·チ
明治	bright + govern = Meiji (period / emperor)	**MEI·JI** メ イ·ジ

COMPONENT #425

RATTLESNAKE 与 与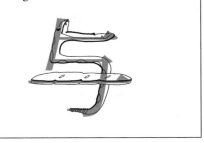

KANJI 425

与 CONFER

一	与	与						

BUILDING THIS KANJI
Rattlesnake 与 + One (hamburger patty) 一
(●) = 与

Meaning
Confer, give.

Remembering this kanji
"I CONFER on you, **rattlesnake**, the prize for best rattling noise. I was going to CONFER it on you, **hamburger patty**, but then I realized you were sizzling instead."

Common Pronunciations
Common **ON** reading: **YO** (ヨ)
Common **kun** reading: **ata** (あた)

Less Common Pronunciations
Less common **ON** reading: none
Less common **kun** reading: none

COMMON WORDS AND COMPOUNDS		
与える	*confer; give*	**ata**·eru あた·える
授与	grant + confer = *conferment; awarding*	**JU·YO** ジュ·ヨ

KANJI 426

昼 DAYTIME

ㄱ	コ	尸	尺	尺	尽	昼	昼	昼

BUILDING THIS KANJI
Measurement 尺(332) + Dawn 旦(183) = 昼

Meaning
Daytime, midday.

Remembering this kanji
It's pointless to make a **measurement** of **dawn**, because really, when does it begin and end? No, a more useful **measurement** would be to calculate the hours of DAYTIME instead.

Common Pronunciations
Common **ON** reading: **CHŪ** (チュウ)
Common **kun** reading: **hiru** (ひる)

Less Common Pronunciations
Less common **ON** reading: none
Less common **kun** reading: none

COMMON WORDS AND COMPOUNDS		
昼	*daytime; midday*	**hiru** ひる
昼間	daytime + interval = *daytime; during the day*	**hiru·ma** ひる・ま
昼食	daytime + eat = *lunch*	**CHŪ·SHOKU** チュウ・ショ

KANJI 427

産 PRODUCE

'	一	立	立	立	产	产	产	产
産	産							

BUILDING THIS KANJI
Vase ☆ + Cliff 厂 + Life 生 (99) = 産

Meaning
Produce, give birth to.

Remembering this kanji
A **vase** teeters on a **cliff**, its **life** in the balance...
What kind of feeling does this PRODUCE in
you?

Common Pronunciations
Common **ON** reading: **SAN** (サン)
Common **kun** reading: **u** (う)

The **kun-yomi** forms the intransitive/transiti
verb pair 産まれる / 産む (**u**·mareru / **u**·n
'to be born / to give birth to'; these verbs ha
the same meaning as the identically pronoun
生まれる / 生む , which we learned back
Entry 99. The **on-yomi** can become voiced in
second position, but only in a few compou
related to childbirth.

Less Common Pronunciations
Less common **ON** reading: none
Less common **kun** reading: **ubu** (うぶ)

IRREGULAR READING		
土産	earth + produce = *souvenir*	**miyage** みやげ

The honorary prefix 'o-' is often attached to t
word: お土産 .

COMMON WORDS AND COMPOUNDS		
産院	produce + institution = *maternity hospital*	**SAN·IN** サン・イ
生産	life + produce = *production*	**SEI·SAN** セイ・サ
水産	water + produce = *marine products*	**SUI·SAN** スイ・サ

COMPONENT #428

RAT

This component is written with three strokes, not two.

KANJI 428

建

CONSTRUCT

7	⊐	⊐	⊒	⊒	聿	律	建	建

BUILDING THIS KANJI

Pitchfork ⊒ + Two 二(4) + Pole │ + Rat 乂
建

Meaning

Construct, build. You may notice that the 'pole' component in this character extends all the way through the kanji for 'two', whereas it stops short in 書 ('write', from Entry 136). The reason for this is simple: the sun burnt off the bottom of the pole in 書.

Remembering this kanji

"So you were able to CONSTRUCT a barn, but you've already got **rats**, huh?"

"Yeah, should I CONSTRUCT a **rat** hotel for them somewhere else so that they'll leave?"

"Well, if you do you'll need **two** objects to get rid of them: a **pitchfork** to scare them out of their hiding spots, and a **pole** to herd them off. It might be cheaper to just CONSTRUCT some **rat** traps for them instead."

Common Pronunciations

Common **ON** reading: **KEN** (ケ ン)
Common **kun** reading: **ta** (た)

As the second example shows, this is another kanji whose verb form can incorporate its **hiragana** ending in certain compounds.

Less Common Pronunciations

Less common **ON** reading: **KON** (コ ン)
Less common **kun** reading: none

COMMON WORDS AND COMPOUNDS		
建てる	*construct; build*	**ta**·teru た·てる
建物	construct + thing = *building*	**tate**·mono たて·もの
建国	construct + country = *founding of a country*	**KEN**·KOKU ケン·コク

KANJI 429

妹

YOUNGER SISTER

女	女	女	女	女	妹	妹

BUILDING THIS KANJI

Woman 女(16) + Not Yet 未(276) = 妹

Meaning

Younger sister.

Remembering this kanji

"What's up with that **woman** over there?"

"They keep telling her it's **not yet** her turn, so she's upset."

"Doesn't she realize what's going to happen?"

"She's been pretty sheltered, so probably not; that's Marie Antoinette's YOUNGER SISTER."

Common Pronunciations
Common **ON** reading: **MAI** (マイ)
Common **kun** reading: **imōto** (いもうと)

Less Common Pronunciations
Less common **ON** reading: none
Less common **kun** reading: none

COMMON WORDS AND COMPOUNDS		
妹	*younger sister*	**imōto** いもう
姉妹	elder sister + younger sister = *sisters*	**SHI·MAI** シ・マイ

 **POND**

`	`	⻊	氵冖	沖	池			

BUILDING THIS KANJI
Splash 氵 + **Huckleberry Finn** 也 = 池

Common Pronunciations
Common **ON** reading: **CHI** (チ)
Common **kun** reading: **ike** (いけ)

Less Common Pronunciations
Less common **ON** reading: none
Less common **kun** reading: none

COMMON WORDS AND COMPOUNDS		
池	*pond*	**ike** いけ
電池	electric + pond = *battery*	**DEN·CHI** デン・チ

Meaning
Pond, reservoir.

Remembering this kanji
"What was that **splash**, **Huckleberry Finn**?"
asked Tom Sawyer. "Did you toss something
into the POND?"
"Uh…yeah, that was it."

COMPONENT #431

CLOWN   市   帀

制 **REGULATION**

ノ	⺅	⻏	乍	告	朱	制	制	制

BUILDING THIS KANJI
Jelly Bean 丶 + **Clown** 市 + **Chisel** 刂 = 制

Meaning
Regulation, control.

~emembering this kanji

~ook, a REGULATION is a REGULATION —
~u have to get rid of the big **jelly bean**."

~ut why?" asked the **clown**. "Mr. **Jelly Bean** has
~ways been the highlight of my act."

~nd that's the issue. You've had it so long it's
~vered in mold; you're going to need a **chisel**
~ get it off your hat."

~eez, who would have thought I was breaking
~ health REGULATION?"

Common Pronunciations

Common **ON** reading: **SEI** (セイ)
Common **kun** reading: none

Less Common Pronunciations

Less common **ON** reading: none
Less common **kun** reading: none

COMMON WORDS AND COMPOUNDS		
自制	self + regulation = *self-control*	**JI·SEI** ジ·セイ
制服	regulation + clothes = *uniform*	**SEI·FUKU** セイ·フク
制度	regulation + degree = *system*	**SEI·DO** セイ·ド

~ANJI 432

 運

TRANSPORT

㇐	㇕	㇌	㇗	㇘	㇙	㇚	軍
軍	渾	運					

~UILDING THIS KANJI

~rmy 軍(260) + Seal ⻌ = 運

~eaning

~ransport. A second important meaning (as can
~ seen in the final example below) relates to
~ck.

~emembering this kanji

~The **army** is furious with you. Didn't you get
~e navy **seals** to TRANSPORT the weapons?"

~Oops, I thought you wanted me to get real **seals**
~ TRANSPORT them."

Common Pronunciations

Common **ON** reading: **UN** (ウン)
Common **kun** reading: **hako** (はこ)

Create your **on-yomi** keyword and enter it in the
table at the back of the book. Then, after creating
your **kun-yomi** keyword, write your sentence to
remember the **on-yomi** and **kun-yomi** readings in
the box below.

Less Common Pronunciations

Less common **ON** reading: none
Less common **kun** reading: none

COMMON WORDS AND COMPOUNDS		
運ぶ	*transport; carry*	**hako·bu** はこ·ぶ
運送	transport + send = *transportation; shipping*	**UN·SŌ** ウン·ソウ
不運	not + transport (luck) = *bad luck; misfortune*	**FU·UN** フ·ウン

KANJI 433

 MECHANISM

一	十	才	木	术	札	松	松	松
松	機	機	機	機	機	機		

BUILDING THIS KANJI
Tree 木(13) + **How Many** 幾(400) = 機

Meaning
The general sense is of mechanisms and things employing some type of mechanistic action (the final compound below provides an interesting example). This kanji also conveys the idea of 'opportunity' or 'chance' in some of the compounds in which it appears (as in the first compound). This is, incidentally, the only time in the general-use kanji that the character for 'how many' figures as a component in another character.

Remembering this kanji
Whenever DaVinci looked at a **tree** he imagine **how many** MECHANISMS it could yield; clock MECHANISM, a loom MECHANISM and a gear MECHANISM, for example.

Common Pronunciations
Common **ON** reading: **KI** (キ)
Common **kun** reading: none

Less Common Pronunciations
Less common **ON** reading: none
Less common **kun** reading: **hata** (は た)

COMMON WORDS AND COMPOUNDS		
機会	mechanism + meet = *chance; opportunity*	**KI·KAI** キ·カイ
電動機	electric + move + mechanism = *electric motor*	**DEN·DŌ·KI** デン·ドウ·ｷ
有機体	have + mechanism + body = *organism*	**YŪ·KI·TAI** ユウ·キ·タ ｨ

KANJI 434

 **STRONG**

フ	コ	弓	弘	弘	弘	弘	強	強
強	強							

BUILDING THIS KANJI
Bow 弓 (143) + **Broken Crutch** ム + **Insect** 虫 (391) = 強

Meaning
Strong.

Remembering this kanji
I took out my **bow** but couldn't scare it. whacked it with my crutch, but this only le me with a **broken crutch**. I had only one though as the **insect** came closer: "Wow, this insect i STRONG."

Common Pronunciations
Common **ON** reading: **KYŌ** (キ ョ ウ)
Common **kun** reading: **tsuyo** (つ よ)

The **kun-yomi** is usually voiced when in second position.

Less Common Pronunciations
Less common **ON** reading: **GŌ** (ゴ ウ)
Less common **kun** reading: **shi** (し)

This **on-yomi** usually appears in words that carry a violent or negative connotation.

COMMON WORDS AND COMPOUNDS		
強い	*strong*	**tsuyo·i** つよ・い
強化	strong + change = *strengthening; intensification*	**KYŌ·KA** キョウ・カ
強制	strong + regulation = *compulsion; coercion*	**KYŌ·SEI** キョウ・セイ

COMPONENT #435

ROCKET LAUNCH   ヽ l ／

KANJI 435

光   SHIN E

1	ヽ	ソ	⺌	光	光		

BUILDING THIS KANJI
Rocket Launch ヽ l ／ + **One (hamburger patty)**
一 (3) + **Ballet** 儿 = 光

Meaning
Shine, light.

Remembering this kanji
"What a **rocket launch**," she said. "Look at the SHINE coming off the rocket!"
"It's even making the grease on my **hamburger patty** SHINE," he said.
"You're right. It's shining just like the sequins on my **ballet** outfit."

Common Pronunciations
Common **ON** reading: **KŌ** (コ ウ)
Common **kun** reading: **hika** (ひ か);
hikari (ひ か り)

Less Common Pronunciations
Less common **ON** reading: none
Less common **kun** reading: none

COMMON WORDS AND COMPOUNDS		
光る	*shine*	**hika·ru** ひか・る
光	*light; ray*	**hikari** ひかり
日光	sun + shine = *sunshine; sunlight*	**NIK·KŌ** ニッ・コウ

KANJI 436

難 DIFFICULT

一	十	艹	艹	芑	苫	苫	莒	莫
茣	堇	菓	剚	歎	歎	難	難	難

BUILDING THIS KANJI
Wreath ⁺⁺ + Girl with a Hula Hoop 茣 +
Squirrels 隹 = 難

Meaning
Difficult.

Remembering this kanji
"Is it DIFFICULT to put a wreath on a girl **with
a hula hoop**?"

"It's a bit DIFFICULT, because you have to
watch for the hula hoop spinning about. But at
least it's easier than doing it to those **squirrels**
on that brick wall over there; they're so DIFFI-
CULT they won't even let the **wreath** appear
above them in this kanji."

Common Pronunciations
Common **ON** reading: **NAN** (ナ ン)
Common **kun** reading: **muzuka** (む ず か) ;
kata (か た)

It's only fitting that this kanji is a bit difficu[lt].
NAN, however, is by far the most common rea[d]-
ing, and the two **kun-yomi** form adjectives. Wh[en]
in the second position, **kata** becomes voiced a[nd]
makes an adjective of the type shown in t[he]
second example below.

IRREGULAR READING		
有 り 難 う	have + difficult = *Thank you; Thanks*	a·ri **gatō** あ·り が と· [う]

Less Common Pronunciations
Less common **ON** reading: none
Less common **kun** reading: none

COMMON WORDS AND COMPOUNDS		
難しい	*difficult*	**muzuka**·shii むずか·しい
言い難い	say + difficult = *difficult to say*	i·i **gata**·i い·い がた·[い]
難民	difficult + people = *refugees*	**NAN·MIN** ナン·ミン

KANJI 437

社 COMPANY

`	フ	ァ	ネ	ネ-	礻	社		

BUILDING THIS KANJI
Whittling 礻 + Earth 土(87) = 社

Meaning
Company. This kanji also refers to Shinto
shrines; note how the second compound below
can encompass both meanings.

Remembering this kanji
"My COMPANY? Oh, it's involved in whi[t]-
tling earth."

"So you've got a landscaping COMPAN[Y]
then?"

"There's no need to be rude. We prefer to call [it]
a **whittling earth** COMPANY."

Common Pronunciations

Common **ON** reading: **SHA** (シャ)
Common **kun** reading: none

The final compound below is the only instance in which the **on-yomi** becomes voiced.

Less Common Pronunciations

Less common **ON** reading: none
Less common **kun** reading: **yashiro** (やしろ)

COMMON WORDS AND COMPOUNDS		
会社	meet + company = *company; corporation*	KAI·SHA カイ・シャ
本社	main + company = *head office; main temple*	HON·SHA ホン・シャ
神社	god + company = *Shinto shrine*	JIN·JA ジン・ジャ

KANJI 438

LAUGH

ノ	⺮	⺭	⺮	⺮	竺	竺	竿
笑							

BUILDING THIS KANJI

Machine Guns ⺮⺮ + 1950's Rock Star 天 = 笑

Meaning

Laugh.

Remembering this kanji

"So that's when he started performing with **machine guns**?"

"Yeah, I suppose he was desperate. Nobody wanted to listen to a **1950's rock star** any more."

"How did he react when the crowd began to LAUGH?"

"Well, it was a little dicey for a while—I mean, he did have **machine guns**—but fortunately he ended up as a comedian. It turns out he enjoyed making others LAUGH."

Common Pronunciations

Common **ON** reading: **SHŌ** (ショウ)
Common **kun** reading: **wara** (わら)

Less Common Pronunciations

Less common **ON** reading: none
Less common **kun** reading: **e** (え)

COMMON WORDS AND COMPOUNDS		
笑う	*laugh; smile*	**wara**·u わら・う
高笑い	tall + laugh = *loud laughter*	taka **wara**·i たか わら・い
失笑	lose + laugh = *burst out laughing*	SHIS·SHŌ シッ・ショウ

COMPONENT #439

ECCENTRIC PROFESSOR 侴 侴

As befits an eccentric, this fellow will have an umbrella no matter what the weather.

KANJI 439

験 **TEST**

丨	厂	丌	丌	丐	馬	馬	馬	馬
馬	馭	馯	駘	験	験	験	験	験

BUILDING THIS KANJI
Horse 馬 (144) + Eccentric Professor 侴 = 験

Meaning
Test, examine.

Remembering this kanji
Bolting into the classroom on a **horse**, the **eccentric professor** threw out the TEST. "This is an important TEST," he said. "It will TEST if you can pass a TEST in the presence of a **horse**."

Common Pronunciations
Common **ON** reading: **KEN** (ケン)
Common **kun** reading: none

Less Common Pronunciations
Less common **ON** reading: **GEN** (ゲン)
Less common **kun** reading: none

COMMON WORDS AND COMPOUNDS		
試験	try + test = *test; examination*	SHI·**KEN** シ・ケン
受験	receive + test = *take an examination*	JU·**KEN** ジュ・ケン
実験	actual + test = *experiment*	JIK·**KEN** ジッ・ケン

KANJI 440

史 **HISTORY**

丶	冖	口	史	史			

BUILDING THIS KANJI
Mouth (vampire) 口 (8) + Piranha 人 = 史

Meaning
History. It's worth taking a moment to see clearly that this kanji does <u>not</u> function as a component in 更 ('anew', from Entry 373).

Remembering this kanji
"Excuse me, I'm looking for a book about **vampires** and **piranhas**."
"What's it called?"
"'Scary Stuff That Bites: A HISTORY'."

Common Pronunciations

Common **ON** reading: **SHI** (シ)
Common **kun** reading: none

Note that the first two kanji in the final compound mean 'literature' when taken together.

Less Common Pronunciations

Less common **ON** reading: none
Less common **kun** reading: none

	COMMON WORDS AND COMPOUNDS	
史学	history + study = *history; historical studies*	**SHI·GAKU** シ・ガク
史料	history + fee (materials) = *historical materials/records*	**SHI·RYŌ** シ・リョウ
文学史	literature + history = *literary history*	**BUN·GAKU·SHI** ブン・ガク・シ

CHAPTER 19 REVIEW EXERCISES

A. Please match the following kanji to their meanings.

1.	泳	a.	Travel
2.	験	b.	What
3.	妹	c.	Test
4.	何	d.	Busy
5.	料	e.	Mechanism
6.	旅	f.	Produce
7.	機	g.	Younger sister
8.	難	h.	Fee
9.	忙	i.	Difficult
10.	産	j.	Swim

B. Please match the following meanings to their kanji, and these to their **on-** or **kun-yomi**.

1.	Dish	a. 昼	1.	**GYŌ**(ギョウ)
2.	Regulation	b. 遅	2.	**UN**(ウン)
3.	Pond	c. 飲	3.	**IN**(イン)
4.	Shine	d. 制	4.	**ike**(いけ)
5.	Slow	e. 皿	5.	**hikari**(ひかり)
6.	Drink	f. 運	6.	**SHI**(シ)
7.	Daytime	g. 光	7.	**oso**(おそ)
8.	History	h. 業	8.	**sara**(さら)
9.	Business	i. 史	9.	**SEI**(セイ)
10.	Transport	j. 池	10.	**hiru**(ひる)

C. Please choose the best answer(s) to the following questions.

1. Which of the following kanji has the most number of strokes?
   a. 強   b. 旅   c. 答   d. 料   e. 産

2. Which of the following readings apply to the kanji 治?
   a. **CHI**(チ)   b. **osa**(おさ)   c. **JI**(ジ)
   d. **SHI**(シ)   e. **nao**(なお)

3. He fell in the pond, and she couldn't help but _____ .
   a. 光   b. 旅   c. 研   d. 笑   e. 与

4. Which of the following readings apply to the kanji 黄?
   a. **KŌ**(コウ)   b. **SHŌ**(ショウ)
   c. **ku**(く)   d. **Ō**(オウ)
   e. **ki**(き)

5. Which is the correct reading of 遅れる?
   a. **aka·reru**(あか・れる)
   b. **chika·reru**(ちか・れる)
   c. **oku·reru**(おく・れる)
   d. **hama·reru**(はま・れる)

D. Please match the following compounds to their meanings and pronunciations.

1. 神社   a. Sunshine

2. 強化   b. Travel

3. 料理   c. Shinto shrine

4. 難民   d. Refugees

5. 建物   e. Cooking / Food

6. 日光   f. Yellow

7. 電池   g. Battery

8. 研究   h. Research

9. 黄色   i. Strengthening

10. 旅行   j. Building

1. **NAN·MIN**
    (ナン・ミン)

2. **RYŌ·RI**
    (リョウ・リ)

3. **ki·iro**
    (き・いろ)

4. **RYŌ·KŌ**
    (リョ・コウ)

5. **NIK·KŌ**
    (ニッ・コウ)

6. **DEN·CHI**
    (デン・チ)

7. **tate·mono**
    (たて・もの)

8. **JIN·JA**
    (ジン・ジャ)

9. **KEN·KYŪ**
    (ケン・キュウ)

10. **KYŌ·KA**
    (キョウ・カ)

E. Please read the passage below and answer the questions that follow.

"今何時ですか。"
"二時半です。バスが遅れていますね。"
"そうですね。先週から大通りで工事をしています。"
"ああ〜忘れていました。いつまでですか。"
"年末まで続きます"

1. What did the first person initially want to know
2. For what form of transportation are these two people waiting?
3. Why is it running late?
4. When had this work begun?
5. For how long will it continue?

KANJI 441

階 **FLOOR**

阝	阝	阝ー	阝ヒ	阝ヒ'	阝ヒヒ	阝ヒヒ	阝ヒヒ
皆	階	階					

BUILDING THIS KANJI
Novice Yodeler 阝 + All 皆 (344) = 階

Meaning
Floor, story (of a building). Related to this idea of layers, 階 can also refer to the rank or social stratum to which a person or group of people belong.

Remembering this kanji
The **novice yodeler yodeled**, and was so terrible that **all** of them dropped to the FLOOR. And not just those on the FLOOR he on, I'm talking everyone on **all** the FLOORS in the building.

Common Pronunciations
Common **ON** reading: **KAI** (カイ)
Common **kun** reading: none

Less Common Pronunciations
Less common **ON** reading: none
Less common **kun** reading: none

COMMON WORDS AND COMPOUNDS		
一階	one + floor = *first floor; ground floor*	IK·KAI イッ・カイ
階上	floor + upper = *upstairs*	KAI·JŌ カイ・ジョウ
階下	floor + lower = *downstairs*	KAI·KA カイ・カ

KANJI 442

点 **POINT**

l	ㅏ	丶	占	占	占	点	点	点

BUILDING THIS KANJI
Occupy 占 (255) + Gas Stove 灬 = 点

Meaning
Point, mark.

Remembering this kanji
"Organization is everything," our chef told us before the exam, "so have your frying pan nicely **occupy** the top of the **gas stove**. You will get maximum POINTS for doing this, and may even earn a bonus POINT."

Common Pronunciations
Common **ON** reading: **TEN** (テ ン)
Common **kun** reading: none

Less Common Pronunciations
Less common **ON** reading: none
Less common **kun** reading: none

COMMON WORDS AND COMPOUNDS		
点火	point + fire = *ignition*	**TEN·KA** テン·カ
重点	heavy + point = *important point; emphasis*	**JŪ·TEN** ジュウ·テン
氷点	ice + point = *freezing point*	**HYŌ·TEN** ヒョウ·テン

COMPONENT #443

BUNK BEDS 臼

KANJI 443

官 **OFFICIAL**

' 宀 宀 宀 官 官 官 官

BUILDING THIS KANJI
Pincers 宀 + Bunk Beds 臼 = 官

Meaning
Official, government. This kanji is often used as a suffix to indicate an official with some sort of governmental or bureaucratic authority.

Remembering this kanji
The refugees looked on as an OFFICIAL watched a set of **pincers** offload **bunk beds**. "I've heard he's the OFFICIAL in charge of **pincers**," one of them said.
"Really? Why isn't the **bunk bed** OFFICIAL here then?" asked another.
"Oh, she's over there, talking with the mattress OFFICIAL and the bed frame OFFICIAL," replied the first.

Common Pronunciations
Common **ON** reading: **KAN** (カ ン)
Common **kun** reading: none

Recall that the first two kanji of the secon compound mean 'test' or 'examination' (fro Entry 439), and that the first two kanji of the fir compound mean 'foreign policy' (from Ent 185) when taken together.

Less Common Pronunciations
Less common **ON** reading: none
Less common **kun** reading: none

COMMON WORDS AND COMPOUNDS		
教官	teach + official = *instructor*	**KYŌ·KAN** キョウ·カン
試験官	examination + official = *examiner*	**SHI·KEN·KAN** シ·ケン·カン
外交官	foreign policy + official = *diplomat*	**GAI·KŌ·KAN** ガイ·コウ·カン

KANJI 444

羽 **FEATHER**

| ┐ | ㇆ | ㇇ | 羽 | 羽 | 羽 | 羽 | | | |

BUILDING THIS KANJI
Crane ┐ + Pinball ⸝ + Crane ┐ + Pinball ⸝
= 羽

Meaning
Feather. This kanji can also refer to the wings of birds, insects and airplanes, etc.

Remembering this kanji
"Look what I found, grandpa!"
"That's a FEATHER, sweetheart."
"Really? What can you do with it?"
"Well, you can have a FEATHER pillow and a FEATHER duvet, for instance. You wouldn't want a FEATHER crane, though, as even a couple of those would be pretty useless. Oh, and I wouldn't want a pair of FEATHER pinball flippers either, as that would really ruin the game."

Common Pronunciations
Common **ON** reading: none
Common **kun** reading: **ha** (は); **hane** (はね)

hane tends to be the reading used when the kanji appears on its own, while **ha** is the more common in compounds. Note that the odd word in the final example below uses one of the less common **on-yomi** of 合 (**KA-** / カ ツ); this is the only time 合 is read with this pronunciation.

Less Common Pronunciations
Less common **ON** reading: **U** (ウ)
Less common **kun** reading: none

COMMON WORDS AND COMPOUNDS		
羽	*feather; wing*	**hane** はね
合羽	match + feather = *raincoat*	KAP·pa カ ッ·ぱ

KANJI 445

温 **WARM**

| ` | ⸌ | ⸍ | ⸍l | ⸍冂 | 汩 | 沪 | 沪 | 沪 | 浭 |
| 浭 | 温 | 温 | | | | | | | |

BUILDING THIS KANJI
Splash ⸍ + Sun 日 (6) + Dish 皿 (423) = 温

Meaning
Warm.

Remembering this kanji
"Whew! It's really WARM isn't it?"
"It sure is. Let me **splash** this on you."
"OK…oh yuck, what did you just **splash** me with?"
"Relax, it's only butter; the **sun** melted it in the **dish**. Do you feel how WARM it is?"

Common Pronunciations
Common **ON** reading: **ON** (オン)
Common **kun** reading: **atata** (あたた)

Less Common Pronunciations
Less common **ON** reading: none
Less common **kun** reading: none

COMMON WORDS AND COMPOUNDS		
温かい	*warm*	**atata**·kai あたた·かい
気温	spirit + warm = *(air) temperature*	**KI·ON** キ·オン
温泉	warm + springs = *hot spring; spa*	**ON·SEN** オン·セン

COMPONENT #446

TIC TAC TOE

KANJI 446

寒 **COLD**

`	宀	宀	宀	宀	宀	宀	宀	宀
寒	寒	寒						

BUILDING THIS KANJI
Pincers 宀 + Tic Tac Toe 井 + Seesaw 一 +
Jelly Bean ヽ + Jelly Bean ヽ = 寒

Meaning
Cold.

Remembering this kanji
"Aren't you COLD out here?"
"Sure I'm COLD, but what of it? I couldn't pick
up a date in that club if I had **pincers**."
"What about that girl you had a game of **tic tac
toe** with? She seemed nice."
"She was until I won. Then she turned COLD."
"Well you can't just sit here on this **seesaw**, staring at a couple of discarded **jelly beans** no one
will ever care for. I mean, that even makes me
feel COLD."

Common Pronunciations
Common **ON** reading: **KAN** (カン)
Common **kun** reading: **samu** (さむ)

Note that the second compound below can also
be read as (**samu**·KE / さむ·ケ); meaning 'chil
(from a sickness, etc)', it uses the less commo
on-yomi of 気.

Less Common Pronunciations
Less common **ON** reading: none
Less common **kun** reading: none

COMMON WORDS AND COMPOUNDS		
寒い	*cold*	**samu**·i さむ·い
寒気	cold + spirit = *coldness; the cold*	**KAN·KI** カン·キ
寒冷前線	cold + cool + before + line = *cold front*	**KAN·REI·ZEN·SEN** カン·レイ·ゼン·セン

ANJI 447

勉 DILIGENCE

UILDING THIS KANJI
xemption 免(311) + **Strength** 力(63) = 勉

leaning
iligence. This is the only one of the general-se kanji in which the character for exemption stretched out in such a way; the story and lustration takes this into account.

emembering this kanji
le got an **exemption** because of his **strength**, ut stressed that it was also due to his DILI-ENCE. "**Strength** alone," he said, "could not ave done this. It took forever, and I could not ave stretched out the kanji for '**exemption**' the vay I have without a lot of DILIGENCE."

Common Pronunciations
Common **ON** reading: **BEN** (ベン)
Common **kun** reading: none

Create your **on-yomi** keyword and enter it in the table at the back of the book. After that, write your sentence to remember the **on-yomi** reading in the box below.

Less Common Pronunciations
Less common **ON** reading: none
Less common **kun** reading: none

COMMON WORDS AND COMPOUNDS		
勉学	diligence + study = *diligent study*	**BEN**·GAKU ベン·ガク
勉強	diligence + strong = *studying*	**BEN**·KYŌ ベン·キョウ

ANJI 448

術 TECHNIQUE

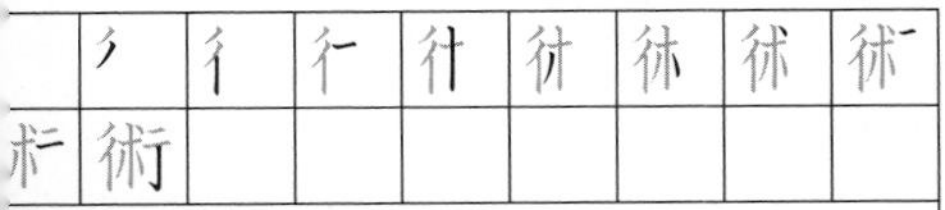

UILDING THIS KANJI
o 行(173) + **Zombie** 朮 + **Jelly Bean** ヽ = 術

Meaning
Technique, skill. The most striking thing about this kanji is that the character for 'go' is split in half. 行 is, in fact, unusual in this respect, for with the exception of its appearance in one obscure kanji [桁* (keta·けた) "beam; girder"] it is the only character in the general-use list that always does this when functioning as a component in other kanji. As a result, it will be the only one that retains its original meaning despite breaking apart in this way.

Remembering this kanji

"**Go!**" she said to the **zombie**, but of course it wouldn't leave.

"TECHNIQUE…" it said, "…practice…"

"Oh, all right," she sighed. "I'll toss the **jelly bean**, you catch it. I still don't understand why you want to master this silly TECHNIQUE, though."

Common Pronunciations

Common **ON** reading: **JUTSU** (ジュツ)
Common **kun** reading: none

Create your **on-yomi** keyword and enter it in the table at the back of the book. After that, write your sentence to remember the **on-yomi** read in the box below.

Less Common Pronunciations

Less common **ON** reading: none
Less common **kun** reading: none

COMMON WORDS AND COMPOUNDS		
美術	beautiful + technique = *art; the fine arts*	**BI·JUTSU** ビ・ジュツ
手術	hand + technique = *surgical operation*	**SHU·JUTSU** シュ・ジュツ
話術	speak + technique = *storytelling*	**WA·JUTSU** ワ・ジュツ

KANJI 449

身

PERSONAL

BUILDING THIS KANJI
Self 自 (33) + Comet 一 = 身

Meaning

This odd-looking kanji has to do with things 'personal', in the sense of someone's own body (as in the first compound) or a specific thing's characteristics (as in the third). Take care with the stroke order here; though deformed by the comet, the kanji is written in the order of the components as listed.

Remembering this kanji

"No, it's not your PERSONAL affair, **come** Your behavior is affecting other kanji in a ver PERSONAL way. I mean, look what you'v done to '**self**' here by blazing across it like thi you've made the Cyclops drop his club!"

"Hey, the jelly bean's still there."

"So what? I'm telling you, the other kanji a talking, and it's going to get PERSONAL."

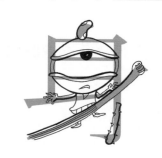

Common Pronunciations

Common **ON** reading: **SHIN** (シン)
Common **kun** reading: **mi** (み)

u will encounter both readings frequently,
hough **mi** predominates in the first position
d **SHIN** in the second.

ss **Common Pronunciations**
ss common **ON** reading: none
ss common **kun** reading: none

COMMON WORDS AND COMPOUNDS		
身体	personal + body = *the body; physical*	**SHIN**·TAI シン・タイ
出身	exit + body = *one's hometown*	SHUS·**SHIN** シュッ・シン
中身	middle + body = *contents*	naka·**mi** なか・み

1ATADOR

nsure that you can see the difference
etween this component and 扌, our component
or 'whittling' introduced prior to Entry 253.

KANJI 450

 BEGINNING

ﾌ	ﾈ	ﾈ	ﾈ	初	初		

BUILDING THIS KANJI
Matador 衤 + Sword 刀(117) = 初

Meaning
Beginning.

Remembering this kanji
We watched as the **matador** drew his **sword**.
"It's BEGINNING!" she yelled to me over the
oar of the crowd. "It's finally BEGINNING!"

Common Pronunciations
Common **ON** reading: SHO (ショ)
Common **kun** reading: **haji**(はじ); **hatsu**(はつ)

SHO is the most common of these three readings.
haji appears only in the initial word below and
one other: 初めて (**haji**·mete / はじ・めて) 'for
the first time'. **hatsu** tends to have a more poetic
shade of meaning and appears with only a few
compounds in the first position.

Less Common Pronunciations
Less common **ON** reading: none
Less common **kun** reading: **so** (そ)

COMMON WORDS AND COMPOUNDS		
初め	*beginning; outset*	**haji**·me はじ・め
初雪	beginning + snow = *first snowfall of the year*	**hatsu**·yuki はつ・ゆき
初日	beginning + sun (day) = *first day; opening day*	**SHO**·NICHI ショ・ニチ

KANJI 451

DISTRESS

| 丨 | 冂 | 冂 | 闬 | 困 | 闭 | 困 | 困 |

BUILDING THIS KANJI
Prison 囗 + **Tree** 木(13) = 困

Meaning
Distress.

Remembering this kanji
I'm never in more DISTRESS than when I catch
sight of a **tree** in **prison**. I mean, the thought of
it being rooted to one spot while the other cons
stroll about the yard chatting…I can't imagine
the DISTRESS it must feel.

Common Pronunciations
Common **ON** reading: **KON** (コ ン)
Common **kun** reading: koma (こ ま)

Less Common Pronunciations
Less common **ON** reading: none
Less common **kun** reading: none

COMMON WORDS AND COMPOUNDS		
困る	*be distressed; suffer*	**koma**·ru こ ま・る
困難	distress + difficult = *distress; difficulty*	**KON·NAN** コ ン・ナ ン

KANJI 452

PUT

| 丶 | 冖 | 冖 | 罒 | 罒 | 罒 | 罒 | 罒 | 罘 |
| 罘 | 置 | 置 | 置 | | | | | |

BUILDING THIS KANJI
Bandage 罒 + **Straight** 直(407) = 置

Meaning
Put, place, leave behind. It's worth spending a
moment to ensure that you can clearly see the
differences between this kanji and two others
learned earlier: 直 ('straight', Entry 407) and
真 ('true', Entry 358).

Remembering this kanji
"PUT it on! PUT it on!"
"Calm down. I want the **bandage** to be nice and
straight."
"Who cares? PUT it on before I lose conscious-
ness!"

Common Pronunciations
Common **ON** reading: **CHI** (チ)
Common **kun** reading: **o** (お)

The **kun-yomi** is invariably the reading in th[
first position, with the **on-yomi** more commo[
in the second. As you can see from the middl[
compound below, this is another kanji that ca[
absorb its accompanying **hiragana**.

Less Common Pronunciations
Less common **ON** reading: none
Less common **kun** reading: none

COMMON WORDS AND COMPOUNDS		
置く	*put; place; leave*	**o**·ku お・く
置場	put + place = *place (for something)*	**oki**·ba お き・ば
配置	distribute + put = *arrangement; layout*	**HAI·CHI** ハ イ・チ

個 **SOLO**

	イ	仁	们	佢	佢	佢	佢	個
固								

BUILDING THIS KANJI

Giraffe イ + Hard 固(361) = 個

Meaning

This kanji emphasizes the separateness of individual objects (including people). It is, in fact, used as a general counter for 'pieces'—the final compound shows this aspect of its meaning.

Remembering this kanji

"What with predators about," he said, " a **giraffe** had better be **hard** if he's gonna graze SOLO."

Common Pronunciations

Common **ON** reading: **KO** (コ)
Common **kun** reading: none

Less Common Pronunciations

Less common **ON** reading: none
Less common **kun** reading: none

COMMON WORDS AND COMPOUNDS		
個人	solo + person = *an individual*	**KO**·JIN コ·ジン
個別	solo + different = *individually; one by one*	**KO**·BETSU コ·ベツ
三個	three + solo = *three (pieces)*	SAN·**KO** サン·コ

PIRATE 戊 戊

Here we have the fourth member of our special family of components. As with 弋 'spilling coffee' and 戈 'killer bee', the stroke order is broken here by anything that appears underneath the horizontal line (the following kanji provides an example). And finally, don't ever forget to include the doubloon with this component—the pirate is known to become very angry if someone takes away his money.

成 **BECOME**

ノ	厂	万	成	成	成			

BUILDING THIS KANJI
Pirate 戊 + Crane フ = 成

Meaning

Become. Pay close attention to the stroke order of this kanji, as the sword of the pirate is always written <u>before</u> the horizontal line (thus making these initial strokes the opposite of 厂, the "cliff" learned prior to Entry 287. Remember also that the crane breaks the stroke order of the pirate by following immediately after the horizontal line.

Remembering this kanji

"If you want to BECOME a **pirate** these days," Blackbeard told me, "you'll need to have a **crane**."

"Why's that?" I asked.

"Well, have you seen the size of those supertankers? You even attempt to scale one of those with ropes and you'll BECOME a laughingstock."

Common Pronunciations
Common **ON** reading: **SEI** (セイ)
Common **kun** reading: **na** (な)

The **kun-yomi** can incorporate its **hiragana** ending in certain compounds.

Less Common Pronunciations
Less common **ON** reading: **JŌ** (ジョウ)
Less common **kun** reading: none

COMMON WORDS AND COMPOUNDS		
成る	*become*	**na**·ru な・る
成年	become + year = *adult; age of majority*	**SEI**·**NEN** セイ・ネ〉
成立	become + stand = *formation*	**SEI**·**RITSU** セイ・リ〉

KANJI 455

 **WORK**

ノ	イ	イ´	仁	仨	仹	信	信	俥
俥	偅	働	働					

BUILDING THIS KANJI
Giraffe イ + Move 動(318) = 働

Meaning
Work.

Remembering this kanji
"Do you ever notice that **giraffes** always seem to be on the **move**?"
"That's because a lot of them are unemployed. They're looking for WORK."

Common Pronunciations
Common **ON** reading: none
Common **kun** reading: **hatara** (はたら)

Less Common Pronunciations
Less common **ON** reading: **DŌ** (ドウ)
Less common **kun** reading: none

COMMON WORDS AND COMPOUNDS		
働く	*work*	**hatara**·ku はたら・く
働き口	work + mouth = *job; position*	**hatara**·ki guchi はたら・き ぐち

OMPONENT #456

RAB WITH A MOHAWK ⺍

his is a good place to review a number of milar-looking components. In addition to the esent one, ensure that you are able to easily entify 'pincers', 'UFO', "claw", 'weightlifter', 'stroller', 'quick-nd', and 'rocket launch'.

ANJI 456

堂 HALL

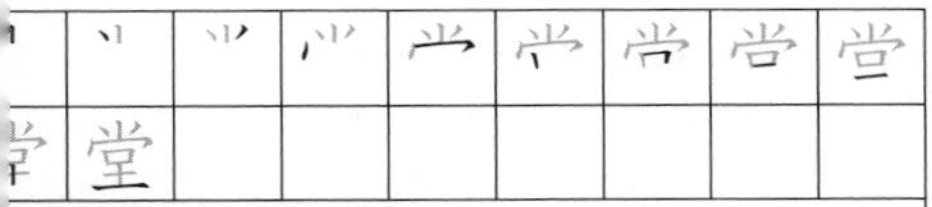

UILDING THIS KANJI

rab With a Mohawk ⺍ + **Mouth (vampire)** 口(8) + **Earth** 土(87) = 堂

eaning

his kanji refers to a larger-sized hall, usually a public building.

Remembering this kanji

The HALL was in a bloodthirsty uproar, as the **crab with a mohawk** had unexpectedly pinned the **vampire**. Moments later, however, the HALL fell silent, and we watched as the **crab** helped the **vampire** to his feet and brushed the **earth** from his cape. I was not alone in feeling ashamed, for no one in that HALL had ever witnessed such sportsmanship.

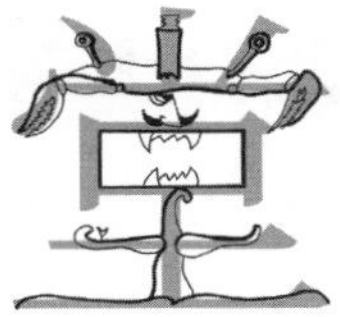

Common Pronunciations

Common **ON** reading: **DŌ** (ドウ)

Common **kun** reading: none

Less Common Pronunciations

Less common **ON** reading: none

Less common **kun** reading: none

COMMON WORDS AND COMPOUNDS		
食堂	eat + hall = *dining hall; cafeteria*	SHOKU·**DŌ** ショク·ドウ
本堂	main + hall = *main hall; main temple*	HON·**DŌ** ホン·ドウ

ANJI 457

組 ASSOCIATION

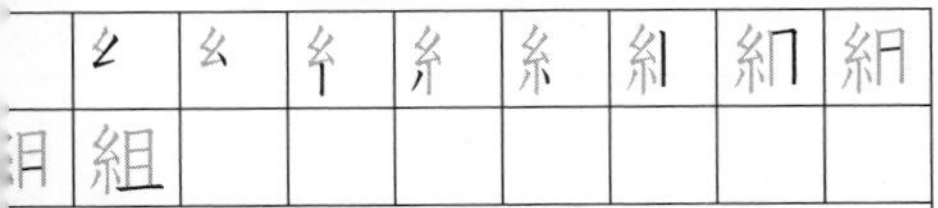

UILDING THIS KANJI

hread 糸(196) + **Besides (filing cabinet)** 且 293) = 組

ssociation, set. This kanji has to do with things oming together or being put together in groups.

Remembering this kanji

"**Thread**?" she said. "Yes, of course we do. I'll get you some from the **filing cabinet** over there."

And so, she thought, it goes on…will I ever get free from the clutches of the Quilter's ASSOCIATION?

Common Pronunciations

Common **ON** reading: none

Common **kun** reading: **ku** (く); **kumi** (くみ)

These readings become voiced in the second position according to the rules we learned for 付 in Entry 226. Note the mix of **on-** and **kun-yomi** in the final compound.

Less Common Pronunciations
Less common **ON** reading: **SO** (ソ)
Less common **kun** reading: none

COMMON WORDS AND COMPOUNDS		
組む	*put together; form*	**ku·mu** く・む
組合	association + match = *association; (labor) union*	**kumi·ai** く・み・あい
番組	order + association = *a program*	BAN·**gumi** バン・ぐみ

KANJI 458

起 **ARISE**

一	十	土	千	耂	走	走	起	起
起								

BUILDING THIS KANJI
Run 走(212) + **Oneself (whip)** 己(214) = 起

Meaning
Arise, get up, happen. The kanji for 'run' always stretches out like this when appearing on the left of another character as a component.

Remembering this kanji
If you **run** with a **whip** and yell 'ARISE!', it's pretty likely that something or someone will in fact ARISE.

Common Pronunciations
Common **ON** reading: **KI** (キ)
Common **kun** reading: **o** (お)

The first two examples below function as a normal intransitive/transitive verb pair.

Less Common Pronunciations
Less common **ON** reading: none
Less common **kun** reading: none

COMMON WORDS AND COMPOUNDS		
起こる (intr)	*to happen; come to pass*	**o·koru** お・こる
起こす (tr)	*to bring about; raise up*	**o·kosu** お・こす
起きる (intr)	*to get up / rise*	**o·kiru** お・きる
起点	arise + point = *starting point*	**KI·TEN** キ・テン

KANJI 459

争 **DISPUTE**

ノ	ク	ク	与	马	争		

BUILDING THIS KANJI
Little Red Riding Hood ⺈ + **Pitchfork** ⺕ + **Harpoon** ∫ = 争

Meaning
Dispute, argue.

Remembering this kanji
Little Red Riding Hood is a country girl, so it was natural that she'd grab a **pitchfork**. What was odd, though, was how she managed to get a **harpoon**...had she really gone down to the docks? Anyway, what was beyond DISPUTE was that she was finally ready for any DISPUTE.

ommon Pronunciations

ommon **ON** reading: **SŌ** (ソ ウ)
ommon **kun** reading: **araso** (あ ら そ)

ess Common Pronunciations

ess common **ON** reading: none
ess common **kun** reading: none

COMMON WORDS AND COMPOUNDS		
争 う	*dispute; contend*	**araso·u** あ ら そ ・ う
争 点	dispute + point = *point of dispute*	**SŌ·TEN** ソ ウ ・ テ ン
内 争	inside + dispute = *internal dispute*	**NAI·SŌ** ナ イ ・ ソ ウ

COMPONENT #460

UCLEAR REACTOR

here's no need to be concerned about what's
eaking out of the right-hand side of the reac-
or here; this is only an illustration.

ANJI 460

風 **WIND**

几	几	几	凡	凤	風	風	風

UILDING THIS KANJI

Nuclear Reactor 几 + Comet 一 + Insect 虫
391) = 風

leaning

Vind (as in breeze). An important secondary
neaning relates to the ideas of style and appear-
nce; the final compound provides an example.

Remembering this kanji

You expect me to believe that the **nuclear reac-
or** was struck by a **comet**?" I asked.
Look, pal," said the giant mutating **insect**, "I'm
nly suggesting you might want to stay ahead
f the WIND."

ommon Pronunciations

ommon **ON** reading: **FŪ** (フ ウ)
ommon **kun** reading: **kaza** (か ざ); **kaze** (か ぜ)

FŪ is the more common of the three readings,
while **kaza** appears only in the first position. **kaze**
is the reading used when the kanji stands on its
own; it rarely occurs in the first position but is
as common as **FŪ** when this character is the last
in a compound. **FŪ** is the reading used in those
compounds relating to style and appearance.

Create your **on-yomi** keyword and write it in the
table at the back of the book. Then, after creating
your **kun-yomi** keywords, write your sentence to
remember the on-yomi and kun-yomi readings
in the box below.

Less Common Pronunciations

Less common **ON** reading: **FU** (フ)
Less common **kun** reading: none

This reading is primarily useful for its appearance
in the well-known Japanese word for 'bath': 風
呂 * (**FU·RO** / フ ・ ロ), from the kanji 'wind' and
'spine'. The latter character, incidentally, is not
presented in this book, but can be easily remembered as a straight pictogram of a spine, or as a
pair of *katakana* **RO** (ロ) strung together.

COMMON WORDS AND COMPOUNDS		
風	*wind*	**kaze** か ぜ
風 車	wind + car = *windmill*	**kaza·guruma** か ざ ・ ぐ る ま
台 風	platform + wind = *typhoon*	**TAI·FŪ** タ イ ・ フ ウ
日 本 風	Japan + wind (style) = *Japanese style*	**NI·HON·FŪ** ニ ・ ホ ン ・ フ ウ

KANJI 461

痛 **PAIN**

`	一	广	广	广	疒	疒	疒	疒
疒	疒	痛						

BUILDING THIS KANJI
Lemmings 疒 + Dentist Light マ + Utilize 用 (270) = 痛

Meaning
Pain.

Remembering this kanji
I watched as the **lemmings** carefully positioned the **dentist light** above me. At least they're able to **utilize** that, I thought. Nevertheless, I couldn't shake the feeling that my root canal was about to leave me in a lot of PAIN.

Common Pronunciations
Common **ON** reading: **TSŪ** (ツ ウ)
Common **kun** reading: **ita** (い た)

Recall from Entry 303 that the final compou[nd] below uses a less common **on-yomi** for 頭.

Less Common Pronunciations
Less common **ON** reading: none
Less common **kun** reading: none

COMMON WORDS AND COMPOUNDS		
痛い	*painful*	**ita·i** い た・い
痛み止め	pain + stop = *painkiller*	**ita·mi do·me** い た・み ど・め
頭痛	head + pain = *headache*	**ZU·TSŪ** ズ・ツ ウ

KANJI 462

吏 **OFFICER**

一	厂	一	三	吏	吏			

BUILDING THIS KANJI
One (hamburger patty) 一 (3) + History 史 (440) = 吏

Meaning
An officer or official, typically one of lower standing. We will find more use for this kanji as a component than as a character on its own.

Remembering this kanji
"What is it I do? I'm a **hamburger patty histor**[y] OFFICER."
"Is that so?"
"Yes, well the **hamburger patty** has an interes[t]ing **history**. I mean, anything that's gone fro[m] a slab of gristle-clogged beef to the status [of] culinary icon needs someone to tell its story. Who else is more qualified than a **hamburge**[r] **patty history** OFFICER?"

Common Pronunciations
Common **ON** reading: **RI** (リ)
Common **kun** reading: none

ess Common Pronunciations
ss common **ON** reading: none
ss common **kun** reading: none

COMPONENT #463

| UGGLER | |

KANJI 463

寝

SLEEP

丶	ﾉ	宀	宀	宀	宀	宀	宀	宀
宀	宀	寝	寝					

BUILDING THIS KANJI

Pincers 宀 + **Juggler** ﾖ + **Comb** ヨ + **UFO**
宀 + **Again (ironing board)** 又(159) = 寝

Meaning

Sleep.

Remembering this kanji

The stress of a modern lifestyle, it seemed, was
starting to be too much.

"SLEEP...SLEEP..." he said softly.

"But I can't SLEEP!" she exclaimed. "I've got
so much to do, I feel like there's a huge set of
pincers hovering over me. I mean, I'm like a
juggler! I always have to keep up my appearance
with this **comb**..."

"Just SLEEP..."

"But how can I? Since the aliens in the **UFO**
gave me the **ironing board** and told me to take
better care of the family..."

"Sssshhh...you just need to SLEEP..."

Common Pronunciations
Common **ON** reading: **SHIN** (シ ン)
Common **kun** reading: **ne** (ね)

The **kun-yomi** is the more common reading here.

Less Common Pronunciations
Less common **ON** reading: none
Less common **kun** reading: none

COMMON WORDS AND COMPOUNDS

寝る	*sleep*	**ne**·ru ね・る
昼寝	daytime + sleep = *afternoon nap*	hiru·**ne** ひる・ね
寝室	sleep + room = *bedroom*	**SHIN**·SHITSU シン・シツ

KANJI 464

 関 CHECKPOINT

| 丨 | 冂 | 冖 | 冃 | 冃¹ | 門 | 門 | 門 | 門 |
| 門 | 門 | 閂 | 閔 | 関 | | | | |

BUILDING THIS KANJI
Gate 門(96) + Opera Singer 关 = 関

Meaning
Checkpoint, barrier.

Remembering this kanji
We approached the **gate** but found our way blocked by an **opera singer**. "This is a CHECKPOINT," she said.
I was frightened, but you were not. "I'm not sure I understand," you replied. "Is the **gate** the CHECKPOINT, or are you the CHECKPOINT?"

Common Pronunciations
Common **ON** reading: **KAN** (カ ン)
Common **kun** reading: **seki** (せ き)

Less Common Pronunciations
Less common **ON** reading: none
Less common **kun** reading: none

COMMON WORDS AND COMPOUNDS		
·関	*checkpoint; barrier*	**seki** せき
機関	mechanism + checkpoint = *engine; organization*	**KI·KAN** キ・カン
関係	checkpoint + connection = *relationship; connection*	**KAN·KEI** カン・ケイ

KANJI 465

側 SIDE

| ノ | 亻 | 亻 | 刂 | 俏 | 伹 | 佃 | 倶 | 俱 |
| 側 | 側 | | | | | | | |

BUILDING THIS KANJI
Giraffe 亻 + Rule 則(382) = 側

Meaning
Side.

Remembering this kanji
"**Giraffes** have a **rule**," he said. "When the graze, everyone else has to step to the SIDE It's always been like that here on the savanna."
"Well, you might be happy to watch from th SIDE," she said, "but I'm not. Those arrogan **giraffes** and their **rules** won't force me to th SIDE forever."

Common Pronunciations
Common **ON** reading: **SOKU** (ソ ク)
Common **kun** reading: **gawa** (が わ)

...ess Common Pronunciations

...ess common **ON** reading: none

...ess common **kun** reading: none

COMMON WORDS AND COMPOUNDS		
側	*side*	**gawa** がわ
左側	left + side = *left side*	hidari·**gawa** ひだり·がわ
側近	side + near = *close associate*	**SOK·KIN** ソッ·キン

CHAPTER 20 REVIEW EXERCISES

. Please match the following kanji to their meanings.

1.	困	a.	Cold
2.	寒	b.	Point
3.	点	c.	Personal
4.	働	d.	Dispute
5.	争	e.	Pain
6.	痛	f.	Warm
7.	組	g.	Feather
8.	身	h.	Distress
9.	羽	i.	Work
10.	温	j.	Association

. Please match the following meanings to their kanji, and these to their on- or kun-yomi.

1.	Checkpoint	a. 置	1.	**KAI** (カイ)
2.	Become	b. 堂	2.	**kaze** (かぜ)
3.	Arise	c. 術	3.	**DŌ** (ドウ)
	(on-yomi)			
4.	Side	d. 関	4.	**JUTSU** (ジュツ)
5.	Sleep	e. 起	5.	**KI** (キ)
6.	Put	f. 成	6.	**seki** (せき)
	(kun-yomi)			
7.	Wind	g. 風	7.	**gawa** (がわ)
8.	Technique	h. 階	8.	**o** (お)
9.	Floor	i. 側	9.	**ne** (ね)
10.	Hall	j. 寝	10.	**na** (な)

C. Please choose the best answer(s) to the following questions.

1. Which is the correct reading of 働く?
   a. **hara·ku** (はら·く)
   b. **hatara·ku** (はたら·く)
   c. **kotara·ku** (こたら·く)
   d. **hikera·ku** (ひけら·く)

2. Which of the following readings apply to the kanji 初?
   a. **haji** (はじ)　　　b. **SHO** (ショ)
   c. **SHŌ** (ショウ)　　d. **ha** (は)
   e. **hatsu** (はつ)

3. Rembrandt's _____ is known for its subtlety.
   a. 側　　b. 風　　c. 官　　d. 術　　e. 羽

4. Which is the correct reading of 寒い?
   a. **ubu·i** (うぶ·い)
   b. **kamu·i** (かむ·い)
   c. **samu·i** (さむ·い)
   d. **kayu·i** (かゆ·い)

5. Which of the following kanji has the most number of strokes?
   a. 風　　b. 身　　c. 官　　d. 困　　e. 初

D. Please match the following compounds to their meanings and pronunciations.

1. 台風　a. Headache
2. 勉強　b. An individual
3. 個人　c. Afternoon nap
4. 温泉　d. Point of dispute
5. 頭痛　e. Typhoon
6. 関係　f. Connection
7. 番組　g. Hot spring / Spa
8. 出身　h. A program
9. 争点　i. Studying
10. 昼寝　j. One's hometown

1. **ZU·TSŪ** (ズ·ツウ)
2. **BAN·gumi** (バン·ぐみ)
3. **KO·JIN** (コ·ジン)
4. **SŌ·TEN** (ソウ·テン)
5. **TAI·FŪ** (タイ·フウ)
6. **SHUS·SHIN** (シュッ·シン)
7. **ON·SEN** (オン·セン)
8. **BEN·KYŌ** (ベン·キョウ)
9. **KAN·KEI** (カン·ケイ)
10. **hiru·ne** (ひる·ね)

E. Please read the passage below and answer t questions that follow.

科学の勉強をしている時に気温が下がって初雪が降りました。寒いのでクラスの後、温泉に行く事に決めました。二人の友達と行って楽しかったです。

1. What was this person studying?
2. What happened during this time?
3. What did this person decide to do after class?
4. With whom did this person go?
5. What made them decide to do this?

Kanji #466—490

荷 **CARGO**

一	十	艹	芍	芢	芢	荶	荷	荷
荷								

BUILDING THIS KANJI

Wreath 艹 + What 何 (411) = 荷

Meaning

Cargo, burden. As mentioned in Entry 411, this is the only general-use kanji in which the character for 'what' appears as a component. As there, it will be highlighted in the story below by a string of exclamation and question marks.

Remembering this kanji

"A **wreath**," she said quietly.

"**What**!!!???"

"I couldn't believe it either. We looked everywhere, but that was the only CARGO."

Common Pronunciations

Common **ON** reading: **KA** (カ)

Common **kun** reading: **ni** (に)

The **kun-yomi** is by far the more common reading. Note that the second compound (a combination of **on-** and **kun-yomi**) uses the less common **on-yomi** of 物 ("thing", from Entry 125).

Less Common Pronunciations

Less common **ON** reading: none

Less common **kun** reading: none

COMMON WORDS AND COMPOUNDS		
重荷	heavy + cargo = *heavy burden / load*	omo·**ni** おも・に
荷物	cargo + thing = *luggage; baggage*	**ni**·MOTSU に・モツ
出荷	exit + cargo = *shipment; shipping*	SHUK·**KA** シュッ・カ

KANJI 467

 PORT

丶	氵	氵	汢	汢	汢	洪	洪	洪
洪	港	港						

BUILDING THIS KANJI
Splash 氵 + **Together** 共 (409) + **Oneself (whip)**
己 (214) = 港

Meaning
Port, harbor.

Remembering this kanji
I was woken by a **splash** and looked up; we were still **together** on the raft, but the elements were lashing us like a **whip**. The PORT, I thought, would we ever make it to the PORT?

Common Pronunciations
Common **ON** reading: **KŌ** (コウ)
Common **kun** reading: **minato** (みなと)

Less Common Pronunciations
Less common **ON** reading: none
Less common **kun** reading: none

COMMON WORDS AND COMPOUNDS		
港	*port; harbor*	**minato** みなと
入港	enter + port = *entering port; arrival*	NYŪ·KŌ ニュウ・コウ
空港	empty (sky) + port = *airport*	KŪ·KŌ クウ・コウ

KANJI 468

 HIT

一	丁	扌	扌	打				

BUILDING THIS KANJI
Finger 扌 + **Block** 丁 (165) = 打

Meaning
Hit, strike.

Remembering this kanji
"It's rough here, so for goodness sakes don't wag your **finger** at anyone in this **block**. You'll get HIT."

Common Pronunciations
Common **ON** reading: **DA** (ダ)
Common **kun** reading: **u** (う)

u is the more common reading. This is anothe kanji that will often incorporate its accompanying **hiragana** when forming nouns.

Create your **on-yomi** keyword and enter it in the table at the back of the book. Then, after creating your **kun-yomi** keyword, write your sentence to remember the **on-yomi** and **kun-yomi** readings in the box below.

ss Common Pronunciations
ss common **ON** reading: none
ss common **kun** reading: none

COMMON WORDS AND COMPOUNDS		
打つ	hit; strike	**u·**tsu う・つ
打ち切る	hit + cut = *stop doing something; break off*	**u·**chi ki·ru う・ち き・る
打者	hit + individual = *batter; hitter (in baseball)*	**DA·**SHA ダ・シャ

COMPONENT #469

UNGLEMAN   歹   歹

KANJI 469

列   **ROW**

ー	フ	歹	歹	列	列		

BUILDING THIS KANJI
Jungleman 歹 + Chisel 刂 = 列

Meaning
Row (as in a row of objects).

Remembering this kanji
"It really bugs me that it's so messy here in
the jungle," said the **jungleman**, "and since it
can be easy to misplace stuff because of that,
it's important that I keep everything tidy and
D my possessions with this **chisel**. Here, for
instance, are my spears: you'll notice they're
nicely arranged in a ROW. Over there are my
animal skulls—also in a ROW—and of course
my leopard-skin shorts. And yes, those are in a
ROW, too."

Common Pronunciations
Common **ON** reading: **RETSU** (レ ツ)
Common **kun** reading: none

Create your **on-yomi** keyword and enter it in the
table at the back of the book. After that, write
your sentence to remember the **on-yomi** reading
in the box below.

Less Common Pronunciations
Less common **ON** reading: none
Less common **kun** reading: none

COMMON WORDS AND COMPOUNDS		
列島	row + island = *island chain; archipelago*	**RET·**TŌ レッ・トウ
列車	row + car = *train*	**RES·**SHA レッ・シャ
系列	system + row = *series; corporate group*	**KEI·**RETSU ケイ・レツ

KANJI 470

丸 **ROUND**

ノ	九	丸						

BUILDING THIS KANJI
Nine 九(39) + **Jelly Bean** ﹨ = 丸

Meaning
Round. By extension are the ideas of completion and wholeness, etc.

Remembering this kanji
"Yes, I realize you're dressed to the **nines** and look great. But if you keep eating one **jelly bean** after another like this…I'm telling you, you're going to get ROUND."

Common Pronunciations
Common **ON** reading: none
Common **kun** reading: **maru** (ま る)

Less Common Pronunciations
Less common **ON** reading: **GAN** (ガ ン)
Less common **kun** reading: none

COMMON WORDS AND COMPOUNDS		
丸 い	*round*	**maru·i** ま る・い
丸 め る	*to make round*	**maru·meru** ま る・め る
日 の 丸	*sun + round* = *the Japanese (rising sun) flag*	hi no **maru** ひ の ま る

KANJI 471

館 **MANOR**

ノ	𠆢	𠂉	今	今	会	食	食	食’
食’	館	館	館	館	館	館		

BUILDING THIS KANJI
Umbrella 𠆢 + Glutton 𝄕 + Official 官 (443) = 館

Meaning
Manor, although this kanji can appear in compounds referring to anything from stately embassies to simple country inns.

Remembering this kanji
Though an **umbrella** was covering the **glutton**, the **official** at the MANOR was not fooled. "I'm not letting you in," she said. "This wine and cheese is only for **officials** who have been invited to the MANOR."

Common Pronunciations
Common **ON** reading: **KAN** (カ ン)
Common **kun** reading: none

·call from Entry 448 that the first two kanji of the
al compound mean 'art' when taken together.

·ss Common Pronunciations
·ss common **ON** reading: none
·ss common **kun** reading: none

COMMON WORDS AND COMPOUNDS		
旅館	travel + manor = *Japanese-style inn*	RYO·**KAN** リョ・カン
図書館	diagram + write + manor = *library*	TO·SHO·**KAN** ト・ショ・カン
美術館	art + manor = *art museum*	BI·JUTSU·**KAN** ビ・ジュツ・カン

OMPONENT #472

·UMMINGBIRD

·ANJI 472

飛 **FLY**

乁 乁 飞 飞 飞 飞 飛 飛 飛

·UILDING THIS KANJI
·lummingbird 飞 + **Pole** | + **Giraffe** ⺅ +
·lummingbird 飞 = 飛

·leaning
·ly. You will need to take care with the stroke
·rder of this very unusual-looking character; it
·nay help when writing it to think of your pen
·noving in the odd pattern of left to right, back
·o left, and once again to right.

·lemembering this kanji
·A couple of **hummingbirds** can obviously FLY,
·ut what about a **pole**? Well, it can FLY through
·he air if you toss it, right? And don't even bring
··p the **giraffe**; anyone who looks at its shape in
·his kanji can tell that it's FLYING.

Common Pronunciations
Common **ON** reading: **HI** (ヒ)
Common **kun** reading: to (と)

The **kun-yomi** can absorb its accompanying **hira-gana** when forming nouns. When taken together, the first two kanji in the final compound mean 'flight' or 'flying'.

Less Common Pronunciations
Less common **ON** reading: none
Less common **kun** reading: none

COMMON WORDS AND COMPOUNDS		
飛ぶ	*fly*	**to**·bu と・ぶ
飛び出す	fly + exit = *fly out; jump out*	**to**·bi da·su と・び だ・す
飛行機	flight + mechanism = *airplane*	**HI**·KŌ·KI ヒ・コウ・キ

KANJI 473

 **NUMBER**

丶	丷	丄	半	米	米	米	米	米
数	数	数	数					

BUILDING THIS KANJI
Rice 米(32) + Woman 女(16) + Cheerleaders 文 = 数

Meaning
Number. When in the first position, this kanji will sometimes carry the meaning of 'several' of whatever is indicated by the character following (years, persons, days, etc.).

Remembering this kanji
"The NUMBER of rice grains that you can stack on this **woman** is very important," she said. "It will determine which of you **cheerleaders** pass the tryout."

"Uh, excuse me?" said the **woman**. "What kind of ridiculous job is this? I'm supposed to just sit here and get covered with **rice**? No wonder a NUMBER of **women** told me not to apply."

Common Pronunciations
Common **ON** reading: **SŪ** (スウ)
Common **kun** reading: **kazu** (かず); **kazo** (かぞ

SŪ is the most common reading, and the one use to express the idea of 'several' mentioned abov **kazu** is the general word for 'number' and form only a few compounds, while **kazo** is a verb ste (for the verb in the second example below). O rare occasions the **on-yomi** can become voice the final compound is an example.

Create your **on-yomi** keyword and write it in th table at the back of the book. Then, after creatin your **kun-yomi** keywords, write your sentence remember the **on-yomi** and **kun-yomi** readings the box below.

Less Common Pronunciations
Less common **ON** reading: **SU** (ス)
Less common **kun** reading: none

COMMON WORDS AND COMPOUNDS		
数	*number*	**kazu** かず
数える	*count*	**kazo·eru** かぞ·える
数学	number + study = *mathematics*	**SŪ·GAKU** スウ·ガク
人数	person + number = *number of persons*	**NIN·ZŪ** ニン·ズ

KANJI 474

 LEARN

フ	ヨ	ヨ	ヨ1	羽	羽	羽	羽	羽
習	習							

BUILDING THIS KANJI
Feather 羽(444) + White 白(7) = 習

Meaning
Learn. Take care not to confuse this kanji with 皆 ('all', from Entry 344).

emembering this kanji

f you drop a **feather** on something **white**," said
e guru. "What will you LEARN? Assuming
e **feather** is **white**, of course."

couldn't care less," he said.

Oh. Well you obviously have much to LEARN."

Common Pronunciations
Common **ON** reading: **SHŪ** (シュウ)
Common **kun** reading: **nara** (なら)

Less Common Pronunciations
Less common **ON** reading: none
Less common **kun** reading: none

COMMON WORDS AND COMPOUNDS		
習う	*learn; take lessons*	**nara·u** なら・う
自習	self + learn = *learning by oneself*	**JI·SHŪ** ジ・シュウ
習字	learn + character = *penmanship*	**SHŪ·JI** シュウ・ジ

LAYGROUND

s this is the last of several similar-looking
omponents, it's now a good idea for us to
ompare it to the others: 呆 'sherpa', 仐
sprinter', 仈 'crossing gate'.

KANJI 475

展 **DISPLAY**

フ	⁊	尸	尸	尸	屏	屏	屈	展	展
展									

UILDING THIS KANJI

'lag 尸 + Wreath 艹 + Playground 㐅 = 展

Meaning

Display, spread.

Remembering this kanji
"DISPLAY the **flag**! She's here!"
And we did so without complaint, for this
was our champion, her victory **wreath** on full
DISPLAY. Even those in the **playground**, it must
be said, were unable to swing or slide, being
awestruck by the entire DISPLAY.

Common Pronunciations
Common **ON** reading: **TEN** (テン)
Common **kun** reading: none

Less Common Pronunciations
Less common **ON** reading: none
Less common **kun** reading: none

COMMON WORDS AND COMPOUNDS		
展開	display + open = *unfolding; development*	**TEN·KAI** テン・カイ
展示	display + show = *display; exhibition*	**TEN·JI** テン・ジ
発展	discharge + display = *development; expansion*	**HAT·TEN** ハッ・テン

KANJI 476

面 **MASK**

一	一	厂	厂	而	而	而	面	面

Meaning

Mask, aspect, face. Underlying the meaning of this character is a sense of the surface appearance of things. You've no doubt seen enough kanji by now to realize what a unique-looking character we're dealing with here; you'll need to take your time with the stroke order, as it's unlike any other kanji you'll meet.

Common Pronunciations

Common **ON** reading: **MEN** (メン)
Common **kun** reading: **omote** (おもて);
omo (おも)

MEN is the far more common reading.

Less Common Pronunciations

Less common **ON** reading: none
Less common **kun** reading: **tsura** (つら)

IRREGULAR READING		
真面目	true + mask + eye = *honest; earnest*	ma·**ji**·me ま・じ・め

COMMON WORDS AND COMPOUNDS		
面	*surface; face*	**omote** おもて
面白い	mask + white = *interesting*	**omo** shiro·i おも しろ・い
面接	mask + join = *interview*	**MEN**·SETSU メン・セツ

KANJI 477

選 **SELECT**

ﾚ	ｺ	己	己ﾞ	弖	弖	弓	弛	弛
巽	巽	巽	巽	選	選			

BUILDING THIS KANJI

Oneself (whip) 己 (214) + **Oneself (whip)** 己
(214) + **Together** 共 (409) + **Seal** ⻌ = 選

Meaning

Select, choose.

Remembering this kanji

It was my turn to SELECT, but just like the oth
rookies I could only do it with a couple of **whip**
The herd, of course, attempted to stick **togeth**
at first, but I was eventually able to force a **sea**
to stray from the rest. Quite honestly, though,
should have been able to SELECT a better one

mmon Pronunciations

mmon **ON** reading: **SEN** (セ ン)

mmon **kun** reading: **era** (え ら)

ss Common Pronunciations

s common **ON** reading: none

s common **kun** reading: none

COMMON WORDS AND COMPOUNDS		
選ぶ	*select; choose*	**era**·bu え ら·ぶ
選手	select + hand = *athlete*	**SEN**·SHU セ ン·シュ
特選	special + select = *special selection*	TOKU·**SEN** ト ク·セ ン

OMPONENT #478

HILI PEPPER

ANJI 478

帰

HOMEWARD

リ	リ⁻	リ⁻	リ⁻	尸	尸	帰	帰	帰
帰								

JILDING THIS KANJI

hili Pepper リ + Comb ヨ + UFO ⌐ + Cloth
(162) = 帰

eaning

omeward, in the sense of going back or return-
g.

emembering this kanji

glance HOMEWARD…

m a **chili pepper** in a foreign land, and they
e looking for those like me with a fine-toothed
mb. They call me an alien, and I feel, some-
nes, as if I *had* dropped here from a **UFO**. And
t I am needed here, to draw a **cloth** across my
veating brow doing jobs that others feel are
neath them. It is unbearable, and yet for the
ke of my loved ones, I cannot turn HOME-
ARD…

Common Pronunciations

Common **ON** reading: **KI** (キ)

Common **kun** reading: **kae** (か え)

The **kun-yomi** becomes voiced (as in the second
compound) according to the same rules as those
for 付 (Entry 226).

Less Common Pronunciations

Less common **ON** reading: none

Less common **kun** reading: none

COMMON WORDS AND COMPOUNDS		
帰る	*go back*	**kae**·ru か え·る
日帰り	sun (day) + homeward = *day trip*	hi **gae**·ri ひ が え·り
帰国	homeward + country = *go back to one's country*	**KI**·KOKU キ·コ ク

KANJI 479

 部 SECTION

`	一	宀	宀	立	立	音	音	音⁷
音阝	部							

BUILDING THIS KANJI
Stand 立(112) + Mouth (vampire) 口 (8) +
Veteran Yodeler 阝 = 部

Meaning
Section, department, category.

Remembering this kanji
"Why can't I **stand** in this SECTION?" asked
the **vampire**. "I'd prefer to be…"
He was interrupted by a yodel. A magnificent,
soaring, yodel.
"I'm so sorry," he said. "I didn't realize this was
the **veteran yodeler** SECTION."

Common Pronunciations
Common **ON** reading: **BU** (ブ)
Common **kun** reading: none

Create your **on-yomi** keyword and enter it in
table at the back of the book. After that, w
your sentence to remember the **on-yomi** read
in the box below.

Less Common Pronunciations
Less common **ON** reading: none
Less common **kun** reading: none

IRREGULAR READING		
部屋	section + roof = *room (of a house, etc.)*	he·ya へ・や

COMMON WORDS AND COMPOUNDS		
全部	complete + section = *all; the whole*	ZEN·BU ゼン・ブ
上部	upper + section = *upper section / part*	JŌ·BU ジョウ・ブ
部分	section + part = *part; portion*	BU·BUN ブ・ブン

KANJI 480

 題 TOPIC

`	冂	冃	日	旦	早	昻	昻	是
是	是	题	題	題	題	題	題	題

BUILDING THIS KANJI
Approve 是 (406) + Guy Wearing a Barrel 頁
= 題

Meaning
Topic, theme. This is the only instance in t
general-use kanji in which the character f
'approve' is stretched out; the story takes th
into account.

Remembering this kanji

"What's the TOPIC?"

It's 'Do you **approve** of a **guy wearing a barrel** being a component in kanji?'"

"Hmmm. That's a troubling TOPIC, given he way he's so rudely distorting the **approve** omponent in TOPIC."

Common Pronunciations
Common **ON** reading: **DAI** (ダイ)
Common **kun** reading: none

Less Common Pronunciations
Less common **ON** reading: none
Less common **kun** reading: none

COMMON WORDS AND COMPOUNDS		
問題	question + topic = *problem; issue*	MON·**DAI** モン・ダイ
宿題	lodging + topic = *homework*	SHUKU·**DAI** シュク・ダイ
主題	primary + topic = *theme; subject*	SHU·**DAI** シュ・ダイ

COMPONENT #481

PARFAIT   其   其

Like any good parfait, there are three layers of ice cream here: chocolate, strawberry and vanilla (or whichever others you may prefer).

KANJI 481

期 **PERIOD**

一	十	艹	吐	甘	其	其	其	其
期	期	期						

BUILDING THIS KANJI
Parfait 其 + Moon 月 (11) = 期

Meaning
Period (of time).

Remembering this kanji

"**Parfaits**?" said the **moon**. "Yes, there's a PERIOD in a month when I binge on them until I'm full. But after that it seems I can't bear to look at them, and for an equal PERIOD I just waste away."

Common Pronunciations
Common **ON** reading: **KI** (キ)
Common **kun** reading: none

Less Common Pronunciations
Less common **ON** reading: **GO** (ゴ)
Less common **kun** reading: none

COMMON WORDS AND COMPOUNDS		
期間	period + interval = *period of time*	**KI**·KAN キ・カン
期待	period + wait = *expectation*	**KI**·TAI キ・タイ
定期	fixed + period = *fixed period*	TEI·**KI** テイ・キ

KANJI 482

授 **GRANT**

一	十	扌	护	护	护	护	护	护
授	授							

BUILDING THIS KANJI
Finger 扌 + Receive 受(191) = 授

Meaning
To grant, impart.

Remembering this kanji
She watched nervously as one **finger** after another was scrutinized; would she finally **receive** the manicure? At last the famous beautician looked up. "Yes," she said, "I will GRANT it."

Common Pronunciations
Common **ON** reading: **JU** (ジュ)
Common **kun** reading: none

Less Common Pronunciations
Less common **ON** reading: none
Less common **kun** reading: **sazu** (さず)

COMMON WORDS AND COMPOUNDS		
授業	grant + business = *lesson; instruction*	**JU·GYŌ** ジュ・ギョウ
授与	grant + confer = *awarding; conferring*	**JU·YO** ジュ・ヨ
教授	teach + grant = *teaching; a professor*	**KYŌ·JU** キョウ・ジュ

KANJI 483

便 **DELIVERY**

ノ	イ	イ	仁	佰	佰	佰	伊	便

BUILDING THIS KANJI
Giraffe イ + Anew 更(373) = 便

Meaning
This character has an array of meanings, from postal services, convenience and opportunity to—believe it or not—bodily functions such as defecation and urination. Underlying everything, when you think about it though, is a sense of (ahem) 'delivering' things or of things being delivered in some way.

Remembering this kanji
The **giraffe** was suffering **anew**. "Has th DELIVERY truck been here yet?" she aske the clerk hoarsely. "I'm really hoping you g that DELIVERY of throat lozenges today."

Common Pronunciations
Common **ON** reading: **BEN** (シン);
BIN (ビン)
Common **kun** reading: none

BEN is the reading used in compounds related both convenience and bodily functions (as in t first two examples below), while **BIN** appears compounds having to do with mail (such as in t final example) and opportunity. Recall from En that the first two kanji in the final compound an 'urgent' when taken together.

eate your **on-yomi** keyword for **BIN** (ビン) d enter it in the table at the back of the book. ter that, write your sentence to remember the -yomi readings in the box below.

Less Common Pronunciations

Less common **ON** reading: none
Less common **kun** reading: **tayo** (たよ)

COMMON WORDS AND COMPOUNDS		
便利	delivery + profit = *convenient; handy*	**BEN·RI** ベン・リ
便所	delivery + location = *toilet; lavatory*	**BEN·JO** ベン・ジョ
至急便	urgent + delivery = *express (mail)*	**SHI·KYŪ·BIN** シ・キュウ・ビン

歳 ANNUAL

| ١ | ۲ | ۱۴ | ۱۴ | 一 | 广 | 产 | 岸 | 虍 |

| 声 | 歳 | 歳 | 歳 |

BUILDING THIS KANJI

top 止(43) + **Pirate** 戊 + **One (hamburger patty)** 一(3) + **Small** 小(20) = 歳

Meaning

Annual, year, age. When used as a suffix (as in he final example below), this kanji translates as '…years old'. Pay close attention to the intricate troke order of this character, keeping in mind hat anything underneath the horizontal line of he pirate component is always written immediately after it.

Remembering this kanji

If we intend to **stop** this **pirate**," he said, "we hould offer him a **hamburger patty**."

But he won't care about that," she said. "It's way too **small**."

Hmmm. You're right. I'm sure he has a lot of ANNUAL expenses, but his ANNUAL income s still probably more than my ANNUAL salary."

Common Pronunciations

Common **ON** reading: **SAI** (サイ)
Common **kun** reading: none

The famous word in the second example is the only time this reading becomes voiced; recall from Entry 89 that 万 is read with its less common **on-yomi** here. Recall as well from Entry 411 that 何 (in the first compound) can express the idea of 'how many' in addition to 'what'.

Less Common Pronunciations

Less common **ON** reading: **SEI** (セイ)
Less common **kun** reading: none

IRREGULAR READING		
二十歳	twenty + annual = *twenty years old*	**hatachi** はたち

COMMON WORDS AND COMPOUNDS		
何歳	what + annual = *how many years old*	nan·**SAI** なん・サイ
万歳	ten thousand + annual = *Hurrah!*	**BAN·ZAI** バン・ザイ
五歳	five + annual = *five years old*	**GO·SAI** ゴ・サイ

COMPONENT #485

CHURCH

KANJI 485

専 EXCLUSIVE

BUILDING THIS KANJI
Church 甫 + Tiny (soccer player) 寸(103) = 専

Meaning
Exclusive.

Remembering this kanji
"I'd ask you into our **church**," said the **tin** **soccer player**, "but unfortunately it's EXCLU SIVE."
"Oh, I'm sorry. I didn't realize there was **church** for **tiny soccer players**."
"Yes, but don't worry. There's an EXCLUSIV church for medium-sized soccer players dow the street."

Common Pronunciations
Common **ON** reading: **SEN** (セン)
Common **kun** reading: none

Less Common Pronunciations
Less common **ON** reading: none
Less common **kun** reading: **moppa** (もっぱ)

COMMON WORDS AND COMPOUNDS		
専門	exclusive + gate = *specialty*	**SEN·MON** セン·モン
専用	exclusive + utilize = *exclusive use; private use*	**SEN·YŌ** セン·ヨウ
専有	exclusive + have = *exclusive possession*	**SEN·YŪ** セン·ユウ

KANJI 486

向 ORIENT

BUILDING THIS KANJI
Jelly Bean ヽ + Gorilla 冂 + Mouth (vampire) 口(8) = 向

Meaning
To orient, to look on. The overall sense is o things either orienting themselves or being oriented in a literal or figurative direction. Wher used as a suffix as in the second compound below, the meaning becomes 'intended for' o 'suited to'. Take care not to confuse this kanj with 同 'same' from Entry 197.

emembering this kanji

nce **jelly beans** are a **gorilla's** favorite party ood, you can always ORIENT one toward the aack table by placing some there. Attempting to RIENT a **vampire**, however, will be a lot more .cky and dangerous, but then, I keep telling you at you shouldn't even invite one.

mmon Pronunciations

mmon **ON** reading: **KŌ** (コ ウ)
mmon **kun** reading: **mu** (む)

though the **kun-yomi** usually acts as a verb m (as in the first example below), it's worth ing aware that the word 向こう (**mu**·kō / む· う) is actually a noun meaning 'the other side/ rty' or 'beyond'.

Less Common Pronunciations

Less common **ON** reading: none
Less common **kun** reading: none

COMMON WORDS AND COMPOUNDS		
向かう	face on; be opposite	**mu**·kau む﹑かう
夏向き	summer + orient = *for summer*	natsu **mu**·ki なつ む﹑き
向学心	orient + study + heart = *love of learning*	**KŌ**·GAKU·SHIN コウ﹑ガク﹑シン

KANJI 487

練 **TRAIN**

⼣	⼂	⼻	⼻	⼩	⼩	⼩	⼩
⼩	綗	紳	練	練			

BUILDING THIS KANJI

Thread 糸(196) + **East** 東(76) = 練

Meaning

o train, knead.

Remembering this kanji

o I grabbed my **thread** and headed off to he **East**. If I wanted to be a kimono maker, I hought, where better to TRAIN?

Common Pronunciations

ommon **ON** reading: **REN** (レ ン)
ommon **kun** reading: **ne** (ね)

Create your **on-yomi** keyword and enter it in the table at the back of the book. Then, after creating your kun-yomi keyword, write your sentence to remember the **on-yomi** and **kun-yomi** readings in the box below.

Less Common Pronunciations

Less common **ON** reading: none
Less common **kun** reading: none

COMMON WORDS AND COMPOUNDS		
練る	*to train; knead*	**ne**·ru ね﹑る
練習	train + learn = *practice; exercise*	**REN**·SHŪ レン﹑シュウ
訓練	instruction + train = *training; discipline*	KUN·**REN** クン﹑レン

COMPONENT #488

MERMAID

KANJI 488

育 **RAISE**

| ' | 一 | 云 | 六 | 亠 | 方 | 育 | 育 | |

BUILDING THIS KANJI
Mermaid 云 + Moon 月 (21) = 育

Meaning
To raise, bring up (as in children).

Remembering this kanji
I was unsure if I could RAISE a family, so I thought I'd practice first with a **mermaid**. Unfortunately, it didn't turn out well, as she'd flip her tail and disappear whenever I approached. So I attempted to RAISE the **moon** instead, but this was even worse; it would never stay home, and paid no attention to me at all. Darn it. I'm obviously not fit to RAISE anything.

Common Pronunciations
Common **ON** reading: **IKU** (イ ク)
Common **kun** reading: **soda** (そ だ)

Create your **on-yomi** keyword and enter it in the table at the back of the book. Then, after creating your **kun-yomi** keyword, write your sentence to remember the **on-yomi** and **kun-yomi** readings in the box below.

Less Common Pronunciations
Less common **ON** reading: none
Less common **kun** reading: none

COMMON WORDS AND COMPOUNDS		
育てる	*raise; bring up*	soda·teru そだ·てる
教育	teach + raise = *education*	KYŌ·IKU キョウ·イク
体育	body + raise = *physical education*	TAI·IKU タイ·イク

KANJI 489

考 **CONSIDER**

| 一 | 十 | 土 | 少 | 耂 | 考 | | | |

BUILDING THIS KANJI
Earth 土 (87) + Comet 一 + Rattlesnake 与
= 考

Meaning
Consider, think about.

Remembering this kanji

CONSIDER this: there was nothing else to do but pile **earth** on top of the **rattlesnake** after the **comet** crashed through this kanji. Should you be shocked? Hardly, when you CONSIDER that the **rattlesnake** was so horribly squashed that its head needs to be written from right to left here. What to do with this troublesome **comet**? Fine it? Scold it? It appears we'll have to CONSIDER everything.

Common Pronunciations

Common **ON** reading: **KŌ** (コ ウ)
Common **kun** reading: **kanga** (か ん が)

Less Common Pronunciations

Less common **ON** reading: none
Less common **kun** reading: none

COMMON WORDS AND COMPOUNDS		
考える	consider; think about	**kanga**·eru かんが・える
思考	think + consider = *thinking; consideration*	**SHI·KŌ** シ・コウ
考古学	consider + old + study = *archaeology*	**KŌ·KO·GAKU** コウ・コ・ガク

KANJI 490

員

MEMBER

'	⌐	◻	⼝	冂	冃	肙	肙	肙	員
員									

BUILDING THIS KANJI
Mouth (vampire) 口 (8) + Shellfish 貝 (21) = 員

Meaning
Member.

Remembering this kanji

"I wish to be a MEMBER," said the **vampire**. "Um…this is the **Shellfish** Club," she said, "and I can't imagine you have anything in common with **shellfish**."

"Well, I shut myself up in my coffin like a **shellfish**."

"Oh, you're right. In that case, fine. We'd be happy to have you as a MEMBER."

Common Pronunciations

Common **ON** reading: **IN** (イ ン)
Common **kun** reading: none

Less Common Pronunciations

Less common **ON** reading: none
Less common **kun** reading: none

COMMON WORDS AND COMPOUNDS		
全員	complete + member = *all members; the whole staff*	**ZEN·IN** ゼン・イン
店員	shop + member = *clerk; store assistant*	**TEN·IN** テン・イン
社員	company + member = *employee; member*	**SHA·IN** シャ・イン

CHAPTER 21 REVIEW EXERCISES

A. Please match the following kanji to their meanings.

1.	飛	a.	Consider
2.	歳	b.	Manor
3.	考	c.	To train
4.	港	d.	Period
5.	帰	e.	Fly
6.	展	f.	Homeward
7.	期	g.	Port
8.	練	h.	Row
9.	館	i.	Display
10.	列	j.	Annual

B. Please match the following meanings to their kanji, and these to their **on-** or **kun-yomi**.

1.	Number	a. 授	1.	**BU**（ブ）
2.	Topic	b. 育	2.	**SHŪ**（シュウ）
3.	Grant	c. 部	3.	**u**（う）
4.	Member	d. 向	4.	**JU**（ジュ）
5.	Orient	e. 打	5.	**IN**（イン）
6.	Learn	f. 丸	6.	**soda**（そだ）
7.	Hit	g. 数	7.	**maru**（まる）
8.	Round	h. 員	8.	**mu**（む）
9.	Section	i. 題	9.	**DAI**（ダイ）
10.	Raise	j. 習	10.	**kazu**（かず）

C. Please choose the best answer(s) to the following questions.

1. Which of the following readings apply to the kanji 面?
   a. **omo**（おも）
   b. **MEN**（メン）
   c. **omote**（おもて）
   d. **MON**（モン）
   e. **omono**（おもの）

2. Which is the correct reading of 数える?
   a. **kama·eru**（かま・える）
   b. **kita·eru**（きた・える）
   c. **kazo·eru**（かぞ・える）
   d. **kota·eru**（こた・える）

3. Which of the following kanji has the mo number of strokes?
   a. 港   b. 授   c. 飛   d. 歳   e. 期

4. Grandma went down to the dockyard, as seemed her ____ had just come in.
   a. 館   b. 打   c. 題   d. 育   e. 荷

5. Which of the following readings apply t the kanji 便?
   a. **BON**（ボン）
   b. **BIN**（ビン）
   c. **KAN**（カン）
   d. **BEN**（ベン）
   e. **HIN**（ヒン）

D. Please match the following compounds to the meanings and pronunciations.

1.	数学	a. Specialty	1.	**TEN·JI**（テン・ジ）
2.	専門	b. Expectation	2.	**KŪ·KŌ**（クウ・コウ）
3.	荷物	c. Airport	3.	**ni·MOTSU**（に・モツ）
4.	展示	d. Display / Exhibition	4.	**SEN·SHU**（セン・シュ）
5.	選手	e. Mathematics	5.	**SŪ·GAKU**（スウ・ガク）
6.	空港	f. Inn / Hotel	6.	**RYO·KAN**（リョ・カン）
7.	練習	g. Practice / Exercise	7.	**KYŌ·IKU**（キョウ・イク）
8.	期待	h. Education	8.	**REN·SHŪ**（レン・シュウ）
9.	教育	i. Luggage / Baggage	9.	**SEN·MON**（セン・モン）
10.	旅館	j. Athlete	10.	**KI·TAI**（キ・タイ）

E. Please read the passage below and answer the
   questions that follow.

図書館で美術の本を読むのが大好
きです。一番好きなのは、古い日
本画です。色が美しいし、形と顔
がとても面白いと思います。

1. What does this person really like to do?
2. Where do they go to do this?
3. Which type of art do they like most?
4. What do they find beautiful about it?
5. How do they feel about the forms and faces?

Kanji #491—520

KANJI 491

写 **COPY**

BUILDING THIS KANJI
UFO ⼍ + Confer 与 (425) = 写

Meaning
Copy, photograph.

Remembering this kanji
The UFO hovered overhead as the alien stepped forward to **confer** the award. "With this COPY," it began, "we would…"
"Hang on a sec," she interrupted. "This is a COPY? Where's the real one?"

Common Pronunciations
Common **ON** reading: **SHA** (シャ)
Common **kun** reading: **utsu** (うつ)

Less Common Pronunciations
Less common **ON** reading: none
Less common **kun** reading: none

COMMON WORDS AND COMPOUNDS		
写す	*copy; take a photograph*	**utsu·su** うつ・す
写真	copy + true = *photograph*	**SHA·SHIN** シャ・シン
写生	copy + life = *sketch; sketching*	**SHA·SEI** シャ・セイ

COMPONENT #492

JACK IN THE BOX

Compare the jack in the box to 关, the 'opera singer' preceding Entry 313, and 夭, the '1950's rock star' preceding Entry 326 so as to solidify the differences between these similar-looking components.

KANJI 492

廷   **COURT**

| 一 | 二 | 千 | 壬 | ⁷壬 | 廷 | 廷 | |

BUILDING THIS KANJI
Jack in the Box 壬 + Rat 廴 = 廷

Meaning
Court. This kanji can refer to courts of law (as in the initial two compounds below) and imperial courts (as in the last).

Remembering this kanji
Suddenly, the **jack in the box** popped up and pointed right at the **rat**.
"How dare you **rat** me out!" the **rat** squealed.
There was chaos in the COURT.

Common Pronunciations
Common **ON** reading: **TEI** (シン)
Common **kun** reading: none

Less Common Pronunciations
Less common **ON** reading: none
Less common **kun** reading: none

COMMON WORDS AND COMPOUNDS		
法廷	law + court = *law court*	HŌ·TEI ホウ·テイ
出廷	exit + court = *appear in court*	SHUT·TEI シュッ·テイ
朝廷	morning (dynasty) + court = *the imperial court*	CHŌ·TEI チョウ·テイ

KANJI 493

横   **SIDEWAYS**

| 一 | 十 | 才 | 木 | 朾 | 朾 | 柑 | 柑 | 柑 |
| 柑 | 梼 | 横 | 横 | 横 | 横 | | | |

BUILDING THIS KANJI
Tree 木(13) + Yellow 黄 (420) = 横

Meaning
Sideways, horizontal.

Remembering this kanji
I had given it only a SIDEWAYS glance, but realized in an instant that something in the **tree** was **yellow**. A lemon, perhaps? I carefully turned SIDEWAYS to make sure…

Common Pronunciations
Common **ON** reading: **Ō** (オ ウ)
Common **kun** reading: **yoko** (よ こ)

The **kun-yomi** is the more common reading.

Less Common Pronunciations

Less common **ON** reading: none
Less common **kun** reading: none

COMMON WORDS AND COMPOUNDS		
横	*sideways; horizontal*	**yoko** よこ
横切る	sideways + cut = *go across; traverse*	**yoko** gi·ru よこ ぎ·る
横転	sideways + roll = *turn sideways;* *barrel roll*	**Ō**·TEN オウ·テン

 **CERTAIN**

`	ソ	必	必	必			

BUILDING THIS KANJI
Heart 心(25) + Comet 一 = 必

Meaning

Certain, sure. Despite its simplicity, writing this kanji is difficult due to 'heart' being written in an entirely different stroke order.

Remembering this kanji

This much is CERTAIN: when a **comet** goes through a **heart** there will be a major disruption. In the case of the kanji for 'heart', this means that its stroke order gets totally scrambled. Given how our **comet** has been behaving, it was pretty much CERTAIN that this would happen.

Common Pronunciations

Common **ON** reading: **HITSU** (ヒ ツ)
Common **kun** reading: **kanara** (か な ら)

Create your **on-yomi** keyword and enter it in th[e] table at the back of the book. Then, after creati[ng] your **kun-yomi** keyword, write your sentence [to] remember the on-yomi and kun-yomi readings [in] the box below.

Less Common Pronunciations

Less common **ON** reading: none
Less common **kun** reading: none

COMMON WORDS AND COMPOUNDS		
必ず	*certain; for sure*	**kanara**·zu かなら·ず
必要	certain + essential = *essential; necessary*	**HITSU**·**YŌ** ヒ ツ·ヨ ウ
必死	certain + death = *certain death; desperate*	**HIS**·**SHI** ヒ ッ·シ

POLO

Ensure that you can see the difference between this component and 冫 (the 'ice hockey' component that was introduced prior to Entry 271), and ⼎, the "pinball" component that first appeared before Entry 308.

 **WITH**

¹	∠	レ	ソ	以			

BUILDING THIS KANJI
Polo 以 + Person 人(2) = 以

Meaning

This odd-looking but useful character works together with the kanji that follows it, and with its companion sets some type of condition on the kanji preceding them (you can see how it functions in the compounds below). As with the kanji for 'what' (Entry 411) we will distinguish this character from all other occurrences of the word 'with' by a string of exclamation or question marks.

Common Pronunciations

Common **ON** reading: **I** (イ)

Common **kun** reading: none

Less Common Pronunciations

Less common **ON** reading: none

Less common **kun** reading: none

COMMON WORDS AND COMPOUNDS		
六十 以上	sixty + with + upper = *more than sixty*	ROKU·JU·I·JŌ ロク・ジュウ・ イ・ジョウ
十度 以内	ten + degree + with + inside = *within ten degrees*	JŪ·DO·I·NAI ジュウ・ド・ イ・ナイ
私以外	private (I) + with + outside = *except for me*	watashi·I·GAI わたし・イ・ガイ

Remembering this kanji

"You mean…you want a game of **polo**…but it has to be *with* a **person**?"

"That's right."

"WITH!!!???"

"Yes, for goodness sakes, WITH!!!"

KANJI 496

単

SINGLE

丶	丶丶	丷	丷	丷丷	単	単	単	単

BUILDING THIS KANJI

Claw 丷 + Sun 日 (6) + Ten (scarecrow) 十 (28) = 単

Meaning

Single, simple. Take care when writing this character to have the scarecrow be in <u>front</u> of the sun (not under it as in 早 , 'early' from Entry 29). The story below emphasizes this point.

Remembering this kanji

"Did you realize," said the **scarecrow**, "that it's a SINGLE **claw** that brings up the **sun**?"

"There isn't a SINGLE bit of truth in that," she said. "And anyway, how could you tell? Everything happens behind you."

There was just no impressing her, the **scarecrow** thought. She wasn't believing a SINGLE statement he made.

Common Pronunciations
Common **ON** reading: **TAN** (タ ン)
Common **kun** reading: none

Less Common Pronunciations
Less common **ON** reading: none
Less common **kun** reading: none

COMMON WORDS AND COMPOUNDS		
単語	single + words = *word*	**TAN·GO** タン・ゴ
単数	single + number = *singular* *(opposite of plural)*	**TAN·SŪ** タン・スウ
単刀 直入	single + sword + straight + enter = *straight to the* *point; frank*	**TAN·TŌ·CHOKU·** **NYŪ** タン・トウ・チョク・ ニュウ

KANJI 497

 VERSUS

¹	一	ナ	文	文一	対	対		

BUILDING THIS KANJI
Police 一 + Banana Peels メ + Tiny (soccer
player) 寸(103) = 対

Meaning
Versus. The general sense is of things opposing
each other in a confrontational way, or simply
facing each other in a more neutral manner.

Remembering this kanji
Then one of the **police** threw down a **banana
peel**, but the **tiny soccer player's** cleats prevented
him from skidding. The game was getting nasty,
as it always did when it was **police** VERSUS **tiny
soccer players**.

Common Pronunciations
Common **ON** reading: **TAI** (タ イ)
Common **kun** reading: none

Less Common Pronunciations
Less common **ON** reading: **TSUI** (ツ イ)
Less common **kun** reading: none

COMMON WORDS AND COMPOUNDS		
対立	versus + stand = *opposition; confrontation*	**TAI·RITSU** タイ・リツ
対比	versus + compare = *comparison; contrast*	**TAI·HI** タイ・ヒ
反対	against + versus = *opposite; contrary*	**HAN·TAI** ハン・タイ

KANJI 498

 MEAL

ノ	人	入	今	今	食	食	食	食一
飣	飵	飯						

BUILDING THIS KANJI
Umbrella へ + Glutton 良 + Against 反(287)
= 飯

Meaning
Meal, (cooked) rice.

Remembering this kanji

Unable to sneak in under his **umbrella**, the **glutton** lowered it and spoke. "Why are you always **against** me?" he asked.

"Look," we said. "This is a buffet, and we have to make sure that everyone gets a MEAL."

Common Pronunciations

Common **ON** reading: **HAN** (ハン)
Common **kun** reading: **meshi** (めし)

Note that ' ご ' in the second example below can also be written with the honorific prefix 御* (not included in this book).

Less Common Pronunciations

Less common **ON** reading: none
Less common **kun** reading: none

COMMON WORDS AND COMPOUNDS		
飯	*meal; (cooked) rice*	**meshi** めし
ご飯	*meal; (cooked) rice*	go·**HAN** ご・ハン

LIGHTNING

KANJI 499

号

TITLE

口	口	므	号			

BUILDING THIS KANJI
Mouth (vampire) 口 (8) + Lightning 万 = 号

Meaning

Title, sign. This is a versatile kanji that can refer to everything from traffic signals to newspaper editions. The idea of a title or sign, however, is usually present in some way.

Remembering this kanji

The **vampire** swooped down like **lightning**. "I am Count Dracula," he said. "What is *your* TITLE?"

"Uh…I'm a librarian."

"Wonderful. Tell me, then, do you have this TITLE?"

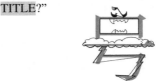

Common Pronunciations

Common **ON** reading: **GŌ** (ゴウ)
Common **kun** reading: none

Less Common Pronunciations

Less common **ON** reading: none
Less common **kun** reading: none

COMMON WORDS AND COMPOUNDS		
信号	trust + title = *signal*	SHIN·**GŌ** シン・ゴウ
番号	order + title = *number*	BAN·**GŌ** バン・ゴウ
年号	year + title = *name of an era*	NEN·**GŌ** ネン・ゴウ

KANJI 500

卒 **GRADUATE**

'	一	广	亡	方	亥	亢	卒

BUILDING THIS KANJI
Police 亠 + Person 人(2) + Person 人(2) +
Ten (scarecrow) 十(28) = 卒

Meaning
Graduate, come to an end. A secondary meaning
relates to soldiers.

Remembering this kanji
"You have earned the right," said the **police**
chief, "to GRADUATE from the academy."
First one **person** then another **person** marched
by, but when the **scarecrow** attempted to do so he
was held back by being tied to his boards. "I'm
sorry," he was told, "but unless you can get up
here, you can't GRADUATE."

Common Pronunciations
Common **ON** reading: **SOTSU** (シ ツ)
Common **kun** reading: none

Note that the second compound below is a short-
ening of 大学卒業者 (DAI·GAKU·SOTS
GYŌ·SHA/ ダイ・ガク・ソツ・ギョウ・シャ
from 'university', 'graduation', and 'individua
This type of word creation is a common featur
of Japanese.

Create your **on-yomi** keyword and enter it in t
table at the back of the book. After that, wri
your sentence to remember the **on-yomi** readi
in the box below.

Less Common Pronunciations
Less common **ON** reading: none
Less common **kun** reading: none

COMMON WORDS AND COMPOUNDS		
卒業	graduate + business = *graduation*	SOTSU·GYŌ ソツ・ギョウ
大卒	large + graduate = *university graduate*	DAI·SOTSU ダイ・ソツ

KANJI 501

枚 **SHEET**

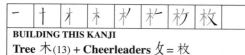

BUILDING THIS KANJI
Tree 木(13) + Cheerleaders 攵 = 枚

Meaning
Sheet. This is the counting word that Japanese
uses for flat, thin objects.

Remembering this kanji
"Yay, **tree**!" cheered the **cheerleaders**, holdin
up a SHEET.

That seems really weird, she thought, watchin
the scene nervously from a distance. Maybe I'
be able to figure out what they're up to if I ca
make out what's on that SHEET…

Common Pronunciations
Common **ON** reading: **MAI** (マ イ)
Common **kun** reading: none

Less Common Pronunciations
Less common **ON** reading: none
Less common **kun** reading: none

COMMON WORDS AND COMPOUNDS		
百枚	hundred + sheet = *one hundred sheets*	HYAKU·MAI ヒャク・マイ
枚数	sheet + number = *number of sheets*	MAI·SŪ マイ・スウ

KANJI 502

 HOT

丶	冂	冃	冃	曰	旦	早	星	昇	昇
暑	暑	暑							

BUILDING THIS KANJI
Sun 日 (6) + Individual 者 (93) = 暑

Common Pronunciations
Common **ON** reading: **SHO** (ショ)
Common **kun** reading: **atsu** (あつ)

Less Common Pronunciations
Less common **ON** reading: none
Less common **kun** reading: none

COMMON WORDS AND COMPOUNDS		
暑い	*hot (weather)*	atsu·i あつ・い
暑がる	*suffer from the heat*	atsu·garu あつ・がる
暑中	hot + middle = *height of summer; hot season*	SHO·CHŪ ショ・チュウ

Meaning
Hot. This kanji relates solely to air temperature and weather; it's opposite is thus 寒 , 'cold' (Entry 446).

Remembering this kanji
If the **sun** is hovering this closely over an **individual**, the conditions for them are probably pretty HOT. 'Cause the **sun**, from what I've been told, is always HOT.

COMPONENT #503

TORII

This component represents the famous gateway to a Shinto shrine. Note that its two straight legs distinguish it from 开 , our 'picnic table'.

KANJI 503

 **RIDE**

BUILDING THIS KANJI
Comet 一 + Torii 禾 + Tree 木 (13) = 乗

Meaning
Ride. A secondary meaning relates to deceiving someone or being deceived oneself (think of 'being taken for a ride'). Take care to write this character in the order of the components as listed above.

Remembering this kanji

She could hardly believe it, but there it was as the legend had foretold: a **comet** was passing over the **torii**! Scrambling down from the **tree**, she was rushing off on her bicycle moments later. "RIDE," was her only thought. "RIDE!"

Common Pronunciations

Common **ON** reading: **JŌ** (ジョウ)
Common **kun** reading: **no** (の)

The **kun-yomi** can incorporate its hiragana ending in certain compounds.

Less Common Pronunciations

Less common **ON** reading: none
Less common **kun** reading: none

COMMON WORDS AND COMPOUNDS		
乗る	*ride; get onto*	**no·ru** の・る
乗り場	ride + place = *(bus) stop; place to get on*	**no·ri ba** の・り ば
同乗	same + ride = *ride together; share a ride*	**DŌ·JŌ** ド ウ・ジ ョ ウ

KANJI 504

婦 **LADY**

く	女	女	女⁷	女⁼	女ヨ	女ヨ	女ヨ	婦
婦	婦							

BUILDING THIS KANJI
Woman 女 (16) + Comb ⦀ + UFO ⌒ + Cloth 巾 (162) = 婦

Meaning

Lady, woman. It's worthwhile to see how this kanji differs visually from 寝 'sleep' (Entry 463), and 帰 'homeward' (Entry 478).

Remembering this kanji

"Hey, **woman**!"
She was so stunned that she turned with the **comb** still in her hair. "Who do you think you are?" she said. "That's no way to get my attention!"
"Forgive me," said the alien, fidgeting with a **cloth**. "I just came down from that **UFO** up there, and thought it was the custom on your planet to pick up a **woman's cloth** when she dropped it."
"Well, I don't care what you thought," she said. "I'm a LADY, understand? And you don't talk like that to a LADY."

Common Pronunciations

Common **ON** reading: **FU** (フ)
Common **kun** reading: none

Recall from Entry 315 that the final example below is one of the only instances where 夫 i read with its less common **on-yomi** of FŪ.

Less Common Pronunciations

Less common **ON** reading: none
Less common **kun** reading: none

	COMMON WORDS AND COMPOUNDS		
婦人	lady + person = *lady; woman*	**FU·JIN** フ・ジン	
婦人用	lady + person + utilize = *for ladies; women's*	**FU·JIN·YŌ** フ・ジン・ヨ ウ	
夫婦	husband + lady = *husband and wife*	**FŪ·FU** フウ・フ	

KANJI 505

 NATURE

ノ	ク	タ	タ	タ｀	タ丶	外	狄	妖
然	然	然						

BUILDING THIS KANJI
Moon 月 (11) + Dog 犬 (171) + Gas Stove ⺗
= 然

Meaning

Nature. This kanji emphasizes the nature or personality of the character preceding it.

Remembering this kanji

"Isn't NATURE intricate?"
"What do you mean?"
"Well, when the **moon** is out like this your **dog** howls. It's in his NATURE. And then, it's the NATURE of that **gas stove** there to have cooked your hot **dog**."
"Uh…is it in your NATURE to be this weird?"

Common Pronunciations

Common **ON** reading: **ZEN** (ゼ ン)
Common **kun** reading: none

Note that the second compound features the only instance of 自 being read with its less common **on-yomi** of SHI.

Less Common Pronunciations

Less common **ON** reading: **NEN** (ネ ン)
Less common **kun** reading: none

You are only likely to meet this reading in one compound (it's commonly used, however): 天 然 (**TEN·NEN** / テ ン・ネ ン) 'natural', from the kanji 'heaven' and 'nature'.

	COMMON WORDS AND COMPOUNDS	
全然	complete + nature = *entirely; (not) at all*	**ZEN·ZEN** ゼ ン・ゼ ン
自然	self + nature = *nature*	**SHI·ZEN** シ・ゼ ン

KANJI 506

 TONE

`	＾	ニ	言	言	言	言	訁	訂
訂	調	調	調	調	調			

BUILDING THIS KANJI
Say 言 (80) + Around 周 (120) = 調

Meaning

Tone, tune. As an extension to toning and tuning comes the ideas of investigation, checking and preparation of things.

Remembering this kanji

"Just **say** it. There's nobody **around** but us."
"OK then, I will. He has no TONE, so tell him to TONE it down."

Common Pronunciations
Common **ON** reading: **CHŌ** (チョウ)
Common **kun** reading: **shira** (しら)

Less Common Pronunciations
Less common **ON** reading: none
Less common **kun** reading: **totono** (ととの)

COMMON WORDS AND COMPOUNDS		
調べる	*investigate; inspect*	**shira**·beru しら·べる
強調	strong + tone = *emphasis; stress*	KYŌ·CHŌ キョウ·チョウ
単調	single + tone = *monotonous; dull*	TAN·CHŌ タン·チョウ

COMPONENT #507

YOGA

Take a moment to compare this component with
匚 , our 'coat rack' introduced prior to Entry
234.

KANJI 507

 KEEP

´	㇄	𠂉	𠂉㇆	𠂉㇆	𠂉㇆	留	留	留
留								

BUILDING THIS KANJI
Yoga 𠃌 + **Sword** 刀 (117) + **Rice Field** 田 (73)
= 留

Meaning
Keep, detain.

Remembering this kanji
He did **yoga** to KEEP in top shape, but would
also KEEP a **sword** at the ready. Because after
what almost happened in the **rice field**…well,
he realized he had to KEEP his wits about him.

Common Pronunciations
Common **ON** reading: **RYŪ** (リュウ)
Common **kun** reading: **to** (と)

The two verbs listed below have some overlap
with an identically pronounced pair we learned
back in Entry 43 (止まる / 止める). The two
here, however, have more of a sense of keeping
in place or being kept in place.

Create your **on-yomi** keyword and enter it in the
table at the back of the book. Then, after creating
your kun-yomi keyword, write your sentence to
remember the **on-yomi** and **kun-yomi** readings
in the box below.

Less Common Pronunciations
Less common **ON** reading: **RU** (ル)
Less common **kun** reading: none

COMMON WORDS AND COMPOUNDS		
留まる (intr)	*to be kept in place*	**to**·maru と·まる
留める (tr)	*keep in place; detain*	**to**·meru と·める
留置	keep + put = *detention; custody*	**RYŪ**·CHI リュウ·チ

KANJI 508

熱 HEAT

-	+	土	尹	尧	坴	幸	坴	刲
丸	刲	刲	熱	熱	熱			

BUILDING THIS KANJI
Earth 土(87) + Ballet ⼉ + Earth 土(87) +
Round 丸(470) + Gas Stove 灬 = 熱

Meaning
Heat, hot (in aspects other than weather), and the ideas of enthusiasm and passion. The opposite to this kanji is 冷 , 'cool' (Entry 362). Note that the kanji for earth appears above and below the ballet component (the story takes this into account) and that certain fonts will 'round off' the right-hand end of the kanji for 'round'.

Remembering this kanji
In the HEAT of their anger, the audience threw **earth** at the **ballet dancer** from above and below the stage. Once they had covered him with a **round** pile, they began to HEAT it with a **gas stove**. "Maybe this will generate a bit of HEAT in his performance," someone muttered.

Common Pronunciations
Common **ON** reading: **NETSU** (ネ ツ)
Common **kun** reading: **atsu** (あ つ)

Create your **on-yomi** keyword and enter it in the table at the back of the book. Then, after creating your **kun-yomi** keyword, write your sentence to remember the **on-yomi** and **kun-yomi** readings in the box below.

Less Common Pronunciations
Less common **ON** reading: none
Less common **kun** reading: none

COMMON WORDS AND COMPOUNDS		
熱	*heat; a fever*	**NETSU** ネツ
熱い	*hot (to the touch); heated*	**atsu·i** あつ·い
熱愛	heat + love = *passionate love; devotion*	**NETSU·AI** ネツ·アイ

KANJI 509

使 USE

ノ	亻	亻	仁	仨	佰	伊	使

BUILDING THIS KANJI
Giraffe 亻 + Officer 吏 (462) = 使

Meaning
Use. This is the last of a group of five kanji that we can now review as a whole. The building pattern for the present character has been as follows: 史 'history'(Entry 440), to 吏 'officer' (Entry 462), to 使 . A pair of similar-looking but unrelated kanji were constructed in this way: 更 'anew' (Entry 373), to 便 'delivery' (Entry 483).

Remembering this kanji

The **giraffe** sauntered up to the **officer**. "I wish to USE you," it said.

"For what?"

"Isn't it obvious? Something for which it's best to USE an **officer**."

Less Common Pronunciations

Less common **ON** reading: none
Less common **kun** reading: none

COMMON WORDS AND COMPOUNDS		
使う	*use*	**tsuka·u** つか・う
使用	use + utilize = *use; utilize*	**SHI·YŌ** シ・ヨウ
天使	heaven + use = *angel*	**TEN·SHI** テン・シ

Common Pronunciations

Common **ON** reading: **SHI** (シ)
Common **kun** reading: **tsuka** (つか)

The **kun-yomi** can become voiced in second position, although never when forming verbs.

COMPONENT #510

DANCING SKELETON 麦 麦

Here at last we have the final member of our special component family, who would be well advised, incidentally, to dance with a little less energy given that his left forearm is flying off. Reviewing from the first, we have: 七 'ghost' (preceding Entry 220), 弋 'spilling coffee' (preceding Entry 321), 戈 'killer bee' (preceding Entry 400), 戊 'pirate' (preceding Entry 454), and the present addition. Remember that the stroke order of the middle three is broken by anything appearing underneath their respective horizontal lines.

KANJI 510

 **REMAIN**

一	丁	歹	歹	歹	歹	歼	残	残
残								

BUILDING THIS KANJI
Jungleman 歹 + **Dancing Skeleton** 麦 = 残

Meaning

Remain. In an interesting connection, a second ary meaning relates to cruelty.

Remembering this kanji

The **jungleman** adjusts his leopard-skin shor and exchanges an awkward glance with th **dancing skeleton**. The ball is over, and yet the REMAIN...

Common Pronunciations

Common **ON** reading: **ZAN** (ザン)
Common **kun** reading: **noko** (のこ)

Note the mix of on and **kun-yomi** in the fin compound (and the voicing of 高).

reate your **on-yomi** keyword and enter it in the
ble at the back of the book. Then, after creating
ur **kun-yomi** keyword, write your sentence to
member the **on-yomi** and **kun-yomi** readings in
e box below.

Less Common Pronunciations

Less common **ON** reading: none
Less common **kun** reading: none

COMMON WORDS AND COMPOUNDS		
残る	*remain; be left*	**noko·ru** のこ・る
残業	remain + business = *overtime work*	**ZAN·GYŌ** ザン・ギョウ
残高	remain + tall = *(account) balance*	**ZAN·daka** ザン・だか

 **QUIET**

ー	十	土	主	圭	青	青	青	青
靑	静	静	静	静				

BUILDING THIS KANJI
Blue 青 (86) + **Dispute** 争 (459) = 静

Meaning
Quiet.

Remembering this kanji
"They're feeling **blue**," she said, "so any **dispute**
hey have will be fairly QUIET."

Common Pronunciations
Common **ON** reading: **SEI** (セイ)
Common **kun** reading: **shizu** (しず)

Less Common Pronunciations
Less common **ON** reading: **JŌ** (ジョウ)
Less common **kun** reading: none

COMMON WORDS AND COMPOUNDS		
静か	*quiet; peaceful*	**shizu·ka** しず・か
安静	ease + quiet = *rest; repose*	**AN·SEI** アン・セイ
静物画	quiet + thing + painting = *still life*	**SEI·BUTSU·GA** セイ・ブツ・ガ

 GIFT

BUILDING THIS KANJI
Shellfish 貝 (21) + **Rabbit** ` ′ + **Rice Field** 田
(73) + **Sun** 日 (6) = 贈

Meaning
Gift, present.

Remembering this kanji

"I gave a GIFT of **shellfish**,
to a **rabbit** in a **rice field**,
that sparkled in the **sun**."

"Well, that's my poem so far. Do you like it?"
"It's OK, I guess. But what's with the **shellfish**
for a **rabbit**? I mean, that's just a totally useless
GIFT."

Common Pronunciations

Common **ON** reading: none
Common **kun** reading: **oku** (おく)

Less Common Pronunciations

Less common **ON** reading: **ZŌ** (ゾウ);
SŌ (ソウ)
Less common **kun** reading: none

COMMON WORDS AND COMPOUNDS		
贈る	*present (a gift)*	**oku·ru** おく・る
贈り物	gift + thing = *gift; present*	**oku·ri mono** おく・り もの

KANJI 513

 **VEGETABLE**

一	十	艹	艻	艻	芓	苎	苎	莯
莯	菜							

BUILDING THIS KANJI
Wreath 艹 + Appearance 采 (259) = 菜

Meaning
Vegetable.

Remembering this kanji

"In order to get the champion's **wreath** at a
county fair, any VEGETABLE realizes that its
appearance must be flawless. A carrot must be
a sturdy and orange VEGETABLE, and a beet
must be a plump and purple VEGETABLE, for
example."

Common Pronunciations

Common **ON** reading: **SAI** (サイ)
Common **kun** reading: none

Less Common Pronunciations

Less common **ON** reading: none
Less common **kun** reading: **na** (な)

COMMON WORDS AND COMPOUNDS		
野菜	field + vegetable = *vegetables*	**YA·SAI** ヤ・サイ
菜食	vegetable + eat = *vegetarian diet*	**SAI·SHOKU** サイ・ショク
菜園	vegetable + garden = *vegetable garden*	**SAI·EN** サイ・エン

KANJI 514

 **MISCELLANEOUS**

ノ	九	九	卆	杂	杂	杂'	杂	杂'
杂	新	雑	雑	雑				

BUILDING THIS KANJI
Nine 九 (39) + Tree 木 (13) + Squirrels 隹 = 雑

Meaning
Miscellaneous.

emembering this kanji

)id you realize that **99%** of **trees** have **squirrels**
them? And not only that, there are MISCEL-
ANEOUS **trees** and MISCELLANEOUS
quirrels!"

3eez, I'm getting tired of you and your
IISCELLANEOUS facts."

ommon Pronunciations

•mmon **ON** reading: **ZATSU** (ザ ツ)
•mmon **kun** reading: none

eate your **on-yomi** keyword and enter it in the
ıle at the back of the book. After that, write
ur sentence to remember the **on-yomi** reading
the box below.

Less Common Pronunciations

Less common **ON** reading: **ZŌ** (ゾ ウ)
Less common **kun** reading: none

COMMON WORDS AND COMPOUNDS		
雑音	miscellaneous + sound = *noise; interference*	**ZATSU·ON** ザ ツ・オ ン
雑事	miscellaneous + matter = *miscellaneous affairs*	**ZATSU·JI** ザ ツ・ジ
雑用	miscellaneous + utilize = *miscellaneous things to do*	**ZATSU·YŌ** ザ ツ・ヨ ウ

COMPONENT #515

PIDER

KANJI 515

無 **WITHOUT**

ー	二	午	午	缶	無	無	無
無	無	無					

BUILDING THIS KANJI

ipider + Gas Stove ハ ハ = 無

Meaning

Without. This is another important negating
anji, along with 不 not' (Entry 186) and 非
ın-' (Entry 320). It imparts a sense of '-less'
r '-free' in many of the compounds in which
appears.

Remembering this kanji

"I was tired of always dining of raw food," said
the **spider**, "and so I got myself a **gas stove**.
I mean, I can get by WITHOUT furniture or
WITHOUT air con...but WITHOUT a **gas
stove**? No, I can't imagine being WITHOUT
one."

Common Pronunciations

Common **ON** reading: **MU** (ム); **BU** (ブ)
Common **kun** reading: **na** (な)

MU is by far the more common of these readings, although **BU** figures in a few important
compounds as well. Except when it appears on
its own (as in the first example below), **na** will be
found only in the second or third position.

Create your **on-yomi** keyword for **MU** (ム) and enter it in the table at the back of the book. Then, after creating your **kun-yomi** keyword, write your sentence to remember the **on-yomi** and **kun-yomi** readings in the box below.

Less Common Pronunciations
Less common **ON** reading: none
Less common **kun** reading: none

COMMON WORDS AND COMPOUNDS		
無い	*there is no…*	**na·i** な・い
無料	without + fee = *free of charge*	**MU·RYŌ** ム・リョ
無事	without + matter = *without incident; safe and sound*	**BU·JI** ブ・ジ

KANJI 516

 **YARD**

'	一	广	广	庐	庄	庄	庭	庭
庭								

BUILDING THIS KANJI
Cliff Diver 广 + Court 廷(492) = 庭

Meaning
Yard, garden.

Remembering this kanji
"I swear I never meant to dive into that YARD," the **cliff diver** told the **court**. "I simply misjudged where I would land. Believe me, it's not very fun to miss the pool and crash into a YARD full of rose bushes when you're in a bathing suit."

Common Pronunciations
Common **ON** reading: **TEI** (テイ)
Common **kun** reading: **niwa** (にわ)

Less Common Pronunciations
Less common **ON** reading: none
Less common **kun** reading: none

COMMON WORDS AND COMPOUNDS		
庭	*yard; garden*	**niwa** にわ
庭園	yard + garden = *garden*	**TEI·EN** テイ・エ〉
家庭	house + yard = *home; household*	**KA·TEI** カ・テイ

ANJI 517

相 **RECIPROCAL**

| 十 | 才 | 木 | 朾 | 机 | 朾 | 相 | 相 |

UILDING THIS KANJI

ree 木(13) + **Eye (Cyclops)** 目(15) = 相

eaning

eciprocal, each other. An important secondary eaning is present when this kanji appears as e final character in certain compounds; in such stances it can indicate a government minister s in the final example below).

emembering this kanji

sn't it interesting what goes on between a **tree** d a **Cyclops**? Until the **tree** gives up its wood r the **Cyclops'** club, he keeps an **eye** on it." You're right. Their relationship is wonderfully ECIPROCAL."

Common Pronunciations

Common **ON** reading: **SŌ** (ソ ウ);
SHŌ (ショ ウ)
Common **kun** reading: **ai** (あ い)

SŌ is the most common reading here, with **SHŌ** only used outside of first position to indicate government ministers.

Less Common Pronunciations

Less common **ON** reading: none
Less common **kun** reading: none

COMMON WORDS AND COMPOUNDS		
相手	reciprocal + hand = *the other party; opponent*	**ai**·te あい·て
相続	reciprocal + continue = *inheritance; succession*	**SŌ**·ZOKU ソ ウ·ゾ ク
首相	neck (leader) + reciprocal (minister) = *prime minister*	SHU·**SHŌ** シ ュ·ショ ウ

COMPONENT #518

OOTHBRUSH

ou may wish to compare the final component f this book to ヨ, our 'comb' from Entry 95.

ANJI 518

長 **LONG**

| 「 | 下 | F | 上 | 토 | 長 | 長 |

UILDING THIS KANJI

oothbrush ⺆ + **Playground** ⺇ = 長

eaning

ong. This kanji can also refer to the 'chief' or ead' of entities such as cities and companies he final compound provides an example).

Remembering this kanji

"Tough day?"
"Yeah. Boss gave me a **toothbrush** and told me to clean the **playground**."
"Yikes!"
"No kidding. The swings were easy enough, but some of those slides are really LONG."

Common Pronunciations

Common **ON** reading: **CHŌ** (チ ョ ウ)
Common **kun** reading: **naga** (な が)

Recall from Entry 384 that the identically pronounced 永い (naga·i / なが·い) refers to 'long' in terms of time.

Less Common Pronunciations
Less common ON reading: none
Less common kun reading: none

COMMON WORDS AND COMPOUNDS		
長い	long	**naga·i** なが·い
長期	long + period = *long-term*	**CHŌ·KI** チョウ·キ
社長	company + long (chief) = *company president*	**SHA·CHŌ** シャ·チョ

KANJI 519

 **COURTESY**

Common Pronunciations
Common ON reading: **REI** (レイ)
Common kun reading: none

Less Common Pronunciations
Less common ON reading: **RAI** (ライ)
Less common kun reading: none

`	ラ	ネ	ネ	礼			

BUILDING THIS KANJI
Whittling ネ + Hook し = 礼

COMMON WORDS AND COMPOUNDS		
失礼	lose + courtesy = *discourtesy; rudeness*	**SHITSU·R** シツ·レイ
無礼	without + courtesy = *impoliteness; rudeness*	**BU·REI** ブ·レイ
礼服	courtesy + clothes = *formal dress*	**REI·FUKU** レイ·フク

Meaning
Courtesy, politeness.

Remembering this kanji
"You're really terrible at **whittling**. I'm surprised it would **hook** you like this."
"You're not much for COURTESY, are you?"

KANJI 520

 FINISH

Meaning
Finish.

し	ぇ	ㄠ	幺	糸	糸	糸	糽	終
終	終							

BUILDING THIS KANJI
Thread 糸 (196) + Winter 冬 (60) = 終

Remembering this kanji
They had followed the **thread** through th seasons, but when it ran out in **winter** the wondered: is it here that we must FINISH?

ommon Pronunciations

ommon **ON** reading: **SHŪ** (シュウ)

ommon **kun** reading: **o** (お)

ess Common Pronunciations

ess common **ON** reading: none

ess common **kun** reading: none

COMMON WORDS AND COMPOUNDS		
終わる	*finish; come to an end*	**o·waru** お・わる
終結	finish + bind = *conclusion; end*	**SHŪ·KETSU** シュウ・ケツ
終点	finish + point = *last stop; end of the line*	**SHŪ·TEN** シュウ・テン

CHAPTER 22 REVIEW EXERCISES

. Please match the following kanji to their meanings.

1.	長	a.	Ride
2.	熱	b.	Heat
3.	卒	c.	Court
4.	乗	d.	Vegetable
5.	静	e.	Nature
6.	必	f.	Quiet
7.	対	g.	Versus
8.	菜	h.	Certain
9.	廷	i.	Long
10.	然	j.	Graduate

. Please match the following meanings to their kanji, and these to their on- or kun-yomi.

1.	Meal	a. 横	1.	**yoko** (よこ)
2.	Hot	b. 暑	2.	**I** (イ)
3.	With	c. 以	3.	**RYŪ** (リュウ)
4.	Sideways	d. 庭	4.	**GŌ** (ゴウ)
5.	Remain	e. 枚	5.	**ZAN** (ザン)
6.	Title	f. 残	6.	**tsuka** (つか)
7.	Sheet	g. 使	7.	**MAI** (マイ)
8.	Keep	h. 留	8.	**TEI** (テイ)
9.	Yard	i. 号	9.	**HAN** (ハン)
10.	Use	j. 飯	10.	**atsu** (あつ)

. Please choose the best answer(s) to the following questions.

1. Which of the following readings apply to the kanji 無?
   a. **BU** (ブ)   b. **GU** (グ)
   c. **MU** (ム)   d. **CHŪ** (チュウ)
   e. **SU** (ス)

2. Which is the correct reading of 静か?
   a. **sazo·ka** (さぞ・か)
   b. **shizu·ka** (しず・か)
   c. **kazo·ka** (かぞ・か)
   d. **tazo·ka** (たぞ・か)

3. Which of the following kanji has the most number of strokes?
   a. 残   b. 然   c. 菜   d. 婦   e. 終

4. We have to be very ____ or we'll wake up that werewolf.
   a. 菜   b. 贈   c. 長   d. 横   e. 静

5. Which is the correct reading of 必ず?
   a. **tomura·zu** (とむら・ず)
   b. **manaka·zu** (まなか・ず)
   c. **chikara·zu** (ちから・ず)
   d. **kanara·zu** (かなら・ず)

D. Please match the following compounds to their meanings and pronunciations.

1.	雑音	a. Nature	1.	**FU·JIN** (フ・ジン)
2.	無礼	b. Opposite	2.	**SHA·SHIN** (シャ・シン)
3.	写真	c. Conclusion	3.	**SOTSU·GYŌ** (ソツ・ギョウ)
4.	婦人	d. Photograph	4.	**SHŪ·KETSU** (シュウ・ケツ)
5.	相手	e. Lady / Woman	5.	**TAN·CHŌ** (タン・チョウ)

6. 反対   f. Graduation

7. 終結   g. Noise /
              Interference

8. 自然   h. The other
              party

9. 単調   i. Monotonous

10. 卒業   j. Impoliteness

6. **HAN·TAI**
   （ハン・タイ）

7. **SHI·ZEN**
   （シ・ゼン）

8. **ZATSU·ON**
   （ザツ・オン）

9. **ai·te**
   （あい・て）

10. **BU·REI**
    （ブ・レイ）

"家庭菜園の野菜は美味しいで
すね。"

"はい、そうですね。でも一番
良いのは無料な事です。"

社長夫人はお金が大好きな人だ。

E. Please read the passage below and answer the
   questions that follow.

今朝、社長夫人と話しました。。。

1. With whom did this person speak?
2. When did they speak with her?
3. What do they think is delicious?
4. What does the company president's wife like mo
   about them?
5. What kind of person is the company president
   wife?

CUMULATIVE REVIEW EXERCISES FOR
CHAPTERS 1 - 22

A. Please match the following kanji to their meanings.

1. 辞   a. Back

2. 笑   b. Possible

3. 背   c. Resign

4. 初   d. Forget

5. 忘   e. Degree

6. 可   f. Exclusive

7. 選   g. Laugh

8. 比   h. Compare

9. 専   i. Beginning

10. 度   j. Select

B. Which kanji does not belong in the group?

1. a.鼻   b.指   c.顔   d.頭   e.民

2. a.妹   b.夫   c.兄   d.姉   e.弟

3. a.橋   b.屋   c.戸   d.風   e.口

4. a.菜   b.酒   c.石   d.茶   e.豆

5. a.熱   b.温   c.暑   d.氷   e.日

6. a.笑   b.困   c.病   d.悪   e.痛

7. a.虫   b.婦   c.魚   d.医   e.地

8. a.利   b.社   c.商   d.業   e.飲

9. a.池   b.堂   c.氷   d.泉   e.洋

10. a.則   b.法   c.晴   d.制   e.治

C. Identify the kanji in each group having th
   most number of strokes.

1. a.定   b.育   c.始   d.是   e.身

2. a.館   b.雑   c.静   d.熱   e.絵

3. a.重   b.建   c.幾   d.婚   e.免

4. a. 永　b. 虫　c. 氷　d. 払　e. 令

5. a. 氏　b. 弔　c. 比　d. 区　e. 民

6. a. 薬　b. 顔　c. 機　d. 頭　e. 横

7. a. 無　b. 漢　c. 様　d. 園　e. 節

8. a. 色　b. 向　c. 両　d. 廷　e. 成

9. a. 働　b. 続　c. 痛　d. 歳　e. 銀

10. a. 都　b. 通　c. 弱　d. 乗　e. 特

D. Please list the following kanji in the order indicated (alphabetical).

1. Court / Original / Shop / Wide / Yard
   a. 原　b. 店　c. 廷　d. 庭　e. 広

2. Anew / Delivery / History / Officer / Use
   a. 史　b. 更　c. 吏　d. 便　e. 使

3. Business / Heavy / Move / Ride / Work
   a. 業　b. 働　c. 乗　d. 動　e. 重

4. Lend / People / Substitute / Surname / Type
   a. 民　b. 式　c. 代　d. 氏　e. 貸

5. All / Compare / Feather / Floor / Learn
   a. 羽　b. 階　c. 皆　d. 比　e. 習

6. Annual / Become / How many / Mechanism / Remain
   a. 残　b. 幾　c. 機　d. 歳　e. 成

7. Command / Match / Now / Orient / Same
   a. 向　b. 同　c. 今　d. 合　e. 令

8. Each / Lucky / Occupy / Platform / Stone
   a. 石　b. 台　c. 吉　d. 各　e. 占

9. Prefecture / Put / Straight / Tool / True
   a. 置　b. 真　c. 県　d. 具　e. 直

10. Display / Far / Garden / Long / Travel
    a. 旅　b. 展　c. 園　d. 遠　e. 長

E. Please choose the best answer to the following questions.

1. I really love the ____ of your eyes.
   a. 黄　b. 病　c. 束　d. 動　e. 色

2. The head chef served her creation in a beautiful ____ .
   a. 亜　b. 両　c. 皿　d. 申　e. 由

3. What will it take for people to live together in ____ ?
   a. 魚　b. 氷　c. 和　d. 菜　e. 画

4. The tiny country didn't have a chance against the ____ of its larger neighbor.
   a. 池　b. 紙　c. 酒　d. 味　e. 軍

5. You've really planted some fantastic flowers in your ____.
   a. 顔　b. 矢　c. 婚　d. 園　e. 争

F. Please choose the best answer to the following questions.

1. As 軽 is to 重 , 速 is to ____.
   a. 起　b. 遠　c. 遅　d. 達　e. 送

2. As 冷 is to 温 , 寒 is to ____.
   a. 場　b. 鼻　c. 旨　d. 暑　e. 単

3. As 兄 is to 弟 , 姉 is to ____.
   a. 婦　b. 婚　c. 数　d. 始　e. 妹

4. As 食 is to 飲 , 貸 is to ____.
   a. 昔　b. 是　c. 借　d. 共　e. 黄

5. As 強 is to 弱 , 長 is to ____.
   a. 豆　b. 頭　c. 矢　d. 短　e. 医

G. Please choose the best answer to the following questions.

1. Which is the correct reading of 土産?
   a. **karage** (からげ)　b. **samage** (さまげ)
   c. **miyage** (みやげ)　d. **takagi** (たかぎ)

2. Which is the correct reading of 今朝?
   a. **kyō** (きょう)　　b. **kesa** (けさ)
   c. **sage** (さげ)　　　d. **kosu** (こす)

3. Which is the correct reading of 風呂?
    a. **KA·RO** (カ·ロ)   b. **MA·RO** (マ·ロ)
    c. **TA·RO** (タ·ロ)   d. **FU·RO** (フ·ロ)

4. Which is the correct reading of 天然?
    a. **TEN·KEN** (テン·ケン)
    b. **TEN·NEN** (テン·ネン)
    c. **SE·KEN** (セ·ケン)
    d. **SEN·NEN** (セン·ネン)

5. Which is the correct reading of 今年?
    a. **ko·toshi** (こ·とし)
    b. **ki·toshi** (き·とし)
    c. **ma·NEN** (ま·ネン)
    d. **ke·NEN** (け·ネン)

6. Which is the correct reading of 兄弟?
    a. **SAI·DAI** (サイ·ダイ)
    b. **NEN·DAI** (ネン·ダイ)
    c. **SHŌ·TAI** (ショウ·タイ)
    d. **KYŌ·DAI** (キョウ·ダイ)

7. Which is the correct reading of 合羽?
    a. **KI·ha** (キ·は)
    b. **KOP·pa** (コッ·ぱ)
    c. **mop·pa** (もっ·ぱ)
    d. **KAP·pa** (カッ·ぱ)

8. Which is the correct reading of 弟子?
    a. **DE·SHI** (デ·シ)   b. **KO·SHI** (コ·シ)
    c. **ta·ko** (た·こ)   d. **TAI·ko** (タイ·こ)

9. Which is the correct reading of 今日?
    a. **shō** (しょう)   b. **mō** (もう)
    c. **kyō** (きょう)   d. **kyū** (きゅう)

10. Which is the correct reading of 頭痛?
    a. **TO·TSŪ** (ト·ツウ)
    b. **ZU·TSŪ** (ズ·ツウ)
    c. **KA·TSŪ** (カ·ツウ)
    d. **SHI·TSŪ** (シ·ツウ)

H. Please match the following compounds to their meanings and pronunciations.

1. 暗示   a. Drinking   1. **BEN·RI**
            alcohol   (ベン·リ)

2. 去年   b. Peace   2. **HITSU·YŌ**
                                 (ヒツ·ヨウ

3. 昼食   c. Last year   3. **KAI·SHA**
                                 (カイ·シャ

4. 住民   d. Convenient   4. **IN·SHU**
                                 (イン·シュ

5. 便利   e. Festival   5. **KEK·**
            day   **KYOKU**
                                 (ケッ·
                                 キョク)

6. 自己   f. After all   6. **AN·JI**
                                 (アン·ジ)

7. 祭日   g. Essential   7. **CHŪ·**
                                 SHOKU
                                 (チュウ·
                                 ショク)

8. 必要   h. Hint   8. **JIS·SAI**
                                 (ジッ·サイ

9. 遊泳   i. Company /   9. **JI·KO**
            Corporation   (ジ·コ)

10. 平和   j. Oneself   10. **YŪ·EI**
                                 (ユウ·エイ

11. 実際   k. Lunch   11. **KYO·NEN**
                                 (キョ·ネン

12. 無料   l. Residents   12. **MU·RYŌ**
                                 (ム·リョウ

13. 飲酒   m. In actuality   13. **SAI·JITSU**
                                 (サイ·ジツ

14. 会社   n. Swimming   14. **JŪ·MIN**
                                 (ジュウ·
                                 ミン)

15. 結局   o. Free of   15. **HEI·WA**
            charge   (ヘイ·ワ)

ANSWER KEY FOR EXERCISES

CHAPTER 1

Section A

e	2. c	3. g	4. i	5. b
f	7. a	8. j	9. h	10. d

Section B

g – 8	2. j – 5	3. a – 10	4. i – 7
b – 3	6. h – 9	7. c – 1	8. f – 2
d – 6	10. e – 4		

Section C

b/c/d	2. c	3. d/e	4. a/d	5. a/d/e

Section D

d	2. e	3. b	4. d	5. b

Section E

f – 4	2. j – 9	3. a – 6	4. e – 5
b – 10	6. i – 2	7. h – 1	8. d – 7
c – 3	10. g - 8		

CHAPTER 2

Section A

c	2. j	3. f	4. h	5. e
a	7. i	8. g	9. d	10. b

Section B

d – 10	2. f – 4	3. a – 2	4. j – 9	5. h – 1
b – 3	7. g – 8	8. e – 7	9. c – 6	10. i – 5

Section C

a/b/d	2. a/b/d/e	3. b/d	4. d	5. a/b/c/d/e

Section D

b	2. c	3. a	4. d	5. c

Section E

g – 1	2. j – 6	3. a – 10	4. f – 3
i – 7	6. c – 2	7. h – 9	8. d – 5
b – 8	10. e - 4		

CHAPTER 3

Section A

d	2. h	3. j	4. b	5. i
g	7. c	8. f	9. a	10. e

Section B

i – 10	2. f – 2	3. d – 3	4. c – 7
a – 1	6. g – 8	7. b – 9	8. j – 4
h – 5	10. e – 6		

Section C

a/d	2. e	3. c/d	4. a/b/d	5. b/c/d

Section D

1. b	2. b	3. a	4. c	5. d

Section E

1. d – 6	2. b – 4	3. h – 2	4. j – 7
5. c – 9	6. f – 1	7. i – 5	8. g – 10
9. e – 3	10. a – 8		

CHAPTER 4

Section A

1. c	2. j	3. f	4. h	5. b
6. g	7. d	8. i	9. a	10. e

Section B

1. f – 4	2. c – 9	3. i – 2	4. g – 8
5. a – 6	6. j – 3	7. e – 7	8. d – 1
9. h – 5	10. b – 10		

Section C

1. a/b	2. b/c	3. a/d/e	4. d	5. b/e

Section D

1. d	2. b	3. c	4. d	5. a

Section E

1. c – 9	2. h – 6	3. f – 8	4. a – 3
5. j – 1	6. e – 10	7. i – 4	8. d – 7
9. g – 2	10. b – 5		

CHAPTER 5

Section A

1. h	2. b	3. e	4. g	5. c
6. j	7. f	8. i	9. d	10. a

Section B

1. d – 10	2. e – 5	3. a – 1	4. j – 3	5. g – 8
6. i – 6	7. b – 4	8. f – 9	9. h – 2	10. c – 7

Section C

1. c/e	2. a/b/d	3. e	4. d	5. b/d/e

Section D

1. b	2. c	3. d	4. b	5. d

Section E

1. f – 4	2. d – 7	3. h – 3	4. a – 9	5. c – 6
6. j – 8	7. e – 10	8. g – 1	9. b – 5	10. i – 2

CUMULATIVE REVIEW FOR CHAPTERS 1 - 5

Section A

1. f	2. d	3. i	4. a	5. h
6. c	7. j	8. e	9. g	10. b

Section B

1. c (not a body part)
2. a (not a person)
3. b (not something found in nature)
4. e (not a plant or animal)
5. a (not a direction)
6. d (not a number)
7. b (not a number)
8. c (not of water)
9. a (not a verb of motion)
10. h (not one of the kanji for days of the week)

Section C

1. b	2. d	3. a	4. d	5. e
6. c	7. a	8. b	9. e	10. c

Section D

1. d/c/a/e/b	2. b/d/a/e/c
3. c/e/d/a/b	4. c/b/e/a/d
5. a/e/d/c/b	6. b/c/d/e/a
7. e/c/a/d/b	8. a/d/b/e/c
9. c/b/d/a/e	10. b/a/d/e/c

Section E

1. e	2. b	3. d	4. d	5. c

Section F

1. a/b/e	2. a/b/d/e/f/g	3. a/b/c
4. a/b/c/d/e/g	5. a/b/c/e	

Section G

1. b	2. a	3. d	4. d	5. b
6. c	7. a	8. c	9. b	10. d

Section H

1. k – 3	2. e – 10	3. h – 14	4. m – 6
5. b – 12	6. f – 4	7. c – 9	8. n – 15
9. 1 – 7	10. g – 13	11. i – 2	12. o – 8
13. a – 5	14. j – 11	15. d – 1	

CHAPTER 6

Section A

1. f	2. c	3. g	4. a	5. b
6. e	7. i	8. j	9. d	10. h

Section B

1. i – 7	2. f – 2	3. h – 6	4. c – 10
5. a – 5	6. j – 3	7. d – 8	8. e – 9
9. g – 4	10. b – 1		

Section C

1. b/e	2. a/d	3. c	4. d/e	5. a/c

Section D

1. d	2. c	3. a	4. a	5. b/d

Section E

1. g – 3	2. d – 10	3. h – 1	4. j – 7
5. i – 5	6. b – 6	7. a – 4	8. e – 8
9. f – 2	10. c – 9		

CHAPTER 7

Section A

1. a	2. f	3. j	4. c	5. h
6. e	7. d	8. i	9. b	10. g

Section B

1. c – 5	2. h – 4	3. f – 1	4. i – 10
5. a – 7	6. j – 3	7. b – 9	8. d – 2
9. g – 8	10. e – 6		

Section C

1. b/c	2. a/e	3. c/d	4. d	5. a/e

Section D

1. b	2. d	3. c	4. a	5. a

Section E

1. i – 4	2. g – 9	3. e – 1	4. a – 7
5. c – 5	6. b – 8	7. f – 3	8. d – 10
9. j – 2	10. h – 6		

CHAPTER 8

Section A

1. b	2. d	3. a	4. i	5. g
6. j	7. f	8. c	9. e	10. h

Section B

1. j – 10	2. b – 1	3. f – 9	4. h – 4
5. c – 8	6. e – 7	7. a – 5	8. i – 3
9. d – 6	10. g – 2		

Section C

1. b/e	2. d	3. a/c	4. d/e	5. a/c/d

Section D

1. d	2. b	3. a	4. a	5. c

Section E

1. b – 5	2. h – 3	3. a – 9	4. f – 1
5. j – 6	6. d – 10	7. g – 8	8. i – 2
9. c – 4	10. e – 7		

CHAPTER 9

Section A

1. g	2. b	3. f	4. j	5. h
6. c	7. i	8. d	9. e	10. a

Section B

1. a – 8	2. b – 2	3. i – 9	4. g – 4
5. c – 1	6. h – 10	7. f – 6	8. e – 5
9. j – 3	10. d – 7		

Section C

1. a/c	2. b/e	3. b/d	4. c	5. a/b/c

Section D
1. d	2. a	3. b	4. c	5. d

Section E
1. j – 8	2. d – 3	3. g – 2	4. c – 10
5. a – 5	6. i – 9	7. h – 4	8. e – 6
9. f – 1	10. b – 7		

CHAPTER 10

Section A
1. h	2. i	3. e	4. b	5. c
6. j	7. a	8. g	9. f	10. d

Section B
1. d – 9	2. j – 3	3. a – 6	4. g – 10
5. h – 5	6. c – 2	7. i – 4	8. e – 7
9. b – 1	10. f – 8		

Section C
1. d/e	2. a/d	3. e	4. b/c	5. a/b/d/e

Section D
1. c	2. a	3. d	4. b	5. d

Section E
1. i – 7	2. h – 10	3. e – 1	4. g – 3
5. b – 8	6. a – 6	7. j – 2	8. d – 9
9. c – 4	10. f – 5		

CUMULATIVE REVIEW FOR CHAPTERS 1 - 10

Section A
1. f	2. e	3. g	4. c	5. i
6. b	7. h	8. j	9. a	10. d

Section B
1.   d (not a time measurement)
2.   b (not a color)
3.   c (not a season)
4.   c (not a population center)
5.   a (not an animal)
6.   e (not a direction)
7.   b (not a body part)
8.   a (not a time of the day)
9.   d (not a man-made object)
10. e (not a positive thing)

Section C
1. e	2. c	3. a	4. d	5. c
6. d	7. b	8. d	9. e	10. b

Section D
1. b/c/d/a/e	2. a/d/e/b/c
3. c/b/a/d/e	4. c/a/b/d/e
5. e/c/d/b/a	6. e/d/c/b/a
7. c/d/a/e/b	8. d/b/a/c/e
9. b/e/c/d/a	10. d/c/b/e/a

Section E
1. e	2. c	3. e	4. d	5. a

Section F
1. a	2. d	3. b	4. e	5. b

Section G
1. b	2. d	3. a	4. a	5. c
6. d	7. a	8. c	9. b	10. d

Section H
1. c – 8	2. h – 1	3. a – 11	4. f – 14
5. o – 5	6. k – 7	7. m – 4	8. d – 12
9. i – 3	10. e – 15	11. n – 6	12. g – 13
13. b – 9	14. l – 2	15. j – 10	

CHAPTER 11

Section A
1. e	2. a	3. j	4. i	5. b
6. d	7. h	8. c	9. g	10. f

Section B
1. c – 2	2. f – 9	3. h – 1	4. g – 4
5. j – 6	6. a – 10	7. e – 3	8. b – 8
9. d – 7	10. i – 5		

Section C
1. b	2. b/c/d	3. d	4. c	5. a

Section D
1. a – 8	2. e – 5	3. g – 10	4. j – 2
5. c – 3	6. f – 1	7. b – 6	8. h – 9
9. d – 4	10. i – 7		

Section E
1. At 9AM.
2. To the university.
3. Their parents.
4. At the gate in front of the university.
5. By bicycle.

CHAPTER 12

Section A
1. f	2. j	3. g	4. e	5. c
6. b	7. i	8. d	9. a	10. h

Section B
1. f – 7	2. b – 9	3. a – 3	4. h – 1
5. e – 8	6. i – 2	7. g – 4	8. c – 6
9. j – 10	10. d – 5		

Section C
1. a/b/e	2. d	3. b	4. a	5. a

Section D
1. e – 7	2. f – 9	3. j – 6	4. c – 5
5. h – 1	6. b – 3	7. g – 2	8. a – 8
9. i – 10	10. d – 4		

Section E

1. At a bank.
2. Reception work.
3. Ten minutes.
4. An important interview.
5. At noon.

CHAPTER 13

Section A

1. e	2. j	3. c	4. g	5. d
6. h	7. f	8. i	9. b	10. a

Section B

1. d – 4	2. a – 9	3. i – 5	4. e – 7
5. g – 1	6. c – 8	7. b – 3	8. j – 2
9. h – 10	10. f – 6		

Section C

1. b	2. d	3. a/d/e	4. c	5. b/d

Section D

1. h – 5	2. j – 9	3. a – 7	4. b – 3
5. f – 1	6. i – 6	7. d – 4	8. e – 10
9. g – 8	10. c – 2		

Section E

1. Tea ceremony.
2. On the weekend.
3. On Kyushu.
4. Saturday.
5. By train.

CHAPTER 14

Section A

1. e	2. c	3. h	4. j	5. d
6. i	7. b	8. a	9. g	10. f

Section B

1. a – 5	2. j – 7	3. g – 4	4. c – 6
5. b – 9	6. h – 10	7. e – 2	8. i – 1
9. d – 8	10. f – 3		

Section C

1. d	2. c/e	3. a	4. d	5. c/d/e

Section D

1. f – 5	2. d – 10	3. j – 1	4. g – 6
5. a – 8	6. b – 7	7. e – 3	8. i – 4
9. h – 9	10. c – 2		

Section E

1. A festival.
2. In Kyoto.
3. There's a school trip.
4. No.
5. Some important business.

CHAPTER 15

Section A

1. a	2. h	3. f	4. d	5. g
6. i	7. c	8. b	9. j	10. e

Section B

1. d – 5	2. i – 4	3. f – 10	4. b – 7
5. c – 1	6. h – 6	7. e – 3	8. a – 2
9. g – 9	10. j – 8		

Section C

1. a/e	2. c	3. d	4. d	5. b

Section D

1. d – 8	2. h – 10	3. e – 1	4. g – 6
5. c – 7	6. i – 4	7. f – 9	8. j – 5
9. a – 2	10. b – 3		

Section E

1. He got married.
2. Last weekend.
3. They've been friends since elementary school.
4. That he worked as a newspaper reporter.
5. He's a doctor.

CHAPTER 16

Section A

1. c	2. i	3. b	4. a	5. g
6. e	7. h	8. d	9. j	10. f

Section B

1. c – 5	2. e – 10	3. i – 7	4. b – 2
5. h – 1	6. d – 3	7. g – 8	8. j – 6
9. a – 9	10. f – 4		

Section C

1. c	2. a/e	3. d	4. b	5. c

Section D

1. j – 5	2. e – 4	3. a – 6	4. g – 9
5. f – 2	6. i – 1	7. b – 10	8. h – 8
9. d – 3	10. c – 7		

Section E

1. To Hiroshima.
2. Her husband.
3. The prefectural zoo.
4. Hiked in the nearby mountains.
5. To Hokkaido.

CUMULATIVE REVIEW FOR CHAPTER 1 - 16

Section A

1. i	2. c	3. j	4. a	5. b
6. g	7. e	8. h	9. d	10. f

Section B
 (not something found in nature)
 (not an animal)
 (not a verb of motion)
 (not a family member)
 (not something sad)
 (not something with a connection to water)
 (not an adjective)
 (not something positive)
 (not a body part)
 e (not something to do with time)

Section C
| | 2. e | 3. c | 4. b | 5. b |
| | 7. c | 8. a | 9. b | 10. e |

Section D
/e/b/d/a	2. a/c/b/d/e	3. c/a/e/d/b
/b/a/c/d	5. b/a/e/c/d	6. d/e/a/c/b
/d/b/e/c	8. e/a/d/b/c
/e/c/d/a	10. a/d/c/e/b

Section E
| | 2. e | 3. e | 4. b | 5. d |

Section F
| | 2. a | 3. c | 4. d | 5. b |

Section G
| | 2. b | 3. d | 4. c | 5. a |
| | 7. b | 8. a | 9. d | 10. c |

Section H
e – 6	2. g – 9	3. n – 1	4. b – 15
k – 13	6. f – 2	7. a – 12	8. o – 5
m – 8	10. h – 7	11. i – 14	12. c – 11
l – 3	14. j – 10	15. d – 4

CHAPTER 17

Section A
| b | 2. h | 3. f | 4. g | 5. j |
| c | 7. i | 8. d | 9. e | 10. a |

Section B
d – 10	2. a – 8	3. b – 9	4. e – 2
j – 1	6. f – 6	7. c – 5	8. i – 3
h – 7	10. g – 4

Section C
| c/d/e | 2. b | 3. c | 4. b | 5. c |

Section D
g – 1	2. b – 9	3. c – 4	4. a – 5
i – 8	6. f – 10	7. j – 7	8. e – 6
h – 3	10. d – 2

Section E
| A cold rain fell. | 2. Late autumn. |
| No, it's small. | 4. Black birds have gathered |
| No, I'm once again alone. |

CHAPTER 18

Section A
| 1. e | 2. f | 3. j | 4. h | 5. c |
| 6. d | 7. i | 8. a | 9. b | 10. g |

Section B
1. c – 10	2. j – 5	3. g – 4	4. a – 9
5. b – 2	6. e – 1	7. f – 8	8. h – 7
9. i – 3	10. d – 6

Section C
| 1. c | 2. c | 3. b | 4. a/d | 5. d |

Section D
1. h – 8	2. e – 3	3. i – 10	4. c – 1
5. f – 9	6. b – 4	7. j – 6	8. g – 2
9. a – 7	10. d – 5

Section E
1. A television.
2. A shop in front of Shinjuku statiion.
3. The new television that has just come on sale.
4. 250,000 yen.
5. I asked my younger brother for a loan.

CHAPTER 19

Section A
| 1. j | 2. c | 3. g | 4. b | 5. h 6. a |
| 7. e | 8. i | 9. d | 10. f |

Section B
1. e – 8	2. d – 9	3. j – 4	4. g – 5
5. b – 7	6. c – 3	7. a – 10	8. i – 6
9. h – 1	10. f – 2

Section C
| 1. c | 2. a/b/c/e | 3. d | 4. a/d/e | 5. c |

Section D
1. c – 8	2. i – 10	3. e – 2	4. d – 1
5. j – 7	6. a – 5	7. g – 6	8. h – 9
9. f – 3	10. b – 4

Section E
1. What time it was.
2. A bus.
3. Because of construction on the main road.
4. The week before.
5. Until the end of the year.

CHAPTER 20

Section A
| 1. h | 2. a | 3. b | 4. i | 5. d |
| 6. e | 7. j | 8. c | 9. g | 10. f |

Section B

1. d – 6	2. f – 10	3. e – 5	4. i – 7
5. j – 9	6. a – 8	7. g – 2	8. c – 4
9. h – 1	10. b – 3		

Section C

1. b	2. a/b/e	3. d	4. c	5. a

Section D

1. e – 5	2. i – 8	3. b – 3	4. g – 7
5. a – 1	6. f – 9	7. h – 2	8. j – 6
9. d – 4	10. c – 10		

Section E

1. Science.
2. The temperature dropped, and the first snow of the year fell.
3. To go to a hot spring resort.
4. Two friends.
5. Because it was cold.

CHAPTER 21

Section A

1. e	2. j	3. a	4. g
5. f	6. i	7. d	8. c
9. b	10. h		

Section B

1. g – 10	2. i – 9	3. a – 4	4. h – 5
5. d – 8	6. j – 2	7. e – 3	8. f – 7
9. c – 1	10. b – 6		

Section C

1. a/b/c	2. c	3. d	4. e	5. b/d

Section D

1. e – 5	2. a – 9	3. i – 3	4. d – 1
5. j – 4	6. c – 2	7. g – 8	8. b – 10
9. h – 7	10. f – 6		

Section E

1. Read art books.
2. The library.
3. Old Japanese paintings.
4. The colors.
5. That they're very interesting.

CHAPTER 22

Section A

1. i	2. b	3. j	4. a	5. f
6. h	7. g	8. d	9. c	10. e

Section B

1. j – 9	2. b – 10	3. c – 2	4. a – 1
5. f – 5	6. i – 4	7. e – 7	8. h – 3
9. d – 8	10. g – 6		

Section C

1. a/c	2. b	3. b	4. e	5. d

Section D

1. g – 8	2. j – 10	3. d – 2	4. e – 1
5. h – 9	6. b – 6	7. c – 4	8. a – 7
9. i – 5	10. f – 3		

Section E

1. The company president's wife.
2. This morning.
3. Vegetables from the household vegetable garden.
4. That they're free.
5. Someone who really likes money.

CUMULATIVE REVIEW FOR CHAPTER 1 - 22

Section A

1. c	2. g	3. a	4. i	5. d
6. b	7. j	8. h	9. f	10. e

Section B

1. e (not a body part)
2. b (not a brother or sister)
3. d (not a man-made object)
4. c (not a food or drink)
5. d (not something hot or warm)
6. a (not something negative)
7. e (not something that lives)
8. e (not something related to business)
9. b (not something related to water)
10. c (not something related to governance)

Section C

1. d	2. a	3. c	4. b	5. e
6. b	7. c	8. d	9. e	10. a

Section D

1. c/a/b/e/d	2. b/d/a/c/e	3. a/e/d/c/b
4. e/a/c/d/b	5. c/d/a/b/e	6. d/e/b/c/a
7. e/d/c/a/b	8. d/c/e/b/a	9. c/a/e/d/b
10. b/d/c/e/a		

Section E

1. e	2. c	3. c	4. e	5. d

Section F

1. c	2. d	3. e	4. c	5. d

Section G

1. c	2. b	3. d	4. b	5. a
6. d	7. d	8. a	9. c	10. b

Section H

1. h – 6	2. c – 11	3. k – 7	4. l – 14
5. d – 1	6. j – 9	7. e – 13	8. g – 2
9. n – 10	10. b – 15	11. m – 8	12. o – 12
13. a – 4	14. i – 3	15. f – 5	

INDEX 1: STROKE COUNT

1 Stroke
一 3

2 Strokes
人 2　二 4　八 19　九 28　十 39　七 44　力 63　入 94　刀 117　又 159　丁 165

3 Strokes
山 1　三 5　口 8　女 16　大 17　小 20　上 30　下 31　工 47　子 56　千 65　川 70　干 81　士 84　土 87　万 89　寸 103　夕 108　弓 143　巾 162　己 214　亡 254　与 425　丸 470

4 Strokes
日 6　月 11　木 13　五 14　中 18　六 22　王 23　心 25　内 34　止 43　少 45　円 52　元 53　火 59　水 61　手 67　化 69　父 79　牛 100　切 118　天 123　分 124　斤 126　引 146　公 161　友 166　犬 171　不 186　太 189　凶 192　午 198　文 202　戸 205　方 223　弔 228　氏 234　比 240　欠 246　介 263　斗 278　反 287　予 299　夫 315　尺 332　今 383　区 398

5 Strokes
白 7　四 10　目 15　右 24　半 35　左 38　古 48　冬 58　本 60　北 68　田 72　出 73　外 98　立 99　母 109　央 112　失 130　甲 140　市 142　主 148　民 163　正 164　付 183　由 208　申 220　示 222　仕 226　可 236　占 237　世 247　台 248　用 252　未 255　末 256　矢 264　且 270　払 276　代 277　平 285　令 293　広 314　石 321　丙 333　去 337　永 339　340　370　375　384

6 Strokes
回 9　全 27　早 29　米 32　自 33　有 36　肉 37　百 51　好 57　安 62　休 66　耳 78　寺 104　先 105　舌 110　西 116　名 129　多 134　会 138　気 149　年 155　団 167　毎 168　死 172　字 173　交 176　系 185　同 196　両 197　至 219　旨 239　合 244　羊 250　州 262　吉 266　次 269　各 271　地 282　伝 328　式 329　虫 353　色 391　共 404　忙 409　池 413　光 430　羽 435　成 444　争 454　吏 459　列 462　向 469　考 486　489

7 Strokes
貝 21　見 42　体 71　男 74　言 80　売 92　図 111　花 128　私 131　近 141　来 156　赤 160　町 170　村 175　車 180　足 190　走 195　声 212　住 224　辛 225　低 267　孝 272　利 273　豆 275　形 280　良 283　忘 288　完 291　医 292　別 324　即 342　束 345　冷 356　究 359　更 362　系 364　亜 373　作 374　弟 377　決 380　何 389　社 397　身 411　初 437　困 449　廷 450　対 451　492　497

8 Strokes
明 12　国 26　京 41　歩 55　東 76　金 82　青 86　雨 90　者 93　門 96　周 120　物 125　夜 132　英 152　押 154　学 157　空 169　取 174　具 177　注 178　林 181　受 191　事 206　泣 229　若 235　所 242　画 251　定 257　采 259　姉 261　服 268　的 284　和 301　実 305　免 311　非 320　味 331　店 346　固 352　昔 361　法 363　知 386　始 395　直 405　泳 407　治 417　妹 424　制 429　官 431　有 443　卒 488　枚 500　使 501　長 509　518

9 Strokes
春 40　南 46　首 54　思 77　美 101　星 114　秋 115　前 133　持 135　音 137　秒 147　品 179　後 187　海 193　信 201　待 207　県 209　洗 210　要 213　計 238　重 241　神 249　軍 253　急 260　茶 265　界 274　指 281　活 286　送 298　変 300　食 313　泉 316　映 317　319　323　洋 325　度 334　皆 344　昨 355　則 382　科 388　発 399　室 401　是 406　研 412　昼 418　建 426　点 428　風 442　飛 460　面 472　便 476　専 483　単 485　乗 496　相 517

10 Strokes
高 49　夏 64　家 75　島 102　書 136　馬 144　時 150　訓 153　校 194　酒 204　紙 258　配 289　降 295　弱 308　記 322　院 347　原 349　通 354　特 357　真 358　借 396　病 403　料 408　旅 415　笑 422　勉 438　個 447　起 453　荷 458　展 466　帰 475　員 478　留 490　残 507　庭 510　516

11 Strokes
掛 88　雪 95　鳥 107　週 145　黒 184　進 203　転 215　理 217　問 231　第 243　都 294　婚 296　祭 297　経 302　魚 304　動 318　現 327　野 338　族 368　教 369　宿 371　接 378　商 393　悪 394　黄 420　産 427　強 434　術 448　堂 456　組 457　側 465　習 474　部 479　授 482　婦 504　菜 513　終 520

12 Strokes
買 50　朝 85　間 97　開 106　道 122　森 182　最 188　番 211　軽 218　絵 227　着 233　遊 245　達 279　短 306　結 309　貫 330　登 336　晩 348　絡 350　集 351　場 360　幾 387　落 400　答 402　運 414　階 419　温 421　寒 432　痛 441　港 445　期 446　飯 461　暑 467　然 481　無 498　502　505　515

13 Strokes
電 91　新 127　話 151　意 158　愛 199　楽 216　暗 232　遠 290　続 307　辞 310　漢 341　園 343　試 372　節 381　業 416　置 452　働 455　寝 463　数 473　歳 484

14 Strokes
語 83　読 121　聞 139　銀 230　歌 312　際 335　鼻 376　説 379　様 390　駅 392　関 464　練 487　静 511　雑 514

15 Strokes
質 221　線 366　選 477　横 493　調 506　熱 508

16 Strokes
親 113　頭 303　橋 326　薬 365　機 433　館 471

18 Strokes
曜 119　離 200　顔 367　難 436　験 439　題 480　贈 512

19 Strokes
願 410

INDEX 2: KANJI NAMES

ari 係 418	ki 着 245	koto 言 80	MEI 明 12	naka 中 18	omo 面 476
KU 画 251	ki 利 275	koto 事 206	MEI 名 129	naka 半 38	omote 表 352
KU 各 282	ki 決 397	kowa 声 224	MEN 免 311	nama 生 99	omote 面 476
ai 上 30	ki 黄 420	ku 来 156	MEN 面 476	nan 何 411	ON 音 137
ai 神 253	KI 気 149	ku 食 317	meshi 飯 498	NAN 南 46	ON 遠 290
ai 紙 258	KI 己 214	ku 組 457	mi 三 5	NAN 男 74	ON 温 445
N 神 253	KI 記 322	KU 口 8	mi 見 305	NAN 難 436	ON 同 197
N 干 81	KI 幾 400	KU 九 39	mi 実 305	nana 七 44	ona 女 16
N 間 97	KI 機 433	KU 工 47	mi 身 449	nani 何 411	onna 女 16
N 甲 148	KI 起 458	KU 公 161	MI 未 276	nano 七 44	onoono 各 282
N 完 292	KI 帰 478	KU 区 398	MI 味 331	nao 直 407	onore 己 214
N 漢 341	KI 期 481	KŪ 空 169	mi- 三 5	nao 治 424	osa 治 424
N 官 443	KICHI 吉 269	kuba 配 289	michi 道 122	nara 習 474	oshi 教 369
N 寒 446	KIN 金 82	kubi 首 54	migi 右 35	natsu 夏 64	oso 教 369
N 関 464	KIN 斤 126	kuchi 口 8	mijika 短 309	ne 音 137	oso 遅 414
N 館 471	KIN 近 141	kuda 下 31	mimi 耳 78	ne 寝 463	oto 音 137
a 金 82	KIN 巾 162	kumi 組 457	MIN 明 12	ne 練 487	otōto 弟 389
ara 必 494	KIN 今 383	KUN 訓 153	MIN 民 220	nega 願 410	otoko 男 74
e 金 82	kita 北 72	kuni 国 26	mina 皆 344	NEN 年 155	otto 夫 315
ga 考 489	KITSU 吉 269	kura 暗 232	minami 南 46	NEN 然 508	oya 親 113
顔 367	kiwa 際 335	kura 比 240	minato 港 467	NETSU 熱 508	oyo 泳 417
a 空 169	kiwa 究 364	kuro 黒 184	mino 実 305	ni 荷 466	RAI 来 156
a 辛 267	ko 木 13	kuruma 車 190	mise 店 346	NI 二 4	RAI 礼 519
a 絡 351	ko 小 20	kusuri 薬 365	miyako 都 294	NICHI 日 5	RAKU 楽 216
ada 体 71	ko 子 56	KYO 去 375	mizu 水 61	nii 新 127	RAKU 絡 351
o 軽 227	ko 黄 420	KYO 京 41	mizuka 自 33	NIKU 肉 37	RAKU 落 402
u 軽 227	KO 古 58	KYŌ 凶 192	mo 持 135	NIN 人 2	REI 令 337
a 重 249	KO 戸 205	KYŌ 兄 208	mō 申 237	nishi 西 116	REI 冷 362
hira 頭 303	KO 己 214	KYŌ 経 302	MŌ 亡 254	niwa 庭 516	REI 礼 519
a 語 83	KO 固 361	KYŌ 橋 326	mochi 用 270	no 野 338	REN 練 487
a 方 223	KO 去 375	KYŌ 教 369	MOKU 木 13	no 飲 419	RETSU 列 469
a 形 283	KO 個 453	KYŌ 共 409	MOKU 目 15	no 乗 503	RI 里 180
a 固 361	kō 神 253	KYŌ 強 434	MON 門 96	nobo 上 31	RI 離 200
a 難 436	KŌ 口 8	KYOKU 局 359	MON 聞 139	nobo 登 348	RI 理 217
achi 形 283	KŌ 工 47	KYŪ 九 39	MON 文 202	nochi 後 187	RI 利 275
ana 刀 117	KŌ 高 49	KYŪ 休 66	MON 問 231	noko 残 510	RI 吏 462
ari 語 83	KŌ 好 57	KYŪ 弓 143	mono 者 93	nushi 主 164	RIKI 力 63
TSU 活 300	KŌ 甲 148	KYŪ 泣 229	mono 物 125	NYAKU 若 235	RIKU 六 22
va 川 70	KŌ 公 161	KYŪ 急 265	moppa 専 485	NYO 女 16	RIN 林 181
a 通 354	KŌ 行 173	KYŪ 究 364	mori 森 182	NYŌ 女 16	RITSU 立 112
za 風 460	KŌ 交 185	ma 目 15	moto 下 31	NYŪ 入 94	ROKU 六 22
ke 風 460	KŌ 後 187	ma 間 97	moto 元 53	o 小 20	RU 留 507
zo 数 473	KŌ 校 194	ma 馬 144	moto 本 188	o 下 31	RYO 旅 422
zu 数 473	KŌ 孝 273	ma 交 185	MOTSU 物 125	o 生 99	RYŌ 両 219
化 69	KŌ 降 295	ma 待 207	motto 最 188	o 押 154	RYŌ 良 288
家 75	KŌ 広 339	ma 真 358	mu 六 22	o 降 295	RYŌ 料 415
気 149	KŌ 更 373	machi 町 97	mu 向 486	o 落 452	RYOKU 力 63
京 41	KŌ 黄 420	mae 前 133	MU 無 515	o 置 452	RYŪ 立 112
CI 兄 208	KŌ 光 435	MAI 米 32	mu- 六 22	o 起 458	RYŪ 留 507
CI 軽 227	KŌ 港 467	MAI 毎 168	mui 六 22	o 終 520	sa 下 31
CI 計 241	KŌ 向 486	MAI 妹 429	mukashi 昔 363	O 和 301	sa 指 298
CI 形 283	KŌ 考 489	MAI 枚 501	mune 旨 175	O 悪 394	sa 冷 362
CI 経 302	kōri 氷 385	maji 交 185	mura 村 401	ō 大 17	sa 去 375
CI 系 374	koe 声 224	mame 豆 280	muro 室 401	ō 多 134	SA 左 48
CI 係 418	kokono 九 39	MAN 万 89	mushi 虫 391	Ō 王 23	SA 茶 274
CN 見 42	kokoro 心 25	mana 学 89	musu 結 330	Ō 央 154	SA 作 380
CN 間 97	kokoro 試 372	manuka 免 311	muzuka 難 436	Ō 押 154	sada 定 257
CN 犬 171	KOKU 国 26	maru 円 52	MYŌ 明 12	Ō 黄 420	SAI 西 116
CN 県 209	KOKU 黒 184	maru 丸 470	MYŌ 名 129	Ō 横 493	SAI 切 118
CN 研 412	KOKU 石 340	masa 正 222	na 名 129	ōyake 公 161	SAI 最 188
CN 建 428	koma 困 451	mata 又 229	na 泣 229	okona 行 173	SAI 采 259
CN 験 439	kome 米 32	mato 的 284	na 亡 254	oku 後 187	SAI 祭 297
TSU 欠 246	KON 金 82	matsu 祭 297	na 成 454	oku 送 313	SAI 際 335
TSU 結 330	KON 婚 296	MATSU 末 277	na 菜 513	oku 遅 414	SAI 歳 484
TSU 決 397	KON 今 383	matta 全 27	na 無 515	oku 贈 510	SAI 菜 513
木 13	KON 建 428	matto 全 27	na 永 515	OKU 屋 281	saka 酒 204
生 99	KON 困 451	mawa 回 9	naga 永 384	omo 思 77	sakana 魚 304
切 118	kono 好 57	me 目 15	naga 長 518	omo 主 164	saké 酒 204
聞 139	koro 転 215	me 女 16	nago 和 301	omo 重 249	saki 先 105
来 156	kota 答 421		NAI 内 34		

INDEX 3

ON-YOMI KEYWORD TABLE

ON-YOMI		KEYWORD(s)	ON-YOMI		KEYWORD(s)
A	ア		GYO	ギョ	
AI	アイ		GYŌ	ギョウ	
AKU	アク		GYOKU	ギョク	
AN	アン		GYŪ	ギュウ	
BA	バ		HA-	ハッ	
BAI	バイ		HACHI	ハチ	
BAN	バン		HAI	ハイ	
BATSU	バツ		HAKU	ハク	
BEI	ベイ		HAN	ハン	
BEN	ベン		HATSU	ハツ	
BETSU	ベツ		HEI	ヘイ	
BI	ビ		HEN	ヘン	
BIN	ビン		HI	ヒ	
BO	ボ		HIN	ヒン	
BŌ	ボウ		HITSU	ヒツ	
BOKU	ボク		HO	ホ	
BU	ブ		HO-	ホッ	
BUN	ブン		HŌ	ホウ	
BUTSU	ブツ		HOKU	ホク	
BYAKU	ビャク		HON	ホン	
BYŌ	ビョウ		HOTSU	ホツ	
CHA	チャ		HYAKU	ヒャク	
CHAKU	チャク		HYŌ	ヒョウ	
CHI	チ		I	イ	
CHŌ	チョウ		ICHI	イチ	
CHOKU	チョク		IKU	イク	
CHŪ	チュウ		IN	イン	
DA	ダ		ITSU	イツ	
DAI	ダイ		JAKU	ジャク	
DAN	ダン		JI	ジ	
DE	デ		JIKI	ジキ	
DEN	デン		JIN	ジン	
DO	ド		JITSU	ジツ	
DŌ	ドウ		JO	ジョ	
DOKU	ドク		JŌ	ジョウ	
E	エ		JU	ジュ	
EI	エイ		JŪ	ジュウ	
EKI	エキ		JUTSU	ジュツ	
EN	エン		KA	カ	
FU	フ		KA-	カッ	
FŪ	フウ		KAI	カイ	
FUKU	フク		KAKU	カク	
FUN	フン		KAN	カン	
FUTSU	フツ		KATSU	カツ	
GA	ガ		KE	ケ	
GA-	ガッ		KEI	ケイ	
GAI	ガイ		KEN	ケン	
GAKU	ガク		KETSU	ケツ	
GAN	ガン		KI	キ	
GATSU	ガツ		KICHI	キチ	
GE	ゲ		KIN	キン	
GEN	ゲン		KITSU	キツ	
GETSU	ゲツ		KO	コ	
GIN	ギン		KŌ	コウ	
GO	ゴ		KOKU	コク	
GŌ	ゴウ		KON	コン	
GON	ゴン		KU	ク	
GU	グ		KŪ	クウ	
GUN	グン		KUN	クン	

ON-YOMI		KEYWORD(s)	ON-YOMI		KEYWORD(s)
KYO	キョ		SETSU	セツ	
KYŌ	キョウ		SHA	シャ	
KYOKU	キョク		SHAKU	シャク	
KYŪ	キュウ		SHI	シ	
MAI	マイ		SHICHI	シチ	
MAN	マン		SHIKI	シキ	
MATSU	マツ		SHIN	シン	
MEI	メイ		SHITSU	シツ	
MEN	メン		SHO	ショ	
MI	ミ		SHŌ	ショウ	
MIN	ミン		SHOKU	ショク	
MŌ	モウ		SHU	シュ	
MOKU	モク		SHŪ	シュウ	
MON	モン		SHUKU	シュク	
MOTSU	モツ		SHUN	シュン	
MU	ム		SHUTSU	シュツ	
MYŌ	ミョウ		SO	ソ	
NAI	ナイ		SŌ	ソウ	
NAN	ナン		SOKU	ソク	
NEN	ネン		SON	ソン	
NETSU	ネツ		SOTSU	ソツ	
NI	ニ		SU	ス	
NICHI	ニチ		SŪ	スウ	
NIKU	ニク		SUI	スイ	
NIN	ニン		SUN	スン	
NYAKU	ニャク		TA	タ	
NYO	ニョ		TAI	タイ	
NYŌ	ニョウ		TAKU	タク	
NYŪ	ニュウ		TAN	タン	
O	オ		TATSU	タツ	
Ō	オウ		TEI	テイ	
OKU	オク		TEKI	テキ	
ON	オン		TEN	テン	
RAI	ライ		TO	ト	
RAKU	ラク		TŌ	トウ	
REI	レイ		TOKU	トク	
REN	レン		TON	トン	
RETSU	レツ		TSU	ツ	
RI	リ		TSŪ	ツウ	
RIKI	リキ		TSUI	ツイ	
RIKU	リク		U	ウ	
RIN	リン		UN	ウン	
RITSU	リツ		WA	ワ	
ROKU	ロク		YA	ヤ	
RU	ル		YAKU	ヤク	
RYO	リョ		YO	ヨ	
RYŌ	リョウ		YŌ	ヨウ	
RYOKU	リョク		YU	ユ	
RYŪ	リュウ		YŪ	ユウ	
SA	サ		YUI	ユイ	
SAI	サイ		ZAN	ザン	
SAKU	サク		ZATSU	ザツ	
SAN	サン		ZE	ゼ	
SATSU	サツ		ZEI	ゼイ	
SE	セ		ZEN	ゼン	
SECHI	セチ		ZETSU	ゼツ	
SEI	セイ		ZŌ	ゾウ	
SEKI	セキ		ZOKU	ゾク	
SEN	セン		ZU	ズ	